THE ODYSSEY READER

IDEAS AND STYLE
SHORTER EDITION

THE ODYSSEY READER

IDEAS AND STYLE

SHORTER EDITION

Newman P. Birk & Genevieve B. Birk

TUFTS UNIVERSITY

A Division of The
**BOBBS-MERRILL EDUCATIONAL PUBLISHING
Indianapolis**

Copyright © 1969 by The Bobbs-Merrill Company, Inc.

Printed in the United States of America

All rights reserved. No part of this book shall be reproduced or transmitted in any form or by any means, electronic or mechanical, including photocopying, recording, or by any information or retrieval system, without written permission from the Publisher:

>The Bobbs-Merrill Company, Inc.
>4300 West 62nd Street
>Indianapolis, Indiana 46268

Fifth Printing—1978
Library of Congress Catalog Card Number: 68-57964
ISBN 0-672-63075-3 (pbk.)

Cover photograph and design by Ursula Suess.

The authors are grateful to the following writers, publishers, and literary agents for permission to use the materials listed below.

Appleton-Century-Crofts, Inc.: "The Intrinsic Value of Art" from *The Principles of Aesthetics*, Second Edition, by DeWitt H. Parker. Copyright 1920, 1946 by F. S. Crofts & Co., Inc. Reprinted by permission of Appleton-Century-Crofts. Passage from *Science and Christian Tradition* by Thomas Henry Huxley.

Edward Arnold, Ltd.: passage from *The Human Situation* by W. Macneile Dixon.

The Atlantic Monthly: "A Reasonable Life in a Mad World" by Irwin Edman, "Grammar for Today" by Bergen Evans. Copyright © March 1949/March 1960 by The Atlantic Monthly Company, Boston, Mass. 02116. Reprinted with permission.

Beacon Press: "Notes of a Native Son" from *Notes of a Native Son* by James Baldwin, reprinted by permission of the Beacon Press, copyright © 1955 by James Baldwin.

Brandt & Brandt: "The Principles of Newspeak" from *Nineteen Eighty-four* by George Orwell.

The Clarendon Press: passage from *The Manual of Epictetus* (translated by P. E. Matheson).

Norman Cousins: "The Computer and the Poet" in *Saturday Review*, July 23, 1966.

Doubleday and Company, Inc.: selections from *The Theatre of the Absurd*, copyright © 1961 by Martin Esslin, reprinted by permission of Doubleday & Company, Inc.

Les Éditions Nagel: passage from *L'Existentialisme Est un Humanisme* by Jean-Paul Sartre (trans. Philip Mairet).

Estate of Irwin Edman: "A Reasonable Life in a Mad World" by Irwin Edman in *The Atlantic Monthly*, March, 1949, copyright © 1960 by The Atlantic Monthly Company, Boston, Mass. 02116. Reprinted with permission.

Bergen Evans: "Grammar for Today" in *The Atlantic Monthly*, March, 1960. Copyright © March 1960 by The Atlantic Monthly Company, Boston, Mass. 02116. Reprinted with permission.

Farrar, Straus & Giroux, Inc.: "My Negro Problem—and Ours" from *Doings and Undoings* by Norman Podhoretz. Copyright © 1963 by Norman Podhoretz. Reprinted with permission of Farrar, Straus & Giroux, Inc. "Settling the Colonel's Hash," reprinted with permission of Farrar, Straus & Giroux, Inc. from *On the*

ACKNOWLEDGMENTS

Contrary by Mary McCarthy. Copyright © 1961 by Mary McCarthy.

John Fischer: "Substitutes for Violence." Copyright © 1965 by Harper's Magazine, Inc. Reprinted from the January, 1966, issue of Harper's Magazine by permission of the author.

Harcourt, Brace & World, Inc.: "Why I Write" from *Such, Such Were the Joys* by George Orwell, copyright, 1945, 1952, 1953, by Sonia Brownell Orwell. Reprinted by permission of Harcourt, Brace & World, Inc. "The Genesis of a Mood" from *The Modern Temper* by Joseph Wood Krutch, copyright, 1929, by Harcourt, Brace & World, Inc.; renewed, 1957, by Joseph Wood Krutch. Reprinted by permission of the publishers.

Harper & Row, Publishers, Inc.: "Calculating Machine" from *The Second Tree from the Corner* by E. B. White. Copyright 1951 by E. B. White. "Walden" from *One Man's Meat* by E. B. White. Copyright 1939 by E. B. White. "The Ideal of Individual Fulfillment" from *Excellence: Can We Be Equal and Excellent Too?* by John W. Gardner. Copyright © by John W. Gardner. All reprinted by permission of Harper & Row, Publishers.

Harper's Magazine: "Substitutes for Violence" by John Fischer. Copyright © 1965, by Harper's Magazine, Inc. Reprinted from the January, 1966, issue of Harper's Magazine by permission of the author.

Harvard University Press: "The Idea of a Multiversity." Reprinted by permission of the publishers from Clark Kerr, *The Uses of the University.*

A. M. Heath & Company, Limited: "The Principles of Newspeak" from *Nineteen Eighty-four* by George Orwell. Reprinted by permission of Miss Sonia Brownell; Martin Secker & Warburg, Limited; A. M. Heath & Company, Limited.

Holt, Rinehart and Winston, Inc.: excerpts from *The Sane Society* by Erich Fromm. Copyright © 1955 by Erich Fromm. Reprinted by permission of Holt, Rinehart and Winston, Inc.

Houghton Mifflin Company: "The Crisis of American Masculinity" from *The Politics of Hope* by Arthur M. Schlesinger, Jr.

Leon H. Keyserling: "Something for Everybody" in *The New York Times Book Review*, February 27, 1966. © by The New York Times Company. Reprinted by permission.

Joseph Wood Krutch: "Life, Liberty, and the Pursuit of Welfare," 1961.

John Lear: "Men, Moonships, and Morality" in *Saturday Review*, January 7, 1967.

Longmans, Green & Company, Inc.: passage from *The Will to Believe* by William James.

F. L. Lucas: "On the Fascination of Style." Reprinted by special permission of the author and Holiday, copyright 1960, by The Curtis Publishing Co.

John Lukacs: "It's Halfway to 1984" in *The New York Times Magazine*, January 2, 1966. © 1966 by The New York Times Company. Reprinted by permission.

McGraw-Hill Book Company: "What If We Succeed?" from *We Are Not Alone* by Walter Sullivan. Copyright © 1964, 1966 by Walter Sullivan. Used by permission.

Julian Messner: "The Creative Mind," reprinted by permission of Julian Messner, Division of Simon and Schuster, Inc., from *Science and Human Values* by J. Bronowski. Copyright © 1956, by J. Bronowski.

Emmanuel G. Mesthene: "Learning to Live with Science" in *Saturday Review*, July 17, 1965.

vi Acknowledgments

Methuen and Company, Ltd.: passage from *Existentialism and Humanism* by Jean-Paul Sartre, translated by Philip Mairet.

The Michigan Quarterly Review: "Two Heresies" by Geoffrey Crowther in *The Michigan Alumnus Quarterly Review*, LXVI (Summer 1960), 266–271. Reprinted by permission of the University of Michigan and *The Michigan Quarterly Review*, successor to *The Michigan Alumnus Quarterly Review*.

Elting E. Morison: "It's Two-Thirds of a Century—We've Made It, So Far" in *The New York Times Magazine*, April 24, 1966. © 1966 by The New York Times Company. Reprinted by permission.

Lewis Mumford: "The American Way of Death." Reprinted from *The New York Review of Books*, copyright © 1966, Lewis Mumford.

The New York Times Book Review: "Something for Everybody" by Leon H. Keyserling, February 27, 1966. © 1966 by The New York Times Company. Reprinted by permission.

The New York Times Magazine: "It's Halfway to 1984" by John Lukacs in the *Times Magazine*, January 2, 1966; "It's Two-Thirds of a Century—We've Made It, So Far" by Elting E. Morison, April 24, 1966. © 1966 by The New York Times Company.

Mario Pei: "The Dictionary as a Battlefront" by Mario Pei in *Saturday Review* Education Supplement, July 21, 1962.

Philosophical Library, Inc.: "Science and Religion" from *Out of My Later Years* by Albert Einstein; "Does Human Nature Change?" by John Dewey, first published in *The Rotarian* and later in *Problems of Men*. Reprinted by permission.

Princeton University Press: "The Anti-Hero" from *Radical Innocence: Studies in the Contemporary American Novel* by Ihab Hassan. Reprinted by permission of Princeton University Press. © 1961.

Random House, Inc.: William Faulkner's Nobel Prize Address.

St. Martin's Press, Inc.: passage from *The Human Situation* by W. Macneile Dixon.

Saturday Review, Inc.: "The Dictionary as a Battlefront" by Mario Pei in the Education Supplement of *Saturday Review*, July 21, 1962; "Learning to Live with Science" by Emmanuel G. Mesthene, July 17, 1965; "The Computer and the Poet" by Norman Cousins, July 23, 1966; "Men, Moonships, and Morality" by John Lear, January 7, 1967.

Martin Secker & Warburg, Ltd.: passage from *Nineteen Eighty-four* by George Orwell, reprinted by permission of Miss Sonia Brownell and Secker & Warburg.

Simon and Schuster, Inc.: "The Monster" from *Of Men and Music* by Deems Taylor, copyright 1937 by Deems Taylor. Reprinted by permission of Simon and Schuster, Inc. "Prospects in the Arts and Sciences" from *The Open Mind* by J. Robert Oppenheimer, copyright © 1955 by J. Robert Oppenheimer. Reprinted by permission of Simon and Schuster, Inc.

Estate of James Thurber: "Which" from *Ladies' and Gentlemen's Guide to Modern English Usage*. Copr. © 1931, 1959 James Thurber. From *The Owl In the Attic*, published by Harper & Row. Originally printed in *The New Yorker*.

Nils Y. Wessell: "The Opportunity for Change," Matriculation Speech, 1965, Tufts University.

Yale University Press: "The Ideal Democracy" from *Modern Democracy* by Carl L. Becker. Copyright © 1941 by Yale University Press.

PREFACE

This shorter edition of *The Odyssey Reader: Ideas and Style* is designed to meet the needs of teachers who build their courses around several types of writing and who can assign only a brief period to nonfictional prose. At the same time, the shorter version attempts both to follow much of the plan and to achieve many of the objectives of the longer book.

The first of these objectives is to provide a real intellectual experience for the inquiring student receptive to the thought and the wisdom of great and good minds, past and present. A number of the readings have been chosen to give an enlarged understanding of our intellectual heritage and of the contemporary world. Another objective is not only to stir the vital, questioning young mind but also to offer a choice of answers; the diversity in points of view in these readings will, it is hoped, stimulate the student to examine his own beliefs and attitudes and help him choose meaningful values on which to build a personal philosophy. Finally, the study, analysis, and judgment of rhetorical principles and techniques in good prose should improve students' writing: students become more aware of rhetorical choices open to them when they write, and newly aware, as they read, of the importance of the way ideas are phrased and developed. This volume, like the longer *Odyssey Reader*, repeatedly stresses the oneness of content and form, mind and manner, ideas and style.

Different teachers will, of course, use this book differently. Students should probably read carefully the "Introduction to Rhetorical Analysis," the purpose of which is to supply tools for analysis and suggestions about reading. "Part One, Ways of Ordering Ideas and Experience" is designed to emphasize organization and to give clear examples of some ways of ordering material. Comments and questions following each reading stress organization and techniques of coherence and development within the larger patttern; but they deal too (as do comments and questions throughout the book) with the writer's ideas and with other aspects of his style and tone. The essays in Part One need not be read in the sequence in which they appear; in general, however, the arrangement is from material most easily read to material more complex in content and organization. Readings in "Part Two, Ideas and Values" are grouped by theme; numbers after each subsection in the table of contents refer to other readings relevant to the theme or to the authors represented in the unit. The instructor, perhaps using these cross-references, may wish to depart from the plan shown in the "Contents" and to combine or relate the readings in different ways.

It has been possible to retain in this shorter edition, in several instances, more than one sample of an author's writing. Three selections from Plato give students some acquaintance with the Socratic-Platonic philosophy and provide some background for references to Greek thought that occur in other readings. For rather different reasons, Joseph Wood Krutch, George Orwell, and E. B. White, as skillful modern writers, are each represented by two selections. Comparison and contrast of the ideas, style, and persona in more than one sample of an author's work may be fruitful subjects for discussion or writing.

As indicated earlier, comments and questions follow each reading in the book. Although some teachers may find this sort of critical-analytical apparatus an encumbrance, we have found that most students profit from it: well-planned questions will often lead students to notice what, without guidance, they might have missed, and so may make them more perceptive and judicious readers and eventually more conscious and effective writers. Such analytical apparatus may also free the teacher to go his own way in class, assuming that his students have worked and thought through the questions and that he need not cover the same ground. Teachers who prefer not to use the Comment and Questions can, of course, ignore them, even tell their students to ignore them.

The questions and the arrangement of material in the text should not bind the instructor. They suggest, rather, possible approaches and still allow the instructor flexibility in planning his assignments and following his own bent in teaching ideas and style.

GENEVIEVE B. BIRK

CONTENTS

AN INTRODUCTION TO RHETORICAL ANALYSIS   1

PART ONE | Ways of Ordering Ideas and Experience

THESIS AND EXAMPLES   21
    [1] *James Thurber:* Which   21

THESIS AND REASONS   24
    [2] *Geoffrey Crowther:* Two Heresies   24

GENERALIZATIONS AND QUALIFICATION   33
    [3] *Nils Y. Wessell:* The Opportunity for Change   33

NARRATION   39
    [4] *E. B. White:* Walden, 1939   39

ANALYSIS   46
    [5] *George Orwell:* Why I Write   46

CONTRAST AND COMPARISON   54
    [6] *John Lukacs:* It's Halfway to 1984   54

CAUSE AND EFFECT   64
    [7] *Erich Fromm:* Alienation: Quantification, Abstractification   64

QUESTION-TO-ANSWER OR PROBLEM-TO-SOLUTION   73

[8] *Arthur M. Schlesinger, Jr.:* The Crisis of American Masculinity   73

DEFINITION   83

[9] *Carl L. Becker:* The Ideal Democracy   83

PART TWO | Ideas and Values

EDUCATION AND THE INQUIRING MIND   99

[10] *Plato:* Apology   99
[11] *Plato:* The Myth of the Cave   121
[12] *John Stuart Mill:* On the Liberty of Thought and Discussion   128
[13] *John Henry Newman:* Enlargement of Mind   152
[14] *Clark Kerr:* The Idea of a Multiversity   161
[15] *John W. Gardner:* Excellence: The Ideal of Individual Fulfillment   168

SEE ALSO: 2, 3, 16, 22, 24, 27, 42, 44, 52

THE QUEST FOR VALUES   176

[16] *Plato:* from the Symposium   176
[17] *Epicurus:* Letter to a Friend   183
[18] The Stoic View   186
    Epictetus: The Quiet Mind   187
    Marcus Aurelius: from the Meditations   193
[19] *Jesus:* Sermon on the Mount   200
[20] *Thomas Henry Huxley:* Agnosticism and Christianity   208
[21] *William James:* Religious Faith   213
[22] *Albert Einstein:* Science and Religion   221
[23] *Jean-Paul Sartre:* Existentialism   227

SEE ALSO: 2, 3, 4, 7, 8, 10, 11, 12, 13, 15, 24, 25, 26, 27, 28, 31, 35, 37, 40, 42, 43, 44, 45, 47, 50, 52

HUMAN NATURE AND THE HUMAN SITUATION   238

[24] *John Dewey:* Does Human Nature Change?   238
[25] *W. Macneile Dixon:* Human Nature and the Human Situation   246

CONTENTS xi

[26] *Joseph Wood Krutch:* The Genesis of a Mood 260
[27] *Joseph Wood Krutch:* Life, Liberty, and the Pursuit of Welfare 272
[28] *Irwin Edman:* A Reasonable Life in a Mad World 284

SEE ALSO: 4, 6, 7, 8, 11, 21, 23, 36, 37, 41, 43, 44, 45, 46, 47, 49, 50

LANGUAGE 291

[29] *Bergen Evans:* Grammar for Today 291
[30] *Mario Pei:* The Dictionary as a Battlefront: English Teachers' Dilemma 299
[31] *E. B. White:* Calculating Machine 308
[32] *George Orwell:* The Principles of Newspeak 310
[33] *F. L. Lucas:* On the Fascination of Style 321

SEE ALSO: 1, 4, 5, 6, 7, 34, 37

LITERATURE AND THE ARTS 331

[34] *Joseph Conrad:* Preface to The Nigger of the Narcissus 331
[35] *William Faulkner:* Remarks on Receiving the Nobel Prize 336
[36] *Ihab Hassan:* The Anti-Hero 338
[37] *Martin Esslin:* The Significance of the Absurd 348
[38] *Mary McCarthy:* Settling the Colonel's Hash 357
[39] *Deems Taylor:* The Monster 369
[40] *DeWitt Parker:* The Intrinsic Value of Art 373

SEE ALSO: 5, 31, 41, 42, 45

SCIENCE AND THE MODERN WORLD 383

[41] *J. Bronowski:* The Creative Mind 383
[42] *J. Robert Oppenheimer:* Prospects in the Arts and Sciences 396
[43] *Elting E. Morison:* It's Two-Thirds of a Century—We've Made It, So Far 405
[44] *Emmanuel G. Mesthene:* Learning to Live with Science 413
[45] *Norman Cousins:* The Computer and the Poet 422
[46] *Walter Sullivan:* What If We Succeed? 425

SEE ALSO: 2, 7, 20, 22, 26, 52

CURRENT PROBLEMS AND ATTITUDES 438

[47] *Lewis Mumford:* The American Way of Death 438
[48] *James Baldwin:* Notes of a Native Son 450
[49] *Norman Podhoretz:* My Negro Problem—and Ours 468

[50] *John Fischer:* Substitutes for Violence — 481
[51] *Leon H. Keyserling:* Something for Everybody — 490
[52] *John Lear:* Men, Moonships, and Morality — 498

SEE ALSO: 4, 6, 7, 8, 23, 27, 36, 37, 41, 42, 43, 44, 45, 46

A GLOSSARY OF RHETORICAL TERMS — 507

INDEX — 513

AN INTRODUCTION TO RHETORICAL ANALYSIS

How does a composition come into being? How, as Robert Frost once said of a poem, does it assume direction and end in a clarification? Writers work, of course, in different ways; but, given an idea, a body of information, a set of values, or an experience which a writer wants to communicate, he is likely to be faced, simultaneously, with a number of questions: What general order or arrangement is best suited to my material? How can I make this order clear? How can I develop meaningfully the parts of the material? Answers to such questions usually depend on another question: What kind of audience am I writing for? Consideration of audience leads to still further questions: What shall be my attitude toward my audience and my material? What "voice," or what image of myself, do I wish to project? And, finally—in the actual process of writing—what kind of language and what rhetorical devices will best fit my total purpose in this communication? Shaping a composition involves making choices.

Some of these choices may be inevitable or automatic. For example, if the writer merely wants to give a clear account of a process, then a step-by-step chronological order may seem inevitable; if he knows that he is addressing an audience of nonspecialists, he knows, too, that he must avoid or must explain technical language; and his attitude toward his material may be purely objective. More often, though, the writer's choices are not predetermined by material or situation; he makes them consciously and thoughtfully, guided by his conception of the impact he wants his writing to have on the reader. As a writer or as a perceptive reader, one needs to be aware of possible choices—of organization, of tone, and of modes of expression—which we shall discuss in the following pages.

I. WAYS OF ORDERING IDEAS AND EXPERIENCE

Perhaps we should begin this section by elaborating a statement made earlier. Writers work in different ways; it is therefore difficult, if not impossible, to give an exact account of their procedure in organizing their material. Except in very short and simple pieces, the writer is likely to go through a period of somewhat random thinking, and then of rough planning in which he tentatively fixes on the main divisions of his subject, on a possible sequence of main ideas, on sub-units within the major divisions, and on methods of ordering and developing those smaller units. The process may be in some ways analogous to the arranging of materials in a chest of drawers—deciding what should go into which drawer and how the contents of each are best arranged for order and convenience. Working by trial and error and impelled by sudden new ideas, the writer may make choices and changes that extend from total reorganization to, in the last stages, choices of particular words and even of punctuation marks. By means of a process in itself perhaps disorderly, the successful writer arrives at an orderly presentation; a coherent pattern emerges finally from his struggle with his material.

The classification and description of such final patterns is to some degree artificial because the patterns are often used in combination in a complex piece of writing (or even in a single paragraph) and because the ways of ordering material overlap: a definition may also be an analysis; narration may be a primary method of showing a cause–effect relationship. What might be called the general or dominant order of ideas frequently splinters into other orders, as when a broad thesis supported by reasons is developed in detail by paragraphs of contrast and comparison. The listing below (and in Part I of the readings) is therefore meant to call the reader's attention to some ways of ordering ideas and to aid him in recognizing and evaluating the pattern or patterns chosen by the authors he reads. What the reader requires is that there be some kind of order, by means of which the writer ends in a clarification.

Thesis and Examples. The writer may state his thesis or generalization early and support it by short or long examples. Or he may start with examples from which he arrives at a thesis or conclusion. Or he may begin and end with general statements, both supported by the examples he supplies. The reader's response to a piece of writing using this organization will depend largely on the intrinsic interest of the examples and their aptness in supporting the thesis.

Thesis and Reasons. Using this order, the writer often states early his belief, judgment, or recommendation (thesis), and then gives reasons for believing as he does. Part of his reasoning may consist of anticipating and countering possible objections to the position he is taking.

Generalization and Qualification. This pattern is akin to Thesis and

Reasons. It occurs when the writer wishes to state a thesis which, taken literally, sounds like a sweeping generalization. He may qualify (that is, modify, limit, or restrict) by defining terms and by negation or exclusion —showing what he does *not* mean by, or what he excludes from, his original generalization. Having qualified and clarified, he usually restates his generalization at the end.

Narration. The most common order in nonfictional narration is chronological arrangement, or the setting down of events in the time-order in which they occur. When events occur simultaneously, in different places, narration may also involve space-order. And, in complex narration, the writer may have reasons (which should be made clear to the reader) for moving about in time and space—for starting his narrative in the middle, for example, or at the end, of a sequence of events.

Analysis. Analysis is the method of dividing a complex subject into its main parts, examining each of the parts, and showing their relationship to each other and to the whole. In a formal analysis, the main parts may in turn be divided, each subdivision may be further divided, and so on down to the last possible unit. When a writer says, "Four problems face the Security Council," or "There are many reasons for unrest on the campus," he is introducing an analysis of a subject too complex to be treated as a whole. The section you are now reading is an analysis of "ways of ordering ideas and experience."

Contrast and Comparison. The writer using this pattern sets side by side two or more people, things, or situations, and considers the differences, or similarities, or differences and similarities between them. One might, for example, compare the passive resistance of Gandhi with that of Martin Luther King, or compare and contrast the relationship of the individual and society in two or more modern novels. If the subjects being compared are complex, the writer may break them by analysis into their main parts and contrast or compare them part by part. He may discuss the topics, or the parts of them, in combination, or he may present one topic first and then compare the other with it.

Cause and Effect. In this pattern of organization a writer discusses the cause of an event or a situation and then the effect—for example, the cause of the growth of large universities and the effect of that growth. Within the general cause–effect order, the writer often uses analysis; that is, he divides "cause" into three or four main causes, and "effect" into three or four main effects. He may also reverse the order, starting with the effects of a development or event, and then discussing its causes.

Question-to-Answer or **Problem-to-Solution.** The writer using this order may need to clarify the question or problem by means of facts, examples, quotations, definition, or analysis. His proposed answer or solution is usually arrived at and supported by examples, reasons, statistics, and other kinds of amplifying detail.

Definition. Extended definition (of a term, an idea, or a mood, for example) attempts, like brief definition, to put the subject into a genus or class and to differentiate it from other members of that class. It also clarifies the subject in one or more of these ways: (1) by giving examples; (2) by comparing the subject with something familiar to the reader; (3) by comparing and contrasting it with related subjects; (4) by tracing its history or development; (5) by negating or excluding—showing what it does not mean or does not include in this context; (6) by restating the essentials of the definition; (7) by analyzing—breaking the subject into its components and examining each part.

As we have suggested earlier, the patterns of organization described above (and we have not exhausted the list of possible patterns, but have merely named the most common ones) are used in developing paragraphs as well as longer pieces of writing; a cause–effect organization may therefore contain paragraphs or even larger units of definition, analysis, contrast and comparison, etc. We might note in passing that many of these ways of ordering material are also used in single sentences. For example, "I believe that objective examinations should be abolished because they often test knowledge of unimportant details and because they do not stimulate thought" is a sentence of thesis and reasons; "Mankind must put an end to war or war will put an end to mankind" is a sentence of contrast or antithesis. Antithetical structures like the last one are also, of course, aspects of a writer's style.

One further point about the ordering of ideas and experience: We have thus far been dealing with logical order. Another consideration for the writer may be psychological order. A writer may be primarily concerned with informing, persuading, convincing, communicating an attitude or experience, or moving to action. In the light of his intention, what arrangement of points, examples, or reasons will be most interesting, pleasing, moving, or convincing? What strategy will be most effective in achieving his aims? We shall return later to this matter of psychological order.

II. CLARITY AND COHERENCE

When the writer has decided on the logical order best suited to his material, he uses four major devices for making that order (and the material) clear to his readers.

1. He may use his title or his opening paragraphs, or both, to signal his organization to the reader. A title like "The Problem of People," for example, suggests definition and analysis of the problem and possibly a proposed solution.

2. The writer uses paragraphs to mark the units of his discourse, to

indicate to the reader that one phase of his discussion has ended and another is beginning. He may use section numbers, headings, or transitional paragraphs to mark off the main divisions of his thought. Often, though certainly not always, the writer begins his paragraphs with topic sentences; when he does, these first sentences provide an outline of the piece of writing. The skillful writer generally develops his paragraphs fully, by using one or more of the ways of ordering ideas discussed in the preceding pages; each paragraph is an organized block in the whole structure of the composition.

3. The writer uses transitional devices to link his paragraphs and to carry the reader smoothly from one unit of the composition into the next. A good writer is like a man who knows just where he is going, attended by a friend who is in a dark and unfamiliar area. In this analogy, transitions are ways of saying "turn right" or "turn left" or "now we go straight ahead for a while," and the reader is like a blind man whose mental steps the writer is directing. One of the marks of the skillful writer is the deft and unobtrusive use of transitions. Common transitional devices are: (a) concluding a paragraph with a sentence which introduces the next phase of the discussion; (b) using in the first sentence of a new paragraph a connective like *therefore, in addition, on the contrary;* (c) beginning a paragraph with a sentence that refers clearly, perhaps by pronoun references or the repetition of key words, or synonyms, to material in the preceding paragraph. The passage below consists of the last two sentences of a paragraph and the opening sentence of the following paragraph. The transitional devices are italicized.

So regarded, the term democracy refers primarily to a form of government, and it has always meant government by the many as opposed to government by the one—government by the people as opposed to government by a tyrant, a dictator, or an absolute monarch. This is the most *general meaning* of the *word* as men have commonly understood *it*.

In *this antithesis* there are, *however*, certain implications, always tacitly understood, which give a *more precise meaning* to *the term*.—CARL L. BECKER, *Modern Democracy*

4. The writer may use brief summaries or restatement to emphasize his central idea, to conclude a major division of his discussion, or to establish the relationship between parts of the material.

Being alert to any such signals which the writer provides will help the reader to follow the development of the composition.

III. AUDIENCE, ASSUMPTIONS, TONE, PERSONA

Sometimes unconsciously, but more often consciously, the writer makes certain assumptions about his audience. His readers are, for example, knowledgeable about his subject or they are uninformed; they consider his subject important or they need to be persuaded that it is important to them; they are likely to be receptive to his ideas or they are likely to be hostile; they will respond to subtleties of wit and irony or they will be confused by such subtleties. Effective communication depends, as Cardinal Newman pointed out, on initial agreements, "tacit understandings," between reader and writer. In so far as he can, the able writer needs to determine what attitudes or shared beliefs or interests he can safely count on and use as a starting point for further discussion. If he anticipates opposition to his ideas, he may try to establish initial agreements of another kind—for example, common interests in other areas, or the agreement that unorthodox ideas deserve a hearing; he may use interest-arousing devices, such as an opening anecdote or a startling initial statement or question to capture the reader's attention and persuade him to read on. When a communication is to be spoken (as some of the readings in this book were), the writer may make further assumptions in the light of the occasion: his audience will expect a formal address, or they will expect an informal discussion; the occasion calls for the establishing of an easy, personal relationship with the audience, or it does not. All such assumptions will help to shape what we have earlier called the psychological order or the strategy of the composition, and they will profoundly influence the writer's style and his tone.

Tone may be defined as the manner of verbal expression that a speaker or writer adopts. It is the expression of his attitudes toward his audience, himself, and his material. For example, his attitude toward his audience may be friendly or reserved; his attitude toward himself may be overconfident or modest; his attitude toward his material may be enthusiastic or indignant, emotional or objective. In expressing his attitude toward his subject a writer consciously or unconsciously slants his material by the way he selects facts, words, and emphasis to produce a favorable or unfavorable response. Slanting, whether blatant and deliberate or subtle and perhaps even unintentional, can be examined by studying the author's bias in selecting or omitting facts, his preference for favorably or unfavorably charged words (a politician may be called a "patriot" or a "demagogue"), and his use of proportion and position in developing his ideas to achieve the desired emphasis.

Related to tone is the *persona*—the "voice," the role, the personality, which, consciously or unconsciously, the writer adopts in a particular communication. The writer, of course, may be, and often is, simply himself, honestly expressing his views. "Self," however, is many-sided; we all have various selves, some consciously, some unconsciously, revealed; we have the capacity for looking at a subject in different ways, with different selves. President Kennedy, for example, parodied his own famous Inaugural Address—"ask not what . . . ask . . . "—at a Democratic fund-raising dinner. His serious address revealed his serious, idealistic side, and his fund-raising speech revealed his sense of humor. Thus a writer, without dishonesty or hypocrisy, may write dispassionately on something about which he has strong feelings: his analytic self dominates his emotional self for the purposes of his communication. An angry man may adopt the role of a reasonable man; he may deliberately understate in order to avoid the appearance of overstating. A writer sometimes assumes a personality wholly unlike his own, seeming to approve when he actually disapproves; in this case he trusts his readers to see through the assumed persona, to perceive and appreciate his irony, and so to share his real attitudes. Persona is the writer's presence in a piece of writing, his revelation of himself, of which the perceptive reader is aware.

IV. STYLE

Style is compounded of many elements, including the writer's personality, his way of thinking, his conscious or unconscious slanting, his tone, his choice of words, his arrangement of words, the length and rhythm of his sentences. We shall suggest here some of the characteristics which the good reader notices as he analyzes a writer's style in relation to the writer's ideas.[1] Many of these aspects of style are interdependent and overlapping; and some may be conspicuously present, subtly present, or even conspicuously absent in a particular piece of writing.

The general formality or informality of the style and its appropriateness to the writer's material. Vocabulary, sentence structure, and length of sentences are important elements in this quality of style. So are the writer's tone and sometimes, specifically, his use of contractions and his use of pronouns (*I, you, we, one*), which are part of the persona. The following passage about a boy and his colt is an example of informal style:

Yes, conceit. I was full of it, and the colt was quite as bad. One day my chum Hjalmar came into town on his Black Bess, blanketed. She had had a great fistula cut out of her shoulder and had to be kept warm. I expected to see her weak and dull, but no, the good old mare was champing and dancing, like my colt.

"What is it makes her so?" I asked, and Hjalmar said he didn't know, but he thought she was proud of the blanket. A great idea. I had a gaudy horse blanket. I put it on the colt, and I could hardly hold her. We rode down the main street together, both horses, and both boys, so full of vanity that everybody stopped to smile. We thought they admired, and maybe they did. But some boys on the street gave us another angle. They, too, stopped and looked, and as we passed, one of them said, "Think you're hell, don't you?"

Spoilsport!

[1] Any unfamiliar terms used in this discussion are defined in the Glossary, pages 507–511.

We did, as a matter of fact; we thought we were hell.—*The Autobiography of Lincoln Steffens*

The following paragraph, on a very different subject, illustrates a much more formal style. The author uses longer sentences, a more formal vocabulary, and, particularly, more complex sentence structures, including sustained parallelism and appositive structures.

In the long history of man on earth there comes a time when he remembers something of what has been, anticipates something that will be, knows the country he has traversed, wonders what lies beyond—the moment when he becomes aware of himself as a lonely, differentiated item in the world. Sooner or later there emerges for him the most devastating of all facts, namely, that in an indifferent universe which alone endures, he alone aspires, endeavors to attain, and attains only to be defeated in the end. From that moment his immediate experience ceases to be adequate, and he endeavors to project himself beyond it by creating ideal worlds of semblance, Utopias of other time or place in which all has been, may be, or will be well.—CARL L. BECKER, *Modern Democracy*

Sentence length and variety in length. In the first of the passages quoted above, the sentences are either very short or are of medium length; in the second, the sentences are consistently long. The able writer usually varies his sentence length, not necessarily in a single passage, but in the whole composition, and often for purposes of emphasis. A short sentence among long ones, for example, is given emphasis by contrast. In the following passage, a complex sentence of more than seventy words is followed by a simple six-word sentence.

Were nature constant in her intentions we might hope to understand them, but how at odds with herself this Lady Bountiful, mother of all living, when she counsels one species of her own creation, providing an armoury the most ingenious, claws and fangs and suckers, instruments of death, that one tribe of her offspring might the better murder the members of another, a device, to our poor uninstructed vision, neither lovely nor divine. Nature is no believer in disarmament.—W. MACNEILE DIXON, *The Human Situation*

Sentence structure and variety in structure. Variety in structure as well as in length is illustrated in the preceding passage. Skillful writers avoid monotony; they vary their structures by intermingling loose and periodic sentences; by using parallel and balanced constructions as a change from simpler constructions; by use and arrangement of subordinate clauses, modifiers, and appositive structures; by occasional departures from the normal subject–verb–object order of English sentences. Conspicuous use of any of these rhetorical techniques can be a distinguishing mark of a writer's style.

The first of the following sentences about the Emperor Marcus Aurelius, an example of formal nineteenth-century prose, is an elaborate periodic sentence; the second is a simple loose sentence with a short introductory modifier:

Inasmuch then as the theology of Christianity did not appear to him true or of divine origin; inasmuch as this strange history of a crucified God was not credible to him, and a system which purported to rest entirely upon a foundation to him so wholly unbelievable, could not be foreseen by him to be that renovating agency which, after all abatements, it has in fact proved to be; the gentlest and most amiable of philosophers and rulers, under a solemn sense of duty, authorized the persecution of Christianity. To my mind this is one of the most tragical facts in all history.—JOHN STUART MILL, *On Liberty*

In the following passage, an example of less formal modern style, the first and third sentences begin with subject–verb; the second, longer sentence has three parallel phrases and begins with a subordinate clause:

I am not able, and I do not want, completely to abandon the world view that I acquired in childhood. So long as I remain alive and well I shall continue to feel strongly about prose style, to love the surface of the earth, and to take a pleasure in solid objects and scraps of useless information. It is no use trying to suppress that side of myself.—GEORGE ORWELL, "Why I Write"

The following sentence, part of Winston Churchill's report on the evacuation of Dunkirk in World War II, further illustrates parallel phrasing and also a high degree of subordination and modification:

I have, myself, full confidence that if all do their duty, if nothing is neglected, and if the best arrangements are made, as they are being made, we shall prove ourselves once again able to defend our Island home, to ride out the storm of war, and to outlive the menace of tyranny, if necessary for years, if necessary alone.

Triple parallel constructions, called triads, which are more characteristic of formal than of informal style, are noticeable in the preceding sentence in the three *if* clauses (*if all* . . . , *if nothing* . . . , *if the best arrangements* . . . .) and in the three infinitive phrases (*to defend* . . . , *to ride* . . . , *to outlive* . . . .).

In the passage below, the first three sentences are similarly constructed, on a pattern of contrast or antithesis. The last two sentences illustrate inversion, or departure from conventional sentence order: three objects (*almanac, solstice, equinox*) precede the subject and verb. The whole passage builds effectively to a climax with the three clauses in the last sentence and the figure of speech at the end.

The civilized man has built a coach, but has lost the use of his feet. He is supported on crutches, but lacks so much support of muscle. He has a fine Geneva watch, but he fails of the skill to tell the hour by the sun. A Greenwich nautical almanac he has, and so being sure of the information when he wants it, the man in the street does not know a star in the sky. The solstice he does not observe, the equinox he knows as little; and the whole bright calendar of the year is without a dial in his mind.—RALPH WALDO EMERSON, "Self-Reliance"

The first of the three sentences below begins, not with the subject, but with an adverb and part of the verb, and ends with parallel phrases. The second is an example of balance and antithesis. In the third, the main verb and the object twice precede the subject. Words taken out of their normal order and placed at the beginning or the end of a sentence are given emphasis by their unconventional position. Try rearranging the sentence elements in this passage, beginning each sentence or clause with its subject and verb, to see what emphasis is gained by the inverted order.

Never have the nations of the world had so much to lose or so much to gain. Together we shall save our planet or together we shall perish in its flames. Save it we can, and save it we must, and then shall we earn the eternal thanks of mankind and, as peacemakers, the eternal blessing of God.—JOHN F. KENNEDY, Address to the United Nations, September 25, 1961.

It is possible, of course, to overuse some of the rhetorical devices we have been illustrating. An appropriate simplicity can also be a characteristic of good style.

Repetition. Needless and wordy repetition of words or ideas is the mark of the incompetent rather than the competent writer. Skillful repetition, however, can impress key words and phrases on the reader's mind, bind together the parts of a paragraph or composition, and create emotional effects. Skillful repetition of words is illustrated in the passage above from President Kennedy's address to the United Nations: *so much ... so much, Together ... together, Save it ... save it, eternal ... eternal.* Parallel structures and effectively repeated sentence patterns are also techniques of repetition for emphasis and rhythm.

In the passage below, the author doubly emphasizes his main idea of simplicity by the repetition of words in very short sentences. (This passage is a good example, too, of variety in sentence length and sentence structure.)

Our life is frittered away by detail. An honest man has hardly need to count more than his ten fingers, or in extreme cases he may add his ten toes, and lump the rest. Simplicity, simplicity, simplicity! I say, let your affairs be as two or three, and not a hundred or a thousand; instead of a million count half a dozen, and keep your accounts on your thumb-nail. In the midst of this chopping sea of civilized life, such are the clouds and storms and quicksands and thousand-and-one items to be allowed for, that a man has to live, if he would not founder and go to the bottom and not make his port at all, by dead reckoning, and he must be a great calculator indeed who succeeds. Simplify, simplify.

Instead of three meals a day, if it be necessary eat but one; instead of a hundred dishes, five; and reduce other things in proportion.—HENRY DAVID THOREAU, *Walden*

Repetition of words and structures is used for a different effect in the following paragraph; the sentence rhythms imitate the "tick-tock deliberation" of the clock:

In many a country cottage over the land, a tall old clock in a quiet corner told time in a tick-tock deliberation. Whether the orchard branches hung with pink-spray blossoms or icicles of sleet, whether the outside news was seedtime or harvest, rain or drought, births or deaths, the swing of the pendulum was right and left and right and left in a tick-tock deliberation.—CARL SANDBURG, *Abraham Lincoln: The War Years*

The prose writer, like the poet, may also use repeated patterns of sound, such as alliteration,.for special effects; a brief example is the repetition of *l* sounds in this excerpt from President Kennedy's Inaugural Address: "*l*et us go forth to *l*ead the *l*and we *l*ove."

Abstract and concrete language. Abstract words generally name qualities (*intelligence, honor*), concepts (*evolution, scientific method*), and conditions (*poverty, insanity*). Concrete words generally refer to things that exist in the physical world and can be perceived by the senses: *chair, apple, light bulb, rose bush*. Abstract words are necessary in language for expressing general ideas and arriving at judgments and conclusions; frequently, however, they do not have the same meaning for different people, and highly abstract language may leave the reader with only a vague impression of what the writer had in mind. Concrete words and details give supporting facts, statistics, reasons, and examples; they answer such questions as: What kind? What color? How large? How far? How many? Why? In what way? What is an illustration? The good writer therefore communicates his meaning by judicious choice and combination of abstract and concrete language. The good reader judges the effectiveness of the details by which abstractions are supported, clarified, illustrated, or defined.

Figurative language is often used to make a general and abstract idea clear and vivid by associating it with something concrete and familiar. The most common figures of speech are simile—a nonliteral comparison usually introduced by *like* or *as*: "Still we live meanly, *like ants*"; metaphor—an implied nonliteral comparison: "Time is *but the stream I go a-fishing in*"; and analogy—a sustained comparison of two dissimilar ideas or situations. Adlai E. Stevenson, on hearing of the death of Eleanor Roosevelt, said:

She would rather light candles than curse the darkness, and her glow has warmed the world.

The figurative statement, with its extension of the meaning of *light* in *glow* and *warmed*, evokes images and feeling; it concentrates meaning. Compare a literal and colorless statement like "She was not content to complain about things as they are and do nothing about them; she worked successfully in small ways to benefit the world." Figurative language is a marked trait of some styles and not of others; but it is more common in good prose, and a greater contributor to good prose, than many people realize.

Diction. This large term may cover much of what we have been discussing in the preceding pages. We shall use it here to refer to the writer's choice of words: the exactness of his words in denotation and connotation; the economy of his expression—economy not in the sense of brevity but in the sense of his choice of words that work, that warrant the space they take in the sentence; his fresh combinations of words; his use of factual or of emotionally charged language and its appropriateness to content; his choice of words for purposes of wit, humor, or irony.

Diction must be judged, of course, in the context of the whole composition and of the author's intention and tone; but even in brief passages the reader may have an immediate sense of the rightness of the author's words. We have quoted earlier a passage from Carl L. Becker, part of which is "the moment when he [man] becomes aware of himself as a lonely, differentiated item in the world." *Lonely* and *differentiated* do not have the same meaning: *lonely* suggests man's emotion, his unhappiness in his isolation, *differentiated* his sense of difference from other species; together the words carry complex meaning; and *item*, in addition to continuing the idea of separateness in *differentiated*, further connotes insignificance and depersonalization. When Winston Churchill said, ". . . we shall prove ourselves once again able to defend our Island home," *prove ourselves* (rather than "find ourselves") suggested meeting a test and establishing a truth; *once again* was a reminder that the British people had met tests before; and *Island home* had a deeper emotional meaning than "country" or "land," and also suggested, perhaps, the presence of the sea as a protective barrier. In the sentences below, spoken at a memorial service for Winston Churchill, one of the eloquent speakers of the twentieth century paid tribute to another. One feels that the words, the combinations of words, and the image at the end all are exactly right.

We shall hear no longer the remembered eloquence and wit, the old courage and defiance, the robust serenity of indomitable faith. Our world is thus poorer, our political dialogue is diminished, and the sources of public inspiration run more thinly for all of us. There is a lonesome place against the sky.—ADLAI E. STEVENSON, January 28, 1965

Emphasis. We have mentioned earlier several techniques of emphasis: the use of slanting and charged language; the use of the emphatic short sentence among longer ones; the emphasis given a word when it is moved from its normal position to the beginning or end of a sentence; and controlled repetition of structures, words, or ideas.

In general, beginnings and endings are important. A classic piece of advice to inexperienced writers is: "Strike out your first paragraph, strike out your last paragraph, and strike out your favorite sentence." *Favorite sentence* refers to the falsely eloquent or pretentious sentence of which the writer may be unjustly proud; and the advice about paragraphs usually means that the conclusion is a weak summary of the content of a short paper and that the opening paragraph is a dull and wasted leading up to the subject. Experienced writers use their beginning paragraphs for one or more of these purposes: to launch vigorously and directly into the subject, to arouse interest, to establish an appropriate tone or writer–audience relationship. Although some of the readings in this book are excerpts from longer works, many of them are complete essays and addresses; when they are, the author's beginning, and his probable reasons for using the emphatic opening position as he does, are worth particular consideration.

The end-position is usually even more emphatic than the beginning. The strongest sentences build to a climax; the writer uses the ending, followed by the period-pause, for a word, a phrase, or an idea which he wishes to emphasize. Good paragraphs, too, are likely to end strongly; and chapters and whole compositions end with the idea—sometimes a restatement of the main theme—which the writer wants to impress on the reader's mind. Part of analytical reading is noting the writer's ending, considering his emphasis, and thinking about how logically his conclusion is derived from the preceding material or for what psychological reasons he gave major emphasis to his concluding statements.

Within sections of the composition, too, one may observe a climactic order. If the author is giving a series of arguments or examples, why has he arranged them as he has? Is his arrangement dictated by logic, or is it the most emphatic psychological order?

Emphasis is also achieved by proportion—by the amount of space, the length of development, given to parts of the material. The writer generally gives something like equal development to ideas or aspects of the subject which seem to him of equal significance and the fullest development to his most significant ideas. The attentive reader is aware of proportion; at times he may ask himself why the writer has chosen to give emphasis by development to certain parts of the material and whether his reasons are primarily logical or psychological.

In the analysis of narrative writing, the term *pace* is commonly used to refer to the proportions of summary and presentation. Summary is general statement which gives the net result of action; presentation is the dramatic development of scenes, in which characters, in a setting, speak and act. The skillful writer of narrative usually quickens his pace by summarizing, and so de-emphasizing, unimportant events; he slows his pace to present and give emphasis to significant actions and experiences. In a somewhat different sense, one may speak of the pace or movement of a piece of expository writing. When, for example, the writer develops an illustration at length or supplies numerous instances or concrete details to support a generalization, he may do so in order to be clear, interesting, or convincing; but he is also emphasizing the point to which he is giving this full development.

V. READING FOR IDEAS AND STYLE

Some of the most able students who come to college have read widely but superficially. They have not had the experience of reading in depth; and, called upon to do close analytical reading of complex material, they may have one or more of these difficulties: missing main ideas or confusing minor points with major points; failing to see the connections between points and being unclear about the broad development of the theme or idea; not understanding, or misunderstanding, the author's vocabulary and so missing the meaning of sections of the material. Although no simple remedy can be prescribed for these weaknesses, many students improve their reading when they adopt a systematic method of reading for study. One practical method consists of two stages. The first is reading the material through to see the whole development, without stopping to puzzle long over difficult passages, to look up words, to underline, or to take notes. (Students sometimes block themselves in reading—and also lose the thread of thought—by delaying over a passage that will be clarified by the later context; and they are not in a good position to underline or to take notes until they know what ideas are most significant.) This first reading should be as rapid as is consistent with the student's general comprehension of the material, and the reading should be continuous, to give a sense of the sequence and relationship of ideas. The second step is careful re-reading, in which the student examines the development of the main ideas, studies the texture of thought, is attentive to the author's language and tone, and works out the meaning of difficult passages. He may need to consult his dictionary in order to understand the author's words or allusions; more often he needs to study the context and the author's explanation of troublesome terms. If the reader is using his own book, he may be wise in this stage of reading to underline important ideas or to develop a system of marginal notation or numbering which shows the relationship between ideas. Part of this attentive re-reading should be active thought about the material presented.

Another common difficulty in reading comes from twisting the writer's words, distorting the meaning because it is alien or uncongenial to the reader. Not able to believe that anyone could hold such views, the reader reads what he wants to read instead of what is written. Reading Plato's *Symposium* without understanding the Greek attitude toward homosexual love, or reading an essay based on the assumption that "God is dead," or reading a discussion of the unreality of the phenomenal world, students have at times been led by their disbelief or disapproval into reading something the author has not intended and has not said. This difficulty stems, basically, less from habits of reading than from attitudes, habits of mind.

What are the attitudes, the obligations, and the pleasures or satisfactions of the good reader?

His first attitude should be curiosity, openness to new points of view, and willingness to suspend judgment until he has understood and thought about the writer's ideas. His first obligation, therefore, is to be fair to the writer and to make a real effort to understand exactly what is said. In trying to understand, he will be aided by a method of study like the one suggested early in this section. He may also find it helpful to outline complex pieces of writing and to form the habit of summarizing in his own words the writer's central ideas and the sequence of ideas. Sometimes a piece of writing (usually argument or persuasion) can be very briefly summarized in the form of a syllogism or a series of syllogisms. A syllogism is a three-part statement consisting of two premises and a conclusion drawn from the premises. For example:

> Men cut off from the past lose a sense of personal identity. (Major premise)
> Modern man is cut off from the past. (Minor premise)
> Therefore, modern man has lost a sense of personal identity. (Conclusion)

Phrasing such syllogisms, when it is possible to do so, may clarify the author's argument and also enable the reader to think about how, and how convincingly, the writer has established his premises and how valid his conclusion is.

Full understanding of a piece of writing may depend, however, on more than an ability to summarize the factual content, important though that is. Understanding may depend, for example, on awareness of the context of circumstances—the time, the occasion, the type of audience for whom the communication was written.[2] Such knowledge may help to explain the author's assumptions, the kind of language and illustration he chooses, and his tone. The reader also, in so far as he can, needs to determine the author's intention. On the surface, the author may be analyzing or giving information; but he may at the same time want his readers to respond in

[2] In the headnotes to the readings we have supplied some of this information.

certain ways, and he uses words to evoke feelings and attitudes as well as to inform. "Serious" writing is not always consistently serious in tone; the writer may use humor, irony, overstatement, or understatement as devices of persuasion. The reader misreads when he misunderstands the full intention and takes with deadly literalness what is meant to be facetious, ironical, or deliberately extravagant.

If, after his best efforts to understand a piece of writing, the reader still finds himself perplexed by parts of it, he may well consider another attitude and obligation of the good reader. The poet Coleridge phrased this "golden rule": "Until you understand a writer's ignorance, presume yourself ignorant of his understanding." Coleridge, reading one of Plato's Dialogues, found unintelligible passages in it and thought of dismissing the meaningless portions as Platonic jargon. But then he recalled his delight with the wisdom in Plato's other writing; he remembered passages in Plato, now thoroughly comprehensible, which had once seemed equally unintelligible; and he considered the reverence accorded Plato by the numerous great men who had studied his works. Unable to resolve the inconsistency of Plato's genius and a use of meaningless words, Coleridge wrote, "Therefore, utterly baffled in all my attempts to understand the ignorance of Plato, *I conclude myself ignorant of his understanding.*"[3] In marked contrast is the pronouncement of a college freshman: "Plato is dull."

The good reader, then, is receptive and willing to credit the writer with having something to say that is worth understanding; but he is also critical in his reading. He judges the fundamental clarity (as distinct from the immediate transparency), the interest, and the logic of the writer's presentation. He knows that good logicians do not make sweeping statements without needed qualifications; do not base generalizations on too few examples; do not rest their cases on unsupported assumptions that an audience is unlikely to accept; do not use words in special senses without defining them; do not distort meaning by taking statements out of their context; do not use analogies (excellent devices for clarifying or persuading) as substitutes for solid argument or proof. The critical reader considers the appropriateness and effectiveness of language, examples, tone, and emphasis, in the light of what he knows of the circumstances and the author's intention. Finally, having understood as fully as possible and thought about the material, the reader makes a personal evaluation—of the appeal, the interest, the worth, or the truth of this communication for him.

We have not spoken directly of the pleasures or satisfactions of good reading, though some of them have been implied: the satisfaction of understanding; the satisfaction of encountering ideas which may give

[3] *Biographia Literaria,* Chapter XII.

form to the unexpressed thoughts of the reader or which may challenge him, disturb him, but open new vistas of thought; the satisfaction of arriving at sound judgments, of weighing conflicting values and making choices of one's own—for awareness of alternatives increases freedom of choice; the pleasure in language used well. Above all, perhaps, the good reader has the pleasure, even excitement, of seeing a mind at work— a clever, or good, or great mind, thinking; ordering ideas; qualifying, supporting, amplifying; selecting the words, the sentence patterns, the tone, and the emphasis to communicate his meaning to another mind. The reader may be chiefly impressed by a writer's thought, or chiefly impressed by his personality or his craft or art. The very best prose reflects the whole man—reason, imagination, character, and feeling; in it the good reader discovers a harmonious fusion of mind and manner, ideas and style.

PART ONE

*Ways of Ordering Ideas
and Experience*

THESIS AND EXAMPLES

[1] *James Thurber*: Which

JAMES THURBER (1894–1961) was an American essayist, well known, particularly to readers of *The New Yorker*, for his witty and satiric prose pieces and drawings. His books include *My Life and Hard Times, The Middle-Aged Man on the Flying Trapeze, Let Your Mind Alone, Fables for Our Time, My World—and Welcome to It, Thurber Country*, and *Alarms and Diversions*. "Which" is a section of "Ladies' and Gentlemen's Guide to Modern English Usage," published in 1929 in *The New Yorker*. The reference to Fowler in the opening sentences is to H. W. Fowler, whose *Dictionary of Modern English Usage* Thurber is quoting.

[1] The relative pronoun "which" can cause more trouble than any other word, if recklessly used. Foolhardy persons sometimes get lost in which-clauses and are never heard of again. My distinguished contemporary, Fowler, cites several tragic cases, of which the following is one: "It was rumoured that Beaconsfield intended opening the Conference with a speech in French, his pronunciation of which language leaving everything to be desired . . ." That's as much as Mr. Fowler quotes because, at his age, he was afraid to go any farther. The young man who originally got into that sentence was never found. His fate, however, was not as terrible as that of another adventurer who became involved in a remarkable which-mire. Fowler has followed his devious course as far as he safely could on foot: "Surely what applies to games should also apply to racing, the leaders of which being the very people from whom an example might well be looked for . . ." Not even Henry James could have successfully emerged from a sentence with "which," "whom," and "being"

21

in it. The safest way to avoid such things is to follow in the path of the American author, Ernest Hemingway. In his youth he was trapped in a which-clause one time and barely escaped with his mind. He was going along on solid ground until he got into this: "It was the one thing of which, being very much afraid—for whom has not been warned to fear such things—he . . ." Being a young and powerfully built man, Hemingway was able to fight his way back to where he had started, and begin again. This time he skirted the treacherous morass in this way: "He was afraid of one thing. This was the one thing. He had been warned to fear such things. Everybody has been warned to fear such things." Today Hemingway is alive and well, and many happy writers are following along the trail he blazed.

[2] What most people don't realize is that one "which" leads to another. Trying to cross a paragraph by leaping from "which" to "which" is like Eliza crossing the ice. The danger is in missing a "which" and falling in. A case in point is this: "He went up to a pew which was in the gallery, which brought him under a colored window which he loved and always quieted his spirit." The writer, worn out, missed the last "which"—the one that should come just before "always" in that sentence. But supposing he had got it in! We would have: "He went up to a pew which was in the gallery, which brought him under a colored window which he loved and which always quieted his spirit." Your inveterate whicher in this way gives the effect of tweeting like a bird or walking with a crutch, and is not welcome in the best company.

[3] It is well to remember that one "which" leads to two and that two "whiches" multiply like rabbits. You should never start out with the idea that you can get by with one "which." Suddenly they are all around you. Take a sentence like this: "It imposes a problem which we either solve, or perish." On a hot night, or after a hard day's work, a man often lets himself get by with a monstrosity like that, but suppose he dictates that sentence bright and early in the morning. It comes to him typed out by his stenographer and he instantly senses that something is the matter with it. He tries to reconstruct the sentence, still clinging to the "which," and gets something like this: "It imposes a problem which we either solve, or which, failing to solve, we must perish on account of." He goes to the water cooler, gets a drink, sharpens his pencil, and grimly tries again. "It imposes a problem which we either solve or which we don't solve and . . ." He begins once more: "It imposes a problem which we either solve, or which we do not solve, and from which . . ." The more times he does it the more "whiches" he gets. The way out is simple: "We must either solve this problem, or perish." Never monkey with "which." Nothing except getting tangled up in a typewriter ribbon is worse.

‑‑∙₰(COMMENT AND QUESTIONS)₰∙‑‑

1. The author states his general thesis in his opening sentence and restates it in his final sentences. What particular kinds of trouble with *which* do his further statements and his examples emphasize or clarify?
2. What assumptions is Thurber making about the readers of this essay?
3. Examine the diction in paragraph 1. What is the effect of the expressions *recklessly, foolhardy, tragic cases, His fate . . . was not as terrible, barely escaped with his mind?* "Foolhardy persons sometimes get lost in which-clauses" introduces a sustained figure of speech. What is the implied comparison, and what expressions carry it through the paragraph?
4. Is the comparison at the beginning of paragraph 2 related to the sustained figure in paragraph 1? Explain.
5. How might the illustrative sentence in paragraph 2 (*He went up to a pew . . . .*) be improved?
6. Examine the last sentence of paragraph 2. What are the connotations of *inveterate whicher?* What are the suggestions of *tweeting like a bird* and *walking with a crutch?* Does the sentence end strongly?
7. *Multiply like rabbits* in the first sentence of paragraph 3 is ordinarily a cliché. What keeps it from seeming trite in this context?
8. In paragraph 3 Thurber shifts to direct address to the reader (*You should never*) and to imperative mood (*Take a sentence . . . . Never monkey with "which"*). In the sentence beginning *On a hot night*, however, he shifts to third person. Why do you think he makes these shifts?
9. What is the effect of the final sentence of the essay?
10. Revise the following which-mire:
    This article, which comes from *Ladies' and Gentlemen's Guide to Modern English Usage*, which was published in 1929, was written by James Thurber, who was a contributor to *The New Yorker* in which magazine appeared many of his stories and drawings which depict human beings who are caught in a society which is frustrating.

THESIS AND REASONS

[2] *Geoffrey Crowther*: Two Heresies

SIR GEOFFREY CROWTHER (1907–) is an English economist and journalist, former editor of *The Economist*, and Chairman of the Central Advisory Council for Education (in England) from 1956 to 1960. In June, 1960, he received an honorary LL.D. degree from the University of Michigan and delivered, on that occasion, the following commencement address.

[1] Mr. President, Regents of the University, members of the faculty, fellow graduates, ladies and gentlemen: I have been coming to Ann Arbor, on and off, for more than thirty years. I have made many friendships here. I have played some part in sending you a steady stream of graduate students from my own country. I have watched with affection and amazement the gigantic growth of this great institution. Of all the state universities of America, this is the one where I feel most at home.

[2] Yet never in my wildest moments did I dream that I should be admitted to the dignity of becoming an honorary graduate of The University of Michigan, and I am still overwhelmed by it. It is impossible to stand here, in this great stadium, before such a gathering, surrounded as we are by the spreading buildings of a great campus, without feelings of deep emotion, of humility, but also of pride, to know that one is to be a member of your body. I know that in this I can speak for all my fellow honorary graduates. In the words of the Prayer Book, for being made partakers in all this, we give you most humble and hearty thanks.

[3] On me you have conferred the supreme privilege of being permitted

to address you. I would not for the world miss the honor. But it carries a very heavy burden with it. For what can be said in a commencement address that has not been said a thousand times before? Shall I extol the glories of the tradition of learning that leads from the monks' cells of the Middle Ages to the great universities of today? Those glories would gain nothing from anything I could say. Shall I sound the alarm for academic freedom? It seems to me to be in less danger today than at many other times. Should I perhaps address myself exclusively to the graduating class? Should I preach the ancient moral virtues to you? It would be an impertinence. Should I remind you of your duty to the community that has done so much for you? It would be an insult. Should I take the oldest and most shopworn theme of all, and remind you that this is a commencement, a beginning, not an ending? You wouldn't listen to me if I did. Should I try to give you the only thing that the old can give to the young—that is, the fruits of experience? But the chief thing you learn from experience is that no one will learn from other people's experience. No, members of the class of 1960, I can do nothing for you. The campuses of the country have been ringing all week long with high moral sentiments, and I haven't the heart to try to add to them.

[4] I must presume, Mr. President, that you had some deliberate purpose in choosing for your speaker this afternoon a foreigner—and one, moreover, who has been engaged for some years past in an intensive study of the educational system of his own country. I read in that a hint that you wanted to hear something of what an American university looks like from the outside to one who has been put by chance in the position to make some comparison between American universities and those of other countries. If that is your wish, I shall try to comply.

[5] But even then my dilemma is not quite resolved. Should I speak only of what I admire in the American university? That, indeed, would be easy. The words would come quickly to my mouth, because I spend so much of my time when I am at home in England pressing on our own universities some of your practices. I admire so much your generosity—not only your generosity of money, but your generosity of spirit, your deep sense of service to the community, the way you convince the individual—be he freshman or doctor—that you exist to serve him, not he to serve the institution. I admire the way you are forever breaking down the barriers between you and the rest of the community—not hiding behind hedges of aloofness and superiority, as too many of the academic institutions in my own country do. I admire the eagerness with which the pursuit of knowledge is carried on here. In Europe one is sometimes made to feel that the pursuit is over, that knowledge has been caught and tamed and made to live comfortably ever after. I admire the structure of graduate schools superimposed on a liberal arts college—a structure that, in my opinion, we should do well to adopt in England.

[⁶] There is so much to admire. But it would be a poor compliment to you to assume that all you wanted to hear was praise. The purpose of an address, after all, is communication from one mind to another, and if I am to succeed in setting you thinking, I must give you something to think about. So as I pondered what I would say to you this afternoon, I slowly screwed up my courage to the conviction that I can best return the compliment you pay me by telling of some of the things in the American university to which, in my opinion, you should be giving your serious critical attention. Having so often landed into trouble at home for singing the praises of the American university too loud, I had better run the risk of getting into trouble here for the opposite reason. So I determined to pick out this afternoon a couple of points on which I find myself beset with doubts. I am the more emboldened to do this because they are points which, so far as I can observe, do not seem to disturb you. That is why I gave myself the title of "Two Heresies" because I am going to challenge what is usually taken for granted.

[⁷] Let me state my two heresies quite bluntly so that you will see what I am getting at, and then I will try to defend them one after the other. My first heresy is to think that there are too many college students. And my second heresy is to think that they work too hard.

[⁸] When I say that there are too many college students, I don't mean here, at Michigan. There are, indeed, a goodly number here, but I would not presume to say that there are too many. There is a great deal to be said for the small college. And there is a great deal also to be said for the big college—though it is less often said. From what I know of Michigan, I would not say that it is too big—not yet. In any case, that is not my argument. I am not arguing about big colleges and small colleges. I am asking whether, in the United States, as a whole, there are not too many college students altogether—whether the proportion of the population that goes to college is not too large.

[⁹] Now I know that it has always been one of the fundamental doctrines of the American people that there must be no special privileges, no select class, that every boy and girl has a right to go to college if he or she can make the grade and can find, borrow, or earn enough money to stay alive for four years. I am not challenging that great American principle. Heretic though I may be, I am not trying to preach any old-world doctrine of a privileged aristocracy. No, I am trying, now that I am to be admitted to your society, to be a good American democrat (with a small "d"). Certainly, the right exists. But then it always has existed. What is new within the past decade or so—what is new and different and doubtful —is the doctrine that almost every American boy or girl should be encouraged and assisted to claim his right. There is also a right to travel freely on the highway. But even in Michigan you can't all do it at once. Indeed, if you try to claim this right all at once the only result is that nobody gets any benefit from it. It is possible to believe passionately in the existence of a right, and yet to hope that not everyone will claim it.

[10] Where is the process of universal education to stop? Is everyone to go to school until he is twenty-five or thirty—or thirty-five? I have had no opportunity to go back to the statistics, but my impression is that college going, as a percentage of the age group, is now in this country just about where high-school going was two generations ago. Now you know what has happened to the high school. I believe the nation-wide figure is that 85 per cent of the eighteen-year-olds are in high school. The same thing is now visibly happening to college going. If you include the junior colleges, it won't be long before the proportion reaches the halfway mark, and there is no reason to suppose that it will stop there.

[11] In my observation most Americans seem to take it for granted that this is a good thing. Perhaps it is—but not self-evidently so. There must, after all, be a limit somewhere. There must be some age at which universal education—the keeping of everyone in school—should stop. Is it not conceivable that the limit has been reached?

[12] Why do I say this? Chiefly because of the effect this movement towards universal college education is having on the colleges themselves. I will single out two of its effects. The first is that it must be lowering the average intellectual standard of the colleges of the country as a whole. That follows almost mathematically. If the process goes on until every boy and girl is in college, then the average standard of intelligence in the colleges in the country as a whole will be an I.Q. of exactly 100, which is a great deal lower than it has been hitherto. I am no mathematician, and it is a matter of constant surprise to me to discover that as many as half of all the people in the country are below average in intelligence. I am completely assured, however, that it is so. And what is more, that even with all the resources of modern science, there is nothing that can be done about it.

[13] It cannot help the colleges if more and more of their students come to them not because of any genuine desire to continue their education in any real sense of the word, but because it is socially the thing to do. If this is the general picture, then colleges, like this one, which want to maintain and even improve their standards, are forced into being more and more selective. Every good college in the country is besieged by applicants and at its wit's end to know how to choose among them. I do not think that it is good for the front-rank colleges if everyone who gets in has the feeling that he has succeeded in going through the eye of the needle to get there. And I do not think it is good for the country. Thus this great democratic principle of everyone having a college education is in fact creating a new privileged class—those who manage to get a good college education.

[14] The second consequence is this—that if nearly everybody goes to college, then increasingly all those who aspire to enter the professions or the higher ranks of business and administration—in a word all those who want to follow one of the careers for which college used to be the preparation—all these are now forced to go to a graduate school as well. Now, as I said before, I have nothing but admiration for the graduate schools. But they were never intended to serve 15 or 20 per cent of the age group. Moreover, what will happen to them when more and more of their students are there, not because they have any real interest in more study, not even because what they learn will really be useful to them, but simply because they are under some compulsion to appear better educated—which is taken to mean longer educated—than the mass, simply because they can't get the sort of job they want without a second set of letters after their names?

[15] More and more careers, for this reason, and among the highest careers, cannot begin until the age of twenty-four—or even twenty-six or twenty-seven if there is selective service to be done. Now think what this means. I suppose one can say that active life—that is, the life of the conscious mind—begins at or about the age of six or seven when one learns to read. At the other end, retirement from gainful occupation is more and more being pushed down towards sixty. In other words, in the normal life, there are not much more than fifty years or so between infancy and retirement. Is it really good sense that for the intellectual leaders of the country—the most intelligent quarter of the whole—as many as twenty out of those fifty-plus years should be spent in learning and only a bit more than thirty in doing? Is that really a rational employment of the scarcest of all scarce resources—human talent? Isn't there something to be said for the view that there should be less preparation for life and more living? Is America right to keep its young longer and longer on the leash, and to rely for the productive work of the nation more and more on the middle-aged? Only a very rich country could do it at all. But is it a wise application of your riches? When it comes to fighting, the job has to be done by the young. Is war the only activity in which the qualities of youth are needed? Must we in everything else be studied, overtrained, and elderly?

[16] Let me quickly turn, before the brickbats begin to fly, to my second heresy. In saying that the student of today has to work too hard, I can, I think, reasonably anticipate the sympathy of at least part of my audience. But perhaps I don't mean quite what they think I mean.

[17] I was speaking just a moment ago of the pressure that the good colleges are under to defend their standards. It is their duty to do so. If it is a privilege to be admitted to one of these institutions of the first rank, then no student should be allowed to remain there who does not continue

to measure up to the highest standards. I am not criticizing this concern for standards. Indeed, I am supporting it.

[18] But how, by what means, have the standards been enforced and maintained? From what I see and hear, I suspect that far too many colleges are doing it by what is the easy way for them—by demanding an ever higher total of hours put in—of hours, what is more, that have to be devoted to doing what the professor says must be done. Assignments become heavier and are more rigorously enforced. I have no doubt at all that the student of today who wants to secure a good average has to work for much longer hours than he did thirty years ago, when I first knew the American colleges. I don't mean that the student of the last generation led an easy life. His mind was active for as many hours a day as now: But I do think that he didn't have his nose held so close to the grindstone of requirements. He was freer to roam and follow his fancy. Now, it seems to me, he goes very much more in harness. Indeed, I have heard the head of a famous institution—not in Michigan—openly boast that they weed out the weaklings in the first year, not by any considerations of intellectual capacity or promise, but by deliberately setting an almost impossibly heavy schedule of assigned study in order to see who can take it.

[19] Now this all seems to me to be a mistake. Let us indeed have high standards, the highest possible. But high standards of what? Of diligence? Or of intelligence? The two are by no means the same thing. Indeed, they can be, and I suspect often are, at variance with each other, since the high intelligence, the really original mind, is likely to be the first to revolt against a drudgery which, in his case at least, is pointless and unnecessary.

[20] Let us get back to the fundamentals. What does a university exist for? What is the purpose of education? Is it to absorb a defined quantity of instruction? Or to learn how to think? Is it to accumulate knowledge? Or to acquire understanding? No doubt you know the old comparison between the two different ways of regarding the student's mind. You can think of it either as a pitcher that has to be filled up with factual knowledge or as a fire that has to be set alight. Put it in that way, and the right choice, I think, immediately becomes clear. The proper question for educators to be asking themselves every day is not "Am I cramming my students with the proper facts?" but "Am I succeeding in setting their minds ablaze?" And we all know that what is needed for a good roaring blaze is plenty of fresh air.

[21] Please don't misunderstand me. I am not asking for soft options. I don't want the students to live lives of leisure. I want them to be under the heaviest pressure. I want them to lead the most vigorous and rigorous lives. I want them to have to meet the severest tests. But let them be tests of intellect, of understanding, of expression, of imagination, of judgment, of purpose—and not just of the ability to stay awake.

[22] I have one special reason for this plea. We hear a great deal nowadays of the danger of overspecialization, of the confining of the world of learning within narrow compartments which are unable, or unwilling, to say anything to each other. This is a real danger. There has been much discussion in my own country of the emergence of two cultures, the scientific and the humanitarian, which are increasingly separate from, and even hostile to, each other. I think this is an understatement of the danger. It is not two cultures with which we are threatened, but twenty-two. There is nothing in the world of learning more urgent than to find means of breaking down this separatism and moving back, so far as we can, to the time when educated men could travel in each other's territories without passports or interpreters. This is the authentic university tradition. It is indeed what the word means. Let us never forget that this great institution is a university. It ought not to be allowed to become a diversity.

[23] Now I am simple enough to believe that the way to get a meeting of minds is to let them meet. You cannot solve the problem by prescribing courses, chemistry for the historian, or aesthetics for the engineer. You can prescribe the course all right but you can't prescribe the interest in the subject which alone makes it worthwhile. The only way you can get a real cross-fertilization between the different disciplines is to give a generous allowance of time for people of varying interests to explore each other's minds. I would plead that everyone in a university, from the freshman to the president, should make himself much less busy. He will find as a result—of this I am sure—that his mind is much more active.

[24] I hope that I shall be forgiven for asking you to think about my two heresies. Of course, I have exaggerated them. I have been trying to use that powerful stimulus to thought, indignation. But why, after all, should I try to make you cross? There is, I repeat, so very much more to admire than to criticize. It is precisely because so much depends on the American universities that one wants to see them perfect. It is on you, more than on anyone else, that the hopes of liberal civilization in the world rest. You will remember that during the war the United States was often described as the arsenal of freedom—and how rightly. But the moral is in the long run so much more important than the material, and what will in the end determine the shape of the world in which our grandchildren live is not how many rockets or space ships or tanks America can build but the ideas to which Americans attach their faith. You attract to yourselves in your universities, and nowhere more than here in Michigan, so much of the best in the outside world and you give it back with such generosity. It is here that the links are forged that bind the free world together.

[25] So you must not think of me, I hope, as a critic, or even as a candid friend, but simply as the newest of your graduates, full of ambition for the growth in grace and power of his Alma Mater. My prayer for this

great university is the prayer that A. C. Benson uttered for his native country:

> Land of Hope and Glory, Mother of the Free!
> How can we extol thee, who are born of thee?
> Wider yet and wider may thy bounds be set,
> God, who made thee mighty, make thee mightier yet.

COMMENT AND QUESTIONS

1. Any commencement address is governed, in part, by certain established conventions: the speaker, in his introductory remarks, is expected to pay tribute to the college or university, to express gratitude for the honorary degree he is receiving, and to comment on the honor of being chosen to give the commencement address. Crowther observes all of these conventions, certainly, but he goes beyond them—both in the depth and extent of his expression of appreciation and in the extent of his introductory remarks: six paragraphs, approximately a fourth of the speech, precede the actual statement of his thesis. These paragraphs are in part logical preparation for the two heresies, but they also establish a psychological relationship with his audience. This is particularly important because the speaker, an Englishman, an outsider, proposes to criticize some theories and practices in American education. What kind of speaker–audience relationship is established in the first two paragraphs?
2. What is the purpose of paragraph 3—the enumeration of subjects that Crowther might discuss but will not?
3. Paragraphs 4 and 5 make an approach to the speaker's topic and also make a significant contribution to tone. What are the purposes in these paragraphs of the various references to the English system of education? Four sentences in paragraph 5 begin with "I admire." What keeps the sentences in this paragraph from being monotonous?
4. In paragraph 6, what attitudes toward his audience does the speaker express and imply? What attitudes toward himself? What persona has been revealed by the end of the first six paragraphs?
5. What possible misunderstandings of his first heresy is Crowther careful to remove? Comment on the effectiveness of his analogy of the right to go to college and the right to travel.
6. What are Crowther's reasons for thinking that the time may have come for the process of universal college education to stop? Much of this section of the speech has a cause–effect development. What are the effects of universal education as Crowther sees them? Why does he use repeated question-patterns at the end of paragraph 15 instead of making his points in declarative sentences?

7. Are Crowther's reasons for believing that there are too many college students convincing to you? The trend toward universal college education has, of course, increased in the years since this address was given. Would it be desirable to stop or to reverse the trend? Would it be practically possible to do so?
8. With his second heresy, as with his first, the speaker takes pains to correct possible misinterpretations. What kinds of high standards does he think the colleges have been inclined to adopt and enforce? What different high standards would he establish? What are his reasons for urging less busyness? What desirable effects would it produce? Do you find anything especially deft in the last two sentences of paragraph 22?
9. What is the purpose of education, according to Crowther, and what is "the authentic university tradition"? Do you think that decreased assigned work would indeed have the results he foresees?
10. Crowther's style is interesting and good in many ways. Examine paragraphs 19 and 21 to see one of his techniques of repeating and yet varying his sentence length and structure.
11. The last two paragraphs turn from criticism and return to the tone of the opening section of the address. What additional tribute does Crowther pay to American universities in paragraph 24? The closing prayer of A. C. Benson (an English writer, 1862–1925) was probably selected for its tone and the relationship of *Mother* and *Alma Mater*. What part of the prayer is also directly relevant to the central ideas of the address?
12. As you think about the whole speech, do you see any logical or psychological reasons for the order in which Crowther presents his two heresies?

GENERALIZATION
AND QUALIFICATION

[3] *Nils Y. Wessell*: The Opportunity for Change

NILS Y. WESSELL (1914–), whose doctoral degree is in psychology, was president of Tufts University from 1953 to 1966, and is now president of the Sloan Foundation. "The Opportunity for Change" was a matriculation address, given in September, 1965, to the entering members of the Tufts classes of 1969.

[1] If we were to assemble here this evening all of the joys and worries, all of the concerns and enthusiasms, and all of the hopes and doubts that have marked the months and years between your individual decisions to apply to Tufts and your arrival on this campus this week, they would fill this room and the cage beyond to overflowing. Add to these what your teachers and parents and other members of your family have experienced and all of the buildings of this University would not provide capacity enough. There is excitement in your finally being here, for all of us, your teachers and counselors who are the faculty and administration of Tufts, as well as for you. The reason is simple. Great hope and great promise combine as you begin an adventure which you have in your own power to make the most meaningful of your lives.

[2] I grant that some limits will be set on your accomplishments by factors not now possible of substantial modification, but I would urge you tonight and in the next year or two ahead of you that you seek to uncover

those ways in which your growth has not been predestined by what has gone before. This does not mean that I have cast off a bias of the last twenty-five years of my life which gives the nod to nature over nurture, to biology over psychology, to heredity over environment in the development of human traits and in the setting of goals and standards of achievement. What I am attempting to say is that even with whatever predestination you bring with you, biological or otherwise, there are opportunities for growth and maturation and achievement which, if anything, go beyond your present expectations.

[3] One form of predestination never did provide for me a compelling case. This is the Freudian notion that the experiences, traumatic and otherwise, of the first three or four years of life determine adult personality in a substantial and almost irrevocable way—at least irrevocable without psychoanalysis. I do not mean to denigrate early childhood experiences. In fact, there is much we need yet to learn about their role. What I do say is that such influences during infancy do not make impossible at age eighteen significant changes for the better and the development of personal qualities during the college years of a mature and healthy sort. In short, do not assume that it is too late to make fundamental changes in the level of your intellectual achievement or in your personal traits or in your sense of values or in your commitment to ideals. Granted that the change may be negative as well as positive. In the academic community, however, to quote the popular song of a generation ago, we "accentuate the positive."

[4] It is quite possible for you who are shy to develop social poise and confidence; for you who are a bit too arrogant to learn that a measure of humility is both more effective and more attractive; for you who are self-centered to learn the nobler pursuits stemming from a sense of social concern; for you who consider yourself fated to save the world to learn you must save yourself first; for you who would conform completely to the social and personal code of your contemporaries to know the rewards of some individuality; for you who bristle at the slightest imposition of authority to discover that freedom is really the opportunity for self discipline; and for you who have but parroted back what your teachers have taught you to experience the joy and the excitement of personal discovery and invention.

[5] These are but a few illustrations of the potential for change which is within you and it is during the next two years that much of the change can be accomplished. You do not come to college fully formed. Neither computers nor human intuition can define exactly and predict completely your personal and intellectual qualities and the limits of their development.

[6] Your heredity, your early childhood, your home life over the last

eighteen years, and the role of your teachers in influencing you are of course still important. To make sure I am not misunderstood let me turn the coin over for a minute and examine the other side.

[7] The role of heredity in determining many of your traits and characteristics and capacities is real even though not fully understood. Molecular biology and biochemistry however are on the threshold of startling breakthroughs in our understanding of genetic mechanisms. Clearly some of you are blessed with greater potential than others, whether that potential involves quantitative reasoning or verbal facility or physical size and attractiveness or speed of foot. You would be wise to seek the most objective appraisal you can get of what your abilities in any or all of these areas are, provided you do not then set for yourself ceilings of achievement that are arbitrary and fixed or premature.

[8] If you are presently five feet, two inches tall or weigh one hundred twenty pounds or take twenty-two seconds to run the one hundred yard dash, it is most unlikely that you will ever become a professional basketball or football player. If you scored eight hundred on the verbal part of the scholastic aptitude test all three times you took it, and between 350 and 400 on the quantitative part on the same three occasions, and if the scores are reflected also in your grades over the last several years, then engineering or physics might well not be the best choice of a major field you can make. It is not true that anyone can do anything he wants to provided he is sufficiently motivated. If you do not agree with me, I suggest you try flying to the moon without benefit of rocket or capsule.

[9] Of course, all these illustrations are exaggerated by design. They are cited to make sure that you do not interpret my remarks to mean that there are no bounds to what you can achieve intellectually or personally. Trusting that this simple but important point has been made, I turn to my main thesis which is to persuade and to remind you that there is much indeed you can accomplish and that the next two years are critical in determining what your levels of aspiration will be.

[10] As many college teachers will testify, the change that takes place in students from freshman to senior year seems to defy generalization and analysis. Individual differences in students seem to cover so wide a range that anything meaningful and valid and inclusive is difficult to state. But I am willing to try, for I believe that the most important thing I can provide assurance about as you begin your college career is that change— important change—is very much within your power to achieve.

[11] There is evidence that people differ widely in the age at which they reach their ceilings of mental ability. Substantial gains can be made in certain intellectual characteristics, such as reasoning, even after the age of thirty. There is also evidence that the more intelligent persons of a particular age are not only increasing in measured ability at a faster

rate than less intelligent persons of the same age, but also have farther to go in reaching their maximum ability. Your developing your ability to the full is, of course, your first goal and ours to assist you in attaining.

[12] Just as there is evidence that intellectual development does not reach a ceiling by age fifteen or sixteen, so is there evidence to contradict the notion that personality development reaches its fixed characteristics by a similar age. Your personalities are not fully formed by the time you enter college.

[13] The college environment is one which is highly favorable to change. Learning is change and learning is our chief concern. Entering college students face a high degree of independence in comparison with their prior school and home experiences. College students have yet to take on the commitments and the encumbrances typical of young people immediately after the age of twenty-two.

[14] Your attitudes as college students toward change are also somewhat contradictory in that your confidence frequently does not match your aspiration. You look upon college as being a circumstance which by some magic process will bring about the realization of many of your dreams. Somehow college will do this to you and for you. Actually, any of your dreams that are realized will be realized because of your own efforts and not because of some mysterious process which exerts its influence through your mere passive attendance at college.

[15] Your coming to a fuller realization of the potential for change that is within you and subject to your own efforts, your intimate familiarity with change, and your grasp of the factors which make for change grow in importance almost daily, for the world in general is evolving at an accelerated pace. A few decades ago the curve of knowledge could be described as a gently rising plateau. This is no longer so. The line seems to be approaching the vertical. The individual who has not learned to live with change and to effect change in himself will be obsolete the day he receives his diploma. If college graduates are not so educated and prepared, who else in society will be? The unpredictability of the physical world is clearly being matched by the unpredictability of the political and social world.

[16] There are two cautions and a hope I would express as you face the opportunity for change and the prospect of change which will mark your college years. The first is that you avoid being premature in the new commitments you make with respect to intellectual or moral or personal standards. New concepts with respect to such standards should be studied and weighed and discussed and evaluated and even some of them in time made deeply and unequivocally your own. However, I do suggest that you postpone for a while at least the complete identification and the complete espousal of a cause or standard or way of life until you have satisfied yourself that you have brought all the objectivity you can muster to

the issues involved and have examined fairly and carefully more than one point of view. Commitment should come and will come in time, and will before the end of four undergraduate years on many issues in many cases; but do not cast the die too early in your college career.

[17] My second caution is that you do not permit rebellion to be the chief architect of your way of life and of your standards of behavior. Of course it is natural that you should consider yourself more responsible and more prepared to exercise freedom than your parents believe you to be, but beware of the easy trap into which you can fall of determining all of your attitudes on the basis of rebellion to constituted authority or the older generation. May I remind you that you will all too soon be the older generation yourselves and that the generation now called older by you was not too long ago aged eighteen to twenty-two. But more than this, your standards and your ideas and your aspirations should be positive and not reactionary, should be built out of your own experience as contributing, maturing individuals. Living a life only of protest makes no more personal sense than taking in each other's laundry makes economic sense. Protest, yes, injustice and indignity. But you will find only futility in protesting the fact that there are people older than you.

[18] And finally may I express a hope, a hope that in this university and in American society generally there will develop a sense of community out of which will come a realization to the full of the true dignity of the individual and of the common goals and aspirations of all persons of good will, whether they be eighteen or twenty-two or thirty-five or sixty-four and whether they be called students or faculty or administration or the younger generation or the Establishment or what-have-you. That sense of community will enable us to realize to the maximum the potential in all of us, will make of the intellectual experience that is college something both exciting and satisfying, and will result in our personal relations being characterized by mutual respect, confidence and warmth.

[19] By many roads you have traveled to this campus. In a real sense you are all equals in the opportunities now before you and in the potential you possess to capitalize upon these opportunities. It is truly an adventure that awaits you, to prepare yourself for change by changing yourself.

COMMENT AND QUESTIONS

1. How would you describe the tone of the opening paragraph? What relationship with his audience is the speaker establishing?
2. In each of the first three paragraphs, Wessell states and restates parts of

his central thesis: ". . . you begin an adventure which you have in your own power to make the most meaningful of your lives" (paragraph 1); ". . . there are opportunities for growth and maturation and achievement which, if anything, go beyond your present expectations" (paragraph 2); ". . . do not assume that it is too late to make fundamental changes in the level of your intellectual achievement or in your personal traits or in your sense of values or in your commitment to ideals" (paragraph 3). In the second and third paragraphs, how does he qualify these generalizations?

3. Paragraph 4 is a paragraph of examples of possible changes. Notice that the paragraph is a single sentence, with sustained parallel phrasing. Is there a logical or a psychological order, or both, in the arrangement of the examples?

4. Paragraph 5 restates the central idea: "You do not come to college fully formed," and paragraph 6 introduces further qualifications. What are the qualifications, and how are they developed in paragraphs 7 and 8?

5. What is the function of paragraph 9?

6. Paragraph 10 ends with another assurance that important change is possible. Do you find any qualifications in this paragraph?

7. Paragraph 13 states that the college environment is highly favorable to change. In what sense is paragraph 14 a qualification of 13?

8. What does paragraph 15 contribute to the development of the main idea of the speech?

9. What are Wessell's two cautions, and how are they related to the central theme of change? Are there qualifications here too (paragraphs 16 and 17)?

10. Do you think that paragraph 18 was included chiefly for content or for tone? Explain.

11. Examine the final paragraph of the composition. How is "By many roads" related to the earlier content? The author has granted that the students he is addressing are not equal in heredity, background, and potential. In what sense is the second sentence of the last paragraph true? In what ways is the last sentence an effective ending?

NARRATION

[4] *E. B. White*: Walden, 1939

E. B. WHITE (1899–), one of the best of contemporary American essayists, has written regularly for *Harper's Magazine* and for *The New Yorker*. In July, 1963, John F. Kennedy named him in the first group to receive the new Presidential Medal of Freedom, an award to those "who contribute significantly to the quality of American life." E. B. White's books include *One Man's Meat, The Wild Flag, Here Is New York, The Second Tree from the Corner,* and *The Points of My Compass*. The following narrative essay is from *One Man's Meat*.

Miss Nims, take a letter to Henry David Thoreau.

[1] Dear Henry: I thought of you the other afternoon as I was approaching Concord doing fifty on Route 62. That is a high speed at which to hold a philosopher in one's mind, but in this century we are a nimble bunch.

[2] On one of the lawns in the outskirts of the village a woman was cutting the grass with a motorized lawn mower. What made me think of you was that the machine had rather got away from her, although she was game enough, and in the brief glimpse I had of the scene it appeared to me that the lawn was mowing the lady. She kept a tight grip on the handles, which throbbed violently with every explosion of the one-cylinder motor, and as she sheered around bushes and lurched along at a reluctant trot behind her impetuous servant, she looked like a puppy who had grabbed something that was too much for him. Concord hasn't

39

changed much, Henry; the farm implements and the animals still have the upper hand.

[3] I may as well admit that I was journeying to Concord with the deliberate intention of visiting your woods; for although I have never knelt at the grave of a philosopher nor placed wreaths on moldy poets, and have often gone a mile out of my way to avoid some place of historical interest, I have always wanted to see Walden Pond. The account which you left of your sojourn there is, you will be amused to learn, a document of increasing pertinence; each year it seems to gain a little headway, as the world loses ground. We may all be transcendental yet, whether we like it or not. As our common complexities increase, any tale of individual simplicity (and yours is the best written and the cockiest) acquires a new fascination; as our goods accumulate, but not our well-being, your report of an existence without material adornment takes on a certain awkward credibility.

[4] My purpose in going to Walden Pond, like yours, was not to live cheaply or to live dearly there, but to transact some private business with the fewest obstacles. Approaching Concord, doing forty, forty-five, doing fifty, the steering wheel held snug in my palms, the highway held grimly in my vision, the crown of the road now serving me (on the righthand curves), now defeating me (on the lefthand curves), I began to rouse myself from the stupefaction which a day's motor journey induces. It was a delicious evening, Henry, when the whole body is one sense, and imbibes delight through every pore, if I may coin a phrase. Fields were richly brown where the harrow, drawn by the stripped Ford, had lately sunk its teeth; pastures were green; and overhead the sky had that same everlasting great look which you will find on Page 144 of the Oxford pocket edition. I could feel the road entering me, through tire, wheel, spring, and cushion; shall I not have intelligence with earth too? Am I not partly leaves and vegetable mold myself?—a man of infinite horsepower, yet partly leaves.

[5] Stay with me on 62 and it will take you into Concord. As I say, it was a delicious evening. The snake had come forth to die a bloody S on the highway, the wheel upon its head, its bowels flat now and exposed. The turtle had come up too to cross the road and die in the attempt, its hard shell smashed under the rubber blow, its intestinal yearning (for the other side of the road) forever squashed. There was a sign by the wayside which announced that the road had a "cotton surface." You wouldn't know what that is, but neither, for that matter, did I. There is a cryptic ingredient in many of our modern improvements—we are awed and pleased without knowing quite what we are enjoying. It is something to be traveling on a road with a cotton surface.

[6] The civilization round Concord to-day is an odd distillation of city, village, farm, and manor. The houses, yards, fields look not quite subur-

ban, not quite rural. Under the bronze beech and the blue spruce of the departed baron grazes the milch goat of the heirs. Under the porte-cochère stands the reconditioned station wagon; under the grape arbor sit the puppies for sale. (But why do men degenerate ever? What makes families run out?)

[7] It was June and everywhere June was publishing her immemorial stanza; in the lilacs, in the syringa, in the freshly edged paths and the sweetness of moist beloved gardens, and the little wire wickets that preserve the tulips' front. Farmers were already moving the fruits of their toil into their yards, arranging the rhubarb, the asparagus, the strictly fresh eggs on the painted stands under the little shed roofs with the patent shingles. And though it was almost a hundred years since you had taken your ax and started cutting out your home on Walden Pond, I was interested to observe that the philosophical spirit was still alive in Massachusetts; in the center of a vacant lot some boys were assembling the framework of a rude shelter, their whole mind and skill concentrated in the rather inauspicious helter-skeleton of studs and rafters. They too were escaping from town, to live naturally, in a rich blend of savagery and philosophy.

[8] That evening, after supper at the inn, I strolled out into the twilight to dream my shapeless transcendental dreams and see that the car was locked up for the night (first open the right front door, then reach over, straining, and pull up the handles of the left rear and the left front till you hear the click, then the handle of the right rear, then shut the right front but open it again, remembering that the key is still in the ignition switch, remove the key, shut the right front again with a bang, push the tiny keyhole cover to one side, insert key, turn, and withdraw). It is what we all do, Henry. It is called locking the car. It is said to confuse thieves and keep them from making off with the laprobe. Four doors to lock behind one robe. The driver himself never uses a laprobe, the free movement of his legs being vital to the operation of the vehicle; so that when he locks the car it is a pure and unselfish act. I have in my life gained very little essential heat from laprobes, yet I have ever been at pains to lock them up.

[9] The evening was full of sounds, some of which would have stirred your memory. The robins still love the elms of New England villages at sundown. There is enough of the thrush in them to make song inevitable at the end of day, and enough of the tramp to make them hang round the dwellings of men. A robin, like many another American, dearly loves a white house with green blinds. Concord is still full of them.

[10] Your fellow-townsmen were stirring abroad—not many afoot, most of them in their cars; and the sound which they made in Concord at evening was a rustling and a whispering. The sound lacks steadfastness and is wholly unlike that of a train. A train, as you know who lived so

near the Fitchburg line, whistles once or twice sadly and is gone, trailing a memory in smoke, soothing to ear and mind. Automobiles, skirting a village green, are like flies that have gained the inner ear—they buzz, cease, pause, start, shift, stop, halt, brake, and the whole effect is a nervous polytone curiously disturbing.

[11] As I wandered along, the toc toc of ping pong balls drifted from an attic window. In front of the Reuben Brown house a Buick was drawn up. At the wheel, motionless, his hat upon his head, a man sat, listening to Amos and Andy on the radio (it is a drama of many scenes and without an end). The deep voice of Andrew Brown, emerging from the car, although it originated more than two hundred miles away, was unstrained by distance. When you used to sit on the shore of your pond on Sunday morning, listening to the church bells of Acton and Concord, you were aware of the excellent filter of the intervening atmosphere. Science has attended to that, and sound now maintains its intensity without regard for distance. Properly sponsored, it goes on forever.

[12] A fire engine, out for a trial spin, roared past Emerson's house, hot with readiness for public duty. Over the barn roofs the martins dipped and chittered. A swarthy daughter of an asparagus grower, in culottes, shirt, and bandanna, pedaled past on her bicycle. It was indeed a delicious evening, and I returned to the inn (I believe it was your house once) to rock with the old ladies on the concrete veranda.

[13] Next morning early I started afoot for Walden, out Main Street and down Thoreau, past the depot and the Minuteman Chevrolet Company. The morning was fresh, and in a bean field along the way I flushed an agriculturist, quietly studying his beans. Thoreau Street soon joined Number 126, an artery of the State. We number our highways nowadays, our speed being so great we can remember little of their quality or character and are lucky to remember their number. (Men have an indistinct notion that if they keep up this activity long enough all will at length ride somewhere, in next to no time.) Your pond is on 126.

[14] I knew I must be nearing your woodland retreat when the Golden Pheasant lunchroom came into view—Sealtest ice cream, toasted sandwiches, hot frankfurters, waffles, tonics, and lunches. Were I the proprietor, I should add rice, Indian meal, and molasses—just for old time's sake. The Pheasant, incidentally, is for sale: a chance for some nature lover who wishes to set himself up beside a pond in the Concord atmosphere and live deliberately, fronting only the essential facts of life on Number 126. Beyond the Pheasant was a place called Walden Breezes, an oasis whose porch pillars were made of old green shutters sawed into lengths. On the porch was a distorting mirror, to give the traveler a comical image of himself, who had miraculously learned to gaze in an ordinary glass without smiling. Behind the Breezes, in a sun-parched clearing, dwelt your philosophical descendants in their trailers, each

trailer the size of your hut, but all grouped together for the sake of congeniality. Trailer people leave the city, as you did, to discover solitude and in any weather, at any hour of the day or night, to improve the nick of time; but they soon collect in villages and get bogged deeper in the mud than ever. The camp behind Walden Breezes was just rousing itself to the morning. The ground was packed hard under the heel, and the sun came through the clearing to bake the soil and enlarge the wry smell of cramped housekeeping. Cushman's bakery truck had stopped to deliver an early basket of rolls. A camp dog, seeing me in the road, barked petulantly. A man emerged from one of the trailers and set forth with a bucket to draw water from some forest tap.

[15] Leaving the highway I turned off into the woods toward the pond, which was apparent through the foliage. The floor of the forest was strewn with dried old oak leaves and *Transcripts*. From beneath the flattened popcorn wrapper (*granum explosum*) peeped the frail violet. I followed a footpath and descended to the water's edge. The pond lay clear and blue in the morning light, as you have seen it so many times. In the shallows a man's waterlogged shirt undulated gently. A few flies came out to greet me and convoy me to your cove, past the No Bathing signs on which the fellows and the girls had scrawled their names. I felt strangely excited suddenly to be snooping around your premises, tiptoeing along watchfully, as though not to tread by mistake upon the intervening century. Before I got to the cove I heard something which seemed to me quite wonderful: I heard your frog, a full clear *troonk*, guiding me, still hoarse and solemn, bridging the years as the robins had bridged them in the sweetness of the village evening. But he soon quit, and I came on a couple of young boys throwing stones at him.

[16] Your front yard is marked by a bronze tablet set in a stone. Four small granite posts, a few feet away, show where the house was. On top of the tablet was a pair of faded blue bathing trunks with a white stripe. Back of it is a pile of stones, a sort of cairn, left by your visitors as a tribute I suppose. It is a rather ugly little heap of stones, Henry. In fact the hillside itself seems faded, browbeaten; a few tall skinny pines, bare of lower limbs, a smattering of young maples in suitable green, some birches and oaks, and a number of trees felled by the last big wind. It was from the bole of one of these fallen pines, torn up by the roots, that I extracted the stone which I added to the cairn—a sentimental act in which I was interrupted by a small terrier from a nearby picnic group, who confronted me and wanted to know about the stone.

[17] I sat down for a while on one of the posts of your house to listen to the bluebottles and the dragonflies. The invaded glade sprawled shabby and mean at my feet, but the flies were tuned to the old vibration. There were the remains of a fire in your ruins, but I doubt that it was yours; also two beer bottles trodden into the soil and become part of

earth. A young oak had taken root in your house, and two or three ferns, unrolling like the ticklers at a banquet. The only other furnishings were a DuBarry pattern sheet, a page torn from a picture magazine, and some crusts in wax paper.

[18] Before I quit I walked clear round the pond and found the place where you used to sit on the northeast side to get the sun in the fall, and the beach where you got sand for scrubbing your floor. On the eastern side of the pond, where the highway borders it, the State has built dressing rooms for swimmers, a float with diving towers, drinking fountains of porcelain, and rowboats for hire. The pond is in fact a State Preserve, and carries a twenty-dollar fine for picking wild flowers, a decree signed in all solemnity by your fellow-citizens Walter C. Wardwell, Erson B. Barlow, and Nathaniel I. Bowditch. There was a smell of creosote where they had been building a wide wooden stairway to the road and the parking area. Swimmers and boaters were arriving; bodies plunged vigorously into the water and emerged wet and beautiful in the bright air. As I left, a boatload of town boys were splashing about in mid-pond, kidding and fooling, the young fellows singing at the top of their lungs in a wild chorus:

>Amer-ica, Amer-i-ca, God shed his grace on thee,
>And crown thy good with brotherhood
>From sea to shi-ning sea!

[19] I walked back to town along the railroad, following your custom. The rails were expanding noisily in the hot sun, and on the slope of the roadbed the wild grape and the blackberry sent up their creepers to the track.

[20] The expense of my brief sojourn in Concord was:

Canvas shoes	$1.95
Baseball bat	.25
Left-handed fielder's glove	1.25
Hotel and meals	4.25
In all	$7.70

(Baseball bat, Left-handed fielder's glove) } gifts to take back to a boy

As you see, this amount was almost what you spent for food for eight months. I cannot defend the shoes or the expenditure for shelter and food: they reveal a meanness and grossness in my nature which you would find contemptible. The baseball equipment, however, is the kind of impediment with which you were never on even terms. You must remember that the house where you practiced the sort of economy which I respect was haunted only by mice and squirrels. You never had to cope with a shortstop.

──❦{ COMMENT AND QUESTIONS }❧──

This essay is both a tribute by one writer to another, and a commentary on modern society. To one who has read Henry David Thoreau's *Walden*, E. B. White's essay is rich in allusions to and echoes of Thoreau's work. For example, the end of paragraph 4 echoes a passage in which Thoreau, writing about the beneficence of Nature and his sense of oneness with Nature, asks, "Shall I not have intelligence with the earth? Am I not partly leaves and vegetable mould myself?" And E. B. White's record of his expenses in paragraph 20 recalls Thoreau's meticulous records in *Walden*—in all, a cost of $28.12½ for building his house; a profit of $8.71½ from his beans, etc.

1. What does White gain, first by writing his essay as a letter, and second by suggesting that he is dictating the letter?
2. Narrating his visit to Concord and Walden Pond, White follows a generally chronological order. One departure from this order is in paragraph 3, where, leaving the drive to Concord, he goes back in time to the reason for the visit. Point out examples of the devices used to keep clear to the reader the sequence and relationship of events.
3. Why do you think the author has included each of the following: the woman and the lawn mower (paragraph 2); the death of the snake and the turtle (paragraph 5); the "cotton surface" of the road (paragraph 5); the business of locking the car (paragraph 8); the numbering of highways (paragraph 13); the trailer camp (paragraph 14)?
4. Comment on the style of sentence 2 in paragraph 4. What is the effect of the last sentence of that paragraph?
5. Examine the structure of the first sentence of paragraph 8. How does the structure help to communicate meaning? Comment on the structure and diction of the last sentence of paragraph 10.
6. This essay has a wealth of concrete detail, and White is very skillful in arranging the details. Notice that in paragraph 15, for example, he brings together contrasting items: oak leaves and *Transcripts* (copies of a Boston newspaper), the popcorn wrapper and the violet. Point out other examples of juxtaposing incongruous details. What is the effect of this technique?
7. As the author leaves, the boys splashing in the pond are singing part of "America the Beautiful." Do you think that White included this detail simply because he was recording everything he saw and heard or that he had a special reason for including it?
8. Does White state explicitly his judgment of present-day civilization and progress? What particular passages or what parts of the essay seem to you best to convey his judgment?
9. How would you describe the tone of the essay? For example, is the author sad, cynical, bitter, good-humored, resigned, or nostalgic for a way of life no longer possible? Or is the tone complex?
10. When White speaks in the last paragraph of "the sort of economy which I respect," what might he mean besides economy with money?

ANALYSIS

[5] *George Orwell*: Why I Write

GEORGE ORWELL (1903–1950), whose real name was Eric Blair, was an English author and critic, probably best known for his novel *Nineteen Eighty-Four*. The following essay, from *Such, Such Were the Joys*, was written in 1947, the year before Orwell wrote *Nineteen Eighty-Four*.

[¹] From a very early age, perhaps the age of five or six, I knew that when I grew up I should be a writer. Between the ages of about seventeen and twenty-four I tried to abandon this idea, but I did so with the consciousness that I was outraging my true nature and that sooner or later I should have to settle down and write books.
[²] I was the middle child of three, but there was a gap of five years on either side, and I barely saw my father before I was eight. For this and other reasons I was somewhat lonely, and I soon developed disagreeable mannerisms which made me unpopular throughout my schooldays. I had the lonely child's habit of making up stories and holding conversations with imaginary persons, and I think from the very start my literary ambitions were mixed up with the feeling of being isolated and undervalued. I knew that I had a facility with words and a power of facing unpleasant facts, and I felt that this created a sort of private world in which I could get my own back for my failure in everyday life. Nevertheless the volume of serious—*i.e.* seriously intended—writing which I produced all through my childhood and boyhood would not amount to half a dozen pages. I wrote my first poem at the age of four or five, my mother taking it down to dictation. I cannot remember anything about it except that it was about

a tiger and the tiger had "chair-like teeth"—a good enough phrase, but I fancy the poem was a plagiarism of Blake's "Tiger, Tiger." At eleven, when the war of 1914–18 broke out, I wrote a patriotic poem which was printed in the local newspaper, as was another, two years later, on the death of Kitchener. From time to time, when I was a bit older, I wrote bad and usually unfinished "nature poems" in the Georgian style. I also, about twice, attempted a short story which was a ghastly failure. That was the total of the would-be serious work that I actually set down on paper during all those years.

[3] However, throughout this time I did in a sense engage in literary activities. To begin with there was the made-to-order stuff which I produced quickly, easily and without much pleasure to myself. Apart from school work, I wrote *vers d'occasion*, semi-comic poems which I could turn out at what now seems to me astonishing speed—at fourteen I wrote a whole rhyming play, in imitation of Aristophanes, in about a week—and helped to edit school magazines, both printed and in manuscript. These magazines were the most pitiful burlesque stuff that you could imagine, and I took far less trouble with them than I now would with the cheapest journalism. But side by side with all this, for fifteen years or more, I was carrying out a literary exercise of a quite different kind: this was the making up of a continuous "story" about myself, a sort of diary existing only in the mind. I believe this is a common habit of children and adolescents. As a very small child I used to imagine that I was, say, Robin Hood, and picture myself as the hero of thrilling adventures, but quite soon my "story" ceased to be narcissistic in a crude way and became more and more a mere description of what I was doing and the things I saw. For minutes at a time this kind of thing would be running through my head: "He pushed the door open and entered the room. A yellow beam of sunlight, filtering through the muslin curtains, slanted on to the table, where a matchbox, half open, lay beside the inkpot. With his right hand in his pocket he moved across to the window. Down in the street a tortoise-shell cat was chasing a dead leaf," etc., etc. This habit continued till I was about twenty-five, right through my non-literary years. Although I had to search, and did search, for the right words, I seemed to be making this descriptive effort almost against my will, under a kind of compulsion from outside. The "story" must, I suppose, have reflected the styles of the various writers I admired at different ages, but so far as I remember it always had the same meticulous descriptive quality.

[4] When I was about sixteen I suddenly discovered the joy of mere words, *i.e.* the sounds and associations of words. The lines from *Paradise Lost*—

So hee with difficulty and labour hard
Moved on: with difficulty and labour hee,

which do not now seem to me so very wonderful, sent shivers down my backbone; and the spelling "hee" for "he" was an added pleasure. As for the need to describe things, I knew all about it already. So it is clear what kind of books I wanted to write, in so far as I could be said to want to write books at that time. I wanted to write enormous naturalistic novels with unhappy endings, full of detailed descriptions and arresting similes, and also full of purple passages in which words were used partly for the sake of their sound. And in fact my first completed novel, *Burmese Days*, which I wrote when I was thirty but projected much earlier, is rather that kind of book.

[5] I give all this background information because I do not think one can assess a writer's motives without knowing something of his early development. His subject matter will be determined by the age he lives in—at least this is true in tumultuous, revolutionary ages like our own—but before he ever begins to write he will have acquired an emotional attitude from which he will never completely escape. It is his job, no doubt, to discipline his temperament and avoid getting stuck at some immature stage, or in some perverse mood: but if he escapes from his early influences altogether, he will have killed his impulse to write. Putting aside the need to earn a living, I think there are four great motives for writing, at any rate for writing prose. They exist in different degrees in every writer, and in any one writer the proportions will vary from time to time, according to the atmosphere in which he is living. They are:

[6] (1) Sheer egoism. Desire to seem clever, to be talked about, to be remembered after death, to get your own back on grownups who snubbed you in childhood, etc., etc. It is humbug to pretend that this is not a motive, and a strong one. Writers share this characteristic with scientists, artists, politicians, lawyers, soldiers, successful businessmen—in short, with the whole top crust of humanity. The great mass of human beings are not acutely selfish. After the age of about thirty they abandon individual ambition—in many cases, indeed, they almost abandon the sense of being individuals at all—and live chiefly for others, or are simply smothered under drudgery. But there is also the minority of gifted, wilful people who are determined to live their own lives to the end, and writers belong in this class. Serious writers, I should say, are on the whole more vain and self-centred than journalists, though less interested in money.

[7] (2) Esthetic enthusiasm. Perception of beauty in the external world, or, on the other hand, in words and their right arrangement. Pleasure in the impact of one sound on another, in the firmness of good prose or the rhythm of a good story. Desire to share an experience which one feels is valuable and ought not to be missed. The esthetic motive is very feeble in a lot of writers, but even a pamphleteer or a writer of textbooks will have pet words and phrases which appeal to him for non-utilitarian reasons; or he may feel strongly about typography, width of

margins, etc. Above the level of a railway guide, no book is quite free from esthetic considerations.

[8] (3) Historical impulse. Desire to see things as they are, to find out true facts and store them up for the use of posterity.

[9] (4) Political purpose—using the word "political" in the widest possible sense. Desire to push the world in a certain direction, to alter other people's idea of the kind of society that they should strive after. Once again, no book is genuinely free from political bias. The opinion that art should have nothing to do with politics is itself a political attitude.

[10] It can be seen how these various impulses must war against one another, and how they must fluctuate from person to person and from time to time. By nature—taking your "nature" to be the state you have attained when you are first adult—I am a person in whom the first three motives would outweigh the fourth. In a peaceful age I might have written ornate or merely descriptive books, and might have remained almost unaware of my political loyalties. As it is I have been forced into becoming a sort of pamphleteer. First I spent five years in an unsuitable profession (the Indian Imperial Police, in Burma), and then I underwent poverty and the sense of failure. This increased my natural hatred of authority and made me for the first time fully aware of the existence of the working classes, and the job in Burma had given me some understanding of the nature of imperialism: but these experiences were not enough to give me an accurate political orientation. Then came Hitler, the Spanish civil war, etc. By the end of 1935 I had still failed to reach a firm decision. I remember a little poem that I wrote at that date, expressing my dilemma:

> A happy vicar I might have been
> Two hundred years ago,
> To preach upon eternal doom
> And watch my walnuts grow;
>
> But born, alas, in an evil time,
> I missed that pleasant haven,
> For the hair has grown on my upper lip
> And the clergy are all clean-shaven.
>
> And later still the times were good,
> We were so easy to please,
> We rocked our troubled thoughts to sleep
> On the bosoms of the trees.
>
> All ignorant we dared to own
> The joys we now dissemble;
> The greenfinch on the apple bough
> Could make my enemies tremble.

> But girls' bellies and apricots,
> Roach in a shaded stream,
> Horses, ducks in flight at dawn,
> All these are a dream.
>
> It is forbidden to dream again;
> We maim our joys or hide them;
> Horses are made of chromium steel
> And little fat men shall ride them.
>
> I am the worm who never turned,
> The eunuch without a harem;
> Between the priest and the commissar
> I walk like Eugene Aram;[1]
>
> And the commissar is telling my fortune
> While the radio plays,
> But the priest has promised an Austin Seven,
> For Duggie always pays.[2]
>
> I dreamed I dwelt in marble halls,
> And woke to find it true;
> I wasn't born for an age like this;
> Was Smith? Was Jones? Were you?

The Spanish war and other events in 1936-7 turned the scale and thereafter I knew where I stood. Every line of serious work that I have written since 1936 has been written directly or indirectly, *against* totalitarianism and *for* democratic socialism, as I understand it. It seems to me nonsense, in a period like our own, to think that one can avoid writing of such subjects. Everyone writes of them in one guise or another. It is simply a question of which side one takes and what approach one follows. And the more one is conscious of one's political bias, the more chance one has of acting politically without sacrificing one's esthetic and intellectual integrity.

[11] What I have most wanted to do throughout the past ten years is to make political writing into an art. My starting point is always a feeling of partisanship, a sense of injustice. When I sit down to write a book, I do not say to myself, "I am going to produce a work of art." I write it because there is some lie that I want to expose, some fact to which I want to draw attention, and my initial concern is to get a hearing. But I could not do the work of writing a book, or even a long magazine article, if it were not also an esthetic experience. Anyone who cares to examine my work will see that even when it is downright propaganda it contains much that a full-time politician would consider irrelevant. I am not able,

---

[1] Eugene Aram (1704-1757) was an English schoolmaster and a murderer.
[2] A common British saying, used ironically; "Duggie" is an expression equivalent to our "bookie."

and I do not want, completely to abandon the world-view that I acquired in childhood. So long as I remain alive and well I shall continue to feel strongly about prose style, to love the surface of the earth, and to take a pleasure in solid objects and scraps of useless information. It is no use trying to suppress that side of myself. The job is to reconcile my ingrained likes and dislikes with the essentially public, nonindividual activities that this age forces on all of us.

[12] It is not easy. It raises problems of construction and of language, and it raises in a new way the problem of truthfulness. Let me give just one example of the cruder kind of difficulty that arises. My book about the Spanish civil war, *Homage to Catalonia,* is, of course, a frankly political book, but in the main it is written with a certain detachment and regard for form. I did try very hard in it to tell the whole truth without violating my literary instincts. But among other things it contains a long chapter, full of newspaper quotations and the like, defending the Trotskyists who were accused of plotting with Franco. Clearly such a chapter, which after a year or two would lose its interest for any ordinary reader, must ruin the book. A critic whom I respect read me a lecture about it. "Why did you put in all that stuff?" he said. "You've turned what might have been a good book into journalism." What he said was true, but I could not have done otherwise. I happened to know, what very few people in England had been allowed to know, that innocent men were being falsely accused. If I had not been angry about that I should never have written the book.

[13] In one form or another this problem comes up again. The problem of language is subtler and would take too long to discuss. I will only say that of late years I have tried to write less picturesquely and more exactly. In any case I find that by the time you have perfected any style of writing, you have always outgrown it. *Animal Farm* was the first book in which I tried, with full consciousness of what I was doing, to fuse political purpose and artistic purpose into one whole. I have not written a novel for seven years, but I hope to write another fairly soon. It is bound to be a failure, every book is a failure, but I do know with some clarity what kind of book I want to write.

[14] Looking back through the last page or two, I see that I have made it appear as though my motives in writing were wholly public-spirited. I don't want to leave that as the final impression. All writers are vain, selfish and lazy, and at the very bottom of their motives there lies a mystery. Writing a book is a horrible, exhausting struggle, like a long bout of some painful illness. One would never undertake such a thing if one were not driven on by some demon whom one can neither resist nor understand. For all one knows that demon is simply the same instinct that makes a baby squall for attention. And yet it is also true that one can write nothing readable unless one constantly struggles to efface one's own

personality. Good prose is like a window pane. I cannot say with certainty which of my motives are the strongest, but I know which of them deserve to be followed. And looking back through my work, I see that it is invariably where I lacked a *political* purpose that I wrote lifeless books and was betrayed into purple passages, sentences without meaning, decorative adjectives and humbug generally.

COMMENT AND QUESTIONS

1. This essay has three major divisions: (a) background information—an account of Orwell's "nonliterary years" (paragraphs 1–4); (b) an analysis of the four great motives for writing (paragraphs 5–9); (c) an analysis of the author's primarily political motive in writing (paragraphs 10–14). Material in the first of these divisions is roughly, but not wholly, chronological in arrangement. What departures from chronological order do you find in paragraphs 1–4? What are the principal transitional devices by which Orwell links the experiences and activities of his early years? Examine with particular care the sentences in paragraph 3 to see how the author links ideas within a paragraph.
2. The first four paragraphs of the essay might be called an analysis within a larger analysis. In paragraphs 2–4, what particular experiences, attitudes, and habits contribute to what Orwell later calls the world-view acquired in childhood? How do these experiences determine the kind of book (paragraph 4) which, at the age of about twenty-five, he wanted to write?
3. What are Orwell's attitudes toward himself and toward his early literary activities (paragraphs 1–4)? How are the attitudes expressed?
4. At the end of his example, in paragraph 3, of the descriptive story he told himself (and again in paragraph 6), the author uses *etc., etc.*—a practice frequently discouraged by teachers of composition because the expression may be a substitute for thoughtful or accurate detail. Can you justify Orwell's *etc., etc.*? What tone, or attitude toward his audience and material, does it communicate?
5. Paragraph 5 serves the double purpose of explaining why the author has given the background information and of introducing the four motives for writing. How are the background and the motives related? What examples of qualification do you find in paragraph 5?
6. In the analysis of motives (paragraphs 6–9), how do you account for the fact that the first two motives—sheer egoism and esthetic enthusiasm—are given considerably more development than the last two?
7. Notice the sentence structure in paragraphs 6–9. What is the effect of the incomplete sentences following each of the headings? In paragraph 6, Orwell's sentences are notably varied in structure and in length. What is

the effect of this variety? What words or combinations of words seem particularly well selected?

8. The beginning of paragraph 10 restates in different terms what Orwell has said near the end of paragraph 5 about the fluctuations of the four impulses or motives. How is his statement that "by nature" he was one "in whom the first three motives would outweigh the fourth" supported by what we already know of his early experience?

9. Paragraphs 10–14 might be regarded as different levels of analysis: paragraphs 10 and 11 analyze Orwell's political purpose (the last of the four central motives), first by giving the causes or reasons for its development, and second by explaining his desire to make political writing into an art; paragraphs 12 and 13 are an analysis of the problems involved in making political writing an art; and paragraph 14 is a final appraisal of his motives and his writing. What were the reasons (paragraph 10) for his decision to write politically? In what ways does the poem included in paragraph 10 help the reader to understand the difficulty of his choice? (The first line of the last stanza is a near-quotation of a line from Balfe's opera *The Bohemian Girl*. In the song, the marble halls are part of lost wealth and social position. What do the marble halls appear to mean in Orwell's poem?) How does the last sentence of paragraph 10 make an emphatic ending and at the same time lead into the next paragraph?

10. What aspects of the world-view acquired in childhood are referred to in paragraph 11?

11. At the beginning of paragraph 12, Orwell says that combining political and artistic purposes raises problems of construction, language, and truthfulness. Which problems are chiefly emphasized in the example in paragraph 12? In the material in paragraph 13?

12. What is the tone of paragraph 13?

13. What seems to be the purpose of the last paragraph of the essay? What is the meaning of the sentence "Good prose is like a window pane," and how is it related to the baby squalling for attention? In the next-to-last sentence of the paragraph, Orwell says that although he cannot be sure which of his motives are strongest, he knows which deserve to be followed. The *which* in the last part of the sentence is plural; in the context of the whole essay, what does *which* refer to? The last sentence of the paragraph emphasizes, rightly of course, the importance of the political purpose. In the last clause of that last sentence, why is *betrayed* a well-chosen word? How are the four parallel phrases ending the sentence and the essay related to earlier content?

14. What is your impression of the persona, the total personality, revealed in this essay?

CONTRAST
AND COMPARISON

[6]   *John Lukacs*: It's Halfway to 1984

JOHN LUKACS is an essayist, teacher, and historian, author of *A History of the Cold War* and *Decline and Rise of Europe*. The following essay was published in *The New York Times Magazine,* January 2, 1966.

[1] We are now halfway to 1984. George Orwell, the author of "1984," finished his book in 1948. That was 18 years ago, and it is not more than another 18 years before that ominous date rolls around.

[2] It is *ominous,* in every sense of that antique adjective. There is reason to believe that 18 years from now thousands of people will experience a feeling of uneasiness, perhaps a light little shudder of trepidation, as they first encounter that new year's numerals in print. In the English-speaking world, at least, "1984" has become a household term, suggesting some kind of inhuman totalitarian nightmare. And since millions who have not read the book now recognize the term, it is reasonable to assume that both the theme and the title of the book have corresponded to an emerging consciousness among many people in the otherwise progressive-minded English-speaking democracies, to the effect that things are *not* getting better all the time—no, not at all.

[3] The plot of "1984" is well-known but it may be useful to sum it up briefly. By 1984 most of the world has been divided by three super-states—Oceania, Eurasia and Eastasia. They are perpetually at war with one other, but no one of them is completely able to subdue the others.

This state of war enables the rulers of these states (the ruler of Oceania being Big Brother) to keep their peoples both ignorant and submissive. This is achieved by totalitarian and technical methods, by the absoluteness of one-party rule and by a kind of censorship that controls not only the behavior but even the thinking process of individuals. The hero of "1984," Winston Smith, born in 1945 (both the date and the first name are significant), is a simple party member and a functionary of the Ministry of Truth in London, which is the chief city of Airstrip One, for that is what Britain became after she had been absorbed by the United States to form Oceania. (Continental Europe, having been absorbed by the Soviet Union, had become Eurasia.)

[4] Winston is a weak and forlorn intellectual who, however, is sickened not only by the dreary living conditions in 1984 but by the prevalence of official lying and the almost complete absence of personal privacy. One day he stumbles into a love affair, which in itself is a dangerous thing since the party punishes illicit relationships severely. Winston experiences happiness and a sense of personal fulfillment, especially as Julia shares his hatred of the existing system.

[5] There is a high official in the Ministry of Truth, O'Brien, whom Winston instinctively trusts. He and Julia confide in O'Brien. They are deceived. All along, O'Brien has set a trap for them: they are arrested in their secret little room. They are tortured. Winston, despite his strong residue of convictions, not only confesses to everything imaginable, but in the end, faced by an especially horrible torture, he even betrays Julia. He is finally released; he is a completely broken man; he has even come to believe in the almightiness and goodness of Big Brother.

[6] But it is not this plot, it is rather Orwell's description of everyday life in 1984 that is the principal matter of the novel and, one may suppose, the principal matter of interest to its readers. Life in 1984 is a mixture of horror and dreariness. What is horrible is not so much war as the shriveling of personal freedoms and privacy with the planners of the superstate controlling vast portions of once-independent lives. What is dreary is that within these totalitarian conditions the living standards of masses of people in what were once civilized and prosperous countries are reduced: Food and drink are little better than standardized slop; mass entertainments are primitive and vulgar; personal property has virtually disappeared.

[7] One of the profound differences between "1984" and Aldous Huxley's "Brave New World" (published in 1932, the latter still had many of the marks of the light-headed twenties; its philosophy compared with that of "1984" is a rather irresponsible *jeu d'esprit*) lies in Orwell's view of the past rather than of the future. Looking back from 1984, conditions in the early, capitalistic portion of the 20th century seem romantic and almost idyllic to Winston Smith, so much so that on a solemn occasion he

offers a toast "to the past." Unemployment, revolutions, Fascism and, to some extent, even Nazism and Communism are lesser evils than what is going on in Oceania in 1984, since by that time the rulers of the state have perfected brainwashing and thought-control to the point that the memories of entire generations, and hence their opinions about the past, have been eliminated.

[8] This, of course, does not happen overnight: It is a brutal but gradual development. In "1984," Orwell set the decisive turning point in the middle sixties, "the period of the great purges in which the original leaders of the Revolution were wiped out once and for all. By 1970 none of them was left, except Big Brother himself."

[9] Let us keep in mind that "1984" is the work of a novelist and not of a prophet; Orwell ought not be criticized simply because some of his visions have not been borne out. On the other hand, Orwell was concerned in the late forties with certain tendencies of evil portent; and "1984" was a publishing success because around 1950, for great numbers of people, the picture of a society such as he described was not merely fantastic but to some extent plausible.

[10] It is still plausible today, but not quite in the way in which Orwell envisaged the future 18 years ago. Halfway to 1984 we can say, fortunately, that most of Orwell's visions have proved wrong. It is true that the United States, the Soviet Union and China correspond to some extent to the superpowers Oceania, Eurasia and Eastasia. But the United States has not annexed Britain, the Soviet Union has fallen far short of conquering all of Europe, and even China does not extend much beyond her traditional boundaries.

[11] What is more important, the superpowers are not at war with one another. It is true that during the so-called cold war between the United States and the Soviet Union many of the practices of traditional and civilized diplomacy were abandoned; but the cold war has given place to something like a cold peace between these two superpowers. Even the dreadful and ominous war in Asia is marked by the reluctance of the United States and China directly to attack each other.

[12] Orwell proved correct in saying that "war . . . is no longer the desperate, annihilating struggle that it was in the early decades of the 20th century. It is a warfare of limited aims between combatants who are unable to destroy one another. . . ." Yet Orwell was interested principally not in international but in internal developments. For example, in "1984" the peoples of Oceania are isolated; travel is forbidden except for a small minority of the élite; and the press is controlled to the extent that no meaningful information from the outside world is available to the public.

[13] But now, halfway to 1984, the opposite has been happening. It is not warfare but torrents of automobiles and mass tourism that threaten

to destroy entire landscapes and cityscapes; great amounts of information are available to us about an undigestible variety of matters; and at times it seems that the cultural traditions of great Western nations are endangered less by the persistence of isolationism than by a phony internationalism drummed up by a kind of pervasive publicity that drowns out the once truer music of the arts.

[14] Also, in the world of "1984" most people are ill-fed, badly clothed, run-down. But this, too, has not happened. Now, halfway to 1984, almost everywhere in the world, living standards have risen, and the danger is not, as Orwell envisaged it, that entire generations of once-prosperous countries will no longer know such things as wine, oranges, lemons and chocolate; it is, rather, that our traditional tastes and table habits may be washed away by a flood of frozen and synthetic foods of every possible kind, available to us every hour of the day.

[15] The reasons why Orwell's visions of 1984 have been wrong seem to be bound up with the time and the circumstances of the book's conception. About the circumstances Orwell himself was supposed to have said that "1984" "wouldn't have been so gloomy if I had not been so ill." He wrote most of the book in self-imposed isolation on a rain-shrouded Scottish island, finishing it in an English country hospital in late 1948. Shortly thereafter, he was moved to a hospital in London, where in January, 1950, he died. As for the time of writing, in the late nineteen-forties Orwell's imagination succumbed, at least in part, to the temptation of conceiving the future as an increasingly acute continuation of what seems to be going on at the present. (In one of his earlier essays, Orwell had criticized the American writer James Burnham for this very fault.) Around 1949, when most intellectuals had come around to recognizing that Stalin's tyranny was hardly better than Hitler's, many of them concluded that it is in the nature of totalitarianism to become more and more tyrannical as time goes on. Indeed, some of them established their reputations by the ponderous books they produced on this theme. (Hannah Arendt's "The Origins of Totalitarianism" is an example.) Yet only a few years later, events in Eastern Europe and in Russia showed that history is unpredictable and that the projections of intellectuals are often oversimplified. But this Orwell did not live to see.

[16] He foresaw the horrible features of 1984 as the consequences of totalitarianism, of political tyranny, of the despotism of a dictator. But halfway to 1984 we can see, for example, that the era of totalitarian dictatorship is sliding away, into the past. Even the Soviet Union seems to be moving in the direction of what one may call "post-totalitarian"; all over Eastern Europe (though not yet in Asia) we can perceive regimes that, though dictatorial, are no longer totalitarian. The danger for us is, rather, the obverse: the possibility of totalitarian democracy.

[17] Totalitarian democracy? The words seem paradoxical; our eyes

and ears are unaccustomed to the sight and the sound of them in combination. Yet I believe that we ought to accustom our imaginations to the possibility of a democratic society in which universal popular suffrage exists while freedom of speech, press and assembly are hardly more than theoretical possibilities for the individual, whose life and ideas, whose rights to privacy, to family autonomy and to durable possessions are regimented by government and rigidly molded by mass production and by mass communications.

[18] Let me, at this point, fall back on a personal illustration. For a long time the term "1984" evoked, to me, the image of a police state of the Eastern European type. But when I think of 1984 now, the image that swims into my mind is that of a gigantic shopping center and industrial complex—something like the one which has been erected a few miles from where I live in eastern Pennsylvania.

[19] The undulating rural landscape around Valley Forge, with its bright dots of houses and its crossroads, has been transformed. There is now the eerie vastness of the General Electric Space Center whose square edifices spread across hundreds of acres. Beyond it stand other flat windowless blocks of buildings—the King of Prussia shopping center, around the trembling edges of which bulldozers roar from morning to night, boring their brutal tracks into the clayey soil which they must churn to mud before it can be covered by concrete. The predominant material is concrete, horizontal and vertical concrete. Twice a day, thousands of people pour into and out of this compound, in a tremendous metallic flow. But no one lives there. At night and on Sundays, these hundreds of acres resemble a deserted airport, with a few automobiles clustering here and there, or slowly cruising on one of the airstrips, occasionally peered at by uniformed guards. Why fly to the moon? Stand on a cold January night in the middle of a parking lot in a large shopping center in the American North. It is a man-made moonscape. This is how the moon will look after our Herculean efforts, after we reach it, colonize it, pour concrete over it.

[20] This is how 1984 looks to me, in the middle sixties, but I know and feel that this view is neither solitary nor unusual. There are millions of Americans who, passing a similar space-age complex of buildings, will say "1984," covering up their resignation with a thin coat of defensive humor. What strikes us is not just the ugliness of the buildings but something else, something that is not so much the reaction of middle-aged earthmen against brave new worlds as it is the expression of a feeling which is, alas, close to the Orwellian nightmare vision: a sense of impersonality together with a sense of powerlessness.

[21] The impersonality is there, in the hugeness of the Organization and in the anonymous myriads of the interchangeable human beings who make up most of their personnel. The powerlessness is the feeling which I share with so many of my neighbors—that we cannot stop what in

America is called the March of Progress, the cement trucks coming toward us any day from across the hill; the knowledge that our voices, our votes, our appeals, our petitions amount to near-nothing at a time when people have become accustomed to accepting the decisions of planners, experts and faraway powerful agencies. It is a sickening inward feeling that the essence of self-government is becoming more and more meaningless at the very time when the outward and legal forms of democracy are still kept up.

[22] Let us not fool ourselves: Now, halfway to 1984, with all of the recent advances of civil rights, with all of the recent juridical extensions of constitutional freedoms, we *are* facing the erosion of privacy, of property and—yes—even of liberty. This has nothing to do with the Communist Conspiracy or with Ambitious Government Bureaucrats—that is where our New Conservatives go wrong. It has nothing to do with Creeping Socialism. It has very much to do with Booming Technology. The dangers which our modern societies in the West, and particularly the United States, face now, halfway to 1984, are often new kinds of dangers, growing out of newly developing conditions. What ought to concern us is the rootlessness of a modern, technological, impersonal society, with interchangeable people, on all levels of education.

[23] We ought to dwell less on the possibility of unemployment arising out of automation, in a society which, after all, feels obligated to produce full employment; rather, we ought to consider the growing purposelessness of occupations in a society where by now more people are employed in administration that in production. And in such a society we ought to prattle less about the need for more "creative leisure" when the problem is that work becomes less and less creative. We ought to worry not about the insufficient availability of products but about the increasing impermanence of possessions. We ought to think deeply not so much about the growth of the public sectors of the public economy at the expense of private enterprise (which, at any rate, is no longer very "private"), but rather, about the cancerous growth of the public sectors of our existence at the expense of the private autonomy of our personal lives.

[24] We ought to concern ourselves less with the depreciation of money and more with the depreciation of language; with the breakdown of interior, even more than with the state of exterior, communications—or, in other words, with the increasing practices of Orwell's Doubletalk and Doublethink, and with their growing promotion not so much by political tyrannies as by all kinds of techniques, in the name of Progress.

[25] I cannot—and, perhaps, I need not—explain or illustrate these concerns in greater detail. They are, in any event, 1966 concerns about the future, not 1948 ones. Still, while many of the phantoms that haunted Orwell's readers 18 years ago have not materialized, the public currency of the term 1984 has lost none of its poignancy. The tone of our literature,

indeed of our entire cultural atmosphere, is far more pessimistic than it was 18 years ago. "Alienation" and "hopelessness" are no longer Central European words; they are very American. This broad, and often near-nihilistic, cultural apathy and despair is relatively new on the American (and also on the British) scene. Its existence suggests that, despite the errors of Orwell's visions, the nightmare quality of "1984" continues to obsess our imagination, and not merely as the sickly titillation of a horror story. It haunts millions who fear that life may become an Orwellian nightmare even without the political tyranny that Orwell had predicted.

[26] "It is by his political writings," Bertrand Russell once wrote, "that Orwell will be remembered." If this is so—and at this moment, halfway to 1984, it still seems so—he will be remembered for the wrong reasons, and one can only hope that the slow corrective tides of public opinion in the long run will redress the balance.

[27] Orwell was not so much concerned with the degeneration of justice as with the degeneration of truth. For Orwell, both in the beginning and in the end was The Word. This is true of "1984," too, which had three levels. On the top level there is the "plot," the love affair of Winston and Julia, which is really flat and inconsequential. On the second level there is the political vision which, as we have seen, sometimes holds up, sometimes not. It is the third level, of what is happening to words and to print, to speech and to truth in 1984, which agitated Orwell the most. Indeed, this spare and economical writer chose to end the novel "1984" by adding an appendix on "The Principles of Newspeak." Orwell was frightened less by the prospects of censorship than by the potential falsification of history, and by the mechanization of speech.

[28] The first of these protracted practices would mean that the only possible basis for a comparison with conditions other than the present would disappear; the second, that the degeneration of traditional language would lead to a new kind of mechanical talk and print which would destroy the meaning of private communications between persons. This prospect haunted Orwell throughout the last 12 years of his life. Some of his best essays dealt with this theme of falsifications of truth—even more than totalitarianism, this was his main concern. As long as people can talk to one another meaningfully, as long as they have private beliefs, as long as people retain some of the qualities of Winston Smith's mother (she had not been an "unusual woman, still less an intelligent one; and yet she had possessed a kind of nobility, a kind of purity, simply because the standards she obeyed were private ones. Her feelings were her own, and could not be altered from the outside . . ."), tyranny was vulnerable; it could not become total.

[29] Orwell was wrong in believing that the development of science was incompatible with totalitarianism (by 1984, "science, in the old sense, has almost ceased to exist. In Newspeak there is no word for science").

As we have seen, he foresaw a decay of technology ("the fields are cultivated by horse-ploughs while books are written by machinery"). This is not what has happened; now, halfway to 1984, the fields are cultivated by bulldozers while books are written by machine-men. But Orwell was right in drawing attention to Doublethink, "the power of holding two contradictory beliefs in one's mind simultaneously, and accepting both of them," and to the desperate prospects of Doubletalk, of the degeneration of standards of language through varieties of supermodern jargon, practiced by political pitchmen as well as by professional intellectuals. There is reason to believe that, were he alive today, Orwell would have modified his views on the nature of the totalitarian menace; and that, at the same time, he would be appalled by many of the present standards and practices in mass communications, literature and publishing, even in the West, and perhaps especially in the United States.

[30] In short, the 1984 that we ought to fear is now, in 1966, different from the 1948 version. Politically speaking, Tocqueville saw further in the eighteen-thirties than Orwell in the nineteen-forties. The despotism which democratic nations had to fear, Tocqueville wrote, would be different from tyranny: "It would be more extensive and more mild; it would degrade men without tormenting them. . . . The same principle of equality which facilitates despotism tempers its rigor." In an eloquent passage Tocqueville described some of the features of such a society: Above the milling crowds "stands an immense and tutelary power, which takes upon itself alone to secure their gratifications and to watch over their fate. That power is absolute, minute, regular, provident and mild. . . ." But when such a government, no matter how provident and mild, becomes omnipotent, "what remains but to spare [people] all the care of thinking and all the trouble of living?"

[31] Orwell's writing is as timely as Tocqueville's not when he is concerned with forms of polity but when he is concerned with evil communication. In this regard the motives of this English Socialist were not at all different from the noble exhortation with which Tocqueville closed one of his chapters in "Democracy in America": "Let us, then, look forward to the future with that salutary fear which makes men keep watch and ward for freedom, not with that faint and idle terror which depresses and enervates the heart." Present and future readers of "1984" may well keep this distinction in mind.

Contrast and Comparison

COMMENT AND QUESTIONS

1. The first two paragraphs of the essay elaborate the title and discuss the meaning that the term 1984 has for millions of people in the English-speaking world. The date 1984 is *ominous*, the author says, "in every sense of that antique adjective." What are the senses of *ominous*?
2. At the end of paragraph 2, Lukacs states an assumption: the theme and title of Orwell's book have corresponded to an emerging consciousness that things are *not* getting better all the time. Does this assumption follow logically from the preceding material? Explain.
3. Paragraphs 3–5 summarize the plot of *Nineteen Eighty-Four*. Is the summary useful even though, as Lukacs says, the plot is well known? What is the significance (paragraph 4) of the birth-date and the first name of Winston Smith? In paragraph 5, the author uses a number of short sentences and short independent clauses—a departure from the style of the two preceding paragraphs of summary. What is the purpose of these simpler structures?
4. The opening sentence of paragraph 6 makes a transition from the plot to the quality of everyday life in 1984, which is developed in paragraphs 6–8. What distinction is made between the horror and the dreariness of life in 1984? What purpose is served by the brief contrast, in paragraph 7, of Aldous Huxley's and Orwell's views? In what way does paragraph 8 conclude direct discussion of Orwell's novel and mark a return to the central idea of Lukacs' essay?
5. Paragraph 9 introduces the idea that some of Orwell's visions of the future have not been borne out and so prepares for the analysis (paragraphs 10–16) of the world of 1966, halfway to 1984, in comparison to the world Orwell envisaged. This section of the essay is predominantly a series of contrasts, carefully qualified, between what Orwell foresaw and what has happened. In what specific ways have Orwell's visions proved wrong? What explanations does the author give for Orwell's failure as a prophet?
6. In this section of contrast (paragraphs 10–16), what suggestions do you find that developments opposite to those foreseen by Orwell are not in themselves desirable?
7. The end of paragraph 16 introduces the possibility of totalitarian democracy, which is described in paragraph 17. What does this totalitarian democracy have in common with the society of *Nineteen Eighty-four*?
8. In the illustration (paragraphs 18–19) of the author's image of 1984, what words and details best convey his attitudes toward this image of the future world? What devices of emphasis does Lukacs use?
9. Paragraph 20 states directly what has been stated indirectly before: that the Orwellian nightmare vision is already to some extent a reality. Paragraphs 17–25, in fact, deal with both similarities and differences between 1966 and *Nineteen Eighty-Four*. What characteristics of the Orwellian

nightmare are developed in paragraphs 20 and 21? Do the details Lukacs gives adequately support his generalizations?

10. Paragraph 22, developed by restatement and by cause–effect, introduces a series of new problems that should concern us now, halfway to 1984. What are these concerns (paragraphs 22–24)? At the beginning of paragraph 25, the author says that he cannot and perhaps need not explain or illustrate the concerns in greater detail. Would more illustration and detail have helped to clarify his ideas? Can you supply examples of each of these matters of concern?

11. Although the problems facing us in the nineteen-sixties are in many ways unlike the problems of *Nineteen Eighty-Four*, what relationship does the author see between the concept of 1984 and pessimism and "alienation" today? To what extent is the last sentence of paragraph 25 a summary of the content of the essay thus far?

12. Paragraph 26 makes a transition to the last main section of the essay— a discussion of Orwell's primary concern with the degeneration of language and the falsification of truth. If you have read Orwell's essay "Why I Write" (page 46), consider this question: Lukacs says that if Orwell is remembered for his political writing, he will be remembered for the wrong reasons. Does Lukacs mean by "political writing" exactly what Orwell himself meant?

13. Point out examples of contrast and comparison in the last section of the essay (paragraphs 27–31).

14. What are the purposes of the quotations from Tocqueville (paragraphs 30 and 31)? What, precisely, is the "distinction" referred to in the last sentence of the essay? Why is it emphasized by its position at the end of the essay?

CAUSE AND EFFECT

[7] *Erich Fromm*: Alienation: Quantification, Abstractification

ERICH FROMM (1900–), a German-born, naturalized-American psychoanalyst, has taught and lectured at a number of American colleges. His books include *Escape from Freedom, Man for Himself, Psychoanalysis and Religion, The Sane Society, The Art of Loving, May Man Prevail,* and *The Heart of Man.* The following selection is part of Chapter Five of *The Sane Society.* "The alienated person," Fromm says, "is out of touch with himself as he is out of touch with any other person. He, like the others, is experienced as things are experienced; with the senses and with common sense, but at the same time without being related to oneself and to the world outside productively."

[1] We must introduce the discussion of alienation by speaking of one of the fundamental economic features of Capitalism, the process of *quantification* and *abstractification.*
[2] The medieval artisan produced goods for a relatively small and known group of customers. His prices were determined by the need to make a profit which permitted him to live in a style traditionally commensurate with his social status. He knew from experience the costs of production, and even if he employed a few journeymen and apprentices, no elaborate system of bookkeeping or balance sheets was required for the operation of his business. The same held true for the production of the peasant, which required even less quantifying abstract methods. In

64

contrast, the modern business enterprise rests upon its balance sheet. It cannot rest upon such concrete and direct observation as the artisan used to figure out his profits. Raw material, machinery, labor costs, as well as the product can be expressed in the same money value, and thus made comparable and fit to appear in the balance equation. All economic occurrences have to be strictly quantifiable, and only the balance sheets, the exact comparison of economic processes quantified in figures, tell the manager whether and to what degree he is engaged in a profitable, that is to say, a meaningful business activity.

[3] This transformation of the concrete into the abstract has developed far beyond the balance sheet and the quantification of the economic occurrences in the sphere of production. The modern businessman not only deals with millions of dollars, but also with millions of customers, thousands of stockholders, and thousands of workers and employees; all these people become so many pieces in a gigantic machine which must be controlled, whose effects must be calculated; each man eventually can be expressed as an abstract entity, as a figure, and on this basis economic occurrences are calculated, trends are predicted, decisions are made.

[4] Today, when only about 20 per cent of our working population is self-employed, the rest work for somebody else, and a man's life is dependent on someone who pays him a wage or a salary. But we should say "something," instead of "someone," because a worker is hired and fired by an institution, the managers of which are impersonal parts of the enterprise, rather than people in personal contact with the men they employ. Let us not forget another fact: in precapitalistic society, exchange was to a large extent one of goods and services; today, all work is rewarded with money, the abstract expression of work—that is to say, we receive different quantities of the same for different qualities; and we give money for what we receive—again exchanging only different quantities for different qualities. Practically nobody, with the exception of the farm population, could live for even a few days without receiving and spending money, which stands for the abstract quality of concrete work.

[5] Another aspect of capitalist production which results in increasing abstractification is the increasing division of labor. Division of labor as a whole exists in most known economic systems, and, even in most primitive communities, in the form of division of labor between the sexes. What is characteristic of capitalistic production is the degree to which this division has developed. While in the medieval economy there was a division of labor let us say between agricultural production and the work of the artisan, there was little such division within each sphere of production itself. The carpenter making a chair or table made the whole chair or the whole table, and even if some preparatory work was done by his apprentices, he was in control of the production, overseeing it in its entirety. In the modern industrial enterprise, the worker is not in touch

with the whole product at any point. He is engaged in the performance of one specialized function, and while he might shift in the course of time from one function to another, he is still not related to the concrete product *as a whole*. He develops a specialized function, and the tendency is such, that the function of the modern industrial worker can be defined as working in a machinelike fashion in activities for which machine work has not yet been devised or which would be costlier than human work. The only person who is in touch with the whole product is the manager, but to him the product is an abstraction, whose essence is exchange value, while the worker, for whom it is concrete, never works on it as a whole.

[6] Undoubtedly without quantification and abstractification modern mass production would be unthinkable. But in a society in which economic activities have become the main preoccupation of man, this process of quantification and abstractification has transcended the realm of economic production, and spread to the attitude of man to things, to people, and to himself.

[7] In order to understand the abstractification process in modern man, we must first consider the ambiguous function of abstraction in general. It is obvious that abstractions in themselves are not a modern phenomenon. In fact, an increasing ability to form abstractions is characteristic of the cultural development of the human race. If I speak of "a table," I am using an abstraction; I am referring, not to a specific table in its full concreteness, but to the genus "table" which comprises all possible concrete tables. If I speak of "a man" I am not speaking of this or that person, in his concreteness and uniqueness, but of the genus "man," which comprises all individual persons. In other words, I make an abstraction. The development of philosophical or scientific thought is based on an increasing ability for such abstractification, and to give it up would mean to fall back into the primitive way of thinking.

[8] However, there are *two* ways of relating oneself to an object: one can relate oneself to it in its full concreteness; then the object appears with all its specific qualities, and there is no other object which is identical with it. And one can relate oneself to the object in an abstract way, that is, emphasizing only those qualities which it has in common with all other objects of the same genus, and thus accentuating some and ignoring other qualities. The full and productive relatedness to an object comprises this polarity of perceiving it in its uniqueness, and at the same time in its generality; in its concreteness, and at the same time in its abstractness.

[9] In contemporary Western culture this polarity has given way to an almost exclusive reference to the abstract qualities of things and people, and to a neglect of relating oneself to their concreteness and uniqueness. Instead of forming abstract concepts where it is necessary and useful, everything, including ourselves, is being abstractified; the concrete reality of people and things to which we can relate with the reality of our own

person, is replaced by abstractions, by ghosts that embody different qualities.

[¹⁰] It is quite customary to talk about a "three-million-dollar bridge," a "twenty-cent cigar," a "five-dollar watch," and this not only from the standpoint of the manufacturer or the consumer in the process of buying it, but as the essential point in the description. When one speaks of the "three-million-dollar bridge," one is not primarily concerned with its usefulness or beauty, that is, with its concrete qualities, but one speaks of it as of a commodity, the main quality of which is its exchange value, expressed in a quantity, that of money. This does not mean, of course, that one is not concerned also with the usefulness or beauty of the bridge, but it does mean that its concrete (use) value is *secondary* to its abstract (exchange) value in the way the object is experienced. The famous line by Gertrude Stein "a rose is a rose is a rose," is a protest against this abstract form of experience; for most people a rose is just *not* a rose, but a flower in a certain price range, to be bought on certain social occasions; even the most beautiful flower, provided it is a wild one, costing nothing, is not experienced in its beauty, compared to that of the rose, because it has no exchange value.

[¹¹] In other words, things are experienced as commodities, as embodiments of exchange value, not only while we are buying or selling, but in our attitude toward them when the economic transaction is finished. A thing, even after it has been bought, never quite loses its quality as a commodity in this sense; it is expendable, always retaining its exchange-value quality. A good illustration of this attitude is to be found in a report of the Executive Secretary of an important scientific organization as to how he spent a day in his office. The organization had just bought and moved into a building of their own. The Executive Secretary reports that during one of the first days after they had moved into the building, he got a call from a real estate agent, saying that some people were interested in buying the building and wanted to look at it. Although he knew that it was most unlikely that the organization would want to sell the building a few days after they had moved in, he could not resist the temptation to know whether the value of the building had risen since they had bought it, and spent one or two valuable hours in showing the real estate agent around. He writes: "very interested in fact we can get an offer for more than we have put in building. Nice coincidence that offer comes while treasurer is in the office. All agree it will be good for Board's morale to learn that the building will sell for a good deal more than it cost. Let's see what happens." In spite of all the pride and pleasure in the new building, it had still retained its quality as a commodity, as something expendable, and to which no full sense of possession or use is attached. The same attitude is obvious in the relationship of people to the cars they buy; the car never becomes fully a thing to which one is attached, but retains its quality as a commodity to be exchanged in a successful bargain; thus, cars are sold after a year or two, long before their use value is exhausted or even considerably diminished.

[12] This abstractification takes place even with regard to phenomena which are not commodities sold on the market, like a flood disaster; the newspapers will headline a flood, speaking of a "million-dollar catastrophe," emphasizing the abstract quantitative element rather than the concrete aspects of human suffering.

[13] But the abstractifying and quantifying attitude goes far beyond the realm of things. People are also experienced as the embodiment of a quantitative exchange value. To speak of a man as being "worth one million dollars," is to speak of him not any more as a concrete human person, but as an abstraction, whose essence can be expressed in a figure. It is an expression of the same attitude when a newspaper headlines an obituary with the words "Shoe Manufacturer Dies." Actually a *man* has died, a man with certain human qualities, with hopes and frustrations, with a wife and children. It is true that he manufactured shoes, or rather, that he owned and managed a factory in which workers served machines manufacturing shoes; but if it is said that a "Shoe Manufacturer Dies," the richness and concreteness of a human life is expressed in the abstract formula of economic function.

[14] The same abstractifying approach can be seen in expressions like "Mr. Ford produced so many automobiles," or this or that general "conquered a fortress"; or if a man has a house built for himself, he says, "I built a house." Concretely speaking, Mr. Ford did not manufacture the automobiles; he directed automobile production which was executed by thousands of workers. The general never conquered the fortress; he was sitting in his headquarters, issuing orders, and his soldiers did the conquering. The man did not build a house; he paid the money to an architect who made the plans and to workers who did the building. All this is not said to minimize the significance of the managing and directing operations, but in order to indicate that in this way of experiencing things, sight of what goes on concretely is lost, and an abstract view is taken in which one function, that of making plans, giving orders, or financing an activity, is identified with the whole concrete process of production, or of fighting, or of building, as the case may be.

[15] The same process of abstractification takes place in all other spheres. The New York *Times* recently printed a news item under the heading: "B.Sc. + Ph.D. = $40,000." The information under this somewhat baffling heading was that statistical data showed that a student of engineering who had acquired his Doctor's degree will earn, in a lifetime, $40,000 more than a man who has only the degree of Bachelor of Sciences. As far as this is a fact it is an interesting socioeconomic datum, worth while reporting. It is mentioned here because the way of expressing

the fact as an equation between a scientific degree and a certain amount of dollars is indicative of the abstractifying and quantifying thinking in which knowledge is experienced as the embodiment of a certain exchange value on the personality market. It is to the same point when a political report in a news magazine states that the Eisenhower administration feels it has so much "capital of confidence" that it can risk some unpopular measures, because it can "afford" to lose some of that confidence capital. Here again, a human quality like confidence is expressed in its abstract form, as if it were a money investment to be dealt with in terms of a market speculation. How drastically commercial categories have entered even religious thinking is shown in the following passage by Bishop Sheen, in an article on the birth of Christ. "Our reason tells us," so writes the author, "that if anyone of the claimants (for the role of God's son) came from God, the least that God could do to support His Representative's claim would be to preannounce His coming. Automobile manufacturers tell us when to expect a new model."[1] Or, even more drastically, Billy Graham, the evangelist, says: "I am selling the greatest product in the world; why shouldn't it be promoted as well as soap?"[2]

[16] The process of abstractification, however, has still deeper roots and manifestations than the ones described so far, roots which go back to the very beginning of the modern era; to the *dissolution* of any *concrete frame of reference* in the process of life.

[17] In a primitive society, the "world" is identical with the tribe. The tribe is in the center of the Universe, as it were; everything outside is shadowy and has no independent existence. In the medieval world, the Universe was much wider; it comprised this globe, the sky and the stars above it; but it was seen with the earth as the center and man as the purpose of Creation. Everything had its fixed place, just as everybody had his fixed position in feudal society. With the fifteenth and sixteenth centuries, new vistas opened up. The earth lost its central place, and became one of the satellites of the sun; new continents were found, new sea lanes discovered; the static social system was more and more loosened up; everything and everybody was moving. Yet, until the end of the nineteenth century, nature and society had not lost their concreteness and definiteness. Man's natural and social world was still manageable, still had definite contours. But with the progress in scientific thought, technical discoveries and the dissolution of all traditional bonds, this definiteness and concreteness is in the process of being lost. Whether we think of our new cosmological picture, or of theoretical physics, or of atonal music, or abstract art—the concreteness and definiteness of our frame of reference is disappearing. We are not any more in the center of the Universe, we are not

---

[1] From *Collier's* magazine, 1953. (Fromm)
[2] *Time* Magazine, October 25, 1954. (Fromm)

any more the purpose of Creation, we are not any more the masters of a manageable and recognizable world—we are a speck of dust, we are a nothing, somewhere in space—without any kind of concrete relatedness to anything. We speak of millions of people being killed, of one third or more of our population being wiped out if a third World War should occur; we speak of billions of dollars piling up as a national debt, of thousands of light years as interplanetary distances, of interspace travel, of artificial satellites. Tens of thousands work in one enterprise, hundreds of thousands live in hundreds of cities.

[18] The dimensions with which we deal are figures and abstractions; they are far beyond the boundaries which would permit of any kind of concrete experience. There is no frame of reference left which is manageable, observable, which is adapted to *human dimensions*. While our eyes and ears receive impressions only in humanly manageable proportions, our concept of the world has lost just that quality; it does not any longer correspond to our human dimensions.

[19] This is especially significant in connection with the development of modern means of destruction. In modern war, one individual can cause the destruction of hundreds of thousands of men, women and children. He could do so by pushing a button; he may not feel the emotional impact of what he is doing, since he does not know the people whom he kills; it is almost as if his act of pushing the button and their death had no real connection. The same man would probably be incapable of even slapping, not to speak of killing, a helpless person. In the latter case, the concrete situation arouses in him a conscience reaction common to all normal men; in the former, there is no such reaction, because the act and his object are alienated from the doer, his act is not *his* any more, but has, so to speak, a life and a responsibility of its own.

[20] Science, business, politics, have lost all foundations and proportions which make sense humanly. We live in figures and abstractions; since nothing is concrete, nothing is real. Everything is possible, factually and morally. Science fiction is not different from science fact, nightmares and dreams from the events of next year. Man has been thrown out from any definite place whence he can overlook and manage his life and the life of society. He is driven faster and faster by the forces which originally were created by him. In this wild whirl he thinks, figures, busy with abstractions, more and more remote from concrete life.

ERICH FROMM 71

❧ COMMENT AND QUESTIONS ☙

1. One way of analyzing this selection is to examine its different levels of cause–effect relationships. In the large pattern, the "process of quantification and abstractification" is a cause of the alienation of man in modern Western society. This process of quantification and abstractification, in turn, has several causes: (a) the characteristics of capitalist mass production; (b) the related habit of applying the values of economic production to things which are not actually commodities; (c) the deeper cause of a changing concept of the world in which a concrete human frame of reference is lost. The effect of all this is that modern man lives in a "wild whirl . . . busy with abstractions, more and more remote from concrete life."
   Fromm's opening paragraph indicates that he is using the terms *quantification* and *abstractification* to refer to a single phenomenon: ". . . one of the fundamental economic features . . . *the process* of quantification and abstractification." What is the difference in meaning of the two words? Why does Fromm use both of the rather cumbersome terms instead of only one?
2. Paragraph 2 is developed by contrast. What are the significant differences between medieval production and modern business enterprise?
3. In paragraphs 3 and 4, how has the transformation of the concrete into the abstract developed beyond the balance sheet? What words and phrases does Fromm use to emphasize the loss of concrete and personal experience in economic relations?
4. In what specific ways does increasing division of labor (paragraph 5) result in greater abstractification, and, eventually, in alienation?
5. Paragraph 6 is transitional. What connection does it establish between mass production and a changed attitude toward things and people?
6. In the discussion of abstractness and concreteness (paragraphs 7–9), what, according to Fromm, is the value of abstraction? What is the best, or most productive, way of relating oneself to an object? What kind of relating is characteristic of contemporary Western culture? What is the reason for the emphasis, at the end of paragraph 9, on the difference between quantity and quality?
7. What central idea is developed by means of the examples in paragraphs 10–12?
8. In what way does paragraph 12 lead into paragraph 13?
9. Paragraphs 13–15 are developed largely by examples. What slightly different points are made by the examples in each of the three paragraphs?
10. Paragraph 16 introduces a deeper cause of the process of abstractification, which is developed in paragraphs 17–19. What method or methods of development are used in paragraph 17? What does Fromm mean by saying that we have "no frame of reference . . . adapted to *human dimensions*"?

What idea is further developed by the discussion of modern war in paragraph 19?

11. This selection is part of a chapter "Man in Capitalistic Society," an analysis of the socio-economic conditions which create the social character of modern Western man and which are responsible for disturbances in his mental health. Are the statements made in paragraph 20 (the conclusion of one section of the chapter) adequately supported by the preceding material in this selection, or do some of them depend for meaning on a larger context?

12. Look back at the paragraph beginnings in "Alienation: Quantification and Abstractification." How does Fromm use his paragraph beginnings to establish transitions and to keep his organization clear?

QUESTION-TO-ANSWER OR PROBLEM-TO-SOLUTION

[8] *Arthur M. Schlesinger, Jr.*: The Crisis of American Masculinity

ARTHUR M. SCHLESINGER, JR. (1917–   ) has been a professor of history at Harvard and a special assistant to President Kennedy; he is now Albert Schweitzer Professor of the Humanities, City University of New York. Among his books are *The Age of Jackson*, winner of the 1945 Pulitzer Prize for history; *The Vital Center;* three volumes of *The Age of Roosevelt* (*The Crisis of the Old Order, 1919–1933, The Coming of the New Deal, The Politics of Upheaval*); and *A Thousand Days: John F. Kennedy in the White House,* which received the 1965 Pulitzer Prize for biography and the National Book Award in history and biography. The following essay, first published in *Esquire* in November, 1958, was later reprinted in *The Politics of Hope,* a collection of Schlesinger's essays on American politics and culture.

[1] What has happened to the American male? For a long time, he seemed utterly confident in his manhood, sure of his masculine role in society, easy and definite in his sense of sexual identity. The frontiersmen of James Fenimore Cooper, for example, never had any concern about masculinity; they were men, and it did not occur to them to think twice about it. Even well into the twentieth century, the heroes of Dreiser, of Fitzgerald, of Hemingway remain men. But one begins to detect a new theme emerging in some of these authors, especially in Hemingway: the

theme of the male hero increasingly preoccupied with proving his virility to himself. And by mid-century, the male role had plainly lost its rugged clarity of outline. Today men are more and more conscious of maleness not as a fact but as a problem. The ways by which American men affirm their masculinity are uncertain and obscure. There are multiplying signs, indeed, that something has gone badly wrong with the American male's conception of himself.

[²] On the most superficial level, the roles of male and female are increasingly merged in the American household. The American man is found as never before as a substitute for wife and mother—changing diapers, washing dishes, cooking meals and performing a whole series of what once were considered female duties. The American woman meanwhile takes over more and more of the big decisions, controlling them indirectly when she cannot do so directly. Outside the home, one sees a similar blurring of function. While men design dresses and brew up cosmetics, women become doctors, lawyers, bank cashiers and executives. "Women now fill many 'masculine' roles," writes the psychologist, Dr. Bruno Bettelheim, "and expect their husbands to assume many of the tasks once reserved for their own sex." They seem an expanding, aggressive force, seizing new domains like a conquering army, while men, more and more on the defensive, are hardly able to hold their own and gratefully accept assignments from their new rulers. A recent book bears the stark and melancholy title *The Decline of the American Male*.

[³] Some of this evidence, it should be quickly said, has been pushed too far. The willingness of a man to help his wife around the house may as well be evidence of confidence in masculinity as the opposite; such a man obviously does not have to cling to masculine symbols in order to keep demonstrating his maleness to himself. But there is more impressive evidence than the helpful husband that this is an age of sexual ambiguity. It appears no accident, for example, that the changing of sex—the Christine Jorgensen phenomenon—so fascinates our newspaper editors and readers; or that homosexuality, that incarnation of sexual ambiguity, should be enjoying a cultural boom new in our history. Such developments surely express a deeper tension about the problem of sexual identity.

[⁴] Consider the theatre, that faithful mirror of a society's preoccupations. There have been, of course, popular overt inquiries into sexual ambiguities, like *Compulsion* or *Tea and Sympathy*. But in a sense these plays prove the case too easily. Let us take rather two uncommonly successful plays by the most discussed young playwrights of the United States and Great Britain—Tennessee Williams's *Cat On A Hot Tin Roof* and John Osborne's *Look Back in Anger*. Both deal with the young male in a singular state of confusion and desperation. In *Cat On A Hot Tin Roof*, Brick Pollitt, the professional football player, refuses to sleep with his wife because of guilty memories of his relations with a dead team mate. In *Look Back in Anger,* Jimmy Porter, the embittered young intellectual who can sustain a relationship with his wife only by pretending they are furry animals together, explodes with hatred of women and finds his moments of happiness rough-housing around the stage with a male pal.

[5] Brick Pollitt and Jimmy Porter are all too characteristic modern heroes. They are, in a sense, castrated; one is stymied by fear of homosexuality, the other is an unconscious homosexual. Neither is capable of dealing with the woman in his life: Brick surrenders to a strong woman, Jimmy destroys a weak one. Both reject the normal female desire for full and reciprocal love as an unconscionable demand and an intolerable burden. Now not many American males have been reduced to quite the Pollitt-Porter condition. Still the intentness with which audiences have watched these plays suggests that exposed nerves are being plucked—that the Pollitt-Porter dilemma expresses in vivid and heightened form something that many spectators themselves feel or fear.

[6] Or consider the movies. In some ways, the most brilliant and influential American film since the war is *High Noon.* That remarkable movie, which invested the Western with the classic economy of myth, can be viewed in several ways: as an existentialist drama, for example, or as a parable of McCarthyism. It can also be viewed as a mordant comment on the effort of the American woman to emasculate the American man. The sheriff plainly did not suffer from Brick Pollitt's disease. But a large part of the story dealt with the attempt of his girl to persuade him not to use force—to deny him the use of his pistol. The pistol is an obvious masculine symbol, and, in the end, it was the girl herself, in the modern American manner, who used the pistol and killed a villain. (In this connection, one can pause and note why the Gary Coopers, Cary Grants, Clark Gables and Spencer Tracys continue to play romantic leads opposite girls young enough to be their daughters; it is obviously because so few of the younger male stars can project a convincing sense of masculinity.)

[7] Psychoanalysis backs up the theatre and the movies in emphasizing the obsession of the American male with his manhood. "Every psychoanalyst knows," writes one of them, "how many emotional difficulties are due to those fears and insecurities of neurotic men who are unconsciously doubting their masculinity." "In our civilization," Dr. Theodor Reik says, "men are afraid that they will not be men enough." Reik adds significantly: "And women are afraid that they might be considered only women." Why is it that women worry, not over whether they can fill the feminine role, but whether filling that role is enough, while men worry whether they can fill the masculine roll at all? How to account for this rising tide of male anxiety? What has unmanned the American man?

[8] There is currently a fashionable answer to this question. Male anxiety, many observers have declared, is simply the result of female ag-

gression: what has unmanned the American man is the American woman. The present male confusion and desperation, it is contended, are the inevitable consequence of the threatened feminization of American society. The victory of women is the culmination of a long process of masculine retreat, beginning when Puritanism made men feel guilty about sex and the frontier gave women the added value of scarcity. Fleeing from the reality of femininity, the American man, while denying the American woman juridical equality, transformed her into an ideal of remote and transcendent purity with overriding authority over the family, the home, the school and culture. This habit of obeisance left the male psychologically disarmed and vulnerable when the goddess stepped off the pedestal and demanded in addition equal economic, political and legal rights. In the last part of the nineteenth century, women won their battle for equality. They gained the right of entry into one occupation after another previously reserved for males. Today they hold the key positions of personal power in our society and use this power relentlessly to consolidate their mastery. As mothers, they undermine masculinity through the use of love as a technique of reward and punishment. As teachers, they prepare male children for their role of submission in an increasingly feminine world. As wives, they complete the work of subjugation. Their strategy of conquest is deliberately to emasculate men—to turn them into Brick Pollitts and Jimmy Porters.

[9] Or so a standard indictment runs; and no doubt there is something in it. American women have unquestionably gained through the years a place in our society which American men have not been psychologically prepared to accept. Whether because of Puritanism or the frontier, there has been something immature in the traditional American male attitude toward women—a sense of alarm at times amounting to panic. Almost none of the classic American novels, for example, presents the theme of mature and passionate love. Our nineteenth-century novelists saw women either as unassailable virgins or abandoned temptresses—never simply as women. One looks in vain through *Moby Dick* and *The Adventures of Huckleberry Finn*, through Cooper and Poe and Whitman, for an adult portrayal of relations between men and women. "Where," Leslie Fiedler has asked, "is the American *Madame Bovary, Anna Karenina, Wuthering Heights,* or *Vanity Fair?*"

[10] Yet the implication of the argument that the American man has been unmanned by the emancipation of the American woman is that the American man was incapable of growing up. For the nineteenth-century sense of masculinity was based on the psychological idealization and the legal subjection of women; masculinity so spuriously derived could never—and should never—have endured. The male had to learn to live at some point with the free and equal female. Current attempts to blame "the decline of the American male" on the aggressiveness of the

American female amount to a confession that, under conditions of free competition, the female was bound to win. Simple observation refutes this supposition. In a world of equal rights, some women rise; so too do some men; and no pat generalization is possible about the sexual future of society. Women have gained power in certain ways; in others, they have made little progress. It is safe to predict, for example, that we will have a Roman Catholic, perhaps even a Jew, for President before we have a woman. Those amiable prophets of an impending American matriarchy (all men, by the way) are too pessimistic.

[11] Something more fundamental is involved in the unmanning of American men than simply the onward rush of American women. Why is the American man so unsure today about his masculine identity? The basic answer to this is surely because he is so unsure about his identity in general. Nothing is harder in the whole human condition than to achieve a full sense of identity—than to know who you are, where you are going, and what you mean to live and die for. From the most primitive myths to the most contemporary novels—from Oedipus making the horrified discovery that he had married his mother, to Leopold Bloom and Stephen Dedalus searching their souls in Joyce's Dublin and the haunted characters of Kafka trying to make desperate sense out of an incomprehensible universe—the search for identity has been the most compelling human problem. That search has always been ridden with trouble and terror. And it can be plausibly argued that the conditions of modern life make the quest for identity more difficult than it has ever been before.

[12] The pre-democratic world was characteristically a world of status in which people were provided with ready-made identities. But modern western society—free, equalitarian, democratic—has swept away all the old niches in which people for so many centuries found safe refuge. Only a few people at any time in human history have enjoyed the challenge of "making" themselves; most have fled from the unendurable burden of freedom into the womblike security of the group. The new age of social mobility may be fine for those strong enough to discover and develop their own roles. But for the timid and the frightened, who constitute the majority in any age, the great vacant spaces of equalitarian society can become a nightmare filled with nameless horrors. Thus mass democracy, in the very act of offering the individual new freedom and opportunity, offers new moral authority to the group and thereby sets off a new assault on individual identity. Over a century ago Alexis de Tocqueville, the perceptive Frenchman who ruminated on the contradictions of equality as he toured the United States in the Eighteen Thirties, pointed to the "tyranny of the majority" as a central problem of democracy. John Stuart Mill, lamenting the decline of individualism in Great Britain, wrote: "That so few now dare to be eccentric marks the chief danger of the time." How much greater that danger seems a century later!

[13] For our own time has aggravated the assault on identity by adding economic and technological pressures to the political and social pressures of the nineteenth century. Modern science has brought about the growing centralization of the economy. We work and think and live and even dream in larger and larger units. William H. Whyte, Jr., has described the rise of "the organization man," working by day in immense business concerns, sleeping by night in immense suburban developments, deriving his fantasy life from mass-produced entertainments, spending his existence, not as an individual, but as a member of a group and coming in the end to feel guilty and lost when he deviates from his fellows. Adjustment rather than achievement becomes the social ideal. Men no longer fulfill an inner sense of what they *must be;* indeed, with the cult of the group, that inner sense itself begins to evaporate. Identity consists, not of self-realization, but of smooth absorption into the group. Nor is this just a matter of passive acquiescence. The group is aggressive, imperialistic, even vengeful, forever developing new weapons with which to overwhelm and crush the recalcitrant individual. Not content with disciplining the conscious mind, the group today is even experimenting with means of violating the subconscious. The subliminal invasion represents the climax of the assault on individual identity.

[14] It may seem a long way from the loss of the sense of self to the question of masculinity. But if people do not know *who* they are, it is hardly surprising that they are no longer sure what sex they are. Nigel Dennis's exuberant novel, *Cards of Identity,* consists of a series of brilliant variations on the quest for identity in contemporary life. It reaches one of its climaxes in the tale of a person who was brought up by enlightened parents to believe that there was no such thing as pure male or female— everyone had elements of both—and who accepted this proposition so rigorously that he (she) could not decide what his (her) own sex was. "In what identity do you intend to face the future?" someone asks. "It seems that nowadays," comes the plaintive reply, "one must choose between being a woman who behaves like a man, and a man who behaves like a woman. In short, I must choose to be one in order to behave like the other." If most of us have not yet quite reached that condition of sexual chaos, yet the loss of a sense of identity is obviously a fundamental step in the decay of masculinity. And the gratification with which some American males contemplate their own decline should not obscure the fact that women, for all their recent legal and economic triumphs, are suffering from a loss of identity too. It is not accidental that the authors of one recent book described modern woman as the "lost sex."

[15] If this is true, then the key to the recovery of masculinity does not lie in any wistful hope of humiliating the aggressive female and restoring the old masculine supremacy. Masculine supremacy, like white supremacy, was the neurosis of an immature society. It is good for men as well

as for women that women have been set free. In any case, the process is irreversible; that particular genie can never be put back into the bottle. The key to the recovery of masculinity lies rather in the problem of identity. When a person begins to find out *who* he is, he is likely to find out rather soon what sex he is.

[16] For men to become men again, in short, their first task is to recover a sense of individual spontaneity. And to do this a man must visualize himself as an individual apart from the group, whatever it is, which defines his values and commands his loyalty. There is no reason to suppose that the group is always wrong: to oppose the group automatically is nearly as conformist as to surrender to it automatically. But there is every necessity to recognize that the group is one thing and the individual— oneself—is another. One of the most sinister of present-day doctrines is that of *togetherness*. The recovery of identity means, first of all, a new belief in apartness. It means a determination to resist the overpowering conspiracy of blandness, which seeks to conceal all tension and conflict in American life under a blanket of locker-room affability. And the rebirth of spontaneity depends, at bottom, on changes of attitude *within* people— changes which can perhaps be described, without undue solemnity, as moral changes. These changes will no doubt come about in as many ways as there are individuals involved. But there are some general suggestions that can be made about the techniques of liberation. I should like to mention three such techniques: satire, art, and politics.

[17] Satire means essentially the belief that nothing is sacred—that there is no person or institution or idea which cannot but benefit from the exposure of comedy. Our nation in the past has reveled in satire; it is, after all, the nation of Abraham Lincoln, of Mark Twain, of Finley Peter Dunne, of H. L. Mencken, of Ring Lardner. Indeed, the whole spirit of democracy is that of satire; as Montaigne succinctly summed up the democratic faith: "Sit he on never so high a throne, a man still sits on his own bottom." Yet today American society can only be described as a pompous society, at least in its official manifestations. Early in 1958 Mort Sahl, the night-club comedian, made headlines in New York because he dared make a joke about J. Edgar Hoover! It was not an especially good joke, but the fact that he made it at all was an encouraging sign. One begins to feel that the American people can only stand so much reverence —that in the end our native skepticism will break through, sweep aside the stuffed shirts and the stuffed heads and insist that platitudes are platitudinous and the great are made, among other things, to be laughed at. Irony is good for our rulers; and it is even better for ourselves because it is a means of dissolving the pomposity of society and giving the individual a chance to emerge.

[18] If irony is one source of spontaneity, art is another. Very little can so refresh our vision and develop our vision and develop our values as

the liberating experience of art. The mass media have cast a spell on us: the popular addiction to prefabricated emotional clichés threatens to erode our capacity for fresh and direct aesthetic experience. Individual identity vanishes in the welter of machine-made reactions. But thoughtful exposure to music, to painting, to poetry, to the beauties of nature, can do much to restore the inwardness, and thereby the identity, of man. There is thus great hope in the immense cultural underground of our age—the paper-bound books, the long-playing records, the drama societies, the art festivals, the new interest in painting and sculpture. All this represents a disdain for existing values and goals, a reaching out for something more exacting and more personal, an intensified questing for identity.

[19] And politics in a true sense can be a means of liberation—not the banal politics of rhetoric and self-congratulation, which aims at burying all real issues under a mass of piety and platitude; but the politics of responsibility, which tries to define the real issues and present them to the people for decision. Our national politics have become boring in recent years because our leaders have offered neither candid and clear-cut formulations of the problems nor the facts necessary for intelligent choice. A virile political life will be definite and hardhitting, respecting debate and dissent, seeking clarity and decision.

[20] As the American male develops himself by developing his comic sense, his aesthetic sense and his moral and political sense, the lineaments of personality will at last begin to emerge. The achievement of identity, the conquest of a sense of self—these will do infinitely more to restore American masculinity than all the hormones in the test tubes of our scientists. "Whoso would be a *man*," said Emerson, "must be a nonconformist"; and, if it is the present writer who adds the italics, nonetheless one feels that no injustice is done to Emerson's intention. How can masculinity, femininity, or anything else survive in a homogenized society, which seeks steadily and benignly to eradicate all differences between the individuals who compose it? If we want to have *men* again in our theatres and our films and our novels—not to speak of in our classrooms, our business offices and our homes—we must first have a society which encourages each of its members to have a distinct identity.

COMMENT AND QUESTIONS

1. Schlesinger's essay has four main parts: the first section (paragraphs 1–7), which begins and ends with similar questions, develops a problem; the second section (paragraphs 8–10) supplies one current answer to the ques-

tions, an answer which the author considers inadequate; the third section (paragraphs 11–15) explores a deeper cause of the problem; and the last section (paragraphs 16–20) suggests a solution. Within this framework of problem-to-solution, Schlesinger uses contrast and comparison as well as cause–effect development.

Examine paragraph 1 of the essay. What makes it an effective beginning? How is the paragraph developed? How are the sentences within the paragraph linked? Why is *rugged* ("*rugged* clarity of outline," sentence 4) a better word than, for example, "unmistakable"? What are the two functions of the last sentence of paragraph 1?

2. Paragraphs 2–7 support the author's thesis that the American male is uncertain of his masculinity. What kinds of evidence does Schlesinger give? What examples of qualification do you find in this section (see especially paragraphs 3, 5, and 6)?
3. What contrasts and comparisons are used to develop paragraph 5?
4. What is the currently fashionable answer to the question of what has unmanned the American man? What are Schlesinger's reasons (paragraphs 9–10) for finding this answer not wholly satisfactory?
5. Paragraph 9 explicitly introduces the idea of some deficiency in American men themselves. In paragraphs 9 and 10, what direct and indirect references do you find to the idea of immaturity in the American man's attitude toward women?
6. Examine the organization and the transitions in the first two divisions of the essay (paragraphs 1–10) by re-reading, and perhaps underlining, the following sentences: the first and last sentences of paragraph 1; the first and fourth sentences of paragraph 2; the first and third sentences of paragraph 3; the first sentences of paragraphs 4, 5, and 6; the first and last sentences of paragraph 7; the first two sentences of paragraph 8; the first two sentences of paragraph 9; and the first sentence of paragraph 10. What are Schlesinger's principal devices for keeping the sequence of ideas and the relationship of ideas clear?
7. Paragraph 11 states a new thesis (a "basic answer" to the problem of American masculinity), supported in paragraphs 12 and 13. What is the thesis? What contrasts are used in paragraph 12? How is paragraph 12 linked to paragraph 13? How is paragraph 13 developed?
8. What is the function of paragraph 14? Do the concluding sentences, about women, violate the unity of the paragraph and of the essay on masculinity?
9. What is the reference of *this* ("If *this* is true") at the beginning of paragraph 15? Paragraph 15 is largely summary and restatement. What ideas and themes discussed earlier are drawn together in this paragraph?
10. Paragraph 16 introduces a solution to the problem of lost identity and, at the end, introduces three techniques for recovery of self. Comment on Schlesinger's diction in this paragraph; specifically, what are the connotations and contributions to tone of *spontaneity, sinister* (applied to "togetherness"), *overpowering conspiracy of blandness, blanket of locker-room affability, liberation*? What instances of qualification do you find in the paragraph?
11. In paragraphs 17–19, exactly what does Schlesinger mean by satire, art,

and politics? How may each of these help to restore identity? Are they related to the idea of maturity (or immaturity) discussed earlier in the essay? In recommending satire, art, and politics, is the author addressing the average American man, or a particular kind of American man? Would you add other "techniques of liberation" to the three he suggests?

12. Examine the sentences in paragraphs 18 and 19. What distinctive traits of style do you notice? In paragraph 18, why does Schlesinger use the term "immense cultural *underground*" in reference to paperback books, records, etc.? In the last sentence of paragraph 19, what words are particularly well chosen to fit the context of the whole essay?

13. What are the functions of the first two sentences of paragraph 20? In the next-to-last sentence of paragraph 20, why does the author mention femininity as well as masculinity? What are the connotations of *homogenized society*? What is the effect of the compounded adverbs *steadily and benignly*?

14. The structure of the concluding sentence gives major emphasis to having men in theatres, films, and novels, and less emphasis to having men in classrooms, offices, and homes. Does this emphasis follow logically from the content of the essay?

DEFINITION

[9]   *Carl L. Becker*: The Ideal Democracy

CARL L. BECKER (1873–1945) was a distinguished American historian who taught at Pennsylvania State College, Dartmouth, the Universities of Kansas and Minnesota, and after 1917 at Cornell. Among his books are *The Heavenly City of the Eighteenth Century Philosophers, Every Man His Own Historian, New Liberties for Old, How New Will the Better World Be?* and *Modern Democracy*, from which this selection is taken. "The Ideal Democracy" was originally delivered as a lecture at the University of Virginia in 1940. References to then-current world affairs date the essay in minor ways, but it remains contemporary as an illuminating definition and discussion of the historical development of democracy.

[1] Democracy, like liberty or science or progress, is a word with which we are all so familiar that we rarely take the trouble to ask what we mean by it. It is a term, as the devotees of semantics say, which has no "referent" —there is no precise or palpable thing or object which we all think of when the word is pronounced. On the contrary, it is a word which connotes different things to different people, a kind of conceptual Gladstone bag which, with a little manipulation, can be made to accommodate almost any collection of social facts we may wish to carry about in it. In it we can as easily pack a dictatorship as any other form of government. We have only to stretch the concept to include any form of government supported by a majority of the people, for whatever reasons and by whatever means of expressing assent, and before we know it the empire of Napoleon, the Soviet regime of Stalin, and the Fascist systems of

Mussolini and Hitler are all safely in the bag. But if this is what we mean by democracy, then virtually all forms of government are democratic, since virtually all governments, except in times of revolution, rest upon the explicit or implicit consent of the people. In order to discuss democracy intelligently it will be necessary, therefore, to define it, to attach to the word a sufficiently precise meaning to avoid the confusion which is not infrequently the chief result of such discussions.

[2] All human institutions, we are told, have their ideal forms laid away in heaven, and we do not need to be told that the actual institutions conform but indifferently to these ideal counterparts. It would be possible then to define democracy either in terms of the ideal or in terms of the real form—to define it as government of the people, by the people, for the people; or to define it as government of the people, by the politicians, for whatever pressure groups can get their interests taken care of. But as a historian, I am naturally disposed to be satisfied with the meaning which, in the history of politics, men have commonly attributed to the word—a meaning, needless to say, which derives partly from the experience and partly from the aspirations of mankind. So regarded, the term democracy refers primarily to a form of government, and it has always meant government by the many as opposed to government by the one—government by the people as opposed to government by a tyrant, a dictator, or an absolute monarch. This is the most general meaning of the word as men have commonly understood it.

[3] In this antithesis there are, however, certain implications, always tacitly understood, which give a more precise meaning to the term. Peisistratus, for example, was supported by a majority of the people, but his government was never regarded as a democracy for all that. Caesar's power derived from a popular mandate, conveyed through established republican forms, but that did not make his government any less a dictatorship. Napoleon called his government a democratic empire, but no one, least of all Napoleon himself, doubted that he had destroyed the last vestiges of the democratic republic. Since the Greeks first used the term, the essential test of democratic government has always been this: the source of political authority must be and remain in the people and not in the ruler. A democratic government has always meant one in which the citizens, or a sufficient number of them to represent more or less effectively the common will, freely act from time to time, and according to established forms, to appoint or recall the magistrates and to enact or revoke the laws by which the community is governed. This I take to be the meaning which history has impressed upon the term democracy as a form of government. It is, therefore, the meaning which I attach to it in these lectures.

[4] The most obvious political fact of our time is that democracy as thus defined has suffered an astounding decline in prestige. Fifty years

ago it was not impossible to regard democratic government, and the liberties that went with it, as a permanent conquest of the human spirit. In 1886 Andrew Carnegie published a book entitled *Triumphant Democracy*. Written without fear and without research, the book was not an achievement of the highest intellectual distinction perhaps; but the title at least expressed well enough the prevailing conviction—the conviction that democracy had fought the good fight, had won the decisive battles, and would inevitably, through its inherent merits, presently banish from the world the most flagrant political and social evils which from time immemorial had afflicted mankind. This conviction could no doubt be most easily entertained in the United States, where even the tradition of other forms of government was too remote and alien to color our native optimism. But even in Europe the downright skeptics, such as Lecky, were thought to be perverse, and so hardheaded a historian as J. B. Bury could proclaim with confidence that the long struggle for freedom of thought had finally been won.

[5] I do not need to tell you that within a brief twenty years the prevailing optimism of that time has been quite dispelled. One European country after another has, willingly enough it seems, abandoned whatever democratic institutions it formerly enjoyed for some form of dictatorship. The spokesmen of Fascism and Communism announce with confidence that democracy, a sentimental aberration which the world has outgrown, is done for; and even the friends of democracy support it with declining conviction. They tell us that democracy, so far from being triumphant, is "at the crossroads" or "in retreat," and that its future is by no means assured. What are we to think of this sudden reversal in fortune and prestige? How explain it? What to do about it?

- II -

[6] One of the presuppositions of modern thought is that institutions, in order to be understood, must be seen in relation to the conditions of time and place in which they appear. It is a little difficult for us to look at democracy in this way. We are so immersed in its present fortunes that we commonly see it only as a "close-up," filling the screen to the exclusion of other things to which it is in fact related. In order to form an objective judgment of its nature and significance, we must therefore first of all get it in proper perspective. Let us then, in imagination, remove from the immediate present scene to some cool high place where we can survey at a glance five or six thousand years of history, and note the part which democracy has played in human civilization. The view, if we have been accustomed to take democratic institutions for granted, is a bit bleak and disheartening. For we see at once that in all this long time, over the habitable globe, the great majority of the human race has neither known nor apparently much cared for our favorite institutions.

[⁷] Civilization was already old when democracy made its first notable appearance among the small city states of ancient Greece, where it flourished brilliantly for a brief century or two and then disappeared. At about the same time something that might be called democracy appeared in Rome and other Italian cities, but even in Rome it did not survive the conquest of the world by the Roman Republic, except as a form of local administration in the cities of the empire. In the twelfth and thirteenth centuries certain favorably placed medieval cities enjoyed a measure of self-government, but in most instances it was soon replaced by the dictatorship of military conquerors, the oligarchic control of a few families, or the encroaching power of autocratic kings. The oldest democracy of modern times is the Swiss Confederation, the next oldest is the Dutch Republic. Parliamentary government in England does not antedate the late seventeenth century, the great American experiment is scarcely older. Not until the nineteenth century did democratic government make its way in any considerable part of the world—in the great states of continental Europe, in South America, in Canada and Australia, in South Africa and Japan.

[⁸] From this brief survey it is obvious that, taking the experience of mankind as a test, democracy has as yet had but a limited and temporary success. There must be a reason for this significant fact. The reason is that democratic government is a species of social luxury, at best a delicate and precarious adventure which depends for success upon the validity of certain assumptions about the capacities and virtues of men, and upon the presence of certain material and intellectual conditions favorable to the exercise of these capacities and virtues. Let us take the material conditions first.

[⁹] It is a striking fact that until recently democracy never flourished except in very small states—for the most part in cities. It is true that in both the Persian and the Roman empires a measure of self-government was accorded to local communities, but only in respect to purely local affairs; in no large state as a whole was democratic government found to be practicable. One essential reason is that until recently the means of communication were too slow and uncertain to create the necessary solidarity of interest and similarity of information over large areas. The principle of representation was well enough known to the Greeks, but in practice it proved impracticable except in limited areas and for special occasions. As late as the eighteenth century it was still the common opinion that the republican form of government, although the best ideally, was unsuited to large countries, even to a country no larger than France. This was the view of Montesquieu, and even of Rousseau. The view persisted into the nineteenth century, and English conservatives, who were opposed to the extension of the suffrage in England, consoled themselves with the notion that the American Civil War would confirm it—would demonstrate that government by and for the people would perish, if not from off the earth at least from large countries. If their hopes were confounded the reason is that the means of communication, figuratively speaking, were making large countries small. It is not altogether fanciful to suppose that, but for the railroad and the telegraph, the United States would today be divided into many small republics maneuvering for advantage and employing war and diplomacy for maintaining an unstable balance of power.

[10] If one of the conditions essential to the success of democratic government is mobility, ease of communication, another is a certain measure of economic security. Democracy does not flourish in communities on the verge of destitution. In ancient and medieval times democratic government appeared for the most part in cities, the centers of prosperity. Farmers in the early Roman Republic and in the Swiss Cantons were not wealthy to be sure, but equality of possessions and of opportunity gave them a certain economic security. In medieval cities political privilege was confined to the prosperous merchants and craftsmen, and in Athens and the later Roman Republic democratic government was found to be workable only on condition that the poor citizens were subsidized by the government or paid for attending the assemblies and the law courts.

[11] In modern times democratic institutions have, generally speaking, been most successful in new countries, such as the United States, Canada, and Australia, where the conditions of life have been easy for the people; and in European countries more or less in proportion to their industrial prosperity. In European countries, indeed, there has been a close correlation between the development of the industrial revolution and the emergence of democratic institutions. Holland and England, the first countries to experience the industrial revolution, were the first also (apart from Switzerland, where certain peculiar conditions obtained) to adopt democratic institutions; and as the industrial revolution spread to France, Belgium, Germany, and Italy, these countries in turn adopted at least a measure of democratic government. Democracy is in some sense an economic luxury, and it may be said that in modern times it has been a function of the development of new and potentially rich countries, or of the industrial revolution which suddenly dowered Europe with unaccustomed wealth. Now that prosperity is disappearing round every next corner, democracy works less well than it did.

[12] So much for the material conditions essential for the success of democratic government. Supposing these conditions to exist, democratic government implies in addition the presence of certain capacities and virtues in its citizens. These capacities and virtues are bound up with the assumptions on which democracy rests, and are available only in so

far as the assumptions are valid. The primary assumption of democratic government is that its citizens are capable of managing their own affairs. But life in any community involves a conflict of individual and class interests, and a corresponding divergence of opinion as to the measures to be adopted for the common good. The divergent opinions must be somehow reconciled, the conflict of interests somehow compromised. It must then be an assumption of democratic government that its citizens are rational creatures, sufficiently so at least to understand the interests in conflict; and it must be an assumption that they are men of good will, sufficiently so toward each other at least to make those concessions of individual and class interest required for effecting workable compromises. The citizens of a democracy should be, as Pericles said the citizens of Athens were, if not all originators at least all sound judges of good policy.

[13] These are what may be called the minimum assumptions and the necessary conditions of democratic government anywhere and at any time. They may be noted to best advantage, not in any state, but in small groups within the state—in clubs and similar private associations of congenial and like-minded people united for a specific purpose. In such associations the membership is limited and select. The members are, or may easily become, all acquainted with each other. Everyone knows, or may easily find out, what is being done and who is doing it. There will of course be differences of opinion, and there may be disintegrating squabbles and intrigues. But on the whole, ends and means being specific and well understood, the problems of government are few and superficial; there is plenty of time for discussion; and since intelligence and good will can generally be taken for granted there is the disposition to make reasonable concessions and compromises. The analogy must be taken for what it is worth. States may not be the mystical blind Molochs of German philosophy, but any state is far more complex and intangible than a private association, and there is little resemblance between such associations and the democracies of modern times. Other things equal, the resemblance is closest in very small states, and it is in connection with the small city states of ancient Greece that the resemblance can best be noted.

[14] The Greek states were limited in size, not as is often thought solely or even chiefly by the physiography of the country, but by some instinctive feeling of the Greek mind that a state is necessarily a natural association of people bound together by ties of kinship and a common tradition of rights and obligations. There must then, as Aristotle said, be a limit:

For if the citizens of a state are to judge and distribute offices according to merit, they must know each other's characters; where they do not possess this knowledge, both the elections to offices and the decisions in the law courts will go wrong. Where the population is very large they are manifestly settled by haphazard, which clearly ought not to be. Besides, in over-populous states foreigners and metics will readily acquire citizenship, for who will find them out?

It obviously did not occur to Aristotle that metics and foreigners should be free to acquire citizenship. It did not occur to him, or to any Greek of his time, or to the merchants of the self-governing medieval city, that a state should be composed of all the people inhabiting a given territory. A state was rather an incorporated body of people within, but distinct from, the population of the community.

[15] Ancient and medieval democracies had thus something of the character of a private association. They were, so to speak, purely pragmatic phenomena, arising under very special conditions, and regarded as the most convenient way of managing the affairs of people bound together by community of interest and for the achievement of specific ends. There is no suggestion in Aristotle that democracy (polity) is intrinsically a superior form of government, no suggestion that it derives from a special ideology of its own. If it rests upon any superiority other than convenience, it is the superiority which it shares with any Greek state, that is to say, the superiority of Greek over barbarian civilization. In Aristotle's philosophy it is indeed difficult to find any clear-cut distinction between the democratic form of government and the state itself; the state, if it be worthy of the name, is always, whatever the form of government, "the government of freemen and equals," and in any state it is always necessary that "the freemen who compose the bulk of the people should have absolute power in some things." In Aristotle's philosophy the distinction between good and bad in politics is not between good and bad types of government, but between the good and the bad form of each type. Any type of government—monarchy, aristocracy, polity—is good provided the rulers aim at the good of all rather than at the good of the class to which they belong. From Aristotle's point of view neither democracy nor dictatorship is good or bad in itself, but only in the measure that it achieves, or fails to achieve, the aim of every good state, which is that "the inhabitants of it should be happy." It did not occur to Aristotle that democracy (polity), being in some special sense in harmony with the nature of man, was everywhere applicable, and therefore destined by fate or the gods to carry throughout the world a superior form of civilization.

[16] It is in this respect chiefly that modern democracy differs from earlier forms. It rests upon something more than the minimum assumptions. It is reinforced by a full-blown ideology which, by endowing the individual with natural and imprescriptible rights, sets the democratic form of government off from all others as the one which alone can achieve the good life. What then are the essential tenets of the modern democratic faith?

– III –

[17] The liberal democratic faith, as expressed in the works of eighteenth- and early nineteenth-century writers, is one of the formulations

of the modern doctrine of progress. It will be well, therefore, to note briefly the historical antecedents of that doctrine.

[18] In the long history of man on earth there comes a time when he remembers something of what has been, anticipates something that will be, knows the country he has traversed, wonders what lies beyond—the moment when he becomes aware of himself as a lonely, differentiated item in the world. Sooner or later there emerges for him the most devastating of all facts, namely, that in an indifferent universe which alone endures, he alone aspires, endeavors to attain, and attains only to be defeated in the end. From that moment his immediate experience ceases to be adequate, and he endeavors to project himself beyond it by creating ideal worlds of semblance, Utopias of other time or place in which all has been, may be, or will be well.

[19] In ancient times Utopia was most easily projected into the unknown past, pushed back to the beginning of things—to the time of P'an Ku and the celestial emperors, to the Garden of Eden, or the reign of King Chronos when men lived like gods free from toil and grief. From this happy state of first created things there had obviously been a decline and fall, occasioned by disobedience and human frailty, and decreed as punishment by fate or the angry gods. The mind of man was therefore afflicted with pessimism, a sense of guilt for having betrayed the divine purpose, a feeling of inadequacy for bringing the world back to its original state of innocence and purity. To men who felt insecure in a changing world, and helpless in a world always changing for the worse, the future had little to offer. It could be regarded for the most part only with resignation, mitigated by individual penance or well-doing, or the hope of some miraculous intervention by the gods, or the return of the god-like kings, to set things right again, yet with little hope that from this setting right there would not be another falling away.

[20] This pervasive pessimism was gradually dispelled in the Western world, partly by the Christian religion, chiefly by the secular intellectual revolution occurring roughly between the fifteenth and the eighteenth centuries. The Christian religion gave assurance that the lost golden age of the past would be restored for the virtuous in the future, and by proclaiming the supreme worth of the individual in the eyes of God enabled men to look forward with hope to the good life after death in the Heavenly City. Meantime, the secular intellectual revolution, centering in the matter-of-fact study of history and science, gradually emancipated the minds of men from resignation to fate and the angry gods. Accumulated knowledge of history, filling in time past with a continuous succession of credible events, banished all lost golden ages to the realm of myth, and enabled men to live without distress in a changing world since it could be regarded as not necessarily changing for the worse. At the same time,

a more competent observation and measurement of the action of material things disclosed an outer world of nature, indifferent to man indeed, yet behaving, not as the unpredictable sport of the gods, but in ways understandable to human reason and therefore ultimately subject to man's control.

[21] Thus the conditions were fulfilled which made it possible for men to conceive of Utopia, neither as a lost golden age of the past nor as a Heavenly City after death prepared by the gods for the virtuous, but as a future state on earth of man's own devising. In a world of nature that could be regarded as amenable to man's control, and in a world of changing social relations that need not be regarded as an inevitable decline and fall from original perfection, it was possible to formulate the modern doctrine of progress: the idea that, by deliberate intention and rational direction, men can set the terms and indefinitely improve the conditions of their mundane existence.

[22] The eighteenth century was the moment in history when men first fully realized the engaging implications of this resplendent idea, the moment when, not yet having been brought to the harsh appraisal of experience, it could be accepted with unclouded optimism. Never had the universe seemed less mysterious, more open and visible, more eager to yield its secrets to common-sense questions. Never had the nature of man seemed less perverse, or the mind of man more pliable to the pressure of rational persuasion. The essential reason for this confident optimism is that the marvels of scientific discovery disclosed to the men of that time a God who still functioned but was no longer angry. God the Father could be conceived as a beneficient First Cause who, having performed his essential task of creation, had withdrawn from the affairs of men, leaving them competently prepared and fully instructed for the task of achieving their own salvation. In one tremendous sentence Rousseau expressed the eighteenth-century world view of the universe and man's place in it. "Is it simple," he exclaimed, "is it natural that God should have gone in search of Moses in order to speak to Jean Jacques Rousseau?"

[23] God had indeed spoken to Rousseau, he had spoken to all men, but his revelation was contained, not in Holy Writ interpreted by Holy Church, but in the great Book of Nature which was open for all men to read. To this open book of nature men would go when they wanted to know what God had said to them. Here they would find recorded the laws of nature and of nature's God, disclosing a universe constructed according to a rational plan; and that men might read these laws aright they had been endowed with reason, a bit of the universal intelligence placed within the individual to make manifest to him the universal reason implicit in things and events. "Natural law," as Volney so clearly and confidently put it, "is the regular and constant order of facts by which God rules the

universe; the order which his wisdom presents to the sense and reason of men, to serve them as an equal and common rule of conduct, and to guide them, without distinction of race or sect, toward perfection and happiness." Thus God had devised a planned economy, and had endowed men with the capacity for managing it: to bring his ideas, his conduct, and his institutions into harmony with the universal laws of nature was man's simple allotted task.

[24] At all times political theory must accommodate itself in some fashion to the prevailing world view, and liberal-democratic political theory was no exception to this rule. From time immemorial authority and obedience had been the cardinal concepts both of the prevailing world view and of political and social theory. From time immemorial men had been regarded as subject to overruling authority—the authority of the gods, and the authority of kings who were themselves gods, or descended from gods, or endowed with divine authority to rule in place of gods; and from time immemorial obedience to such divine authority was thought to be the primary obligation of men. Even the Greeks, who were so little afraid of their gods that they could hob-nob with them in the most friendly and engaging way, regarded mortals as subject to them; and when they lost faith in the gods they deified the state as the highest good and subordinated the individual to it. But the eighteenth-century world view, making man the measure of all things, mitigated if it did not destroy this sharp contrast between authority and obedience. God still reigned but he did not govern. He had, so to speak, granted his subjects a constitution and authorized them to interpret it as they would in the supreme court of reason. Men were still subject to an overruling authority, but the subjection could be regarded as voluntary because self-imposed, and self-imposed because obedience was exacted by nothing more oppressive than their own rational intelligence.

[25] Liberal-democratic political theory readily accommodated itself to this change in the world view. The voice of the people was now identified with the voice of God, and all authority was derived from it. The individual instead of the state or the prince was now deified and endowed with imprescriptible rights; and since ignorance or neglect of the rights of man was the chief cause of social evils, the first task of political science was to define these rights, the second to devise a form of government suited to guarantee them. The imprescriptible rights of man were easily defined, since they were self-evident: "All men are created equal, [and] are endowed by their Creator with certain inalienable rights, among which are life, liberty, and the pursuit of happiness." From this it followed that all just governments would remove those artificial restraints which impaired these rights, thereby liberating those natural impulses with which God had endowed the individual as a guide to thought and

conduct. In the intellectual realm, freedom of thought and the competition of diverse opinion would disclose the truth, which all men, being rational creatures, would progressively recognize and willingly follow. In the economic realm, freedom of enterprise would disclose the natural aptitudes of each individual, and the ensuing competition of interests would stimulate effort, and thereby result in the maximum of material advantage for all. Liberty of the individual from social constraint thus turned out to be not only an inherent natural right but also a preordained natural mechanism for bringing about the material and moral progress of mankind. Men had only to follow reason and self-interest: something not themselves, God and Nature, would do whatever else was necessary for righteousness.

[26] Thus modern liberal-democracy is associated with an ideology which rests upon something more than the minimum assumptions essential to any democratic government. It rests upon a philosophy of universally valid ends and means. Its fundamental assumption is the worth and dignity and creative capacity of the individual, so that the chief aim of government is the maximum of individual self-direction, the chief means to that end the minimum of compulsion by the state. Ideally considered, means and ends are conjoined in the concept of freedom: freedom of thought, so that the truth may prevail; freedom of occupation, so that careers may be open to talent; freedom of self-government, so that no one may be compelled against his will.

[27] In the possibility of realizing this ideal the prophets and protagonists of democracy exhibited an unquestioned faith. If their faith seems to us somewhat naïve, the reason is that they placed a far greater reliance upon the immediate influence of good will and rational discussion in shaping the conduct of men than it is possible for us to do. This difference can be conveniently noted in a passage from the *Autobiography* of John Stuart Mill, in which he describes his father's extraordinary faith in two things—representative government and complete freedom of discussion:

So complete was my father's reliance on the influence of reason over the minds of mankind, whenever it was allowed to reach them, that he felt as if all would be gained if the whole population were taught to read, if all sorts of opinions were allowed to be addressed to them by word and writing, and if by means of the suffrage they could nominate a legislature to give effect to the opinions they adopted. He thought that when the legislature no longer represented a class interest, it would aim at the general interest, honestly and with adequate wisdom; since the people would be sufficiently under the guidance of educated intelligence to make in general good choice of persons to represent them, and having done so to leave to those whom they had chosen a liberal discretion. Accordingly, artistocratic rule, the government of the few in any of its shapes, being in his eyes the only thing that stood between mankind and the administration of its affairs by the best wisdom to be found amongst them, was the object of his sternest disapprobation, and a democratic suffrage the principal article of his political creed.

[28] The beliefs of James Mill were shared by the little group of Philosophical Radicals who gathered about him. They were, indeed, the beliefs of all those who in the great crusading days placed their hopes in democratic government as a panacea for injustice and oppression. The actual working of democratic government, as these devoted enthusiasts foresaw it, the motives that would inspire men and the objects they would pursue in that ideal democracy which so many honest men have cherished and fought for, have never been better described than by James Bryce in his *Modern Democracies*. In this ideal democracy, says Bryce,

the average citizen will give close and constant attention to public affairs, recognizing that this is his interest as well as his duty. He will try to comprehend the main issues of policy, bringing them an independent and impartial mind, which thinks first not of its own but of the general interest. If, owing to inevitable differences of opinion as to what are the measures needed for the general welfare, parties become inevitable, he will join one, and attend its meetings, but will repress the impulses of party spirit. Never failing to come to the polls, he will vote for his party candidate only if satisfied by his capacity and honesty. He will be ready to . . . be put forward as a candidate for the legislature (if satisfied of his own competence), because public service is recognized as a duty. With such citizens as electors, the legislature will be composed of upright and capable men, single-minded in their wish to serve the nation. Bribery in constituencies, corruption among public servants, will have disappeared. Leaders may not always be single-minded, nor assemblies always wise, nor administrators efficient, but all will be at any rate honest and zealous, so that an atmosphere of confidence and goodwill will prevail. Most of the causes that make for strife will be absent, for there will be no privileges, no advantages to excite jealousy. Office will be sought only because it gives opportunity for useful public service. Power will be shared by all, and a career open to all alike. Even if the law does not—perhaps it cannot—prevent the accumulation of fortunes, these will be few and not inordinate, for public vigilance will close the illegitimate paths to wealth. All but the most depraved persons will obey and support the law, feeling it to be their own. There will be no excuse for violence, because the constitution will provide a remedy for every grievance. Equality will produce a sense of human solidarity, will refine manners, and increase brotherly kindness.

[29] Such is the ideal form of modern democracy laid away in heaven. I do not need to tell you that its earthly counterpart resembles it but slightly.

--⊰{ COMMENT AND QUESTIONS }⊱--

1. One of the best ways to study the very skillful organization of this essay is to examine the first and last sentences of each paragraph, noticing how they state or emphasize topic ideas, and how they establish transitions between paragraphs and sections. What phase of the subject is treated in each of the three major divisions of the essay, and how are the three divisions related?
2. What methods of definition are used in paragraphs 1–3?
3. Paragraph 4 (developed by contrast and example) states a thesis which is further developed and supported in paragraph 5. What is the thesis? Is it still supportable today, almost thirty years after Becker wrote "The Ideal Democracy"?
4. What is Becker's attitude toward Andrew Carnegie's book (paragraph 4)? What expressions particularly reveal the attitude? How would you describe Becker's tone in this passage?
5. Which of the three questions at the end of section I is most directly answered in section II?
6. The last sentence of paragraph 6 and the first sentence of paragraph 8 state, in different words, a generalization about democracy. How is the generalization supported in paragraph 7?
7. Paragraph 8 introduces reasons for the limited success of democracy in human history. Upon what material conditions does democracy depend (paragraphs 9–11)? What minimum assumptions does democracy make about the capacities and virtues of its citizens (paragraph 12)? Some Americans at the present time find it difficult to understand why people of other countries—the developing nations, for example—have not been and are not enthusiastic about democratic government. In what ways might Becker's discussion of the history of democracy throw light on the fact that the institutions which seem obviously valuable to us are not equally attractive to all people?
8. What are the purposes in the essay of paragraphs 13–16?
9. Paragraphs 18–21 are developed by time-order and by cause and effect. What were the historical causes of (a) man's creation of ideal worlds or Utopias; (b) the pessimism, in ancient times, about the future; (c) the gradual dispelling of this pessimism; (d) the formulation of the modern doctrine of progress?
10. This essay, like all of Carl Becker's writing, is notable for its lucid and polished style. Study the writing in paragraphs 18–21, noticing the rhythm and flow of the sentences and the way the sentences are structured to end strongly. What particular qualities of style seem to you especially effective?
11. Examine the diction in paragraph 22. What words and expressions convey a sense of the magnificence of the eighteenth-century world view? At the same time, how does Becker indicate his own reservations about that optimistic view?

12. What contrasts are established in paragraph 24, and how are the contrasts emphasized? Explain how the world view of the eighteenth century affected political theory and produced the modern democratic ideology (paragraphs 24–26).
13. One way of supporting a thesis or generalization is the use of apt quotation. Comment on Becker's use of quotation in this essay and on the purposes served by the quoted material.
14. Becker ends with an assumption: "I do not need to tell you . . . ." In your opinion, in what marked ways does the "earthly counterpart" of democracy differ from the ideal form?
15. Since "The Ideal Democracy" is the first of three lectures on democracy, it is somewhat inconclusive: the author does not answer all the questions he raises at the end of the first section, and he may leave in doubt his own opinion of democracy as a form of government. That opinion is stated in the following passage from another of Becker's books, *New Liberties for Old:*

> To have faith in the dignity and worth of the individual man as an end in himself, to believe that it is better to be governed by persuasion than by coercion, to believe that fraternal good will is more worthy than a selfish and contentious spirit, to believe that in the long run all values are inseparable from the love of truth and the disinterested search for it, to believe that knowledge and the power it confers should be used to promote the welfare and happiness of all men rather than to serve the interests of those individuals and classes whom fortune and intelligence endow with temporary advantage—these are the values which are affirmed by the traditional democratic ideology. . . . The case for democracy is that it accepts the rational and humane values as ends, and proposes as the means of realizing them the minimum of coercion and the maximum of voluntary assent. We may well abandon the cosmological temple in which the democratic ideology originally enshrined these values without renouncing the faith it was designed to celebrate. The essence of that faith is belief in the capacity of man, as a rational and humane creature, to achieve the good life by rational and humane means. The chief virtue of democracy, and the sole reason for cherishing it, is that with all its faults it still provides the most favorable conditions for achieving that end by those means.

What is meant, in the third-from-the-last sentence in the quotation above, by *"the cosmological temple* in which the democratic ideology originally enshrined these values"? What difference do you see between the view of democracy which Becker expresses in the last two sentences of the quotation above and the view of the writers quoted in the last section of "The Ideal Democracy"?

PART TWO

Ideas and Values

EDUCATION AND THE INQUIRING MIND

[10]   *Plato*: Apology

IN 399 B.C., SOCRATES, Greek philosopher and teacher, was accused of impiety and of corrupting the youth of Athens with false doctrines, and was tried and condemned to death by a court of 501 Athenian citizens. According to Athenian law, the accused acted as his own attorney and spoke to the court in his own behalf. If he was judged guilty of the charges, and if no punishment for the offense was established by Athenian law, his accusers proposed a penalty, and the defendant might propose an alternate penalty; the court then chose between them. The *Apology*, or *Defense* (the Greek word did not imply expression of regret, as our word *apology* may), is Socrates' speech to the court, reported by his pupil Plato. It gives us a picture of a human being, an almost legendary thinker, who has helped to shape Western thought, and whose voice still says over the centuries that wisdom and virtue come only from thought and inquiry, and that the unexamined life is not worth living.

[1] How you, O Athenians, have been affected by my accusers, I cannot tell; but I know that they almost made me forget who I was—so persuasively did they speak; and yet they have hardly uttered a word of truth. But of the many falsehoods told by them, there was one which quite amazed me;—I mean when they said that you should be upon your guard and not allow yourselves to be deceived by the force of my eloquence. To say this, when they were certain to be detected as soon as I opened

This selection was translated by Benjamin Jowett.

my lips and proved myself to be anything but a great speaker, did indeed appear to me most shameless—unless by the force of eloquence they mean the force of truth; for if such is their meaning, I admit that I am eloquent. But in how different a way from theirs! Well, as I was saying, they have scarcely spoken the truth at all; but from me you shall hear the whole truth; not, however, delivered after their manner in a set oration duly ornamented with words and phrases. No, by heaven! but I shall use the words and argument which occur to me at the moment; for I am confident in the justice of my cause: at my time of life I ought not to be appearing before you, O men of Athens, in the character of a juvenile orator—let no one expect it of me. And I must beg of you to grant me a favour:—if I defend myself in my accustomed manner, and you hear me using the words which I have been in the habit of using in the agora, at the tables of the money-changers, or anywhere else, I would ask you not to be surprised, and not to interrupt me on this account. For I am more than seventy years of age, and appearing now for the first time in a court of law, I am quite a stranger to the language of the place; and therefore I would have you regard me as if I were really a stranger, whom you would excuse if he spoke in his native tongue, and after the fashion of his country:—Am I making an unfair request of you? Never mind the manner, which may or may not be good; but think only of the truth of my words, and give heed to that: let the speaker speak truly and the judge decide justly.

[2] And first, I have to reply to the older charges and to my first accusers, and then I will go on to the later ones. For of old I have had many accusers, who have accused me falsely to you during many years; and I am more afraid of them than of Anytus and his associates, who are dangerous, too, in their own way. But far more dangerous are the others, who began when you were children, and took possession of your minds with their falsehoods, telling of one Socrates, a wise man, who speculated about the heaven above, and searched into the earth beneath, and made the worse appear the better cause. The disseminators of this tale are the accusers whom I dread; for their hearers are apt to fancy that such enquirers do not believe in the existence of the gods. And they are many, and their charges against me are of ancient date, and they were made by them in the days when you were more impressible than you are now—in childhood, or it may have been in youth—and the cause when heard went by default, for there was none to answer. And hardest of all, I do not know and cannot tell the names of my accusers; unless in the chance case of a comic poet. All who from envy and malice have persuaded you—some of them having first convinced themselves—all this class of men are most difficult to deal with; for I cannot have them up here, and cross-examine them, and therefore I must simply fight with shadows in my own defence,

and argue when there is no one who answers. I will ask you then to assume with me, as I was saying, that my opponents are of two kinds; one recent, the other ancient: and I hope that you will see the propriety of my answering the latter first, for these accusations you heard long before the others, and much oftener.

[3] Well, then, I must make my defence, and endeavour to clear away in a short time, a slander which has lasted a long time. May I succeed, if to succeed be for my good and yours, or likely to avail me in my cause! The task is not an easy one; I quite understand the nature of it. And so leaving the event with God, in obedience to the law I will now make my defence.

[4] I will begin at the beginning, and ask what is the accusation which has given rise to the slander of me, and in fact has encouraged Meletus to prefer this charge against me. Well, what do the slanderers say? They shall be my prosecutors, and I will sum up their words in an affidavit: "Socrates is an evildoer, and a curious person, who searches into things under the earth and in heaven, and he makes the worse appear the better cause; and he teaches the aforesaid doctrines to others." Such is the nature of the accusation: it is just what you have yourselves seen in the comedy of Aristophanes, who has introduced a man whom he calls Socrates, going about and saying that he walks in air, and talking a deal of nonsense concerning matters of which I do not pretend to know either much or little—not that I mean to speak disparagingly of any one who is a student of natural philosophy. I should be very sorry if Meletus could bring so grave a charge against me. But the simple truth is, O Athenians, that I have nothing to do with physical speculations. Very many of those here present are witnesses to the truth of this, and to them I appeal. Speak then, you who have heard me, and tell your neighbours whether any of you have ever known me hold forth in few words or in many upon such matters. . . . You hear their answer. And from what they say of this part of the charge you will be able to judge of the truth of the rest.

[5] As little foundation is there for the report that I am a teacher and take money; this accusation has no more truth in it than the other. Although, if a man were really able to instruct mankind, to receive money for giving instruction would, in my opinion, be an honour to him. There is Gorgias of Leontium, and Prodicus of Ceos, and Hippias of Elis, who go the round of the cities, and are able to persuade the young men to leave their own citizens by whom they might be taught for nothing, and come to them whom they not only pay, but are thankful if they may be allowed to pay them. There is at this time a Parian philosopher residing in Athens, of whom I have heard; and I came to hear of him in this way:—I came across a man who has spent a world of money on the Sophists, Callias, the son of Hipponicus, and knowing that he had sons, I asked

him: "Callias," I said, "if your two sons were foals or calves, there would be no difficulty in finding some one to put over them; we should hire a trainer of horses, or a farmer, probably, who would improve and perfect them in their own proper virtue and excellence; but as they are human beings, whom are you thinking of placing over them? Is there any one who understands human and political virtue? You must have thought about the matter, for you have sons; is there any one?" "There is," he said. "Who is he?" said I; "and of what country? and what does he charge?" "Evenus the Parian," he replied; "he is the man, and his charge is five minae." Happy is Evenus, I said to myself, if he really has this wisdom, and teaches at such a moderate charge. Had I the same, I should have been very proud and conceited; but the truth is that I have no knowledge of the kind.

[6] I dare say, Athenians, that some one among you will reply, "Yes, Socrates, but what is the origin of these accusations which are brought against you; there must have been something strange which you have been doing? All these rumours and this talk about you would never have arisen if you had been like other men: tell us, then, what is the cause of them, for we should be sorry to judge hastily of you." Now, I regard this as a fair challenge, and I will endeavor to explain to you the reason why I am called wise and have such an evil fame. Please to attend then. And although some of you may think that I am joking, I declare that I will tell you the entire truth. Men of Athens, this reputation of mine has come of a certain sort of wisdom which I possess. If you ask me what kind of wisdom, I reply, wisdom such as may perhaps be attained by man, for to that extent I am inclined to believe that I am wise; whereas the persons of whom I was speaking have a superhuman wisdom, which I may fail to describe, because I have it not myself; and he who says that I have, speaks falsely, and is taking away my character. And here, O men of Athens, I must beg you not to interrupt me, even if I seem to say something extravagant. For the word which I will speak is not mine. I will refer you to a witness who is worthy of credit; that witness shall be the God of Delphi—he will tell you about my wisdom, if I have any, and of what sort it is. You must have known Chaerephon; he was early a friend of mine, and also a friend of yours, for he shared in the recent exile of the people, and returned with you. Well, Chaerephon, as you know, was very impetuous in all his doings, and he went to Delphi and boldly asked the oracle to tell him whether—as I was saying, I must beg you not to interrupt—he asked the oracle to tell him whether any one was wiser than I was, and the Pythian prophetess answered, that there was no man wiser. Chaerephon is dead himself; but his brother, who is in court, will confirm the truth of what I am saying.

[7] Why do I mention this? Because I am going to explain to you why I have such an evil name. When I heard the answer, I said to myself,

What can the God mean? and what is the interpretation of his riddle? for I know that I have no wisdom, small or great. What then can he mean when he says that I am the wisest of men? And yet he is a god, and cannot lie; that would be against his nature. After long consideration, I thought of a method of trying the question. I reflected that if I could only find a man wiser than myself, then I might go to the god with a refutation in my hand. I should say to him, "Here is a man who is wiser than I am; but you said that I was the wisest." Accordingly I went to one who had the reputation of wisdom, and observed him—his name I need not mention; he was a politician whom I selected for examination—and the result was as follows: When I began to talk with him, I could not help thinking that he was not really wise, although he was thought wise by many, and still wiser by himself; and thereupon I tried to explain to him that he thought himself wise, but was not really wise; and the consequence was that he hated me, and his enmity was shared by several who were present and heard me. So I left him, saying to myself, as I went away: Well, although I do not suppose that either of us knows anything really beautiful and good, I am better off than he is—for he knows nothing, and thinks that he knows; I neither know nor think that I know. In this latter particular, then, I seem to have slightly the advantage of him. Then I went to another who had still higher pretensions to wisdom, and my conclusion was exactly the same. Whereupon I made another enemy of him, and of many others besides him.

[8] Then I went to one man after another, being not unconscious of the enmity which I provoked, and I lamented and feared this: but necessity was laid upon me,—the word of God, I thought, ought to be considered first. And I said to myself, Go I must to all who appear to know, and find out the meaning of the oracle. And I swear to you, Athenians, by the dog I swear!—for I must tell you the truth—the result of my mission was just this: I found that the men most in repute were all but the most foolish; and that others less esteemed were really wiser and better. I will tell you the tale of my wanderings and of the "Herculean" labours, as I may call them, which I endured only to find at last the oracle irrefutable. After the politicians, I went to the poets; tragic, dithyrambic, and all sorts. And there, I said to myself, you will be instantly detected; now you will find out that you are more ignorant than they are. Accordingly I took them some of the most elaborate passages in their own writings, and asked what was the meaning of them—thinking that they would teach me something. Will you believe me? I am almost ashamed to confess the truth, but I must say that there is hardly a person present who would not have talked better about their poetry than they did themselves. Then I knew that not by wisdom do poets write poetry, but by a sort of genius and inspiration; they are like diviners or soothsayers who also say many fine things, but do not understand the meaning of them. The poets ap-

peared to me to be much in the same case; and I further observed that upon the strength of their poetry they believed themselves to be the wisest of men in other things in which they were not wise. So I departed, conceiving myself to be superior to them for the same reason that I was superior to the politicians.

[9] At last I went to the artisans. I was conscious that I knew nothing at all, as I may say, and I was sure that they knew many fine things; and here I was not mistaken, for they did know many things of which I was ignorant, and in this they certainly were wiser than I was. But I observed that even the good artisans fell into the same error as the poets;—because they were good workmen they thought that they also knew all sorts of high matters, and this defect in them overshadowed their wisdom; and therefore I asked myself on behalf of the oracle, whether I would like to be as I was, neither having their knowledge nor their ignorance, or like them in both; and I made answer to myself and to the oracle that I was better off as I was.

[10] This inquisition has led to my having many enemies of the worst and most dangerous kind, and has given occasion also to many calumnies. And I am called wise, for my hearers always imagine that I myself possess the wisdom which I find wanting in others; but the truth is, O men of Athens, that God only is wise; and by his answer he intends to show that the wisdom of men is worth little or nothing; he is not speaking of Socrates, he is only using my name by way of illustration, as if he said, He, O men, is the wisest, who, like Socrates, knows that his wisdom is in truth worth nothing. And so I go about the world obedient to the god, and search and make enquiry into the wisdom of any one, whether citizen or stranger, who appears to be wise; and if he is not wise, then in vindication of the oracle I show him that he is not wise; and my occupation quite absorbs me, and I have no time to give either to any public matter of interest or to any concern of my own, but I am in utter poverty by reason of my devotion to the god.

[11] There is another thing:—young men of the richer classes, who have not much to do, come about me of their own accord; they like to hear the pretenders examined, and they often imitate me, and proceed to examine others; there are plenty of persons, as they quickly discover, who think that they know something, but really know little or nothing; and then those who are examined by them instead of being angry with themselves are angry with me: This confounded Socrates, they say; this villainous misleader of youth!—and then if somebody asks them, Why, what evil does he practise or teach? they do not know, and cannot tell; but in order that they may not appear to be at a loss, they repeat the ready-made charges which are used against all philosophers about teaching things up in the clouds and under the earth, and having no gods, and making the worst appear the better cause; for they do not like to confess

that their pretence of knowledge has been detected—which is the truth; and as they are numerous and ambitious and energetic, and are drawn up in battle array and have persuasive tongues, they have filled your ears with their loud and inveterate calumnies. And this is the reason why my three accusers, Meletus and Anytus and Lycon, have set upon me; Meletus, who has a quarrel with me on behalf of the poets; Anytus, on behalf of the craftsmen and politicians; Lycon, on behalf of the rhetoricians: and, as I said at the beginning, I cannot expect to get rid of such a mass of calumny all in a moment. And this, O men of Athens, is the truth and the whole truth; I have concealed nothing, I have dissembled nothing. And yet, I know that my plainness of speech makes them hate me, and what is their hatred but a proof that I am speaking the truth? Hence has arisen the prejudice against me; and this is the reason of it, as you will find out either in this or in any future enquiry.

[12] I have said enough in my defence against the first class of my accusers; I turn to the second class. They are headed by Meletus, that good man and true lover of his country, as he calls himself. Against these, too, I must try to make a defence:—Let their affidavit be read: it contains something of this kind: It says that Socrates is a doer of evil, who corrupts the youth; and who does not believe in the gods of the State, but has other new divinities of his own. Such is the charge; and now let us examine the particular counts. He says that I am a doer of evil, and corrupt the youth; but I say, O men of Athens, that Meletus is a doer of evil, in that he pretends to be in earnest when he is only in jest, and is so eager to bring men to trial from a pretended zeal and interest about matters in which he really never had the smallest interest. And the truth of this I will endeavour to prove to you.

[13] Come hither, Meletus, and let me ask a question of you. You think a great deal about the improvement of youth?

Yes, I do.

Tell the judges, then, who is their improver; for you must know, as you have taken the pains to discover their corrupter, and are citing and accusing me before them. Speak, then, and tell the judges who their improver is.—Observe, Meletus, that you are silent, and have nothing to say. But is not this rather disgraceful, and a very considerable proof of what I was saying, that you have no interest in the matter? Speak up, friend, and tell us who their improver is.

The laws.

But that, my good sir, is not my meaning. I want to know who the person is, who, in the first place, knows the laws.

The judges, Socrates, who are present in court.

What, do you mean to say, Meletus, that they are able to instruct and improve youth?

Certainly they are.

What, all of them, or some only and not others?

All of them.

By the goddess Here, that is good news! There are plenty of improvers, then. And what do you say of the audience,—do they improve them?

Yes, they do.

And the senators?

Yes, the senators improve them.

But perhaps the members of the assembly corrupt them?—or do they improve them?

They improve them.

Then every Athenian improves and elevates them; all with the exception of myself; and I alone am their corrupter? Is that what you affirm?

That is what I stoutly affirm.

I am very unfortunate if you are right. But suppose I ask you a question: How about horses? Does one man do them harm and all the world good? Is not the exact opposite the truth? One man is able to do them good, or at least not many;—the trainer of horses, that is to say, does them good, and others who have to do with them rather injure them? Is not that true, Meletus, of horses, or of any other animal? Most assuredly it is; whether you and Anytus say yes or no. Happy indeed would be the condition of youth if they had one corrupter only, and all the rest of the world were their improvers. But you, Meletus, have sufficiently shown that you never had a thought about the young: your carelessness is seen in your not caring about the very things which you bring against me.

And now, Meletus, I will ask you another question—by Zeus I will: Which is better, to live among bad citizens, or among good ones? Answer, friend, I say; the question is one which may be easily answered. Do not the good do their neighbours good, and the bad do them evil?

Certainly.

And is there any one who would rather be injured than benefited by those who live with him? Answer, my good friend, the law requires you to answer—does any one like to be injured?

Certainly not.

And when you accuse me of corrupting and deteriorating the youth, do you allege that I corrupt them intentionally or unintentionally?

Intentionally, I say.

But you have just admitted that the good do their neighbours good, and the evil do them evil. Now, is that a truth which your superior wisdom has recognized thus early in life, and am I, at my age, in such darkness and ignorance as not to know that if a man with whom I have to live is corrupted by me, I am very likely to be harmed by him; and yet I corrupt him, and intentionally, too—so you say, although neither I nor any other human being is ever likely to be convinced by you. But either I do not corrupt them, or I corrupt them unintentionally; and on either view of the case you lie. If my offence is unintentional, the law has no cognizance of unintentional offences: you ought to have taken me privately, and warned and admonished me; for if I had been better advised, I should have left off doing what I only did unintentionally—no doubt I should; but you would have nothing to say to me and refused to teach me. And now you bring me up in this court, which is a place not of instruction, but of punishment.

It will be very clear to you, Athenians, as I was saying, that Meletus has no care at all, great or small, about the matter. But still I should like to know, Meletus, in what I am affirmed to corrupt the young. I suppose you mean, as I infer from your indictment, that I teach them not to acknowledge the gods which the State acknowledges, but some other new divinities or spiritual agencies in their stead. These are the lessons by which I corrupt the youth, as you say.

Yes, that I say emphatically.

Then, by the gods, Meletus, of whom we are speaking, tell me and the court, in somewhat plainer terms, what you mean! For I do not as yet understand whether you affirm that I teach other men to acknowledge some gods, and therefore that I do believe in gods, and am not an entire atheist—this you do not lay to my charge,—but only you say that they are not the same gods which the city recognizes—the charge is that they are different gods. Or, do you mean that I am an atheist simply, and a teacher of atheism?

I mean the latter—that you are a complete atheist.

What an extraordinary statement! Why do you think so, Meletus? Do you mean that I do not believe in the godhead of the sun or moon, like other men?

I assure you judges, that he does not: for he says that the sun is stone, and the moon earth.

Friend Meletus, you think that you are accusing Anaxagoras: and you have but a bad opinion of the judges, if you fancy them illiterate to such a degree as not to know that these doctrines are found in the books of Anaxagoras the Clazomenian, which are full of them. And so, forsooth, the youth are said to be taught them by Socrates, when there are not infrequently exhibitions of them at the theatre (price of admission one drachma at the most); and they might pay their money, and laugh at Socrates if he pretends to father these extraordinary views. And so, Meletus, you really think that I do not believe in any god?

I swear by Zeus that you believe absolutely in none at all.

Nobody will believe you, Meletus, and I am pretty sure that you do not believe yourself. I cannot help thinking, men of Athens, that Meletus is reckless and impudent, and that he has written this indictment in a spirit of mere wantonness and youthful bravado. Has he not compounded a riddle, thinking to try me? He said to himself:—I shall see whether the wise Socrates will discover my facetious contradiction, or whether I shall be able to deceive him and the rest of them. For he certainly does appear to me to contradict himself in the indictment as much as if he said that Socrates is guilty of not believing in the gods, and yet of believing in them—but this is not like a person who is in earnest.

I should like you, O men of Athens, to join me in examining what I conceive to be his inconsistency; and do you, Meletus, answer. And I must remind the audience of my request that they would not make a disturbance if I speak in my accustomed manner:

Did ever man, Meletus, believe in the existence of human things, and not of human beings? . . . I wish, men of Athens, that he would answer, and not be always trying to get up an interruption. Did ever any man believe in horsemanship, and not in horses? or in flute-playing, and not in flute-players? No, my friend; I will answer to you and to the court, as you refuse to answer for yourself. There is no man who ever did. But now please to answer the next question: Can a man believe in spiritual and divine agencies, and not in spirits or demigods?

He cannot.

How lucky I am to have extracted that answer, by the assistance of the court! But then you swear in the indictment that I teach and believe in divine or spiritual agencies (new or old, no matter for that); at any rate, I believe in spiritual agencies,—so you say and swear in the affidavit; and yet if I believe in divine beings, how can I help believing in spirits or demigods;—must I not? To be sure I must; and therefore I may assume that your silence gives consent. Now what are spirits or demigods? are they not either gods or the sons of gods?

Certainly they are.

But this is what I call the facetious riddle invented by you: the demigods or spirits are gods, and you say first that I do not believe in gods, and then again that I do believe in gods; that is, if I believe in demigods. For if the demigods are the illegitimate sons of gods, whether by the nymphs or by any other mothers, of whom they are said to be the sons—what human being will ever believe that there are no gods if they are the sons of Gods? You might as well affirm the existence of mules, and deny that of horses and asses. Such nonsense, Meletus, could only have been intended by you to make trial of me. You have put this into the indictment because you had nothing real of which to accuse me. But no one who has a particle of understanding will ever be convinced by you that the same men can believe in divine and superhuman things, and yet not believe that there are gods and demigods and heroes.

[14] I have said enough in answer to the charge of Meletus: any elaborate defence is unnecessary; but I know only too well how many are the enmities which I have incurred, and this is what will be my destruction if I am destroyed;—not Meletus, nor yet Anytus, but the envy and detrac-

tion of the world, which has been the death of many good men, and will probably be the death of many more; there is no danger of my being the last of them.

[15] Some one will say: And are you not ashamed, Socrates, of a course of life which is likely to bring you to an untimely end? To him I may fairly answer: There you are mistaken: a man who is good for anything ought not to calculate the chance of living or dying; he ought only to consider whether in doing anything he is doing right or wrong—acting the part of a good man or of a bad. Whereas, upon your view, the heroes who fell at Troy were not good for much, and the son of Thetis above all, who altogether despised danger in comparison with disgrace; and when he was so eager to slay Hector, his goddess mother said to him, that if he avenged his companion Patroclus, and slew Hector, he would die himself—"Fate," she said, in these or the like words, "waits for you next after Hector"; he, receiving this warning, utterly despised danger and death, and instead of fearing them, feared rather to live in dishonour, and not to avenge his friend. "Let me die forthwith," he replied, "and be avenged of my enemy, rather than abide here by the beaked ships, a laughingstock and a burden of the earth." Had Achilles any thought of death and danger? For wherever a man's place is, whether the place which he has chosen or that in which he has been placed by a commander, there he ought to remain in the hour of danger; he should not think of death or of anything but of disgrace. And this, O men of Athens, is a true saying.

[16] Strange, indeed, would be my conduct, O men of Athens, if I, who, when I was ordered by the generals whom you chose to command me at Potidaea and Amphipolis and Delium, remained where they placed me, like any other man, facing death—if now, when, as I conceive and imagine, God orders me to fulfill the philosopher's mission of searching into myself and other men, I were to desert my post through fear of death, or any other fear; that would indeed be strange, and I might justly be arraigned in court for denying the existence of the gods, if I disobeyed the oracle because I was afraid of death, fancying that I was wise when I was not wise. For the fear of death is indeed the pretence of wisdom, and not real wisdom, being a pretence of knowing the unknown; and no one knows whether death, which men in their fear apprehend to be the greatest evil, may not be the greatest good. Is not this ignorance of a disgraceful sort, the ignorance which is the conceit that a man knows what he does not know? And in this respect only I believe myself to differ from men in general, and may perhaps claim to be wiser than they are:—that whereas I know but little of the world below, I do not suppose that I know: but I do know that injustice and disobedience to a better, whether God or man, is evil and dishonourable, and I will never fear or avoid a possible good rather than a certain evil. And therefore if you let me go now, and are not convinced by Anytus, who said that since I had been

prosecuted I must be put to death; (or if not that I ought never to have been prosecuted at all); and that if I escape now, your sons will all be utterly ruined by listening to my words—if you say to me, Socrates, this time we will not mind Anytus, and you shall be let off, but upon one condition, that you are not to enquire and speculate in this way any more, and that if you are caught doing so again you shall die;—if this was the condition on which you let me go, I should reply: Men of Athens, I honour and love you; but I shall obey God rather than you, and while I have life and strength I shall never cease from the practice and teaching of philosophy, exhorting any one whom I meet and saying to him after my manner: You, my friend,—a citizen of the great and mighty and wise city of Athens,—are you not ashamed of heaping up the greatest amount of money and honour and reputation, and caring so little about wisdom and truth and the greatest improvement of the soul, which you never regard or heed at all? And if the person with whom I am arguing, says: Yes, but I do care; then I do not leave him or let him go at once; but I proceed to interrogate and examine and cross-examine him, and if I think that he has no virtue in him, but only says that he has, I reproach him with undervaluing the greater, and overvaluing the less. And I shall repeat the same words to every one whom I meet, young and old, citizen and alien, but especially to the citizens, inasmuch as they are my brethren. For know that this is the command of God; and I believe that no greater good has ever happened in the State than my service to the God. For I do nothing but go about persuading you all, old and young alike, not to take thought for your persons or your properties, but first and chiefly to care about the greatest improvement of the soul. I tell you that virtue is not given by money, but that from virtue comes money and every other good of man, public as well as private. This is my teaching, and if this is the doctrine which corrupts the youth, I am a mischievous person. But if any one says that this is not my teaching, he is speaking an untruth. Wherefore, O men of Athens, I say to you, do as Anytus bids or not as Anytus bids, and either acquit me or not; but whichever you do, understand that I shall never alter my ways, not even if I have to die many times.

[17] Men of Athens, do not interrupt, but hear me; there was an understanding between us that you should hear me to the end: I have something more to say, at which you may be inclined to cry out; but I believe that to hear me will be good for you, and therefore I beg that you will not cry out. I would have you know, that if you kill such an one as I am, you will injure yourselves more than you will injure me. Nothing will injure me, not Meletus nor yet Anytus—they cannot, for a bad man is not permitted to injure a better than himself. I do not deny that Anytus may, perhaps, kill him, or drive him into exile, or deprive him of civil

rights; and he may imagine, and others may imagine, that he is inflicting a great injury upon him: but there I do not agree. For the evil of doing as he is doing—the evil of unjustly taking away the life of another—is greater far.

[18] And now, Athenians, I am not going to argue for my own sake, as you may think, but for yours, that you may not sin against the God by condemning me, who am his gift to you. For if you kill me you will not easily find a successor to me, who, if I may use such a ludicrous figure of speech, am a sort of gadfly, given to the State by God; and the State is a great and noble steed who is tardy in his motions owing to his very size, and requires to be stirred into life. I am that gadfly which God has attached to the State, and all day long and in all places am always fastening upon you, arousing and persuading and reproaching you. You will not easily find another like me, and therefore I would advise you to spare me. I dare say that you may feel out of temper (like a person who is suddenly awakened from sleep), and you think that you might easily strike me dead as Anytus advises, and then you would sleep on for the remainder of your lives, unless God in his care of you sent you another gadfly. When I say that I am given to you by God, the proof of my mission is this:—if I had been like other men, I should not have neglected all my own concerns or patiently seen the neglect of them during all these years, and have been doing yours, coming to you individually like a father or elder brother, exhorting you to regard virtue; such conduct, I say, would be unlike human nature. If I had gained anything, or if my exhortations had been paid, there would have been some sense in my doing so; but now, as you will perceive, not even the impudence of my accusers dares to say that I have ever exacted or sought pay of any one; of that they have no witness. And I have a sufficient witness to the truth of what I say—my poverty.

[19] Some one may wonder why I go about in private giving advice and busy myself with the concerns of others, but do not venture to come forward in public and advise the State. I will tell you why. You have heard me speak at sundry times and in divers places of an oracle or sign which comes to me, and is the divinity which Meletus ridicules in the indictment. This sign, which is a kind of voice, first began to come to me when I was a child; it always forbids but never commands me to do anything which I am going to do. This is what deters me from being a politician. And rightly, as I think. For I am certain, O men of Athens, that if I had engaged in politics, I should have perished long ago, and done no good either to you or to myself. And do not be offended at my telling you the truth: for the truth is, that no man who goes to war with you or any other multitude, honestly striving against the many lawless and unrighteous deeds which are done in a state, will save his life; he who will fight for

the right, if he would live even for a brief space, must have a private station and not a public one.

[20] I can give you convincing evidence of what I say, not words only, but what you value far more—actions. Let me relate to you a passage of my own life which will prove to you that I should never have yielded to injustice from any fear of death and that "as I should have refused to yield" I must have died at once. I will tell you a tale of the courts, not very interesting perhaps, but nevertheless true. The only office of State which I ever held, O men of Athens, was that of senator: the tribe Antiochis, which is my tribe, had the presidency at the trial of the generals who had not taken up the bodies of the slain after the battle of Arginusae; and you proposed to try them in a body, contrary to law, as you all thought afterwards; but at the time I was the only one of the Prytanes who was opposed to the illegality, and I gave my vote against you; and when the orators threatened to impeach and arrest me, and you called and shouted, I made up my mind that I would run the risk, having law and justice with me, rather than take part in your injustice because I feared imprisonment and death. This happened in the days of the democracy. But when the oligarchy of the Thirty was in power, they sent for me and four others into the rotunda, and bade us bring Leon the Salaminian from Salamis, as they wanted to put him to death. This was a specimen of the sort of commands which they were always giving with the view of implicating as many as possible in their crimes; and then I showed, not in word only but in deed, that, if I may be allowed to use such an expression, I cared not a straw for death, and that my great and only care was lest I should do an unrighteous or unholy thing. For the strong arm of that oppressive power did not frighten me into doing wrong; and when we came out of the rotunda the other four went to Salamis and fetched Leon, but I went quietly home. For which I might have lost my life, had not the power of the Thirty shortly afterwards come to an end. And many will witness to my words.

[21] Now, do you really imagine that I could have survived all these years, if I had led a public life, supposing that like a good man I had always maintained the right and had made justice, as I ought, the first thing? No, indeed, men of Athens, neither I nor any other man. But I have been always the same in all my actions, public as well as private, and never have I yielded any base compliance to those who are slanderously termed my disciples, or to any other. Not that I have any regular disciples. But if any one likes to come and hear me while I am pursuing my mission, whether he be young or old, he is not excluded. Nor do I converse only with those who pay; but any one, whether he be rich or poor, may ask and answer me and listen to my words; and whether he turns out to be a bad man or a good one, neither result can be justly imputed to me; for

I never taught or professed to teach him anything. And if any one says that he has ever learned or heard anything from me in private which all the world has not heard, let me tell you that he is lying.

[22] But I shall be asked, Why do people delight in continually conversing with you? I have told you already, Athenians, the whole truth about this matter: they like to hear the cross-examination of the pretenders to wisdom; there is amusement in it. Now, this duty of cross-examining other men has been imposed upon me by God; and has been signified to me by oracles, visions, and in every way in which the will of divine power was ever intimated to any one. This is true, O Athenians; or, if not true, would be soon refuted. If I am or have been corrupting the youth, those of them who are now grown up and have become sensible that I gave them bad advice in the days of their youth should come forward as accusers, and take their revenge; or if they do not like to come themselves, some of their relatives, fathers, brothers, or other kinsmen, should say what evil their families have suffered at my hands. Now is their time. Many of them I see in the court. There is Crito, who is of the same age and of the same deme with myself, and there is Critobulus his son, whom I also see. Then again there is Lysanias of Sphettus, who is the father of Aeschines—he is present; and also there is Antiphon of Cephisus, who is the father of Epigenes; and there are the brothers of several who have associated with me. There is Nicostratus the son of Theosdotides, and the brother of Theodotus (now Theodotus himself is dead, and therefore he, at any rate, will not seek to stop him); and there is Paralus the son of Demodocus, who had a brother Theages; and Adeimantus the son of Ariston, whose brother Plato is present; and Aeantodorus, who is the brother of Apollodorus, whom I also see. I might mention a great many others, some of whom Meletus should have produced as witnesses in the course of his speech; and let him still produce them, if he has forgotten— I will make way for him. And let him say, if he has any testimony of the sort which he can produce. Nay, Athenians, the very opposite is the truth. For all these are ready to witness on behalf of the corrupter, of the injurer of their kindred, as Meletus and Anytus call me; not the corrupted youth only—there might have been a motive for that—but their uncorrupted elder relatives. Why should they too support me with their testimony? Why, indeed, except for the sake of truth and justice, and because they know that I am speaking the truth, and that Meletus is a liar.

[23] Well, Athenians, this and the like of this is all the defence which I have to offer. Yet a word more. Perhaps there may be some one who is offended at me, when he calls to mind how he himself on a similar, or even a less serious occasion, prayed and entreated the judges with many tears, and how he produced his children in court, which was a moving spectacle, together with a host of relations and friends; whereas I, who am

probably in danger of my life, will do none of these things. The contrast may occur to his mind, and he may be set against me, and vote in anger because he is displeased at me on this account. Now, if there be such a person among you,—mind, I do not say that there is,—to him I may fairly reply: My friend, I am a man, and like other men, a creature of flesh and blood, and not "of wood or stone," as Homer says; and I have a family, yes, and sons, O Athenians, three in number, one almost a man, and two others who are still young; and yet I will not bring any of them hither in order to petition you for an acquittal. And why not? Not from any self-assertion or want of respect for you. Whether I am or am not afraid of death is another question, of which I will not now speak. But, having regard to public opinion, I feel that such conduct would be discreditable to myself, and to you, and to the whole State. One who has reached my years, and who has a name for wisdom, ought not to demean himself. Whether this opinion of me be deserved or not, at any rate the world has decided that Socrates is in some way superior to other men. And if those among you who are said to be superior in wisdom and courage, and any other virtue, demean themselves in this way, how shameful is their conduct! I have seen men of reputation, when they have been condemned, behaving in the strangest manner; they seem to fancy that they were going to suffer something dreadful if they died, and that they could be immortal if you only allowed them to live; and I think that such are a dishonour to the State, and that any stranger coming in would have said of them that the most eminent men of Athens, to whom the Athenians themselves give honour and command, are no better than women. And I say that these things ought not to be done by those of us who have a reputation; and if they are done, you ought not to permit them; you ought rather to show that you are far more disposed to condemn the man who gets up a doleful scene and makes the city ridiculous, than him who holds his peace.

[24] But, setting aside the question of public opinion, there seems to be something wrong in asking a favour of a judge, and thus procuring an acquittal, instead of informing and convincing him. For his duty is, not to make a present of justice, but to give judgment; and he has sworn that he will judge according to the laws, and not according to his own good pleasure; and we ought not to encourage you, nor should you allow yourselves to be encouraged, in this habit of perjury—there can be no piety in that. Do not then require me to do what I consider dishonourable and impious and wrong, especially now, when I am being tried for impiety on the indictment of Meletus. For if, O men of Athens, by force of persuasion and entreaty I could overpower your oaths, then I should be teaching you to believe that there are no gods, and in defending should simply convict myself of the charge of not believing in them. But that it is not so—far otherwise. For I do believe that there are gods, and in a sense higher

than that in which any of my accusers believe in them. And to you and to God I commit my cause, to be determined by you as is best for you and me.

[*The vote is taken and Socrates is convicted.*]

[25] There are many reasons why I am not grieved, O men of Athens, at the vote of condemnation. I expected it, and am only surprised that the votes are so nearly equal; for I had thought that the majority against me would have been far larger; but now, had thirty votes gone over to the other side, I should have been acquitted. And I may say, I think, that I have escaped Meletus. I may say more; for without the assistance of Anytus and Lycon, any one may see that he would not have had a fifth part of the votes, as the law requires, in which case he would have incurred a fine of a thousand drachmae.

[26] And so he proposes death as the penalty. And what shall I propose on my part, O men of Athens? Clearly that which is my due. And what is my due? What returns shall be made to the man who has never had the wit to be idle during his whole life; but has been careless of what the many care for—wealth, and family interests, and military offices, and speaking in the assembly, and magistracies, and plots, and parties. Reflecting that I was really too honest a man to be a politician and live, I did not go where I could do no good to you or to myself; but where I could do the greatest good privately to every one of you, thither I went, and sought to persuade every man among you that he must look to himself, and seek virtue and wisdom before he looks to his private interests, and look to the State before he looks to the interests of the State; and that this should be the order which he observes in all his actions. What shall be done to such an one? Doubtless some good thing, O men of Athens, if he has his reward; and the good should be of a kind suitable to him. What would be a reward suitable to a poor man who is your benefactor, and who desires leisure that he may instruct you? There can be no reward so fitting as maintenance in the Prytaneum, O men of Athens, a reward which he deserves far more than the citizen who has won the prize at Olympia in the horse or chariot race, whether the chariots were drawn by two horses or by many. For I am in want, and he has enough; and he only gives you the appearance of happiness, and I give you the reality. And if I am to estimate the penalty fairly, I should say that maintenance in the Prytaneum is the just return.

[27] Perhaps you think that I am braving you in what I am saying now, as in what I said before about the tears and prayers. But this is not so. I speak rather because I am convinced that I never intentionally wronged any one, although I cannot convince you—the time has been too short; if there were a law at Athens, as there is in other cities, that a capital cause should not be decided in one day, then I believe that I should have con-

vinced you. But I cannot in a moment refute great slanders; and, as I am convinced that I never wronged another, I will assuredly not wrong myself. I will not say of myself that I deserve any evil, or propose any penalty. Why should I? Because I am afraid of the penalty of death which Meletus proposes? When I do not know whether death is a good or an evil, why should I propose a penalty which would certainly be an evil? Shall I say imprisonment? And why should I live in prison, and be the slave of the magistrate of the year—of the Eleven? Or shall the penalty be a fine, imprisonment until the fine is paid? There is the same objection. I should have to lie in prison, for money I have none, and cannot pay. And if I say exile (and this may possibly be the penalty which you will affix), I must indeed be blinded by the love of life, if I am so irrational as to expect that when you, who are my own citizens, cannot endure my discourses and words, and have found them so grievous and odious that you will have no more of them, others are likely to endure me. No, indeed, men of Athens, that is not very likely. And what a life should I lead, at my age, wandering from city to city, ever changing my place of exile, and always being driven out! For I am quite sure that wherever I go, there, as here, the young men will flock to me; and if I drive them away, their elders will drive me out at their request; and if I let them come, their fathers and friends will drive me out for their sakes.

[28] Some one will say: Yes, Socrates, but cannot you hold your tongue, and then you may go into a foreign city, and no one will interfere with you? Now, I have great difficulty in making you understand my answer to this. For if I tell you that to do as you say would be a disobedience to the God, and therefore that I cannot hold my tongue, you will not believe that I am serious; and if I say again that daily to discourse about virtue, and of those other things about which you hear me examining myself and others is the greatest good of man, and that the unexamined life is not worth living, you are still less likely to believe me. Yet I say what is true, although a thing of which it is hard for me to persuade you. Also, I have never been accustomed to think that I deserve to suffer any harm. Had I money I might have estimated the offence at what I was able to pay, and not have been much the worse. But I have none, and therefore I must ask you to proportion the fine to my means. Well, perhaps I could afford a mina, and therefore I propose that penalty: Plato, Crito, Critobulus, and Apollodorus, my friends here, bid me say thirty minae, and they will be the sureties. Let thirty minae be the penalty; for which sum they will be ample security to you.

[*Socrates is condemned to death.*]

[29] Not much time will be gained, O Athenians, in return for the evil name which you will get from the detractors of the city, who will say that you killed Socrates, a wise man; for they will call me wise, even though I

am not wise, when they want to reproach you. If you had waited a little while, your desire would have been fulfilled in the course of nature. For I am far advanced in years, as you may perceive, and not far from death. I am speaking now not to all of you, but only to those who have condemned me to death. And I have another thing to say to them: You think that I was convicted because I had no words of the sort which would have procured my acquittal—I mean, if I had thought fit to leave nothing undone or unsaid. Not so; the deficiency which led to my conviction was not of words—certainly not. But I had not the boldness or impudence or inclination to address you as you would have liked me to do, weeping and wailing and lamenting, and saying and doing many things which you have been accustomed to hear from others, and which, as I maintain, are unworthy of me. I thought at the time that I ought not to do anything common or mean when in danger: nor do I now repent of the style of my defence; I would rather die having spoken after my manner, than speak in your manner and live. For neither in war nor yet at law ought I or any man to use every way of escaping death. Often in battle there can be no doubt that if a man will throw away his arms, and fall on his knees before his pursuers, he may escape death; and in other dangers there are other ways of escaping death; if a man is willing to say and do anything. The difficulty, my friends, is not to avoid death, but to avoid unrighteousness; for that runs faster than death. I am old and move slowly, and the slower runner has overtaken me, and my accusers are keen and quick, and the faster runner, who is unrighteousness, has overtaken them. And now I depart hence condemned by you to suffer the penalty of death,—they too go their ways condemned by the truth to suffer the penalty of villainy and wrong; and I must abide by my award—let them abide by theirs. I suppose that these things may be regarded as fated,—and I think that they are well.

[30] And now, O men who have condemned me, I would fain prophesy to you; for I am about to die, and in the hour of death men are gifted with prophetic power. And I prophesy to you who are my murderers, that immediately after my departure punishment far heavier than you have inflicted on me will surely await you. Me you have killed because you wanted to escape the accuser, and not to give an account of your lives. But that will not be as you suppose: far otherwise. For I say that there will be more accusers of you than there are now; accusers whom hitherto I have restrained: and as they are younger they will be more inconsiderate with you, and you will be more offended at them. If you think that by killing men you can prevent some one from censuring your evil lives, you are mistaken; that is not a way of escape which is either possible or honourable; the easiest and the noblest way is not to be disabling others, but to be improving yourselves. This is the prophecy which I utter before my departure to the judges who have condemned me.

[³¹] Friends, who would have acquitted me, I would like also to talk with you about the thing which has come to pass, while the magistrates are busy, and before I go to the place at which I must die. Stay then a little, for we may as well talk with one another while there is time. You are my friends, and I should like to show you the meaning of this event which has happened to me. O my judges—for you I may truly call judges —I should like to tell you of a wonderful circumstance. Hitherto the divine faculty of which the internal oracle is the source has constantly been in the habit of opposing me even about trifles, if I was going to make a slip or error in any matter; and now as you see there has come upon me that which may be thought, and is generally believed to be, the last and worst evil. But the oracle made no sign of opposition, either when I was leaving my house in the morning, or when I was on my way to the court, or while I was speaking, at anything which I was going to say; and yet I have often been stopped in the middle of a speech, but now in nothing I either said or did touching the matter in hand has the oracle opposed me. What do I take to be the explanation of this silence? I will tell you. It is an intimation that what has happened to me is a good, and that those of us who think that death is an evil are in error. For the customary sign would surely have opposed me had I been going to evil and not to good.

[³²] Let us reflect in another way, and we shall see that there is great reason to hope that death is a good; for one of two things—either death is a state of nothingness and utter unconsciousness, or, as men say, there is a change and migration of the soul from this world to another. Now, if you suppose that there is no consciousness, but a sleep like the sleep of him who is undisturbed even by dreams, death will be an unspeakable gain. For if a person were to select the night in which his sleep was undisturbed even by dreams, and were to compare with this the other days and nights of his life, and then were to tell us how many days and nights he had passed in the course of his life better and more pleasantly than this one, I think that any man, I will not say a private man, but even the great king will not find many such days or nights, when compared with the others. Now, if death be of such a nature, I say that to die is gain; for eternity is then only a single night. But if death is the journey to another place, and there, as men say, all the dead abide, what good, O my friends and judges, can be greater than this? If, indeed, when the pilgrim arrives in the world below, he is delivered from the professors of justice in this world, and finds the true judges who are said to give judgment there, Minos and Rhadamanthus and Aeacus and Triptolemus, and other sons of God who were righteous in their own life, that pilgrimage will be worth making. What would not a man give if he might converse with Orpheus and Musaeus and Hesiod and Homer? Nay, if this be true, let me die again and again. I myself, too, shall have a wonderful interest in there meeting and conversing with Palamedes, and Ajax the son of Telamon, and any other ancient hero who has suffered death through an unjust judgment; and there will be no small pleasure, as I think, in comparing my own sufferings with theirs. Above all, I shall then be able to continue my search into true and false knowledge; as in this world, so also in the next; and I shall find out who is wise, and who pretends to be wise, and is not. What would not a man give, O judges, to be able to examine the leader of the great Trojan expedition; or Odysseus or Sisyphus, or numberless others, men and women too! What infinite delight would there be in conversing with them and asking them questions! In another world they do not put a man to death for asking questions; assuredly not. For besides being happier than we are, they will be immortal, if what is said is true.

[33] Wherefore, O judges, be of good cheer about death, and know of a certainty, that no evil can happen to a good man, either in life or after death. He and his are not neglected by the gods; nor has my own approaching end happened by mere chance. But I see clearly that the time had arrived when it was better for me to die and be released from trouble; wherefore the oracle gave no sign. For which reason, also, I am not angry with my condemners, or with my accusers; they have done me no harm, although they did not mean to do me any good; and for this I may gently blame them.

[34] Still, I have a favour to ask of them. When my sons are grown up, I would ask you, O my friends, to punish them; and I would have you trouble them, as I have troubled you, if they seem to care about riches, or anything, more than about virtue; or if they pretend to be something when they are really nothing,—then reprove them, as I have reproved you, for not caring about that for which they ought to care, and thinking that they are something when they are really nothing. And if you do this, both I and my sons will have received justice at your hands.

[35] The hour of departure has arrived, and we go our ways—I to die, and you to live. Which is better God only knows.

COMMENT AND QUESTIONS

1. The opening paragraph of the *Apology* is an interesting study in speaker–audience relationship. What is Socrates' attitude toward his audience? What persuasive facts does he give about himself, and what impressions does he give of himself and of his accusers?

2. Socrates believes that more dangerous to him than the immediate accusations of Meletus, Anytus, and Lycon is the body of rumor and misapprehension about him which has grown over a period of time. What false ideas about himself does he attempt to correct in the opening section of his defense?
3. Exactly what did the oracle say about Socrates? What, according to Socrates, did the oracle mean? What is the special character of Socrates' wisdom?
4. In paragraph 12 Socrates states the charges brought against him by Meletus and the second class of his accusers. He replies to these charges by countercharges against Meletus which describe the latter as "a doer of evil, in that he pretends to be earnest when he is only in jest, and is so eager to bring men to trial from a pretended zeal and interest about matters in which he really never had the smallest interest." In your judgment (see paragraph 13 and the many short paragraphs following) how successful is Socrates in supporting the charges he makes against Meletus? Does Socrates use any questionable reasoning in exposing his accuser? If so, where?
5. Socrates asks Meletus who is the improver of the youth. What answer would you give to this question about the youth of the present day?
6. Read again paragraphs 14–35. What are the three or four most important topics Socrates is discussing? What are his main ideas about each topic?
7. Socrates sometimes makes skillful use of comparisons or figures of speech— for example, the youth–horses analogy in his questioning of Meletus, the comparison of the good man's duty to a man's duty in war (paragraph 15), the gadfly analogy (paragraph 18), the figure of unrighteousness as a fast runner, faster than death (paragraph 29), and the comparison of death and sleep (paragraph 32). Which of these figures and comparisons seem to you most apt and memorable? Why?
8. One way to analyze the persona or character of Socrates as it appears in the *Apology* is to examine a list of traits and then to consider which ones Socrates notably possesses or does not possess. What judgment do you arrive at about each of the following, and how can you support your opinion?

courage	piety	spite or malice
tact	intractableness	reasonableness
humility	self-respect	didacticism
self-righteousness	humor	fanaticism
false modesty	hatred	open-mindedness in search
self-centeredness	respect for law	of truth
vanity	intolerance	pride
		integrity

9. John Stuart Mill, in "On the Liberty of Thought and Discussion" (page 128), speaks of the conviction of Socrates as one of "those dreadful mistakes which excite the astonishment and horror of posterity." If you had been a member of the jury hearing Socrates' speeches, how do you think you would have voted, and why?

10. Socrates lived some four hundred years before Jesus. In what ways are his ideas and values similar to and different from Christian ideas and values? (Perhaps see the "Sermon on the Mount," page 200.)

[11] *Plato*: The Myth of the Cave

THE FOLLOWING selection from Book VII of *The Republic* by the Greek philosopher Plato (427–347 B.C.) is close to the center of Platonic thought. It touches on Plato's doctrine of Ideas or Forms—the theory that beyond the forms of the physical world there exist ideal Forms or Verities, of which the things of the visible world are only imperfect manifestations. And it discusses the education of Plato's philosopher-kings, the wise men and lovers of wisdom to whom the government of Plato's ideal Republic will be entrusted. Like all myths, "The Myth of the Cave" has a number of closely related applications: describing the education of the philosopher-kings, it also describes the ascent of the soul from the prison-house of the senses to the intellectual world of pure Being; and it may be read as a description of any process of education or enlightenment whereby one moves, at first with pain and confusion, from a world of familiar shadows into a brighter world of new concepts and realities.

[1] And now, I said, let me show in a figure how far our nature is enlightened or unenlightened:—Behold! human beings living in an underground den, which has a mouth open towards the light and reaching all along the den; here they have been from their childhood, and have their legs and necks chained so that they can not move, and can only see before them, being prevented by the chains from turning round their heads. Above and behind them a fire is blazing at a distance, and between the fire and the prisoners there is a raised way; and you will see, if you look, a low wall built along the way, like the screen which marionette players have in front of them, over which they show the puppets.

I see.

And do you see, I said, men passing along the wall carrying all sorts of vessels, and statues and figures of animals made of wood and stone and various materials, which appear over the wall? Some of them are talking, others silent.

This selection was translated by Benjamin Jowett. (We have arbitrarily inserted paragraph numbers here and there to facilitate reference to particular passages.)

You have shown me a strange image, and they are strange prisoners.

[2] Like ourselves, I replied; and they see only their own shadows, or the shadows of one another, which the fire throws on the opposite wall of the cave?

True, he said; how could they see anything but the shadows if they were never allowed to move their heads?

And of the objects which are being carried in like manner they would only see the shadows?

Yes, he said.

And if they were able to converse with one another, would they not suppose that they were naming what was actually before them?

Very true.

And suppose further that the prison had an echo which came from the other side, would they not be sure to fancy when one of the passers-by spoke that the voice which they heard came from the passing shadow?

No question, he replied.

To them, I said, the truth would be literally nothing but the shadows of the images.

That is certain.

[3] And now look again, and see what will naturally follow if the prisoners are released and disabused of their error. At first, when any of them is liberated and compelled suddenly to stand up and turn his neck round and walk and look towards the light, he will suffer sharp pains; the glare will distress him, and he will be unable to see the realities of which in his former state he had seen the shadows; and then conceive some one saying to him, that what he saw before was an illusion, but that now, when he is approaching nearer to being and his eye is turned towards more real existence, he has a clearer vision,—what will be his reply? And you may further imagine that his instructor is pointing to the objects as they pass and requiring him to name them,—will he not be perplexed? Will he not fancy that the shadows which he formerly saw are truer than the objects which are now shown to him?

Far truer.

[4] And if he is compelled to look straight at the light, will he not have a pain in his eyes which will make him turn away to take refuge in the objects of vision which he can see, and which he will conceive to be in reality clearer than the things which are now being shown to him?

True, he said.

[5] And suppose once more, that he is reluctantly dragged up a steep and rugged ascent, and held fast until he is forced into the presence of the sun himself, is he not likely to be pained and irritated? When he approaches the light his eyes will be dazzled, and he will not be able to see anything at all of what are now called realities.

Not all in a moment, he said.

[6] He will require to grow accustomed to the sight of the upper world. And first he will see the shadows best, next the reflections of men and other objects in the water, and then the objects themselves; then he will gaze upon the light of the moon and the stars and the spangled heaven; and he will see the sky and the stars by night better than the sun or the light of the sun by day?

Certainly.

[7] Last of all he will be able to see the sun, and not mere reflections of him in the water, but he will see him in his own proper place, and not in another; and he will contemplate him as he is.

Certainly.

[8] He will then proceed to argue that this is he who gives the season and the years, and is the guardian of all that is in the visible world, and in a certain way the cause of all things which he and his fellows have been accustomed to behold.

Clearly, he said, he would first see the sun and then reason about him.

[9] And when he remembered his old habitation, and the wisdom of the den and his fellow-prisoners, do you not suppose that he would felicitate himself on the change, and pity them?

Certainly, he would.

And if they were in the habit of conferring honors among themselves on those who were quickest to observe the passing shadows and to remark which of them went before, and which followed after, and which were together; and who were therefore best able to draw conclusions as to the future, do you think that he would care for such honors and glories, or envy the possessors of them? Would he not say with Homer,

"Better to be the poor servant of a poor master,"

and to endure anything, rather than think as they do and live after their manner?

Yes, he said, I think that he would rather suffer anything than entertain these false notions and live in this miserable manner.

Imagine once more, I said, such an one coming suddenly out of the sun to be replaced in his old situation; would he not be certain to have his eyes full of darkness?

To be sure, he said.

And if there were a contest, and he had to compete in measuring the shadows with the prisoners who had never moved out of the den, while his sight was still weak, and before his eyes had become steady (and the time which would be needed to acquire this new habit of sight might be very considerable), would he not be ridiculous? Men would say of him that up he went and down he came without his eyes; and that it was better not even to think of ascending; and if any one tried to loose another and lead him up to the light, let them only catch the offender, and they would put him to death.

No question, he said.

[10] This entire allegory, I said, you may now append, dear Glaucon, to the previous argument; the prisonhouse is the world of sight, the light of the fire is the sun, and you will not misapprehend me if you interpret the journey upwards to be the ascent of the soul into the intellectual world according to my poor belief, which, at your desire, I have expressed—whether rightly or wrongly God knows. But, whether true or false, my opinion is that in the world of knowledge the idea of good appears last of all, and is seen only with an effort; and, when seen, is also inferred to be the universal author of all things beautiful and right, parent of light and of the lord of light in this visible world, and the immediate source of reason and truth in the intellectual; and that this is the power upon which he who would act rationally either in public or private life must have his eye fixed.

I agree, he said, as far as I am able to understand you.

[11] Moreover, I said, you must not wonder that those who attain to this beatific vision are unwilling to descend to human affairs; for their souls are ever hastening into the upper world where they desire to dwell; which desire of theirs is very natural, if our allegory may be trusted.

Yes, very natural.

And is there anything surprising in one who passes from divine contemplations to the evil state of man, misbehaving himself in a ridiculous manner; if, while his eyes are blinking and before he has become accustomed to the surrounding darkness, he is compelled to fight in courts of law, or in other places, about the images or the shadows of images of justice, and is endeavoring to meet the conceptions of those who have never yet seen absolute justice?

Anything but surprising, he replied.

[12] Any one who has common sense will remember that the bewilderments of the eyes are of two kinds, and arise from two causes, either from coming out of the light or from going into the light, which is true of the mind's eye, quite as much as of the bodily eye; and he who remembers this when he sees any one whose vision is perplexed and weak, will not be too ready to laugh; he will first ask whether that soul of man has come out of the brighter life, and is unable to see because unaccustomed to the dark, or having turned from darkness to the day is dazzled by excess of light. And he will count the one happy in his condition and state of being, and he will pity the other; or, if he have a mind to laugh at the soul which comes from below into the light, there will be more reason in this than in the laugh which greets him who returns from above out of the light into the den.

That, he said, is a very just distinction.

But then, if I am right, certain professors of education must be wrong when they say that they can put a knowledge into the soul which was not there before, like sight into blind eyes.

They undoubtedly say this, he replied.

[13] Whereas, our argument shows that the power and capacity of learning exists in the soul already; and that just as the eye was unable to turn from darkness to light without the whole body, so too the instrument of knowledge can only by the movement of the whole soul be turned from the world of becoming into that of being, and learn by degrees to endure the sight of being, and of the brightest and best of being, or in other words, of the good.

Very true.

And must there not be some art which will effect conversion in the easiest and quickest manner; not implanting the faculty of sight, for that exists already, but has been turned in the wrong direction, and is looking away from the truth?

Yes, he said, such an art may be presumed.

[14] And whereas the other so-called virtues of the soul seem to be akin to bodily qualities, for even when they are not originally innate they can be implanted later by habit and exercise, the virtue of wisdom more than anything else contains a divine element which always remains, and by this conversion is rendered useful and profitable; or, on the other hand, hurtful and useless. Did you never observe the narrow intelligence flashing from the keen eye of a clever rogue—how eager he is, how clearly his paltry soul sees the way to his end; he is the reverse of blind, but his keen eye-sight is forced into the service of evil, and he is mischievous in proportion to his cleverness?

Very true, he said.

[15] But what if there had been a circumcision of such natures in the days of their youth; and they had been severed from those sensual pleasures, such as eating and drinking, which, like leaden weights, were attached to them at their birth, and which drag them down and turn the vision of their souls upon the things that are below—if, I say, they had been released from these impediments and turned in the opposite direction, the very same faculty in them would have seen the truth as keenly as they see what their eyes are turned to now.

Very likely.

[16] Yes, I said; and there is another thing which is likely, or rather a necessary inference from what has preceded, that neither the uneducated and uninformed of the truth, nor yet those who never make an end of their education, will be able ministers of State; not the former, because they have no single aim of duty which is the rule of all their actions, private as well as public; nor the latter, because they will not act at all

except upon compulsion, fancying that they are already dwelling apart in the islands of the blest.

Very true, he replied.

[17] Then, I said, the business of us who are the founders of the State will be to compel the best minds to attain that knowledge which we have already shown to be the greatest of all—they must continue to ascend until they arrive at the good; but when they have ascended and seen enough we must not allow them to do as they do now.

What do you mean?

[18] I mean that they remain in the upper world: but this must not be allowed; they must be made to descend again among the prisoners in the den, and partake of their labors and honors, whether they are worth having or not.

But is not this unjust? he said; ought we to give them a worse life, when they might have a better?

[19] You have again forgotten, my friend, I said, the intention of the legislator, who did not aim at making any one class in the State happy above the rest; the happiness was to be in the whole State, and he held the citizens together by persuasion and necessity, making them benefactors of the State, and therefore benefactors of one another; to this end he created them, not to please themselves, but to be his instruments in binding up the State.

True, he said, I had forgotten.

[20] Observe, Glaucon, that there will be no injustice in compelling our philosophers to have a care and providence of others; we shall explain to them that in other States, men of their class are not obliged to share in the toils of politics: and this is reasonable, for they grow up at their own sweet will, and the government would rather not have them. Being self-taught, they can not be expected to show any gratitude for a culture which they have never received. But we have brought you into the world to be rulers of the hive, kings of yourselves and of the other citizens, and have educated you far better and more perfectly than they have been educated, and you are better able to share in the double duty. Wherefore each of you, when his turn comes, must go down to the general underground abode, and get the habit of seeing in the dark. When you have acquired the habit, you will see ten thousand times better than the inhabitants of the den, and you will know what the several images are, and what they represent, because you have seen the beautiful and just and good in their truth. And thus our State, which is also yours, will be a reality, and not a dream only, and will be administered in a spirit unlike that of other States, in which men fight with one another about shadows only and are distracted in the struggle for power, which in their eyes is a great good. Whereas the truth is that the State in which the rulers are

most reluctant to govern is always the best and most quietly governed, and the State in which they are most eager, the worst.

Quite true, he replied.

COMMENT AND QUESTIONS

1. In this dialogue, Socrates, the principal speaker, leads Glaucon, by a series of planned steps and questions, to arrive at certain foreseen conclusions. This progressive question–answer mode of teaching and discussion, used by Socrates in his informal teaching and by Plato in his Dialogues, is called "the Socratic method." How is it like or different from the methods of teaching to which you are accustomed? What are its advantages and disadvantages?
2. Socrates says that he is attempting to "show in a figure how far our nature is enlightened or unenlightened." He makes his meaning clear by elaborating and interweaving two basic figures, the figures of light and the figures of ascent and descent. Listed on the left below are items from "The Myth of the Cave" which have symbolic meaning. Listed on the right, not in order, are meanings which the items represent. Think through the myth, and try to pair the symbols in the left-hand column with the ideas in the right-hand column. Does it seem to you that any of the symbolic meanings are unclear, or are inaccurately stated? Explain.

the prisoners	philosophers
the shadows of images seen by the prisoners	the process of education
	illusions, false notions
the firelight	unenlightened people
the steep ascent	the reality of the physical world
the upper world	the intellectual world of reality
the sun	the good, author of all things beautiful and right
freed prisoners who have become adjusted to the upper world	

3. What is the experience of the prisoner when he is first turned around and then dragged up out of the den?
4. What is the reaction of the cave-dwellers to the freed prisoner when he first returns to the cave?
5. According to Socrates, what kind of wisdom or knowledge is possessed by each of the following: (a) the chained prisoners in the cave; (b) the "clever rogue" described in paragraphs 14 and 15; (c) the philosopher who returns to serve the State (paragraph 20)?
6. For what two reasons may one's vision be perplexed and weak?
7. Why must the enlightened ones, in Plato's ideal State, descend to the den once more? What can they accomplish there?

8. Can you apply the allegory of the cave to any intellectual or spiritual experience of your own?
9. If you have read Nils Y. Wessell's "The Opportunity for Change," page 33, what agreements and disagreements about the nature of education do you find between Plato and Wessell?
10. If you have read John Dewey's "Does Human Nature Changs?" page 238, do you think that Dewey and Plato are in agreement on the changeability of human nature? Do the two educators, separated in time by more than two thousand years, agree on the nature of the educative process? Explain.

[12] *John Stuart Mill*: On the Liberty of Thought and Discussion

THE FOLLOWING selection is a sustained logical argument in favor of freedom of thought and opinion. Although most students will need to spend at least three hours on the essay in order to follow the close reasoning and understand the clear but very complex structure of the argument, the time will be well spent. John Stuart Mill (1806–1873) was an English writer, economist, and logician who has been called "the saint of rationalism." "On the Liberty of Thought and Discussion" is Chapter Two of his famous essay *On Liberty*, published in 1859.

[1] The time, it is to be hoped, is gone by, when any defence would be necessary of the "liberty of the press" as one of the securities against corrupt or tyrannical government. No argument, we may suppose, can now be needed, against permitting a legislature or an executive, not identified in interest with the people, to prescribe opinions to them, and determine what doctrines or what arguments they shall be allowed to hear. This aspect of the question, besides, has been so often and so triumphantly enforced by preceding writers, that it needs not be specially insisted on in this place. Though the law of England, on the subject of the press, is as servile to this day as it was in the time of the Tudors, there is little danger of its being actually put in force against political discussion, except during some temporary panic, when fear of insurrection drives ministers and judges from their propriety; and, speaking generally, it is not, in constitutional countries, to be apprehended that the government, whether completely responsible to the people or not, will often attempt to control the expression of opinion, except when in doing

so it makes itself the organ of the general intolerance of the public. Let us suppose, therefore, that the government is entirely at one with the people, and never thinks of exerting any power of coercion unless in agreement with what it conceives to be their voice. But I deny the right of the people to exercise such coercion, either by themselves or by their government. The power itself is illegitimate. The best government has no more title to it than the worst. It is as noxious, or more noxious, when exerted in accordance with public opinion, than when in opposition to it. If all mankind minus one were of one opinion, and only one person were of the contrary opinion, mankind would be no more justified in silencing that one person, than he, if he had the power, would be justified in silencing mankind. Were an opinion a personal possession of no value except to the owner; if to be obstructed in the enjoyment of it were simply a private injury, it would make some difference whether the injury was inflicted only on a few persons or on many. But the peculiar evil of silencing the expression of an opinion is, that it is robbing the human race; posterity as well as the existing generation; those who dissent from the opinion, still more than those who hold it. If the opinion is right, they are deprived of the opportunity of exchanging error for truth: if wrong, they lose, what is almost as great a benefit, the clearer perception and livelier impression of truth, produced by its collision with error.

[2] It is necessary to consider separately these two hypotheses, each of which has a distinct branch of the argument corresponding to it. We can never be sure that the opinion we are endeavouring to stifle is a false opinion; and if we were sure, stifling it would be an evil still.

[3] First: the opinion which it is attempted to suppress by authority may possibly be true. Those who desire to suppress it, of course deny its truth; but they are not infallible. They have no authority to decide the question for all mankind, and exclude every other person from the means of judging. To refuse a hearing to an opinion, because they are sure that it is false, is to assume that *their* certainty is the same thing as *absolute* certainty. All silencing of discussion is an assumption of infallibility. Its condemnation may be allowed to rest on this common argument, not the worse for being common.

[4] Unfortunately for the good sense of mankind, the fact of their fallibility is far from carrying the weight in their practical judgment which is always allowed to it in theory; for while every one well knows himself to be fallible, few think it necessary to take any precautions against their own fallibility, or admit the supposition that any opinion, of which they feel very certain, may be one of the examples of the error to which they acknowledge themselves to be liable. Absolute princes, or others who are accustomed to unlimited deference, usually feel this complete confidence in their own opinions on nearly all subjects. People more happily situated,

who sometimes hear their opinions disputed, and are not wholly unused to be set right when they are wrong, place the same unbounded reliance only on such of their opinions as are shared by all who surround them, or to whom they habitually defer; for in proportion to a man's want of confidence in his own solitary judgment, does he usually repose, with implicit trust, on the infallibility of "the world" in general. And the world, to each individual, means the part of it with which he comes in contact; his party, his sect, his church, his class of society; the man may be called, by comparison, almost liberal and large-minded to whom it means anything so comprehensive as his own country or his own age. Nor is his faith in this collective authority at all shaken by his being aware that other ages, countries, sects, churches, classes, and parties have thought, and even now think, the exact reverse. He devolves upon his own world the responsibility of being in the right against the dissentient worlds of other people; and it never troubles him that mere accident has decided which of these numerous worlds is the object of his reliance, and that the same causes which make him a Churchman in London, would have made him a Buddhist or a Confucian in Pekin. Yet it is as evident in itself, as any amount of argument can make it, that ages are no more infallible than individuals; every age having held many opinions which subsequent ages have deemed not only false but absurd; and it is as certain that many opinions now general will be rejected by future ages, as it is that many, once general, are rejected by the present.

[5] The objection likely to be made to this argument would probably take some such form as the following. There is no greater assumption of infallibility in forbidding the propagation of error, than in any other thing which is done by public authority on its own judgment and responsibility. Judgment is given to men that they may use it. Because it may be used erroneously, are men to be told that they ought not to use it all? To prohibit what they think pernicious, is not claiming exemption from error, but fulfilling the duty incumbent on them, although fallible, of acting on their conscientious conviction. If we were never to act on our opinions, because those opinions may be wrong, we should leave all our interests uncared for, and all our duties unperformed. An objection which applies to all conduct can be no valid objection to any conduct in particular. It is the duty of governments, and of individuals, to form the truest opinions they can; to form them carefully, and never impose them upon others unless they are quite sure of being right. But when they are sure (such reasoners may say), it is not conscientiousness but cowardice to shrink from acting on their opinions, and allow doctrines which they honestly think dangerous to the welfare of mankind, either in this life or in another, to be scattered abroad without restraint, because other people, in less enlightened times, have persecuted opinions now believed to be true. Let us take care, it may be said, not to make the same mistake: but govern-

ments and nations have made mistakes in other things, which are not denied to be fit subjects for the exercise of authority: they have laid on bad taxes, made unjust wars. Ought we therefore to lay on no taxes, and, under whatever provocation, make no wars? Men, and governments, must act to the best of their ability. There is no such thing as absolute certainty, but there is assurance sufficient for the purposes of human life. We may, and must, assume our opinion to be true for the guidance of our own conduct: and it is assuming no more when we forbid bad men to pervert society by the propagation of opinions which we regard as false and pernicious.

[6] I answer, that it is assuming very much more. There is the greatest difference between presuming an opinion to be true, because, with every opportunity for contesting it, it has not been refuted, and assuming its truth for the purpose of not permitting its refutation. Complete liberty of contradicting and disproving our opinion is the very condition which justifies us in assuming its truth for purposes of action; and on no other terms can a being with human faculties have any rational assurance of being right.

[7] When we consider either the history of opinion, or the ordinary conduct of human life, to what is it to be ascribed that the one and the other are no worse than they are? Not certainly to the inherent force of the human understanding; for, on any matter not self-evident, there are ninety-nine persons totally incapable of judging of it for one who is capable; and the capacity of the hundredth person is only comparative; for the majority of the eminent men of every past generation held many opinions now known to be erroneous, and did or approved numerous things which no one will now justify. Why is it, then, that there is on the whole a preponderance among mankind of rational opinions and rational conduct? If there really is this preponderance—which there must be unless human affairs are, and have always been, in an almost desperate state—it is owing to a quality of the human mind, the source of everything respectable in man either as an intellectual or as a moral being, namely, that his errors are corrigible. He is capable of rectifying his mistakes, by discussion and experience. Not by experience alone. There must be discussion, to show how experience is to be interpreted. Wrong opinions and practices gradually yield to fact and argument; but facts and arguments, to produce any effect on the mind, must be brought before it. Very few facts are able to tell their own story, without comments to bring out their meaning. The whole strength and value, then, of human judgment, depending on the one property, that it can be set right when it is wrong, reliance can be placed on it only when the means of setting it right are kept constantly at hand. In the case of any person whose judgment is really deserving of confidence, how has it become so? Because he has kept his mind open to criticism of his opinions and conduct. Because it has been his practice to

listen to all that could be said against him; to profit by as much of it as was just, and expound to himself, and upon occasion to others, the fallacy of what was fallacious. Because he has felt, that the only way in which a human being can make some approach to knowing the whole of a subject, is by hearing what can be said about it by persons of every variety of opinion, and studying all modes in which it can be looked at by every character of mind. No wise man ever acquired his wisdom in any mode but this; nor is it in the nature of human intellect to become wise in any other manner. The steady habit of correcting and completing his own opinion by collating it with those of others, so far from causing doubt and hesitation in carrying it into practice, is the only stable foundation for a just reliance on it: for, being cognizant of all that can, at least obviously, be said against him, and having taken up his position against all gainsayers—knowing that he has sought for objections and difficulties, instead of avoiding them, and has shut out no light which can be thrown upon the subject from any quarter—he has a right to think his judgment better than that of any person, or any multitude, who have not gone through a similar process.

[8] It is not too much to require that what the wisest of mankind, those who are best entitled to trust their own judgment, find necessary to warrant their relying on it, should be submitted to by that miscellaneous collection of a few wise and many foolish individuals, called the public. The most intolerant of churches, the Roman Catholic Church, even at the canonisation of a saint, admits, and listens patiently to, a "devil's advocate." The holiest of men, it appears, cannot be admitted to posthumous honours, until all that the devil could say against him is known and weighed. If even the Newtonian philosophy were not permitted to be questioned, mankind could not feel as complete assurance of its truth as they now do. The beliefs which we have most warrant for have no safeguard to rest on, but a standing invitation to the whole world to prove them unfounded. If the challenge is not accepted, or is accepted and the attempt fails, we are far enough from certainty still; but we have done the best that the existing state of human reason admits of; we have neglected nothing that could give the truth a chance of reaching us: if the lists are kept open, we may hope that if there be a better truth, it will be found when the human mind is capable of receiving it; and in the meantime we may rely on having attained such approach to truth as is possible in our own day. This is the amount of certainty attainable by a fallible being, and this the sole way of attaining it.

[9] Strange it is, that men should admit the validity of the arguments for free discussion, but object to their being "pushed to an extreme"; not seeing that unless the reasons are good for an extreme case, they are not good for any case. Strange that they should imagine that they are not assuming infallibility, when they acknowledge that there should be free

discussion on all subjects which can possibly be *doubtful,* but think that some particular principle or doctrine should be forbidden to be questioned because it is so *certain,* that is, because *they are certain* that it is certain. To call any proposition certain, while there is any one who would deny its certainty if permitted, but who is not permitted, is to assume that we ourselves, and those who agree with us, are the judges of certainty, and judges without hearing the other side.

[10] In the present age—which has been described as "destitute of faith, but terrified at scepticism"—in which people feel sure, not so much that their opinions are true, as that they should not know what to do without them—the claims of an opinion to be protected from public attack are rested not so much on its truth, as on its importance to society. There are, it is alleged, certain beliefs so useful, not to say indispensable, to well-being that it is as much the duty of governments to uphold those beliefs, as to protect any other of the interests of society. In a case of such necessity, and so directly in the line of their duty, something less than infallibility may, it is maintained, warrant, and even bind, governments to act on their own opinion, confirmed by the general opinion of mankind. It is also often argued, and still oftener thought, that none but bad men would desire to weaken these salutary beliefs; and there can be nothing wrong, it is thought, in restraining bad men, and prohibiting what only such men would wish to practise. This mode of thinking makes the justification of restraints on discussion not a question of the truth of doctrines, but of their usefulness; and flatters itself by that means to escape the responsibility of claiming to be an infallible judge of opinions. But those who thus satisfy themselves, do not perceive that the assumption of infallibility is merely shifted from one point to another. The usefulness of an opinion is itself a matter of opinion: as disputable, as open to discussion, and requiring discussion as much as the opinion itself. There is the same need of an infallible judge of opinions to decide an opinion to be noxious, as to decide it to be false, unless the opinion condemned has full opportunity of defending itself. And it will not do to say that the heretic may be allowed to maintain the utility or harmlessness of his opinion, though forbidden to maintain its truth. The truth of an opinion is part of its utility. If we would know whether or not it is desirable that a proposition should be believed, is it possible to exclude the consideration of whether or not it is true? In the opinion, not of bad men, but of the best men, no belief which is contrary to truth can be really useful: and can you prevent such men from urging that plea, when they are charged with culpability for denying some doctrine which they are told is useful, but which they believe to be false? Those who are on the side of received opinions never fail to take all possible advantage of this plea; you do not find *them* handling the question of utility as if it could be completely abstracted from that of truth: on the contrary, it is, above all, because their doctrine

is "the truth," that the knowledge or the belief of it is held to be so indispensable. There can be no fair discussion of the question of usefulness when an argument so vital may be employed on one side, but not on the other. And in point of fact, when law or public feeling do not permit the truth of an opinion to be disputed, they are just as little tolerant of a denial of its usefulness. The utmost they allow is an extenuation of its absolute necessity, or of the positive guilt of rejecting it.

[11] In order more fully to illustrate the mischief of denying a hearing to opinions because we, in our own judgment, have condemned them, it will be desirable to fix down the discussion to a concrete case; and I choose, by preference, the cases which are least favourable to me—in which the argument against freedom of opinion, both on the score of truth and on that of utility, is considered the strongest. Let the opinions impugned be the belief in a God and in a future state, or any of the commonly received doctrines of morality. To fight the battle on such ground gives a great advantage to an unfair antagonist; since he will be sure to say (and many who have no desire to be unfair will say it internally), Are these the doctrines which you do not deem sufficiently certain to be taken under the protection of law? Is the belief in a God one of the opinions to feel sure of which you hold to be assuming infallibility? But I must be permitted to observe, that it is not the feeling sure of a doctrine (be it what it may) which I call an assumption of infallibility. It is the undertaking to decide that question *for others*, without allowing them to hear what can be said on the contrary side. And I denounce and reprobate this pretension not the less, if put forth on the side of my most solemn convictions. However positive any one's persuasion may be, not only of the falsity but of the pernicious consequences—not only of the pernicious consequences, but (to adopt expressions which I altogether condemn) the immorality and impiety of an opinion; yet if, in pursuance of that private judgment, though backed by the public judgment of his country or his contemporaries, he prevents the opinion from being heard in its defence, he assumes infallibility. And so far from the assumption being less objectionable or less dangerous because the opinion is called immoral or impious, this is the case of all others in which it is most fatal. These are exactly the occasions on which the men of one generation commit those dreadful mistakes which excite the astonishment and horror of posterity. It is among such that we find the instances memorable in history, when the arm of the law has been employed to root out the best men and the noblest doctrines; with deplorable success as to the men, though some of the doctrines have survived to be (as if in mockery) invoked in defence of similar conduct towards those who dissent from *them*, or from their received interpretation.

[12] Mankind can hardly be too often reminded, that there was once a man named Socrates, between whom and the legal authorities and pub-

lic opinion of his time there took place a memorable collision. Born in an age and country abounding in individual greatness, this man has been handed down to us by those who best knew both him and the age, as the most virtuous man in it; while *we* know him as the head and prototype of all subsequent teachers of virtue, the source equally of the lofty inspiration of Plato and the judicious utilitarianism of Aristotle, "*i maëstri di color che sanno,*" the two headsprings of ethical as of all other philosophy. This acknowledged master of all the eminent thinkers who have since lived—whose fame, still growing after more than two thousand years, all but outweighs the whole remainder of the names which make his native city illustrious—was put to death by his countrymen, after a judicial conviction, for impiety and immorality. Impiety, in denying the gods recognised by the State; indeed his accuser asserted (see the "Apologia") that he believed in no gods at all. Immorality, in being, by his doctrines and instructions, a "corrupter of youth." Of these charges the tribunal, there is every ground for believing, honestly found him guilty, and condemned the man who probably of all then born had deserved best of mankind, to be put to death as a criminal.

[13] To pass from this to the only other instance of judicial iniquity, the mention of which, after the condemnation of Socrates, would not be an anti-climax: the event which took place on Calvary rather more than eighteen hundred years ago. The man who left on the memory of those who witnessed his life and conversation such an impression of his moral grandeur that eighteen subsequent centuries have done homage to him as the Almighty in person, was ignominiously put to death, as what? As a blasphemer. Men did not merely mistake their benefactor; they mistook him for the exact contrary of what he was, and treated him as that prodigy of impiety which they themselves are now held to be for their treatment of him. The feelings with which mankind now regard these lamentable transactions, especially the latter of the two, render them extremely unjust in their judgment of the unhappy actors. These were, to all appearance, not bad men—not worse than men commonly are, but rather the contrary; men who possessed in a full, or somewhat more than a full measure, the religious, moral, and patriotic feelings of their time and people: the very kind of men who, in all times, our own included, have every chance of passing through life blameless and respected. The high-priest who rent his garments when the words were pronounced, which, according to all the ideas of his country, constituted the blackest guilt, was in all probability quite as sincere in his horror and indignation as the generality of respectable and pious men now are in the religious and moral sentiments they profess; and most of those who now shudder at his conduct, if they had lived in his time, and been born Jews, would have acted precisely as he did. Orthodox Christians who are tempted to think that those who stoned to death the first martyrs must have been worse

men than they themselves are, ought to remember that one of those persecutors was Saint Paul.

[14] Let us add one more example, the most striking of all, if the impressiveness of an error is measured by the wisdom and virtue of him who falls into it. If ever any one, possessed of power, had grounds for thinking himself the best and most enlightened among his contemporaries, it was the Emperor Marcus Aurelius.[1] Absolute monarch of the whole civilized world, he preserved through life not only the most unblemished justice, but what was less to be expected from his Stoical breeding, the tenderest heart. The few failings which are attributed to him, were all on the side of indulgence: while his writings, the highest ethical product of the ancient mind, differ scarcely perceptibly, if they differ at all, from the most characteristic teachings of Christ. This man, a better Christian in all but the dogmatic sense of the word, than almost any of the ostensibly Christian sovereigns who have since reigned, persecuted Christianity. Placed at the summit of all the previous attainments of humanity, with an open, unfettered intellect, and a character which led him of himself to embody in his moral writings the Christian ideal, he yet failed to see that Christianity was to be a good and not an evil to the world, with his duties to which he was so deeply penetrated. Existing society he knew to be in a deplorable state. But such as it was, he saw, or thought he saw, that it was held together, and prevented from being worse, by belief and reverence of the received divinities. As a ruler of mankind, he deemed it his duty not to suffer society to fall in pieces; and saw not how, if its existing ties were removed, any others could be formed which could again knit it together. The new religion openly aimed at dissolving these ties: unless, therefore, it was his duty to adopt that religion, it seemed to be his duty to put it down. Inasmuch then as the theology of Christianity did not appear to him true or of divine origin; inasmuch as this strange history of a crucified God was not credible to him, and a system which purported to rest entirely upon a foundation to him so wholly unbelievable, could not be foreseen by him to be that renovating agency which, after all abatements, it has in fact proved to be; the gentlest and most amiable of philosophers and rulers, under a solemn sense of duty, authorized the persecution of Christianity. To my mind this is one of the most tragical facts in all history. It is a bitter thought, how different a thing the Christianity of the world might have been, if the Christian faith had been adopted as the religion of the empire under the auspices of Marcus Aurelius instead of those of Constantine. But it would be equally unjust to him and false to truth, to deny, that no one plea which can be urged for punishing anti-Christian teaching, was wanting to Marcus Aurelius for punishing, as he did, the propagation of Christianity. No Christian more

---

[1] See the selection from the *Meditations* of Marcus Aurelius, page 193.

firmly believes that Atheism is false, and tends to the dissolution of society, than Marcus Aurelius believed the same things of Christianity; he who, of all men then living, might have been thought the most capable of appreciating it. Unless any one who approves of punishment for the promulgation of opinions, flatters himself that he is a wiser and better man than Marcus Aurelius—more deeply versed in the wisdom of his time, more elevated in his intellect above it—more earnest in his search for truth, or more singleminded in his devotion to it when found; let him abstain from that assumption of the joint infallibility of himself and the multitude, which the great Antoninus made with so unfortunate a result. . . .[2]

[15] But, indeed, the dictum that truth always triumphs over persecution is one of those pleasant falsehoods which men repeat after one another till they pass into commonplaces, but which all experience refutes. History teems with instances of truth put down by persecution. If not suppressed for ever, it may be thrown back for centuries. To speak only of religious opinions: the Reformation broke out at least twenty times before Luther, and was put down. Arnold of Brescia was put down. Fra Dolcino was put down. Savonarola was put down. The Albigeois were put down. The Vaudois were put down. The Lollards were put down. The Hussites were put down. Even after the era of Luther, whatever persecution was persisted in, it was successful. In Spain, Italy, Flanders, the Austrian empire, Protestantism was rooted out; and, most likely, would have been so in England, had Queen Mary lived, or Queen Elizabeth died. Persecution has always succeeded, save where the heretics were too strong a party to be effectually persecuted. No reasonable person can doubt that Christianity might have been extirpated in the Roman Empire. It spread, and became predominant, because the persecutions were only occasional, lasting but a short time, and separated by long intervals of almost undisturbed propagandism. It is a piece of idle sentimentality that truth, merely as truth, has any inherent power denied to error of prevailing against the dungeon and the stake. Men are not more zealous for truth than they often are for error, and a sufficient application of legal or even of social penalties will generally succeed in stopping the propagation of either. The real advantage which truth has consists in this, that when an opinion is true, it may be extinguished once, twice, or many times, but in the course of ages there will generally be found persons to rediscover it, until some one of its reappearances falls on a time when from favourable circumstances it escapes persecution until it has made such head as to withstand all subsequent attempts to suppress it. . . .

[2] We have made occasional cuts in Mill's chapter. In the passage omitted here, Mill discusses the objection that "persecution is an ordeal through which truth ought to pass, and always passes successfully." Paragraph 15 is Mill's answer to this objection.

[16] Let us now pass to the second division of the argument, and dismissing the supposition that any of the received opinions may be false, let us assume them to be true, and examine into the worth of the manner in which they are likely to be held, when their truth is not freely and openly canvassed. However unwillingly a person who has a strong opinion may admit the possibility that his opinion may be false, he ought to be moved by the consideration that, however true it may be, if it is not fully, frequently, and fearlessly discussed, it will be held as a dead dogma, not a living truth.

[17] There is a class of persons (happily not quite so numerous as formerly) who think it enough if a person assents undoubtingly to what they think true, though he has no knowledge whatever of the grounds of the opinion, and could not make a tenable defence of it against the most superficial objections. Such persons, if they can once get their creed taught from authority, naturally think that no good, and some harm, comes of its being allowed to be questioned. Where their influence prevails, they make it nearly impossible for the received opinion to be rejected wisely and considerately, though it may still be rejected rashly and ignorantly; for to shut out discussion entirely is seldom possible, and when it once gets in, beliefs not grounded on conviction are apt to give way before the slightest semblance of an argument. Waiving, however, this possibility—assuming that the true opinion abides in the mind, but abides as a prejudice, a belief independent of, and proof against, argument—this is not the way in which truth ought to be held by a rational being. This is not knowing the truth. Truth, thus held, is but one superstition the more, accidentally clinging to the words which enunciate a truth.

[18] If the intellect and judgment of mankind ought to be cultivated, a thing which Protestants at least do not deny, on what can these faculties be more appropriately exercised by any one, than on the things which concern him so much that it is considered necessary for him to hold opinions on them? If the cultivation of the understanding consists in one thing more than in another, it is surely in learning the grounds of one's own opinions. Whatever people believe, on subjects on which it is of the first importance to believe rightly, they ought to be able to defend against at least the common objections. But, some one may say, "Let them be *taught* the grounds of their opinions. It does not follow that opinions must be merely parroted because they are never heard controverted. Persons who learn geometry do not simply commit the theorems to memory, but understand and learn likewise the demonstrations; and it would be absurd to say that they remain ignorant of the grounds of geometrical truths, because they never hear any one deny, and attempt to disprove them." Undoubtedly: and such teaching suffices on a subject like mathematics, where there is nothing at all to be said on the wrong side of the ques-

tion. The peculiarity of the evidence of mathematical truths is that all the argument is on one side. There are no objections, and no answers to objections. But on every subject on which difference of opinion is possible, the truth depends on a balance to be struck between two sets of conflicting reasons. Even in natural philosophy, there is always some other explanation possible of the same facts; some geocentric theory instead of heliocentric, some phlogiston instead of oxygen; and it has to be shown why that other theory cannot be the true one: and until this is shown, and until we know how it is shown, we do not understand the grounds of our opinion. But when we turn to subjects infinitely more complicated, to morals, religion, politics, social relations, and the business of life, three-fourths of the arguments for every disputed opinion consist in dispelling the appearance which favour some opinion different from it. The greatest orator, save one, of antiquity, has left it on record that he always studied his adversary's case with as great, if not still greater, intensity than even his own. What Cicero practised as the means of forensic success requires to be imitated by all who study any subject in order to arrive at the truth. He who knows only his own side of the case, knows little of that. His reasons may be good, and no one may have been able to refute them. But if he is equally unable to refute the reasons on the opposite side; if he does not so much as know what they are, he has no ground for preferring either opinion. The rational position for him would be suspension of judgment, and unless he contents himself with that, he is either led by authority, or adopts, like the generality of the world, the side to which he feels most inclination. Nor is it enough that he should hear the arguments of adversaries from his own teachers, presented as they state them, and accompanied by what they offer as refutations. That is not the way to do justice to the arguments, or bring them into real contact with his own mind. He must be able to hear them from persons who actually believe them; who defend them in earnest, and do their very utmost for them. He must know them in their most plausible and persuasive form; he must feel the whole force of the difficulty which the true view of the subject has to encounter and dispose of; else he will never really possess himself of the portion of truth which meets and removes that difficulty. Ninety-nine in a hundred of what are called educated men are in this condition; even of those who can argue fluently for their opinions. Their conclusion may be true, but it might be false for anything they know: they have never thrown themselves into the mental position of those who think differently from them, and considered what such persons may have to say; and consequently they do not, in any proper sense of the word, know the doctrine which they themselves profess. They do not know those parts of it which explain and justify the remainder; the considerations which show that a fact which seemingly conflicts with another is reconcilable with it, or that, of two apparently strong reasons, one and not the other ought to be preferred. All that part of the truth which turns the scale, and decides the judgment of a completely informed mind, they are strangers to; nor is it ever really known, but to those who have attended equally and impartially to both sides, and endeavoured to see the reasons of both in the strongest light. So essential is this discipline to a real understanding of moral and human subjects, that if opponents of all important truths do not exist, it is indispensable to imagine them, and supply them with the strongest arguments which the most skilful devil's advocate can conjure up.

[19] To abate the force of these considerations, an enemy of free discussion may be supposed to say, that there is no necessity for mankind in general to know and understand all that can be said against or for their opinions by philosophers and theologians. That it is not needful for common men to be able to expose all the misstatements or fallacies of an ingenious opponent. That it is enough if there is always somebody capable of answering them, so that nothing likely to mislead uninstructed persons remains unrefuted. That simple minds, having been taught the obvious grounds of the truths inculcated on them, may trust to authority for the rest, and being aware that they have neither knowledge nor talent to resolve every difficulty which can be raised, may repose in the assurance that all those which have been raised have been or can be answered, by those who are specially trained to the task.

[20] Conceding to this view of the subject the utmost that can be claimed for it by those most easily satisfied with the amount of understanding of truth which ought to accompany the belief of it; even so, the argument for free discussion is no way weakened. For even this doctrine acknowledges that mankind ought to have a rational assurance that all objections have been satisfactorily answered; and how are they to be answered if that which requires to be answered is not spoken? or how can the answer be known to be satisfactory, if the objectors have no opportunity of showing that it is unsatisfactory? If not the public, at least the philosophers and theologians who are to resolve the difficulties, must make themselves familiar with those difficulties in their most puzzling form; and this cannot be accomplished unless they are freely stated, and placed in the most advantageous light which they admit of. The Catholic Church has its own way of dealing with this embarrassing problem. It makes a broad separation between those who can be permitted to receive its doctrines on conviction, and those who must accept them on trust. Neither, indeed, are allowed any choice as to what they will accept; but the clergy, such at least as can be fully confided in, may admissibly and meritoriously make themselves acquainted with the arguments of opponents, in order to answer them, and may, therefore, read heretical books; the laity, not unless by special permission, hard to be obtained. This discipline recognises a knowledge of the enemy's case as beneficial to the

teachers, but finds means, consistent with this, of denying it to the rest of the world: thus giving to the *élite* more mental culture, though not more mental freedom, than it allows to the mass. By this device it succeeds in obtaining the kind of mental superiority which its purposes require; for though culture without freedom never made a large and liberal mind, it can make a clever *nisi prius* advocate of a cause. But in countries professing Protestantism, this resource is denied; since Protestants hold, at least in theory, that the responsibility for the choice of a religion must be borne by each for himself, and cannot be thrown off upon teachers. Besides, in the present state of the world, it is practically impossible that writings which are read by the instructed can be kept from the uninstructed. If the teachers of mankind are to be cognizant of all that they ought to know, everything must be free to be written and published without restraint.

[21] If, however, the mischievous operation of the absence of free discussion, when the received opinions are true, were confined to leaving men ignorant of the grounds of those opinions, it might be thought that this, if an intellectual, is no moral evil, and does not affect the worth of the opinions, regarded in their influence on the character. The fact, however, is, that not only the grounds of the opinion are forgotten in the absence of discussion, but too often the meaning of the opinion itself. The words which convey it cease to suggest ideas, or suggest only a small portion of those they were originally employed to communicate. Instead of a vivid conception and a living belief, there remain only a few phrases retained by rote; or, if any part, the shell and husk only of the meaning is retained, the finer essence being lost. The great chapter in human history which this fact occupies and fills, cannot be too earnestly studied and meditated on.

[22] It is illustrated in the experience of almost all ethical doctrines and religious creeds. They are all full of meaning and vitality to those who originate them, and to the direct disciples of the originators. Their meaning continues to be felt in undiminished strength, and is perhaps brought out into even fuller consciousness, so long as the struggle lasts to give the doctrine or creed an ascendancy over other creeds. At last it either prevails, and becomes the general opinion, or its progress stops; it keeps possession of the ground it has gained, but ceases to spread further. When either of these results has become apparent, controversy on the subject flags, and gradually dies away. The doctrine has taken its place, if not as a received opinion, as one of the admitted sects or divisions of opinion: those who hold it have generally inherited, not adopted it; and conversion from one of these doctrines to another, being now an exceptional fact, occupies little place in the thoughts of their professors. Instead of being, as at first, constantly on the alert either to defend themselves against the world, or to bring the world over to them, they have subsided into

acquiescence, and neither listen, when they can help it, to arguments against their creed, nor trouble dissentients (if there be such) with arguments in its favour. From this time may usually be dated the decline in the living power of the doctrine. We often hear the teachers of all creeds lamenting the difficulty of keeping up in the minds of believers a lively apprehension of the truth which they nominally recognise, so that it may penetrate the feelings, and acquire a real mastery over the conduct. No such difficulty is complained of while the creed is still fighting for its existence: even the weaker combatants then know and feel what they are fighting for, and the difference between it and other doctrines; and in that period of every creed's existence, not a few persons may be found, who have realised its fundamental principles in all the forms of thought, have weighed and considered them in all their important bearings, and have experienced the full effect on the character which belief in that creed ought to produce in a mind thoroughly imbued with it. But when it has come to be an hereditary creed, and to be received passively, not actively —when the mind is no longer compelled, in the same degree as at first, to exercise its vital powers on the questions which its belief presents to it, there is a progressive tendency to forget all of the belief except the formularies, or to give it a dull and torpid assent, as if accepting it on trust dispensed with the necessity of realising it in consciousness, or testing it by personal experience, until it almost ceases to connect itself at all with the inner life of the human being. Then are seen the cases, so frequent in this age of the world as almost to form the majority, in which the creed remains as it were outside the mind, incrusting and petrifying it against all other influences addressed to the higher parts of our nature; manifesting its power by not suffering any fresh and living conviction to get in, but itself doing nothing for the mind or heart except standing sentinel over them to keep them vacant.

[23] To what an extent doctrines intrinsically fitted to make the deepest impression upon the mind may remain in it as dead beliefs, without being ever realized in the imagination, the feelings, or the understanding, is exemplified by the manner in which the majority of believers hold the doctrines of Christianity. By Christianity I here mean what is accounted such by all churches and sects—the maxims and precepts contained in the New Testament. These are considered sacred, and accepted as laws, by all professing Christians. Yet it is scarcely too much to say that no one Christian in a thousand guides or tests his individual conduct by reference to those laws. The standard to which he does refer it, is the custom of his nation, his class, or his religious profession. He has thus, on the one hand, a collection of ethical maxims, which he believes to have been vouchsafed to him by infallible wisdom as rules for his government; and on the other, a set of everyday judgments and practices, which go a certain length with some of those maxims, not so great a length with others,

stand in direct opposition to some, and are, on the whole, a compromise between the Christian creed and the interests and suggestions of worldly life. To the first of these standards he gives his homage; to the other his real allegiance. All Christians believe that the blessed are the poor and humble, and those who are ill-used by the world; that it is easier for a camel to pass through the eye of a needle than for a rich man to enter the kingdom of heaven; that they should judge not, lest they be judged; that they should swear not at all; that they should love their neighbor as themselves; that if one take their cloak, they should give him their coat also; that they should take no thought for the morrow; that if they would be perfect, they should sell all that they have and give it to the poor. They are not insincere when they say that they believe these things. They do believe them, as people believe what they have always heard lauded and never discussed. But in the sense of that living belief which regulates conduct, they believe these doctrines just up to the point to which it is usual to act upon them. The doctrines in their integrity are serviceable to pelt adversaries with; and it is understood that they are to be put forward (when possible) as the reasons for whatever people do that they think laudable. But any one who reminded them that the maxims require an infinity of things which they never even think of doing, would gain nothing but to be classed among those very unpopular characters who affect to be better than other people. The doctrines have no hold on ordinary believers—are not a power in their minds. They have an habitual respect for the sound of them, but no feeling which spreads from the words to the things signified, and forces the mind to take *them* in, and make them conform to the formula. Whenever conduct is concerned, they look round for Mr. A and B to direct them how far to go in obeying Christ....

[24] It still remains to speak of one of the principal causes which make diversity of opinion advantageous, and will continue to do so until mankind shall have entered a stage of intellectual advancement which at present seems at an incalculable distance. We have hitherto considered only two possibilities: that the received opinion may be false, and some other opinion, consequently, true; or that, the received opinion being true, a conflict with the opposite error is essential to a clear apprehension and deep feeling of its truth. But there is a commoner case than either of these; when the conflicting doctrines, instead of being one true and the other false, share the truth between them; and the nonconforming opinion is needed to supply the remainder of the truth, of which the received doctrine embodies only a part. Popular opinions, on subjects not palpable to sense, are often true, but seldom or never the whole truth. They are a part of the truth; sometimes a greater, sometimes a smaller part, but exaggerated, distorted, and disjointed from the truths by which they ought to be accompanied and limited. Heretical opinions, on the other hand, are

generally some of these suppressed and neglected truths, bursting the bonds which kept them down, and either seeking reconciliation with the truth contained in the common opinion, or fronting it as enemies, and setting themselves up, with similar exclusiveness, as the whole truth. The latter case is hitherto the most frequent, as, in the human mind, one-sidedness has always been the rule, and many-sidedness the exception. Hence, even in revolutions of opinion, one part of the truth usually sets while another rises. Even progress, which ought to superadd, for the most part only substitutes, one partial and incomplete truth for another; improvement consisting chiefly in this, that the new fragment of truth is more wanted, more adapted to the needs of the time, than that which it displaces. Such being the partial character of prevailing opinions, even when resting on a true foundation, every opinion which embodies somewhat of the portion of truth which the common opinion omits, ought to be considered precious, with whatever amount of error and confusion that truth may be blended. No sober judge of human affairs will feel bound to be indignant because those who force on our notice truths which we should otherwise have overlooked, overlook some of those which we see. Rather, he will think that so long as popular truth is one-sided, it is more desirable than otherwise that unpopular truth should have one-sided assertors too; such being usually the most energetic, and the most likely to compel reluctant attention to the fragment of wisdom which they proclaim as if it were the whole.

[25] Thus, in the eighteenth century, when nearly all the instructed, and all those of the uninstructed who were led by them, were lost in admiration of what is called civilisation, and of the marvels of modern science, literature, and philosophy, and while greatly overrating the amount of unlikeness between the men of modern and those of ancient times, indulged the belief that the whole of the difference was in their own favour; with what a salutary shock did the paradoxes of Rousseau explode like bombshells in the midst, dislocating the compact mass of one-sided opinion, and forcing its elements to recombine in a better form and with additional ingredients. Not that the current opinions were on the whole farther from the truth than Rousseau's were; on the contrary, they were nearer to it; they contained more of positive truth, and very much less of error. Nevertheless there lay in Rousseau's doctrine, and has floated down the stream of opinion along with it, a considerable amount of exactly those truths which the popular opinion wanted; and these are the deposit which was left behind when the flood subsided. The superior worth of simplicity of life, the enervating and demoralising effect of the trammels and hypocrisies of artificial society, are ideas which have never been entirely absent from cultivated minds since Rousseau wrote; and they will in time produce their due effect, though at present needing to

be asserted as much as ever, and to be asserted by deeds, for words, on this subject, have nearly exhausted their power.

[26] In politics, again, it is almost a commonplace, that a party of order or stability, and a party of progress or reform, are both necessary elements of a healthy state of political life; until the one or the other shall have so enlarged its mental grasp as to be a party equally of order and of progress, knowing and distinguishing what is fit to be preserved from what ought to be swept away. Each of these modes of thinking derives its utility from the deficiencies of the other; but it is in a great measure the opposition of the other that keeps each within the limits of reason and sanity. Unless opinions favourable to democracy and to aristocracy, to property and to equality, to co-operation and to competition, to luxury and to abstinence, to sociality and individuality, to liberty and discipline, and all the other standing antagonisms of practical life, are expressed with equal freedom, and enforced and defended with equal talent and energy, there is no chance of both elements obtaining their due; one scale is sure to go up, and the other down. Truth, in the great practical concerns of life, is so much a question of the reconciling and combining of opposites, that very few have minds sufficiently capacious and impartial to make the adjustment with an approach to correctness, and it has to be made by the rough process of a struggle between combatants fighting under hostile banners. On any of the great open questions just enumerated, if either of the two opinions has a better claim than the other, not merely to be tolerated, but to be encouraged and countenanced, it is the one which happens at the particular time and place to be in a minority. That is the opinion which, for the time being, represents the neglected interests, the side of human well-being which is in danger of obtaining less than its share. I am aware that there is not, in this country, any intolerance of differences of opinion on most of these topics. They are adduced to show, by admitted and multiplied examples, the universality of the fact, that only through diversity of opinion is there, in the existing state of human intellect, a chance of fair play to all sides of the truth. When there are persons to be found who form an exception to the apparent unanimity of the world on any subject, even if the world is in the right, it is always probable that dissentients have something worth hearing to say for themselves, and that truth would lose something by their silence.

[27] It may be objected, "But *some* received principles, especially on the highest and most vital subjects, are more than half-truths. The Christian morality, for instance, is the whole truth on that subject, and if any one teaches a morality which varies from it, he is wholly in error." As this is of all cases the most important in practice, none can be fitter to test the general maxim. But before pronouncing what Christian morality is or is not, it would be desirable to decide what is meant by Christian moral-

ity. If it means the morality of the New Testament, I wonder that any one who derives his knowledge of this from the book itself, can suppose that it was announced, or intended, as a complete doctrine of morals. The Gospel always refers to a pre-existing morality, and confines its precepts to the particulars in which that morality was to be corrected, or superseded by a wider and higher; expressing itself, moreover, in terms most general, often impossible to be interpreted literally, and possessing rather the impressiveness of poetry or eloquence than the precision of legislation. To extract from it a body of ethical doctrine, has never been possible without eking it out from the Old Testament, that is, from a system elaborate indeed, but in many respects barbarous, and intended only for a barbarous people. St. Paul, a declared enemy to this Judaical mode of interpreting the doctrine and filling up the scheme of his Master, equally assumes a pre-existing morality, namely that of the Greeks and Romans; and his advice to Christians is in a great measure a system of accommodation to that; even to the extent of giving an apparent sanction to slavery. What is called Christian, but should rather be termed theological, morality, was not the work of Christ or the Apostles, but is of much later origin, having been gradually built up by the Catholic Church of the first five centuries, and though not implicitly adopted by moderns and Protestants, has been much less modified by them than might have been expected. For the most part, indeed, they have contented themselves with cutting off the additions which had been made to it in the Middle Ages, each sect supplying the place by fresh additions, adapted to its own character and tendencies. That mankind owe a great debt to this morality, and to its early teachers, I should be the last person to deny; but I do not scruple to say of it that it is, in many important points, incomplete and one-sided, and that unless ideas and feelings, not sanctioned by it, had contributed to the formation of European life and character, human affairs would have been in a worse condition than they now are. Christian morality (so called) has all the characters of a reaction; it is, in great part, a protest against Paganism. Its ideal is negative rather than positive; passive rather than active; Innocence rather than Nobleness; Abstinence from Evil, rather than energetic Pursuit of Good; in its precepts (as has been well said) "thou shalt not" predominates unduly over "thou shalt." In its horror of sensuality, it made an idol of asceticism, which has been gradually compromised away into one of legality. It holds out the hope of heaven and the threat of hell, as the appointed and appropriate motives to a virtuous life: in this falling far below the best of the ancients, and doing what lies in it to give to human morality an essentially selfish character, by disconnecting each man's feelings of duty from the interests of his fellow-creatures, except so far as a self-interested inducement is offered to him for consulting them. It is essentially a doctrine of passive obedience; it inculcates submission to all authorities found established; who indeed are not to be actively obeyed when they command what religion forbids, but who are not to be resisted, far less rebelled against, for any amount of wrong to ourselves. And while, in the morality of the best Pagan nations, duty to the State holds even a disproportionate place, infringing on the just liberty of the individual; in purely Christian ethics, that grand department of duty is scarcely noticed or acknowledged. It is in the Koran, not the New Testament, that we read the maxim—"A ruler who appoints any man to an office, when there is in his dominions another man better qualified for it, sins against God and against the State." What little recognition the idea of obligation to the public obtains in modern morality is derived from Greek and Roman sources, not from Christian; as, even in the morality of private life, whatever exists of magnanimity, highmindedness, personal dignity, even the sense of honour, is derived from the purely human, not the religious part of our education, and never could have grown out of a standard of ethics in which the only worth, professedly recognised, is that of obedience.

[28] I am as far as any one from pretending that these defects are necessarily inherent in the Christian ethics in every manner in which it can be conceived, or that the many requisites of a complete moral doctrine which it does not contain do not admit of being reconciled with it. Far less would I insinuate this of the doctrines and precepts of Christ himself. I believe that the sayings of Christ are all that I can see any evidence of their having been intended to be; that they are irreconcilable with nothing which a comprehensive morality requires; that everything which is excellent in ethics may be brought within them, with no greater violence to their language than has been done to it by all who have attempted to deduce from them any practical system of conduct whatever. But it is quite consistent with this to believe that they contain, and were meant to contain, only a part of the truth; that many essential elements of the highest morality are among the things which are not provided for, nor intended to be provided for, in the recorded deliverances of the Founder of Christianity, and which have been entirely thrown aside in the system of ethics erected on the basis of those deliverances by the Christian Church. And this being so, I think it a great error to persist in attempting to find in the Christian doctrine that complete rule for our guidance which its author intended it to sanction and enforce, but only partially to provide. I believe, too, that this narrow theory is becoming a grave practical evil, detracting greatly from the moral training and instruction which so many well-meaning persons are now at length exerting themselves to promote. I much fear that by attempting to form the mind and feelings on an exclusively religious type, and discarding those secular standards (as for want of a better name they may be called) which

heretofore coexisted with and supplemented the Christian ethics, receiving some of its spirit, and infusing into it some of theirs, there will result, and is even now resulting, a low, abject, servile type of character, which, submit itself as it may to what it deems the Supreme Will, is incapable of rising to or sympathising in the conception of Supreme Goodness. I believe that other ethics than any which can be evolved from exclusively Christian sources, must exist side by side with Christian ethics to produce the moral regeneration of mankind; and that the Christian system is no exception to the rule, that in an imperfect state of the human mind the interests of truth require a diversity of opinions. It is not necessary that in ceasing to ignore the moral truths not contained in Christianity men should ignore any of those which it does contain. Such prejudice, or oversight, when it occurs, is altogether an evil; but it is one from which we cannot hope to be always exempt, and must be regarded as the price paid for an inestimable good. The exclusive pretension made by a part of the truth to be the whole, must and ought to be protested against; and if a reactionary impulse should make the protestors unjust in their turn, this one-sidedness, like the other, may be lamented, but must be tolerated. If Christians would teach infidels to be just to Christianity, they should themselves be just to infidelity. It can do truth no service to blink the fact, known to all who have the most ordinary acquaintance with literary history, that a large portion of the noblest and most valuable moral teaching has been the work, not only of men who did not know, but of men who knew and rejected, the Christian faith.

[29] I do not pretend that the most unlimited use of the freedom of enunciating all possible opinions would put an end to the evils of religious or philosophical sectarianism. Every truth which men of narrow capacity are in earnest about, is sure to be asserted, inculcated, and in many ways even acted on, as if no other truth existed in the world, or at all events none that could limit or qualify the first. I acknowledge that the tendency of all opinions to become sectarian is not cured by the freest discussion, but is often heightened and exacerbated thereby; the truth which ought to have been, but was not, seen, being rejected all the more violently because proclaimed by persons regarded as opponents. But it is not on the impassioned partisan, it is on the calmer and more disinterested bystander, that this collision of opinions works its salutary effect. Not the violent conflict between parts of the truth, but the quiet suppression of half of it, is the formidable evil; there is always hope when people are forced to listen to both sides; it is when they attend only to one that errors harden into prejudices, and truth itself ceases to have the effect of truth, by being exaggerated into falsehood. And since there are few mental attributes more rare than that judicial faculty which can sit in intelligent judgment between two sides of a question, of which only one is represented by an advocate before it, truth has no chance but in proportion as

every side of it, every opinion which embodies any fraction of the truth, not only finds advocates, but is so advocated as to be listened to.

[30] We have now recognised the necessity to the mental well-being of mankind (on which all their other well-being depends) of freedom of opinion, and freedom of the expression of opinion, on four distinct grounds; which we will now briefly recapitulate.

[31] First, if any opinion is compelled to silence, that opinion may, for aught we can certainly know, be true. To deny this is to assume our own infallibility.

[32] Secondly, though the silenced opinion be an error, it may, and very commonly does, contain a portion of truth; and since the general or prevailing opinion on any subject is rarely or never the whole truth, it is only by the collision of adverse opinions that the remainder of the truth has any chance of being supplied.

[33] Thirdly, even if the received opinion be not only true, but the whole truth; unless it is suffered to be, and actually is, vigorously and earnestly contested, it will, by most of those who receive it, be held in the manner of a prejudice, with little comprehension or feeling of its rational grounds. And not only this, but, fourthly, the meaning of the doctrine itself will be in danger of being lost, or enfeebled, and deprived of its vital effect on the character and conduct: the dogma becoming a mere formal profession, inefficacious for good, but cumbering the ground, and preventing the growth of any real and heartfelt conviction, from reason or personal experience. . . .

COMMENT AND QUESTIONS

1. In the first paragraph, which should be read very carefully, Mill limits the subject, states his point of view, and introduces the first two major sections of the essay. Then he proceeds to support his opinion by presenting arguments in favor of it and by anticipating and refuting objections which might be raised. In the last paragraphs of this selection he summarizes his case. What assumptions is Mill making about his audience? How do his assumptions influence his tone and his choice of material?
2. The following rough outline was written by an able student. Not intended to be a model outline, it illustrates the kind of notes an intelligent reader may take as an aid to understanding the development and main ideas of a complex piece of writing. Such notes are of value, too, when one wishes to review material previously read. The outline is printed here to illustrate one type of note-taking, and to give a general view of the content of the

essay. As you read it, recall the detailed development of each point, and read again parts of the essay that you remember only vaguely.

Evil of silencing opinion is that it robs the human race. If opinion is right, people are deprived of opportunity of exchanging error for truth. If opinion is wrong, they lose the clearer perception of truth produced by collision with error.

I. Opinion to be suppressed may be true.
   A. People who want to suppress it say it is false, but people and ages are not infallible.
   B. Man is capable of rectifying his mistakes only through experience and discussion.
      1. Beliefs can be relied on only when there has been a standing invitation to prove them wrong.
      2. Even RC church has devil's advocate.
      3. The lists must be kept open, to give a chance of receiving a better truth.
   C. Poor argument that "useful" beliefs should be protected.
      1. Usefulness of an opinion is itself a matter of opinion.
      2. Truth of an opinion is part of its utility.
   D. Illustrations of mischief of denying a hearing to opinions because we condemn them. When the opinion is called impious or immoral, men of one generation most often make dreadful mistakes which horrify posterity.
      1. Socrates—impiety and immorality.
      2. Jesus—blasphemy.
      3. Christianity itself—dissolution of society.
   E. Idea that truth triumphs over persecution is false. It can be put down. Truth has only this advantage—in the course of ages it will generally be rediscovered in more favorable circumstances.
II. Opinion to be suppressed may not be true; but consider how beliefs are held if discussion on them is not allowed.
   A. If not fearlessly discussed, a belief becomes a dead dogma.
   B. Blind belief, proof against argument, is prejudice, superstition; this is not the way truth should be held by a rational being.
   C. He who knows only his side of the case knows little of that. One really knows a doctrine by knowing the arguments against it.
   D. Not knowing grounds of opinion is a moral evil as well as an intellectual one: in the absence of discussion, not only the grounds of the belief but the meaning of it is forgotten. New creeds have meaning in the lives and characters of members; later, when hereditary and passively accepted, the belief is outside the mind, encrusting it against other perhaps more vital influences. Doctrines of Christianity used as an example here.
III. Conflicting doctrines often share the truth between them.
   A. We should consider precious, dissenting doctrines which contain some portion of the truth.

B. Since popular truth is one-sided, unpopular truth should have one-sided assertors too.
  C. Rousseau in 18th century emphasized a neglected side of truth.
  D. Minority opinion needs to be heard; it represents neglected interests.
  E. Argument that Christian morality is not the whole truth of morality.
    1. What is it?
      a. New Testament refers to pre-existent morality of Old Testament, in many respects barbarous.
      b. St. Paul assumes pre-existing morality of Greece and Rome (slavery).
      c. Morality actually built up by Catholic Church in first five centuries.
    2. Christian morality is negative, passive, obedient, selfish—not social.
    3. Sayings of Christ contain and were meant to contain only part of truth.
    4. Ethics derived from other sources must exist with Christian ethics for moral regeneration of mankind.
  F. There is always hope when people are forced to listen to both sides; when they hear only one, error hardens into prejudice and truth is exaggerated into falsehood.
IV. Conclusion.
  A. Opinion compelled to silence may be true. To deny this is to assume infallibility.
  B. Though silenced opinion be error, it may contain a portion of the truth.
  C. Even if popular opinion is true, without discussion it will be held as prejudice, with no comprehension of rational grounds.
  D. The meaning of the uncontested doctrine will be lost or enfeebled, deprived of any vital effect on character or conduct.

3. In the last sentence of paragraph 4, Mill speaks of opinions once generally accepted and now thought false. What examples of such opinions can you give from your knowledge of history, science, and the like?
4. How is Mill's discussion of the canonization of a saint (paragraph 8) relevant to his argument?
5. In paragraph 10 and elsewhere, what does Mill mean by "received opinions"? What are examples of received opinions in our own society?
6. What distinction does Mill make between feeling sure of a doctrine and assuming infallibility? What is his attitude toward each?
7. What fact is Mill attempting to establish in his discussion of Socrates (paragraph 12) and of Jesus (paragraph 13)? Has Mill chosen effective examples to prove his point? Explain. Comment on the last sentence in paragraph 13.
8. What further or different point is he making in his discussion of Marcus

Aurelius (paragraph 14)? Has he shown skill in choosing an example? Can you reduce the last sentence of the paragraph to a syllogism?

9. In paragraph 15, how does Mill support his idea that truth does not always triumph over persecution? How does he explain the survival of persecuted truth?
10. In paragraphs 21–23, Mill discusses the "decline in the living power of the [uncontested] doctrine." Just what does he mean? How does he support his thesis? Is his supporting material convincing to you?
11. In paragraph 25, Mill speaks favorably of Rousseau. Why? And how is Rousseau related to Mill's main argument?
12. Summarize the views of Christian morality expressed in paragraphs 27–28. See the "Sermon on the Mount," page 200. Do you find evidence that Mill has been unfair in his comments? Explain.
13. What is the major premise for Mill's whole argument? (See Mill's summary, paragraphs 30–33.)
14. In one or two sentences, phrase your own very brief summary of Mill's essay.
15. To what extent do you agree with Mill's argument in favor of complete freedom of thought and expression? If you disagree with, or have reservations about, any parts of Mill's position, exactly where do you disagree, and how would you justify your position?

[13] *John Henry Newman*: Enlargement of Mind

STUDENTS COME to college, we say, to get an education. But what should the nature of this education be? To this question, from the time of Plato to the present, there have been many answers. In *The Idea of a University*, originally a series of lectures given in 1852, John Henry Newman (1801–1890) analyzed the scope and nature of university education; Walter Pater called his work "the perfect handling of a theory." The following excerpt from Newman's sixth lecture, "Knowledge Viewed in Relation to Learning," defines what he considers the essence, the *sine qua non*, of a liberal education.

Churchman, theologian, educator, leader of the Oxford Movement in the Anglican Church and later cardinal in the Roman Catholic Church, Newman was one of the intellectual leaders in the nineteenth century and was perhaps the greatest prose stylist in a period of great writers of prose. The good reader will attend not only to what Newman has to say but to his manner of saying it.

[¹] I suppose the *primâ-facie* view which the public at large would take of a University, considering it as a place of Education, is nothing more or less than a place for acquiring a great deal of knowledge on a great many subjects. Memory is one of the first developed of mental faculties; a boy's business when he goes to school is to learn, that is, to store up things in his memory. For some years his intellect is little more than an instrument for taking in facts, or a receptacle for storing them; he welcomes them as fast as they come to him; he lives on what is without; he has his eyes ever about him; he has a lively susceptibility of impressions; he imbibes information of every kind; and little does he make his own in a true sense of the word, living rather upon his neighbors all around him. He has opinions, religious, political, and literary, and, for a boy, is very positive in them and sure about them; but he gets them from his schoolfellows, or his masters, or his parents, as the case may be. Such as he is in his other relations, such also is he in his school exercises; his mind is observant, sharp, ready, retentive; he is almost passive in the acquisition of knowledge. I say this in no disparagement of the idea of a clever boy. Geography, chronology, history, language, natural history, he heaps up the matter of these studies as treasures for a future day. It is the seven years of plenty with him; he gathers in by handfuls, like the Egyptians, without counting; and though, as time goes on, there is exercise for his argumentative powers in the Elements of Mathematics, and for his taste in the Poets and Orators, still, while at school, or at least, till quite the last years of his time, he acquires, and little more; and when he is leaving for the University, he is mainly the creature of foreign influences and circumstances, and made up of accidents, homogeneous or not, as the case may be. Moreover, the moral habits, which are a boy's praise, encourage and assist this result; that is, diligence, assiduity, regularity, despatch, persevering application; for these are the direct conditions of acquisition, and naturally lead to it. Acquirements, again, are emphatically producible, and at a moment; they are a something to show, both for master and scholar; an audience, even though ignorant themselves of the subjects of an examination, can comprehend when questions are answered and when they are not. Here again is a reason why mental culture is in the minds of men identified with the acquisition of knowledge.

[²] The same notion possesses the public mind, when it passes on from the thought of a school to that of a University: and with the best of reasons so far as this, that there is no true culture without acquirements, and that philosophy presupposes knowledge. It requires a great deal of reading, or a wide range of information, to warrant us in putting forth our opinions on any serious subject; and without such learning the most original mind may be able indeed to dazzle, to amuse, to refute, to perplex, but not to come to any useful result or any trustworthy conclusion. There are indeed persons who profess a different view of the matter, and even act upon it. Every now and then you will find a person of vigorous or fertile mind, who relies upon his own resources, despises all former authors, and gives the world, with the utmost fearlessness, his views upon religion, or history, or any other popular subject. And his works may sell for a while; he may get a name in his day; but this will be all. His readers are sure to find in the long run that his doctrines are mere theories, and not the expression of facts, that they are chaff instead of bread, and then his popularity drops as suddenly as it rose.

[3] Knowledge then is the indispensable condition of expansion of mind, and the instrument of attaining to it; this cannot be denied; it is ever to be insisted on; I begin with it as a first principle; however, the very truth of it carries men too far, and confirms to them the notion that it is the whole of the matter. A narrow mind is thought to be that which contains little knowledge; and an enlarged mind, that which holds a great deal; and what seems to put the matter beyond dispute is, the fact of the great number of studies which are pursued in a University, by its very profession. Lectures are given on every kind of subject; examinations are held; prizes awarded. There are moral, metaphysical, physical Professors; Professors of languages, of history, of mathematics, of experimental science. Lists of questions are published, wonderful for their range and depth, variety and difficulty; treatises are written, which carry upon their very face the evidence of extensive reading or multifarious information; what then is wanting for mental culture to a person of large reading and scientific attainments? what is grasp of mind but acquirement? where shall philosophical repose be found, but in the consciousness and enjoyment of large intellectual possessions?

[4] And yet this notion is, I conceive, a mistake, and my present business is to show that it is one, and that the end of a Liberal Education is not mere knowledge, or knowledge considered in its *matter;* and I shall best attain my object, by actually setting down some cases, which will be generally granted to be instances of the process of enlightenment or enlargement of mind, and others which are not, and thus, by the comparison, you will be able to judge for yourselves, Gentlemen, whether Knowledge, that is, acquirement, is after all the real principle of the enlargement, or whether that principle is not rather something beyond it.

[5] For instance, let a person, whose experience has hitherto been confined to the more calm and unpretending scenery of these islands, ... go for the first time into parts where physical nature puts on her wilder and more awful forms, whether at home or abroad, as into mountainous districts; or let one, who has ever lived in a quiet village, go for the first time to a great metropolis,—then I suppose he will have a sensation which perhaps he never had before. He has a feeling not in addition or

increase of former feelings, but of something different in its nature. He will perhaps be borne forward, and find for a time that he has lost his bearings. He has made a certain progress, and he has a consciousness of mental enlargement; he does not stand where he did, he has a new centre, and a range of thoughts to which he was before a stranger.

[6] Again, the view of the heavens which the telescope opens upon us, if allowed to fill and possess the mind, may almost whirl it round and make it dizzy. It brings in a flood of ideas, and is rightly called an intellectual enlargement, whatever is meant by the term.

[7] And so again, the sight of beasts of prey and other foreign animals, their strangeness, the originality (if I may use the term) of their forms and gestures and habits and their variety and independence of each other, throw us out of ourselves into another creation, and as if under another Creator, if I may so express the temptation which may come on the mind. We seem to have new faculties, or a new exercise for our faculties, by this addition to our knowledge; like a prisoner, who, having been accustomed to wear manacles or fetters, suddenly finds his arms and legs free.

[8] Hence Physical Science generally, in all its departments, as bringing before us the exuberant riches and resources, yet the orderly course of the Universe, elevates and excites the student, and at first, I may say, almost takes away his breath, while in time it exercises a tranquilizing influence upon him.

[9] Again, the study of history is said to enlarge and enlighten the mind, and why? because, as I conceive, it gives it a power of judging of passing events, and of all events, and a conscious superiority over them, which before it did not possess.

[10] And in like manner, what is called seeing the world, entering into active life, going into society, travelling, gaining acquaintance with the various classes of the community, coming into contact with the principles and modes of thought of various parties, interests, and races, their views, aims, habits and manners, their religious creeds and forms of worship,—gaining experience how various yet how alike men are, how low-minded, how bad, how opposed, yet how confident in their opinions; all this exerts a perceptible influence upon the mind, which it is impossible to mistake, be it good or be it bad, and is popularly called its enlargement.

[11] And then again, the first time the mind comes across the arguments and speculations of unbelievers, and feels what a novel light they cast upon what he has hitherto accounted sacred; and still more, if it gives into them and embraces them, and throws off as so much prejudice what it has hitherto held, and, as if waking from a dream, begins to realize to its imagination that there is now no such thing as law and the transgression of law, that sin is a phantom, and punishment a bugbear, that it is free to sin, free to enjoy the world and the flesh; and still further, when it does enjoy them, and reflects that it may think and hold just

what it will, that "the world is all before it where to choose," and what system to build up as its own private persuasion; when this torrent of wilful thoughts rushes over and inundates it, who will deny that the fruit of the tree of knowledge, or what the mind takes for knowledge, has made it one of the gods, with a sense of expansion and elevation,—an intoxication in reality, still, so far as the subjective state of the mind goes, an illumination? Hence the fanaticism of individuals or nations, who suddenly cast off their Maker. Their eyes are opened; and, like the judgment-stricken king in the Tragedy, they see two suns, and a magic universe, out of which they look back upon their former state of faith and innocence with a sort of contempt and indignation, as if they were then but fools, and the dupes of imposture.

[12] On the other hand, Religion has its own enlargement, and an enlargement, not of tumult, but of peace. It is often remarked of uneducated persons, who have hitherto thought little of the unseen world, that, on their turning to God, looking into themselves, regulating their hearts, reforming their conduct, and meditating on death and judgment, heaven and hell, they seem to become, in point of intellect, different beings from what they were. Before, they took things as they came, and thought no more of one thing than another. But now every event has a meaning; they have their own estimate of whatever happens to them; they are mindful of times and seasons, and compare the present with the past; and the world, no longer dull, monotonous, unprofitable, and hopeless, is a various and complicated drama, with parts and an object, and an awful moral.

[13] Now from these instances, to which many more might be added, it is plain, first, that the communication of knowledge certainly is either a condition or the means of that sense of enlargement or enlightenment, of which at this day we hear so much in certain quarters: this cannot be denied; but next, it is equally plain, that such communication is not the whole of the process. The enlargement consists, not merely in the passive reception into the mind of a number of ideas hitherto unknown to it, but in the mind's energetic and simultaneous action upon and towards and among those new ideas, which are rushing in upon it. It is the action of a formative power, reducing to order and meaning the matter of our acquirements; it is a making the objects of our knowledge subjectively our own, or, to use a familiar word, it is a digestion of what we receive, into the substance of our previous state of thought; and without this no enlargement is said to follow. There is no enlargement, unless there be a comparison of ideas one with another, as they come before the mind, and a systematizing of them. We feel our minds to be growing and expanding *then*, when we not only learn, but refer what we learn to what we know already. It is not the mere addition to our knowledge that is the illumination; but the locomotion, the movement onwards, of that

mental centre, to which both what we know, and what we are learning, the accumulating mass of our acquirements, gravitates. And therefore a truly great intellect, and recognized to be such by the common opinion of mankind, such as the intellect of Aristotle, or of St. Thomas, or of Newton, or of Goethe, . . . is one which takes a connected view of old and new, past and present, far and near, and which has an insight into the influence of all these one on another; without which there is no whole, and no centre. It possesses the knowledge, not only of things, but also of their mutual and true relations; knowledge, not merely considered as acquirement but as philosophy.

[14] Accordingly, when this analytical, distributive, harmonizing process is away, the mind experiences no enlargement, and is not reckoned as enlightened or comprehensive, whatever it may add to its knowledge. For instance, a great memory, as I have already said, does not make a philosopher, any more than a dictionary can be called a grammar. There are men who embrace in their minds a vast multitude of ideas, but with little sensibility about their real relations towards each other. These may be antiquarians, annalists, naturalists; they may be learned in the law; they may be versed in statistics; they are most useful in their own place; I should shrink from speaking disrespectfully of them; still, there is nothing in such attainments to guarantee the absence of narrowness of mind. If they are nothing more than well-read men, or men of information, they have not what specially deserves the name of culture of mind, or fulfills the type of Liberal Education.

[15] In like manner, we sometimes fall in with persons who have seen much of the world, and of the men who, in their day, have played a conspicuous part in it, but who generalize nothing, and have no observation, in the true sense of the word. They abound in information, in detail, curious and entertaining, about men and things; and, having lived under the influence of no very clear or settled principles, religious or political, they speak of every one and every thing, only as so many phenomena, which are complete in themselves, and lead to nothing, not discussing them, or teaching any truth, or instructing the hearer, but simply talking. No one would say that these persons, well informed as they are, had attained to any great culture of intellect or to philosophy.

[16] The case is the same still more strikingly where the persons in question are beyond dispute men of inferior powers and deficient education. Perhaps they have been much in foreign countries, and they receive, in a passive, otiose, unfruitful way, the various facts which are forced upon them there. Seafaring men, for example, range from one end of the earth to the other; but the multiplicity of external objects, which they have encountered, forms no symmetrical and consistent picture upon their imagination; they see the tapestry of human life, as it were on the wrong side, and it tells no story. They sleep, and they rise up, and they find

themselves, now in Europe, now in Asia; they see visions of great cities and wild regions; they are in the marts of commerce, or amid the islands of the South; they gaze on Pompey's Pillar, or on the Andes; and nothing which meets them carries them forward or backward, to any idea beyond itself. Nothing has a drift or relation; nothing has a history or a promise. Every thing stands by itself, and comes and goes in its turn, like the shifting scenes of a show, which leave the spectator where he was. Perhaps you are near such a man on a particular occasion, and expect him to be shocked or perplexed at something which occurs; but one thing is much the same to him as another, or, if he is perplexed, it is not knowing what to say, whether it is right to admire, or to ridicule, or to disapprove, while conscious that some expression of opinion is expected from him; or in fact he has no standard of judgment at all, and no landmarks to guide him to a conclusion. Such is mere acquisition, and, I repeat, no one would dream of calling it philosophy.

[17] Instances, such as these, confirm, by the contrast, the conclusion I have already drawn from those which preceded them. That only is true enlargement of mind which is the power of viewing many things at once as one whole, of referring them severally to their true place in the universal system, of understanding their respective values, and determining their mutual dependence. Thus is that form of Universal Knowledge, of which I have on a former occasion spoken, set up in the individual intellect, and constitutes its perfection. Possessed of this real illumination, the mind never views any part of the extended subject-matter of Knowledge without recollecting that it is but a part, or without the associations which spring from this recollection. It makes every thing in some sort lead to every thing else; it would communicate the image of the whole to every separate portion, till that whole becomes in imagination like a spirit, every where pervading and penetrating its component parts, and giving them one definite meaning. Just as our bodily organs, when mentioned, recall their function in the body, as the word "creation" suggests the Creator, and "subjects" a sovereign, so, in the mind of the Philosopher, as we are abstractedly conceiving of him, the elements of the physical and moral world, sciences, arts, pursuits, ranks, offices, events, opinions, individualities, are all viewed as one, with correlative functions, and as gradually by successive combinations converging, one and all, to the true centre.

[18] To have even a portion of this illuminative reason and true philosophy is the highest state to which nature can aspire, in the way of intellect; it puts the mind above the influences of chance and necessity, above anxiety, suspense, unsettlement, and superstition, which is the lot of the many. Men whose minds are possessed with some one object, take exaggerated views of its importance, are feverish in the pursuit of it, make it the measure of things which are utterly foreign to it, and are

startled and despond if it happens to fail them. They are ever in alarm or in transport. Those on the other hand who have no object or principle whatever to hold by, lose their way, every step they take. They are thrown out, and do not know what to think or say, at every fresh juncture; they have no view of persons, or occurrences, or facts, which come suddenly upon them, and they hang upon the opinion of others, for want of internal resources. But the intellect which has been disciplined to the perfection of its powers, which knows, and thinks while it knows, which has learned to leaven the dense mass of facts and events with the elastic force of reason, such an intellect cannot be partial, cannot be exclusive, cannot be impetuous, cannot be at a loss, cannot but be patient, collected, and majestically calm, because it discerns the end in every beginning, the origin in every end, the law in every interruption, the limit in each delay; because it ever knows where it stands, and how its path lies from one point to another. It is the τετράγωνος of the Peripatetic,[1] and has the "nil admirari"[2] of the Stoic,—

> Felix qui potuit rerum cognoscere causas,
> Atque metus omnes, et inexorabile fatum
> Subjecit pedibus, strepitumque Acherontis avari.[3]

There are men who, when in difficulties, originate at the moment vast ideas or dazzling projects; who, under the influence of excitement, are able to cast a light, almost as if from inspiration, on a subject or course of action which comes before them; who have a sudden presence of mind equal to any emergency, rising with the occasion, and an undaunted magnanimous bearing, and an energy and keenness which is but made intense by opposition. This is genius, this is heroism; it is the exhibition of a natural gift, which no culture can teach, at which no Institution can aim; here, on the contrary, we are concerned, not with mere nature, but with training and teaching. That perfection of the Intellect, which is the result of Education, and its *beau ideal*, to be imparted to individuals in their respective measures, is the clear, calm, accurate vision and comprehension of all things, as far as the finite mind can embrace them, each in its place, and with its own characteristics upon it. It is almost prophetic from its knowledge of history; it is almost heart-searching from its knowledge of human nature; it has almost supernatural charity from its freedom from littleness and prejudice; it has almost the repose of faith, because nothing can startle it; it has almost the beauty and harmony of heavenly contemplation, so intimate is it with the eternal order of things and the music of the spheres.

[1] An allusion to Aristotle's *Ethics*—the good and *foursquare* man.
[2] To be amazed at nothing.
[3] Happy the man who can understand the causes of things, and thus spurn all fear and inexorable fate and the roar of greedy Acheron.

COMMENT AND QUESTIONS

1. In this selection Newman's essential purpose is to define an abstract concept—what he calls mental enlargement, mental illumination, or philosophical knowledge—and to persuade the reader that the achieving of such mental enlargement is the true end of education. In the "Introduction to Rhetorical Analysis" we have said that extended definitions, like brief definitions, put the subject into a genus or class, and differentiate it from other members of its class with which it might be confused. Extended definitions also clarify the subject in one or more of these ways: (a) by giving examples; (b) by comparing the subject with something familiar to the reader; (c) by comparing and contrasting it with related subjects; (d) by tracing its history or development; (e) by negating or excluding—showing what it does not mean or does not include as the author is using it; (f) by restating in different words the essentials of the definition; (g) by analyzing—breaking the subject into its components, and examining each part.
    Which of these methods of definition has Newman used? Where, in your judgment, has he used one or more of the methods most effectively?
2. Do you agree that enlargement of mind should be the chief end of education? What other aims or ends might be considered equally important?
3. To see Newman's skill in organizing his thought, read the first sentences only in paragraphs 1, 2, 3, 13, 14, 17, 18. Note that these sentences provide the framework upon which the development rests and also supply a kind of sentence outline and summary of the essay.
4. Now look at the development more closely by examining paragraphs 5 through 12. What makes these paragraphs a unit? How has the author secured transitions from one paragraph to another? Newman is famous for his ability to see various sides of a question—an ability illustrated in paragraphs 11 and 12. Considering his strong religious beliefs, do you see a reason why paragraph 12 follows rather than precedes paragraph 11? Is paragraph 12 more effective because it is preceded by paragraph 11? Explain your answer.
5. Follow in detail the development of the thought in paragraphs 13 through 17. What is the unifying idea? What purpose is served by each paragraph?
6. In the last paragraph (18) Newman makes certain claims for the kind of education he has been describing and also admits that there are some powers which are beyond the reach of such an education. Just what claims does he make? Do the admissions add to or detract from his whole argument in favor of liberal education?
7. Some aspects of Newman's style which are particularly worthy of notice are his use of sustained parallelism to make his long sentences perfectly clear, his use of balance and antithesis and climactic arrangement, the varied pace and rhythm of his sentences, the subtle use of alliteration, the

choice of figures of speech (the tapestry figure in paragraph 16, for example). Can you find examples of these stylistic traits in this selection?
8. Plato in "The Myth of the Cave" is also writing about education. If you have read this selection, what major points of agreement and disagreement do you find between Newman and Plato?

[14] *Clark Kerr*: The Idea of a Multiversity

CLARK KERR (1911–   ), an economist and author of a number of books on industrial relations, was president of the University of California from 1958 to 1967 and is now head of the Carnegie Study of Higher Education. The following selection consists of two sections of the opening chapter of *The Uses of the University*, published in 1963.

[1] The university started as a single community—a community of masters and students. It may even be said to have had a soul in the sense of a central animating principle. Today the large American university is, rather, a whole series of communities and activities held together by a common name, a common governing board, and related purposes. This great transformation is regretted by some, accepted by many, gloried in, as yet, by few. But it should be understood by all.
[2] The university of today can perhaps be understood, in part, by comparing it with what it once was—with the academic cloister of Cardinal Newman, with the research organism of Abraham Flexner.[1] Those are the ideal types from which it has derived, ideal types which still constitute the illusions of some of its inhabitants. The modern American university, however, is not Oxford nor is it Berlin; it is a new type of institution in the world. As a new type of institution, it is not really private and it is not really public; it is neither entirely of the world nor entirely apart from it. It is unique.
[3] "The Idea of a University" was, perhaps, never so well expressed as by Cardinal Newman when engaged in founding the University of Dublin a little over a century ago. His views reflected the Oxford of his day whence he had come. A university, wrote Cardinal Newman, is "the high protecting power of all knowledge and science, of fact and principle, of inquiry and discovery, of experiment and speculation; it maps out the

[1] An American educator, director of the Institute for Advanced Study at Princeton in 1930.

territory of the intellect, and sees that . . . there is neither encroachment nor surrender on any sides." He favored "liberal knowledge," and said that "useful knowledge" was a "deal of trash."

[4] Newman was particularly fighting the ghost of Bacon who some 250 years before had condemned "a kind of adoration of the mind . . . by means whereof men have withdrawn themselves too much from the contemplation of nature, and the observations of experience, and have tumbled up and down in their own reason and conceits." Bacon believed that knowledge should be for the benefit and use of men, that it should "not be as a courtesan, for pleasure and vanity only, or as a bond-woman, to acquire and gain to her master's use; but as a spouse, for generation, fruit and comfort."

[5] To this Newman replied that "Knowledge is capable of being its own end. Such is the constitution of the human mind, that any kind of knowledge, if it really be such, is its own reward." And in a sharp jab at Bacon he said: "The Philosophy of Utility, you will say, Gentlemen, has at least done its work; and I grant it—it aimed low, but it has fulfilled its aim." Newman felt that other institutions should carry on research, for "If its object were scientific and philosophical discovery, I do not see why a University should have any students"—an observation sardonically echoed by today's students who often think their professors are not interested in them at all but only in research. A University training, said Newman, "aims at raising the intellectual tone of society, at cultivating the public mind, at purifying the national taste, at supplying true principles to popular enthusiasm and fixed aims to popular aspirations, at giving enlargement and sobriety to the ideas of the age, at facilitating the exercise of political powers, and refining the intercourse of private life." It prepares a man "to fill any post with credit, and to master any subject with facility."

[6] This beautiful world was being shattered forever even as it was being so beautifully portrayed. By 1852, when Newman wrote, the German universities were becoming the new model. The democratic and industrial and scientific revolutions were all well underway in the western world. The gentleman "at home in any society" was soon to be at home in none. Science was beginning to take the place of moral philosophy, research the place of teaching.

[7] "The Idea of a Modern University," to use Flexner's phrase, was already being born. "A University," said Flexner in 1930, "is not outside, but inside the general social fabric of a given era. . . . It is not something apart, something historic, something that yields as little as possible to forces and influences that are more or less new. It is on the contrary . . . an expression of the age, as well as an influence operating upon both present and future."

[8] It was clear by 1930 that "Universities have changed profoundly—

and commonly in the direction of the social evolution of which they are part." This evolution had brought departments into universities, and still new departments; institutes and ever more institutes; created vast research libraries; turned the philosopher on his log into a researcher in his laboratory or the library stacks; taken medicine out of the hands of the profession and put it into the hands of the scientists; and much more. Instead of the individual student, there were the needs of society; instead of Newman's eternal "truths in the natural order," there was discovery of the new; instead of the generalist, there was the specialist. The university became, in the words of Flexner, "an institution consciously devoted to the pursuit of knowledge, the solution of problems, the critical appreciation of achievement and the training of men at a really high level." No longer could a single individual "master any subject"—Newman's universal liberal man was gone forever.

[9] But as Flexner was writing of the "Modern University," it, in turn, was ceasing to exist. The Berlin of Humboldt[2] was being violated just as Berlin had violated the soul of Oxford. The universities were becoming too many things. Flexner himself complained that they were "secondary schools, vocational schools, teacher-training schools, research centers, 'uplift' agencies, businesses—these and other things simultaneously." They engaged in "incredible absurdities," "a host of inconsequential things." They "needlessly cheapened, vulgarized and mechanized themselves." Worst of all, they became "'service stations' for the general public."

[10] Even Harvard. "It is clear," calculated Flexner, "that of Harvard's total expenditures not more than one-eighth is devoted to the *central* university disciplines at the level at which a university ought to be conducted." He wondered: "Who has forced Harvard into this false path? No one. It does as it pleases; and this sort of thing pleases." It obviously did not please Flexner. He wanted Harvard to disown the Graduate School of Business and let it become, if it had to survive at all, the "Boston School of Business." He would also have banished all Schools of Journalism and Home Economics, football, correspondence courses, and much else.

[11] It was not only Harvard and other American universities, but also London. Flexner asked "in what sense the University of London is a university at all." It was only "a federation."

[12] By 1930, American universities had moved a long way from Flexner's "Modern University" where "The heart of a university is a graduate school of arts and sciences, the solidly professional schools (mainly, in America, medicine and law) and certain research institutes." They were becoming less and less like a "genuine university," by which

[2] Wilhelm von Humboldt (1767–1835) was a German philologist and statesman who was instrumental in founding the University of Berlin in 1810.

Flexner meant "an organism, characterized by highness and definiteness of aim, unity of spirit and purpose." The "Modern University" was as nearly dead in 1930 when Flexner wrote about it, as the old Oxford was in 1852 when Newman idealized it. History moves faster than the observer's pen. Neither the ancient classics and theology nor the German philosophers and scientists could set the tone for the really modern university—the multiversity.

[13] "The Idea of a Multiversity" has no bard to sing its praises; no prophet to proclaim its vision; no guardian to protect its sanctity. It has its critics, its detractors, its transgressors. It also has its barkers selling its wares to all who will listen—and many do. But it also has its reality rooted in the logic of history. It is an imperative rather than a reasoned choice among elegant alternatives.

[14] President Nathan Pusey wrote in his latest annual report to the members of the Harvard Board of Overseers that the average date of graduation of the present Board members was 1924; and much has happened to Harvard since 1924. Half of the buildings are new. The faculty has grown five-fold, the budget nearly fifteen-fold. "One can find almost anywhere one looks similar examples of the effect wrought in the curriculum and in the nature of the contemporary university by widening international awareness, advancing knowledge, and increasingly sophisticated methods of research. . . . Asia and Africa, radio telescopes, masers and lasers and devices for interplanetary exploration unimagined in 1924 —these and other developments have effected such enormous changes in the intellectual orientation and aspiration of the contemporary university as to have made the university we knew as students now seem a strangely underdeveloped, indeed a very simple and an almost unconcerned kind of institution. And the pace of change continues."

[15] Not only at Harvard. The University of California last year had operating expenditures from all sources of nearly half a billion dollars, with almost another 100 million for construction; a total employment of over 40,000 people, more than IBM and in a far greater variety of endeavors; operations in over a hundred locations, counting campuses, experiment stations, agricultural and urban extension centers, and projects abroad involving more than fifty countries; nearly 10,000 courses in its catalogues; some form of contact with nearly every industry, nearly every level of government, nearly every person in its region. Vast amounts of expensive equipment were serviced and maintained. Over 4,000 babies were born in its hospitals. It is the world's largest purveyor of white mice. It will soon have the world's largest primate colony. It will soon also have 100,000 students—30,000 of them at the graduate level; yet much less than one third of its expenditures are directly related to teaching. It already has nearly 200,000 students in extension courses—including

one out of every three lawyers and one out of every six doctors in the state. And Harvard and California are illustrative of many more.

[16] Newman's "Ideal of a University" still has its devotees—chiefly the humanists and the generalists and the undergraduates. Flexner's "Idea of a Modern University" still has its supporters—chiefly the scientists and the specialists and the graduate students. "The Idea of a Multiversity" has its practitioners—chiefly the administrators, who now number many of the faculty among them, and the leadership groups in society at large. The controversies are still around in the faculty clubs and the student coffee houses; and the models of Oxford and Berlin and modern Harvard all animate segments of what was once a "community of masters and students" with a single vision of its nature and purpose. These several competing visions of true purpose, each relating to a different layer of history, a different web of forces, cause much of the malaise in the university communities of today. The university is so many things to so many different people that it must, of necessity, be partially at war with itself.

[17] How did the multiversity happen? No man created it; in fact, no man visualized it. It has been a long time coming about and it has a long way to go. What is its history? How is it governed? What is life like within it? What is its justification? Does it have a future?

LIFE IN THE MULTIVERSITY

[18] The "Idea of a University" was a village with its priests. The "Idea of a Modern University" was a town—a one-industry town—with its intellectual oligarchy. "The Idea of a Multiversity" is a city of infinite variety. Some get lost in the city; some rise to the top within it; most fashion their lives within one of its many subcultures. There is less sense of community than in the village but also less sense of confinement. There is less sense of purpose than within the town but there are more ways to excel. There are also more refuges of anonymity—both for the creative person and the drifter. As against the village and the town, the "city" is more like the totality of civilization as it has evolved and more an integral part of it; and movement to and from the surrounding society has been greatly accelerated. As in a city, there are many separate endeavors under a single rule of law.

[19] The students in the "city" are older, more likely to be married, more vocationally oriented, more drawn from all classes and races than the students in the village; and they find themselves in a most intensely competitive atmosphere. They identify less with the total community and more with its subgroups. Burton R. Clark and Martin Trow have a particularly interesting typology of these subcultures: the "collegiate" of the fraternities and sororities and the athletes and activities majors; the

"academic" of the serious students; the "vocational" of the students seeking training for specific jobs; and the "nonconformist" of the political activists, the aggressive intellectuals, and the bohemians. These subcultures are not mutually exclusive, and some of the fascinating pageantry of the multiversity is found in their interaction one on another.

[20] The multiversity is a confusing place for the student. He has problems of establishing his identity and sense of security within it. But it offers him a vast range of choices, enough literally to stagger the mind. In this range of choices he encounters the opportunities and the dilemmas of freedom. The casualty rate is high. The walking wounded are many. *Lernfreiheit*—the freedom of the student to pick and choose, to stay or to move on—is triumphant.

[21] Life has changed also for the faculty member. The multiversity is in the mainstream of events. To the teacher and the researcher have been added the consultant and the administrator. Teaching is less central than it once was for most faculty members; research has become more important. This has given rise to what has been called the "non-teacher" —"the higher a man's standing, the less he has to do with students"— and to a threefold class structure of what used to be "the faculty": those who only do research, those who only teach (and they are largely in an auxiliary role), and those who still do some of both. In one university I know, the proportions at the Ph.D. level or its equivalent are roughly one researcher to two teachers to four who do both.

[22] Consulting work and other sources of additional income have given rise to what is called the "affluent professor," a category that does include some but by no means all of the faculty. Additionally, many faculty members, with their research assistants and teaching assistants, their departments and institutes, have become administrators. A professor's life has become, it is said, "a rat race of business and activity, managing contracts and projects, guiding teams and assistants, bossing crews of technicians, making numerous trips, sitting on committees for government agencies, and engaging in other distractions necessary to keep the whole frenetic business from collapse."

[23] The intellectual world has been fractionalized as interests have become much more diverse; and there are fewer common topics of conversation at the faculty clubs. Faculty government has become more cumbersome, more the avocation of active minorities; and there are real questions whether it can work effectively on a large scale, whether it can agree on more than preservation of the status quo. Faculty members are less members of the particular university and more colleagues within their national academic discipline groups.

[24] But there are many compensations. "The American professoriate" is no longer, as Flexner once called it, "a proletariat." Salaries and status have risen considerably. The faculty member is more a fully participating

member of society, rather than a creature on the periphery; some are at the very center of national and world events. Research opportunities have been enormously increased. The faculty member within the big mechanism and with all his opportunities has a new sense of independence from the domination of the administration or his colleagues; much administration has been effectively decentralized to the level of the individual professor. In particular, he has a choice of roles and mixtures of roles to suit his taste as never before. He need not leave the Groves for the Acropolis unless he wishes; but he can, if he wishes. He may even become, as some have, essentially a professional man with his home office and basic retainer on the campus of the multiversity but with his clients scattered from coast to coast. He can also even remain the professor of old, as many do. There are several patterns of life from which to choose. So the professor too has greater freedom. *Lehrfreiheit,* in the old German sense of the freedom of the professor to do as he pleases, also is triumphant.

[25] What is the justification of the modern American multiversity? History is one answer. Consistency with the surrounding society is another. Beyond that, it has few peers in the preservation and dissemination and examination of the eternal truths; no living peers in the search for new knowledge; and no peers in all history among institutions of higher learning in serving so many of the segments of an advancing civilization. Inconsistent internally as an institution, it is consistently productive. Torn by change, it has the stability of freedom. Though it has not a single soul to call its own, its members pay their devotions to truth.

[26] The multiversity in America is perhaps best seen at work, adapting and growing, as it responded to the massive impact of federal programs beginning with World War II. A vast transformation has taken place without a revolution, for a time almost without notice being taken. The multiversity has demonstrated how adaptive it can be to new opportunities for creativity; how responsive to money; how eagerly it can play a new and useful role; how fast it can change while pretending that nothing has happened at all; how fast it can neglect some of its ancient virtues. . . .

COMMENT AND QUESTIONS

1. Look again at the opening paragraph of the selection (also the opening paragraph of Kerr's book). What words and phrases in the first two sentences are echoed later in the selection? How are the choice and arrangement of words in the last two sentences effective?
2. What purposes are served by Kerr's historical approach, beginning in

paragraph 2, to the university of today? What appear to be his attitudes toward the works of Newman and Flexner?
3. Examine paragraph 13. What is its function? What characteristics of style and tone do you notice?
4. What is the purpose, in paragraphs 14–15, of the detailed cataloguing of developments and activities at Harvard and, particularly, at the University of California?
5. What techniques of style and of paragraph development are noteworthy in paragraph 18?
6. Does life for the student in the multiversity, as Kerr describes it in paragraphs 19–20, seem attractive to you? Explain.
7. In the discussion of life for the faculty member in the multiversity (paragraphs 21–24) are there any implications that the student's educational experience is adversely affected? Support your answer with references to what Kerr says.
8. Paragraph 25 is well written. By what means does the author make it a good paragraph?
9. Kerr is notably fair in presenting the advantages and disadvantages of the multiversity. What is your response to the multiversity as he describes it?

[15] *John W. Gardner*: Excellence: The Ideal of Individual Fulfillment

JOHN W. GARDNER (1912–) has been a college teacher, president of the Carnegie Corporation and of the Carnegie Foundation for the Advancement of Teaching, and Secretary of the Department of Health, Education and Welfare; in 1964 he received the Presidential Medal of Freedom. The following selection is Chapter XIII of a book published in 1961, *Excellence: Can We Be Equal and Excellent Too?*

THE PERSON ONE COULD BE

[1] Some years ago I had a memorable conversation with the ten-year-old son of one of my fellow professors. I was walking to class and he was headed for his violin lesson. We fell into conversation, and he complained that he couldn't play any real pieces on the violin yet—only those tiresome exercises. I suggested that this would be remedied as he improved, which led him to respond with melancholy: "But I don't want to improve. I expect I may even get worse."

[²] The idea of excellence is attractive to most people and inspiring to some. But taken alone it is a fairly abstract notion. It is not the universally powerful moving force that one might wish. We must therefore ask ourselves what are the moving and meaningful ideas that will inspire and sustain people as they strive for excellence.

[³] In our own society one does not need to search far for an idea of great vitality and power which can and should serve the cause of excellence. It is our well-established ideal of individual fulfillment. This ideal is implicit in our convictions concerning the worth of the individual. It undergirds our belief in equality of opportunity. It is expressed in our conviction that every individual should be enabled to achieve the best that is in him.

[⁴] The chief instrument we have devised to further the ideal of individual fulfillment is the educational system. But in our understandable preoccupation with perfecting that instrument, we have tended to forget the broader objectives it was designed to serve. Most Americans honor education; few understand its larger purposes. Our thinking about the aims of education has too often been shallow, constricted and lacking in reach or perspective. Our educational purposes must be seen in the broader framework of our convictions concerning the worth of the individual and the importance of individual fulfillment.

[⁵] Education in the formal sense is only a part of the society's larger task of abetting the individual's intellectual, emotional and moral growth. *What we must reach for is a conception of perpetual self-discovery, perpetual reshaping to realize one's best self, to be the person one could be.*

[⁶] This is a conception which far exceeds formal education in scope. It includes not only the intellect but the emotions, character and personality. It involves not only the surface, but deeper layers of thought and action. It involves adaptability, creativeness and vitality.

[⁷] And it involves moral and spiritual growth. We say that we wish the individual to fulfill his potentialities, but obviously we do not wish to develop great criminals or great rascals. Learning for learning's sake isn't enough. Thieves learn cunning, and slaves learn submissiveness. We may learn things that constrict our vision and warp our judgment. We wish to foster fulfillment within the framework of rational and moral strivings which have characterized man at his best. In a world of huge organizations and vast social forces that dwarf and threaten the individual, we must range ourselves whenever possible on the side of individuality; but we cannot applaud an irresponsible, amoral or wholly self-gratifying individuality.

[⁸] America's greatness has been the greatness of a free people who shared certain moral commitments. Freedom without moral commitment is aimless and promptly self-destructive. It is an ironic fact that as individuals in our society have moved toward conformity in their outward behavior, they have moved away from any sense of deeply-shared purposes. We must restore *both* a vigorous sense of individuality *and* a sense of shared purposes. Either without the other leads to consequences abhorrent to us.

[9] To win our deepest respect the individual must both find himself and lose himself. This is not so contradictory as it sounds. We respect the man who places himself at the service of values which transcend his own individuality—the values of his profession, his people, his heritage, and above all the religious and moral values which nourished the ideal of individual fulfillment in the first place. But this "gift of himself" only wins our admiration if the giver has achieved a mature individuality and if the act of giving does not involve an irreparable crippling of that individuality. We cannot admire faceless, mindless servants of The State or The Cause or The Organization who were never mature individuals and who have sacrificed all individuality to the Corporate Good.

WASTE ON A MASSIVE SCALE

[10] In our society today, large numbers of young people never fulfill their potentialities. Their environment may not be such as to stimulate such fulfillment, or it may actually be such as to stunt growth. The family trapped in poverty and ignorance can rarely provide the stimulus so necessary to individual growth. The neighborhood in which delinquency and social disintegration are universal conditions cannot create an atmosphere in which educational values hold a commanding place. In such surroundings, the process by which talents are blighted begins long before kindergarten, and survives long afterward.

[11] The fact that large numbers of American boys and girls fail to attain their full development must weigh heavily on our national conscience. And it is not simply a loss to the individual. At a time when the nation must make the most of its human resources, it is unthinkable that we should resign ourselves to this waste of potentialities. Recent events have taught us with sledge hammer effectiveness the lesson we should have learned from our own tradition—that our strength, creativity and further growth as a society depend upon our capacity to develop the talents and potentialities of our people.

[12] Any adequate attack on this problem will reach far beyond formal educational institutions. It will involve not only the school but the home, the church, the playground and all other institutions which shape the individual. The child welfare society, the adoption service, the foundlings' home, the hospital and clinic—all play their part. And so do slum clearance projects and social welfare programs that seek to create the kind of family and neighborhood environment which fosters normal growth.

[13] But it is not only in childhood that we face obstacles to individual

fulfillment. Problems of another sort emerge at a later stage in the life span.

[14] Commencement speakers are fond of saying that education is a lifelong process. And yet that is something that no young person with a grain of sense needs to be told. Why do the speakers go on saying it? It isn't that they love sentiments that are well worn with reverent handling (though they do). It isn't that they underestimate their audience. The truth is that they know something their young listeners do not know—something that can never be fully communicated. No matter how firm an intellectual grasp the young person may have on the idea that education is a lifelong process, he can never know it with the poignancy, with the deeply etched clarity, with the overtones of satisfaction and regret that an older person knows it. The young person has not yet made enough mistakes that cannot be repaired. He has not yet passed enough forks in the road that cannot be retraced.

[15] The commencement speaker may give in to the temptation to make it sound as though the learning experiences of the older generation were all deliberate and a triumph of character—character that the younger generation somehow lacks. We can forgive him that. It is not easy to tell young people how unpurposefully we learn, how life tosses us head over heels into our most vivid learning experiences, how intensely we resist many of the increments in our own growth.

[16] But we cannot forgive him as readily if he leaves out another part of the story. And that part of the story is that the process of learning through life is by no means continuous and by no means universal. If it were, age and wisdom would be perfectly correlated, and there would be no such thing as an old fool—a proposition sharply at odds with common experience. The sad truth is that for many of us the learning process comes to an end very early indeed. And others learn the wrong things.

[17] The differences among people in their capacity for continued growth are so widely recognized that we need not dwell on them. They must not be confused with differences in the degree of success—as the world measures success—which individuals achieve. Many whom the world counts as unsuccessful have continued learning and growing throughout their lives; and some of our most prominent people stopped learning literally decades ago.

[18] We still have a very imperfect understanding of why some people continue to learn and grow while others do not. Sometimes one can point to adverse circumstances as the cause of a leveling off of individual growth. But we cannot identify the conditions which have hindered or fostered development.

[19] Of course, people are never quite as buffeted by circumstance as they appear to be. The man who experiences great personal growth as a result of some accidental circumstance may have been ready to grow in

any case. Pasteur said that chance favors the prepared mind. The man defeated by circumstance might have triumphed had he been made of other stuff. We all know individuals whose growth and learning can only be explained in terms of an inner drive, a curiosity, a seeking and exploring element in their personalities. Captain Cook said, "I . . . had ambition not only to go farther than any man had ever been before, but as far as it was possible for a man to go." Just as Cook's restless seeking led him over the face of the earth, so other men embark on Odysseys of the mind and spirit.

[20] It is a concern both for the individual and for the nation that moves the commencement speaker. Perhaps many men will always fall into ruts. Perhaps many will always let their talents go to waste. But the waste now exists on such a massive scale that sensible people cannot believe that it is all inevitable.

[21] Unfortunately, the conception of individual fulfillment and lifelong learning which animates the commencement speaker finds no adequate reflection in our social institutions. For too long we have paid pious lip service to the idea and trifled with it in practice. Like those who confine their religion to Sunday and forget it the rest of the week, we have segregated the idea of individual fulfillment into one compartment of our national life, and neglect it elsewhere. We have set "education" off in a separate category from the main business of life. It is something that happens in schools and colleges. It happens to young people between the ages of six and twenty-one. It is not something—we seem to believe—that need concern the rest of us in our own lives.

[22] This way of thinking is long overdue for a drastic change. If we believe what we profess concerning the worth of the individual, then the idea of individual fulfillment within a framework of moral purpose must become our deepest concern, our national preoccupation, our passion, our obsession. We must think of education as relevant for everyone everywhere—at all ages and in all conditions of life.

[23] Aside from our formal educational system there is little evidence of any such preoccupation. Some religious groups are doing excellent work. Our libraries and museums are a legitimate source of pride. Adult education programs have become increasingly effective. Certain of our organizations concerned with social welfare and with mental health play profoundly important roles.

[24] But what about moving pictures, radio and television, with their great possibilities for contributing to the growth of the individual? It would be fair to say that these possibilities have not dominated the imagination of the men who control these media. On the contrary, these media have all too often permitted the triumph of cupidity over every educational value. And what about newspapers and magazines, with their obvious potentialities for furthering the intellectual and moral growth

of the individual? At best, a small fraction of the publishers accepts such a responsibility. Book publishers are less vulnerable to criticism, but they are not without fault.

[25] Serious pursuit of the goal of individual fulfillment will carry us even farther afield. Unions, lodges, professional organizations and social clubs can all contribute importantly to individual growth and learning if they are so inclined. Only sporadically have they been so inclined. There are innumerable opportunities open to the employer who is willing to acknowledge his responsibility for furthering the individual development of men and women in his employ. Some forward-looking companies have made a highly significant beginning in accepting that responsibility.

[26] What we are suggesting is that every institution in our society should contribute to the fulfillment of the individual. Every institution must, of course, have its own purposes and preoccupations, but over and above everything else that it does, it should be prepared to answer this question posed by society: "What is the institution doing to foster the development of the individuals within it?"

[27] Now what does all of this mean? It means that we should very greatly enlarge our ways of thinking about education. We should be painting a vastly greater mural on a vastly more spacious wall. What we are trying to do is nothing less than to build a greater and more creative civilization. We propose that the American people accept as a universal task the fostering of individual development within a framework of rational and moral values. We propose that they accept as an all-encompassing goal the furtherance of individual growth and learning at every age, in every significant situation, in every conceivable way. By doing so we shall keep faith with our ideal of individual fulfillment and at the same time insure our continued strength and creativity as a society.

[28] If we accept this concern for individual fulfillment as an authentic national preoccupation, the schools and colleges will then be the heart of a national endeavor. They will be committed to the furthering of a national objective and not—as they now often find themselves—swimming upstream against the interests of a public that thinks everything else more urgent. The schools and colleges will be greatly strengthened if their task is undergirded by such a powerful public conception of the goal to be sought.

[29] And both schools and colleges will be faced with a challenge beyond anything they have yet experienced. We have said that much will depend upon the individual's attitude toward learning and toward his own growth. This defines the task of the schools and colleges. Above all they must equip the individual for a never-ending process of learning; they must gird his mind and spirit for the constant reshaping and reexamination of himself. They cannot content themselves with the time-honored process of stuffing students like sausages or even the possibly

more acceptable process of training them like seals. It is the sacred obligation of the schools and colleges to instill in their students the attitudes toward growth and learning and creativity which will in turn shape the society. With other institutions at work on other parts of this task, the schools and colleges must of course give particular attention to the intellectual aspects of growth. This is uniquely their responsibility.

[30] If we accept without reservation these implications of our traditional belief in individual fulfillment, we shall have enshrined a highly significant purpose at the heart of our national life—a purpose that will lift all American education to a new level of meaning. We shall have accepted a commitment which promises pervasive consequences for our way of thinking about the purpose of democratic institutions. And we shall have embraced a philosophy which gives a rich personal meaning to the pursuit of excellence.

COMMENT AND QUESTIONS

1. What is the relationship of the ideas in the three opening paragraphs of this selection? Could the sequence of material in the three paragraphs be changed?
2. The author says in paragraph 4: "Our thinking about the aims of education has too often been shallow, constricted and lacking in reach or perspective." What are the different shades of meaning in the three descriptive terms? Where and in what ways does Gardner expand and clarify this sentence?
3. In what ways do paragraphs 7–9 qualify a central thesis about the importance of individual fulfillment?
4. What two major wastes of potentialities does Gardner discuss in the second section of his chapter? To which does he give greater emphasis by development? Can you see a reason for this emphasis?
5. What appear to be the author's attitudes toward the commencement speakers (paragraph 14 and the paragraphs following)?
6. What is the purpose of the distinction made in paragraph 17 between growth and success? Can you think of examples to support the statement in the last sentence of that paragraph?
7. Summarize as clearly as you can Gardner's criticism of our social institutions. Does the criticism seem to you justified? Gardner's book was published in 1961. Do you know of changes in the direction he is recommending that have occurred since then?
8. Paragraph 27 is perhaps the most complete statement of the central ideas of the selection. What techniques of style and of emphasis do you find in the paragraph?

9. What will be the new position and the clearly defined responsibility of the schools and colleges in the more excellent society Gardner hopes for? To what extent do you think that the schools and colleges are now occupying that position and assuming that responsibility? Explain.
10. If you have read the selections about education preceding this one, what similarities and what differences in ideas or emphasis do you find between Gardner and other writers concerned with education?

THE
QUEST FOR VALUES

[16] *Plato*: from the Symposium

THE FOLLOWING excerpt from the *Symposium* (or Banquet) presents Plato's idea of love. Although the term "Platonic love" as it is generally used carries little of Plato's meaning, it is derived from his concept of love as a bridge between the material and the spiritual, by which one moves from the love of earthly objects to the love of absolute beauty. The situation that Plato establishes in the dialogue is this: Socrates and his friends, assembled for a banquet, decide to devote the evening to conversation and to speeches in honor of Love. When it is Socrates' turn to speak, he tells the company that he learned of love from a wise woman, Diotima of Mantineia, and that he will repeat what she said to him. In the dialogue that follows, Diotima asks the questions, and Socrates answers. (For further notes on Plato, see pages 99 and 121.)

[1] "For there is nothing which men love but the good. Is there anything?" "Certainly, I should say, that there is nothing." "Then," she said, "the simple truth is, that men love the good." "Yes," I said. "To which must be added that they love the possession of the good?" "Yes, that must be added." "And not only the possession, but the everlasting possession of the good?" "That must be added too." "Then love," she said, "may be described generally as the love of the everlasting possession of the good?" "That is most true."

This selection was translated by Benjamin Jowett.

[²] "Then if this be the nature of love, can you tell me further," she said, "what is the manner of the pursuit? What are they doing who show all this eagerness and heat which is called love? and what is the object which they have in view? Answer me." "Nay, Diotima," I replied, "if I had known, I should not have wondered at your wisdom, neither should I have come to learn from you about this very matter." "Well," she said, "I will teach you:—The object which they have in view is birth in beauty, whether of body or soul." "I do not understand you," I said; "the oracle requires an explanation." "I will make my meaning clearer," she replied. "I mean to say, that all men are bringing to the birth in their bodies and in their souls. There is a certain age at which human nature is desirous of procreation—procreation which must be in beauty and not in deformity; and this procreation is the union of man and woman, and is a divine thing; for conception and generation are an immortal principle in the mortal creature, and in the inharmonious they can never be. But the deformed is always inharmonious with the divine, and the beautiful harmonious. Beauty, then, is the destiny or goddess of parturition who presides at birth, and therefore, when approaching beauty, the conceiving power is propitious, and diffusive, and benign, and begets and bears fruit: at the sight of ugliness she frowns and contracts and has a sense of pain, and turns away, and shrivels up, and not without a pang refrains from conception. And this is the reason why, when the hour of conception arrives, and the teeming nature is full, there is such a flutter and ecstasy about beauty whose approach is the alleviation of the pain of travail. For love, Socrates, is not, as you imagine, the love of the beautiful only." "What then?" "The love of generation and of birth in beauty." "Yes," I said. "Yes, indeed," she replied. "But why of generation?" "Because to the mortal creature, generation is a sort of eternity and immortality," she replied; "and if, as has been already admitted, love is of the everlasting possession of the good, all men will necessarily desire immortality together with good: Wherefore love is of immortality."

[³] All this she taught me at various times when she spoke of love. And I remember her once saying to me, "What is the cause, Socrates, of love, and the attendant desire? See you not how all animals, birds, as well as beasts, in their desire of procreation, are in agony when they take the infection of love, which begins with the desire of union; whereto is added the care of offspring, on whose behalf the weakest are ready to battle against the strongest even to the uttermost, and to die for them, and will let themselves be tormented with hunger or suffer anything in order to maintain their young? Man may be supposed to act thus from reason; but why should animals have these passionate feelings? Can you tell me why?" Again I replied that I did not know. She said to me: "And do you expect ever to become a master in the art of love, if you do not know this?" "But I have told you already, Diotima, that my ignorance is the reason why I come to you; for I am conscious that I want a teacher; tell me then the cause of this and of the other mysteries of love." "Marvel not," she said, "if you believe that love is of the immortal, as we have several times acknowledged; for here again, and on the same principle too, the mortal nature is seeking as far as is possible to be everlasting and immortal: and this is only to be attained by generation, because generation always leaves behind a new existence in the place of the old. Nay, even in the life of the same individual there is succession and not absolute unity: a man is called the same, and yet in the short interval which elapses between youth and age, and in which every animal is said to have life and identity, he is undergoing a perpetual process of loss and reparation—hair, flesh, bones, blood, and the whole body are always changing. Which is true not only of the body, but also of the soul, whose habits, tempers, opinions, desires, pleasures, pains, fears, never remain the same in any one of us, but are always coming and going; and equally true of knowledge, and what is still more surprising to us mortals, not only do the sciences in general spring up and decay, so that in respect of them we are never the same; but each of them individually experiences a like change. For what is implied in the word 'recollection,' but the departure of knowledge, which is ever being forgotten, and is renewed and preserved by recollection, and appears to be the same although in reality now, according to that law of succession by which all mortal things are preserved, not absolutely the same, but by substitution, the old worn-out mortality leaving another new and similar existence behind—unlike the divine, which is always the same and not another? And in this way, Socrates, the mortal body, or mortal anything, partakes of immortality; but the immortal in another way. Marvel not then at the love which all men have of their offspring; for that universal love and interest is for the sake of immortality."

[4] I was astonished at her words, and said: "Is this really true, O thou wise Diotima?" And she answered with all the authority of an accomplished Sophist: "Of that, Socrates, you may be assured;—think only of the ambition of men, and you will wonder at the senselessness of their ways, unless you consider how they are stirred by the love of an immortality of fame. They are ready to run all risks greater far than they would have run for their children, and to spend money and undergo any sort of toil, and even to die, for the sake of leaving behind them a name which shall be eternal. Do you imagine that Alcestis would have died to save Admetus, or Achilles to avenge Patroclus, or your own Codrus in order to preserve the kingdom for his sons, if they had not imagined that the memory of their virtues, which still survive among us, would be immortal? Nay," she said, "I am persuaded that all men do all things, and the better they are the more they do them, in hope of the glorious fame of immortal virtue; for they desire the immortal.

[5] "Those who are pregnant in the body only, betake themselves to

women and beget children—this is the character of their love; their offspring, as they hope, will preserve their memory and give them the blessedness and immortality which they desire in the future. But souls which are pregnant—for there certainly are men who are more creative in their souls than in their bodies—conceive that which is proper for the soul to conceive or contain. And what are these conceptions?—wisdom and virtue in general. And such creators are poets and all artists who are deserving of the name inventor. But the greatest and fairest sort of wisdom by far is that which is concerned with the ordering of states and families, and which is called temperance and justice. And he who in youth has the seed of these implanted in him and is himself inspired, when he comes to maturity desires to beget and generate. He wanders about seeking beauty that he may beget offspring—for in deformity he will beget nothing—and naturally embraces the beautiful rather than the deformed body; above all, when he finds a fair and noble and well-nurtured soul, he embraces the two in one person, and to such an one he is full of speech about virtue and the nature and pursuits of a good man; and he tries to educate him; and at the touch of the beautiful which is ever present to his memory, even when absent, he brings forth that which he had conceived long before, and in company with him tends that which he brings forth; and they are married by a far nearer tie and have a closer friendship than those who beget mortal children, for the childen who are their common offspring are fairer and more immortal. Who, when he thinks of Homer and Hesiod and other great poets, would not rather have their children than ordinary human ones? Who would not emulate them in the creation of children such as theirs, which have preserved their memory and given them everlasting glory? Or who would not have such children as Lycurgus left behind him to be the saviours, not only of Lacedaemon, but of Hellas, as one may say? There is Solon, too, who is the revered father of Athenian laws; and many others there are in many other places, both among Hellenes and barbarians, who have given to the world many noble works, and have been the parents of virtue of every kind; and many temples have been raised in their honour for the sake of children such as theirs; which were never raised in honour of any one, for the sake of his mortal children.

[6] "These are the lesser mysteries of love, into which even you, Socrates, may enter; to the greater and more hidden ones which are the crown of these, and to which, if you pursue them in a right spirit, they will lead, I know not whether you will be able to attain. But I will do my utmost to inform you, and do you follow if you can. For he who would proceed aright in this matter should begin in youth to visit beautiful forms; and first, if he be guided by his instructor aright, to love one such form only—out of that he should create fair thoughts; and soon he will of himself perceive that the beauty of one form is akin to the beauty of

another; and then if beauty of form in general is his pursuit, how foolish would he be not to recognize that the beauty in every form is one and the same! And when he perceives this he will abate his violent love of the one, which he will despise and deem a small thing, and will become a lover of all beautiful forms; in the next stage he will consider that the beauty of the mind is more honourable than the beauty of the outward form. So that if a virtuous soul have but a little comeliness, he will be content to love and tend him, and will search out and bring to the birth thoughts which may improve the young, until he is compelled to contemplate and see the beauty of institutions and laws, and to understand that the beauty of them all is of one family, and that personal beauty is a trifle; and after laws and institutions he will go on to the sciences, that he may see their beauty, being not like a servant in love with the beauty of one youth or man or institution, himself a slave mean and narrow-minded, but drawing towards and contemplating the vast sea of beauty, he will create many fair and noble thoughts and notions in boundless love of wisdom; until on that shore he grows and waxes strong, and at last the vision is revealed to him of a single science, which is the science of beauty everywhere. To this I will proceed; please to give me your very best attention:

[7] "He who has been instructed thus far in the things of love, and who has learned to see the beautiful in due order and succession, when he comes towards the end will suddenly perceive a nature of wondrous beauty (and this, Socrates, is the final cause of all our former toils)— a nature which in the first place is everlasting, not growing and decaying, or waxing and waning; secondly, not fair in one point of view and foul in another, or at one time or in one relation or at one place fair, at another time or in another relation or at another place foul, as if fair to some and foul to others, or in the likeness of a face or hands or any other part of the bodily frame, or in any form of speech or knowledge, or existing in any other being, as, for example, in an animal, or in heaven, or in earth, or in any other place, but beauty absolute, separate, simple, and everlasting, which without diminution and without increase, or any change, is imparted to the ever-growing and perishing beauties of all other things. He who from these ascending under the influence of true love, begins to perceive that beauty, is not far from the end. And the true order of going, or being led by another, to the things of love, is to begin from the beauties of earth and mount upwards for the sake of that other beauty, using these as steps only, and from one going on to two, and from two to all fair forms, and from fair forms to fair practices, and from fair practices to fair notions, until from fair notions he arrives at the notion of absolute beauty, and at last knows what the essence of beauty is. This, my dear Socrates," said the stranger of Mantineia, "is that life above all others which man should live, in the contemplation of beauty absolute;

a beauty which if you once beheld, you would see not to be after the measure of gold, and garments, and fair boys and youths, whose presence now entrances you; and you and many an one would be content to live seeing them only and conversing with them without meat or drink, if that were possible—you only want to look at them and to be with them. But what if man had eyes to see the true beauty—the divine beauty, I mean, pure and clear and unalloyed, not clogged with the pollutions of mortality and all the colours and vanities of human life—thither looking, and holding converse with the true beauty simple and divine? Remember how in that communion only, beholding beauty with the eye of the mind, he will be enabled to bring forth, not images of beauty, but realities (for he has hold not of an image but of a reality), and bringing forth and nourishing true virtue to become the friend of God and be immortal, if mortal man may. Would that be an ignoble life?"

COMMENT AND QUESTIONS

In the pages of the *Symposium* preceding the excerpt printed here, Diotima has told Socrates that love is a spirit who mediates between gods and men, that love is the offspring of Poverty and Plenty, and that love is love of the beautiful and good. In the selection printed here, the wise woman further explains that since love is of the everlasting possession of the beautiful and good, it is necessarily of the love of immortality, or of generation and birth in beauty, which to mortal creatures is a sort of eternity and immortality. The creative body inspired by love will produce children who provide one kind of immortality; the creative soul inspired by love will produce works of art and works of wisdom and virtue, fairer and more immortal than mortal children. All these things, Diotima says, are the lesser mysteries of love. The greater mystery and the highest experience of love is the experience of moving upward from the love of material objects to the love of spiritual things and finally to a perception of perfect Beauty and Good.

Below are four translations of the short passage in which Diotima summarizes the ascent, step by step, to the highest vision of love. Reading it in somewhat different language may help to clarify this key idea:

1. And the true order of going, or being led by another to the things of love is to begin from the beauties of earth and mount upwards for the sake of that other beauty, using these as steps only, and from one going on to two, and from two to all fair forms, and from fair forms to fair practices, and from fair practices to fair notions, until from fair notions he arrives at the notion of absolute beauty, and at last knows what the essence of beauty is.

2. For such as discipline themselves upon this system, or are conducted

by another begin to ascend through these transitory objects which are beautiful, towards that which is beauty itself, proceeding as on steps from the love of one form to that of two, and from that of two, to that of all forms which are beautiful; and from beautiful forms to beautiful habits and institutions, and from institutions to beautiful doctrines; until, from the meditation of many doctrines, they arrive at that which is nothing else than the doctrine of the supreme beauty itself, in the knowledge and contemplation of which at length they repose.

3. For let me tell you, the right way to approach the things of love, or to be led there by another, is this: beginning from these beautiful things, to mount for that beauty's sake ever upwards, as by a flight of steps, from one to two, and from two to all beautiful bodies, and from beautiful bodies to beautiful pursuits and practices, and from practices to beautiful learnings, so that from learnings he may come at last to that perfect learning which is the learning solely of that beauty itself, and may know at last that which is the perfection of beauty.

4. Those who learn the order of love, or are led by another, beginning with beautiful objects will move upward to beauty itself, proceeding as by steps from one fair form to all fair forms, from all fair forms to all fair actions, from all fair actions to all fair ideas, and thence, from the contemplation of fair ideas, to the knowledge of the very essence of beauty.

1. When Plato's idea is clear to you, give concrete examples of the steps or stages in this progression of love.
2. A less important part of Diotima's teaching is her comment on change. Examine the passage beginning in the middle of paragraph 3 with "Nay, even in the life of the same individual there is succession . . . ," and consider whether or not you agree with the statements made.
3. What particular parts of Diotima's discourse on "the lesser mysteries of love" (paragraphs 1–5) do you find interesting? Do you disagree with anything she says? Explain.
4. The words *sciences* and *science* used in this translation do not have the meaning we commonly assign to them. Examine the use of the words in the passage referred to in question 2 and in the next-to-last sentence of paragraph 6, and try to determine their meaning from context.
5. A. E. Taylor, an authority on Plato, says that the *Symposium* describes "the travel of the soul from temporality to eternity." What does this statement mean? Does it seem accurate to you? Explain your answer.
6. If you have read Plato's "Myth of the Cave," what parallels and what differences do you see between the ascent from the cave to the upper world and the ascent to a knowledge of perfect beauty?

[17] *Epicurus*: Letter to a Friend

EPICURUS (340?–270 B.C.) was a Greek philosopher who founded the Epicurean school. The following letter expresses and explains the central idea of his philosophy, that happiness or pleasure is the greatest good of life—an idea simplified and corrupted by followers who called themselves Epicureans.

[1] We must consider that of desires some are natural, others empty; that of the natural some are necessary, others not; and that of the necessary some are necessary for happiness, others for bodily comfort, and others for life itself. A right understanding of these facts enables us to direct all choice and avoidance toward securing the health of the body and tranquility of the soul; this being the final aim of a blessed life. For the aim of all actions is to avoid pain and fear; and when this is once secured for us the tempest of the soul is entirely quelled, since the living animal no longer needs to wander as though in search of something he lacks, hunting for that by which he can fulfill some need of soul or body. We feel a need of pleasure only when we grieve over its absence; when we stop grieving we are in need of pleasure no longer. Pleasure, then, is the beginning and end of the blessed life.[1] For we recognize it as a good which is both primary and kindred to us. From pleasure we begin every act of choice and avoidance; and to pleasure we return again, using the feeling as the standard by which to judge every good.

[2] Now since pleasure is the good that is primary and most natural to us, for that very reason we do not seize all pleasures indiscriminately; on the contrary we often pass over many pleasures, when greater discomfort accrues to us as a result of them. Similarly we not infrequently judge pains better than pleasures, when the long endurance of a pain yields us a greater pleasure in the end. Thus every pleasure because of its natural kinship to us is good, yet not every pleasure is to be chosen; just as every pain also is an evil, yet that does not mean that all pains are necessarily to be shunned. It is by a scale of comparison and by the consideration of advantages and disadvantages that we must form our

---

From Epicurus' Letter to Menoecius, preserved in Diogenes Laertius, *Lives of the Philosophers*, Bk. X. Translated by Philip Wheelwright in *The Way of Philosophy* (Odyssey Press), pp. 423–25.

[1] I.e., since it is a product of that health of body and tranquility of soul mentioned above.

judgment on these matters. On particular occasions we may have reason to treat the good as bad, and the bad as good.

[³] Independence of circumstances we regard as a great good: not because we wish to dispense altogether with external advantages, but in order that, if our possessions are few, we may be content with what we have, sincerely believing that those enjoy luxury most who depend on it least, and that natural wants are easily satisfied if we are willing to forego superfluities. Plain fare yields as much pleasure as a luxurious table, provided the pain of real want is removed; bread and water can give exquisite delight to hungry and thirsty lips. To form the habit of a simple and modest diet, therefore, is the way to health: it enables us to perform the needful employments of life without shrinking, it puts us in better condition to enjoy luxuries when they are offered, and it renders us fearless of fortune.

[⁴] Accordingly, when we argue that pleasure is the end and aim of life, we do not mean the pleasure of prodigals and sensualists, as some of our ignorant or prejudiced critics persist in mistaking us. We mean the pleasure of being free from pain of body and anxiety of mind. It is not a continual round of drunken debauches and lecherous delights, nor the enjoyment of fish and other delicacies of a wealthy table, which produce a pleasant life; but sober reasoning, searching out the motives of choice and avoidance, and escaping the bondage of opinion, to which the greatest disturbances of spirit are due.

[⁵] The first step and the greatest good is prudence—a more precious thing than philosophy even, for all the other virtues are sprung from it. By prudence we learn that we can live pleasurably only if we live prudently, honorably, and justly, while contrariwise to live prudently, honorably, and justly guarantees a life that is pleasurable as well. The virtues are by nature bound up with a pleasant life, and a pleasant life is inseparable from them in turn.

[⁶] Is there any better and wiser man than he who holds reverent beliefs about the gods, is altogether free from the fear of death, and has serenely contemplated the basic tendencies of natural law? Such a man understands that the limit of good things is easy to attain, and that evils are slight either in duration or in intensity. He laughs at Destiny, which so many accept as all-powerful. Some things, he observes, occur of necessity, others by chance, and still others through our own agency. Necessity is irresponsible, chance is inconstant, but our own actions are free, and it is to them that praise and blame are properly attached. It would be better even to believe the myths about the gods than to submit to the Destiny which the natural philosophers teach. For the old superstitions at least offer some faint hope of placating the gods by worship, but the Necessity of the scientific philosophers is absolutely unyielding. As to chance, the wise man does not deify it as most men do; for if it were divine it would not be without order. Nor will he accept the view that it is a universal cause even though of a wavering kind; for he believes that what chance bestows is not the good and evil that determine a man's blessedness in life, but the starting-points from which each person can arrive at great good or great evil. He esteems the misfortune of the wise above the prosperity of a fool; holding it better that well chosen courses of action should fail than that ill chosen ones should succeed by mere chance.

[7] Meditate on these and like precepts day and night, both privately and with some companion who is of kindred disposition. Thereby shall you never suffer disturbance, waking or asleep, but shall live like a god among men. For a man who lives constantly among immortal blessings is surely more than mortal.

COMMENT AND QUESTIONS

1. Read each sentence in paragraph 1 thoughtfully. What are examples of the different kinds of desires mentioned in the opening sentence? Do you agree that "the final aim of a blessed life" is "securing the health of the body and the tranquility of the soul"? Are you satisfied with the statement that "the aim of all actions is to avoid pain and fear," or do you believe there are other and more valid aims? If so, what are they? If you have read the "Sermon on the Mount," what different aim or aims are implicit in it?
2. Under what circumstances, according to Epicurus, should we choose to endure pain or deny ourselves pleasure? Can you illustrate from your own experience?
3. What is the meaning of "Independence of circumstances" at the beginning of paragraph 3?
4. What particular virtues does Epicurus think necessary for a pleasant life?
5. The *New World Dictionary* defines *epicure* as follows: "1. a person who enjoys and has a discriminating taste for foods and liquors. 2. a person who is especially fond of luxury and sensuous pleasures." It defines the adjective *Epicurean:* "1. of Epicurus or his philosophy. 2. fond of luxury and sensuous pleasure, especially that of eating and drinking. 3. suited to or characteristic of an epicure." Compare these definitions with Epicurus' own statement of his beliefs.
6. Part of Epicurus' teaching was designed to relieve human beings of two common anxieties: fear of the gods and fear of death. The gods, Epicurus believed, did not interfere in human lives; being gods, they were above the

affairs of men; nor was there an inflexible Destiny controlling men, predetermining their lives and fortunes. As to the fear of death, Epicurus argued that death is simply nonexistence; it is the ceasing of sensation, not to be feared because while we live death is not with us, and when death comes we have no sensations with which to experience it. With these ideas in mind, summarize in your own words the main ideas of paragraph 6.

7. It has been said that Epicureanism is a purely personal, and not a social, philosophy. On the basis of this selection do you agree or disagree with that judgment?

8. If you have read the *Apology*, compare and contrast the ideas of Epicurus and of Socrates. Do you think that Epicurus would have approved of the speech and actions of Socrates?

[18]   The Stoic View
Epictetus: The Quiet Mind
Marcus Aurelius: from the Meditations

STOICISM, founded late in the fourth century B.C. by the Greek philosopher Zeno, later became a patchwork of various beliefs. The teaching of Epictetus, however, represented a return to an earlier creed, and Marcus Aurelius read and was profoundly influenced by the *Discourses* of Epictetus. In general, the Stoic philosophy holds that the universe is a vast machine, directed by divine intelligence and ultimately good; all men, part of the great system of nature, are brothers. The wise man keeps his will "in harmony with nature"; he accepts things as they are and regards pleasure, pain, and all external circumstances as matters of indifference; he believes that virtue and perfection of soul are the greatest good of man and that the virtuous man, freed of all passion and desire, is also the happy man.

Epictetus was a Greek philosopher who lived as a slave in Rome in the first century A.D. and later taught in Rome and Epirus. Like Socrates, he left no writing, but his teaching was recorded by his pupil Flavius Arrianus. *The Manual* (or *Enchiridion*), from which the selection we have called "The Quiet Mind" is taken, sets down a brief, sometimes overlapping statement of the main doctrines of Epictetus' philosophy.

The first selection is from *The Manual* of Epictetus, translated by P. E. Matheson. Reprinted with permission of Clarendon Press. The selection from Marcus Aurelius's *Meditations* was translated by George Long.

Marcus Aurelius (121–180) was a Roman Emperor whom John Stuart Mill called "the gentlest and most amiable of philosophers and rulers."[1] The *Meditations* consists of twelve books of short passages which Marcus Aurelius addressed to himself for the purpose of guiding his own conduct. (The original title was *Marcus Aurelius to Himself*.) We have selected from the whole work a number of representative passages.

Epictetus: The Quiet Mind

Of all existing things some are in our power, and others are not in our power. In our power are thought, impulse, will to get and will to avoid, and, in a word, everything which is our own doing. Things not in our power include the body, property, reputation, office, and, in a word, everything which is not our own doing. Things in our power are by nature free, unhindered, untrammelled; things not in our power are weak, servile, subject to hindrance, dependent on others. Remember then that if you imagine that what is naturally slavish is free and what is naturally another's is your own, you will be hampered, you will mourn, you will be put to confusion, you will blame gods and men; but if you think that only your own belongs to you, and that what is another's is indeed another's, no one will ever put compulsion or hindrance on you, you will blame none, you will accuse none, you will do nothing against your will, no one will harm you, you will have no enemy, for no harm can touch you.

1. Aiming then at these high matters, you must remember that to attain them requires more than ordinary effort; you will have to give up some things entirely, and put off others for the moment. And if you would have these also—office and wealth—it may be that you will fail to get them, just because your desire is set on the former, and you will certainly fail to attain those things which alone bring freedom and happiness.

Make it your study then to confront every harsh impression with the words, "You are but an impression, and not at all what you seem to be." Then test it by those rules that you possess; and first by this—the chief test of all—"Is it concerned with what is in our power or with what is not in our power?" And if it is concerned with what is not in our power, be ready with the answer that it is nothing to you.

2. Remember that the will-to-get promises attainment of what you will, and the will-to-avoid promises escape from what you avoid; and he who fails to get what he wills is unfortunate, and he who does not escape what he wills to avoid is miserable. If then you try to avoid only what is unnatural in the region within your control, you will escape from all that

---

[1] For Mill's discussion of Marcus Aurelius see page 136–37.

you avoid; but if you try to avoid disease or death or poverty you will be miserable.

Therefore let your will-to-avoid have no concern with what is not in man's power; direct it only to things in man's power that are contrary to nature. But for the moment you must utterly remove the will-to-get; for if you will to get something not in man's power you are bound to be unfortunate; while none of the things in man's power that you could honourably will to get is yet within your reach. Impulse to act and not to act, these are your concern; yet exercise them gently and without strain, and provisionally.

3. When anything, from the meanest thing upwards, is attractive or serviceable or an object of affection, remember always to say to yourself, "What is its nature?" If you are fond of a jug, say you are fond of a jug; then you will not be disturbed if it be broken. If you kiss your child or your wife, say to yourself that you are kissing a human being, for then if death strikes it you will not be disturbed.

4. When you are about to take something in hand, remind yourself what manner of thing it is. If you are going to bathe put before your mind what happens in the bath—water pouring over some, others being jostled, some reviling, others stealing; and you will set to work more securely if you say to yourself at once: "I want to bathe, and I want to keep my will in harmony with nature," and so in each thing you do; for in this way, if anything turns up to hinder you in your bathing, you will be ready to say, "I did not want only to bathe, but to keep my will in harmony with nature, and I shall not so keep it, if I lose my temper at what happens."

5. What disturbs men's minds is not events but their judgments on events. For instance, death is nothing dreadful, or else Socrates would have thought it so. No, the only dreadful thing about it is men's judgment that it is dreadful. And so when we are hindered, or disturbed, or distressed, let us never lay the blame on others, but on ourselves, that is, on our own judgments. To accuse others for one's own misfortunes is a sign of want of education; to accuse oneself shows that one's education has begun; to accuse neither oneself nor others shows that one's education is complete.

6. Be not elated at an excellence which is not your own. If the horse in his pride were to say, "I am handsome," we could bear with it. But when you say with pride, "I have a handsome horse," know that the good horse is the ground of your pride. You ask then what you can call your own. The answer is—the way you deal with your impressions. Therefore when you deal with your impressions in accord with nature, then you may be proud indeed, for your pride will be in a good which is your own.

7. When you are on a voyage, and your ship is at anchorage, and you disembark to get fresh water, you may pick up a small shellfish or a truffle

by the way, but you must keep your attention fixed on the ship, and keep looking towards it constantly, to see if the Helmsman calls you; and if he does, you have to leave everything, or be bundled on board with your legs tied like a sheep. So it is in life. If you have a dear wife or child given you, they are like the shellfish or the truffle, they are very well in their way. Only, if the Helmsman call, run back to your ship, leave all else, and do not look behind you. And if you are old, never go far from the ship, so that when you are called you may not fail to appear.

8. Ask not that events should happen as you will, but let your will be that events should happen as they do, and you shall have peace.

9. Sickness is a hindrance to the body, but not to the will, unless the will consent. Lameness is a hindrance to the leg, but not to the will. Say this to yourself at each event that happens, for you shall find that though it hinders something else, it will not hinder you.

10. When anything happens to you, always remember to turn to yourself and ask what faculty you have to deal with it. If you see a beautiful boy or a beautiful woman, you will find continence the faculty to exercise there; if trouble is laid on you, you will find endurance; if ribaldry, you will find patience. And if you train yourself in this habit your impressions will not carry you away.

11. Never say of anything, "I lost it," but say, "I gave it back." Has your child died? It was given back. Has your wife died? She was given back. Has your estate been taken from you? Was not this also given back? But you say, "He who took it from me is wicked." What does it matter to you through whom the Giver asked it back? As long as He gives it you, take care of it, but not as your own; treat it as passers-by treat an inn.

12. If you wish to make progress, abandon reasonings of this sort: "If I neglect my affairs I shall have nothing to live on"; "If I do not punish my son, he will be wicked." For it is better to die of hunger, so that you be free from pain and free from fear, than to live in plenty and be troubled in mind. It is better for your son to be wicked than for you to be miserable. Wherefore begin with little things. Is your drop of oil spilt? Is your sup of wine stolen? Say to yourself, "This is the price paid for freedom from passion, this is the price of a quiet mind." Nothing can be had without a price. When you call your slave-boy, reflect that he may not be able to hear you, and if he hears you, he may not be able to do anything you want. But he is not so well off that it rests with him to give you peace of mind.

13. If you wish to make progress, you must be content in external matters to seem a fool and a simpleton; do not wish men to think you know anything, and if any should think you to be somebody, distrust yourself. For know that it is not easy to keep your will in accord with nature and at the same time keep outward things; if you attend to one you must needs neglect the other.

14. It is silly to want your children and your wife and your friends to live for ever, for that means that you want what is not in your control to be in your control, and what is not your own to be yours. In the same way if you want your servant to make no mistakes, you are a fool, for you want vice not to be vice but something different. But if you want not to be disappointed in your will to get, you can attain to that.

Exercise yourself then in what lies in your power. Each man's master is the man who has authority over what he wishes or does not wish, to secure the one or to take away the other. Let him then who wishes to be free not wish for anything or avoid anything that depends on others; or else he is bound to be a slave.

15. Remember that you must behave in life as you would at a banquet. A dish is handed round and comes to you; put out your hand and take it politely. It passes you; do not stop it. It has not reached you; do not be impatient to get it, but wait till your turn comes. Bear yourself thus towards children, wife, office, wealth, and one day you will be worthy to banquet with the gods. But if when they are set before you, you do not take them but despise them, then you shall not only share the gods' banquet, but shall share their rule. For by so doing Diogenes and Heraclitus and men like them were called divine and deserved the name.

16. When you see a man shedding tears in sorrow for a child abroad or dead, or for loss of property, beware that you are not carried away by the impression that it is outward ills that make him miserable. Keep this thought by you: "What distresses him is not the event, for that does not distress another, but his judgment on the event." Therefore do not hesitate to sympathize with him so far as words go, and if it so chance, even to groan with him; but take heed that you do not also groan in your inner being.

17. Remember that you are an actor in a play, and the Playwright chooses the manner of it: if he wants it short, it is short; if long, it is long. If he wants you to act a poor man you must act the part with all your powers; and so if your part be a cripple or a magistrate or a plain man. For your business is to act the character that is given you and act it well; the choice of the cast is Another's.

18. When a raven croaks with evil omen, let not the impression carry you away, but straightway distinguish in your own mind and say, "These portents mean nothing to me; but only to my bit of a body or my bit of property or name, or my children or my wife. But for me all omens are favourable if I will, for, whatever the issue may be, it is in my power to get benefit therefrom."

19. You can be invincible, if you never enter on a contest where victory is not in your power. Beware then that when you see a man raised to honour or great power or high repute you do not let your impression carry you away. For if the reality of good lies in what is in our power,

there is no room for envy or jealousy. And you will not wish to be praetor, or prefect or consul, but to be free; and there is but one way to freedom—to despise what is not in our power.

20. Remember that foul words or blows in themselves are no outrage, but your judgment that they are so. So when any one makes you angry, know that it is your own thought that has angered you. Wherefore make it your first endeavour not to let your impressions carry you away. For if once you gain time and delay, you will find it easier to control yourself.

21. Keep before your eyes from day to day death and exile and all things that seem terrible, but death most of all, and then you will never set your thoughts on what is low and will never desire anything beyond measure.

22. If you set your desire on philosophy you must at once prepare to meet with ridicule and the jeers of many who will say, "Here he is again, turned philosopher. Where has he got these proud looks?" Nay, put on no proud looks, but hold fast to what seems best to you, in confidence that God has set you at this post. And remember that if you abide where you are, those who first laugh at you will one day admire you, and that if you give way to them, you will get doubly laughed at.

23. If it ever happen to you to be diverted to things outside, so that you desire to please another, know that you have lost your life's plan. Be content then always to be a philosopher; if you wish to be regarded as one too, show yourself that you are one and you will be able to achieve it.

24. Let not reflections such as these afflict you: "I shall live without honour, and never be of any account"; for if lack of honour is an evil, no one but yourself can involve you in evil any more than in shame. Is it your business to get office or to be invited to an entertainment?

Certainly not.

Where then is the dishonour you talk of? How can you be "of no account anywhere," when you ought to count for something in those matters only which are in your power, where you may achieve the highest worth?

"But my friends," you say, "will lack assistance."

What do you mean by "lack assistance"? They will not have cash from you and you will not make them Roman citizens. Who told you that to do these things is in our power, and not dependent upon others? Who can give to another what is not his to give?

"Get them then," says he, "that we may have them."

If I can get them and keep my self-respect, honour, magnanimity, show the way and I will get them. But if you call on me to lose the good things that are mine, in order that you may win things that are not good, look how unfair and thoughtless you are. And which do you really prefer? Money, or a faithful, modest friend? Therefore help me rather to keep these qualities, and do not expect from me actions which will make me lose them.

"But my country," says he, "will lack assistance, so far as lies in me."

Once more I ask, What assistance do you mean? It will not owe colonnades or baths to you. What of that? It does not owe shoes to the blacksmith or arms to the shoemaker; it is sufficient if each man fulfils his own function. Would you do it no good if you secured to it another faithful and modest citizen?

"Yes."

Well, then, you would not be useless to it.

"What place then shall I have in the city?"

Whatever place you can hold while you keep your character for honour and self-respect. But if you are going to lose these qualities in trying to benefit your city, what benefit, I ask, would you have done her when you attain to the perfection of being lost to shame and honour?

25. Has some one had precedence of you at an entertainment or a levée or been called in before you to give advice? If these things are good you ought to be glad that he got them; if they are evil, do not be angry that you did not get them yourself. Remember that if you want to get what is not in your power, you cannot earn the same reward as others unless you act as they do. How is it possible for one who does not haunt the great man's door to have equal shares with one who does, or one who does not go in his train equality with one who does; or one who does not praise him with one who does? You will be unjust then and insatiable if you wish to get these privileges for nothing, without paying their price. What is the price of a lettuce? An obol perhaps. If then a man pays his obol and gets his lettuces, and you do not pay and do not get them, do not think you are defrauded. For as he has the lettuces so you have the obol you did not give. The same principle holds good too in conduct. You were not invited to some one's entertainment? Because you did not give the host the price for which he sells his dinner. He sells it for compliments, he sells it for attentions. Pay him the price then, if it is to your profit. But if you wish to get the one and yet not give up the other, nothing can satisfy you in your folly.

What! you say, you have nothing instead of the dinner?

Nay, you have this, you have not praised the man you did not want to praise, you have not had to bear with the insults of his doorstep.

26. It is in our power to discover the will of Nature from those matters on which we have no difference of opinion. For instance, when another man's slave has broken the wine-cup we are very ready to say at once, "Such things must happen." Know then that when your own cup is broken, you ought to behave in the same way as when your neighbour's was broken. Apply the same principle to higher matters. Is another's child or wife dead? Not one of us but would say, "Such is the lot of man"; but when one's own dies, straightway one cries, "Alas! miserable am I,"

But we ought to remember what our feelings are when we hear it of another.

27. As a mark[2] is not set up for men to miss it, so there is nothing intrinsically evil in the world.

Marcus Aurelius: Meditations

1. Begin the morning by saying to thyself, I shall meet with the busybody, the ungrateful, arrogant, deceitful, envious, unsocial. All these things happen to them by reason of their ignorance of what is good and evil. But I who have seen the nature of the good that it is beautiful, and of the bad that it is ugly, and the nature of him who does wrong, that it is akin to me, not only of the same blood or seed, but that it participates in the same intelligence and the same portion of the divinity, I can neither be injured by any of them, for no one can fix on me what is ugly, nor can I be angry with my kinsman, nor hate him. For we are made for co-operation, like feet, like hands, like eyelids, like the rows of the upper and lower teeth. To act against one another then is contrary to nature; and it is acting against one another to be vexed and to turn away.

2. Every moment think steadily as a Roman and a man to do what thou hast in hand with perfect and simple dignity, and feeling of affection, and freedom, and justice; and to give thyself relief from all other thoughts. And thou wilt give thyself relief, if thou doest every act of thy life as if it were the last, laying aside all carelessness and passionate aversion from the commands of reason, and all hypocrisy, and self-love, and discontent with the portion which has been given to thee. Thou seest how few the things are, the which if a man lays hold of, he is able to live a life which flows in quiet, and is like the existence of the gods; for the gods on their part will require nothing more from him who observes these things.

3. Of human life the time is a point, and the substance is in a flux, and the perception dull, and the composition of the whole body subject to putrefaction, and the soul a whirl, and fortune hard to divine, and fame a thing devoid of judgement. And, to say all in a word, everything which belongs to the body is a stream, and what belongs to the soul is a dream and vapour, and life is a warfare and a stranger's sojourn, and after-fame is oblivion. What then is that which is able to conduct a man? One thing and only one, philosophy. But this consists in keeping the daemon[3] within

---

[2] That is, happiness, the result of virtue, is the mark set up for men to aim at.
[3] The inner spirit or spark of divinity in man.

a man free from violence and unharmed, superior to pains and pleasures, doing nothing without a purpose, nor yet falsely and with hypocrisy, not feeling the need of another man's doing or not doing anything; and besides, accepting all that happens, and all that is allotted, as coming from thence, wherever it is, from whence he himself came; and finally, waiting for death with a cheerful mind, as being nothing else than a dissolution of the elements of which every living being is compounded. But if there is no harm to the elements themselves in each continually changing into another, why should a man have any apprehension about the change and dissolution of all the elements? For it is according to nature, and nothing is evil which is according to nature.

4. We ought to observe also that even the things which follow after the things which are produced according to nature contain something pleasing and attractive. For instance, when bread is baked some parts are split at the surface, and these parts which thus open, and have a certain fashion contrary to the purpose of the baker's art, are beautiful in a manner, and in a peculiar way excite a desire for eating. And again, figs, when they are quite ripe, gape open; and in the ripe olives the very circumstance of their being near to rottenness adds a peculiar beauty to the fruit. And the ears of corn bending down, and the lion's eyebrows, and the foam which flows from the mouth of wild boars, and many other things—though they are far from being beautiful, if a man should examine them severally—still, because they are consequent upon the things which are formed by nature, help to adorn them, and they please the mind; so that if a man should have a feeling and deeper insight with respect to the things which are produced in the universe, there is hardly one of those which follow by way of consequence which will not seem to him to be in a manner disposed so as to give pleasure. And so he will see even the real gaping jaws of wild beasts with no less pleasure than those which painters and sculptors show by imitation; and in an old woman and an old man he will be able to see a certain maturity and comeliness; and the attractive loveliness of young persons he will be able to look on with chaste eyes; and many such things will present themselves, not pleasing to every man, but to him only who has become truly familiar with nature and her works.

5. Be like the promontory against which the waves continually break, but it stands firm and tames the fury of the water around it.

Unhappy am I, because this has happened to me.—Not so, but happy am I, though this has happened to me, because I continue free from pain, neither crushed by the present nor fearing the future. For such a thing as this might have happened to every man; but every man would not have continued free from pain on such an occasion. Why then is that rather a misfortune than this a good fortune? And dost thou in all cases call that a man's misfortune, which is not a deviation from man's nature? And does a thing seem to thee to be a deviation from man's nature, when it is not contrary to the will of man's nature? Well, thou knowest the will of nature. Will then this which has happened prevent thee from being just, magnanimous, temperate, prudent, secure against inconsiderate opinions and falsehood; will it prevent thee from having modesty, freedom, and everything else, by the presence of which man's nature obtains all that is its own? Remember too on every occasion which leads thee to vexation to apply this principle: not that this is a misfortune, but that to bear it nobly is good fortune.

6. One man, when he has done a service to another, is ready to set it down to his account as a favour conferred. Another is not ready to do this, but still in his own mind he thinks of the man as his debtor, and he knows what he has done. A third in a manner does not even know what he has done, but he is like a vine which has produced grapes, and seeks for nothing more after it has once produced its proper fruit. As a horse when he has run, a dog when he has tracked the game, a bee when it has made the honey, so a man, when he has done a good act, does not call out for others to come and see, but he goes on to another act, as a vine goes on to produce again the grapes in season.—Must a man then be one of these, who in a manner act thus without observing it?—Yes.

7. In the gymnastic exercises suppose that a man has torn thee with his nails, and by dashing against thy head has inflicted a wound. Well, we neither show any signs of vexation, nor are we offended, nor do we suspect him afterwards as a treacherous fellow; and yet we are on our guard against him, not however as an enemy, nor yet with suspicion, but we quietly get out of his way. Something like this let thy behaviour be in all the other parts of life; let us overlook many things in those who are like antagonists in the gymnasium. For it is in our power, as I said, to get out of the way, and to have no suspicion nor hatred.

8. When thou wishest to delight thyself, think of the virtues of those who live with thee; for instance, the activity of one, and the modesty of another, and the liberality of a third, and some other good quality of a fourth. For nothing delights so much as the examples of the virtues, when they are exhibited in the morals of those who live with us and present themselves in abundance, as far as is possible. Wherefore we must keep them before us.

9. If thou art pained by an external thing, it is not this thing that disturbs thee, but thy own judgement about it. And it is in thy power to wipe out this judgement now. But if anything in thy own disposition gives thee pain, who hinders thee from correcting thy opinion? And even if thou art pained because thou art not doing some particular thing which seems to thee to be right, why dost thou not rather act than complain?— But some insuperable obstacle is in the way?—Do not be grieved then, for the cause of its not being done depends not on thee.

10. Do not despise death, but be well content with it, since this too is one of those things which nature wills. For such as it is to be young and to grow old, and to increase and to reach maturity, and to have teeth and beard and grey hairs, and to beget, and to be pregnant and to bring forth, and all the other natural operations which the seasons of thy life bring, such also is dissolution. This, then, is consistent with the character of a reflecting man, to be neither careless nor impatient nor contemptuous with respect to death, but to wait for it as one of the operations of nature. As thou now waitest for the time when the child shall come out of thy wife's womb, so be ready for the time when thy soul shall fall out of this envelope. But if thou requirest also a vulgar kind of comfort which shall reach thy heart, thou wilt be made best reconciled to death by observing the objects from which thou art going to be removed, and the morals of those with whom thy soul will no longer be mingled. For it is no way right to be offended with men, but it is thy duty to care for them and to bear with them gently; and yet to remember that thy departure will be not from men who have the same principles as thyself. For this is the only thing, if there be any, which could draw us the contrary way and attach us to life, to be permitted to live with those who have the same principles as ourselves. But now thou seest how great is the trouble arising from the discordance of those who live together, so that thou mayest say, Come quick, O death, lest perchance I, too, should forget myself.

11. When thou art offended with any man's shameless conduct, immediately ask thyself, Is it possible, then, that shameless men should not be in the world? It is not possible. Do not, then, require what is impossible. For this man also is one of those shameless men who must of necessity be in the world. Let the same considerations be present to thy mind in the case of the knave, and the faithless man, and of every man who does wrong in any way. For at the same time that thou dost remind thyself that it is impossible that such kind of men should not exist, thou wilt become more kindly disposed towards every one individually. It is useful to perceive this, too, immediately when the occasion arises, what virtue nature has given to man to oppose to every wrongful act. For she has given to man, as an antidote against the stupid man, mildness, and against another kind of man some other power. And in all cases it is possible for thee to correct by teaching the man who is gone astray; for every man who errs misses his object and is gone astray. Besides wherein hast thou been injured? For thou wilt find that no one among those against whom thou art irritated has done anything by which thy mind could be made worse; but that which is evil to thee and harmful has its foundation only in the mind. And what harm is done or what is there strange, if the man who has not been instructed does the acts of an uninstructed man? Consider whether thou shouldst not rather blame thyself, because thou didst not expect such a man to err in such a way. For thou hadst means given thee

by thy reason to suppose that it was likely that he would commit this error, and yet thou hast forgotten and art amazed that he has erred. But most of all when thou blamest a man as faithless or ungrateful, turn to thyself. For the fault is manifestly thy own, whether thou didst trust that a man who had such a disposition would keep his promise, or when conferring thy kindness thou didst not confer it absolutely, nor yet in such way as to have received from thy very act all the profit. For what more dost thou want when thou hast done a man a service? Art thou not content that thou hast done something conformable to thy nature, and dost thou seek to be paid for it? Just as if the eye demand a recompense for seeing, or the feet for walking. For as these members are formed for a particular purpose, and by working according to their several constitutions obtain what is their own; so also as man is formed by nature to acts of benevolence, when he has done anything benevolent or in any other way conducive to the common interest, he has acted conformably to his constitution, and he gets what is his own.

12. When thou hast assumed these names, good, modest, true, rational, a man of equanimity, and magnanimous, take care that thou dost not change these names; and if thou shouldst lose them, quickly return to them. And remember that the term Rational was intended to signify a discriminating attention to every several thing and freedom from negligence; and that Equanimity is the voluntary acceptance of the things which are assigned to thee by the common nature; and that Magnanimity is the elevation of the intelligent part above the pleasurable or painful sensations of the flesh, and above that poor thing called fame, and death, and all such things. If, then, thou maintainest thyself in the possession of these names, without desiring to be called by these names by others, thou wilt be another person and wilt enter on another life. For to continue to be such as thou hast hitherto been, and to be torn in pieces and defiled in such a life, is the character of a very stupid man and one overfond of his life, and like those half-devoured fighters with wild beasts, who though covered with wounds and gore, still intreat to be kept to the following day, though they will be exposed in the same state to the same claws and bites. Therefore fix thyself in the possession of these few names: and if thou art able to abide in them, abide as if thou wast removed to certain islands of the Happy. But if thou shalt perceive that thou fallest out of them and dost not maintain thy hold, go courageously into some nook where thou shalt maintain them, or even depart at once from life, not in passion, but with simplicity and freedom and modesty, after doing this one laudable thing at least in thy life, to have gone out of it thus. In order, however, to the remembrance of these names, it will greatly help thee, if thou rememberest the gods, and that they wish not to be flattered, but wish all reasonable beings to be made like themselves; and if thou rememberest that what does the work of a fig-tree is a fig-tree, and what

does the work of a dog is a dog, and that what does the work of a bee is a bee, and that what does the work of a man is a man.

13. Short is the little time which remains to thee of life. Live as on a mountain. For it makes no difference whether a man lives there or here, if he lives everywhere in the world as in a state (political community). Let men see, let them know a real man who lives according to nature. If they cannot endure him, let them kill him. For that is better than to live thus as men do.

14. The healthy eye ought to see all visible things and not to say, I wish for green things; for this is the condition of a diseased eye. And the healthy hearing and smelling ought to be ready to perceive all that can be heard and smelled. And the healthy stomach ought to be with respect to all food just as the mill with respect to all things which it is formed to grind. And accordingly the healthy understanding ought to be prepared for everything which happens; but that which says, Let my dear children live, and let all men praise whatever I may do, is an eye which seeks for green things, or teeth which seek for soft things.

15. When thou art troubled about anything, thou hast forgotten this, that all things happen according to the universal nature; and forgotten this, that a man's wrongful act is nothing to thee; and further thou hast forgotten this, that everything which happens, always happened so and will happen so, and now happens so everywhere; forgotten this too, how close is the kinship between a man and the whole human race, for it is a community, not of a little blood or seed, but of intelligence. And thou hast forgotten this too, that every man's intelligence is a god, and is an efflux of the deity; and forgotten this, that nothing is a man's own, but that his child and his body and his very soul came from the deity; forgotten this, that everything is opinion; and lastly thou hast forgotten that every man lives the present time only, and loses only this.

16. Man, thou hast been a citizen in this great state (the world): what difference does it make to thee whether for five years (or three)? For that which is conformable to the laws is just for all. Where is the hardship then, if no tyrant nor yet an unjust judge sends thee away from the state, but nature who brought thee into it? The same as if a praetor who has employed an actor dismisses him from the stage.—'But I have not finished the five acts, but only three of them.'—Thou sayest well, but in life the three acts are the whole drama; for what shall be a complete drama is determined by him who was once the cause of its composition, and now of its dissolution: but thou art the cause of neither. Depart then satisfied, for he also who releases thee is satisfied.

--→{ COMMENT AND QUESTIONS }←--

1. Because both of the preceding selections are a series of separate teachings, maxims, or reflections, they have no planned organization, and the numbered sections frequently repeat and overlap. In reviewing each selection, consider what the main ideas of each author are. How could the main ideas of Epictetus be expressed in a related, organized way? How could the main ideas of Marcus Aurelius similarly be expressed? On what matters are the two Stoics most completely in agreement? On what do their ideas and their emphasis appear to differ?
2. What does Epictetus mean in the first sentence of section 1 by "these high matters"?
3. What is the meaning of the word *impression* as Epictetus uses it in the second paragraph of section 1? What is the meaning of the sentence (section 5), "What disturbs men's minds is not events but their judgments on events"? Are the two ideas, about impressions and about judgments on events, similar, or are they the same? Explain.
4. According to Epictetus, with what, in general, is the wise man not concerned? What are some of the particular things and events by which he is not disturbed? What methods does he use to keep himself undisturbed?
5. How does the closing statement of "The Quiet Mind," that there is nothing intrinsically evil in the world, follow logically from the preceding material?
6. It has been said that the coldness and austerity of Stoicism make it a philosophy few men can live by; that it makes almost impossible demands on human nature. What examples or statements in these two selections would seem to you to support that view? On the other hand, do you find in the Stoic philosophy any basic wisdom which might be useful to all men? In considering the last question, think about experiences which have caused you perturbation or unhappiness. Possible examples might be: (a) You have failed to receive an important, expected telephone call or letter. (b) You have fallen behind in your studies; the pressure of work has been enormous, and the situation has seemed hopeless. (c) You have been caught in a rush-hour traffic jam. (d) You have received a low grade on a paper or an examination. (e) You have heard of spiteful gossip directed at you. (f) You have wanted to study, but the dormitory has been noisy. (g) The person you have been in love with has married someone else. How would the Stoic react to these or similar situations?
7. Matthew Arnold called Marcus Aurelius "perhaps the most beautiful figure in history" and said that while the sentences of Epictetus fortify the character, the sentences of Marcus Aurelius touch the soul with the "gentleness and sweetness" of his morality. If you agree with this judgment, what particular examples can you give of the gentleness and sweetness in Marcus Aurelius?

8. The attitudes of Marcus Aurelius toward humanity or human beings in general are complex. What attitudes does he express?
9. Both Epictetus and Marcus Aurelius make skillful use of concrete words and examples and of figurative language. What details and figures of speech in the two selections are most memorable to you?

[19]   *Jesus*: Sermon on the Mount

A HEADNOTE which attempted to state the importance and meaning of the Sermon on the Mount would be presumptuous and unnecessary. We shall merely say that it is the fullest single statement in the Bible of the basic doctrines of Jesus. According to the *New Standard Bible Dictionary*, the Sermon on the Mount is "at any rate in large measure, a compilation of the sayings of Jesus . . . gradually collected and massed in the present elaborate composition," and it constitutes "a general summary of what Matthew understands to have been Jesus' teachings about the disciple's relationship to duty and to God." The translation presented here is that of the King James version; students who prefer to read another version can find this passage in Matthew, chapters 5, 6, and 7.

CHAPTER 5

And seeing the multitudes, he went up into a mountain: and when he was set, his disciples came unto him:

2 And he opened his mouth, and taught them, saying,

3 Blessed *are* the poor in spirit: for theirs is the kingdom of heaven.

4 Blessed *are* they that mourn: for they shall be comforted.

5 Blessed *are* the meek: for they shall inherit the earth.

6 Blessed *are* they which do hunger and thirst after righteousness: for they shall be filled.

7 Blessed *are* the merciful: for they shall obtain mercy.

8 Blessed *are* the pure in heart: for they shall see God.

9 Blessed *are* the peacemakers: for they shall be called the children of God.

10 Blessed *are* they which are persecuted for righteousness' sake: for theirs is the kingdom of heaven.

11 Blessed are ye, when *men* shall revile you, and persecute *you*, and shall say all manner of evil against you falsely, for my sake.

12 Rejoice, and be exceeding glad: for great *is* your reward in heaven: for so persecuted they the prophets which were before you.

13 Ye are the salt of the earth: but if the salt have lost his savour, wherewith shall it be salted? it is thenceforth good for nothing, but to be cast out, and to be trodden under foot of men.

14 Ye are the light of the world. A city that is set on an hill cannot be hid.

15 Neither do men light a candle, and put it under a bushel, but on a candlestick; and it giveth light unto all that are in the house.

16 Let your light so shine before men, that they may see your good works, and glorify your Father which is in heaven.

17 Think not that I am come to destroy the law, or the prophets: I am not come to destroy, but to fulfil.

18 For verily I say unto you, Till heaven and earth pass, one jot or one tittle shall in no wise pass from the law, till all be fulfilled.

19 Whosoever therefore shall break one of these least commandments, and shall teach men so, he shall be called the least in the kingdom of heaven: but whosoever shall do and teach *them*, the same shall be called great in the kingdom of heaven.

20 For I say unto you, That except your righteousness shall exceed *the righteousness* of the scribes and Pharisees, ye shall in no case enter into the kingdom of heaven.

21 Ye have heard that it was said by them of old time, Thou shalt not kill; and whosoever shall kill shall be in danger of the judgment:

22 But I say unto you, That whosoever is angry with his brother without a cause shall be in danger of the judgment: and whosoever shall say to his brother, Raca, shall be in danger of the council: but whosoever shall say, Thou fool, shall be in danger of hell fire.

23 Therefore if thou bring thy gift to the altar, and there rememberest that thy brother hath ought against thee;

24 Leave there thy gift before the altar, and go thy way; first be reconciled to thy brother, and then come and offer thy gift.

25 Agree with thine adversary quickly, whiles thou art in the way with him; lest at any time the adversary deliver thee to the judge, and the judge deliver thee to the officer, and thou be cast into prison.

26 Verily I say unto thee, Thou shalt by no means come out thence, till thou hast paid the uttermost farthing.

27 Ye have heard that it was said by them of old time, Thou shalt not commit adultery:

28 But I say unto you, That whosoever looketh on a woman to lust after her hath committed adultery with her already in his heart.

29 And if thy right eye offend thee, pluck it out, and cast *it* from thee: for it is profitable for thee that one of thy members should perish, and not *that* thy whole body should be cast into hell.

30 And if thy right hand offend thee, cut it off, and cast *it* from thee: for it is profitable for thee that one of thy members should perish, and not *that* thy whole body should be cast into hell.

31 It hath been said, Whosoever shall put away his wife, let him give her a writing of divorcement:

32 But I say unto you, That whosoever shall put away his wife, saving for the cause of fornication, causeth her to commit adultery: and whosoever shall marry her that is divorced committeth adultery.

33 Again, ye have heard that it hath been said by them of old time, Thou shalt not forswear thyself, but shalt perform unto the Lord thine oaths:

34 But I say unto you, Swear not at all; neither by heaven; for it is God's throne:

35 Nor by the earth; for it is his footstool: neither by Jerusalem; for it is the city of the great King.

36 Neither shalt thou swear by thy head, because thou canst not make one hair white or black.

37 But let your communication be, Yea, yea; Nay, nay: for whatsoever is more than these cometh of evil.

38 Ye have heard that it hath been said, An eye for an eye, and a tooth for a tooth:

39 But I say unto you, That ye resist not evil: but whosoever shall smite thee on thy right cheek, turn to him the other also.

40 And if any man will sue thee at the law, and take away thy coat, let him have *thy* cloke also.

41 And whosoever shall compel thee to go a mile, go with him twain.

42 Give to him that asketh thee, and from him that would borrow of thee turn not thou away.

43 Ye have heard that it hath been said, Thou shalt love thy neighbour, and hate thine enemy.

44 But I say unto you, Love your enemies, bless them that curse you, do good to them that hate you, and pray for them which despitefully use you, and persecute you;

45 That ye may be the children of your Father which is in heaven: for he maketh his sun to rise on the evil and on the good, and sendeth rain on the just and on the unjust.

46 For if ye love them which love you, what reward have ye? do not even the publicans the same?

47 And if ye salute your brethren only, what do ye more *than others?* do not even the publicans so?

48 Be ye therefore perfect, even as your Father which is in heaven is perfect.

CHAPTER 6

Take heed that ye do not your alms before men, to be seen of them: otherwise ye have no reward of your Father which is in heaven.

2 Therefore when thou doest *thine* alms, do not sound a trumpet before thee, as the hypocrites do in the synagogues and in the streets, that they may have glory of men. Verily I say unto you, They have their reward.

3 But when thou doest alms, let not thy left hand know what thy right hand doeth:

4 That thine alms may be in secret: and thy Father which seeth in secret himself shall reward thee openly.

5 And when thou prayest, thou shalt not be as the hypocrites *are:* for they love to pray standing in the synagogues and in the corners of the streets, that they may be seen of men. Verily I say unto you, They have their reward.

6 But thou, when thou prayest, enter into thy closet, and when thou hast shut thy door, pray to thy Father which is in secret; and thy Father which seeth in secret shall reward thee openly.

7 But when ye pray, use not vain repetitions, as the heathen *do:* for they think that they shall be heard for their much speaking.

8 Be not ye therefore like unto them: for your Father knoweth what things ye have need of, before ye ask him.

9 After this manner therefore pray ye: Our Father which art in heaven, Hallowed be thy name.

10 Thy kingdom come. Thy will be done in earth, as *it is* in heaven.

11 Give us this day our daily bread.

12 And forgive us our debts, as we forgive our debtors.

13 And lead us not into temptation, but deliver us from evil: For thine is the kingdom, and the power, and the glory, for ever. Amen.

14 For if ye forgive men their trespasses, your heavenly Father will also forgive you:

15 But if ye forgive not men their trespasses, neither will your Father forgive your trespasses.

16 Moreover when ye fast, be not, as the hypocrites, of a sad countenance: for they disfigure their faces, that they may appear unto men to fast. Verily I say unto you, They have their reward.

17 But thou, when thou fastest, anoint thine head, and wash thy face;

18 That thou appear not unto men to fast, but unto thy Father which is in secret: and thy Father, which seeth in secret, shall reward thee openly.

19 Lay not up for yourselves treasures upon earth, where moth and rust doth corrupt, and where thieves break through and steal:

20 But lay up for yourselves treasures in heaven, where neither moth nor rust doth corrupt, and where thieves do not break through nor steal:

21 For where your treasure is, there will your heart be also.

22 The light of the body is the eye: if therefore thine eye be single, thy whole body shall be full of light.

23 But if thine eye be evil, thy whole body shall be full of darkness. If therefore the light that is in thee be darkness, how great *is* that darkness!

24 No man can serve two masters: for either he will hate the one, and love the other; or else he will hold to the one, and despise the other. Ye cannot serve God and mammon.

25 Therefore I say unto you, Take no thought for your life, what ye shall eat, or what ye shall drink; nor yet for your body, what ye shall put on. Is not the life more than meat, and the body than raiment?

26 Behold the fowls of the air: for they sow not, neither do they reap, nor gather into barns; yet your heavenly Father feedeth them. Are ye not much better than they?

27 Which of you by taking thought can add one cubit unto his stature?

28 And why take ye thought for raiment? Consider the lilies of the field, how they grow; they toil not, neither do they spin:

29 And yet I say unto you, That even Solomon in all his glory was not arrayed like one of these.

30 Wherefore, if God so clothe the grass of the field, which to day is, and to morrow is cast into the oven, *shall he* not much more *clothe* you, O ye of little faith?

31 Therefore take no thought, saying, What shall we eat? or, What shall we drink? or, Wherewithal shall we be clothed?

32 (For after all these things do the Gentiles seek:) for your heavenly Father knoweth that ye have need of all these things.

33 But seek ye first the kingdom of God, and his righteousness; and all these things shall be added unto you.

34 Take therefore no thought for the morrow: for the morrow shall take thought for the things of itself. Sufficient unto the day *is* the evil thereof.

CHAPTER 7

Judge not, that ye be not judged.

2 For with what judgment ye judge, ye shall be judged: and with what measure ye mete, it shall be measured to you again.

3 And why beholdest thou the mote that is in thy brother's eye, but considerest not the beam that is in thine own eye?

4 Or how wilt thou say to thy brother, Let me pull out the mote out of thine eye; and, behold, a beam *is* in thine own eye?

5 Thou hypocrite, first cast out the beam out of thine own eye; and then shalt thou see clearly to cast out the mote out of thy brother's eye.

6 Give not that which is holy unto the dogs, neither cast ye your pearls

before swine, lest they trample them under their feet, and turn again and rend you.

7 Ask, and it shall be given you; seek, and ye shall find; knock, and it shall be opened unto you:

8 For every one that asketh receiveth; and he that seeketh findeth; and to him that knocketh it shall be opened.

9 Or what man is there of you, whom if his son ask bread, will he give him a stone?

10 Or if he ask a fish, will he give him a serpent?

11 If ye then, being evil, know how to give good gifts unto your children, how much more shall your Father which is in heaven give good things to them that ask him?

12 Therefore all things whatsoever ye would that men should do to you, do ye even so to them: for this is the law and the prophets.

13 Enter ye in at the strait gate: for wide *is* the gate, and broad *is* the way, that leadeth to destruction, and many there be which go in thereat:

14 Because strait *is* the gate, and narrow *is* the way, which leadeth unto life, and few there be that find it.

15 Beware of false prophets, which come to you in sheep's clothing, but inwardly they are ravening wolves.

16 Ye shall know them by their fruits. Do men gather grapes of thorns, or figs of thistles?

17 Even so every good tree bringeth forth good fruit; but a corrupt tree bringeth forth evil fruit.

18 A good tree cannot bring forth evil fruit, neither *can* a corrupt tree bring forth good fruit.

19 Every tree that bringeth not forth good fruit is hewn down, and cast into the fire.

20 Wherefore by their fruits ye shall know them.

21 Not every one that saith unto me, Lord, Lord, shall enter into the kingdom of heaven; but he that doeth the will of my Father which is in heaven.

22 Many will say to me in that day, Lord, Lord, have we not prophesied in thy name? and in thy name have cast out devils? and in thy name done many wonderful works?

23 And then will I profess unto them, I never knew you: depart from me, ye that work iniquity.

24 Therefore whosoever heareth these sayings of mine, and doeth them, I will liken him unto a wise man, which built his house upon a rock:

25 And the rain descended, and the floods came, and the winds blew, and beat upon that house; and it fell not: for it was founded upon a rock.

26 And every one that heareth these sayings of mine, and doeth them not, shall be likened unto a foolish man, which built his house upon the sand:

27 And the rain descended, and the floods came, and the winds blew, and beat upon that house; and it fell: and great was the fall of it.

28 And it came to pass, when Jesus had ended these sayings, the people were astonished at his doctrine:

29 For he taught them as *one* having authority, and not as the scribes.

COMMENT AND QUESTIONS

Richard G. Moulton, editor of *The Modern Reader's Bible*, states that the Sermon on the Mount, like many sections in the Bible, has a sevenfold structure and "follows a literary form prominent in the Hebrew philosophy we call wisdom literature." Each of these sections consists, he says, of a maxim supported by comment. Students who wish to follow this pattern may find the following outline useful.

Section 1. Matt. 5:3–12; the maxim is 3.
Section 2. Matt. 5:13; the maxim is "Ye are the salt of the earth."
Section 3. Matt. 5:14–16; the maxim is "Ye are the light of the world."
Section 4. Matt. 5:17–48; the maxim is 17.
Section 5. Matt. 6:1–18; the maxim is 1.
Section 6. Matt. 6:19–34; the maxim is 19–20.
Section 7. Matt. 7:1–29 (i.e., the whole of 7); the maxim is 1. Mr. Moulton points out that this seventh section is miscellaneous (another characteristic feature of wisdom literature) and that the number of sayings in it is seven.

1. It has been said that the expression "poor in spirit" (5:3) is a general expression clarified by the statements that follow it. Just what do you take the expression to mean?
2. In 5:13–15 Jesus is using figures of speech to clarify an idea. Explain the figures of speech and their meaning. Whom is Jesus addressing with the pronoun *ye* in these lines?
3. In 5:17 (and again in 7:12) Jesus refers to "the law" and "the prophets." What specific laws and prophets do you think may be referred to?
4. In 6:22–23 Jesus is again using figurative language. What is the literal meaning?
5. In 6:24 it is stated, "Ye cannot serve God and mammon." What is the relationship between this statement and 6:19–21? How does your dictionary define *mammon*? How would you define what is meant by *mammon* in terms of modern life?
6. John Stuart Mill in "On the Liberty of Thought and Discussion," pages 128–49, comments at some length on Christian morality. Do you think that what Mill says there is true of the Sermon on the Mount? Explain.
7. In your opinion, which of the precepts of Jesus are most difficult to follow

in modern living? If you were to follow these precepts strictly, what changes would you have to make in your present way of life?
8. If you have read the *Apology*, what similarities and what differences do you find in the teaching of Socrates and of Jesus?
9. If you have read the selections from Epicurus, Epictetus, and Marcus Aurelius, you are familiar with the basic concepts of three views of life—the Epicurean, the Stoic, and the Christian. Which of these three philosophies do you think it would be most difficult to live by? Which would be most deeply rewarding?

[20] *Thomas Henry Huxley*: Agnosticism and Christianity

THOMAS HENRY HUXLEY (1825–1895) was a distinguished English biologist and teacher, known particularly for his defense of Darwin's theory of evolution, and for his lectures and writings explaining science to general audiences. The following selection is part of the essay "Agnosticism and Christianity," first printed in 1889.

[1] The present discussion has arisen out of the use, which has become general in the last few years, of the terms "Agnostic" and "Agnosticism."

[2] The people who call themselves "Agnostics" have been charged with doing so because they have not the courage to declare themselves "Infidels." It has been insinuated that they have adopted a new name in order to escape the unpleasantness which attaches to their proper denomination. To this wholly erroneous imputation, I have replied by showing that the term "Agnostic" did, as a matter of fact, arise in a manner which negatives it; and my statement has not been, and cannot be refuted. Moreover, speaking for myself, and without impugning the right of any other person to use the term in another sense, I further say that Agnosticism is not properly described as a "negative" creed, nor indeed as a creed of any kind, except in so far as it expresses absolute faith in the validity of a principle which is as much ethical as intellectual. This principle may be stated in various ways, but they all amount to this: that it is wrong for a man to say that he is certain of the objective truth of any proposition unless he can produce evidence which logically justifies that certainty. This is what Agnosticism asserts; and, in my opinion, it is all that is essential to Agnosticism. That which Agnostics deny and repudiate, as immoral, is the contrary doctrine, that there are propositions which men ought to believe, without logically satisfactory evidence; and that reprobation ought to attach to the profession of disbelief in such inadequately supported propositions. The justification of the Agnostic principle lies in the success which follows upon its application, whether in the field of natural, or in that of civil, history; and in the fact that, so far as these topics are concerned, no sane man thinks of denying its validity.

From *Science and Christian Tradition* by Thomas Henry Huxley. Published by Appleton-Century-Crofts, Inc.

[3] Still speaking for myself, I add, that though Agnosticism is not, and cannot be, a creed, except in so far as its general principle is concerned; yet that the application of that principle results in the denial of, or the suspension of judgment concerning, a number of propositions respecting which our contemporary ecclesiastical "gnostics" profess entire certainty. And, in so far as these ecclesiastical persons can be justified in their old-established custom (which many nowadays think more honoured in the breach than the observance) of using opprobrious names to those who differ from them, I fully admit their right to call me and those who think with me "Infidels"; all I have ventured to urge is that they must not expect us to speak of ourselves by that title.

[4] The extent of the region of the uncertain, the number of the problems the investigation of which ends in a verdict of not proven, will vary according to the knowledge and the intellectual habits of the individual Agnostic. I do not very much care to speak of anything as "unknowable." What I am sure about is that there are many topics about which I know nothing; and which, so far as I can see, are out of reach of my faculties. But whether these things are knowable by any one else is exactly one of those matters which is beyond my knowledge, though I may have a tolerably strong opinion as to the probabilities of the case. Relatively to myself, I am quite sure that the region of uncertainty—the nebulous country in which words play the part of realities—is far more extensive than I could wish. Materialism and Idealism; Theism and Atheism; the doctrine of the soul and its mortality or immortality—appear in the history of philosophy like the shades of Scandinavian heroes, eternally slaying one another and eternally coming to life again in a metaphysical "Nifelheim."[1] It is getting on for twenty-five centuries, at least, since mankind began seriously to give their minds to these topics. Generation after generation, philosophy has been doomed to roll the stone uphill; and, just as all the world swore it was at the top, down it has rolled to the bottom again. All this is written in innumerable books; and he who will toil through them will discover that the stone is just where it was when the work began. Hume saw this; Kant saw it; since their time, more and more eyes have been cleaned of the films which prevented them from seeing it; until now the weight and number of those who refuse to be the prey of verbal mystifications has begun to tell in practical life.

[5] It was inevitable that a conflict should arise between Agnosticism and Theology; or rather, I ought to say, between Agnosticism and Ecclesiasticism. For Theology, the science, is one thing; and Ecclesiasticism, the championship of a foregone conclusion as to the truth of a particular form of Theology, is another. With scientific Theology, Agnosticism has no quarrel. On the contrary, the Agnostic, knowing too well the influence

---

[1] Mist home.

of prejudice and idiosyncrasy, even on those who desire most earnestly to be impartial, can wish for nothing more urgently than that the scientific theologian should not only be at perfect liberty to thresh out the matter in his own fashion; but that he should, if he can, find flaws in the Agnostic position; and, even if demonstration is not to be had, that he should put, in their full force, the grounds of the conclusions he thinks probable. The scientific theologian admits the agnostic principle, however widely his results may differ from those reached by the majority of Agnostics.

[6] But, as between Agnosticism and Ecclesiasticism, or, as our neighbours across the Channel call it, Clericalism, there can be neither peace nor truce. The Cleric asserts that it is morally wrong not to believe certain propositions, whatever the results of a strict scientific investigation of the evidence of these propositions. He tells us that "religious error is, in itself, of an immoral nature." He declares that he has prejudged certain conclusions, and looks upon those who show cause for arrest of judgment as emissaries of Satan. It necessarily follows that, for him, the attainment of faith, not the ascertainment of truth, is the highest aim of mental life. And, on careful analysis of the nature of this faith, it will too often be found to be, not the mystic process of unity with the Divine, understood by the religious enthusiast; but that which the candid simplicity of a Sunday scholar once defined it to be. "Faith," said this unconscious plagiarist of Tertullian, "is the power of saying you believe things which are incredible."

[7] Now I, and many other Agnostics, believe that faith, in this sense, is an abomination; and though we do not indulge in the luxury of self-righteousness so far as to call those who are not of our way of thinking hard names, we do feel that the disagreement between ourselves and those who hold this doctrine is even more moral than intellectual. It is desirable there should be an end of any mistakes on this topic. If our clerical opponents were clearly aware of the real state of the case, there would be an end of the curious delusion, which often appears between the lines of their writings, that those whom they are so fond of calling "Infidels" are people who not only ought to be, but in their hearts are, ashamed of themselves. It would be discourteous to do more than hint the antipodal opposition of this pleasant dream of theirs to facts.

[8] The clerics and their lay allies commonly tell us, that if we refuse to admit that there is good ground for expressing definite convictions about certain topics, the bonds of human society will dissolve and mankind lapse into savagery. There are several answers to this assertion. One is that the bonds of human society were formed without the aid of their theology; and, in the opinion of not a few competent judges, have been weakened rather than strengthened by a good deal of it. Greek science, Greek art, the ethics of old Israel, the social organisation of old Rome, contrived to come into being, without the help of any one who

believed in a single distinctive article of the simplest of the Christian creeds. The science, the art, the jurisprudence, the chief political and social theories, of the modern world have grown out of those of Greece and Rome—not by favour of, but in the teeth of, the fundamental teachings of early Christianity, to which science, art, and any serious occupation with the things of this world, were alike despicable.

[9] Again, all that is best in the ethics of the modern world, in so far as it has not grown out of Greek thought, or Barbarian manhood, is the direct development of the ethics of old Israel. There is no code of legislation, ancient or modern, at once so just and so merciful, so tender to the weak and poor, as the Jewish law; and, if the Gospels are to be trusted, Jesus of Nazareth himself declared that he taught nothing but that which lay implicitly, or explicitly, in the religious and ethical system of his people.

And the scribe said unto him, Of a truth, Teacher, thou hast well said that he is one; and there is none other but he and to love him with all the heart, and with all the understanding, and with all the strength, and to love his neighbour as himself, is much more than all the whole burnt offerings and sacrifices. (Mark xii:32, 33.)

[10] Here is the briefest of summaries of the teaching of the prophets of Israel of the eighth century; does the Teacher, whose doctrine is thus set forth in his presence, repudiate the exposition? Nay; we are told, on the contrary, that Jesus saw that he "answered discreetly," and replied, "Thou are not far from the kingdom of God."

[11] So that I think that even if the creeds, from the so-called "Apostles'" to the so-called "Athanasian," were swept into oblivion; and even if the human race should arrive at the conclusion that, whether a bishop washes a cup or leaves it unwashed, is not a matter of the least consequence, it will get on very well. The causes which have led to the development of morality in mankind, which have guided or impelled us all the way from the savage to the civilized state, will not cease to operate because a number of ecclesiastical hypotheses turn out to be baseless. And, even if the absurd notion that morality is more the child of speculation than of practical necessity and inherited instinct, had any foundation; if all the world is going to thieve, murder, and otherwise misconduct itself as soon as it discovers that certain portions of ancient history are mythical; what is the relevance of such arguments to any one who holds by the Agnostic principle?

[12] Surely, the attempt to cast out Beelzebub by the aid of Beelzebub is a hopeful procedure as compared to that of preserving morality by the aid of immorality. For I suppose it is admitted that an Agnostic may be perfectly sincere, may be competent, and may have studied the question at issue with as much care as his clerical opponents. But, if the Agnostic really believes what he says, the "dreadful consequence" argufier (con-

sistently, I admit, with his own principles) virtually asks him to abstain from telling the truth, or to say what he believes to be untrue, because of the supposed injurious consequences to morality. "Beloved brethren, that we may be spotlessly moral, before all things let us lie," is the sum total of many an exhortation addressed to the "Infidel." Now, as I have already pointed out, we cannot oblige our exhorters. We leave the practical application of the convenient doctrines of "Reserve"[2] and "Non-natural interpretation" to those who invented them.

[13] I trust that I have now made amends for any ambiguity, or want of fulness, in my previous exposition of that which I hold to be the essence of the Agnostic doctrine. Henceforward, I might hope to hear no more of the assertion that we are necessarily Materialists, Idealists, Atheists, Theists, or any other ists, if experience had led me to think that the proved falsity of a statement was any guarantee against its repetition. And those who appreciate the nature of our position will see, at once, that when Ecclesiasticism declares that we ought to believe this, that, and the other, and are very wicked if we don't, it is impossible for us to give any answer but this: We have not the slightest objection to believe anything you like, if you will give us good grounds for belief; but, if you cannot, we must respectfully refuse, even if that refusal should wreck morality and insure our own damnation several times over. We are quite content to leave that to the decision of the future. The course of the past has impressed us with the firm conviction that no good ever comes of falsehood, and we feel warranted in refusing even to experiment in that direction.

COMMENT AND QUESTIONS

1. The agnostic principle, Huxley says, is "that it is wrong for a man to say that he is certain of the objective truth of any proposition unless he can produce evidence which logically justifies that certainty." What is the importance of the word *objective* in this statement of the agnostic position? How does agnosticism differ from atheism? From infidelism?
2. Can you supply examples to support Huxley's statement, at the end of paragraph 2, that outside the area of religion no sane man thinks of denying the validity of the agnostic principle?
3. What are examples of the "propositions" and "topics" about which opponents of agnosticism express certainty, and about which Huxley feels that he knows nothing?

[2] Withholding of perplexities from the lay mind.

4. What are the implications in Huxley's statement in paragraph 4: "I do not very much care to speak of anything as 'unknowable' "?
5. What distinction does Huxley make between theology and ecclesiasticism? Why does agnosticism have no quarrel with the former? Why must it be at war with the latter?
6. What are Huxley's answers to the assertion that mankind would lapse into savagery if certain ecclesiastical propositions were abandoned? On the basis of your reading, to what extent do you agree with his answers?
7. Explain the last sentence of paragraph 11: "And, even if the absurd notion that morality is more the child of speculation than of practical necessity and inherited instinct, had any foundation . . . what is the relevance of such arguments to any one who holds by the Agnostic principle?"
8. In what sense, according to Huxley, is the agnostic position a moral and ethical one? Do you agree with his claims? Explain.
9. How would you describe the tone of this selection and the persona revealed? Can you see reasons for Huxley's tone?

[21] William James: Religious Faith

WILLIAM JAMES (1842–1910) was an American psychologist, philosopher, and distinguished teacher at Harvard. "Religious Faith" is an excerpt from *The Will to Believe*, a collection of essays and lectures published in 1897.

[1] And now, in turning to what religion may have to say to the question,[1] I come to what is the soul of my discourse. Religion has meant many things in human history; but when from now onward I use the word I mean to use it in the supernaturalist sense, as declaring that the so-called order of nature, which constitutes this world's experience, is only one portion of the total universe, and that there stretches beyond this visible world an unseen world of which we now know nothing positive, but in its relation to which the true significance of our present mundane life consists. A man's religious faith (whatever more special items of doctrine it may involve) means for me essentially his faith in the existence of an unseen order of some kind in which the riddles of the natural order may be found explained. In the more developed religions the natural world has always been regarded as the mere scaffolding or vestibule of a truer, more eternal world, and affirmed to be a sphere of

[1] The question of the meaning of life.

education, trial, or redemption. In these religions, one must in some fashion die to the natural life before one can enter into life eternal. The notion that this physical world of wind and water, where the sun rises and the moon sets, is absolutely and ultimately the divinely aimed-at and established thing, is one which we find only in very early religions, such as that of the most primitive Jews. It is this natural religion (primitive still, in spite of the fact that poets and men of science whose goodwill exceeds their perspicacity keep publishing it in new editions tuned to our contemporary ears) that, as I said a while ago, has suffered definitive bankruptcy in the opinion of a circle of persons, among whom I must count myself, and who are growing more numerous every day. For such persons the physical order of nature, taken simply as science knows it, cannot be held to reveal any one harmonious spiritual intent. It is mere *weather,* as Chauncey Wright called it, doing and undoing without end.

[2] Now, I wish to make you feel, if I can in the short remainder of this hour, that we have a right to believe the physical order to be only a partial order; that we have a right to supplement it by an unseen spiritual order which we assume on trust, if only thereby life may seem to us better worth living again. But as such a trust will seem to some of you sadly mystical and execrably unscientific, I must first say a word or two to weaken the veto which you may consider that science opposes to our act.

[3] There is included in human nature an ingrained naturalism and materialism of mind which can only admit facts that are actually tangible. Of this sort of mind the entity called "science" is the idol. Fondness for the word "scientist" is one of the notes by which you may know its votaries; and its short way of killing any opinion that it disbelieves in is to call it "unscientific." It must be granted that there is no slight excuse for this. Science has made such glorious leaps in the last three hundred years, and extended our knowledge of nature so enormously both in general and in detail; men of science, moreover, have as a class displayed such admirable virtues,—that it is no wonder if the worshippers of science lose their head. In this very University, accordingly, I have heard more than one teacher say that all the fundamental conceptions of truth have already been found by science, and that the future has only the details of the picture to fill in. But the slightest reflection on the real conditions will suffice to show how barbaric such notions are. They show such a lack of scientific imagination, that it is hard to see how one who is actively advancing any part of science can make a mistake so crude. Think how many absolutely new scientific conceptions have arisen in our own generation, how many new problems have been formulated that were never thought of before, and then cast an eye upon the brevity of science's career. It began with Galileo, not three hundred years ago.

Four thinkers since Galileo, each informing his successor of what discoveries his own lifetime had seen achieved, might have passed the torch of science into our hands as we sit here in this room. Indeed, for the matter of that, an audience much smaller than the present one, an audience of some five or six score people, if each person in it could speak for his own generation, would carry us away to the black unknown of the human species, to days without a document or monument to tell their tale. Is it credible that such a mushroom knowledge, such a growth overnight as this, *can* represent more than the minutest glimpse of what the universe will really prove to be when adequately understood? No! our science is a drop, our ignorance a sea. Whatever else be certain, this at least is certain,—that the world of our present natural knowledge *is* enveloped in a larger world of *some* sort of whose residual properties we at present can frame no positive idea.

[4] Agnostic positivism, of course, admits this principle theoretically in the most cordial terms, but insists that we must not turn it to any practical use. We have no right, this doctrine tells us, to dream dreams, or suppose anything about the unseen part of the universe, merely because to do so may be for what we are pleased to call our highest interests. We must always wait for sensible evidence for our beliefs; and where such evidence is inaccessible we must frame no hypotheses whatever. Of course this is a safe enough position *in abstracto*. If a thinker had no stake in the unknown, no vital needs, to live or languish according to what the unseen world contained, a philosophic neutrality and refusal to believe either one way or the other would be his wisest cue. But, unfortunately, neutrality is not only inwardly difficult, it is also outwardly unrealizable, where our relations to an alternative are practical and vital. This is because, as the psychologists tell us, belief and doubt are living attitudes, and involve conduct on our part. Our only way, for example, of doubting or refusing to believe, that a certain thing *is*, is continuing to act as if it were *not*. If, for instance, I refuse to believe that the room is getting cold, I leave the windows open and light no fire just as if it still were warm. If I doubt that you are worthy of my confidence, I keep you uninformed of all my secrets just as if you were *unworthy* of the same. If I doubt the need of insuring my house, I leave it uninsured as much as if I believed there were no need. And so if I must not believe that the world is divine, I can only express that refusal by declining ever to act distinctively as if it were so, which can only mean acting on certain critical occasions as if it were *not* so, or in an irreligious way. There are, you see, inevitable occasions in life when inaction is a kind of action, and must count as action, and when not to be for is to be practically against; and in all such cases strict and consistent neutrality is an unattainable thing.

[5] And, after all, is not this duty of neutrality, where only our inner interests would lead us to believe, the most ridiculous of commands? Is

is not sheer dogmatic folly to say that our inner interests can have no real connection with the forces that the hidden world may contain? In other cases divinations based on inner interests have proved prophetic enough. Take science itself! Without an imperious inner demand on our part for ideal logical and mathematical harmonies, we should never have attained to proving that such harmonies lie hidden between all the chinks and interstices of the crude natural world. Hardly a law has been established in science, hardly a fact ascertained, which was not first sought after, often with sweat and blood, to gratify an inner need. Whence such needs come from we do not know: we find them in us, and biological psychology so far only classes them with Darwin's "accidental variations." But the inner need of believing that this world of nature is a sign of something more spiritual and eternal than itself is just as strong and authoritative in those who feel it, as the inner need of uniform laws of causation ever can be in a professionally scientific head. The toil of many generations has proved the latter need prophetic. Why *may* not the former one be prophetic, too? And if needs of ours outrun the visible universe, why *may* not that be a sign that an invisible universe is there? What, in short, has authority to debar us from trusting our religious demands? Science as such assuredly has no authority, for she can only say what is, not what is not; and the agnostic "thou shalt not believe without coercive sensible evidence" is simply an expression (free to any one to make) of private personal appetite for evidence of a certain peculiar kind.

[6] Now, when I speak of trusting our religious demands, just what do I mean by "trusting"? Is the word to carry with it license to define in detail an invisible world, and to anathematize and excommunicate those whose trust is different? Certainly not! Our faculties of belief were not primarily given us to make orthodoxies and heresies withal; they were given us to live by. And to trust our religious demands means first of all to live in the light of them, and to act as if the invisible world which they suggest were real. It is a fact of human nature, that men can live and die by the help of a sort of faith that goes without a single dogma of definition. The bare assurance that this natural order is not ultimate but a mere sign or vision, the eternal staging of a many-storied universe, in which spiritual forces have the last word and are eternal,—this bare assurance is to such men enough to make life seem worth living in spite of every contrary presumption suggested by its circumstances on the natural plane. Destroy this inner assurance, however, vague as it is, and all the light and radiance of existence is extinguished for these persons at a stroke. Often enough the wild-eyed look at life—the suicidal mood—will then set in.

[7] And now the application comes directly home to you and me. Probably to almost everyone of us here the most adverse life would seem well worth living, if we only could be *certain* that our bravery and patience

with it were terminating and eventuating and bearing fruit somewhere in an unseen spiritual world. By granting we are not certain, does it then follow that a bare trust in such a world is a fool's paradise and lubberland, or rather that it is a living attitude in which we are free to indulge? Well, we are free to trust at our own risks anything that is not impossible, and that can bring analogies to bear in its behalf. That the world of physics is probably not absolute, all the converging multitude of arguments that make in favor of idealism tend to prove; and that our whole physical life may lie soaking in a spiritual atmosphere, a dimension of being that we at present have no organ for apprehending, is vividly suggested to us by the analogy of our domestic animals. Our dogs, for example, are in our human life but not of it. They witness hourly the outward body of events whose inner meaning cannot, by any possible operation, be revealed to their intelligence,—events in which they themselves often play the cardinal part. My terrier bites a teasing boy, and the father demands damages. The dog may be present at every step of the negotiations, and see the money paid, without an inkling of what it all means, without a suspicion that it has anything to do with *him;* and he never *can* know in his natural dog's life. Or take another case which used greatly to impress me in my medical-student days. Consider a poor dog whom they are vivisecting in a laboratory. He lies strapped on a board and shrieking at his executioners, and to his own dark consciousness is literally in a sort of hell. He cannot see a single redeeming ray in the whole business; and yet all these diabolical-seeming events are often controlled by human intentions with which, if his poor benighted mind could only be made to catch a glimpse of them, all that is heroic in him would religiously acquiesce. Healing truth, relief to future sufferings of beast and man, are to be bought by them. It may be genuinely a process of redemption. Lying on his back on the board there he may be performing a function incalculably higher than any that prosperous canine life admits of; and yet, of the whole performance, this function is the one portion that must remain absolutely beyond his ken.

[8] Now turn from this to the life of man. In the dog's life we see the world invisible to him because we live in both worlds. In human life, although we only see our world, and his within it, yet encompassing both these worlds a still wider world may be there, as unseen by us as our world is by him; and to believe in that world *may* be the most essential function that our lives in this world have to perform. But "*may* be! *may* be!" one now hears the positivist contemptuously exclaim; "what use can a scientific life have for maybes?" Well, I reply, the "scientific" life itself has much to do with maybes, and human life at large has everything to do with them. So far as man stands for anything, and is productive or originative at all, his entire vital function may be said to have to deal with maybes. Not a victory is gained, not a deed of faithfulness or courage

is done, except upon a maybe; not a service, not a sally of generosity, not a scientific exploration or experiment or text-book, that may not be a mistake. It is only by risking our persons from one hour to another that we live at all. And often enough our faith beforehand in an uncertified result *is the only thing that makes the result come true.* Suppose, for instance, that you are climbing a mountain, and have worked yourself into a position from which the only escape is by a terrible leap. Have faith that you can successfully make it, and your feet are nerved to its accomplishment. But mistrust yourself, and think of all the sweet things you have heard the scientists say of *maybes,* and you will hesitate so long that, at last, all unstrung and trembling, and launching yourself in a moment of despair, you roll in the abyss. In such a case (and it belongs to an enormous class), the part of wisdom as well as of courage is to *believe what is in the line of your needs,* for only by such belief is the need fulfilled. Refuse to believe, and you shall indeed be right, for you shall irretrievably perish. But believe, and again you shall be right, for you shall save yourself. You make one or the other of two possible universes true by your trust or mistrust,—both universes having been only *maybes,* in this particular, before you contributed your act.

[9] Now, it appears to me that the question whether life is worth living is subject to conditions logically much like these. It does, indeed, depend on you *the liver.* If you surrender to the nightmare view and crown the evil edifice by your own suicide, you have indeed made a picture totally black. Pessimism, completed by your act, is true beyond a doubt, so far as your world goes. Your mistrust of life has removed whatever worth your own enduring existence might have given to it; and now, throughout the whole sphere of possible influence of that existence, the mistrust has proved itself to have had divining power. But suppose, on the other hand, that instead of giving way to the nightmare view, you cling to it that this world is not the *ultimatum.* Suppose you find yourself a very wellspring, as Wordsworth says, of—

> Zeal and the virtue to exist by faith
> As soldiers live by courage; as, by strength
> Of heart, the sailor fights with roaring seas.

Suppose, however thickly evils crowd upon you, that your unconquerable subjectivity proves to be their match, and that you find a more wonderful joy than any passive pleasure can bring in trusting ever in the larger whole. Have you not now made life worth living on these terms? What sort of a thing would life really be, with your qualities ready for a tussle with it, if it only brought fair weather and gave these higher faculties of yours no scope? Please remember that optimism and pessimism are definitions of the world, and that our own reactions on the world, small as they are in bulk, are integral parts of the whole thing, and necessarily help to determine the definition. They may even be the decisive elements in determining the definition. A large mass can have its unstable equilibrium overturned by the addition of a feather's weight; a long phrase may have its sense reversed by the addition of the three letters *n-o-t*. This life *is* worth living, we can say, *since it is what we make it, from the moral point of view;* and we are determined to make it from that point of view, so far as we have anything to do with it, a success.

[10] Now, in this description of faiths that verify themselves I have assumed that our faith in an invisible order is what inspires those efforts and that patience which make this visible order good for moral men. Our faith in the seen world's goodness (goodness now meaning fitness for successful moral and religious life) has verified itself by leaning on our faith in the unseen world. But will our faith in the unseen world similarly verify itself? Who knows?

[11] Once more it is a case of *maybe;* and once more *maybes* are the essence of the situation. I confess that I do not see why the very existence of an invisible world may not in part depend on the personal response which any one of us may make to the religious appeal. God himself, in short, may draw vital strength and increase of very being from our fidelity. For my own part, I do not know what the sweat and blood and tragedy of this life mean, if they mean anything short of this. If this life be not a real fight, in which something is eternally gained for the universe by success, it is no better than a game of private theatricals from which one may withdraw at will. But it *feels* like a real fight,—as if there were something really wild in the universe which we, with all our idealities and faithfulnesses, are needed to redeem; and first of all to redeem our own hearts from atheisms and fears. For such a half-wild, half-saved universe our nature is adapted. The deepest thing in our nature is this *Binnenleben* (as a German doctor lately has called it), this dumb region of the heart in which we dwell alone with our willingnesses and unwillingnesses, our faiths and fears. As through the cracks and crannies of caverns those waters exude from the earth's bosom which then form the fountain-heads of springs, so in these crepuscular depths of personality the sources of all our outer deeds and decisions take their rise. Here is our deepest organ of communication with the nature of things; and compared with all these concrete movements of our soul all abstract statements and scientific arguments—the veto, for example, which the strict positivist pronounces upon our faith—sound to us like mere chatterings of the teeth. For here possibilities, not finished facts, are the realities with which we have acutely to deal; and to quote my friend William Salter, of the Philadelphia Ethical Society, "as the essence of courage is to stake one's life on a possibility, so the essence of faith is to believe that the possibility exists."

[12] These, then, are my last words to you: Be *not* afraid of life. Believe that life *is* worth living, and your belief will help create the fact. The

"scientific proof" that you are right may not be clear before the day of judgment (or some stage of being which that expression may serve to symbolize) is reached. But the faithful fighters of this hour, or the beings that then and there will represent them, may turn to the faint-hearted, who here decline to go on, with words like those with which Henry IV greeted the tardy Crillon after a great victory had been gained: "Hang yourself, brave Crillon! we fought at Arques, and you were not there."

COMMENT AND QUESTIONS

1. A pragmatic philosophy—the position that the worth of an idea depends on its practical effects—underlies this selection. Summarize in a sentence James' pragmatic argument for faith in an unseen order.
2. James anticipates objections to his thesis that we have a right to assume on trust an unseen spiritual order. By what means does he attempt to counter the objections?
3. How does James qualify *trusting* in his statement about trusting our religious demands?
4. If you have read Thomas Huxley's "Agnosticism and Christianity," you will see that Huxley and James disagree in some ways about religious faith; indeed, paragraph 4 of James' essay is a direct argument against the agnostic position defended by Huxley. What are James' arguments against (a) agnostic neutrality; (b) reliance on scientific evidence alone? Is there an area of agreement between James and Huxley in their attitudes toward religious orthodoxy? Do they agree on any other matters about science and religion?
5. William James is very skillful in the use of persuasive example and analogy. What point is he making by means of each of the following: the man who does not believe the room is getting cold; the dog in the laboratory; the mountain climber faced with a jump over an abyss?
6. Study the sentence structures and rhythms in paragraph 8, and try to determine by what techniques James achieves a vivid, forceful style.
7. How effectively, in your opinion, does James support his idea that life is worth living? What conditions are necessary for a successful life as he defines it?
8. Examine paragraph 11. What concept of God and of the relationship of God and human beings does James appear to hold?
9. In what ways is paragraph 12 an effective ending for James' lecture?

[22] *Albert Einstein:* Science and Religion

ALBERT EINSTEIN (1879–1955), German-born, naturalized-American theoretical physicist, is well known for his theory of relativity and his later generalized theory of gravitation. The following selection, first printed in 1941, has been reprinted as Part II of a longer essay "Science and Religion" in *Out of My Later Years,* a collection of Einstein's essays and addresses published in 1950.

[1] It would not be difficult to come to an agreement as to what we understand by science. Science is the century-old endeavor to bring together by means of systematic thought the perceptible phenomena of this world into as thoroughgoing an association as possible. To put it boldly, it is the attempt at the posterior reconstruction of existence by the process of conceptualization. But when asking myself what religion is, I cannot think of the answer so easily. And even after finding an answer which may satisfy me at this particular moment, I still remain convinced that I can never under any circumstances bring together, even to a slight extent, all those who have given this question serious consideration.

[2] At first, then, instead of asking what religion is, I should prefer to ask what characterizes the aspirations of a person who gives me the impression of being religious: a person who is religiously enlightened appears to me to be one who has, to the best of his ability, liberated himself from the fetters of his selfish desires and is preoccupied with thoughts, feelings, and aspirations to which he clings because of their super-personal value. It seems to me that what is important is the force of this super-personal content and the depth of the conviction concerning its overpowering meaningfulness, regardless of whether any attempt is made to unite this content with a Divine Being, for otherwise it would not be possible to count Buddha and Spinoza as religious personalities. Accordingly, a religious person is devout in the sense that he has no doubt of the significance and loftiness of those super-personal objects and goals which neither require nor are capable of rational foundation. They exist with the same necessity and matter-of-factness as he himself. In this sense religion is the age-old endeavor of mankind to become clearly and completely conscious of these values and goals and constantly to strengthen and extend their effects. If one conceives of religion and science according to these definitions then a conflict between them appears impossible. For

science can only ascertain what *is*, but not what should be, and outside of its domain value judgments of all kinds remain necessary. Religion, on the other hand, deals only with evaluations of human thought and action; it cannot justifiably speak of facts and relationships between facts. According to this interpretation, the well-known conflicts between religion and science in the past must all be ascribed to a misapprehension of the situation which has been described.

[3] For example, a conflict arises when a religious community insists on the absolute truthfulness of all statements recorded in the Bible. This means an intervention on the part of religion into the sphere of science; this is where the struggle of the Church against the doctrines of Galileo and Darwin belongs. On the other hand, representatives of science have often made an attempt to arrive at fundamental judgments with respect to values and ends on the basis of scientific method, and in this way have set themselves in opposition to religion. These conflicts have all sprung from fatal errors.

[4] Now, even though the realms of religion and science in themselves are clearly marked off from each other, nevertheless there exist between the two, strong reciprocal relationships and dependencies. Though religion may be that which determines the goal, it has, nevertheless, learned from science, in the broadest sense, what means will contribute to the attainment of the goals it has set up. But science can only be created by those who are thoroughly imbued with the aspiration towards truth and understanding. This source of feeling, however, springs from the sphere of religion. To this there also belongs the faith in the possibility that the regulations valid for the world of existence are rational, that is comprehensible to reason. I cannot conceive of a genuine scientist without that profound faith. The situation may be expressed by an image: science without religion is lame, religion without science is blind.

[5] Though I have asserted above, that in truth a legitimate conflict between religion and science cannot exist, I must nevertheless qualify this assertion once again on an essential point, with reference to the actual content of historical religions. This qualification has to do with the concept of God. During the youthful period of mankind's spiritual evolution, human fantasy created gods in man's own image, who, by the operations of their will were supposed to determine, or at any rate to influence, the phenomenal world. Man sought to alter the disposition of these gods in his own favor by means of magic and prayer. The idea of God in the religions taught at present is a sublimation of that old conception of the gods. Its anthropomorphic character is shown, for instance, by the fact that men appeal to the Divine Being in prayers and plead for the fulfilment of their wishes.

[6] Nobody, certainly, will deny that the idea of the existence of an omnipotent, just and omnibeneficent personal God is able to accord man

solace, help, and guidance; also, by virtue of its simplicity the concept is accessible to the most undeveloped mind. But, on the other hand, there are decisive weaknesses attached to this idea in itself, which have been painfully felt since the beginning of history. That is, if this Being is omnipotent, then every occurrence, including every human action, every human thought, and every human feeling and aspiration is also His work; how is it possible to think of holding men responsible for their deeds and thoughts before such an Almighty Being? In giving out punishment and rewards He would to a certain extent be passing judgment on himself. How can this be combined with the goodness and righteousness ascribed to Him?

[7] The main source of the present-day conflicts between the spheres of religion and of science lies in this concept of a personal God. It is the aim of science to establish general rules which determine the reciprocal connection of objects and events in time and space. For these rules, or laws of nature, absolutely general validity is required—not proven. It is mainly a program, and faith in the possibility of its accomplishment in principle is only founded on partial success. But hardly anyone could be found who would deny these partial successes and ascribe them to human self-deception. The fact that on the basis of such laws we are able to predict the temporal behavior of phenomena in certain domains with great precision and certainty, is deeply embedded in the consciousness of the modern man, even though he may have grasped very little of the contents of those laws. He need only consider that planetary courses within the solar system may be calculated in advance with great exactitude on the basis of a limited number of simple laws. In a similar way, though not with the same precision, it is possible to calculate in advance the mode of operation of an electric motor, a transmission system, or of a wireless apparatus, even when dealing with a novel development.

[8] To be sure, when the number of factors coming into play in a phenomenological complex is too large, scientific method in most cases fails us. One need only think of the weather, in which case prediction even for a few days ahead is impossible. Nevertheless no one doubts that we are confronted with a causal connection whose causal components are in the main known to us. Occurrences in this domain are beyond the reach of exact prediction because of the variety of factors in operation, not because of any lack of order in nature.

[9] We have penetrated far less deeply into the regularities obtaining within the realm of living things, but deeply enough nevertheless to sense at least the rule of fixed necessity. One need only think of the systematic order in heredity, and in the effect of poisons, as for instance alcohol on the behavior of organic beings. What is still lacking here is a grasp of connections of profound generality, but not a knowledge of order in itself.

[10] The more a man is imbued with the ordered regularity of all

events, the firmer becomes his conviction that there is no room left by the side of this ordered regularity for causes of a different nature. For him neither the rule of human nor the rule of Divine Will exists as an independent cause of natural events. To be sure, the doctrine of a personal God interfering with natural events could never be *refuted*, in the real sense, by science, for this doctrine can always take refuge in those domains in which scientific knowledge has not yet been able to set foot.

[11] But I am persuaded that such behavior on the part of the representatives of religion would not only be unworthy but also fatal. For a doctrine which is able to maintain itself not in clear light but only in the dark, will of necessity lose its effect on mankind, with incalculable harm to human progress. In their struggle for the ethical good, teachers of religion must have the stature to give up the doctrine of a personal God, that is, give up that source of fear and hope which in the past placed such vast power in the hands of priests. In their labors they will have to avail themselves of those forces which are capable of cultivating the Good, the True, and the Beautiful in humanity itself. This is, to be sure, a more difficult but an incomparably more worthy task. After religious teachers accomplish the refining process indicated, they will surely recognize with joy that true religion has been ennobled and made more profound by scientific knowledge.

[12] If it is one of the goals of religion to liberate mankind as far as possible from the bondage of egocentric cravings, desires, and fears, scientific reasoning can aid religion in yet another sense. Although it is true that it is the goal of science to discover rules which permit the association and foretelling of facts, this is not its only aim. It also seeks to reduce the connections discovered to the smallest possible number of mutually independent conceptual elements. It is in this striving after the rational unification of the manifold that it encounters its greatest successes, even though it is precisely this attempt which causes it to run the greatest risk of falling a prey to illusions. But whoever has undergone the intense experience of successful advances made in this domain, is moved by profound reverence for the rationality made manifest in existence. By way of the understanding he achieves a far-reaching emancipation from the shackles of personal hopes and desires, and thereby attains that humble attitude of mind towards the grandeur of reason incarnate in existence, which, in its profoundest depths, is inaccessible to man. This attitude, however, appears to me to be religious, in the highest sense of the word. And so it seems to me that science not only purifies the religious impulse of the dross of its anthropomorphism, but also contributes to a religious spiritualization of our understanding of life.

[13] The further the spiritual evolution of mankind advances, the more certain it seems to me that the path to genuine religiosity does not lie through the fear of life, and the fear of death, and blind faith, but through

striving after rational knowledge. In this sense I believe that the priest must become a teacher if he wishes to do justice to his lofty educational mission.

COMMENT AND QUESTIONS

1. A religiously enlightened person, Einstein says, is one preoccupied with superpersonal goals and values. What examples can you supply of such superpersonal goals and values?
2. To what extent do you agree or disagree with Einstein's definitions of "a religious person" and "religion"?
3. In paragraph 3 Einstein gives some examples of past conflicts between science and religion—conflicts caused by the intervention of one into the sphere of the other. What further examples can you give of such intervention and conflict?
4. Examine the image at the end of paragraph 4. Would there be a loss if the terms were reversed so that the statement read: science without religion is blind, religion without science is lame?
5. Explain clearly what Einstein means by an anthropomorphic personal God and why he believes that this concept of God is incompatible with scientific knowledge.
6. State as clearly as you can what you think Einstein's intentions were in writing this essay.
7. We have said earlier that the ability to grasp the essentials of a piece of writing and to summarize it in precise, packed language is very useful to a college student. Read carefully the two summaries of Einstein's essay printed below; each was written on a quiz in class, in fifteen minutes, by an able student.

[1] Science is the attempt to associate and explain the phenomena of the world; religion is harder to define. The religiously enlightened man is concerned with and convinced of the importance of super-personal thoughts and goals which neither have nor need a rational basis. The understanding of these thoughts and the achievement of these goals is, then, the purpose of religion.

Viewed thus, science, which deals with what *is*, and religion, which deals with what *should be*, cannot conflict except through the overstepping of their limits. This occurs when religion tries to assume full truth for the Bible and conflicts with, for instance, Darwin, or when science attempts value judgments.

Although religion and science are strictly divided, they are interdependent. Religion needs science to point the way to the achievement of its goals; science needs the desire for truth and the faith in future success that religion gives.

In spite of theoretical absence of conflict, the actual content of present religions presents a great conflict in the doctrine of a personal God, which developed from the ancient conception of one or many almighty beings controlling the world. This idea gives comfort and aid and is easily conceived, but it is logically weak. How can God control the thoughts and actions of all beings, yet hold them responsible for these very thoughts and actions? He is judging Himself.

As science has pursued the determining of natural laws (rules interrelating objects and events in time and space), it has failed only through number and variety of factors, not through lack of order in nature. This increasingly manifest logic rules out control of the world by any other factor, human or Divine. Religious teachers must courageously abandon the powerful doctrine of a personal God, utilizing instead the forces for good extant within humanity itself.

Since the purpose of science is also to reduce natural laws to a few basic concepts, it helps religion in another way, for such achievement brings profound respect for the logic of existence and a resulting uplift to the super-personal thoughts and ideals which are the goal of religion.

Science, then, not only purifies religion by disproving the false concept of a personal God, but also contributes to religious spiritualization in the understanding of the phenomenal world. The road to true religion lies not through blind faith, but through science, the search for rational knowledge.

[2] Science deals with what is—the facts of the physical world and their relationship. Religion is concerned with what should be—super-personal ideals and values. Defined this way, science and religion should not conflict, but should be mutually helpful—religion providing the goals, and science the way of attaining the religious values. They conflict only when one wrongly intrudes into the other's proper realm. At present such conflict occurs when religious groups insist on the idea of a personal anthropomorphic God who intervenes and changes natural law in answer to prayer. Scientific knowledge reveals a great ordered regularity in the universe which allows no room for such independent causes or interference. Religious leaders should therefore give up the idea of the personal God and should work, with the aid of science, to teach reverence for the great rationality manifest in existence, and to cultivate the True, Good and Beautiful in humanity itself.

Both of these summaries are good. Which seems to you better, and why; or do you think that they have different virtues and weaknesses?

8. It is also useful to a student to be able to phrase very briefly the central ideas of a piece of writing. Write a concentrated statement of no more than a sentence or two which does this for Einstein's essay.

9. If you have read the selections preceding this one, compare and contrast the attitudes toward science and religion of Thomas Huxley, James, and Einstein.

[23] *Jean-Paul Sartre*: Existentialism

THE FOLLOWING discussion of existentialism, originally a lecture, is taken from *Existentialism and Humanism*, published in 1948. Jean-Paul Sartre (1905–), French novelist, short story writer, playwright, and philosopher, is a leading spokesman for the philosophy which he is explaining and defending in this selection. Assuming a universe without purpose, in which the individual alone determines what he will be, Sartre considers existentialism a philosophy not of pessimism and passivity, but of optimism and action. Among Sartre's other works are *Being and Nothingness, The Flies, No Exit, Nausea*, and *The Words*.

[1] What, then, is this that we call existentialism? Most of those who are making use of this word would be highly confused if required to explain its meaning. For since it has become fashionable, people cheerfully declare that this musician or that painter is "existentialist." A columnist in *Clartés* signs himself "The Existentialist," and, indeed, the word is now so loosely applied to so many things that it no longer means anything at all. It would appear that, for the lack of any novel doctrine such as that of surrealism, all those who are eager to join in the latest scandal or movement now seize upon this philosophy in which, however, they can find nothing to their purpose. For in truth this is of all teachings the least scandalous and the most austere: it is intended strictly for technicians and philosophers. All the same, it can easily be defined.

[2] The question is only complicated because there are two kinds of existentialists. There are, on the one hand, the Christians, amongst whom I shall name Jaspers and Gabriel Marcel, both professed Catholics; and on the other the existential atheists, amongst whom we must place Heidegger as well as the French existentialists and myself. What they have in common is simply the fact that they believe that *existence* comes before *essence*—or, if you will, that we must begin from the subjective. What exactly do we mean by that?

[3] If one considers an article of manufacture—as, for example, a book or a paper-knife—one sees that it has been made by an artisan who had a conception of it; and he has paid attention, equally, to the conception of a paper-knife and to the pre-existent technique of production which is a part of that conception and is, at bottom, a formula. Thus the paper-

This selection was translated by Philip Mairet.

knife is at the same time an article producible in a certain manner and one which, on the other hand, serves a definite purpose, for one cannot suppose that a man would produce a paper-knife without knowing what it was for. Let us say, then, of the paper-knife that its essence—that is to say the sum of the formulae and the qualities which made its production and its definition possible—precedes its existence. The presence of such-and-such a paper-knife or book is thus determined before my eyes. Here, then, we are viewing the world from a technical standpoint, and we can say that production precedes existence.

[4] When we think of God as the creator, we are thinking of him, most of the time, as a supernal artisan. Whatever doctrine we may be considering, whether it be a doctrine like that of Descartes, or of Leibnitz himself, we always imply that the will follows, more or less, from the understanding or at least accompanies it, so that when God creates he knows precisely what he is creating. Thus, the conception of man in the mind of God is comparable to that of the paper-knife in the mind of the artisan: God makes man according to a procedure and a conception, exactly as the artisan manufactures a paper-knife, following a definition and a formula. Thus each individual man is the realization of a certain conception which dwells in the divine understanding. In the philosophic atheism of the eighteenth century, the notion of God is suppressed, but not, for all that, the idea that essence is prior to existence; something of that idea we still find everywhere, in Diderot, in Voltaire and even in Kant. Man possesses a human nature; that "human nature," which is the conception of human being, is found in every man; which means that each man is a particular example of a universal conception, the conception of Man. In Kant, this universality goes so far that the wild man of the woods, man in the state of nature and the bourgeois are all contained in the same definition and have the same fundamental qualities. Here again, the essence of man precedes that historic existence which we confront in experience.

[5] Atheistic existentialism, of which I am a representative, declares with greater consistency that if God does not exist there is at least one being whose existence comes before its essence, a being which exists before it can be defined by any conception of it. That being is man or, as Heidegger has it, the human reality. What do we mean by saying that existence precedes essence? We mean that man first of all exists, encounters himself, surges up in the world—and defines himself afterwards. If man as the existentialist sees him is not definable, it is because to begin with he is nothing. He will not be anything until later, and then he will be what he makes of himself. Thus, there is no human nature, because there is no God to have a conception of it. Man simply is. Not that he is simply what he conceives himself to be, but he is what he wills, and as he conceives himself after already existing—as he wills to be after

that leap towards existence. Man is nothing else but that which he makes of himself. That is the first principle of existentialism. And this is what people call its "subjectivity," using the word as a reproach against us. But what do we mean to say by this, but that man is of a greater dignity than a stone or a table? For we mean to say that man primarily exists— that man is, before all else, something which propels itself towards a future and is aware that it is doing so. Man is, indeed, a project which possesses a subjective life, instead of being a kind of moss, or a fungus or a cauliflower. Before that projection of the self nothing exists; not even in the heaven of intelligence: man will only attain existence when he is what he purposes to be. Not, however, what he may wish to be. For what we usually understand by wishing or willing is a conscious decision taken— much more often than not—after we have made ourselves what we are. I may wish to join a party, to write a book or to marry—but in such a case what is usually called my will is probably a manifestation of a prior and more spontaneous decision. If, however, it is true that existence is prior to essence, man is responsible for what he is. Thus, the first effect of existentialism is that it puts every man in possession of himself as he is, and places the entire responsibility for his existence squarely upon his own shoulders. And, when we say that man is responsible for himself, we do not mean that he is responsible only for his own individuality, but that he is responsible for all men. The word "subjectivism" is to be understood in two senses, and our adversaries play upon only one of them. Subjectivism means, on the one hand, the freedom of the individual subject and, on the other, that man cannot pass beyond human subjectivity. It is the latter which is the deeper meaning of existentialism. When we say that man chooses himself, we do mean that every one of us must choose himself; but by that we also mean that in choosing for himself he chooses for all men. For in effect, of all the actions a man may take in order to create himself as he wills to be, there is not one which is not creative, at the same time, of an image of man such as he believes he ought to be. To choose between this or that is at the same time to affirm the value of that which is chosen; for we are unable ever to choose the worse. What we choose is always the better; and nothing can be better for us unless it is better for all. If, moreover, existence precedes essence and we will to exist at the same time as we fashion our image, that image is valid for all and for the entire epoch in which we find ourselves. Our responsibility is thus much greater than we had supposed, for it concerns mankind as a whole. If I am a worker, for instance, I may choose to join a Christian rather than a Communist trade union. And if, by that membership, I choose to signify that resignation is, after all, the attitude that best becomes a man, that man's kingdom is not upon this earth, I do not commit myself alone to that view. Resignation is my will for everyone, and my action is, in consequence, a commitment on behalf of all mankind. Or if, to take a more personal case, I decide to marry and to have children, even though this decision proceeds simply from my situation, from my passion or my desire, I am thereby committing not only myself, but humanity as a whole, to the practice of monogamy. I am thus responsible for myself and for all men, and I am creating a certain image of man as I would have him to be. In fashioning myself I fashion man.

[6] This may enable us to understand what is meant by such terms—perhaps a little grandiloquent—as anguish, abandonment and despair. As you will soon see, it is very simple. First, what do we mean by anguish? The existentialist frankly states that man is in anguish. His meaning is as follows—When a man commits himself to anything, fully realizing that he is not only choosing what he will be, but is thereby at the same time a legislator deciding for the whole of mankind—in such a moment a man cannot escape from the sense of complete and profound responsibility. There are many, indeed, who show no such anxiety. But we affirm that they are merely disguising their anguish or are in flight from it. Certainly, many people think that in what they are doing they commit no one but themselves to anything: and if you ask them, "What would happen if everyone did so?" they shrug their shoulders and reply, "Everyone does not do so." But in truth, one ought always to ask oneself what would happen if everyone did as one is doing; nor can one escape from that disturbing thought except by a kind of self-deception. The man who lies in self-excuse, by saying "Everyone will not do it" must be ill at ease in his conscience, for the act of lying implies the universal value which it denies. By its very disguise his anguish reveals itself. This is the anguish that Kierkegaard called "the anguish of Abraham." You know the story: An angel commanded Abraham to sacrifice his son: and obedience was obligatory, if it really was an angel who had appeared and said, "Thou, Abraham, shalt sacrifice thy son." But anyone in such a case would wonder, first, whether it was indeed an angel and secondly, whether I am really Abraham. Where are the proofs? A certain mad woman who suffered from hallucinations said that people were telephoning to her, and giving her orders. The doctor asked, "But who is it that speaks to you?" She replied: "He says it is God." And what, indeed, could prove to her that it was God? If an angel appears to me, what is the proof that it is an angel; or, if I hear voices, who can prove that they proceed from heaven and not from hell, or from my own subconsciousness or some pathological condition? Who can prove that they are really addressed to me?

[7] Who, then, can prove that I am the proper person to impose, by my own choice, my conception of man upon mankind? I shall never find any proof whatever; there will be no sign to convince me of it. If a voice speaks to me, it is still I myself who must decide whether the voice is or is not that of an angel. If I regard a certain course of action as good, it is

only I who choose to say that it is good and not bad. There is nothing to show that I am Abraham: nevertheless I also am obliged at every instant to peform actions which are examples. Everything happens to every man as though the whole human race had its eyes fixed upon what he is doing and regulated its conduct accordingly. So every man ought to say, "Am I really a man who has the right to act in such a manner that humanity regulates itself by what I do." If a man does not say that, he is dissembling his anguish. Clearly, the anguish with which we are concerned here is not one that could lead to quietism or inaction. It is anguish pure and simple, of the kind well known to all those who have borne responsibilities. When, for instance, a military leader takes upon himself the responsibility for an attack and sends a number of men to their death, he chooses to do it and at bottom he alone chooses. No doubt he acts under a higher command, but its orders, which are more general, require interpretation by him and upon that interpretation depends the life of ten, fourteen or twenty men. In making the decision, he cannot but feel a certain anguish. All leaders know that anguish. It does not prevent their acting; on the contrary it is the very condition of their action, for the action presupposes that there is a plurality of possibilities, and in choosing one of these, they realize that it has value only because it is chosen. Now it is anguish of that kind which existentialism describes, and moreover, as we shall see, makes explicit through direct responsibility towards other men who are concerned. Far from being a screen which could separate us from action, it is a condition of action itself.

[8] And when we speak of "abandonment"—a favorite word of Heidegger—we only mean to say that God does not exist, and that it is necessary to draw the consequences of his absence right to the end. The existentialist is strongly opposed to a certain type of secular moralism which seeks to suppress God at the least possible expense. Towards 1880, when the French professors endeavored to formulate a secular morality, they said something like this:—God is a useless and costly hypothesis, so we will do without it. However, if we are to have morality, a society and a law-abiding world, it is essential that certain values should be taken seriously; they must have an *à priori* existence ascribed to them. It must be considered obligatory *à priori* to be honest, not to lie, not to beat one's wife, to bring up children and so forth; so we are going to do a little work on this subject, which will enable us to show that these values exist all the same, inscribed in an intelligible heaven although, of course, there is no God. In other words—and this is, I believe, the purport of all that we in France call radicalism—nothing will be changed if God does not exist; we shall rediscover the same norms of honesty, progress and humanity, and we shall have disposed of God as an out-of-date hypothesis which will die away quietly of itself. The existentialist, on the contrary, finds it extremely embarrassing that God does not exist, for there disappears with

Him all possibility of finding values in an intelligible heaven. There can no longer be any good *à priori*, since there is no infinite and perfect consciousness to think it. It is nowhere written that "the good" exists, that one must be honest or must not lie, since we are now upon the plane where there are only men. Dostoevsky once wrote "If God did not exist, everything would be permitted"; and that, for existentialism, is the starting point. Everything is indeed permitted if God does not exist, and man is in consequence forlorn, for he cannot find anything to depend upon either within or outside himself. He discovers forthwith, that he is without excuse. For if indeed existence precedes essence, one will never be able to explain one's action by reference to a given and specific human nature; in other words, there is no determinism—man is free, man *is* freedom. Nor, on the other hand, if God does not exist, are we provided with any values or commands that could legitimize our behavior. Thus we have neither behind us, nor before us in a luminous realm of values, any means of justification or excuse. We are left alone, without excuse. That is what I mean when I say that man is condemned to be free. Condemned, because he did not create himself, yet is nevertheless at liberty, and from the moment that he is thrown into this world he is responsible for everything he does. The existentialist does not believe in the power of passion. He will never regard a grand passion as a destructive torrent upon which a man is swept into certain actions as by fate, and which, therefore, is an excuse for them. He thinks that man is responsible for his passion. Neither will an existentialist think that a man can find help through some sign being vouchsafed upon earth for his orientation: for he thinks that the man himself interprets the sign as he chooses. He thinks that every man, without any support or help whatever, is condemned at every instant to invent man. As Ponge has written in a very fine article, "Man is the future of man." That is exactly true. Only, if one took this to mean that the future is laid up in Heaven, that God knows what it is, it would be false, for then it would no longer even be a future. If, however, it means that, whatever man may now appear to be, there is a future to be fashioned, a virgin future that awaits him—then it is a true saying. But in the present one is forsaken.

[9] As an example by which you may the better understand this state of abandonment, I will refer to the case of a pupil of mine, who sought me out in the following circumstances. His father was quarrelling with his mother and was also inclined to be a "collaborator";[1] his elder brother had been killed in the German offensive of 1940 and this young man, with a sentiment somewhat primitive but generous, burned to avenge him. His mother was living alone with him, deeply afflicted by the semi-treason of his father and by the death of her eldest son, and her one consolation

---

[1] A Frenchman who cooperated with the Germans in World War II.

was in this young man. But he, at this moment, had the choice between going to England to join the Free French Forces or of staying near his mother and helping her to live. He fully realized that this woman lived only for him and that his disappearance—or perhaps his death—would plunge her into despair. He also realized that, concretely and in fact, every action he performed on his mother's behalf would be sure of effect in the sense of aiding her to live, whereas anything he did in order to go and fight would be an ambiguous action which might vanish like water into sand and serve no purpose. For instance, to set out for England he would have to wait indefinitely in a Spanish camp on the way through Spain; or, on arriving in England or in Algiers he might be put into an office to fill up forms. Consequently, he found himself confronted by two very different modes of action; the one concrete, immediate, but directed towards only one individual; and the other an action addressed to an end infinitely greater, a national collectivity, but for that very reason ambiguous—and it might be frustrated on the way. At the same time, he was hesitating between two kinds of morality; on the one side the morality of sympathy, of personal devotion and, on the other side, a morality of wider scope but of more debatable validity. He had to choose between those two. What could help him to choose? Could the Christian doctrine? No. Christian doctrine says: Act with charity, love your neighbour, deny yourself for others, choose the way which is hardest, and so forth. But which is the harder road? To whom does one owe the more brotherly love, the patriot or the mother? Which is the more useful aim, the general one of fighting in and for the whole community, or the precise aim of helping one particular person to live? Who can give an answer to that *à priori*? No one. Nor is it given in any ethical scripture. The Kantian ethic says, Never regard another as a means, but always as an end. Very well; if I remain with my mother, I shall be regarding her as the end and not as a means: but by the same token I am in danger of treating as means those who are fighting on my behalf; and the converse is also true, that if I go to the aid of the combatants I shall be treating them as the end at the risk of treating my mother as a means.

[10] If values are uncertain, if they are still too abstract to determine the particular, concrete case under consideration, nothing remains but to trust in our instincts. That is what this young man tried to do; and when I saw him he said, "In the end, it is feeling that counts; the direction in which it is really pushing me is the one I ought to choose. If I feel that I love my mother enough to sacrifice everything else for her—my will to be avenged, all my longings for action and adventure—then I stay with her. If, on the contrary, I feel that my love for her is not enough, I go." But how does one estimate the strength of a feeling? The value of his feeling for his mother was determined precisely by the fact that he was standing by her. I may say that I love a certain friend enough to sacrifice such or

such a sum of money for him, but I cannot prove that unless I have done it. I may say, "I love my mother enough to remain with her," if actually I have remained with her. I can only estimate the strength of this affection if I have performed an action by which it is defined and ratified. But if I then appeal to this affection to justify my action, I find myself drawn into a vicious circle.

[11] Moreover, as Gide has very well said, a sentiment which is play-acting and one which is vital are two things that are hardly distinguishable one from another. To decide that I love my mother by staying beside her, and to play a comedy the upshot of which is that I do so—these are nearly the same thing. In other words, feeling is formed by the deeds that one does; therefore I cannot consult it as a guide to action. And that is to say that I can neither seek within myself for an authentic impulse to action, nor can I expect, from some ethic, formulae that will enable me to act. You may say that the youth did, at least, go to a professor to ask for advice. But if you seek counsel—from a priest, for example—you have selected that priest; and at bottom you already knew, more or less, what he would advise. In other words, to choose an adviser is nevertheless to commit oneself by that choice. If you are a Christian, you will say, Consult a priest; but there are collaborationists, priests who are resisters and priests who wait for the tide to turn: which will you choose? Had this young man chosen a priest of the resistance, or one of the collaboration, he would have decided beforehand the kind of advice he was to receive. Similarly, in coming to me, he knew what advice I should give him, and I had but one reply to make. You are free, therefore choose—that is to say, invent. No rule of general morality can show you what you ought to do: no signs are vouchsafed in this world. The Catholics will reply, "Oh, but they are!" Very well; still, it is I myself, in every case, who have to interpret the signs. While I was imprisoned,[2] I made the acquaintance of a somewhat remarkable man, a Jesuit, who had become a member of that order in the following manner. In his life he had suffered a succession of rather servere setbacks. His father had died when he was a child, leaving him in poverty, and he had been awarded a free scholarship in a religious institution, where he had been made continually to feel that he was accepted for charity's sake, and, in consequence, he had been denied several of those distinctions and honors which gratify children. Later, about the age of eighteen, he came to grief in a sentimental affair; and finally, at twenty-two—this was a trifle in itself, but it was the last drop that overflowed his cup—he failed in his military examination. This young man, then, could regard himself as a total failure: it was a sign —but a sign of what? He might have taken refuge in bitterness or despair. But he took it—very cleverly for him—as a sign that he was not intended

---

[2] As a German prisoner of war in World War II.

for secular successes, and that only the attainments of religion, those of sanctity and of faith, were accessible to him. He interpreted his record as a message from God, and became a member of the Order. Who can doubt but that this decision as to the meaning of the sign was his, and his alone? One could have drawn quite different conclusions from such a series of reverses—as, for example, that he had better become a carpenter or a revolutionary. For the decipherment of the sign, however, he bears the entire responsibility. That is what "abandonment" implies, that we ourselves decide our being. And with this abandonment goes anguish.

[12] As for "despair," the meaning of this expression is extremely simple. It merely means that we limit ourselves to a reliance upon that which is within our wills, or within the sum of the probabilities which render our action feasible. Whenever one wills anything, there are always these elements of probability. If I am counting upon a visit from a friend, who may be coming by train or by tram, I presuppose that the train will arrive at the appointed time, or that the tram will not be derailed. I remain in the realm of possibilities; but one does not rely upon any possibilities beyond those that are strictly concerned in one's action. Beyond the point at which the possibilities under consideration cease to affect my action, I ought to disinterest myself. For there is no God and no prevenient design, which can adapt the world and all its possibilities to my will. When Descartes said, "Conquer yourself rather than the world," what he meant was, at bottom, the same—that we should act without hope.

[13] Marxists, to whom I have said this, have answered: "Your action is limited, obviously, by your death; but you can rely upon the help of others. That is, you can count both upon what the others are doing to help you elsewhere, as in China and in Russia, and upon what they will do later, after your death, to take up your action and carry it forward to its final accomplishment which will be the revolution. Moreover you must rely upon this; not to do so is immoral." To this I rejoin, first, that I shall always count upon my comrades-in-arms in the struggle, in so far as they are committed, as I am, to a definite, common cause; and in the unity of a party or a group which I can more or less control—that is, in which I am enrolled as a militant and whose movements at every moment are known to me. In that respect, to rely upon the unity and the will of the party is exactly like my reckoning that the train will run to time or that the tram will not be derailed. But I cannot count upon men whom I do not know, I cannot base my confidence upon human goodness or upon man's interest in the good of society, seeing that man is free and that there is no human nature which I can take as foundational. I do not know where the Russian revolution will lead. I can admire it and take it as an example in so far as it is evident, today, that the proletariat plays a part in Russia which it has attained in no other nation. But I cannot affirm that this will necessarily lead to the triumph of the proletariat: I must confine

myself to what I can see. Nor can I be sure that comrades-in-arms will take up my work after my death and carry it to the maximum perfection, seeing that those men are free agents and will freely decide, tomorrow, what man is then to be. Tomorrow, after my death, some men may decide to establish Fascism, and the others may be so cowardly or so slack as to let them do so. If so, Fascism will then be the truth of man, and so much the worse for us. In reality, things will be such as men have decided they shall be. Does that mean that I should abandon myself to quietism? No. First I ought to commit myself and then act my commitment, according to the time-honored formula that "one need not hope in order to undertake one's work." Nor does this mean that I should not belong to a party, but only that I should be without illusion and that I should do what I can. For instance, if I ask myself "Will the social ideal as such, ever become a reality?" I cannot tell, I only know that whatever may be in my power to make it so, I shall do; beyond that, I can count upon nothing.

[14] Quietism is the attitude of people who say, "let others do what I cannot do." The doctrine I am presenting before you is precisely the opposite of this, since it declares that there is no reality except in action. It goes further, indeed, and adds, "Man is nothing else but what he purposes, he exists only in so far as he realizes himself, he is therefore nothing else but the sum of his actions, nothing else but what his life is." Hence we can well understand why some people are horrified by our teaching. For many have but one resource to sustain them in their misery, and that is to think, "Circumstances have been against me, I was worthy to be something much better than I have been. I admit I have never had a great love or a great friendship; but that is because I never met a man or a woman who were worthy of it; if I have not written any very good books, it is because I had not the leisure to do so; or, if I have had no children to whom I could devote myself it is because I did not find the man I could have lived with. So there remains within me a wide range of abilities, inclinations and potentialities, unused but perfectly viable, which endow me with a worthiness that could never be inferred from the mere history of my actions." But in reality and for the existentialist, there is no love apart from the deeds of love; no potentiality of love other than that which is manifested in loving; there is no genius other than that which is expressed in works of art. The genius of Proust is the totality of the works of Proust; the genius of Racine is the series of his tragedies, outside of which there is nothing. Why should we attribute to Racine the capacity to write yet another tragedy when that is precisely what he did not write? In life, a man commits himself, draws his own portrait and there is nothing but that portrait. No doubt this thought may seem comfortless to one who has not made a success of his life. On the other hand, it puts everyone in a position to understand that reality alone is reliable; that dreams, expectations and hopes serve to define a man only

as deceptive dreams, abortive hopes, expectations unfulfilled; that is to say, they define him negatively, not positively. Nevertheless, when one says, "You are nothing else but what you live," it does not imply that an artist is to be judged solely by his works of art, for a thousand other things contribute no less to his definition as a man. What we mean to say is that a man is no other than a series of undertakings, that he is the sum, the organization, the set of relations that constitute these undertakings.

COMMENT AND QUESTIONS

1. Explain clearly the following existentialist beliefs: (a) that existence precedes essence; (b) that man makes himself; (c) that man is responsible for all men.
2. In paragraph 2 and particularly in paragraph 5, Sartre equates the idea that "existence precedes essence" with the idea of "subjectivity." What does the term *subjectivity* mean in this context?
3. Sartre says in paragraph 5, "To choose between this or that is at the same time to affirm the value of that which is chosen; for we are unable ever to choose the worse." Do you agree or disagree with the logic of this statement? Explain.
4. When Sartre says (at the end of paragraph 5), "In fashioning myself I fashion man" and later (in paragraph 7), "I also am obliged at every instant to perform actions which are examples," is he assuming that there is one truth or one good way of life for all men, or is his meaning different? Explain.
5. What is the relevance of the example of the mad woman, at the end of paragraph 6, to the point Sartre is making?
6. How do *anguish, abandonment,* and *despair,* as Sartre uses the words, differ in meaning? Could one term be used to convey all three meanings? Explain.
7. What does Sartre mean by saying that man is condemned to be free?
8. Explain the statement that "there is no reality except in action."
9. In what sense is existentialism an optimistic philosophy? In what sense does it dignify man?
10. If you have read the selections from Epictetus and Marcus Aurelius (page 186), do you find points of agreement between the Stoic philosophers and Sartre?
11. If you have read the selections from Plato printed in this book, what contrasts do you see between the Socratic or Platonic view and the existentialist view of man? Are there any parallels or similarities between the two philosophies?

HUMAN NATURE
AND THE HUMAN
SITUATION

[24] *John Dewey*: Does Human Nature Change?

JOHN DEWEY (1859–1952) was an American philosopher and educator, a follower of William James, and the founder of the progressive-school movement. "Does Human Nature Change?" is a selection from *Problems of Men*, published in 1946.

[1] I have come to the conclusion that those who give different answers to the question I have asked in the title of this article are talking about different things. This statement in itself, however, is too easy a way out of the problem to be satisfactory. For there is a real problem, and so far as the question is a practical one instead of an academic one, I think the proper answer is that human nature *does* change.

[2] By the practical side of the question, I mean the question whether or not important, almost fundamental, changes in the ways of human belief and action have taken place and are capable of still taking place. But to put this question in its proper perspective, we have first to recognize the sense in which human nature does not change. I do not think it can be shown that the innate needs of men have changed since man became man or that there is any evidence that they will change as long as man is on the earth.

[3] By "needs" I mean the inherent demands that men make because of

their constitution. Needs for food and drink and for moving about, for example, are so much a part of our being that we cannot imagine any condition under which they would cease to be. There are other things not so directly physical that seem to me equally engrained in human nature. I would mention as examples the need for some kind of companionship; the need for exhibiting energy, for bringing one's powers to bear upon surrounding conditions; the need for both coöperation with and emulation of one's fellows for mutual aid and combat alike; the need for some sort of aesthetic expression and satisfaction; the need to lead and to follow, etc.

[4] Whether my particular examples are well chosen or not does not matter so much as does recognition of the fact that there are some tendencies so integral a part of human nature that the latter would not be human nature if they changed. These tendencies used to be called instincts. Psychologists are now more chary of using that word than they used to be. But the word by which the tendencies are called does not matter much in comparison to the fact that human nature has its own constitution.

[5] Where we are likely to go wrong, after the fact is recognized that there is something unchangeable in the structure of human nature, is the inference we draw from it. We suppose that the manifestation of these needs is also unalterable. We suppose that the manifestations we have got used to are as natural and as unalterable as are the needs from which they spring.

[6] The need for food is so imperative that we call the persons insane who persistently refuse to take nourishment. But what kinds of food are wanted and used are a matter of acquired habit influenced by both physical environment and social custom. To civilized people today, eating human flesh is an entirely unnatural thing. Yet there have been peoples to whom it seemed natural because it was socially authorized and even highly esteemed. There are well-accredited stories of persons needing support from others who have refused palatable and nourishing foods because they were not accustomed to them; the alien foods were so "unnatural" they preferred to starve rather than eat them.

[7] Aristotle spoke for an entire social order as well as for himself when he said that slavery existed by nature. He would have regarded efforts to abolish slavery from society as an idle and utopian effort to change human nature where it was unchangeable. For according to him it was not simply the desire to be a master that was engrained in human nature. There were persons who were born with such an inherently slavish nature that it did violence to human nature to set them free.

[8] The assertion that human nature cannot be changed is heard when social changes are urged as reforms and improvements of existing conditions. It is always heard when the proposed changes in institutions or

conditions stand in sharp opposition to what exists. If the conservative were wiser, he would rest his objections in most cases, not upon the unchangeability of human nature, but upon the inertia of custom; upon the resistance that acquired habits offer to change after they are once acquired. It is hard to teach an old dog new tricks and it is harder yet to teach society to adopt customs which are contrary to those which have long prevailed. Conservatism of this type would be intelligent, and it would compel those wanting change not only to moderate their pace, but also to ask how the changes they desire could be introduced with a minimum of shock and dislocation.

[9] Nevertheless, there are few social changes that can be opposed on the ground that they are contrary to human nature itself. A proposal to have a society get along without food and drink is one of the few that are of this kind. Proposals to form communities in which there is no cohabitation have been made and the communities have endured for a time. But they are so nearly contrary to human nature that they have not endured long. These cases are almost the only ones in which social change can be opposed simply on the ground that human nature cannot be changed.

[10] Take the institution of war, one of the oldest, most socially reputable of all human institutions. Efforts for stable peace are often opposed on the ground that man is by nature a fighting animal and that this phase of his nature is unalterable. The failure of peace movements in the past can be cited in support of this view. In fact, however, war is as much a social pattern as is the domestic slavery which the ancients thought to be an immutable fact.

[11] I have already said that, in my opinion, combativeness is a constituent part of human nature. But I have also said that the manifestations of these native elements are subject to change because they are affected by custom and tradition. War does not exist because man has combative instincts, but because social conditions and forces have led, almost forced, these "instincts" into this channel.

[12] There are a large number of other channels in which the need for combat has been satisfied, and there are other channels not yet discovered or explored into which it could be led with equal satisfaction. There is war against disease, against poverty, against insecurity, against injustice, in which multitudes of persons have found full opportunity for the exercise of their combative tendencies.

[13] The time may be far off when men will cease to fulfill their need for combat by destroying each other and when they will manifest it in common and combined efforts against the forces that are enemies of all men equally. But the difficulties in the way are found in the persistence of certain acquired social customs and not in the unchangeability of the demand for combat.

[14] Pugnacity and fear are native elements of human nature. But so are pity and sympathy. We send nurses and physicians to the battlefield and provide hospital facilities as "naturally" as we charge bayonets and discharge machine guns. In early times there was a close connection between pugnacity and fighting, for the latter was done largely with the fists. Pugnacity plays a small part in generating wars today. Citizens of one country do not hate those of another nation by instinct. When they attack or are attacked, they do not use their fists in close combat, but throw shells from a great distance at persons whom they have never seen. In modern wars, anger and hatred come after the war has started; they are effects of war, not the cause of it.

[15] It is a tough job sustaining a modern war; all the emotional reactions have to be excited. Propaganda and atrocity stories are enlisted. Aside from such extreme measures there has to be definite organization, as we saw in the two World Wars, to keep up the morale of even noncombatants. And morale is largely a matter of keeping emotions at a certain pitch; and unfortunately fear, hatred, suspicion, are among the emotions most easily aroused.

[16] I shall not attempt to dogmatize about the causes of modern wars. But I do not think that anyone will deny that they are social rather than psychological, though psychological appeal is highly important in working up a people to the point where they want to fight and in keeping them at it. I do not think, moreover, that anyone will deny that economic conditions are powerful among the social causes of war. The main point, however, is that whatever the sociological causes, they are affairs of tradition, custom, and institutional organization, and these factors belong among the changeable manifestations of human nature, not among the unchangeable elements.

[17] I have used the case of war as a typical instance of what is changeable and what is unchangeable in human nature, in their relation to schemes of social change. I have selected the case because it is an extremely difficult one in which to effect durable changes, not because it is an easy one. The point is that the obstacles in the way are put there by social forces which do change from time to time, not by fixed elements of human nature. This fact is also illustrated in the failures of pacifists to achieve their ends by appeal simply to sympathy and pity. For while, as I have said, the kindly emotions are also a fixed constituent of human nature, the channel they take is dependent upon social conditions.

[18] There is always a great outburst of these kindly emotions in time of war. Fellow feeling and the desire to help those in need are intense during war, as they are at every period of great disaster that comes home to observation or imagination. But they are canalized in their expression; they are confined to those upon our side. They occur simultaneously with manifestation of rage and fear against the other side, if not always in the

same person, at least in the community generally. Hence the ultimate failure of pacifist appeals to the kindly elements of native human nature when they are separated from intelligent consideration of the social and economic forces at work.

[19] William James made a great contribution in the title of one of his essays, *The Moral Equivalent of War*. The very title conveys the point I am making. Certain basic needs and emotions are permanent. But they are capable of finding expression in ways that are radically different from the ways in which they now currently operate.

[20] An even more burning issue emerges when any fundamental change in economic institutions and relations is proposed. Proposals for such sweeping change are among the commonplaces of our time. On the other hand, the proposals are met by the statement that the changes are impossible because they involve an impossible change in human nature. To this statement, advocates of the desired changes are only too likely to reply that the present system or some phase of it is contrary to human nature. The argument *pro* and *con* then gets put on the wrong ground.

[21] As a matter of fact, economic institutions and relations are among the manifestations of human nature that are most susceptible of change. History is living evidence of the scope of these changes. Aristotle, for example, held that paying interest is unnatural, and the Middle Ages reëchoed the doctrine. All interest was usury, and it was only after economic conditions had so changed that payment of interest was a customary and in that sense a "natural" thing, that usury got its present meaning.

[22] There have been times and places in which land was held in common and in which private ownership of land would have been regarded as the most monstrous of unnatural things. There have been other times and places when all wealth was possessed by an overlord and his subjects held wealth, if any, subject to his pleasure. The entire system of credit so fundamental in contemporary financial and industrial life is a modern invention. The invention of the joint-stock company with limited liability of individuals has brought about a great change from earlier facts and conceptions of property. I think the need of owning something is one of the native elements of human nature. But it takes either ignorance or a very lively fancy to suppose that the system of ownership that exists in the United States in 1946, with all its complex relations and its interweaving with legal and political supports, is a necessary and unchangeable product of an inherent tendency to appropriate and possess.

[23] Law is one of the most conservative of human institutions; yet through the cumulative effect of legislation and judicial decisions it changes, sometimes at a slow rate, sometimes rapidly. The changes in human relations that are brought about by changes in industrial and legal institutions then react to modify the ways in which human nature mani-

fests itself, and this brings about still further changes in institutions, and so on indefinitely.

[24] It is for these reasons that I say that those who hold that proposals for social change, even of rather a profound character, are impossible and utopian because of the fixity of human nature confuse the resistance to change that comes from acquired habits with that which comes from original human nature. The savage, living in a primitive society, comes nearer to being a purely "natural" human being than does civilized man. Civilization itself is the product of altered human nature. But even the savage is bound by a mass of tribal customs and transmitted beliefs that modify his original nature, and it is these acquired habits that make it so difficult to transform him into a civilized human being.

[25] The revolutionary radical, on the other hand, overlooks the force of engrained habits. He is right, in my opinion, about the indefinite plasticity of human nature. But he is wrong in thinking that patterns of desire, belief, and purpose do not have a force comparable to the inertia, the resistance to movement, possessed by these same objects when they are at rest. Habit, not original human nature, keeps things moving most of the time, about as they have moved in the past.

[26] If human nature is unchangeable, then there is no such thing as education and all our efforts to educate are doomed to failure. For the very meaning of education is modification of native human nature in formation of those new ways of thinking, of feeling, of desiring, and of believing that are foreign to raw human nature. If the latter were unalterable, we might have training but not education. For training, as distinct from education, means simply the acquisition of certain skills. Native gifts can be trained to a point of higher efficiency without that development of new attitudes and dispositions which is the goal of education. But the result is mechanical. It is like supposing that while a musician may acquire by practice greater technical ability, he cannot rise from one plane of musical appreciation and creation to another.

[27] The theory that human nature is unchangeable is thus the most depressing and pessimistic of all possible doctrines. If it were carried out logically, it would mean a doctrine of predestination from birth that would outdo the most rigid of theological doctrines. For according to it, persons are what they are at birth and nothing can be done about it, beyond the kind of training that an acrobat might give to the muscular system with which he is originally endowed. If a person is born with criminal tendencies, a criminal he will become and remain. If a person is born with an excessive amount of greed, he will become a person living by predatory activities at the expense of others; and so on. I do not doubt at all the existence of differences in natural endowment. But what I am questioning is the notion that they doom individuals to a fixed channel of

expression. It is difficult indeed to make a silk purse out of a sow's ear. But the particular form which, say, a natural musical endowment will take depends upon the social influences to which one is subjected. Beethoven in a savage tribe would doubtless have been outstanding as a musician, but he would not have been the Beethoven who composed symphonies.

[28] The existence of almost every conceivable kind of social institution at some time and place in the history of the world is evidence of the plasticity of human nature. This fact does not prove that all these different social systems are of equal value, materially, morally, and culturally. The slightest observation shows that such is not the case. But the fact in proving the changeability of human nature indicates the attitude that should be taken toward proposals for social changes. The question is primarily whether they, in special cases, are desirable or not. And the way to answer that question is to try to discover what their consequences would be if they were adopted. Then if the conclusion is that they are desirable, the further question is how they can be accomplished with a minimum of waste, destruction, and needless dislocation.

[29] In finding the answer to this question, we have to take into account the force of existing traditions and customs; of the patterns of action and belief that already exist. We have to find out what forces already at work can be reinforced so that they move toward the desired change and how the conditions that oppose change can be gradually weakened. Such questions as these can be considered on the basis of fact and reason.

[30] The assertion that a proposed change is impossible because of the fixed constitution of human nature diverts attention from the question of whether or not a change is desirable and from the other question of how it shall be brought about. It throws the question into the arena of blind emotion and brute force. In the end, it encourages those who think that great changes can be produced offhand and by the use of sheer violence.

[31] When our sciences of human nature and human relations are anything like as developed as are our sciences of physical nature, their chief concern will be with the problem of how human nature is most effectively modified. The question will not be whether it is capable of change, but of how it is to be changed under given conditions. This problem is ultimately that of education in its widest sense. Consequently, whatever represses and distorts the processes of education that might bring about a change in human dispositions with the minimum of waste puts a premium upon the forces that bring society to a state of deadlock, and thereby encourages the use of violence as a means of social change.

COMMENT AND QUESTIONS

1. Dewey qualifies his thesis that human nature does change by means of an analysis of "human nature." What aspects of human nature does he consider unchangeable? What aspects are alterable? What examples does he give of each?
2. How does Dewey support his idea that profound changes in social and economic institutions and relations are not contrary to human nature? What accounts for the fact that such changes are difficult to bring about?
3. Can you think of current proposals for social or economic change that have been resisted on the ground that they are contrary to human nature? What attitude would Dewey recommend that one take toward these proposals?
4. According to the philosophy of pragmatism, to which Dewey subscribed, the worth or validity of an action or an idea is to be judged by the practical results it produces. What evidence can you see in this essay of Dewey's pragmatism?
5. What relationships does Dewey, who devoted much of his life to education, see between education and the changeability of human nature?
6. If you have read Newman's "Enlargement of Mind," compare his ideas and Dewey's on the meaning of education.
7. We have mentioned Dewey's initial qualification of his central thesis. His essay contains many examples of lesser qualifications and of care in avoiding sweeping generalizations. Notice, for example, in paragraph 28, "*almost* every conceivable kind," "*This fact does not prove,*" "The question is *primarily* whether they, *in special cases.*" Point out other examples in the essay of this kind of careful qualification.
8. Understanding a writer's ideas often depends on understanding key words and phrases—terms which he uses to make distinctions or to define, and which he may repeat for purposes of emphasis or unity. Explain clearly how and why Dewey uses each of the following terms: *needs, manifestations, inertia of custom, acquired habits, combativeness, war, social patterns, channel, plasticity of human nature, education, training, waste and dislocation, use of violence.*

[25] W. *Macneile Dixon*: Human Nature and the Human Situation

THE FOLLOWING analysis is part of Chapter IV of a book called *The Human Situation*, which was originally delivered as the Gifford Lectures in the University of Glasgow, 1935-37. This book, available in an inexpensive edition, is one that we should like to recommend to all thoughtful college students. W. Macneile Dixon (1886-1946) was Professor of English Language and Literature in the University of Glasgow, and is the author of a number of books including *Tragedy, The Englishman,* and *An Apology for the Arts*.

[1] The first and fundamental wonder is existence itself. That I should be alive, conscious, a person, a part of the whole, that I should have emerged out of nothingness, that the Void should have given birth not merely to things, but to me. Among the many millions who throughout the centuries have crossed the stage of time, probably not more than a handful have looked about them with astonishment, or found their own presence within the visible scene in any way surprising. Our immediate impressions and requirements, the daily doings, comings and goings of others like ourselves absorb in the years of infancy all our attention. Life steals imperceptibly upon us, without any sudden shock or sense of strangeness. How quietly we accommodate ourselves to the situation! In our early years, when all is fresh and new, we take the miracle for granted, and find abundant occupation and endless variety of interest. We are busy looking about us, and grow accustomed to living, and nothing appears startling to which we are accustomed. Thus it is that in the existence of the world or ourselves there appears for most of us no cause for amazement. So far from asking with Coleridge the unanswerable question, "Why should there be anything at all, any world at all?" we accept life without wonder and without curiosity. One might almost imagine that we were here on well-known ground, and but revisiting a country with which we had a previous acquaintance. Yet let the mind once awake—and distress of mind is the great awakener of mind—and this emergence from the womb of the immeasurable universe rises to its full significance, to tower above all other thoughts, the wonder of wonders, beyond digestion into speech. To find oneself a member of a particular family and society, among innumerable other families and

societies, engaged in a round of activities, to feel, think, love, hate, to eat, drink, sleep, to be involved in all these multitudinous affairs, not knowing in the least why this state of things should be ours, how we came into possession of this peculiar nature, acquired these needs, powers and passions, how or why we were launched upon this most extraordinary adventure—once give way to thoughts like these, and you are a prisoner for life, the prisoner of philosophy. But you will remain one of a negligible minority. And if it be a delusion to suppose that many human beings have been concerned with such musings, it is equally a delusion to suppose they have been spiritually minded, anxious about the state of their souls, eager for communion with God. All but the slenderest of minorities have been immersed in a struggle for existence, for material satisfactions, have sought the pleasures of the senses, or followed after power or wealth. Most have died, whatever their pursuits, in the full vigour of their sensuality, and all in the full tide of their ignorance. If there has been one God, universally acknowledged, universally worshipped, in all ages and countries, it is money.

> What is here?
> 'Gold? yellow, precious, glittering gold?'

The inhabitants of Norwich in 1650 petitioned Parliament to grant them the land and other materials "of that vast and altogether useless cathedral of Norwich" towards the building of a workhouse and repairing piers.

[2] However it came about, here we find ourselves, and in many and most delicately balanced ways, adjusted to the business in hand. Had the adjustment been perfect, had the whole worked without friction, as the earth moves through the heavens without a disturbing ripple, our lives like those of the plants, without desire or pain, possibly a dim sense of happiness, a gentle, unruffled dream might have been ours. Nature appears to have begun, if she ever did begin, her great undertaking with insensate things, and it mattered not at all what she did with them. Whirling suns, seas, mountains, even plants, trees, flowers of all varieties might have come into and passed out of existence without disturbance of the great calm of eternity. But with the entrance upon the scene of that disturbing visitor, the soul, that singular entity which suffers and enjoys, with the coming of beings capable of sharp pains and acute desires, there arose a formidable situation. These entities sought satisfaction for their wishes and avoidance of suffering. They became struggling creatures, in possession of life, but not the life they desired. Every man goes about arm in arm with disappointment. They discovered a harsh limit to their power over things. They found an enemy in the field, an evil thing, figured in all religions as the Adversary, the Opponent, the ἀντίθεόν, Ahriman in the Persian system, Lucifer or Satan in the Christian.

[³] How unfortunate, some theologians tell us, that man gave way to mental curiosity, and so forfeited his happy lot in the Garden of Eden, rising to a level of intelligence above the lowlier, unaspiring animals, content with pasture, with satisfactions of food and sex. They fared better, and ours, but for the great aboriginal catastrophe, would have been a like existence, without expectations or searchings of heart, without souls embittered by fruitless desires. The knowledge of good and evil was the fatal departure from the original design—Nature's error, or, as in the Christian view, the fault of man himself. The pursuit of wisdom brought misery, and to intelligence was attached a penalty.

[⁴] There is a saying that nature does nothing in vain. Yet if she created automatic machines, and some thinkers like the behaviourists insist we are no more, why did she proceed to the blunder, for assuredly a blunder it was, of conferring upon them an unnecessary sensitivity to pain and pleasure? Without sensitivity machines work very well. How much better had she been content with insensate things. But we are not stones or trees, and in making sensitive beings nature went clean out of her way. Consciousness is an unpardonable blot upon her scheme, and for this philosophy an inexplicable enigma. So it is that, in the midst of nature, man appears not as her child, but as a changeling. Exiled from his native home of innocence, elevated to kingly rank in the creation, the bond between mother and son was snapped. She reared a disappointed and rebellious child, a critic of his parent, judging her morals detestable, counselling, as did Huxley, resistance to her rule and defiance of her authority. Cosmic nature, he declares, is "no school of virtue," but the headquarters of its enemy.

[⁵] That the world is not to their mind has never ceased to surprise, if not to exasperate the philosophers. Its pattern displeases them, and they would remould it nearer to their hearts' desire. Some religions think it past mending, but the passion for reforming the world and one's neighbours has afflicted all the schools of thought, nor has it yet been abandoned. Yet the patterns they would substitute have never been divulged. The most dissatisfied are chary of offering alternative and superior worlds, nor does it appear that they know of any with which our own unfavourably compares. By some natural talent they perceive its deficiencies, but the plan of operations is kept a secret. Alfonso the Wise of Spain, indeed, remarked that "he could have suggested improvements in the universe had the Creator consulted him." Unfortunately at that moment a terrible thunderstorm burst over the Alcazar, and there is no record of his proposals, if he had any.

[⁶] The world has been called *theatrum Dei*, God's theatre. And if we were merely players on the stage, repeating words put into our mouths, performing actions assigned to us, and like them really unconcerned, appearing to suffer and yet not suffering, the situation were beyond rebuke.

It is unhappily quite otherwise. Feeling entered the world and let loose a torrent of ills—the sick heart, the ailing body, the distressed mind.

> All thoughts that rive the heart are here, and all are vain,
> Horror, and scorn, and hate, and fear, and indignation.

[7] It is a curious speculation, yet not irrelevant to our enquiry, how human lots are cast, so strangely varied they are. You are born and no reasons given, a man or a woman, an Arab or an Andaman islander, an African pygmy or an Egyptian Pharaoh, a Chinese coolie or an English gentleman, a St. Thomas or an Ivan the Terrible. You are ushered into the world in the Stone Age, the fifth or fifteenth century, a vegetarian or a cannibal, of base or noble stock, the child of half-witted parents or of Viking breed, an imbecile or a fanatic. You inherit, according to the accident of your birth, a family blood-feud, a belief in Voodoo and a string of fantastic fetishes, or a Christian creed of love and charity. You are a warrior or a serf as Heaven decrees, are exposed as an infant born in ancient Sparta, die in middle life bitten by a poisonous snake in India, or live a respectable German merchant to a ripe old age. One of a million million possible lots is yours. Is it accidental, an act of God, or, as some have conjectured, a selection made by yourself in a previous state? How profound a mystery lies behind these so manifestly unequal conditions of human existence! And what justice is it, if one man languishes most of his life on a bed of sickness, and another enjoys health and happiness or sits upon an imperial throne? Nature strews these inequalities of place, time, heredity, circumstances with a monstrous partiality. On what principles you are allotted good looks, a musical ear, a sunny temper, an affectionate disposition, a talent for figures, or denied these qualities does not appear. We are, the maxim runs, as God made us, and there the matter perforce must end.

[8] Nor is it only our nature and disposition that we inherit, but the habits and traditions of some community, a Pagan, a Buddhistic or a Mohammedan creed, the *mos majorum*, the custom of our ancestors; and, with few exceptions, by these our lives are governed. These bodies of ours, as it would seem at haphazard distributed, are not negligible, or to be treated with cavalier indifference. From their tiresome demands and complaints there is no escape. They do very much as they please with us, often lame our best intentions and enforce our most sensual. To keep them in repair is a constant anxiety. What a despot is the stomach, whose caprices make us moody or cheerful, bland or irritable. Listen to the enormous laughter of Rabelais while he recounts the indignities to which the body subjects the mind, making indecency an intimate part of our lives. He mocks at nature, which delights in shaming us. Our pride revolts, we are nauseated by ourselves, as was Swift, or nervously and shamefacedly avert our eyes from the dishonours we must endure.

[⁹] If nature gave us logic, she appears to be singularly lacking in what she bestows. For she herself drives no straight furrow, and exhibits an inconsistency which in a man would be accounted madness. Her habit is to turn upon herself, wound and afflict herself, undoing with her left hand what she has done with her right. What more inharmonious than that she should send hailstones to the destruction of her own blossoms and fruits, tempests upon the crops she has herself ripened to the harvest? The meteorite that, in 1908, fell in Siberia, about 100 tons in weight, destroyed the forest in which it fell for a radius of about forty miles. The lightning splits the tree, and sets the forest aflame. The sand of the desert or the encroaching sea turns fertile fields into barren wastes, and reduces whole populations to distress or starvation. It is her own features which nature thus rends and mangles. Wild beasts destroy 3000 persons every year in India, and 20,000 die of snake-bite. There are 700 million sufferers from malaria in the world. Forty per cent of the children born in Central China perish from cold or famine before they are a year old.

[¹⁰] When people talk of nature, what do they mean? Is it the immensity, the sublimity, the grandeur, or the indifference, the inhumanity she exhibits, of which they are thinking? We know her wonders and splendours, we know also her disorders, her cataclysms, her tempests. Nature is everything we admire and fear, everything we love, and everything we hate. She is "the sum of all phenomena." A perfectly ordered world, exact as a geometrical pattern, is the world desired by the logical mind. But how different the reality. Before its irrationalities reason trembles. The eruption of Krakatoa, in 1783, destroyed 40,000 human beings; the Quito, in 1797, also 40,000; the Lisbon earthquake, in 1755, twice that number. Is human life a bubble? Within the present century, in 1908, and again, in 1920, similar disturbances in Sicily and China eliminated half a million lives in sixty seconds. The eruption of Mount Pelé, in less than a quarter of an hour, laid the capital of Martinique in ruins, with the loss of 30,000 lives. During the Yangtse floods in 1931 over a million perished by drowning. Etna wakes and Messina perishes. Islands are submerged with their human freights, like ships at sea. In 1929 Ninaforu, in the Pacific, simply disappeared with all its inhabitants into the ocean depths. Would these things be "if the King of the universe were our friend"? The larks are not always in the sky on an April morning.

[¹¹] Professor Bosanquet thought it exceedingly improbable that an earthquake would destroy London. His reason for thinking so was not a geological one. It would be, he believed, contrary to "the world-wisdom." Such a preference by nature for London over Tokio or California is indeed very flattering to us as a nation, and very comforting. But what are we to think of a philosopher who says such things? You say nothing: you close his book.

[12] Nature does not seem to know her own mind, or else she speaks an equivocal language. Are her powers, perhaps, limited, and hers an imperium divided among satraps, or governors, not wholly in subordination to her central authority? For if not, why should there be a discord between her animate and inanimate provinces? The human mind looks for unity, yet everywhere in nature's realm contending powers are in conflict. You have the physical world indifferent to living things, unconcerned whether they exist or do not exist. In its turn, upon the insecure foundation of the body, the living organism, rises the mind, incapable, it would seem, of any independent existence. So that thought, love, hope, the soul and its affections, the whole intellectual structure of human life, are perilously poised in a trembling insecurity upon the material elements, themselves in continual flux.

[13] Were nature constant in her intentions we might hope to understand them, but how at odds with herself this Lady Bountiful, mother of all living, when she counsels one species of her own creation, providing an armoury the most ingenious, claws and fangs and suckers, instruments of death, that one tribe of her offspring might the better murder the members of another, a device, to our poor uninstructed vision, neither lovely nor divine. Nature is no believer in disarmament. The bird preys upon the insect and the worm, the glow-worm feeds upon the snail, the ichneumon lays its eggs upon the caterpillar, which, when the grubs emerge, will serve as their food. There are animals which seem an incarnation of malice, like that dweller in darkness, the blood-sucking vampire bat. How difficult to think of Christ as the son of the God of nature! Nature encourages internecine strife. Nor has she any favourites among her creatures, unless it be the insect tribe. There are not less than ten million varieties of them in existence. "In India alone the loss of crops, of timber, and of animal products by insect damage is estimated at over 150 million pounds annually, and the death roll due to insect-borne diseases at over a million and a half lives."[1]

[14] Life is one throughout the universe, yet its parts are in conflict. Nature has her racks and thumbscrews. You cannot instruct her in any of the torturer's or executioner's arts. There is no kindness in the sea, no benevolence in the forest. If you complain that men are a cruel breed, you need not enquire whence they derived the propensity. It is inherited, and from the mother's side.

[15] Perhaps these things should not be mentioned. Truth is a thorny rose. Sentimental writers do not dwell upon this theme. These star-gazers do not remind us of the *bellum omnium contra omnes*.[2] How tiresome are the one-eyed philosophies. There will be brave men born after us who will not attempt to build up their spiritual lives on a diet of lies. All forms of

[1] *The World of Nature*, by H. C. Knapp-Fisher, p. 295.
[2] war of all against all.

life, all organisms in which it is manifested, are engaged in an unceasing struggle to maintain themselves against the disintegrating forces of nature. All are in conflict with each other for the means of life, clan against clan, individual against individual. Each exists at the expense of others, and keeps its foothold only by success over the rest. Here is a telegram from South Australia, dated Nov. 6, 1934. "It is estimated that the farmers in Adelaide will lose at least three-quarters of their crops through the depredations of grass-hoppers, which are advancing in uncontrollable swarms on a front of 250 miles." How deep it goes, this warfare, you may conjecture if you remind yourself that the very trees of the forest are battling with each other for the light of the sun, and that the plants have their defensive armour, the rose and thistle their thorns, the nettle its sting. Make your heart iron within you, when you remember that to live you must kill, either plants or animals. "To live, my Lucilius, is to make war." Hunger for food, hunger for life, of which war is merely the continuation, are the presiding issues.

[16] It is no doubt necessary to think in terms of right and wrong, yet how much more convincing would be our moralists if they began at the beginning, if they could bring themselves to think first in terms of life and death. Who is ignorant that good and evil go everywhere hand in hand, in the closest, indeed inseparable, partnership? The misfortunes of one community make the fortunes of another. If England secures the world markets, they are lost to Germany. If oil becomes the necessary and universal fuel, the oil-producing districts flourish at the expense of those which have none. Among the competitors for a post, or the hand of a lady, one only can prove successful, and not invariably the most deserving. The magistrate and police depend for their livelihood on the swindler and the burglar, the physician upon the sick and disabled. Scarcity of food brings destitution to the poor and high prices to the farmer, and the higher a nation's standard of intellect and skill the worse for the incapable and unintelligent.

[17] We are not sure of what best nourishes, or what damages, the delicate machinery of nerve and brain. We guess at the causes of our physical lassitude. Poisons circulate in our blood from origins unknown. We are surrounded by unseen foes. Nor are our souls less vulnerable than our bodies. Affections spring up in us only to be thwarted or forbidden, or we discover too late that they have been foolishly misplaced and are betrayed. Our very sympathies lead us astray. We are imposed upon by falsehoods and depressed by misunderstandings. The whole region of the emotions is subject to doubts, misgivings, confusion, and those who have shallow natures, feeling little, appear to be best suited for life. Instinct and desire point one way and mature reflection another. Duties conflict not merely with our wishes, but with opposing duties, so that we are in doubt where our loyalty is first due, which cause we should espouse,

to which of the arguing voices we should give ear. And, do what we will, to live at all without inflicting injuries upon others is well-nigh, if not altogether impossible. "A terrible thing is life," says Socrates in the *Gorgias*. He thought it a disease, and left with his friend, Crito, a commission to sacrifice a cock as a thank-offering for his deliverance.

[18] Yet within this "odious scene of violence and cruelty," as Mill, rising to a moral superiority over the universe, called it, there runs a counter current. So that in nature's speech there is an equivocation, an irony, an irony clearly discerned, with that unclouded vision of theirs, by the Greeks, and even by the simpler peoples of the earth. A recent traveller reports the philosophy of an African tribe: "They said that although God is good, and wishes good for everybody, unfortunately he has a half-witted brother, who is always interfering with what he does. This half-witted brother keeps on obtruding himself, and does not give God a chance." How kindly a view of Satan! And what is irony? It is a double-speaking, it is language which, since it is open to two interpretations, hides the speaker's meaning, in which a sense is wrapped other than the obvious sense, language which says one thing and yet means another. There is the irony, too, of circumstances, promising what they do not perform, or it may be performing what they do not promise, or by the event baffling confident expectation. For this ironical language nature has a fondness. Observe that this nature which wars upon herself is the nature which constructs the exquisite fabric of the living organism, and with a physician's arts ministers to the diseases she inflicts, produces in the body anti-toxins to defeat the toxins, administers anaesthetics, and exercises a *vis medicatrix*[3] all her own. How difficult to recognise in the ferocities we see around us the subtle power which made the brain, which elaborated with consummate exactness the mechanism of the heart and lungs, all the devices by which the body maintains its existence! That nature should create a world full of difficulties and dangers, and thereupon proceed to place within it fabrics of an infinite delicacy and complexity to meet these very dangers and difficulties is a contradiction that baffles the understanding. With a cunning past all human thought she solves the problems she has, as it were, absent-mindedly set herself. The flood and the earthquake have no consideration for the plant or animal, yet nature which sends the flood and earthquake has provided, with foresight or in a dream, for the living things they destroy. She both smiles and frowns upon her own creation, and is at once friendly and unfriendly. Like a scarlet thread it runs through her dominion, this inconsistency. Side by side with the undeniable and admirable adjustment between things organic and inorganic, you have the hostility, the discordance. What wonder that men, bewildered by this inexplicable procedure, have supposed her govern-

---

[3] healing power.

ments distributed among a hierarchy of squabbling deities, persecuting or protecting this or that race of men—Zeus the Greeks, Jehovah the Jews? What wonder they supposed even the trees to be the better of protecting deities, the olive Athena, the vine Dionysus? Ah, nature! subtle beyond all human subtlety, enigmatic, profound, life-giver and life-destroyer, nourishing mother and assassin, inspirer of all that is best and most beautiful, of all that is most hideous and forbidding!

[19] That the world is a unity the philosophers and men of science reiterate with a wearisome persistence. That it is united, they have the sense not to proclaim. How the world became disunited they have not told us. Yet in this procession of time and tears it is not so much the rivers of blood which flow through history, it is the broken hearts that appal us. What elicits human horror and indignation is not so much the suffering that the strong may with courage endure as the suffering at random inflicted upon the weak and innocent and defenceless. I read not long since of a child, who trustingly looked up the chimney to see the coming of Santa Claus. Her clothing took fire, and she was burnt to death. A painful world we might school ourselves to combat, were it only rational, but the conjunction of pain and senselessness is hard to bear. Nor would the heroic race of men, "toil-worn since being began," shrink from grief and wounds were it only assigned a noble task. But nature prescribes no tasks. She calls for no volunteers for a great essay. For the asking she might have millions. She points willing climbers to no Everest. The discovery of the goal—by far the most difficult task—she leaves to us. We are mountaineers by nature, but born blind, and must find for ourselves the Himalayan peak, if there be any peak, we are built to ascend, or else while away the time till the great axe falls, and the futilities are done with. Go where you will through nature, you find no directions for travellers. You choose your path, uncounselled and at your own peril, and the unlikely track may prove to be the best. To be clear-sighted is often to be short-sighted, as when the molluscs and crustaceans, protecting themselves with heavy defensive armour, entered with all their care and caution a blind alley, while naked, unaccommodated man, selecting the more dangerous path, advanced to the headship of living creatures.

[20] Life is a unique experience. There is nothing with which to compare it, no measure of its value in terms of some other thing, and money will not purchase it. Yet with this pearl of price we know not what to do. Schopenhauer loves to dwell, in illustration of his pessimistic thesis, upon the boredom of life, and cites card-playing, a kill-time device, as "quite peculiarly an indication of the miserable side of humanity." That mortals should desire immortality, and yet find difficulty in passing an afternoon —if you have a fancy for paradoxes, here is a pretty one. We contemplate eternity without horror, and find an hour of our own society intolerable. "How dreary it is to be alive, gentlemen!" And how poverty-stricken is the

human soul, which, even when armed with supernatural powers, can find no occupation for itself. Marlowe's Faustus, with Mephistopheles to gratify his every wish, can make nothing of his transcendent opportunity.

[21] Tacitus draws a terrible picture of the *taedium vitae*[4] which in imperial times descended upon the Roman aristocracy:

> In his cool hall, with haggard eyes,
>   The Roman noble lay:
> He drove abroad, in furious guise,
>   Along the Appian Way.
>
> He made a feast, drank fierce and fast,
>   And crown'd his head with flowers—
> No easier nor no quicker pass'd
>   The impracticable hours.

Or if, by good fortune, we inherit a nature abundant in resource, which finds every moment full of charm, and think the world a divine playground; another shadow darkens the windows of the soul. As the child, enchanted with the fairy spectacle upon the stage, the joyous bustle and the glittering lights, whispered to its mother—"Mother, this is not going to end soon, is it?" we are startled to discover that

> in the very temple of delight
> Veil'd melancholy has her sovran shrine.

To foresee the end of happiness poisons the springs of happiness. It will end, and soon. We are permitted an hour at the pageant and the curtain falls.

[22] It may be that, although appearances are against her, nature meant well by us, that her powers were limited. She has done what she could, giving us a "second best," since the best was beyond her. It lay within her strength to confer life, but not to preserve it. Yet one cannot refrain from asking, was it necessary that man's superiority should prove his bane, that his aspirations should end in the grave? To create immortal longings in the ephemeral being of an hour, to implant in him passions never to be gratified, for knowledge never to be attained, for understanding never to be fulfilled, to give him imagination, a fatal dowry, poverty of his possessions with the abundance of his cravings— was this necessary? It appears either a refinement of malicious irony, or a promise of fulfilment, but which? The gods are silent.

> Or is it that some Force, too wise, too strong,
> Even for yourselves to conjure or beguile,
> Sweeps earth, and heaven, and men, and gods along,
> Like the broad volume of the insurgent Nile?
> And the great powers we serve, themselves may be
> Slaves of a tyrannous necessity? . . .

---

[4] weariness of life.

Oh, wherefore cheat our youth, if thus it be,
Of one short joy, one lust, one pleasant dream?
Stringing vain words of powers we cannot see,
Blind divinations of a will supreme;
Lost labour! when the circumambient gloom
But hides, if Gods, Gods careless of our doom?

[23] There is, among her inconsistencies, another persuasive artifice of nature, for which, by any mechanical philosophy it is difficult, indeed, to account—the artifice by which she induced men to interest in a future they could not hope to see. She persuades them to self-sacrifice, to loss of life for their offspring, for their race, their country, to martyrdom for their faiths, for shadowy, intangible notions, less substantial than gossamer. By what arrangement of cranks, wheels and levers did she cozen this creature of a day to look beyond his own instant profit, his obvious gain? Why should hope have a place, heroism a place, renunciation a place in this automaton? Is cajolery among her talents? Manifestly the Spartans at Thermopylae were flattered to their ruin by a ridiculous pride of race.

[24] View life as a whole, exert all your powers of fancy, take all history into your account, the embarrassing contradiction remains. On all sides it raises its sphinx-like, ironical countenance. Another and final illustration will suffice. At the heart of existence there lies an undeniable sweetness, which no philosophy has fathomed, and no railing accusation against life can dislodge. The complaints against it are legion. In all ages and societies goes up the bitter cry, "Vanity of vanities, all is vanity." "All that exists," wrote Leopardi, "is evil, that anything exists is an evil; everything exists only to achieve evil; existence itself is an evil, and destined to evil. There is no other good than nonexistence."

[25] So much for life: not a pennyworth of value anywhere. Yet the doctrines and religions, and they are numerous, which condemn existence, offer no adequate explanation of the clinging attraction for a state they censure and profess to despise. From this so undesirable a possession their adherents are, for the most part, curiously unwilling to part. "What sort of a pessimist is this," asks Nietzsche, "who plays the flute?" The pessimists are not alone in vilifying life. They have the support of Christian preachers. "The whole world," says Donne, "is but a universal churchyard, but our common grave." Christianity has little good to say of life, yet how reluctant the best Christians are to become angels. Like the worldlings they, too, are intoxicated with the pleasures of sense. They marry and are given in marriage. They succumb at times to song and laughter. Cheerfulness keeps lurking in odd corners of the horrid gloom. There is some magic at work here. Is it possible that something may be said for this vale of sorrows? Though not to be compared with the ineffable bliss we demand, yet as an alternative to nothing a case for existence can be stated. In fairness to nature you must enter this natural sweetness in the

ledger of your account with her. The ecstasy of lovers, the joy in activity, the glow, the radiance, the sunlight, the perfume—omit these, and it is a caricature you have drawn, not the landscape. There is a music in the air.

> Riding adown the country lanes;
> The larks sang high—
> O heart, for all thy griefs and pains
> Thou shalt be loath to die.

[26] Many philosophers have been defeatists. Diogenes and Zeno, Epictetus and Marcus Aurelius, Schopenhauer and Spinoza. Ἀπάθεια, ἀταραξία, *nil admirari*, indifference, impassivity, passionlessness, they are all one. Stoicism, Epicureanism, Taoism, how many creeds and doctrines are in their essence, withdrawals from life? For them it is not an adventure but a weary pilgrimage. They take no pleasure in it. Sick of time, they take refuge in eternity. And we seem forced to the strange conclusion that Paganism suits world conditions better. Perhaps it should, indeed, be expected. For why should the haters of life be more at home in it than its lovers? The creed of the Northmen, for example, left room for activity and prowess, for skill and enterprise, for courage and adventure. They had a liking for the risks and dangers of existence, which gave a zest to living, and for a worthy antagonist, who put them on their mettle.

[27] Life is like the sea, never at rest, untamed, moody, capricious, perilous. Many a man who knows the sea has sworn, and sworn again, that once on land he would never more embark upon so inclement, so treacherous, so hateful an element. And few who have so sworn have not heard with aching hearts her call, and longed for her bitter and incomparable society. Like life she lays a spell upon them, a spell not resident in her smiles, though smile she can, nor in her calm, though, like life, she, too, has her seasons of calm, her sheltered lagoons and quiet havens. Men are said to love flattery. The sea never flatters. They are said to love ease. She offers toil. Like life, she deals in every form of danger, and many modes of death—famine, thirst, fire, cold, shipwreck. Like life she strips men of their pretensions and vanities, exposes the weakness of the weak and the folly of the fool. Wherein then lies the fascination, against which the soft Lydian airs cannot with men that are men prevail? It flings a challenge and human nature rises to a challenge. Men are by nature striving creatures, heroically stubborn, as is the mind itself.

> Still nursing the unconquerable hope,
> Still clutching the inviolable shade.

They love best what they do for themselves, for what they themselves make they have a great affection; what is given them out of charity they value less. The world seems somehow so made as to suit best the adventurous and courageous, the men who, like Nelson, wear all their stars, like Napoleon's marshals their most splendid uniforms, not that they may be less but more conspicuous and incur greater dangers than their fellows. Leonidas at Thermopylae, resolved to stand and die for his country's cause, wished to save two lads by sending them home with a message to Sparta. He was met by the answer, "We are not here to carry messages, but to fight." However it comes about, such men are more inspiring figures than the defeatists.

[28] Matthew Arnold quotes with admiration Pope's rendering of the passage in Homer in which Sarpedon urges his friend Glaucus into the fight, the passage which in the original Lord Granville quoted on his deathbed.

> Could all our care elude the gloomy grave
> Which claims no less the fearful than the brave,
> For lust of fame I should not vainly dare
> In fighting fields, nor urge thy soul to war;
> But since, alas! ignoble age must come,
> Disease, and death's inexorable doom;
> The life which others pay, let us bestow,
> And give to fame what we to nature owe.

Cogito, ergo sum, said Descartes. "I think, therefore I am." He desired a platform, or rather an undeniable proposition as the foundation of his philosophic thought. His successors have not found it either undeniable or sufficient. They have rejected, too, such alternatives as "I act, therefore I am." "I desire, therefore I am." Let me suggest still another. No philosophers, or men of science, have so far had the hardihood, as far as I know, to deny us our pains. They relieve us of all else. They have taken from us our personality, our freedom, our souls, our very selves. They have, however, left us our sorrows. Let us take, then, as our foundation the proposition "I suffer, therefore I am." And let us add to it the converse and equally true statement, "I am, therefore I suffer." The privilege, if it be a privilege, of existence is ours and we have paid the price required. We have discharged our debts. We have not had something for nothing. We have free minds, and can look around us with a smile. Nothing can any longer intimidate us.

COMMENT AND QUESTIONS

1. The human situation, as Dixon sees it, is full of irony, paradox, contradiction. What irony or irrationality does he find in each of the following: (a) the fact that man has imagination, and is sensitive to pleasure and

pain; (b) the existence of natural phenomena such as floods, earthquakes, and volcanic eruptions; (c) the relationship of the mind and the body; (d) the relationship between species of living things; (e) the fact that nature cures and heals; (f) the human desire for immortality; (g) human self-sacrifice for race or country or a faith; (h) the sweetness of life?
2. The passages below express attitudes toward nature that were very common in the nineteenth century.

> The indescribable innocence and beneficence of Nature,—of sun and wind and rain, of summer and winter,—such health, such cheer, they afford forever! and such sympathy have they ever with our race, that all Nature would be affected and the sun's brightness fade, and the winds would sigh humanely, and the clouds rain tears, and the woods shed their leaves and put on mourning in midsummer, if any man should ever for a just cause grieve.—HENRY DAVID THOREAU, *Walden*

> And I have felt
> A presence that disturbs me with the joy
> Of elevated thoughts; a sense sublime
> Of something far more deeply interfused,
> Whose dwelling is the light of setting suns,
> And the round ocean and the living air,
> And the blue sky, and in the mind of man:
> A motion and a spirit, that impels
> All thinking things, all objects of all thought,
> And rolls through all things. Therefore am I still
> A lover of the meadows and the woods,
> And mountains; and of all that we behold
> From this green earth; of all the mighty world
> Of eye, and ear,—both what they half create,
> And what perceive; well pleased to recognise
> In nature and the language of the sense
> The anchor of my purest thoughts, the nurse,
> The guide, the guardian of my heart, and soul
> Of all my moral being.—WILLIAM WORDSWORTH,
> "Lines Composed a Few Miles Above Tintern Abbey"

Compare Dixon's view of nature with the views held by Thoreau and Wordsworth. Which view are you inclined to hold? Which seems to you more nearly true?
3. "Every man goes about arm in arm with disappointment," the author says. Do you agree or disagree with this statement? Do you think that intelligent men are likely to feel more or less disappointment than unintelligent men; or do you think intelligence has no relevance to disappointment?
4. In paragraph 22, Dixon restates an idea he has touched on earlier: "It may be that, although appearances are against her, nature meant well by us, that her powers were limited." A more conventional idea is that nature (or God) is all-powerful. Does one of these ideas seem to you more satisfying than the other? If so, why?

5. Do you think the author is implying that life is purposeless? Do you think he is implying that it is not worth living? Explain.
6. Given the human situation presented in the essay, what attitudes toward life does the author think an intelligent human being should hold? How should he live?
7. How would you describe Dixon's tone in this essay?
8. Dixon is an interesting stylist. Choose several passages from this selection that seem to you particularly good and analyze them carefully. Notice the sentence structure and variety in length and structure; the use of apt quotations, allusions, and examples; the use of figurative language; the touches of humor and irony; and the diction.

[26]   *Joseph Wood Krutch*: The Genesis of a Mood

JOSEPH WOOD KRUTCH (1893–) has been a professor of dramatic literature at Columbia University and drama critic for *The Nation;* in recent years he has lived in Arizona and has devoted himself exclusively to writing. Among his many books are *The American Drama Since 1918, Henry David Thoreau, The Twelve Seasons, The Desert Year, The Measure of Man,* and *Human Nature and the Human Condition.* The following selection is Chapter One of Krutch's most famous book, *The Modern Temper,* published in 1929. In a preface to a 1956 edition of *The Modern Temper,* Krutch explained that some of his views had changed but that the description he gave of the origin of the modern temper "and the consequences likely to follow from it seem to me as valid as they ever were. It is only my own attitude toward it which is different. What I described and shared in I still describe but no longer accept. Hence the situation which *The Modern Temper* presents as hopeless does not now seem to me entirely so. But by the diagnosis I will still stand." Students will find Krutch's later attitudes expressed in *The Measure of Man* (1954), in *Human Nature and the Human Condition* (1959), and also in the essay following this one.

[1] It is one of Freud's quaint conceits that the child in its mother's womb is the happiest of living creatures. Into his consciousness no conflict has yet entered, for he knows no limitations to his desires and the universe is exactly as he wishes it to be. All his needs are satisfied before even he becomes aware of them, and if his awareness is dim that is but the natural result of a complete harmony between the self and the environment, since, as Spencer pointed out in a remote age, to be omniscient

and omnipotent would be to be without any consciousness whatsoever. The discomfort of being born is the first warning which he receives that any event can be thrust upon him; it is the first limitation of his omnipotence which he perceives, and he is cast upon the shores of the world wailing his protest against the indignity to which he has been subjected. Years pass before he learns to control the expression of enraged surprise which arises within him at every unpleasant fact with which he is confronted, and his parents conspire so to protect him that he will learn only by very slow stages how far is the world from his heart's desire.

[2] The cradle is made to imitate as closely as may be the conditions, both physical and spiritual, of the womb. Of its occupant no effort is demanded, and every precaution is taken to anticipate each need before it can arise. If, as the result of any unforeseen circumstance, any unsatisfied desire is born, he need only raise his voice in protest to cause the entire world in so far as he knows it—his nurse or his parents—to rush to his aid. The whole of his physical universe is obedient to his will and he is justified by his experience in believing that his mere volition controls his destiny. Only as he grows older does he become aware that there are wills other than his own or that there are physical circumstances rebellious to any human will. And only after the passage of many years does he become aware of the full extent of his predicament in the midst of a world which is in very few respects what he would wish it to be.

[3] As a child he is treated as a child, and such treatment implies much more than the physical coddling of which Freud speaks. Not only do those who surround him co-operate more completely than they ever will again to satisfy his wishes in material things, but they encourage him to live in a spiritual world far more satisfactory than their own. He is carefully protected from any knowledge of the cruelties and complexities of life; he is led to suppose that the moral order is simple and clear, that virtue triumphs, and that the world is, as the desires of whole generations of mankind have led them to try to pretend that it is, arranged according to a pattern which would seem reasonable and satisfactory to human sensibilities. He is prevented from realizing how inextricably what men call good and evil are intertwined, how careless is Nature of those values called mercy and justice and righteousness which men have come, in her despite, to value; and he is, besides, encouraged to believe in a vast mythology peopled with figments which range all the way from the Saints to Santa Claus and which represent projections of human wishes which the adult has come to recognize as no more than projections but which he is willing that the child, for the sake of his own happiness, should believe real. Aware how different is the world which experience reveals from the world which the spirit desires, the mature, as though afraid that reality could not be endured unless the mind had been gradually inured to it, allow the child to become aware of it only by slow stages, and little by

little he learns, not only the limitations of his will, but the moral discord of the world. Thus it is, in a very important sense, true that the infant does come trailing clouds of glory from that heaven which his imagination creates, and that as his experience accumulates he sees it fade away into the light of common day.

[4] Now races as well as individuals have their infancy, their adolescence, and their maturity. Experience accumulates not only from year to year but from generation to generation, and in the life of each person it plays a little larger part than it did in the life of his father. As civilization grows older it too has more and more facts thrust upon its consciousness and is compelled to abandon one after another, quite as the child does, certain illusions which have been dear to it. Like the child, it has instinctively assumed that what it would like to be true is true, and it never gives up any such belief until experience in some form compels it to do so. Being, for example, extremely important to itself, it assumes that it is extremely important to the universe also. The earth is the center of all existing things, man is the child and the protégé of those gods who transcend and who will ultimately enable him to transcend all the evils which he has been compelled to recognize. The world and all that it contains were designed for him, and even those things which seem noxious have their usefulness only temporarily hid. Since he knows but little he is free to imagine, and imagination is always the creature of desire.

– II –

[5] The world which any consciousness inhabits is a world made up in part of experience and in part of fancy. No experience, and hence no knowledge, is complete, but the gaps which lie between the solid fragments are filled in with shadows. Connections, explanations, and reasons are supplied by the imagination, and thus the world gets its patterned completeness from material which is spun out of the desires. But as time goes on and experience accumulates there remains less and less scope for the fancy. The universe becomes more and more what experience has revealed, less and less what imagination has created, and hence, since it was not designed to suit man's needs, less and less what he would have it be. With increasing knowledge his power to manipulate his physical environment increases, but in gaining the knowledge which enables him to do so he surrenders insensibly the power which in his ignorance he had to mold the universe. The forces of nature obey him, but in learning to master them he has in another sense allowed them to master him. He has exchanged the universe which his desires created, the universe made for man, for the universe of nature of which he is only a part. Like the child growing into manhood, he passes from a world which is fitted to him into a world for which he must fit himself.

[6] If, then, the world of poetry, mythology, and religion represents

the world as a man would like to have it, while science represents the world as he gradually comes to discover it, we need only compare the two to realize how irreconcilable they appear. For the cozy bowl of the sky arched in a protecting curve above him he must exchange the cold immensities of space and, for the spiritual order which he has designed, the chaos of nature. God he had loved *because* God was anthropomorphic, because He was made in man's own image, with purposes and desires which were human and hence understandable. But Nature's purpose, if purpose she can be said to have, is no purpose of his and is not understandable in his terms. Her desire merely to live and to propagate in innumerable forms, her ruthless indifference to his values, and the blindness of her irresistible will strike terror to his soul, and he comes in the fullness of his experience to realize that the ends which he proposes to himself—happiness and order and reason—are ends which he must achieve, if he achieve them at all, in her despite. Formerly he had believed in even his darkest moments that the universe was rational if he could only grasp its rationality, but gradually he comes to suspect that rationality is an attribute of himself alone and that there is no reason to suppose that his own life has any more meaning than the life of the humblest insect that crawls from one annihilation to another. Nature, in her blind thirst for life, has filled every possible cranny of the rotting earth with some sort of fantastic creature, and among them man is but one—perhaps the most miserable of all, because he is the only one in whom the instinct of life falters long enough to enable it to ask the question "Why?" As long as life is regarded as having been created, creating may be held to imply a purpose, but merely to have come into being is, in all likelihood, merely to go out of it also.

[7] Fortunately, perhaps, man, like the individual child, was spared in his cradle the knowledge which he could not bear. Illusions have been lost one by one. God, instead of disappearing in an instant, has retreated step by step and surrendered gradually his control of the universe. Once he decreed the fall of every sparrow and counted the hairs upon every head; a little later he became merely the original source of the laws of nature, and even today there are thousands who, unable to bear the thought of losing him completely, still fancy that they can distinguish the uncertain outlines of a misty figure. But the rôle which he plays grows less and less, and man is left more and more alone in a universe to which he is completely alien. His world was once, like the child's world, three-quarters myth and poetry. His teleological concepts molded it into a form which he could appreciate and he gave to it moral laws which would make it meaningful, but step by step the outlines of nature have thrust themselves upon him, and for the dream which he made is substituted a reality devoid of any pattern which he can understand.

[8] In the course of this process innumerable readjustments have been

made, and always with the effort to disturb as little as possible the myth which is so much more full of human values than the fact which comes in some measure to replace it. Thus, for example, the Copernican theory of astronomy, removing the earth from the center of the universe and assigning it a very insignificant place among an infinitude of whirling motes, was not merely resisted as a fact but was, when finally accepted, accepted as far as possible without its implications. Even if taken entirely by itself and without the whole system of facts of which it is a part, it renders extremely improbable the assumption, fundamental in most human thought, that the universe has man as its center and is hence understandable in his terms, but this implication was disregarded just as, a little later, the implications of the theory of evolution were similarly disregarded. It is not likely that if man had been aware from the very beginning that his world was a mere detail in the universe, and himself merely one of the innumerable species of living things, he would ever have come to think of himself, as he even now tends to do, as a being whose desires must be somehow satisfiable and whose reason must be matched by some similar reason in nature. But the myth, having been once established, persists long after the assumptions upon which it was made have been destroyed, because, being born of desire, it is far more satisfactory than any fact.

[9] Unfortunately, perhaps, experience does not grow at a constant, but at an accelerated, rate. The Greeks who sought knowledge, not through the study of nature but through the examination of their own minds, developed a philosophy which was really analogous to myth, because the laws which determined its growth were dictated by human desires and they discovered few facts capable of disturbing the pattern which they devised. The Middle Ages retreated still further into themselves, but with the Renaissance man began to surrender himself to nature, and the sciences, each nourishing the other, began their iconoclastic march. Three centuries lay between the promulgation of the Copernican theory and the publication of the *Origin of Species,* but in sixty-odd years which have elapsed since that latter event the blows have fallen with a rapidity which left no interval for recovery. The structures which are variously known as mythology, religion, and philosophy, and which are alike in that each has as its function the interpretation of experience in terms which have human values, have collapsed under the force of successive attacks and shown themselves utterly incapable of assimilating the new stores of experience which have been dumped upon the world. With increasing completeness science maps out the pattern of nature, but the latter has no relation to the pattern of human needs and feelings.

[10] Consider, for example, the plight of ethics. Historical criticism having destroyed what used to be called by people of learning and intelligence "Christian Evidences," and biology having shown how unlikely it is

that man is the recipient of any transcendental knowledge, there remains no foundation in authority for ideas of right and wrong; and if, on the other hand, we turn to the traditions of the human race anthropology is ready to prove that no consistent human tradition has ever existed. Custom has furnished the only basis which ethics have ever had, and there is no conceivable human action which custom has not at one time justified and at another condemned. Standards are imaginary things, and yet it is extremely doubtful if man can live well, either spiritually or physically, without the belief that they are somehow real. Without them society lapses into anarchy and the individual becomes aware of an intolerable disharmony between himself and the universe. Instinctively and emotionally he is an ethical animal. No known race is so low in the scale of civilization that it has not attributed a moral order to the world, because no known race is so little human as not to suppose a moral order so innately desirable as to have an inevitable existence. It is man's most fundamental myth, and life seems meaningless to him without it. Yet, as that systematized and cumulative experience which is called science displaces one after another the myths which have been generated by need, it grows more and more likely that he must remain an ethical animal in a universe which contains no ethical element.

– III –

[11] Mystical philosophers have sometimes said that they "accepted the universe." They have, that is to say, formed of it some conception which answered the emotional needs of their spirit and which brought them a sense of being in harmony with its aims and processes. They have been aware of no needs which Nature did not seem to supply and of no ideals which she too did not seem to recognize. They have felt themselves one with her because they have had the strength of imagination to make her over in their own image, and it is doubtful if any man can live at peace who does not thus feel himself at home. But as the world assumes the shape which science gives it, it becomes more and more difficult to find such emotional correspondences. Whole realms of human feeling, like the realm of ethics, find no place for themselves in the pattern of nature and generate needs for which no satisfaction is supplied. What man knows is everywhere at war with what he wants.

[12] In the course of a few centuries his knowledge, and hence the universe of which he finds himself an inhabitant, has been completely revolutionized, but his instincts and his emotions have remained, relatively at least, unchanged. He is still, as he always was, adjusted to the orderly, purposeful, humanized world which all peoples unburdened by experience have figured to themselves, but that world no longer exists. He has the same sense of dignity to which the myth of his descent from the gods was designed to minister, and the same innate purposefulness

which led him to attribute a purpose to nature, but he can no longer think in terms appropriate to either. The world which his reason and his investigation reveal is a world which his emotions cannot comprehend.

[13] Casually he accepts the spiritual iconoclasm of science, and in the detachment of everyday life he learns to play with the cynical wisdom of biology and psychology, which explain away the awe of emotional experience just as earlier science explained away the awe of conventional piety. Yet, under the stress of emotional crises, knowledge is quite incapable of controlling his emotions or of justifying them to himself. In love, he calls upon the illusions of man's grandeur and dignity to help him accept his emotions, and faced with tragedy he calls upon illusion to dignify his suffering; but lyric flight is checked by the rationality which he has cultivated, and in the world of metabolism and hormones, repressions and complexes, he finds no answer for his needs. He is feeling about love, for example, much as the troubadour felt, but he thinks about it in a very different way. Try as he may, the two halves of his soul can hardly be made to coalesce, and he cannot either feel as his intelligence tells him that he should feel or think as his emotions would have him think, and thus he is reduced to mocking his torn and divided soul. In the grip of passion he cannot, as some romanticist might have done, accept it with a religious trust in the mystery of love, nor yet can he regard it as a psychiatrist, himself quite free from emotion, might suggest—merely as an interesting specimen of psychical botany. Man *qua* thinker may delight in the intricacies of psychology, but man *qua* lover has not learned to feel in its terms; so that, though complexes and ductless glands may serve to explain the feelings of another, one's own still demand all those symbols of the ineffable in which one has long ceased to believe.

[14] Time was when the scientist, the poet, and the philosopher walked hand in hand. In the universe which the one perceived the other found himself comfortably at home. But the world of modern science is one in which the intellect alone can rejoice. The mind leaps, and leaps perhaps with a sort of elation, through the immensities of space, but the spirit, frightened and cold, longs to have once more above its head the inverted bowl beyond which may lie whatever paradise its desires may create. The lover who surrendered himself to the Implacable Aphrodite or who fancied his foot upon the lowest rung of the Platonic ladder of love might retain his self-respect, but one can neither resist nor yield gracefully to a carefully catalogued psychosis. A happy life is a sort of poem, with a poem's elevation and dignity, but emotions cannot be dignified unless they are first respected. They must seem to correspond with, to be justified by, something in the structure of the universe itself; but though it was the function of religion and philosophy to hypostatize some such correspondence, to project a humanity upon nature, or at least to conceive

of a humane force above and beyond her, science finds no justification for such a process and is content instead to show how illusions were born.

[15] The most ardent love of truth, the most resolute determination to follow nature no matter to what black abyss she may lead, need not blind one to the fact that many of the lost illusions had, to speak the language of science, a survival value. Either individuals or societies whose life is imbued with a cheerful certitude, whose aims are clear, and whose sense of the essential rightness of life is strong, live and struggle with an energy unknown to the skeptical and the pessimistic. Whatever the limitations of their intellects as instruments of criticism, they possess the physical and emotional vigor which is, unlike critical intelligence, analogous to the processes of nature. They found empires and conquer wildernesses, and they pour the excess of their energy into works of art which the intelligence of more sophisticated peoples continues to admire even though it has lost the faith in life which is requisite for the building of a Chartres or the carving of a Venus de Milo. The one was not erected to a law of nature or the other designed to celebrate the libido, for each presupposed a sense of human dignity which science nowhere supports.

[16] Thus man seems caught in a dilemma which his intellect has devised. Any deliberately managed return to a state of relative ignorance, however desirable it might be argued to be, is obviously out of the question. We cannot, as the naïve proponents of the various religions, new and old, seem to assume, believe one thing and forget another merely because we happen to be convinced that it would be desirable to do so; and it is worth observing that the new psychology, with its penetrating analysis of the influence of desire upon belief, has so adequately warned the reason of the tricks which the will can play upon it that it has greatly decreased the possibility of beneficent delusion and serves to hold the mind in a steady contemplation of that from which it would fain escape. Weak and uninstructed intelligences take refuge in the monotonous repetition of once living creeds, or are even reduced to the desperate expedient of going to sleep amid the formulae of the flabby pseudo-religions in which the modern world is so prolific. But neither of these classes affords any aid to the robust but serious mind which is searching for some terms upon which it may live.

[17] And if we are, as by this time we should be, free from any teleological delusion, if we no longer make the unwarranted assumption that every human problem is somehow of necessity solvable, we must confess it may be that for the sort of being whom we have described no survival is possible in any form like that which his soul has now taken. He is a fantastic thing that has developed sensibilities and established values beyond the nature which gave him birth. He is of all living creatures the one to whom the earth is the least satisfactory. He has arrived at a point

where he can no longer delude himself as to the extent of his predicament, and should he either become modified or disappear the earth would continue to spin and the grass to grow as it has always done. Of the thousands of living species the vast majority would be as unaware of his passing as they are unaware now of his presence, and he would go as a shadow goes. His arts, his religions, and his civilizations—these are fair and wonderful things, but they are fair and wonderful to him alone. With the extinction of his poetry would come also the extinction of the only sensibility for which it has any meaning, and there would remain nothing capable of feeling a loss. Nothing would be left to label the memory of his discontent "divine," and those creatures who find in nature no lack would resume their undisputed possession of the earth.

[18] Anthropoid in form some of them might continue to be, and possessed as well of all of the human brain that makes possible a cunning adaptation to the conditions of physical life. To them nature might yield up subtler secrets than any yet penetrated; their machines might be more wonderful and their bodies more healthy than any yet known—even though there had passed away, not merely all myth and poetry, but the need for them as well. Cured of his transcendental cravings, content with things as they are, accepting the universe as experience had shown it to be, man would be freed of his soul and, like the other animals, either content or at least desirous of nothing which he might not hope ultimately to obtain.

[19] Nor can it be denied that certain adumbrations of this type have before now come into being. Among those of keener intellect there are scientists to whom the test tube and its contents are all-sufficient, and among those of coarser grain, captains of finance and builders of mills, there are those to whom the acquirement of wealth and power seems to constitute a life in which no lack can be perceived. Doubtless they are not new types; doubtless they have always existed; but may they not be the strain from which Nature will select the coming race? Is not their creed the creed of Nature, and are they not bound to triumph over those whose illusions are no longer potent because they are no longer really believed? Certain philosophers, clinging desperately to the ideal of a humanized world, have proposed a retreat into the imagination. Bertrand Russell in his popular essay, *A Free Man's Worship,* Unamuno and Santayana *passim* throughout their works, have argued that the way of salvation lay in a sort of ironic belief, in a determination to act as though one still believed the things which once were really held true. But is not this a desperate expedient, a last refuge likely to appeal only to the leaders of a lost cause? Does it not represent the last, least substantial, phase of fading faith, something which borrows what little substance it seems to have from a reality of the past? If it seems half real to the sons of those who lived in the spiritual world of which it is a shadow, will it

not seem, a little further removed, only a faint futility? Surely it has but little to oppose to those who come armed with the certitudes of science and united with, not fleeing from, the nature amid which they live.

[20] And if the dilemma here described is itself a delusion it is at least as vividly present and as terribly potent as those other delusions which have shaped or deformed the human spirit. There is no significant contemporary writer upon philosophy, ethics, or aesthetics whose speculations do not lead him to it in one form or another, and even the less reflective are aware of it in their own way. Both our practical morality and our emotional lives are adjusted to a world which no longer exists. In so far as we adhere to a code of conduct, we do so largely because certain habits still persist, not because we can give any logical reason for preferring them, and in so far as we indulge ourselves in the primitive emotional satisfactions—romantic love, patriotism, zeal for justice, and so forth—our satisfaction is the result merely of the temporary suspension of our disbelief in the mythology upon which they are founded. Traditionalists in religion are fond of asserting that our moral codes are flimsy because they are rootless; but, true as this is, it is perhaps not so important as the fact that our emotional lives are rootless too.

[21] If the gloomy vision of a dehumanized world which has just been evoked is not to become a reality, some complete readjustment must be made, and at least two generations have found themselves unequal to the task. The generation of Thomas Henry Huxley, so busy with destruction as never adequately to realize how much it was destroying, fought with such zeal against frightened conservatives that it never took time to do more than assert with some vehemence that all would be well, and the generation that followed either danced amid the ruins or sought by various compromises to save the remains of a few tottering structures. But neither patches nor evasions will serve. It is not a changed world but a new one in which man must henceforth live if he lives at all, for all his premises have been destroyed and he must proceed to new conclusions. The values which he thought established have been swept away along with the rules by which he thought they might be attained.

[22] To this fact many are not yet awake, but our novels, our poems, and our pictures are enough to reveal that a generation aware of its predicament is at hand. It has awakened to the fact that both the ends which its fathers proposed to themselves and the emotions from which they drew their strength seem irrelevant and remote. With a smile, sad or mocking, according to individual temperament, it regards those works of the past in which were summed up the values of life. The romantic ideal of a world well lost for love and the classic ideal of austere dignity seem equally ridiculous, equally meaningless when referred, not to the temper of the past, but to the temper of the present. The passions which swept through the once major poets no longer awaken any profound

response, and only in the bleak, tortuous complexities of a T. S. Eliot does it find its moods given adequate expression. Here disgust speaks with a robust voice and denunciation is confident, but ecstasy, flickering and uncertain, leaps fitfully up only to sink back among the cinders. And if the poet, with his gift of keen perceptions and his power of organization, can achieve only the most momentary and unstable adjustments, what hope can there be for those whose spirit is a less powerful instrument?

[23] And yet it is with such as he, baffled, but content with nothing which plays only upon the surface, that the hope for a still humanized future must rest. No one can tell how many of the old values must go or how new the new will be. Thus, while under the influence of the old mythology the sexual instinct was transformed into romantic love and tribal solidarity into the religion of patriotism, there is nothing in the modern consciousness capable of effecting these transmutations. Neither the one nor the other is capable of being, as it once was, the *raison d'être* of a life or the motif of a poem which is not, strictly speaking, derivative and anachronistic. Each is fading, each becoming as much a shadow as devotion to the cult of purification through self-torture. Either the instincts upon which they are founded will achieve new transformations or they will remain merely instincts, regarded as having no particular emotional significance in a spiritual world which, if it exists at all, will be as different from the spiritual world of, let us say, Robert Browning as that world is different from the world of Cato the Censor.

[24] As for this present unhappy time, haunted by ghosts from a dead world and not yet at home in its own, its predicament is not, to return to the comparison with which we began, unlike the predicament of the adolescent who has not yet learned to orient himself without reference to the mythology amid which his childhood was passed. He still seeks in the world of his experience for the values which he had found there, and he is aware only of a vast disharmony. But boys—most of them, at least—grow up, and the world of adult consciousness has always held a relation to myth intimate enough to make readjustment possible. The finest spirits have bridged the gulf, have carried over with them something of a child's faith, and only the coarsest have grown into something which was not more than finished animality. Today the gulf is broader, the adjustment more difficult, than ever it was before, and even the possibility of an actual human maturity is problematic. There impends for the human spirit either extinction or a readjustment more stupendous than any made before.

COMMENT AND QUESTIONS

1. As the title of his chapter suggests, Krutch uses both a narrative method and a cause–effect development in discussing the genesis of the modern temper. He also makes extensive use of contrast and comparison, notably in the sustained comparison of the child and the human race. What is the purpose, in the first three paragraphs, of developing so fully the experience of the child before and after birth?
2. According to Krutch, how does the world of poetry, mythology, and religion differ from the world revealed by science? What were the values of the myths and illusions which he says man has been forced to abandon?
3. Among Krutch's many skills as a writer is his way of building his paragraphs to strong endings. Re-read the final sentences of paragraphs 1–10 (the first two sections of the chapter). What identical or similar ideas are restated, and so given additional emphasis, in these emphatic end-sentences?
4. In the first two sections (paragraphs 1–10), is Krutch making any assumptions about the experience of the child or of man which you are unable to accept? Explain.
5. Krutch suggests (in paragraph 17 and elsewhere) that man with his developed sensibilities and values, adjusted to a world which no longer exists, has become a "fantastic thing" for whom survival may not be possible. What kind of "dehumanized world" does the author fear?
6. What escapes from the modern dilemma does Krutch reject as unsatisfactory for intelligent men?
7. What is the general tone of the selection? Does Krutch see any hope for a happy or satisfying future for man?
8. Select one or two paragraphs in which the writing seems to you effective, and carefully analyze the author's sentence structures and use of language.
9. Writing in 1929, Krutch concludes his chapter: "There impends for the human spirit either extinction or a readjustment more stupendous than any made before." On the basis of more recent writing (i.e., since 1929) which you have read—in this book or elsewhere—would you say that the human spirit is becoming extinct, or that it is making a readjustment to a new kind of world, or neither?

[27] *Joseph Wood Krutch*: Life, liberty, and the Pursuit of Welfare

FOR A NOTE ON Joseph Wood Krutch, see page 260. The following essay was published in the *Saturday Evening Post*, July 15, 1961.

[¹] "Welfare" is one of the key words of our time. What too many men now seem to desire is not virtue or knowledge or justice, but welfare. To the majority the word sums up the principal object of government and, indeed, of all social institutions.

[²] Had you asked a Greek philosopher what the purpose of government should be, he would have said something about the maintenance of justice. And had you pressed him to say in what justice consists, he would have replied—not very satisfactorily—"In assuring to every man that which is rightfully his."

[³] A medieval theologian would have added something about the City of God and the extent to which a community of mortals might approximate it. On the other hand that brutal seventeenth-century realist, Thomas Hobbes, would have gone to the other extreme. To him the principal aim of government is simply the maintenance of order, the taming of that state of nature which is anarchy or war. And the state of anarchy, he would have added, is so terrible that any government is better than no government.

[⁴] Finally, had you posed the same question to an eighteenth-century philosopher, he would have said something to the effect that the chief purpose of government is not simply the maintenance of order, but the assurance to each man of his inalienable rights. And if you had asked him what these inalienable rights are, he would have answered in some form not too different from that of the Declaration—"Life, liberty and the pursuit of happiness."

[⁵] In any event, it is obvious that none of these formulas is entirely satisfactory to most people today. They do not explicitly reject life, liberty and the pursuit of happiness, but they obviously consider them something less than enough. The invention of the term "welfare state" to describe something more than the democratic state is an expression of this dissatisfaction. It is intended to define a new ideal, which its proponents would call an extension of the ideal of a merely democratic state.

[⁶] If it be objected that the philosophers, theologians and social critics cited above did not actually speak for the masses and that the great majority of the people would always have preferred "welfare" to the less easily understood goods proposed to them, the answer is that even if this be granted, it is not crucial to the argument which follows. The fact remains that the power of the masses is now for the first time decisive and that the sociologists and political scientists most influential today tend both to accept this fact and to concur in regarding "welfare" as the chief legitimate aim of government.

[7] In a broad, general way we all know what welfare so used implies, what specific laws and institutions are called welfare measures, and what are the premises upon which they are advocated. No one would object very much if I said that the welfare state assumes, not only that men should be protected against those who would deprive them of their right to life, liberty and the pursuit of happiness, but that it should go beyond mere protection to something more positive. All men not only must be guaranteed their liberties but also, to a very considerable extent, "looked after." Many of the arguments both for and against the policy of looking after people are too familiar to need mentioning. But certain fundamental questions are seldom asked. What is the ultimate definition of welfare— in what does it consist, and who decides what it is? Or, to put the question in a simpler form: Does the promotion of welfare mean giving people what they want or seem to want or think they want, or does it consist in giving them what they ought to have?

[8] The answer implied in various specific welfare proposals is sometimes the one and sometimes the other. But few have ever dared to put the question boldly and to give a positive answer one way or another. If welfare means that people get what they want, then which wants of which people come first? If welfare means giving them what they ought to have, then who decides what they ought to have, and on the basis of what criteria is the decision made?

[9] This last is a very tough question indeed for an age which has rejected absolutes and enthusiastically embraced both cultural and moral relativism. One of the few bold answers I have ever encountered was given by David Thompson, a lecturer in history at Cambridge University. "The welfare state," said he, "exists to promote whatever the community regards as beneficial and good. If the community regards automobiles, TV sets and football pools as of greater value than better schools, more generous care for old people, and a creative use of leisure, then the democratic state will provide more automobiles, TV sets and football pools."

[10] In the course of the article Mr. Thompson gives the impression that he has preferences of his own and that they are not what he believes to be those of most people. But he does not appear to have his tongue in his cheek when he yields to the only definition of democracy and the only definition of welfare which his relativistic philosophy will permit. Like

most of our contemporaries, he is unwilling to consider the possibility that what the community regards as valuable is not the only possible standard by which values may be judged. Nor, as a matter of fact, can anyone escape such a conviction unless he is willing to assume what most today refuse to assume, namely, that some basis for calling one thing intrinsically and absolutely better or righter or higher than another can be found somewhere: In nature, in reason or in the law of God—all of which are independent of either custom or majority opinion.

[11] Refuse, as most sociologists, psychologists and anthropologists do refuse, to make such an assumption, and you are driven to the conclusion which Mr. Thompson accepts: That nothing is better or more desirable than anything else except insofar as more people want it. Thus he comes to defend democracy not because of any conviction that its decisions are wiser by some independent standards than those arrived at by other forms of government, but simply because any decision which has majority sanction is wise and right by the only possible definition of those terms.

[12] If, as most people seem to assume, the normal is merely the average, if the good life is whatever the majority thinks or has been persuaded to think it is, if what men should do is whatever they do do, then it must follow that the desirable is whatever is most widely desired, and that democracy means that what the majority admires is necessarily to be called excellent. Mr. Thompson himself may prefer what he calls "the creative use of leisure" to TV sets and football pools, but he is too broadminded—as we now call it—to suppose that such a preference is anything more than just another one of those tastes about which there is no disputing.

[13] *Laissez faire* is generally supposed to describe the social theory diametrically opposed to that of the welfare state, but here one sort of *laissez faire* is exchanged for another. Though the economy is to be planned, society is to be allowed to drift intellectually and culturally with whatever economic, technological or other currents may vary in this direction or that.

[14] Under democracy of the older sort the most fundamental right of the citizen was assumed to be the pursuit of happiness. The welfare state substitutes welfare—usually defined in material terms—for happiness. But by way of compensation it assures the citizen that his right is not merely to pursue happiness but to attain welfare; and under this arrangement we lose something as well as, perhaps, gain something. Though we may pursue whatever kind of happiness seems to us most worth pursuing, the welfare which is going to be assured us must be mass-produced, whether it is defined, under a dictatorship, as what the dictator thinks we ought to have, or, as in our society, by what the majority wants or has been persuaded to want.

[15] If I object that to define welfare as whatever most people seem

to want tends to mean more things and fewer ideas and, in general, tends toward the vulgarest possible conception of what constitutes the good life, I will be told that the answer is education—that, given enough schools, and schools that are good enough, the community will want what is truly most desirable; and that, if properly educated, it will provide for itself and ultimately reach a truly acceptable definition of welfare.

[16] But despite all the schooling which Americans get, many of them do not seem to be very effectively learning any ideals or cultivating any interests other than those which seem to prevail among the uneducated. High-school graduates and college graduates also very frequently prefer television and shinier automobiles to any of the more intellectual and less material forms of welfare.

[17] This fact brings us again up against the unanswered question and it suggests that education is failing to help people to achieve an acceptable definition of welfare for the same reason that the ideal of welfare itself is failing—because, in other words, we are unable to give any definition of education except the same kind of definition we give of welfare.

[18] If students do not want classical literature, philosophy or science, if they do want sports, courses in movie appreciation and in the accepted social conventions, then, just as the other things constitute welfare, so these things must constitute education. Once the school, like the church, tended to embody a protest, or at least a countervailing influence, against what the other forces in society tended to make of that society and of man himself. The church held that man undisciplined by religion was wicked. The school held that unless he was educated, he would be ignorant and crass. But both the church and the school seem now to have fallen in love with the world as it is. They talk more and more about adjustment—and by that to mean "adjustment to things as they are."

[19] The church halfheartedly, the school with real enthusiasm, gives up the attempt to direct society and is content to follow it, like the political leader who watches where the mob is going, puts himself at the head of it and says, "Follow me." Educators so-called have said, "Don't teach literary English; teach acceptable English." If, as a New York commission recently has proposed, children are not interested in the classics, don't waste time trying to arouse their interests; give them something they are interested in—teach them how to drive automobiles, how lipstick is best applied or, and this is part of one actual course in a Midwestern institution of learning, how to order groceries over the telephone.

[20] These are the things many of the students will be doing; this is what their lives will be made up of. And if the business of education is to prepare for life, then these are the things that they ought to be taught. But the statement so commonly made, that education should be a

preparation for life, is meaningless unless the kind of life it is supposed to prepare for is specified. If education is properly defined as hardly more than what anthropologists call "acculturation," then it is worth taking account of the fact that most children get much more of their education in this sense from advertisements, moving pictures, television, popular songs and so on, than they do from school. Preparation for life as the schools are tending to define it is much better accomplished by those institutions outside the school system than by those within it.

[21] It would, of course, be inaccurate as well as unfair to leave the impression that there is no protest against the ideals and practices of the schools as typified by the examples just given. During the past few years such protests have grown from a whisper to an outcry. Various organizations, notably the Council for Basic Education, have been formed to combat the prevailing tendencies. The latter especially has conducted a vigorous campaign of propaganda, buttressed by news bulletins, which report both outrageous examples of denatured education and reforms in the directions of which it approves.

[22] Such protests have had their effect. In California, for instance, the recent report of a state-appointed commission puts itself squarely on record as finding the prevailing aims and methods of the school system to be in many instances radically undesirable.

[23] Even more important perhaps is the fact that many parents have expressed their dissatisfaction and called for reform. The National Education Association, a very powerful and well entrenched group, has bitterly resented most such criticisms, but if the tide has not actually turned, it looks as though it might be on the point of turning.

[24] Nevertheless, it is not enough merely to ridicule current extravagances, to call for a return to the three R's and to insist that education does not consist in miscellaneous instruction in such varied specific subjects as safety rules for automobilists, the use of consumer credit and the current conventions governing "dating." Neither is it enough to say only that schools should be concerned primarily with the intellect and that those who talk about "educating the whole child" seem to forget that his head is part of him. Any rational theory must be based upon some conviction that the man of whom the child is the father ought to be in mind, in taste and in convictions something more than what he will be if he is allowed to follow only his simplest inclinations and whatever happens to be the current conventions of his group. In other words, what is necessary is a standard of values. Education is simply not changing people as much as it should.

[25] Many critics of our society have said that we lack standards. This has been said so often by preachers and by the makers of commencement addresses that we have almost stopped asking what, if anything,

it means to say that our society "lacks standards." But that we do lack standards for welfare and standards for education is obvious. Welfare turns into vulgar materialism because we have no standard by which to measure it. Education fails because it also refuses to face the responsibility of saying in what education consists. Both tend to become merely what people seem to want.

[26] To any such complaint most sociologists, psychologists and educators will shrug and say, "Perhaps. But where can you find standards other than those which are set by society itself? Who is arrogant enough to set them up? Where can the authority for such standards be found?"

[27] Most periods of human history have believed that they could be found somewhere outside mere custom. They have usually been sought in one or all of three places: (1) In the revealed will of God; (2) in the operation of right reason, supposedly capable of defining good and evil; (3) in something permanent in human nature itself.

[28] If I say this to the modern relativist, he replies that none of these things will any longer do. (1) God no longer exists. (2) Though man is capable of thinking instrumentally—that is to say, capable of scheming to get what he wants—there is no such thing as pure reason capable of reaching an absolute; and whenever men have thought they were doing so, they were, in fact only rationalizing their desires or the customs of their particular country. (3) What we call "human nature" is merely the result of the conditioning of the individual, either by the society in which he lives or by the peculiar experiences which have happened to be his. Since neither God nor pure reason exists, and since human nature is infinitely variable, it is evident that morals are merely mores, or custom; that right reason is merely a rationalization of the prejudices of the individual or his society; and that human nature is merely what social circumstances have made it.

[29] If all these characteristic modern convictions—or lack of convictions—are sound, then we must agree that whatever most people want is welfare, and that whatever pupils think they would least dislike doing in school is education. It is then useless to ask whether society is going in the right direction or whether men today are leading a good life. Nothing is absolutely better than anything else; things are what they are and will be what they will be, and we cannot control or direct. We must follow where events may lead us.

[30] Before accepting this counsel of despair once and for all, it would be worth while to ask again if it really is certain that all three of the conceivable bases upon which some standard might be founded really are merely illusory. Each of them might be taken up in turn. One might ask again does God exist; one might ask again is right reason a mere figment of the imagination? Does human nature exist?

[31] I here raise only what is perhaps the least difficult of all these

questions—the last one. Granted that man may be conditioned in various ways, is it nevertheless true that there are limits to the extent to which he can be conditioned? Is it true that human nature tends to return to some norm, that it is not limitlessly conditionable? And is it possible that to some extent one thing is better or higher or more valuable than another because human nature tends persistently to think that it is? Or, to put the question in its most general form, is there a good life which might be loosely defined as "that which is in accord with the most fundamental and persistent wants, desires and needs of human nature"?

[32] If ours is the richest and most powerful civilization that has ever existed, but if it is also the most anxious and ill at ease, is that in part because human nature needs something more than the wealth and power it has acquired? Is it possibly because human nature needs to believe just what modern thought has forbidden it to believe—that is, that morals are more than mores and that value judgments are more than merely rationalized prejudices? Once you insist that human nature as such does not exist, all the relativisms of our time—cultural, moral and social—inevitably follow. So, almost in desperation, let us ask again, "How good is the evidence that there is no such thing as human nature, that it is nothing but what experience or culture has made it?"

[33] We must begin by remembering that the theory that human nature is nothing in itself is not actually new. In that enormously influential seventeenth-century book, *Leviathan* by Thomas Hobbes, the theory is already implicit. Hobbes attempts to account for all the phenomena of human life by assuming that there is nothing innate in man except the ability to receive stimuli, the ability to react to them and the desire to experience pleasure. There is, accordingly, nothing in the mind which has not been first in the senses. There are no such things as innate ideas or desires other than the simple desire to experience pleasure or to exercise power, which latter is said to be the same thing. Hence man becomes whatever experience makes him and, to use the phrase which became popular later, he is born with a blank slate upon which anything may be written.

[34] We have enormously complicated this theory. We have drawn from it many deductions. But we have added little if anything essentially new. The whole of modern relativism seems to follow logically from Hobbes. If the human mind begins as a blank slate upon which anything may be written, then morals are only mores, our ideas of what is good or evil, just or unjust, beautiful or ugly, seemly or unseemly, are simply learned from the society in which we grow up. Nothing is eternally or inherently better than anything else—cultures vary from time to time and from place to place, but there is no external standard by which one may be judged as better than another. Incidentally, this complete abandon-

ment of the right to judge we now commonly call "getting rid of our prejudices."

[35] Contemporary anthropologists are fond of pointing out that what was considered right and desirable in one society was not so considered in another. Already by the end of the nineteenth century the historian Lecky could assert in his *History of European Morals* that there is no act which has not at one time or place been commanded as a duty and at another time or place forbidden as a sin—which is to say again that morals are only mores. Or, as a contemporary college textbook on psychology, written by a professor at the University of Southern California, puts it in a very short chapter on morals, "We call a man moral when he acts in accord with the laws and customs of his society"—by which definition, no doubt, a Nazi who took part in the persecution of the Jews would be a moral man, and who did not would be an immoral one.

[36] In a world which has so definitely rejected transcendental sanctions for either codes of morals or standards of value, the question whether human nature itself might supply them becomes enormously important. Is the usual negative answer really justifiable? Shall we one day swing again in a different direction and discover evidence now neglected that human nature is something in itself and does provide certain absolutes, valid at least within the human realm?

[37] Have the anthropologists, for instance, been so preoccupied with the collection of materials to demonstrate the enormous differences between cultures that they have overlooked some things which are common to all? Have the experimental psychologists been so busy conditioning both men and animals that they have paid little attention to the resistance to conditioning which both can put up?

[38] One little breeze in psychological doctrine might seem to point in this direction. Some skeptical psychologists have begun to wonder whether instinct on the one hand and the conditioned reflex on the other really can account for all of the behavior of living organisms. Certain sufficiently obvious facts have recently been re-emphasized.

[39] Consider three of them which seem ludicrously simple. (1) Birds know by instinct how to fly and do not have to be taught, though mother birds sometimes seem to be teaching them. This is an example of instinct. (2) Seals do not instinctively know how to swim, but they learn very easily how to swim when they are taught by their parents. (3) You would have a very hard time indeed teaching most songbirds to swim. In other words, there are not just two classes of animal behavior—that which is inborn and that which is learned. There is also a third and possibly an enormously important one—namely, that behavior which is not inborn, though the ability to learn it easily is.

[40] Considering such facts, some have begun to wonder whether the same might be true not only of skills but throughout the whole psychic

realm of beliefs, tastes, motives, desires and needs. The thesis of the moral relativist is—to take an extreme case—that since no one is born with an innate idea that dishonesty and treachery are evil, then the conviction that they are evil can be nothing but the result of social education, and the opposite could just as easily have been taught, since value judgments are merely the rationalized prejudices of a given culture. May it not be true on the contrary that certain ideas are much more easily learned than others, and that what the eighteenth century called natural law, natural taste and the rest, is real—consisting in those beliefs and tastes which are most readily learned and most productive of health and happiness?

[41] Perhaps you can condition an individual or a society to think and behave unnaturally just as you might possibly teach a robin to swim, but men who have been conditioned to think or behave unnaturally are unhappy—as unhappy and as inefficient as swimming robins. Perhaps Hobbes was right to the extent that no ideas are innate; but if the capacity to entertain readily some ideas and not others is innate, then it comes down to much the same thing. As Alexander Pope wrote nearly two and a half centuries ago, "Nature affords at least a glimmering light; the lines, though touched but faintly, are drawn right"—which is to say that the faint lines on the not quite blank slate constitute the reality behind the idea of a normal human being.

[42] What Pope thought of as a metaphor may be an accurate biological statement. On the not quite blank slate the lines are touched too faintly to constitute an automatic instinct—they may even be destroyed by resolute conditioning and education—but they are rather like a latent image on a photographic plate, imperceptible until developed, though development will reveal only what already exists. If this is true, then there is such a thing as human nature. What we are born with is not a blank slate, but a film bearing already a latent image.

[43] No doubt, as Pope himself said elsewhere, as experimental psychologists prove in the laboratory and as dictators as well as educators have too often demonstrated, the lines may be overlaid, and the unnatural may cease to seem a creature of hideous mien. But the conditioners have to work hard. Men, I suspect, believe much more readily in the reality of good and evil than they accept cultural relativism. Perhaps that means that belief in the reality of good and evil is according to nature and the modern tendency to dismiss them as mere prejudices of culture is fundamentally unnatural.

[44] Such an assumption is at least one which no valid science forbids, and if we make even such a minimum assumption, we can be saved from the nihilism of the present-day social, cultural and moral relativism. We have again some point of reference now lacking in every inquiry

which sets out to determine what kind of society or education or culture would be best for us. One thing is no longer as good as another provided only it can be shown or made to exist. We would no longer need to talk only about what can be done to men or what we might possibly be able to make them into, for we would be able to talk again about what men are in themselves.

[45] We would have the beginning of a basis for a definition of welfare and a definition of education such as we now totally lack. We could say, for example, that welfare is not merely what people at a given moment believe they want, but that which experience has proved to be conducive to health and happiness.

[46] We could say that education is not whatever a pupil thinks he wants in school, but that it is that which experience has shown will lead to a true understanding of his own nature, his own needs and his own wants. We could say the ideal of education is not conformity, not acculturation, but the full development of human nature's potentialities.

[47] We could say that the normal is not the same thing as the average, but rather that the normal is normative—that is to say, that by which a thing is to be judged. And we could add that the normal human being is not the average human being, but the thing to which human nature aspires.

[48] To attempt to determine what is part of permanent human nature is to undertake no easy task. To distinguish between what is truly natural and what is merely conditioned is extremely difficult. But to conclude that the question is actually a meaningful one is already to have concluded something vastly important. We talk much today about the extent to which we can control nature and our destiny, of how we have taken the future of the human race into our hands. But control implies some idea of the direction in which you want to go. We have the power, perhaps, but what good is the power unless we know what we want to do with it? "Give me a fulcrum for my lever, and I will move the world," said Archimedes. But a fulcrum for a lever is exactly what we lack. It implies a point of support which is necessary if you are going to move the world. We are trying to lever society without having any fulcrum on which to rest the lever and, in the absence of any other, we might possibly find it in some understanding of fundamental human nature.

[49] However much there may be still to learn about human nature, certain of its characteristics seem to me obvious enough to suggest some of the ways in which our society has been going wrong.

[50] The first of these permanent characteristics seems to me to be that man is inveterately a maker of value judgments. His idea of what constitutes right and wrong conduct, of what is just or unjust, has been—perhaps will continue to be—extremely diverse. But he has nearly always believed that good and evil, justice and injustice, are realities which it

is of the first importance to define and to cherish, while moral and cultural relativism—the idea that morals are nothing but mores and that one society is not absolutely better than another is so profoundly unnatural a conviction that it has seldom been entertained for long and is destructive of human welfare when it is.

[51] Closely related to the value judgment is the idea of justice. Men have varied enormously, irreconcilably, over the question of what constitutes justice. But they have nearly always believed that there is some such thing and that they should adhere to it. Part of that feeling is, I believe, the conviction that acts should have consequences, and that the way you are treated should be in some degree affected by the way in which you behave. A spoiled child, one who never pays any penalty for his follies or misdeeds, one who is given what some of the modern educators call "uncritical love," is usually an unhappy child because something fundamental in his human nature tells him that acts should have consequences and makes him profoundly uneasy in a world where they do not.

[52] Similarly I believe that a society is unhappy if it holds—as so many sociologists now profess to hold—that no man should be held responsible for his imprudences or his crimes. He may be glad to escape those consequences, but he is finding himself in a world without justice, in a world where the way in which you act has no effect upon the way in which you are treated. And I believe that, like the spoiled child, he is profoundly uneasy in that unnatural situation.

[53] I believe that it is also in accord with fundamental human nature to want some goods other than the material, that a society which defines the good life as merely a high standard of living and then defines the high standard of living in terms of material things alone is one which, in that respect, is denying expression to a fundamental characteristic of man. Few societies, whether primitive or not, have ever accepted the belief that welfare thus narrowly defined is the one and only supreme good. Men have sought all sorts of other things—they have sought God, they have sought beauty, they have sought truth or they have sought glory, militarily or otherwise. They have sought adventure; they have even—so anthropologists tell us—sometimes believed that a large collection of dried human heads was the thing in all the world most worth having. But seldom if ever, so it seems to me, have they confessedly sought only what is now called "welfare."

[54] This is a mere beginning. You may dispute, if you like, even the few general statements I have made about permanent human nature. But if you admit that some things are and some things are not in accord

with human nature, then you have grasped an instrument capable of doing something which few men today seem able to do, namely, attempt a rational criticism of things as they are.

COMMENT AND QUESTIONS

1. What is the purpose, in the first six paragraphs of the essay, of Krutch's discussion of various concepts of the purpose of government? In these opening paragraphs, does Krutch express or imply his own attitudes toward welfare as the chief aim of government?
2. One of Krutch's key terms is *cultural and moral relativism*. In the context of the essay, how is the term defined and clarified? What is the relativist view of what constitutes welfare?
3. Briefly summarize Krutch's reasons (paragraphs 10–15) for believing that welfare, properly defined, should consist of giving people what they ought to have instead of what they want or think they want.
4. Explain the statement (paragraph 17) that "education is failing to help people to achieve an acceptable definition of welfare . . . because . . . we are unable to give any definition of education except the same kind of definition we give of welfare." How does Krutch support this statement? How does he qualify it?
5. In paragraphs 25–30, Krutch discusses our lack of standards and the prevalent opinion that no standards can exist outside of mere custom and conditioning. If you have read "The Genesis of a Mood," what was Krutch's attitude in that selection toward a similar "counsel of despair"? In "Life, Liberty, and the Pursuit of Welfare" (written thirty-two years later) what is his attitude? Where is he looking for standards or values?
6. Krutch introduces, at the end of paragraph 33, the figure of the human mind as a "blank slate" on which anything can be written. Trace the recurrence and development of this figure later in the essay.
7. What is the point of the discussion, beginning in paragraph 39, of birds and seals? What conclusions does Krutch draw from the "simple" facts about animal behavior?
8. Point out examples, in paragraphs 40–44, of the author's qualifications of his statements.
9. What are the characteristics which seem to Krutch a part of, or in accord with, fundamental human nature? In qualifying his assertions about these characteristics, does the author qualify them out of existence; that is, do the assertions seem meaningful and valid to you after they are so fully qualified? What is the relationship of each of the human characteristics to the concept of welfare?
10. Early in the essay (paragraphs 7 and 8), Krutch raises two basic questions: (a) "Does the promotion of welfare mean giving people what they

want or seem to want or think they want, or does it consist in giving them what they ought to have?" and (b) "If welfare means giving them what they ought to have, then who decides what they ought to have, and on the basis of what criteria is the decision made?" In the course of the essay, Krutch gives his answer to the first question. Does he also answer the second? Would you say that the general pattern of the essay is problem-to-solution? Explain.

11. What are your answers to Krutch's two questions quoted above, and how would you support your answers?

12. Krutch in this essay is dealing with a number of abstract ideas (*welfare, relativism, education, values, the good life, human nature,* for example). Study his use of concrete language—concrete words, facts, examples, quotations, allusions, and comparisons—to clarify and develop the abstractions. What instances of concrete language seem to you most effective in making or supporting a point?

[28] *Irwin Edman*: A Reasonable Life in a Mad World

IRWIN EDMAN (1896–1954) was a professor of philosophy at Columbia University; author of *Four Ways of Philosophy, Philosopher's Holiday, Candle in the Dark, Arts and the Man;* and a contributor to *The New Yorker* as well as to scholarly journals. He is one of the most readable and one of the most rewarding of modern writers-on-philosophy. The following essay was published in *The Atlantic Monthly* in 1949.

[1] That the world is mad has been the judgment of self-denominated sane philosophers from the Greeks to the present day. It is not a discovery of our own age that both the public and private lives of human beings are dominated by folly and stupidity. Philosophers pressing the point have brought such charges not against human nature only—that is, the world of human relations—but against that larger universe in which the world of human relations is set. As far back as the Book of Job and probably much further back, for there must have been at least gruntingly articulate Jobs in prehistory, it is not only men who have been declared mad: by any standards of rationality the universe itself has been called irrational, pointless, meaningless, with incidental, unintended overtones of cruelty and injustice.

[2] With the provincialism of each generation, ours imagines that the

causes of cynicism and despair are new in our time. There have, of course, been modern improvements and refinements of stupidity and folly. No previous generation has been by way of organizing itself with insane efficiency for blowing the whole race to smithereens. It does not take a particularly logical mind at the present moment to discover that the world is quite mad, though a great many critics apparently think that the cruel absurdity of technical efficiency combined with moral bankruptcy is a discovery that it took great wit on their part to turn up.

[3] Reputations are being made by reiterating, to the extent of four or five hundred pages, that collective modern man is a technical genius merged with a moral imbecile.

[4] The first encouragement I can bring is the reminder that the kind of madness which we all realize to be the present state of the world is not something new. It is, just like everything else in the modern world, bigger and more streamlined, if not better. It is a pity some of the great satirists are dead; Swift and Voltaire would have given their eyeteeth for the present situation. And Aristophanes would scarcely have believed it. But the essential charges they would bring against the present time and the essential absurdities they would show up are not different in essence now from what they were.

[5] Neither nature nor man appears reasonable by reasonable human standards. So acutely does this seem to many people to be true that in almost exuberant desperation they decide to march crazily in the insane procession. Existentialists make a cult of anxiety and despair and find a kind of wry comfort in saying, Since the world is absurd, let absurdity and irony be our standards. There are others who say—and the currency of an ersatz theological literature shows how epidemic they are—that since the world and mankind at present seem so palpably absurd it simply can't be true, and history, as Toynbee[1] now assures us, moves delightfully and progressively to fulfillment in the Church of God—a kind of quiet, English Church incorporating the best features of Islam, Buddhism, Confucianism, and a little, even, of the Hebrew prophets and the secular sciences.

[6] The excitements and confused urgencies of the present time may seem to make hysteria or mystical narcosis or hedonistic excitement tantamount to a philosophy. But the still, small voice of rationality persists. And the question still remains the same as that propounded by the Greeks long ago: How, in a world certainly not at first acquaintance rational-appearing, is it possible to lead a rational life?

[7] It seems mad now to say that anyone could believe, as the Fabians[2]

[1] Arnold J. Toynbee, contemporary English historian and author of *A Study of History*.

[2] English socialists who aimed to reform society gradually, avoiding revolutionary methods.

did (including such unsentimental people as George Bernard Shaw and Sidney and Beatrice Webb and Graham Wallas and later H. G. Wells), that the world could be transformed into a livable, beautiful, reasonable place by the co-operation of reasonable men. It is not simply that the violent external events of the past generation have revealed to us how precarious were security and comfort, and for how few it obtained at all.

[8] But the psychological sciences have revealed to us the deep sources of violence, confusion, hysteria, and madness in ourselves. What perhaps a generation ago seemed a melodramatic aphorism when Santayana uttered it seems now to be a hitting of the nail on the head: "The normal man holds a lunatic in leash." The definition needs to be amended. In the light of the past twenty-five years, the normal man no longer *does* hold a lunatic in leash. The fact that even talk about a third world war has become standard has practically made lunacy respectable. It is now become a stamp of madness to talk as if one seriously believed that a peaceful and just world were possible.

[9] And yet the sentiment of rationality persists and the hope persists also that it is not impossible, at least in imagination, to dream and in organized effort to work for what seems "an ordered, coherent world society." The most ardent workers for such a world, however, realize that there is plenty of madness left, out of which a third world war may come.

– II –

[10] The persistence of power politics, the greed for privilege, the insane clutching of wealth, the pathological tribalisms of nations, of class, and of race; it is this world in which we are actually living, and the human problem for anyone in it is to discover what is a reasonable life in such a world.

[11] Is it to forget as far as possible and to live only in the moment and to make that moment as brief and bright as possible? Is it to surrender any hope for pleasure or happiness now and give one's dedicated and ruthless devotion to work for a more reasonable world? Is it to seek Nirvana or to seek some salvation in another world? There seems to be some sense in each answer, but which answer one chooses will depend ultimately on how one answers a basic question: Is the world always and necessarily mad? Is it completely mad now, and is it possible even now to understand the madness and, through understanding, to endure or change it?

[12] Let us try as simply as possible to deal with some of these questions. First, is the world always and necessarily mad? By "the world," of course, one means both the processes of nature and the activities of human beings. For "world" in the first sense one had perhaps better use the word "universe." A thoroughly rational universe would be one which was achieving a purpose set down in advance, a purpose which in human

terms made sense and which by human standards made moral sense. A rational universe might be one such as the Deists conceived in the eighteenth century, in which nature was simply reason incarnate or reason embodied in the vast machinery of things.

[13] In one respect at least the advance of knowledge of the physical world has not made the world seem more irrational. It has made it seem orderly and regular. But in another respect an understanding of the causes and consequences of nature by conventional standards made nature seem wholly irrational. "I am what I am," said Jehovah in the Old Testament, as if that announcement were sufficient explanation of his wrathful ways. "It is what it is and it does what it does" may be said to be the conclusions of empirical physical science. It is maddening to rational creatures to discover they were born into a world which is not particularly interested in human purposes, which perhaps permits and sustains these purposes but is innocent of any solicitude concerning them. The rain notoriously falls on the just and the unjust, and the just feel highly put upon. Death is no respecter of persons; plagues fell the virtuous. The most generous and devoted enterprises are washed away by floods along with the conspiracies of the sinister and hateful.

[14] Theologians have spent a good deal of time trying to gloss away the irrationalities of the universe, explaining that God moves in a mysterious or at least salutary way, his morally therapeutic wonders to perform. Job was not greatly impressed by his comforters, and neither are we. But if exasperated humans have criticized the world in general, they have been especially critical of the madness of their fellow men. Voltaire found his greatest weapon of satire in treating cruelty, barbarism, and superstition not as evil but as absurd.

[15] The most serious and damaging charge we can bring against civilization is that by the very standards of civilization it is a ridiculous failure. It takes a high degree of sophistication and technical resources to make such an international shambles as we seem fated to do. It takes something like genius in folly to have millions starving in the midst of plenty, to have technological magic whose fruits are poverty, squalor, anarchy, and death; it takes a refinement of absurdity to use the most generous aphorism of the highest religions to justify or rationalize intolerance, violence, and our established international disorder.

[16] Now about the first irrationality: that of the universe itself. Perhaps the only reasonable attitude is that of resignation and endurance of it. Perhaps it is only the persistence of our childhood wishes and expectations that has led to an assumption that the universe must conform to human purposes and that it is shockingly unreasonable of it not so to conform. We can, within the limits of a world not made for us, make it conform to ideals and values which flower out of nature itself. Part of the life of reason is a contemplation of the unchanging and unchangeable elements

in the world of nature; part of it is a sedulous attempt to discover the ways of changing the world in the interest of human values.

[17] With respect to the world of human activities there has been an accelerated desperation at the present time. In the old days when humor could still flourish in Central Europe it used to be said that the difference between the temper of Berlin and Vienna could be stated as follows: In Berlin when things went wrong it was remarked: "The situation is serious but not hopeless"; in Vienna with smiling deprecation the Viennese used to say: "The situation is hopeless but not serious." The Berlin version seems of late more greatly to have impressed the world.

[18] Though Existentialism may be said to describe the world as being both hopeless and trivial, if one so conceives the realm of human affairs the Epicurean prescription for a reasonable life is perhaps the best that one can find. However clouded and uncertain the future, there is at least possible for the lucky and the prudent a brief, bright interval in which they may find luster and to which their refined sensibilities may give luster. In a world without meaning they may find exquisite nuances of meaning in the arts, in friendship, in love.

[19] The trouble with the Epicurean solution and abdication is that it is always haunted by a scruple of conscience and the shadow of despair. There is something already tarnished in a brightness that declares itself both ultimately meaningless and transient. Sorrow and inhibition and regret dog the footsteps of the Epicurean in a world where folly is no longer a joke but a terrifying threat to all mankind.

[20] There are those, therefore, in our own age who jump to the other extreme. One insists that one *must* give up any hope for present happiness and give one's dedicated and ruthless devotion to work for a better world. I have friends, especially in social or government work or in the social sciences, who regard humor, irony, urbanity, or relaxation with something of the same moral impatience with which a missionary might watch the natives of the Fiji Islands dance or lounge in the sun. There is so little time; it is later than you think; there is no time for comedy. Urbanity is a form of evasion, and laughter is a form of bourgeois or decadent callousness. Let us gird our loins and work together rapidly for the common good or we shall all in common be destroyed. The psychiatric departments of hospitals number among their patients a good many people who in their earnest haste to save the world from destruction ended up by destroying their equilibrium and almost themselves. The tension of moral earnestness, the refusal to permit the enjoyment of even such goods as are possible in a chaotic world, is one of the diseases of our civilization, not a sign of its health. If Epicureanism leads to dismay, unrelieved moral dedication leads to fanaticism. Neither the playboy nor the zealot is a true or adequate incarnation of the life of reason.

[21] Those who recognize the disillusion of a pleasure philosophy or

the destructiveness of a moral fanaticism have begun in our age, as they have in other ages, to turn to otherworldly philosophies. They have tried to seek an inward light unquenchable by external circumstances. They have tried in spirit to follow the Indian saint into the wilderness or the monk into his cell or the mystic into his remote meditation. They have sought Nirvana, or a Oneness with the One, or an Aloneness with the Alone. The follies of society are not cured by the incantations of pure mysticism, and the search for oblivion is really a pathological attempt simply to become oblivious to the actual and remediable conflicts and disorders in society.

[22] There are still others than the pleasure-lovers, the Nirvana-seekers, the devotees of such mystics, who have sought to make a prescription for a reasonable life. Among those others now epidemic are followers of historians and zoologists who with the theological wave of a wand discover that a palpably absurd world is somehow moving toward a cozy fulfillment where, as I heard Mr. Toynbee say, "God is Love." It would seem a strange moment to detect the course of history as the operations of universal love when the world is being filled with universal hate.

[23] No, I do not think any of these ersatz solutions will do. The pressure of events simply confirms again what the life of reason does consist in: a brave contemplation of what things are discoverably like and a resolute attempt to improve the lot of man in the conditions into which he finds himself born. The life of reason must always have a stoic element because there is no sign that either the follies of humanity or the uncaring order of nature will ever be magically transformed.

[24] The life of reason must also contain an element of hope, for it is quite clear, as the history of every improvement in man's estate has shown us, that human intelligence accompanied by human goodwill may profoundly improve the life of mankind. The life of reason must include the pleasure principle also, for what else gives life meaning if not joy and delight of life, and what a folly it would be not to cherish and embrace, not to nourish then, even in a sick society, that which yields the fruit of a quickened, multiplied awareness, the substance of vision and of joy. The universe may be pointless, but there are many good points in it. Our urgencies may be intense, but the world does not end with us or even with our own civilization; nor, if we do not quench intelligence and generosity in ourselves, is it a foregone conclusion that our civilization must end. And the best insurance, perhaps, of maintaining both is to reaffirm the quality of life itself, of its possibility of beauty and its intimations of order and of justice.

COMMENT AND QUESTIONS

1. Edman begins with an assumption—that the world is mad. Would you expect his readers to agree? Do you agree? In the course of the essay, what aspects of the world and of human relations are mentioned in support of the assumption of madness?
2. Edman, in this essay, is frequently ironical and satirical, and he makes use of some highly charged language. Point out examples of irony, satire, and charged words, and comment on their effectiveness in achieving what you take to be the author's purpose.
3. In the last sentence of paragraph 7, in paragraph 8, and in the first half of the single sentence of paragraph 10, Edman makes some general statements about the world of human affairs. Because this essay was written in 1949, the specific events and instances Edman had in mind are not exactly those of the present time. To what extent are his generalizations true today? What concrete examples can you give to support those which do seem true?
4. What seems to be Edman's answer to the question "Is the world always and necessarily mad?"
5. What are the various prescriptions for a reasonable life which the author rejects as "ersatz solutions"? Why does he reject each one?
6. On the basis of your knowledge of exstentialism, Epicureanism, and mysticism, to what extent do you agree with Edman's attitudes toward these philosophies? Explain.
7. For a study of Edman's style, read carefully paragraphs 18–21. What is distinctive in his sentence structures and in his choice and use of words?
8. State in your own words the concept of the reasonable life presented in the last two paragraphs of the essay. Does the author's conclusion follow logically from the ideas and details presented earlier in the essay? Explain.
9. To what extent do you agree or disagree with Edman's idea of the reasonable life, and why?

LANGUAGE

[29] *Bergen Evans:* Grammar for Today

BERGEN EVANS (1904–   ), a professor of English at Northwestern University, is well known as the host and commentator on television and radio programs including "The Last Word" and "Of Many Things." Among his numerous publications are *Natural History of Nonsense, A Dictionary of Contemporary American Usage* (with Cornelia Evans), and *Comfortable Words.* The following article appeared in *The Atlantic Monthly* in March, 1960.

[1] In 1747 Samuel Johnson issued a plan for a new dictionary of the English language. It was supported by the most distinguished printers of the day and was dedicated to the model of all correctness, Philip Dormer Stanhope, Fourth Earl of Chesterfield. Such a book, it was felt, was urgently needed to "fix" the language, to arrest its "corruption" and "decay," a degenerative process which, then as now, was attributed to the influence of "the vulgar" and which, then as now, it was a mark of superiority and elegance to decry. And Mr. Johnson seemed the man to write it. He had an enormous knowledge of Latin, deep piety, and dogmatic convictions. He was also honest and intelligent, but the effect of these lesser qualifications was not to show until later.

[2] Oblig'd by hunger and request of friends, Mr. Johnson was willing to assume the role of linguistic dictator. He was prepared to "fix" the pronunciation of the language, "preserve the purity" of its idiom, brand "impure" words with a "note of infamy," and secure the whole "from being overrun by ... low terms."

[3] There were, however, a few reservations. Mr. Johnson felt it necessary to warn the oversanguine that "Language is the work of man, a being from whom permanence and stability cannot be derived." English "was not formed from heaven ... but was produced by necessity and enlarged by accident." It had, indeed, been merely "thrown together by negligence" and was in such a state of confusion that its very syntax could no longer "be taught by general rules, but [only] by special precedents."

[4] In 1755 the *Dictionary* appeared. The noble patron had been given a great deal more immortality than he had bargained for by the vigor of the kick Johnson had applied to his backside as he booted him overboard. And the *Plan* had been replaced by the *Preface*, a sadder but very much wiser document.

[5] Eight years of "sluggishly treading the track of the alphabet" had taught Johnson that the hopes of "fixing" the language and preserving its "purity" were but "the dreams of a poet doomed at last to wake a lexicographer." In "the boundless chaos of living speech," so copious and energetic in its disorder, he had found no guides except "experience and analogy." Irregularities were "inherent in the tongue" and could not be "dismissed or reformed" but must be permitted "to remain untouched." "Uniformity must be sacrificed to custom ... in compliance with a numberless majority" and "general agreement." One of the pet projects of the age had been the establishment of an academy to regulate and improve style. "I hope," Johnson wrote in the *Preface*, that if "it should be established ... the spirit of English liberty will hinder or destroy [it.]"

[6] At the outset of the work he had flattered himself, he confessed, that he would reform abuses and put a stop to alterations. But he had soon discovered that "sounds are too volatile and subtle for legal restraints" and that "to enchain syllables and to lash the wind are equally undertakings of pride unwilling to measure its desires by its strength." For "the causes of change in language are as much superior to human resistance as the revolutions of the sky or the intumescence of the tide."

[7] There had been an even more profound discovery: that grammarians and lexicographers "do not form, but register the language; do not teach men how they should think, but relate how they have hitherto expressed their thoughts." And with this statement Johnson ushered in the rational study of linguistics. He had entered on his task a medieval pedant. He emerged from it a modern scientist.

[8] Of course his discoveries were not strikingly original. Horace had observed that use was the sole arbiter and norm of speech and Montaigne had said that he who would fight custom with grammar was a fool. Doubtless thousands of other people had at one time or another perceived and said the same thing. But Johnson introduced a new principle. Find-

ing that he could not lay down rules, he gave actual examples to show meaning and form. He offered as authority illustrative quotations, and in so doing established that language is what usage makes it and that custom, in the long run, is the ultimate and only court of appeal in linguistic matters.

[9] This principle, axiomatic today in grammar and lexicography, seems to exasperate a great many laymen who, apparently, find two hundred and five years too short a period in which to grasp a basic idea. They insist that there are absolute standards of correctness in speech and that these standards may be set forth in a few simple rules. To a man, they believe, of course, that they speak and write "correctly" and they are loud in their insistence that others imitate them.

[10] It is useless to argue with such people because they are not, really, interested in language at all. They are interested solely in demonstrating their own superiority. Point out to them—as has been done hundreds of times—that forms which they regard as "corrupt," "incorrect," and "vulgar" have been used by Shakespeare, Milton, and the Bible and are used daily by 180 million Americans and accepted by the best linguists and lexicographers, and they will coolly say, "Well, if they differ from me, they're wrong."

[11] But if usage is not the final determinant of speech, what is? Do the inhabitants of Italy, for example, speak corrupt Latin or good Italian? Is Spanish superior to French? Would the Breton fisherman speak better if he spoke Parisian French? Can one be more fluent in Outer Mongolian than in Inner Mongolian? One has only to ask such questions in relation to languages other than one's own, languages within which our particular snobberies and struggles for prestige have no stake, to see the absurdity of them.

[12] The language that we do speak, if we are to accept the idea of "corruption" and "decay" in language, is a horribly decayed Anglo-Saxon, grotesquely corrupted by Norman French. Furthermore, since Standard English is a development of the London dialect of the fourteenth century, our speech, by true aristocratic standards, is woefully middle-class, commercial, and vulgar. And American speech is lower middle-class, reeking of counter and till. Where else on earth, for instance, would one find crime condemned because it didn't *pay!*

[13] In more innocent days a great deal of time was spent in wondering what was the "original" language of mankind, the one spoken in Eden, the language of which all modern tongues were merely degenerate remnants. Hector Boethius tells us that James I of Scotland was so interested in this problem that he had two children reared with a deaf and dumb nurse on an island in order to see what language they would

"naturally" speak. James thought it would be Hebrew, and in time, to his great satisfaction, it was reported that the chidren were speaking Hebrew!

[14] Despite this experiment, however, few people today regard English as a corruption of Hebrew. But many seem to think it is a corruption of Latin and labor mightily to make it conform to this illusion. It is they and their confused followers who tell us that we can't say "I am mistaken" because translated into Latin this would mean "I am misunderstood," and we can't say "I have enjoyed myself" unless we are egotistical or worse.

[15] It is largely to this group—most of whom couldn't read a line of Latin at sight if their lives depended on it—that we owe our widespread bewilderment concerning *who* and *whom*. In Latin the accusative or dative form would always be used, regardless of the word's position in the sentence, when the pronoun was the object of a verb or a preposition. But in English, for at least four hundred years, this simply hasn't been so. When the pronoun occurs at the beginning of a question, people who speak natural, fluent, literary English use the nominative, regardless. They say "Who did you give it to?" not "Whom did you give it to?" But the semiliterate, intimidated and bewildered, are mouthing such ghastly utterances as a recent headline in a Chicago newspaper: WHOM'S HE KIDDING?

[16] Another group seems to think that in its pure state English was a Laputan tongue, with logic as its guiding principle. Early members of this sect insisted that *unloose* could only mean "to tie up," and present members have compelled the gasoline industry to label its trucks *Flammable* under the disastrous insistence, apparently, that the old *Inflammable* could only mean "not burnable."

[17] It is to them, in league with the Latinists, that we owe the bogy of the double negative. In all Teutonic languages a doubling of the negative merely emphasizes the negation. But we have been told for a century now that two negatives make a positive, though if they do and it's merely a matter of logic, then three negatives should make a negative again. So that if "It doesn't make no difference" is wrong merely because it includes two negatives, then "It doesn't never make no difference" ought to be right again. Both of these groups, in their theories at least, ignore our idiom. Yet idiom—those expressions which defy all logic but are the very essence of a tongue—plays a large part in English. We go to school and college, but we go to *the* university. We buy two dozen eggs but a couple *of* dozen. *Good and* can mean *very* ("I am good and mad!") and "a hot cup of coffee" means that the coffee, not the cup, is to be hot. It makes a world of difference to a condemned man whether his reprieve is *upheld* or *held up*.

[18] There are thousands of such expressions in English. They are the

"irregularities" which Johnson found "inherent in the tongue" and which his wisdom perceived could not and should not be removed. Indeed, it is in the recognition and use of these idioms that skillful use of English lies.

[19] Many words in the form that is now mandatory were originally just mistakes, and many of these mistakes were forced into the language by eager ignoramuses determined to make it conform to some notion of their own. The *s* was put in island, for instance, in sheer pedantic ignorance. The second *r* doesn't belong in *trousers*, nor the *g* in *arraign*, nor the *t* in deviltry, nor the *n* in *passenger* and *messenger*. Nor, so far as English is concerned, does that first *c* in *arctic* which so many people twist their mouths so strenuously to pronounce.

[20] And grammar is as "corrupted" as spelling or pronunciation. "You are" is as gross a solecism as "me am." It's recent, too; you won't find it in the Authorized Version of the Bible. *Lesser, nearer,* and *more* are grammatically on a par with *gooder*. *Crowed* is the equivalent of *knowed* or *growed*, and *caught* and *dug* (for *catched* and *digged*) are as "corrupt" as *squoze* for *squeezed* or *snoze* for *sneezed*.

[21] Fortunately for our peace of mind most people are quite content to let English conform to English, and they are supported in their sanity by modern grammarians and linguists.

[22] Scholars agree with Puttenham (1589) that a language is simply speech "fashioned to the common understanding and accepted by consent." They believe that the only "rules" that can be stated for a language are codified observations. They hold, that is, that language is the basis of grammar, not the other way round. They do not believe that any language can become "corrupted" by the linguistic habits of those who speak it. They do not believe that anyone who is a native speaker of a standard language will get into any linguistic trouble unless he is misled by snobbishness or timidity or vanity.

[23] He may, of course, if his native language is English, speak a form of English that marks him as coming from a rural or an unread group. But if he doesn't mind being so marked, there's no reason why he should change. Johnson retained a Staffordshire burr in his speech all his life. And surely no one will deny that Robert Burns's rustic dialect was just as good as a form of speech as, and in his mouth infinitely better as a means of expression than, the "correct" English spoken by ten million of his southern contemporaries.

[24] The trouble is that people are no longer willing to be rustic or provincial. They all want to speak like educated people, though they don't want to go to the trouble of becoming truly educated. They want to believe that a special form of socially acceptable and financially valuable speech can be mastered by following a few simple rules. And there is no

lack of little books that offer to supply the rules and promise "correctness" if the rules are adhered to. But, of course, these offers are specious because you don't speak like an educated person unless you are an educated person, and the little books, if taken seriously, will not only leave the lack of education showing but will expose the pitiful yearning and the basic vulgarity as well, in such sentences as "Whom are you talking about?"

[25] As a matter of fact, the educated man uses at least three languages. With his family and his close friends, on the ordinary, unimportant occasions of daily life, he speaks, much of the time, a monosyllabic sort of shorthand. On more important occasions and when dealing with strangers in his official or business relations, he has a more formal speech, more complete, less allusive, politely qualified, wisely reserved. In addition he has some acquaintance with the literary speech of his language. He understands this when he reads it, and often enjoys it, but he hesitates to use it. In times of emotional stress hot fragments of it may come out of him like lava, and in times of feigned emotion, as when giving a commencement address, cold, greasy gobbets of it will ooze forth.

[26] The linguist differs from the amateur grammarian in recognizing all of these variations and gradations in the language. And he differs from the snob in doubting that the speech of any one small group among the language's more than 300 million daily users constitutes a model for all the rest to imitate.

[27] The methods of the modern linguist can be illustrated by the question of the grammatical number of *none*. Is it singular or plural? Should one say "None of them is ready" or "None of them are ready"?

[28] The prescriptive grammarians are emphatic that it should be singular. The Latinists point out that *nemo,* the Latin equivalent, is singular. The logicians triumphantly point out that *none* can't be more than one and hence can't be plural.

[29] The linguist knows that he hears "None of them are ready" every day, from people of all social positions, geographical areas, and degrees of education. He also hears "None is." Furthermore, literature informs him that both forms were used in the past. From Malory (1450) to Milton (1650) he finds that *none* was treated as a singular three times for every once that it was treated as a plural. That is, up to three hundred years ago men usually said *None is.* From Milton to 1917, *none* was used as a plural seven times for every four times it was used as a singular. That is, in the past three hundred years men often said *None is,* but they said *None are* almost twice as often. Since 1917, however, there has been a noticeable increase in the use of the plural, so much so that today *None are* is the preferred form.

[30] The descriptive grammarian, therefore, says the while *None is* may still be used, it is becoming increasingly peculiar. This, of course, will not be as useful to one who wants to be cultured in a hurry as a

short, emphatic permission or prohibition. But it has the advantage of describing English as it is spoken and written here and now and not as it ought to be spoken in some Cloud-Cuckoo-Land.

[31] The descriptive grammarian believes that a child should be taught English, but he would like to see the child taught the English actually used by his educated contemporaries, not some pedantic, theoretical English designed chiefly to mark the imagined superiority of the designer.

[32] He believes that a child should be taught the parts of speech, for example. But the child should be told the truth—that these are functions of use, not some quality immutably inherent in this or that word. Anyone, for instance, who tells a child—or anyone else—that *like* is used in English only as a preposition has grossly misinformed him. And anyone who complains that its use as a conjunction is a corruption introduced by Winston cigarettes ought, in all fairness, to explain how Shakespeare, Keats, and the translators of the Authorized Version of the Bible came to be in the employ of the R. J. Reynolds Tobacco Company.

[33] Whether formal grammar can be taught to advantage before the senior year of high school is doubtful; most studies—and many have been made—indicate that it can't. But when it is taught, it should be the grammar of today's English, not the obsolete grammar of yesterday's prescriptive grammarians. By that grammar, for instance, *please* in the sentence "Please reply" is the verb and *reply* its object. But by modern meaning *reply* is the verb, in the imperative, and *please* is merely a qualifying word meaning "no discourtesy intended," a mollifying or de-imperatival adverb, or whatever you will, but not the verb.

[34] This is a long way from saying "Anything goes," which is the charge that, with all the idiot repetition of a needle stuck in a groove, the uninformed ceaselessly chant against modern grammarians. But to assert that usage is the sole determinant in grammar, pronunciation, and meaning is *not* to say that anything goes. Custom is illogical and unreasonable, but it is also tyrannical. The least deviation from its dictates is usually punished with severity. And because this is so, children should be taught what the current and local customs in English are. They should not be taught that we speak a bastard Latin or a vocalized logic. And they should certainly be disabused of the stultifying illusion that after God had given Moses the Commandments He called him back and pressed on him a copy of Woolley's *Handbook of English Grammar*.

[35] The grammarian does not see it as his function to "raise the standards" set by Franklin, Lincoln, Melville, Mark Twain, and hundreds of millions of other Americans. He is content to record what they said and say.

[36] Insofar as he serves as a teacher, it is his business to point out the limits of the permissible, to indicate the confines within which the writer may exercise his choice, to report that which custom and practice

have made acceptable. It is certainly not the business of the grammarian to impose his personal taste as the only norm of good English, to set forth his prejudices as the ideal standard which everyone should copy. That would be fatal. No one person's standards are broad enough for that.

COMMENT AND QUESTIONS

1. In the three opening paragraphs, how does Evans communicate his attitudes toward the kind of dictionary Samuel Johnson proposed to write and toward the people who wish to "fix" language?
2. What purposes are served by the introductory section of the essay (paragraphs 1–7)? What pattern of organization does Evans use in these first seven paragraphs?
3. What is the purpose of paragraphs 8–12? In these paragraphs, how does the author support his central thesis? How successfully, in your opinion, does he support it?
4. What is the purpose of the anecdote in paragraph 13? What is the main idea of the division which it introduces (paragraphs 13–21)?
5. At the end of paragraph 15, Evans is criticizing the newspaper headline for the use of *whom*. On what other ground might one also object to this headline?
6. Look up in your dictionary the words listed in paragraph 19. Do you find support for the point Evans is making in this paragraph?
7. Evans uses some strong language in dealing with those who do not share his views. Point out examples of his verbal assaults. Do they seem to you effective? Explain.
8. What is the difference between prescriptive and descriptive grammar? Comment on Evans' use of the problem of *none* as a persuasive illustration of the methods of the descriptive grammarian.
9. In paragraph 34, Evans says emphatically that the modern grammarian is *not* saying that "anything goes." Does this statement come as a surprise to the reader? Has it been prepared for by anything in the preceding material? Explain.
10. To what extent, and on what particular points, do you agree or disagree with Evans' ideas about language and usage?

[30] *Mario Pei*: The Dictionary as a Battlefront: English Teachers' Dilemma

MARIO PEI (1901–   ) is a noted author and linguist, professor of Romance philology at Columbia University. His many books include *The World's Chief Languages, The Story of Language, Voices of Man,* and *The American Heritage.* The following article, part of the controversy about *Webster's Third New International Dictionary,* appeared in the *Saturday Review,* July 21, 1962.

[1] For some years, there have been more and more insistent rumblings from all sorts of quarters concerning the quality of the English imparted in our schools and colleges. Graduates of our educational institutions, the critics have charged, do not know how to spell, punctuate, or capitalize; to divide a thought concept into phrases, sentences, and paragraphs; or to express themselves, either in speech or writing, in the sort of English that is meaningful and acceptable. As a single sample of the many complaints that have been voiced, I may cite a friend who is a high official in WNBC-TV: "Recently we interviewed over a hundred college graduates to fill a post calling for a knowledge of good English. Not one of them made the grade. None of them knew the rules of good writing, and none of them could express himself or herself in clear, simple, forthright English sentences."

[2] The blame for this state of affairs has consistently been put upon two branches of the educational world: the teachers of English and the progressive educationists. Books such as "Why Johnny Can't Read" are indictments of modern educational practice. A cultured lay writer, J. Donald Adams of the New York *Times Book Review,* said in his column of December 20, 1959:

If more parents who were themselves the recipients of a decent education could be made aware of the asinine statements about the teaching of the English language which are being spewed forth by today's educational theorists, there would be an armed uprising among the Parent-Teacher Associations all over the United States. It would be an uprising armed by common sense and hot indignation, and it would demand and get the scalps of those so-called educators whose indefensible doctrines are rapidly producing a generation of American illiterates . . . The root responsibility for the decline in standards of English rests, I think, with the teachers of English in our primary and secondary schools, and even more so, with the teachers of education who produced them. . . . There is an organization called the National Council of Teachers of English, whose attitudes and activities constitute one of the chief threats to the cultivation of good English in our schools.

[3] What critics of present-day methods of teaching English have in the past failed to realize is that the responsibility for the situation lies deeper than the departments of English and the teachers colleges. The practices of both are merely a reflection of the philosophy and theories of a school of linguistics that is in turn linked with a school of cultural anthropology of the equalitarian persuasion whose views color far more than the teaching of languages in general or English in particular.

[4] As far back as 1948, in a New York *Herald Tribune* book review, Bernard De Voto came out with a blast at the cultural anthropologists for assuming that methods that seem to work with the Ubangi and the Trobriand Islanders will produce dependable results when applied to the English or Americans. But his was a voice crying in the wilderness. Few people were sufficiently specialized, or interested, to perceive the link between theories presented in scholarly books on anthropology or linguistics and practices that affect the daily lives of all of us.

[5] It was only with the appearance of the new third edition of "Webster's Unabridged International Dictionary" late in 1961 that the issues at stake, at least for what concerns languages, became clear to the cultured, educated layman of America. For this there was a deep, underlying reason that reaches down to the grass roots of our mores.

[6] The English language, as is well known, has no set standard and no accepted authority, in the sense that countries such as France, Italy, and Spain have language academies that undertake to tell the speakers what is and what is not good standard practice. Since the days of Dr. Johnson, who refused to embalm the language and thereby destroy liberty, English speakers have submitted to the Doctrine of Usage rather than to the Voice of Authority. But usage has its own canons. In Britain, something called the King's (or Queen's) English has been enshrined over and above local dialects that range from London's Cockney to super-cultivated Oxford, and from the harsh speech of the North Country to the mellifluous accents of Kent. In America there is no President's American, but there is the Dictionary. From the time of Noah Webster, Americans have been wont to dip into a dictionary, the more unabridged the better, to settle questions of usage and proper practice.

[7] It may be stressed at this point that at no time did the compilers of the various editions of the Merriam-Webster, the most comprehensive dictionary of America, set themselves up as authorities or arrogate the right to tell the people what was right and what was wrong in the matter of language. All they did was to record prevailing usage among the more educated classes. They listed and described plenty of variant regional

pronunciations and words. They recorded, too, speech-forms of the lower classes, carefully labeling them "colloquial," "substandard," "vulgar," or "slang." This was not meant to prescribe or proscribe the use of certain forms, but merely to inform the reader as to the distribution of their occurrence. The attitude of the earlier lexicographers seemed to be: "Go ahead and use this form if you want to; but if you do, don't complain if someone says you are using a slang term."

[8] The new 1961 edition of the Merriam-Webster has many features to commend it. Not only does it list the multitude of new terms, technological and otherwise, that have entered the language in recent years; it also has the merit of listing, with full definitions and examples, word combinations that have acquired special connotations not inherent in their component parts. The older Webster's defines both "guilt" and "association"; but the new Webster's also gives you "guilt by association." This means that the new edition is a handier tool than the older.

[9] But the new edition makes one startling innovation which has recommended itself to the attention of all reviewers and of the general public as well. It blurs to the point of obliteration the older distinction between standard, substandard, colloquial, vulgar, and slang. "Ain't," it says, is now used by many cultivated speakers; "who" in the accusative function and "me" after a copulative verb are of far more frequent occurrence than "whom" and "I," and, by implication, should be preferred. This viewpoint goes right down the line. It led the editor of the New York Times to compose a passage that starts:

A passel of double-domes at the G. & C. Merriam Company joint in Springfield, Mass., have been confabbing and yakking for twenty-seven years—which is not intended to infer that they have not been doing plenty work—and now they have finalized Webster's Third New International Dictionary, Unabridged, a new edition of that swell and esteemed word book.

Those who regard the foregoing paragraph as acceptable English prose will find that the new Webster's is just the dictionary for them.

[10] There is more: the older Webster's, insofar as it gave citations, used only established authors, recognized masters of the language. The new Webster's cites profusely from people who are in the public eye, but who can hardly be said to qualify as shining examples of fine speaking or writing. This leads another critic to complain that Churchill, Maritain, Oppenheimer, and Schweitzer are ranged as language sources side by side with Billy Rose, Ethel Merman, James Cagney, and Ted Williams; Shakespeare and Milton with Polly Adler and Mickey Mantle.

[11] Dr. Gove's defense, fully presented in the pages of the same New York Times that had thundered editorially against his product, is both able and forthright: a dictionary's function, he said in substance, is to record the language, not to judge or prescribe it. Language, like prac-

tically everything else, is in a state of constant flux. It is not responsible to expect it to remain static, to retain unchanged forms that were current at one period but are no longer current today. We have changed our point of view in many fields; why not in language? His defense is, in a sense, a counterattack against the forces of purism, conservatism, and reaction. Why disguise the true function of a dictionary by turning it into a tool of prescriptivism, a fortress of a language traditionalism that no one today really wants? Language, after all, is what people speak, not what someone, be it even Webster, thinks they ought to speak.

[12] This both clarifies and restricts the issue. But an issue still remains. Should a dictionary be merely a record of what goes on in language (all language, both high and low), or should it also be not so much a prescriptive tool as a guide for the layman, to not merely what *is* usage, but what is the *best* usage?

[13] A speaking community that has been accustomed for the better part of two centuries to rely upon the dictionary to settle questions of usage balks at finding all usage now set on an identical plane. The contention of the objectors is that there are different, clearly identifiable levels of usage, which it is the duty of the dictionary to define. Without necessarily using the terms "correct" and "incorrect," they still would like to see a distinction made between what is better and what is worse.

[14] In opposition to their stand, the new philosophy, linguistic and otherwise, seems to be summed up in this formula: "What is is good, simply because it is." Good and bad, right and wrong, correct and incorrect no longer exist. Any reference to any of these descriptive adjectives is a value judgment, and unworthy of the scientific attitude, which prescribes that we merely observe and catalogue the facts, carefully refraining from expressing either judgment or preference.

[15] This relativistic philosophy, fully divorced from both ethics and esthetics, is said to be modern, sophisticated, and scientific. Perhaps it is. Some claim that its fruits are to be seen in present-day moral standards, national, international, and personal, as well as in modern so-called art, music, literature, and permissive education.

[16] But we are concerned here only with its reflections on the language. The appearance of the new Webster's International has had several major effects. It has brought the question of permissiveness in language squarely to the attention of millions of educated laymen, who use the dictionary and refer to it for guidance. Without forcing a renunciation of Anglo-American reliance on usage rather than on the Voice of Authority, it has brought into focus the paramount question: "Whose usage? That of the cultivated speakers, or that of the semiliterates?" Finally, it has for the first time brought forth, into the view of the general public, those who are primarily responsible for the shift in attitude and point of view in

matters of language—not the ordinary classroom teachers of English, not the educationists of the teachers colleges, but the followers of the American, anthropological, descriptive, structuralistic school of linguistics, a school which for decades has been preaching that one form of language is as good as another; that there is no such thing as correct or incorrect so far as native speakers of the language are concerned; that at the age of five anyone who is not deaf or idiotic has gained a full mastery of his language; that we must not try to correct or improve language, but must leave it alone; that the only language activity worthy of the name is speech on the colloquial, slangy, even illiterate plane; that writing is a secondary, unimportant activity which cannot be dignified with the name of language; that systems of writing serve only to disguise the true nature of language; and that it would be well if we completely refrained from teaching spelling for a number of years.

[17] If these pronouncements come as a novelty to some of my readers, it is the readers themselves who are at fault. The proponents of these language theories certainly have made no mystery about them; they have been openly, even vociferously advancing them for years, and this can easily be documented from their voluminous writings.

[18] The real novelty of the situation lies in the fact that, through the publication of the new Webster's—compiled in accordance with these principles—the principles themselves and their original formulators, rather than their effects upon the younger generations, now come to the attention of the general public. Lay reviewers generally display their complete awareness.

[19] Dwight MacDonald, reviewing the new Webster extensively in the March 10, 1962 *New Yorker*, after claiming that the "scientific" revolution in linguistics has meshed gears with a trend toward permissiveness, in the name of democracy, that is debasing our language by rendering it less precise and thus less effective as communication, goes on to say:

Dr. Gove and the other makers of 3 are sympathetic to the school of language study that has become dominant since 1934. It is sometimes called Structural Linguistics Science. . . . Dr. Gove and his editors are part of the dominant movement in the professional study of language—one that has in the last few years established strong beachheads in the National Council of Teachers of English and the College English Association. . . . As a scientific discipline, Structural Linguistics can have no truck with values or standards. Its job is to deal only with The Facts.

[20] Max S. Marshall, Professor of Microbiology at the University of California, writing in *Science,* March 2, 1962, says in part:

Opposed to [believers in a standard of quality in English] with several ringleaders at the head, is a group which goes back some thirty years, but has been actively proselytizing only in relatively recent years. These are the advocates of "observing precisely what happens when native speakers speak." These are the self-styled structural linguists, presenting language in a way so foreign that it might be imposed before users of the language discover its existence. . . . Gove declares himself flatly on the side of the structural linguists, calmly assuming, as do their ringleaders, that they are about to take over.

[21] The principles of the American school of linguistics described above may come as a shock to some, but there is no need to be shocked. They are based upon definitely observable historical facts. Language invariably changes. Within our own personal experience we have noticed certain forms and expressions once considered slangy turning into regularly accepted parts of the standard language.

[22] All that the American school of linguistics advocates is that we accept the process of change in language and submit gracefully to its inevitability. If we persist in hanging on to language forms and concepts that are antiquated and superseded, then we are merely subscribing to what they call "the superstitions of the past." We should be forward-looking, and progressive-minded. We renounce imperialism and colonialism in international relations, and admit nations like Ghana and the Congo to full equality with the established countries of Europe; by the same token, we should view the languages of the Arapahoes and the Zulus as being of equal importance with Latin and French. We believe in democracy and majority rule in political elections. Then, if a majority of the speakers of American English use "aint," "knowed," "I'll learn you," "I laid on the bed," "who did you see," "between you and I," "like a cigarette should," these forms are by definition standard usage, and the corresponding minority forms, though sanctioned by traditional grammars, are, if not incorrect, at least obsolescent.

[23] It may be argued, as does our Professor of Microbiology in *Science*, that "weighing the speech of casual speakers with no pretense of expertness on the same IBM card as usages of topnotch writers of past and present is an example of what the modern linguist calls 'science.' Tabulation is not science. Public opinion polls do not settle questions of science, or even of right and wrong. . . . If the guttersnipes of language do more talking than professors of English they get proportionally more votes."

[24] But the structuralistic linguists can easily reply that language is a matter of habit and convention, not of dogma or esthetics, and that if the basic purpose of semantic communication is achieved, it matters little what linguistic form is used. In engineering, calculations as to stresses and structures must be precise and correct, under penalty of seeing the bridge collapse. In medicine, correct dosage is essential, under penalty of seeing your patient die. But in language, the use of a substandard for a standard form seldom leads to irreparable consequences; at the most, as picturesquely stated by a leader of the school, you may not be invited to tea again.

[25] On the other hand, members of the American school of linguistics are not always consistent in the application of their democratic and equalitarian principles. In reply to his critics, Dr. Gove remarked that while comments in lay newspapers and magazines had generally been unfavorable, the learned journals had not yet reviewed the new edition. The implication seemed to be that favorable reviews from a few members of his own clique, read and approved by a small circle of professional structuralistic linguists, would more than offset the generally unfavorable reaction of newspapers like the New York *Times* and magazines like the *New Yorker*, which appeal to large audiences of cultivated laymen. This not only puts the process of democracy into reverse; it comes close to setting up a hierarchy of professional linguists acting as the Voice of Authority for a recalcitrant majority of educated people.

[26] There is no doubt in my mind that widespread localisms, slang, vulgarisms, colloquialisms, even obscenities and improprieties, should be duly noted in a comprehensive dictionary, whose first duty is to record what goes on in the field of language. Should such forms be labeled and described for what they are, not in a spirit of condemnation, but merely for the guidance of the reader? That, too, seems reasonable. If this procedure helps to slow up the inevitable process of language change by encouraging the speakers to use what the older dictionaries call standard forms, and discouraging them from using substandard forms, this impresses me as a distinct advantage. Too rapid and too widespread language change is a hindrance to communications. It lends itself to confusion and misunderstanding. The use of a more or less uniform standard by all members of the speaking community is desirable in the interests of efficiency rather than of esthetics. There is no question that within the next 500 years the English language, along with all other languages spoken today, will be so changed as to be practically unrecognizable. This will happen whether we like it or not. But need we deliberately hasten and amplify the process? Between sudden revolution and stolid reaction there is a middle ground of sound conservatism and orderly change.

[27] Also, without being puristic to the point of ejecting "ain't" and kindred forms from a dictionary of recorded usage, it might be worth while to recognize the existence of a standard language, neither literary nor slangy, which has acceptance and is understood practically everywhere in the country, even if everybody does not use it. Such phrases as "Them dogs is us'uns" and "I'll call you up without I can't," which an American structural linguist claims are good, meaningful language to him, merely because they are uttered by some native American speakers, definitely do not form part of that standard language. By all means let us record them for our own information and amusement, but let us not try to palm them off on the public on the general ground that the native speaker can do no wrong, and that "correct" and "incorrect" are terms that

can be legitimately applied only to the speech of foreigners attempting to use English.

[28] Language is something more than a heritage of sentimental value. It is an indispensable tool of communication and exchange of ideas. The more standardized and universal it is, the more effective it is. The more it is allowed to degenerate into local and class forms, the less effective it becomes. It may be perfectly true that in the past language has been allowed to run its own sweet, unbridled course, with the chips falling where they might. We are now in an age where we no longer believe in letting diseases and epidemics run their natural course, but take active, artificial means to control them. In fact, we endeavor to control natural, physical, and sociological phenomena of all descriptions, from floods to business cycles, from weather to diet, from the monetary system to racial relations. Is it unreasonable for us, far from leaving our language alone, as advocated by the American school of linguistics, to wish to channel it in the directions where it will prove of maximum efficiency for its avowed function, which is that of semantic transfer?

[29] For the concern of that other burning question, standards of writing, as apart from standards of speech, ought we not to recognize that until such a time as tapes, recordings, dictaphones and spoken films altogether replace our system of written communications, the latter should be viewed and treated with respect? Again, we need not let ourselves be led too far afield by purely literary or esthetic considerations. The written language, in a modern civilization, is practically on a par with speech as a communications tool. It is incongruous to see our American structuralistic linguists devote so much painstaking attention to phonetic phenomena like pitch, stress, intonation, and juncture, to the fine distinctions between "a light housekeeper" and "a lighthouse keeper," "an iceman" and "a nice man," and yet shrug their shoulders at correct spelling, punctuation, and capitalization. More misunderstandings have occurred over misplaced commas than over misplaced junctures, and a wrong spelling can be just as fatal as a wrong intonation.

[30] Perhaps the time has come, in language as in other fields, for the return of reason, and its ascendancy over dogma, whether the latter be of the puristic or of the structuralistic variety.

[31] Above all, there is need for sound, scientific consideration of *all* the facts of language, not merely that portion which happens to suit the tastes and inclinations of a small group. Language is more than a set of phonemes, morphemes, junctures, and stresses. It also happens to be our most important instrument of semantic transfer, and the common possession of all of us. If democracy means anything, we, the speakers, have the right to have our say as to how it shall be viewed and used, and not to be forced to subscribe to the prescriptive excesses of what the European professor of linguistics describes as "the God's Truth School."

⇥ COMMENT AND QUESTIONS ⇤

1. The first two paragraphs deal with a decline in the quality of English taught in schools and colleges, and with the placing of blame for this decline on teachers of English and progressive educationists. Does Pei support the statements made in these paragraphs, or does he assume that his readers agree that the situation is as he describes it? What is the relevance of these two paragraphs to the main ideas of the article?
2. For what common reasons do people consult dictionaries? What use of the dictionary is Pei emphasizing?
3. What major differences does Pei find between the older editions and the new *Webster's*? What is the substance of Dr. Gove's defense of *Webster's Third*? To Pei, what central issue still remains?
4. Look up in *Webster's Third New International Dictionary* four or five expressions which you consider either colloquial English or substandard English. Do you find any restrictive labels or comments? Does your research support Pei's statement in paragraph 13 that all usage is "set on an identical plane"?
5. Summarize in your own words what the author is saying in paragraph 15. Does his brief departure from the subject of language seem an irrelevancy in the essay? Explain.
6. Paragraph 16 is a harsh indictment of the American school of structural linguistics, an indictment supported to some extent, at least, by the quotations in paragraphs 19, 20, and 23. Does it seem to you that Pei is overstating in paragraph 16? If you have read the preceding selection by Bergen Evans, do you think that Evans would agree with Pei's summary of the linguistic philosophy?
7. Comment on the last sentence of paragraph 24. Do you agree or disagree with this linguistic stand?
8. On some matters, Pei agrees with the structural linguists. Point out examples of such agreement. How does the author qualify his agreement and emphasize his own point of view?
9. Do you agree with the statement in paragraph 28 that the more standard and universal language is, the more effective it is as a means of communication? How successful is the use of analogy in paragraph 28? Explain.
10. How would you explain the subtitle of this essay—"English Teachers' Dilemma"? What is the dilemma?
11. To what extent do you agree or disagree with Pei's argument that a good dictionary should guide the reader by making a distinction between *usage* and *best usage*?

[31] *E. B. White*: Calculating Machine

THE FOLLOWING short essay if from *The Second Tree from the Corner*, published in 1951. For a note on E. B. White, see page 39.

[1] A publisher in Chicago has sent us a pocket calculating machine by which we may test our writing to see whether it is intelligible. The calculator was developed by General Motors, who, not satisfied with giving the world a Cadillac, now dream of bringing perfect understanding to men. The machine (it is simply a celluloid card with a dial) is called the Reading Ease Calculator and shows four grades of "reading ease"—Very Easy, Easy, Hard, and Very Hard. You count your words and syllables, set the dial, and an indicator lets you know whether anybody is going to understand what you have written. An instruction book came with it, and after mastering the simple rules we lost no time in running a test on the instruction book itself, to see how *that* writer was doing. The poor fellow! His leading essay, the one on the front cover, tested Very Hard.

[2] Our next step was to study the first phrase on the face of the calculator: "How to test Reading-Ease of written matter." There is, of course, no such thing as reading ease of written matter. There is the ease with which matter can be read, but that is a condition of the reader, not of the matter. Thus the inventors and distributors of this calculator get off to a poor start, with a Very Hard instruction book and a slovenly phrase. Already they have one foot caught in the brier patch of English usage.

[3] Not only did the author of the instruction book score badly on the front cover, but inside the book he used the word "personalize" in an essay on how to improve one's writing. A man who likes the word "personalize" is entitled to his choice, but we wonder whether he should be in the business of giving advice to writers. "Whenever possible," he wrote, "personalize your writing by directing it to the reader." As for us, we would as lief Simonize our grandmother as personalize our writing.

[4] In the same envelope with the calculator, we received another training aid for writers—a booklet called "How to Write Better," by Rudolf Flesch. This, too, we studied, and it quickly demonstrated the broncolike ability of the English language to throw whoever leaps cocksurely into the saddle. The language not only can toss a rider but knows a thousand tricks for tossing him, each more gay than the last. Dr. Flesch

stayed in the saddle only a moment or two. Under the heading "Think Before You Write," he wrote, "The main thing to consider is your *purpose* in writing. Why are you sitting down to write?" And Echo answered: Because, sir, it is more comfortable than standing up.

[5] Communication by the written word is a subtler (and more beautiful) thing than Dr. Flesch and General Motors imagine. They contend that the "average reader" is capable of reading only what tests Easy, and that the writer should write at or below this level. This is a presumptuous and degrading idea. There is no average reader, and to reach down toward this mythical character is to deny that each of us is on the way up, is ascending. ("Ascending," by the way, is a word Dr. Flesch advises writers to stay away from. Too unusual.)

[6] It is our belief that no writer can improve his work until he discards the dulcet notion that the reader is feeble-minded, for writing is an act of faith, not a trick of grammar. Ascent is at the heart of the matter. A country whose writers are following a calculating machine downstairs is not ascending—if you will pardon the expression—and a writer who questions the capacity of the person at the other end of the line is not a writer at all, merely a schemer. The movies long ago decided that a wider communication could be achieved by a deliberate descent to a lower level, and they walked proudly down until they reached the cellar. Now they are groping for the light switch, hoping to find the way out.

[7] We have studied Dr. Flesch's instructions diligently, but we return for guidance in these matters to an earlier American, who wrote with more patience, more confidence. "I fear chiefly," he wrote, "lest my expression may not be *extra-vagant* enough, may not wander far enough beyond the narrow limits of my daily experience, so as to be adequate to the truth of which I have been convinced . . . Why level downward to our dullest perception always, and praise that as common sense? The commonest sense is the sense of men asleep, which they express by snoring."

[8] Run that through your calculator! It may come out Hard, it may come out Easy. But it will come out whole, and it will last forever.

COMMENT AND QUESTIONS

1. An informal tone and style are combined with careful use of language in this selection. Because "Calculating Machine" was originally written for *The New Yorker,* White uses the editorial *we* (*us, our*) as a matter of convention; he also, however, uses the informal *you* (in paragraph 1, for example). What other informal expressions do you find in the essay?

2. Numerous touches of humor and of irony occur in "Calculating Machine," and White also uses figurative language, often for purposes of humor or irony. Point out examples that seem to you effective.
3. Do you agree with White's criticisms, in paragraphs 2–4, of the English used on the calculator and in the accompanying books? Explain.
4. Can you accept White's statement in paragraph 5 that there is no average reader? Explain.
5. Examine the writing in paragraph 6. What stylistic traits do you notice?
6. The quotation in paragraph 7 is from Thoreau. What does White appear to mean by saying that the earlier American "wrote with more patience, more confidence"?
7. What techniques has White used to make his ending emphatic?
8. This essay illustrates a method frequently used by E. B. White, and also by other informal essayists: the method of starting with a small, particular experience or event, and proceeding to its larger implications. Briefly summarize the serious things that, for all of his humor and lightness of tone, E. B. White is saying about language and about contemporary society.

[32] *George Orwell*: The Principles of Newspeak

THE FOLLOWING essay was written as an appendix to *Nineteen Eighty-Four,* a novel depicting life in a future totalitarian state made up of countries in Europe and America. For a note on George Orwell see page 51.

[1] Newspeak was the official language of Oceania and had been devised to meet the ideological needs of Ingsoc, or English Socialism. In the year 1984 there was not as yet anyone who used Newspeak as his sole means of communication, either in speech or writing. The leading articles in the *Times* were written in it, but this was a tour de force which could only be carried out by a specialist. It was expected that Newspeak would have finally superseded Oldspeak (or Standard English, as we should call it) by about the year 2050. Meanwhile it gained ground steadily, all Party members tending to use Newspeak words and grammatical constructions more and more in their everyday speech. The version in use in 1984, and embodied in the Ninth and Tenth Editions of the Newspeak dictionary, was a provisional one, and contained many

superfluous words and archaic formations which were due to be suppressed later. It is with the final, perfected version, as embodied in the Eleventh Edition of the dictionary, that we are concerned here.

[2] The purpose of Newspeak was not only to provide a medium of expression for the world-view and mental habits proper to the devotees of Ingsoc, but to make all other modes of thought impossible. It was intended that when Newspeak had been adopted once and for all and Oldspeak forgotten, a heretical thought—that is, a thought diverging from the principles of Ingsoc—should be literally unthinkable, at least so far as thought is dependent on words. Its vocabulary was so constructed as to give exact and often very subtle expression to every meaning that a Party member could properly wish to express, while excluding all other meanings and also the possibility of arriving at them by indirect methods. This was done partly by the invention of new words, but chiefly by eliminating undesirable words and by stripping such words as remained of unorthodox meanings, and so far as possible of all secondary meanings whatever. To give a single example, the word *free* still existed in Newspeak, but it could only be used in such statements as "This dog is free from lice" or "This field is free from weeds." It could not be used in its old sense of "politically free" or "intellectually free," since political and intellectual freedom no longer existed even as concepts, and were therefore of necessity nameless. Quite apart from the suppression of definitely heretical words, reduction of vocabulary was regarded as an end in itself, and no word that could be dispensed with was allowed to survive. Newspeak was designed not to extend but to *diminish* the range of thought, and this purpose was indirectly assisted by cutting the choice of words down to a minimum.

[3] Newspeak was founded on the English language as we now know it, though many Newspeak sentences, even when not containing newly created words, would be barely intelligible to an English-speaker of our own day. Newspeak words were divided into three distinct classes, known as the A vocabulary, the B vocabulary (also called compound words), and the C vocabulary. It will be simpler to discuss each class separately, but the grammatical peculiarities of the language can be dealt with in the section devoted to the A vocabulary, since the same rules held good for all three categories.

[4] *The A vocabulary.* The A vocabulary consisted of the words needed for the business of everyday life—for such things as eating, drinking, working, putting on one's clothes, going up and down stairs, riding in vehicles, gardening, cooking, and the like. It was composed almost entirely of words that we already possess—words like *hit, run, dog, tree, sugar, house, field*—but in comparison with the present-day English vocabulary, their number was extremely small, while their meanings were

far more rigidly defined. All ambiguities and shades of meaning had been purged out of them. So far as it could be achieved, a Newspeak word of this class was simply a staccato sound expressing *one* clearly understood concept. It would have been quite impossible to use the A vocabulary for literary purposes or for political or philosophical discussion. It was intended only to express simple, purposive thoughts, usually involving concrete objects or physical actions.

[⁵] The grammar of Newspeak had two outstanding peculiarities. The first of these was an almost complete interchangebililty between different parts of speech. Any word in the language (in principle this applied even to very abstract words such as *if* or *when*) could be used either as verb, noun, adjective, or adverb. Between the verb and the noun form, when they were of the same root, there was never any variation, this rule of itself involving the destruction of many archaic forms. The word *thought*, for example, did not exist in Newspeak. Its place was taken by *think*, which did duty for both noun and verb. No etymological principle was involved here; in some cases it was the original noun that was chosen for retention, in other cases the verb. Even when a noun and verb of kindred meaning were not etymologically connected, one or other of them was frequently suppressed. There was, for example, no such word as *cut*, its meaning being sufficiently covered by the noun-verb *knife*. Adjectives were formed by adding the suffix *-ful* to the noun-verb, and adverbs by adding *-wise*. Thus, for example, *speedful* meant "rapid" and *speedwise* meant "quickly." Certain of our present-day adjectives, such as *good, strong, big, black, soft,* were retained, but their total number was very small. There was little need for them, since almost any adjectival meaning could be arrived at by adding *-ful* to a noun-verb. None of the now-existing adverbs was retained, except for a very few already ending in *-wise;* the *-wise* termination was invariable. The word *well*, for example, was replaced by *goodwise*.

[⁶] In addition, any word—this again applied in principle to every word in the language—could be negatived by adding the affix *un-*, or could be strengthened by the affix *plus-*, or, for still greater emphasis, *doubleplus-*. Thus, for example, *uncold* meant "warm," while *pluscold* and *doublepluscold* meant, respectively, "very cold" and "superlatively cold." It was also possible, as in present-day English, to modify the meaning of almost any word by prepositional affixes such as *ante-, post-, up-, down-,* etc. By such methods it was found possible to bring about an enormous diminution of vocabulary. Given, for instance, the word *good*, there was no need for such a word as *bad*, since the required meaning was equally well—indeed, better—expressed by *ungood*. All that was necessary, in any case where two words formed a natural pair of opposites, was to decide which of them to suppress. *Dark*, for example, could be replaced by *unlight*, or *light* by *undark*, according to preference.

[⁷] The second distinguishing mark of Newspeak grammar was its regularity. Subject to a few exceptions which are mentioned below, all inflections followed the same rules. Thus, in all verbs the preterite and the past participle were the same and ended in -*ed*. The preterite of *steal* was *stealed,* the preterite of think was *thinked,* and so on throughout the language, all such forms as *swam, gave, brought, spoke, taken,* etc., being abolished. All plurals were made by adding -*s* or -*es* as the case might be. The plurals of *man, ox, life* were *mans, oxes, lifes.* Comparison of adjectives was invariably made by adding -*er,* -*est* (*good, gooder, goodest*), irregular forms and the *more, most* formation being suppressed.

[⁸] The only classes of words that were still allowed to inflect irregularly were the pronouns, the relatives, the demonstrative adjectives, and the auxiliary verbs. All of these followed their ancient usage, except that *whom* had been scrapped as unnecessary, and the *shall, should* tenses had been dropped, all their uses being covered by *will* and *would.* There were also certain irregularities in word-formation arising out of the need for rapid and easy speech. A word which was difficult to utter, or was liable to be incorrectly heard, was held to be ipso facto a bad word; occasionally therefore, for the sake of euphony, extra letters were inserted into a word or an archaic formation was retained. But this need made itself felt chiefly in connection with the B vocabulary. *Why* so great an importance was attached to ease of pronunciation will be made clear later in this essay.

[⁹] *The B vocabulary.* The B vocabulary consisted of words which had been deliberately constructed for political purposes: words, that is to say, which not only had in every case a political implication, but were intended to impose a desirable mental attitude upon the person using them. Without a full understanding of the principles of Ingsoc it was difficult to use these words correctly. In some cases they could be translated into Oldspeak, or even into words taken from the A vocabulary, but this usually demanded a long paraphrase and always involved the loss of certain overtones. The B words were a sort of verbal shorthand, often packing whole ranges of ideas into a few syllables, and at the same time more accurate and forcible than ordinary language.

[¹⁰] The B words were in all cases compound words.[1] They consisted of two or more words, or portions of words, welded together in an easily pronounceable form. The resulting amalgam was always a noun-verb, and inflected according to the ordinary rules. To take a single example: the word *goodthink,* meaning, very roughly, "orthodoxy," or, if one chose to regard it as a verb, "to think in an orthodox manner." This inflected as

[1] Compound words, such as *speakwrite,* were of course to be found in the A vocabulary, but these were merely convenient abbreviations and had no special ideological color.

follows: noun-verb, *goodthink;* past tense and past participle, *goodthinked;* present participle, *goodthinking;* adjective, *goodthinkful;* adverb, *goodthinkwise;* verbal noun, *goodthinker.*

[11] The B words were not constructed on any etymological plan. The words of which they were made up could be any parts of speech, and could be placed in any order and mutilated in any way which made them easy to pronounce while indicating their derivation. In the word *crimethink* (thought-crime), for instance, the *think* came second, whereas in *thinkpol* (Thought Police) it came first, and in the latter word *police* had lost its second syllable. Because of the greater difficulty in securing euphony, irregular formations were commoner in the B vocabulary than in the A vocabulary. For example, the adjectival forms of *Minitrue, Minipax,* and *Miniluv* were, respectively, *Minitruthful, Minipeaceful,* and *Minilovely,* simply because *-trueful, -paxful,* and *-loveful* were slightly awkward to pronounce. In principle, however, all B words could inflect, and all inflected in exactly the same way.

[12] Some of the B words had highly subtilized meanings, barely intelligible to anyone who had not mastered the language as a whole. Consider, for example, such a typical sentence from a *Times* leading article as *Oldthinkers unbellyfeel Ingsoc.* The shortest rendering that one could make of this in Oldspeak would be: "Those whose ideas were formed before the Revolution cannot have a full emotional understanding of the principles of English Socialism." But this is not an adequate translation. To begin with, in order to grasp the full meaning of the Newspeak sentence quoted above, one would have to have a clear idea of what is meant by *Ingsoc.* And, in additon, only a person thoroughly grounded in Ingsoc could apprecate the full force of the word *bellyfeel,* which implied a blind, enthusiastic acceptance difficult to imagine today; or of the word *oldthink,* which was inextricably mixed up with the idea of wickedness and decadence. But the special function of certain Newspeak words, of which *oldthink* was one, was not so much to express meanings as to destroy them. These words, necessarily few in number, had had their meanings extended until they contained within themselves whole batteries of words which, as they were sufficiently covered by a single comprehensive term, could now be scrapped and forgotten. The greatest difficulty facing the compilers of the Newspeak dictionary was not to invent new words, but, having invented them, to make sure what they meant: to make sure, that is to say, what ranges of words they canceled by their existence.

[13] As we have already seen in the case of the word *free,* words which had once borne a heretical meaning were sometimes retained for the sake of convenience, but only with the undesirable meanings purged out of them. Countless other words such as *honor, justice, morality, interna-*

tionalism, democracy, science, and *religion* had simply ceased to exist. A few blanket words covered them, and, in covering them, abolished them. All words grouping themselves round the concepts of liberty and equality, for instance, were contained in the single word *crimethink*, while all words grouping themselves round the concepts of objectivity and rationalism were contained in the single word *oldthink*. Greater precision would have been dangerous. What was required in a Party member was an outlook similar to that of the ancient Hebrew who knew, without knowing much else, that all nations other than his own worshipped "false gods." He did not need to know that these gods were called Baal, Osiris, Moloch, Ashtaroth, and the like; probably the less he knew about them the better for his orthodoxy. He knew Jehovah and the commandments of Jehovah; he knew, therefore, that all gods with other names or other attributes were false gods. In somewhat the same way, the Party member knew what constituted right conduct, and in exceedingly vague, generalized terms he knew what kinds of departure from it were possible. His sexual life, for example was entirely regulated by the two Newspeak words *sexcrime* (sexual immorality) and *goodsex* (chastity). *Sexcrime* covered all sexual misdeeds whatever. It covered fornication, adultery, homosexuality, and other perversions, and, in addition, normal intercourse practiced for its own sake. There was no need to enumerate them separately, since they were all equally culpable, and, in principle, all punishable by death. In the C vocabulary, which consisted of scientific and technical words, it might be necessary to give specialized names to certain sexual aberrations, but the ordinary citizen had no need of them. He knew what was meant by *goodsex*—that is to say, normal intercourse between man and wife, for the sole purpose of begetting children, and without physical pleasure on the part of the woman; all else was *sexcrime*. In Newspeak it was seldom possible to follow a heretical thought further than the perception that is *was* heretical; beyond that point the necessary words were nonexistent.

[14] No word in the B vocabulary was ideologically neutral. A great many were euphemisms. Such words, for instance, as *joycamp* (forced-labor camp) or *Minipax* (Ministry of Peace, i.e., Ministry of War) meant almost the exact opposite of what they appeared to mean. Some words, on the other hand, displayed a frank and contemptuous understanding of the real nature of Oceanic society. An example was *prolefeed*, meaning the rubbishy entertainment and spurious news which the Party handed out to the masses. Other words, again, were ambivalent, having the connotation "good" when applied to the Party and "bad" when applied to its enemies. But in addition there were great numbers of words which at first sight appeared to be mere abbreviations and which derived their ideological color not from their meaning but from their structure.

[15] So far as it could be contrived, everything that had or might have political significance of any kind was fitted into the B vocabulary. The name of every organization, or body of people, or doctrine, or country, or institution, or public building, was invariably cut down into the familiar shape; that is, a single easily pronounced word with the smallest number of syllables that would preserve the original derivation. In the Ministry of Truth, for example, the Records Department, in which Winston Smith worked, was called *Recdep,* the Fiction Department was called *Ficdep,* the Teleprograms Department was called *Teledep,* and so on. This was not done solely with the object of saving time. Even in the early decades of the twentieth century, telescoped words and phrases had been one of the characteristic features of political language; and it had been noticed that the tendency to use abbreviations of this kind was most marked in totalitarian countries and totalitarian organizations. Examples were such words as *Nazi, Gestapo, Comintern, Inprecor, Agitprop.* In the beginning the practice had been adopted as it were instinctively, but in Newspeak it was used with a conscious purpose. It was perceived that in thus abbreviating a name one narrowed and subtly altered its meaning, by cutting out most of the associations that would otherwise cling to it. The words *Communist International,* for instance, call up a composite picture of universal human brotherhood, red flags, barricades, Karl Marx, and the Paris Commune. The word *Comintern,* on the other hand, suggests merely a tightly knit organization and a well-defined body of doctrine. It refers to something almost as easily recognized, and as limited in purpose, as a chair or a table. *Comintern* is a word that can be uttered almost without taking thought, whereas *Communist Internatonal* is a phrase over which one is obliged to linger at least momentarily. In the same way, the associations called up by a word like *Minitrue* are fewer and more controllable than those called up by *Ministry of Truth.* This accounted not only for the habit of abbreviating whenever possible, but also for the almost exaggerated care that was taken to make every word easily pronounceable.

[16] In Newspeak, euphony outweighed every consideration other than exactitude of meaning. Regularity of grammar was always sacrificed to it when it seemed necessary. And rightly so, since what was required, above all for political purposes, were short clipped words of unmistakable meaning which could be uttered rapidly and which roused the minimum of echoes in the speaker's mind. The words of the B vocabulary even gained in force from the fact that nearly all of them were very much alike. Almost invariably these words—*goodthink, Minipax, prolefeed, sexcrime, joycamp, Ingsoc, bellyfeel, thinkpol,* and countless others —were words of two or three syllables, with the stress distributed equally between the first syllable and the last. The use of them encouraged a gabbling style of speech, at once staccato and monotonous. And this was

exactly what was aimed at. The intention was to make speech, and especially speech on any subject not ideologically neutral, as nearly as possible independent of consciousness. For the purposes of everyday life it was no doubt necessary, or sometimes necessary, to reflect before speaking, but a Party member called upon to make a political or ethical judgment should be able to spray forth the correct opinions as automatically as a machine gun spraying forth bullets. His training fitted him to do this, the language gave him an almost foolproof instrument, and the texture of the words, with their harsh sound and a certain willful ugliness which was in accord with the spirit of Ingsoc, assisted the process still further.

[17] So did the fact of having very few words to choose from. Relative to our own, the Newspeak vocabulary was tiny, and new ways of reducing it were constantly being devised. Newspeak, indeed, differed from almost all other languages in that its vocabulary grew smaller instead of larger every year. Each reduction was a gain, since the smaller the area of choice, the smaller the temptation to take thought. Ultimately it was hoped to make articulate speech issue from the larynx without involving the higher brain centers at all. This aim was frankly admitted in the Newspeak word *duckspeak,* meaning "to quack like a duck." Like various other words in the B vocabulary, *duckspeak* was ambivalent in meaning. Provided that the opinions which were quacked out were orthodox ones, it implied nothing but praise, and when the *Times* referred to one of the orators of the Party as a *doubleplusgood duckspeaker* it was paying a warm and valued compliment.

[18] *The C vocabulary.* The C vocabulary was supplementary to the others and consisted entirely of scientific and technical terms. These resembled the scientific terms in use today, and were constructed from the same roots, but the usual care was taken to define them rigidly and strip them of undesirable meanings. They followed the same grammatical rules as the words in the other two vocabularies. Very few of the C words had any currency either in everyday speech or in political speech. Any scientific worker or technician could find all the words he needed in the list devoted to his own specialty, but he seldom had more than a smattering of the words occurring in the other lists. Only a very few words were common to all lists, and there was no vocabulary expressing the function of Science as a habit of mind, or a method of thought, irrespective of its particular branches. There was, indeed, no word for "Science," any meaning that it could possibly bear being already sufficiently covered by the word *Ingsoc.*

[19] From the foregoing account it will be seen that in Newspeak the expression of unorthodox opinions, above a very low level, was well-nigh

impossible. It was of course possible to utter heresies of a very crude kind, a species of blasphemy. It would have been possible, for example, to say *Big Brother is ungood*. But this statement, which to an orthodox ear merely conveyed a self-evident absurdity, could not have been sustained by reasoned argument, because the necessary words were not available. Ideas inimical to Ingsoc could only be entertained in a vague wordless form, and could only be named in very broad terms which lumped together and condemned whole groups of heresies without defining them in doing so. One could, in fact, only use Newspeak for unorthodox purposes by illegitimately translating some of the words back into Oldspeak. For example *All mans are equal* was a possible Newspeak sentence, but only in the same sense in which *All men are redhaired* is a possible Oldspeak sentence. It did not contain a grammatical error, but it expressed a palpable untruth, i.e., that all men are of equal size, weight, or strength. The concept of political equality no longer existed, and this secondary meaning had accordingly been purged out of the word *equal*. In 1984, when Oldspeak was still the normal means of communication, the danger theoretically existed that in using Newspeak words one might remember their original meanings. In practice it was not difficult for any person well grounded in *doublethink* to avoid doing this, but within a couple of generations even the possibility of such a lapse would have vanished. A person growing up with Newspeak as his sole language would no more know that *equal* had once had the secondary meaning of "politically equal," or that *free* had once meant "intellectually free," than, for instance, a person who had never heard of chess would be aware of the secondary meanings attaching to *queen* and *rook*. There would be many crimes and errors which it would be beyond his power to commit, simply because they were nameless and therefore unimaginable. And it was to be foreseen that with the passage of time the distinguishing characteristics of Newspeak would become more and more pronounced—its words growing fewer and fewer, their meanings more and more rigid, and the chance of putting them to improper uses always diminishing.

[20] When Oldspeak had been once and for all superseded, the last link with the past would have been severed. History had already been rewritten, but fragments of the literature of the past survived here and there, imperfectly censored, and so long as one retained one's knowledge of Oldspeak it was possible to read them. In the future such fragments, even if they chanced to survive, would be unintelligible and untranslatable. It was impossible to translate any passage of Oldspeak into Newspeak unless it either referred to some technical process or some very simple everyday action, or was already orthodox (*goodthinkful* would be the Newspeak expression) in tendency. In practice this meant that no book written before approximately 1960 could be translated as a whole. Prerevolutionary literature could only be subjected to ideological trans-

lation—that is, alteration in sense as well as language. Take for example the well-known passage from the Declaration of Independence:

[21] *We hold these truths to be self-evident, that all men are created equal, that they are endowed by their Creator with certain inalienable rights, that among these are life, liberty, and the pursuit of happiness. That to secure these rights, Governments are instituted among men, deriving their powers from the consent of the governed. That whenever any form of Government becomes destructive of these ends, it is the right of the People to alter or abolish it, and to institute new Government . . .*

[22] It would have been quite impossible to render this into Newspeak while keeping to the sense of the original. The nearest one could come to doing so would be to swallow the whole passage up in the single word *crimethink*. A full translation could only be an ideological translation, whereby Jefferson's words would be changed into a panegyric on absolute government.

[23] A good deal of the literature of the past was, indeed, already being transformed in this way. Considerations of prestige made it desirable to preserve the memory of certain historical figures, while at the same time bringing their achievements into line with the philosophy of Ingsoc. Various writers, such as Shakespeare, Milton, Swift, Bryon, Dickens and some others were therefore in process of translation; when the task had been completed, their original writing, with all else that survived of the past, would be destroyed. These translations were a slow and difficult business, and it was not expected that they would be finished before the first or second decade of the twenty-first century. There were also large quantities of merely utilitarian literature—indispensable technical manuals and the like—that had to be treated in the same way. It was chiefly in order to allow time for the preliminary work of translation that the final adoption of Newspeak had been fixed for so late a date as 2050.

---—•❦ COMMENT AND QUESTIONS ❧•—

1. The following questions will check your understanding of the factual content and structure of Orwell's essay: (a) What are the purposes of Newspeak? (b) What are the chief characteristics of each of the three classes of words? (c) Why does the author choose to discuss the grammar of Newspeak in connection with the A vocabulary instead of discussing it in a section preceding his analysis of the three vocabularies? (d) Why is the B vocabulary discussed more fully than the other two; the C vocabu-

lary less fully? (e) Why is easy pronunciation important in Newspeak? (f) What is meant by the ideological translation of older literature? Why is it necessary?

2. The basis of irony is contrast—contrast, for example, between what is said and what is meant, or between what is expected and what actually occurs, or between what is and what seems to be or should be. What kind or kinds of irony do you find in "The Principles of Newspeak"?

3. Consider the language of the following passages:

> Its vocabulary was so constructed as to give *exact and often very subtle expression* to every meaning that a Party member could properly wish to express. . . .

> The B words were a sort of verbal shorthand, often packing whole ranges of ideas into a few syllables, and at the same time *more accurate and forcible than ordinary language.*

> Each reduction [in vocabulary] was *a gain,* since the smaller the area of choice, the smaller the temptation to take thought.

What sort of attitude toward the subject would normally be communicated by the italicized expressions? In the context of the essay, what do these expressions mean? What does the author gain by stating his meaning thus indirectly instead of directly?

4. Point out other examples in Orwell's essay of the kind of ironical expression illustrated in the passages above.

5. Look up in your dictionary the word *euphony.* Do the definitions clarify Orwell's use of the word at the beginning of paragraph 16?

6. Can you determine from context the meaning of *doublethink* in paragraph 19?

7. Does there appear to be a plan in the illustrations the author uses; that is, does he seem to be emphasizing any point or points with his examples comparing Newspeak to Oldspeak?

8. What tendencies toward the kind of language perfected in Newspeak do you see in present-day English? Do any of the simplifications or other changes seem to you sensible or desirable? Do you think that they would to George Orwell?

9. List as many characteristics as you can of the hypothetical society of 1984 as it appears in this selection. What is the relationship of each of these characteristics to the language of Newspeak? Do the attitudes and the practices of 1984 seem wholly remote from those of our society, or are at least some of them extensions of present practices? (If you have read the essay by John Lukacs, "It's Halfway to 1984," consider his comments on the last part of this question.)

10. Summarize what you take to be Orwell's ideas about the relationship between language and thought. To what extent do you agree with his ideas, and why?

[33]   F. L. Lucas: On the Fascination of Style

F. L. LUCAS (1894–) is a British critic, scholar, poet, and fellow and lecturer of King's College, Cambridge. Among his many books are *Authors Dead and Living, Literature and Psychology, Greek Drama for Everyman, Style, Tennyson, The Search for Good Sense,* and *The Drama of Ibsen and Strindberg.* The following essay was published in *Holiday* in March, 1960.

[1] When it was suggested to Walt Whitman that one of his works should be bound in vellum, he was outraged—"Pshaw!" he snorted, "—hangings, curtains, finger bowls, chinaware, Matthew Arnold!" And he might have been equally irritated by talk of style; for he boasted of "my barbaric yawp"—he would *not* be literary; his readers should touch not a book but a man. Yet Whitman took the pains to rewrite *Leaves of Grass* four times, and his style is unmistakable. Samuel Butler maintained that writers who bothered about their style became unreadable but he bothered about his own. "Style" has got a bad name by growing associated with precious and superior persons who, like Oscar Wilde, spend a morning putting in a comma, and the afternoon (so he said) taking it out again. But such abuse of "style" is misuse of English. For the word means merely "a way of expressing oneself, in language, manner, or appearance"; or, secondly, "a *good* way of so expressing oneself"—as when one says, "Her behavior never lacked style."
[2] Now there is no crime in expressing oneself (though to try to impress oneself on others easily grows revolting or ridiculous). Indeed one cannot help expressing oneself, unless one passes one's life in a cupboard. Even the most rigid Communist, or Organization-man, is compelled by Nature to have a unique voice, unique fingerprints, unique handwriting. Even the signatures of the letters on your breakfast table may reveal more than their writers guess. There are blustering signatures that swish across the page like cornstalks bowed before a tempest. There are cryptic signatures, like a scrabble of lightning across a cloud, suggesting that behind is a lofty divinity whom all must know, or an aloof divinity whom none is worthy to know (though, as this might be highly inconvenient, a docile typist sometimes interprets the mystery in a bracket underneath). There are impetuous squiggles implying that the author is a sort of strenuous Sputnik streaking round the globe every eighty minutes. There are florid signatures, all curlicues and danglements and

flamboyance, like the youthful Disraeli (through these seem rather out of fashion). There are humble, humdrum signatures. And there are also, sometimes, signatures that are courteously clear, yet mindful of a certain simple grace and artistic economy—in short, of style.

[3] Since, then, not one of us can put pen to paper, or even open his mouth, without giving something of himself away to shrewd observers, it seems mere common sense to give the matter a little thought. Yet it does not seem very common. Ladies may take infinite pains about having style in their clothes, but many of us remain curiously indifferent about having it in our words. How many women would dream of polishing not only their nails but also their tongues? They may play freely on that perilous little organ, but they cannot often be bothered to tune it. And how many men think of improving their talk as well as their golf handicap?

[4] No doubt strong silent men, speaking only in gruff monosyllables, may despise "mere words." No doubt the world does suffer from an endemic plague of verbal dysentery. But that, precisely, is bad style. And consider the amazing power of mere words. Adolf Hitler was a bad artist, bad statesman, bad general, and bad man. But largely because he could tune his rant, with psychological nicety, to the exact wave length of his audiences and make millions quarrelsome-drunk all at the same time by his command of windy nonsense, skilled statesmen, soldiers, scientists were blown away like chaff, and he came near to rule the world. If Sir Winston Churchill had been a mere speechifier, we might well have lost the war; yet his speeches did quite a lot to win it.

[5] No man was less of a literary aesthete than Benjamin Franklin; yet this tallow-chandler's son, who changed world history, regarded as "a principal means of my advancement" that pungent style which he acquired partly by working in youth over old *Spectators;* but mainly by being Benjamin Franklin. The squinting demagogue, John Wilkes, as ugly as his many sins, had yet a tongue so winning that he asked only half an hour's start (to counteract his face) against any rival for a woman's favor. "Vote for you!" growled a surly elector in his constituency. "I'd sooner vote for the devil!" "But in case your friend should not stand . . . ?" Cleopatra, that ensnarer of world conquerors, owed less to the shape of her nose than to the charm of her tongue. Shakespeare himself has often poor plots and thin ideas; even his mastery of character has been questioned; what does remain unchallenged in his verbal magic. Men are often taken, like rabbits, by the ears. And though the tongue has no bones, it can sometimes break millions of them.

[6] "But," the reader may grumble, "I am neither Hitler, Cleopatra, nor Shakespeare. What is all this to me?" Yet we all talk—often too much; we all have to write letters—often too many. We live not by bread alone but also by words. And not always with remarkable efficiency. Strikes,

lawsuits, divorces, all sorts of public nuisance and private misery, often come just from the gaggling incompetence with which we express ourselves. Americans and British get at cross-purposes because they use the same words with different meanings. Men have been hanged on a comma in a statute. And in the valley of Balaclava a mere verbal ambiguity, about *which* guns were to be captured, sent the whole Light Brigade to futile annihilation.

[7] Words can be more powerful, and more treacherous, than we sometimes suspect; communication more difficult than we may think. We are all serving life sentences of solitary confinement within our own bodies; like prisoners, we have, as it were, to tap in awkward code to our fellow men in their neighboring cells. Further, when A and B converse, there take part in their dialogue not two characters, as they suppose, but six. For there is A's real self—call it A_1; there is also A's picture of himself —A_2; there is also B's picture of A—A_3. And there are three corresponding personalities of B. With six characters involved even in a simple tête-à-tête, no wonder we fall into muddles and misunderstandings.

[8] Perhaps, then, there are five main reasons for trying to gain some mastery of language:

We have no other way of understanding, informing, misinforming, or persuading one another.

Even alone, we think mainly in words; if our language is muddy, so will our thinking be.

By our handling of words we are often revealed and judged. "Has he written anything?" said Napoleon of a candidate for an appointment. "Let me see his *style*."

Without a feeling for language one remains half-blind and deaf to literature.

Our mother tongue is bettered or worsened by the way each generation uses it. Languages evolve like species. They can degenerate; just as oysters and barnacles have lost their heads. Compare ancient Greek with modern. A heavy responsibility, though often forgotten.

[9] Why and how did I become interested in style? The main answer, I suppose, is that I was born that way. Then I was, till ten, an only child running loose in a house packed with books, and in a world (thank goodness) still undistracted by radio and television. So at three I groaned to my mother, "Oh, I *wish* I could read," and at four I read. Now travel among books is the best travel of all, and the easiest, and the cheapest. (Not that I belittle ordinary travel—which I regard as one of the three main pleasures in life.) One learns to write by reading good books, as one learns to talk by hearing good talkers. And if I have learned anything of writing, it is largely from writers like Montaigne, Dorothy Osborne,

Horace Walpole, Johnson, Goldsmith, Montesquieu, Voltaire, Flaubert and Anatole France. Again, I was reared on Greek and Latin, and one can learn much from translating Homer or the Greek Anthology, Horace or Tacitus, if one is thrilled by the originals and tries, however vainly, to recapture some of that thrill in English.

[10] But at Rugby I could *not* write English essays. I believe it stupid to torment boys to write on topics that they know and care nothing about. I used to rush to the school library and cram the subject, like a python swallowing rabbits; then, still replete as a postprandial python, I would tie myself in clumsy knots to embrace those accursed themes. Bacon was wise in saying that reading makes a full man; talking, a ready one; writing, an exact one. But writing from an empty head is futile anguish.

[11] At Cambridge, my head having grown a little fuller, I suddenly found I *could* write—not with enjoyment (it is always tearing oneself in pieces)—but fairly fluently. Then came the War of 1914-18; and though soldiers have other things than pens to handle, they learn painfully to be clear and brief. Then the late Sir Desmond MacCarthy invited me to review for the *New Statesman;* it was a useful apprenticeship, and he was delightful to work for. But I think it was well after a few years to stop; reviewers remain essential, but there are too many books one *cannot* praise, and only the pugnacious enjoy amassing enemies. By then I was an ink-addict—not because writing is much pleasure, but because not to write is pain; just as some smokers do not so much enjoy tobacco as suffer without it. The positive happiness of writing comes, I think, from work when done—decently, one hopes, and not without use—and from the letters of readers which help to reassure, or delude, one that so it is.

[12] But one of my most vivid lessons came, I think, from service in a war department during the Second War. Then, if the matter one sent out was too wordy, the communication channels might choke; yet if it was not absolutely clear, the results might be serious. So I emerged, after six years of it, with more passion than ever for clarity and brevity, more loathing than ever for the obscure and the verbose.

[13] For forty years at Cambridge I have tried to teach young men to write well, and have come to think it impossible. To write really well is a gift inborn; those who have it teach themselves; one can only try to help and hasten the process. After all, the uneducated sometimes express themselves far better than their "betters." In language, as in life, it is possible to be perfectly correct—and yet perfectly tedious, or odious. The illiterate last letter of the doomed Vanzetti was more moving than most professional orators; 18th Century ladies, who should have been spanked for their spelling, could yet write far better letters than most professors of English; and the talk of Synge's Irish peasants seems to me vastly more vivid than the later styles of Henry James. Yet Synge averred

that his characters owed far less of their eloquence to what he invented for them than to what he had overheard in the cottages of Wicklow and Kerry:

CHRISTY. It's little you'll think if my love's a poacher's, or an earl's itself, when you'll feel my two hands stretched around you, and I squeezing kisses on your puckered lips, till I'd feel a kind of pity for the Lord God in all ages sitting lonesome in His golden chair.

PEGEEN. That'll be right fun, Christy Mahon, and any girl would walk her heart out before she'd meet a young man was your like for eloquence, or talk at all.

[14] Well she might! It's not like that they talk in universities—more's the pity.

[15] But though one cannot teach people to write well, one can sometimes teach them to write rather better. One can give a certain number of hints, which often seem boringly obvious—only experience shows they are not.

[16] One can say: Beware of pronouns—they are devils. Look at even Addison, describing the type of pedant who chatters of style without having any:

Upon enquiry I found my learned friend had dined that day with Mr. Swan, the famous punster; and desiring *him* to give me some account of Mr. Swan's conversation, *he* told me that *he* generally talked in the Paronomasia, that *he* sometimes gave it to the Plocé, but that in *his* humble opinion *he* shone most in the Antanaclasis.

What a sluttish muddle of *he* and *him* and *his!* It all needs rewording. Far better repeat a noun, or a name, than puzzle the reader, even for a moment, with ambiguous pronouns. Thou shalt not puzzle thy reader.

[17] Or one can say: Avoid jingles. The B.B.C. news bulletins seem compiled by earless persons, capable of crying round the globe: "The enemy is re*port*ed to have seized this im*port*ant *port*, and reinforcements are hurrying up in sup*port*." Any fool, once told, can hear such things to be insupportable.

[18] Or one can say: Be sparing with relative clauses. Don't string them together like sausages, or jam them inside one another like Chinese boxes or the receptacles of Buddha's tooth. Or one can say: Don't flaunt jargon, like Addison's Mr. Swan, or the type of modern critic who gurgles more technical terms in a page than Johnson used in all his *Lives* or Sainte-Beuve in thirty volumes. But dozens of such snippety precepts, though they may sometimes save people from writing badly, will help them little toward writing well. Are there no general rules of a more positive kind, and of more positive use?

[19] Perhaps. There *are* certain basic principles which seem to me

observed by many authors I admire, which I think have served me and which may serve others. I am not talking of geniuses, who are a law to themselves (and do not always write a very good style, either); nor of poetry, which has different laws from prose; nor of poetic prose, like Sir Thomas Browne's or De Quincey's, which is often more akin to poetry; but of the plain prose of ordinary books and documents, letters and talk.

[20] The writer should respect truth and himself; therefore honesty. He should respect his readers; therefore courtesy. These are two of the cornerstones of style. Confucius saw it, twenty-five centuries ago: "The Master said, The gentleman is courteous, but not pliable: common men are pliable, but not courteous."

[21] First, honesty. In literature, as in life, one of the fundamentals is to find, and be, one's true self. One's true self may indeed be unpleasant (though one can try to better it); but a false self, sooner or later, becomes disgusting—just as a nice plain woman, painted to the eyebrows, can become horrid. In writing, in the long run, pretense does not work. As the police put it, anything you say may be used as evidence against you. If handwriting reveals character, writing reveals it still more. You cannot fool *all* your judges *all* the time.

[22] Most style is not honest enough. Easy to say, but hard to practice. A writer may take to long words, as young men to beards—to impress. But long words, like beards, are often the badge of charlatans. Or a writer may cultivate the obscure, to seem profound. But even carefully muddied puddles are soon fathomed. Or he may cultivate eccentricity, to seem original. But really original people do not have to think about being original—they can no more help it than they can help breathing. They do not need to dye their hair green. The fame of Meredith, Wilde or Bernard Shaw might now shine brighter, had they struggled less to be brilliant; whereas Johnson remains great, not merely because his gifts were formidable but also because, with all his prejudice and passion, he fought no less passionately to "clear his mind of cant."

[23] Secondly, courtesy—respect for the reader. From this follow several other basic principles of style. Clarity is one. For it is boorish to make your reader rack his brains to understand. One should aim at being impossible to misunderstand—though men's capacity for misunderstanding approaches infinity. Hence Molière and Po Chu-i tried their work on their cooks; and Swift his on his men-servants—"which, if they did not comprehend, he would alter and amend, until they understood it perfectly." Our bureaucrats and pundits, unfortunately, are less considerate.

[24] Brevity is another basic principle. For it is boorish, also, to waste your reader's time. People who would not dream of stealing a penny of one's money turn not a hair at stealing hours of one's life. But that does

not make them less exasperating. Therefore there is no excuse for the sort of writer who takes as long as a marching army corps to pass a given point. Besides, brevity is often more effective; the half can say more than the whole, and to imply things may strike far deeper than to state them at length. And because one is particularly apt to waste words on preambles before coming to the substance, there was sense in the Scots professor who always asked his pupils—"Did ye remember to tear up that fir-r-st page?"

[25] Here are some instances that would only lose by lengthening.

It is useless to go to bed to save the light, if the result is twins. (Chinese proverb.)

My barn is burnt down—
Nothing hides the moon. (Complete Japanese poem.)

Je me regrette. (Dying words of the gay Vicomtesse d'Houdetot.)

I have seen their backs before. (Wellington, when French marshals turned their backs on him at a reception.)

Continue until the tanks stop, then get out and walk. (Patton to the Twelfth Corps, halted for fuel supplies at St. Dizier, 8/30/44.)

[26] Or there is the most laconic diplomatic note on record: when Philip of Macedon wrote to the Spartans that, if he came within their borders, he would leave not one stone of their city, they wrote back the one word—"If."

[27] Clarity comes before even brevity. But it is a fallacy that wordiness is necessarily clearer. Metternich when he thought something he had written was obscure would simply go through it crossing out everything irrelevant. What remained, he found, often became clear. Wellington, asked to recommend three names for the post of Commander-in-Chief, India, took a piece of paper and wrote three times—"Napier." Pages could not have been clearer—or as forcible. On the other hand the lectures, and the sentences, of Coleridge became at times bewildering because his mind was often "wiggle-waggle"; just as he could not even walk straight on a path.

[28] But clarity and brevity, though a good beginning, are only a beginning. By themselves, they may remain bare and bleak. When Calvin Coolidge, asked by his wife what the preacher had preached on, replied "Sin," and, asked what the preacher had said, replied, "He was against it," he was brief enough. But one hardly envies Mrs. Coolidge.

[29] An attractive style requires, of course, all kinds of further gifts—such as variety, good humor, good sense, vitality, imagination. Variety means avoiding monotony of rhythm, of language, of mood. One needs to vary one's sentence length (this present article has too many short

sentences; but so vast a subject grows here as cramped as a djin in a bottle); to amplify one's vocabulary; to diversify one's tone. There are books that petrify one throughout, with the rigidly pompous solemnity of an owl perched on a leafless tree. But ceaseless facetiousness can be as bad; or perpetual irony. Even the smile of Voltaire can seem at times a fixed grin, a disagreeable wrinkle. Constant peevishness is far worse, as often in Swift; even on the stage too much irritable dialogue may irritate an audience, without its knowing why.

[30] Still more are vitality, energy, imagination gifts that must be inborn before they can be cultivated. But under the head of imagination two common devices may be mentioned that have been the making of many a style—metaphor and simile. Why such magic power should reside in simply saying, or implying, that A is like B remains a little mysterious. But even our unconscious seems to love symbols; again, language often tends to lose itself in clouds of vaporous abstraction, and simile or metaphor can bring it back to concrete solidity; and, again, such imagery can gild the gray flats of prose with sudden sun-glints of poetry.

[31] If a foreigner may for a moment be impertinent, I admire the native gift of Americans for imagery as much as I wince at their fondness for slang. (Slang seems to me a kind of linguistic fungus; as poisonous, and as shortlived, as toadstools.) When Matthew Arnold lectured in the United States, he was likened by one newspaper to "an elderly macaw pecking at a trellis of grapes"; he observed, very justly, "How lively journalistic fancy is among the Americans!" General Grant, again, unable to hear him, remarked: "Well, wife, we've paid to see the British lion, but as we can't hear him roar, we'd better go home." By simile and metaphor, these two quotations bring before us the slightly pompous, fastidious, inaudible Arnold as no direct description could have done.

[32] Or consider how language comes alive in the Chinese saying that lending to the feckless is "like pelting a stray dog with dumplings," or in the Arab proverb: "They came to shoe the pasha's horse, and the beetle stretched forth his leg"; in the Greek phrase for a perilous cape—"stepmother of ships"; or the Hebrew adage that "as the climbing up a sandy way is to the feet of the aged, so is a wife full of words to a quiet man"; in Shakespeare's phrase for a little England lost in the world's vastness— "in a great Poole, a Swan's nest"; or Fuller's libel on tall men—"Ofttimes such who are built four stories high are observed to have little in their cockloft"; in Chateaubriand's "I go yawning my life"; or in Jules Renard's portrait of a cat, "well buttoned in her fur." Or, to take a modern instance, there is Churchill on dealing with Russia:

> Trying to maintain good relations with a Communist is like wooing a crocodile. You do not know whether to tickle it under the chin or beat it over the head. When it opens its mouth, you cannot tell whether it is trying to smile or preparing to eat you up.

What a miracle human speech can be, and how dull is most that one hears! Would one hold one's hearers, it is far less help, I suspect, to read manuals on style than to cultivate one's own imagination and imagery.

[33] I will end with two remarks by two wise old women of the civilized 18th Century.

[34] The first is from the blind Mme. du Deffand (the friend of Horace Walpole) to that Mlle. de Lespinasse with whom, alas, she was to quarrel so unwisely: "You must make up your mind, my queen, to live with me in the greatest truth and sincerity. You will be charming so long as you let yourself be natural, and remain without pretension and without artifice." The second is from Mme. de Charrière, the Zélide whom Boswell had once loved at Utrecht in vain, to a Swiss girl friend: "Lucinde, my clever Lucinde, while you wait for the Romeos to arrive, you have nothing better to do than become perfect. Have ideas that are clear, and expressions that are simple." ("*Ayez des idées nettes et des expressions simples.*") More than half the bad writing in the world, I believe, comes from neglecting those two very simple pieces of advice.

[35] In many ways, no doubt, our world grows more and more complex; sputniks cannot be simple; yet how many of our complexities remain futile, how many of our artificialities false. Simplicity too can be subtle—as the straight lines of a Greek temple, like the Parthenon at Athens, are delicately curved, in order to look straighter still.

COMMENT AND QUESTIONS

1. What are the purposes of Lucas' first seven paragraphs? The author later recommends brevity and speaks of not wasting words on preambles before coming to the substance. Do you think that the first seven paragraphs might have been briefer? Explain.
2. What point is Lucas making, in paragraph 7, with his analysis of the six characters involved in a dialogue? Does the analysis seem to you accurate?
3. Which of the five main reasons for gaining some mastery of language has the author discussed in the paragraphs preceding paragraph 8? Which of the five reasons seem most important to you, and why?
4. What, in your judgment, were Lucas' reasons for including the biographical information in paragraphs 9–14?
5. Paragraph 18 begins with the precept "Be sparing with relative clauses." Examine the relative clauses in paragraph 19. Could any of them be eliminated without loss?
6. What is the meaning of *pliable* in paragraph 20, and how is the word related to the topic idea of the paragraph?
7. In the discussion of honesty and courtesy, what particular kinds of dis-

honesty and discourtesy is the author criticizing? Why does he devote more space to courtesy than to honesty?
8. What relationships does Lucas see between brevity and clarity?
9. According to the author, what are the values of metaphor and simile? Examine Lucas' figurative language, especially in paragraphs 2, 5, 7, 18, 21, 22, 29, 30, and 35. Which figures seem to you effective, and why?
10. In what ways are the quotations in paragraph 34 well chosen to conclude the essay?
11. One of the noticeable qualities of Lucas' writing is his use, not only of figurative language, but also of quotation and of concrete example and detail. Comment on this use of quotation and illustrative detail. Is there more of it than the author needs or the reader wants? Is Lucas sacrificing brevity to clarity? Or, do you find his use of supporting detail skillful and interesting? Explain.
12. What seem to you the most significant things that Lucas communicates, directly and indirectly, to the young writer interested in improving his style?

LITERATURE
AND THE ARTS

[34] *Joseph Conrad*: Preface to
The Nigger of the Narcissus

JOSEPH CONRAD (1857–1924) was a famous English novelist and short story writer, Polish by birth and originally named Teodor Jozef Konrad Korzeniowski. After spending twenty years at sea, first as a sailor and later as an officer in the British merchant marine, Conrad retired to live in his adopted country and devote himself to writing. The following preface to a novel published in 1897 presents his concept of art and the aims of the serious writer of fiction. Among Conrad's other works are *Almayer's Folly, Lord Jim, Nostromo, Victory, Youth, Typhoon,* and *Heart of Darkness*.

[1] A work that aspires, however humbly, to the condition of art should carry its justification in every line. And art itself may be defined as a single-minded attempt to render the highest kind of justice to the visible universe, by bringing to light the truth, manifold and one, underlying its every aspect. It is an attempt to find in its forms, in its colors, in its light, in its shadows, in the aspects of matter and in the facts of life what of each is fundamental, what is enduring and essential—their one illuminating and convincing quality—the very truth of their existence. The artist, then, like the thinker or the scientist, seeks the truth and makes his appeal. Impressed by the aspect of the world the thinker plunges into

ideas, the scientist into facts—whence, presently, emerging they make their appeal to those qualities of our being that fit us best for the hazardous enterprise of living. They speak authoritatively to our commonsense, to our intelligence, to our desire of peace or to our desire of unrest; not seldom to our prejudices, sometimes to our fears, often to our egoism—but always to our credulity. And their words are heard with reverence, for their concern is with weighty matters: with the cultivation of our minds and the proper care of our bodies, with the attainment of our ambitions, with the perfection of the means and the glorification of our precious aims.

[2] It is otherwise with the artist.

[3] Confronted by the same enigmatical spectacle the artist descends within himself, and in that lonely region of stress and strife, if he be deserving and fortunate, he finds the terms of his appeal. His appeal is made to our less obvious capacities: to that part of our nature which, because of the warlike conditions of existence, is necessarily kept out of sight within the more resisting and hard qualities—like the vulnerable body within a steel armour. His appeal is less loud, more profound, less distinct, more stirring—and sooner forgotten. Yet its effect endures forever. The changing wisdom of successive generations discards ideas, questions facts, demolishes theories. But the artist appeals to that part of our being which is not dependent on wisdom: to that in us which is a gift and not an acquisition—and, therefore, more permanently enduring. He speaks to our capacity for delight and wonder, to the sense of mystery surrounding our lives; to our sense of pity, and beauty, and pain; to the latent feeling of fellowship with all creation—and to the subtle but invincible conviction of solidarity that knits together the loneliness of innumerable hearts, to the solidarity in dreams, in joy, in sorrow, in aspirations, in illusions, in hope, in fear, which binds men to each other, which binds together all humanity—the dead to the living and the living to the unborn.

[4] It is only some such train of thought, or rather of feeling, that can in a measure explain the aim of the attempt, made in the tale which follows, to present an unrestful episode in the obscure lives of a few individuals out of all the disregarded multitude of the bewildered, the simple, and the voiceless. For, if any part of truth dwells in the belief confessed above, it becomes evident that there is not a place of splendour or a dark corner of the earth that does not deserve if only a passing glance of wonder and pity. The motive then, may be held to justify the matter of the work; but this preface, which is simply an avowal of endeavour, cannot end here—for the avowal is not yet complete.

[5] Fiction—if it at all aspires to be art—appeals to temperament. And in truth it must be, like painting, like music, like all art, the appeal of one temperament to all the other innumerable temperaments whose

subtle and resistless power endows passing events with their true meaning, and creates the moral, the emotional atmosphere of the place and time. Such an appeal to be effective must be an impression conveyed through the senses; and, in fact, it cannot be made in any other way, because temperament, whether individual or collective, is not amenable to persuasion. All art, therefore, appeals primarily to the senses, and the artistic aim when expressing itself in written words must make its appeal through the senses, if its high desire is to reach the secret spring of responsive emotions. It must strenuously aspire to the plasticity of sculpture, the color of painting, and to the magic suggestiveness of music—which is the art of arts. And it is only through complete, unswerving devotion to the perfect blending of form and substance; it is only through an unremitting never-discouraged care for the shape and ring of sentences that an approach can be made to plasticity, to color, and that the light of magic suggestiveness may be brought to play for an evanescent instant over the commonplace surface of words: of the old, old words, worn thin, defaced by ages of careless usage.

[6] The sincere endeavour to accomplish that creative task, to go as far on that road as his strength will carry him, to go undeterred by faltering, weariness or reproach, is the only valid justification for the worker in prose. And if his conscience is clear, his answer to those who in the fulness of wisdom which looks for immediate profit, demand specifically to be edified, consoled, amused; who demand to be promptly improved, or encouraged, or frightened, or shocked, or charmed, must run thus:—My task which I am trying to achieve is, by the power of the written word to make you hear, to make you feel—it is, before all, to make you *see*. That—and no more, and it is everything. If I succeed, you shall find there according to your deserts: encouragement, consolation, fear, charm—all you demand—and, perhaps, also that glimpse of truth for which you have forgotten to ask.

[7] To snatch in a moment of courage, from the remorseless rush of time, a passing phase of life, is only the beginning of the task. The task approached in tenderness and faith is to hold up unquestioningly, without choice and without fear, the rescued fragment before all eyes in the light of a sincere mood. It is to show its vibration, its color, its form; and through its movement, its form, and its color, reveal the substance of its truth—disclose its inspiring secret: the stress and passion within the core of each convincing moment. In a single-minded attempt of that kind, if one be deserving and fortunate, one may perchance attain to such clearness of sincerity that at last the presented vision of regret, or pity, of terror or mirth, shall awaken in the hearts of the beholders that feeling of unavoidable solidarity; of the solidarity in mysterious origin, in toil, in joy, in hope, in uncertain fate, which binds men to each other and all mankind to the visible world.

[8] It is evident that he who, rightly or wrongly, holds by the convictions expressed above cannot be faithful to any one of the temporary formulas of his craft. The enduring part of them—the truth which each only imperfectly veils—should abide with him as the most precious of his possessions, but they all: Realism, Romanticism, Naturalism, even the unofficial sentimentalism (which like the poor, is exceedingly difficult to get rid of), all these gods must, after a short period of fellowship, abandon him—even on the very threshold of the temple—to the stammerings of his conscience and to the outspoken consciousness of the difficulties of his work. In that uneasy solitude the supreme cry of Art for Art itself, loses the exciting ring of its apparent immorality. It sounds far off. It has ceased to be a cry, and is heard only as a whisper, often incomprehensible, but at times and faintly encouraging.

[9] Sometimes, stretched at ease in the shade of a roadside tree, we watch the motions of a labourer in a distant field, and after a time, begin to wonder languidly as to what the fellow may be at. We watch the movements of his body, the waving of his arms, we see him bend down, stand up, hesitate, begin again. It may add to the charm of an idle hour to be told the purpose of his exertions. If we know he is trying to lift a stone, to dig a ditch, to uproot a stump, we look with a more real interest at his efforts; we are disposed to condone the jar of his agitation upon the restfulness of the landscape; and even, if in a brotherly frame of mind, we may bring ourselves to forgive his failure. We understood his object, and, after all, the fellow has tried, and perhaps he had not the strength—and perhaps he had not the knowledge. We forgive, go on our way—and forget.

[10] And so it is with the workman of art. Art is long and life is short, and success is very far off. And thus, doubtful of strength to travel so far, we talk a little about the aim—the aim of art, which, like life itself, is inspiring, difficult—obscured by mists. It is not in the clear logic of a triumphant conclusion; it is not in the unveiling of one of those heartless secrets which are called the Laws of Nature. It is not less great, but only more difficult.

[11] To arrest, for the space of a breath, the hands busy about the work of the earth, and compel men entranced by the sight of distant goals to glance for a moment at the surrounding vision of form and color, of sunshine and shadows; to make them pause for a look, for a sigh, for a smile—such is the aim, difficult and evanescent, and reserved only for a very few to achieve. But sometimes, by the deserving and the fortunate, even that task is accomplished. And when it is accomplished—behold!—all the truth of life is there: a moment of vision, a sigh, a smile—and the return to an eternal rest.

COMMENT AND QUESTIONS

1. Examine the definition of art in the second and third sentences of paragraph 1. In that definition and the expansion of it in paragraphs 1–3, what basic assumptions is Conrad making about life and human experience?
2. Although English was not his native language, Conrad is known as a master of English style. Comment on the sentence structures and the use of words in paragraph 1. Point out other passages in the essay in which the writing seems to you notably good, and explain why it is good.
3. Can you reconcile the statements in paragraph 3 that the appeal of the artist is "sooner forgotten" than the appeal of the thinker or the scientist, and yet that the effect of the artist's appeal "endures forever"? What is the difference in meaning between *gift* and *acquisition* in paragraph 3, and what point is Conrad making with his contrast?
4. Where and for what purposes does Conrad return to the contrast, developed in the first three paragraphs, between the thinker or the scientist and the artist?
5. Paragraph 4 briefly refers to the content of *The Nigger of the Narcissus*. How has Conrad justified writing a novel about "an unrestful episode" in a few "obscure lives"? Is his justification convincing to you? Explain.
6. What two points about the writing of fiction is Conrad emphasizing in paragraph 5? Does either principle, or do both, seem applicable to other kinds of writing? Explain.
7. A statement in paragraph 6 is often quoted: "My task which I am trying to achieve. . . ." Think of one or more novels or short stories that have impressed you. Have they made you hear, feel, and, before all, *see*? Would you make any additions to Conrad's statement about the creative writer's task?
8. In this essay, is Conrad following his precept of making the reader hear, feel, and see? Explain.
9. What are the implications of *the very threshold of the temple* in paragraph 8?
10. In paragraph 9, what is the purpose of the experience described and commented on?
11. In paragraphs 3, 7, and 11, Conrad uses the combination of *deserving* and *fortunate* in talking about the artistic writer. What does *deserving* appear to mean or to imply?
12. Summarize in your own words what Conrad means by *art*. To what extent do you agree or disagree with his concept? Explain.

[35] *William Faulkner*: Remarks on Receiving the Nobel Prize

WILLIAM FAULKNER (1897–1962) is regarded by many critics as the most brilliant American short story writer and novelist of the twentieth century. Among his novels are *The Sound and the Fury; As I Lay Dying; Light in August; Absalom, Absalom; Intruder in the Dust; A Fable; The Hamlet; The Town; The Mansion;* and *The Reivers.* Faulkner gave the following short address in Stockholm, Sweden, in December, 1950, when he accepted the award of the 1949 Nobel Prize for Literature.

[1] I feel that this award was not made to me as a man but to my work —a life's work in the agony and sweat of the human spirit, not for glory and least of all for profit, but to create out of the materials of the human spirit something which did not exist before. So this award is only mine in trust. It will not be difficult to find a dedication for the money part of it commensurate with the purpose and significance of its origin. But I would like to do the same with the acclaim too, by using this moment as a pinnacle from which I might be listened to by the young men and women already dedicated to the same anguish and travail, among whom is already that one who will some day stand here where I am standing.

[2] Our tragedy today is a general and universal physical fear so long sustained by now that we can even bear it. There are no longer problems of the spirit. There is only the question: when will I be blown up? Because of this, the young man or woman writing today has forgotten the problems of the human heart in conflict with itself which alone can make good writing because only that is worth writing about, worth the agony and the sweat.

[3] He must learn them again. He must teach himself that the basest of all things is to be afraid; and, teaching himself that, forget it forever, leaving no room in his workshop for anything but the old verities and truths of the heart, the old universal truths lacking which any story is ephemeral and doomed—love and honor and pity and pride and compassion and sacrifice. Until he does so he labors under a curse. He writes not of love but of lust, of defeats in which nobody loses anything of value, of victories without hope, and worst of all, without pity or compassion.

His griefs grieve on no universal bones, leaving no scars. He writes not of the heart but of the glands.

[4] Until he relearns these things he will write as though he stood alone and watched the end of man. I decline to accept the end of man. It is easy enough to say that man is immortal simply because he will endure; that when the last ding-dong of doom has clanged and faded from the last worthless rock hanging tideless in the last red and dying evening, that even then there will still be one more sound: that of his puny inexhaustible voice, still talking. I refuse to accept this. I believe that man will not merely endure: he will prevail. He is immortal, not because he alone among creatures has an inexhaustible voice, but because he has a soul, a spirit capable of compassion and sacrifice and endurance. The poet's, the writer's, duty is to write about these things. It is his privilege to help man endure by lifting his heart, by reminding him of the courage and honor and hope and pride and compassion and pity and sacrifice which have been the glory of his past. The poet's voice need not merely be the record of man, it can be one of the props, the pillars to help him endure and prevail.

COMMENT AND QUESTIONS

1. In what phrases in the first two paragraphs does Faulkner stress the suffering a writer must endure? Why should the suffering be necessary?
2. Do the first three sentences of paragraph 2 seem to you to be true today? Explain.
3. What does Faulkner appear to mean, in paragraph 2, by "the problems of the human heart in conflict with itself"?
4. What is the meaning of *workshop* in paragraph 3? What is the literal meaning of the next-to-last sentence of this paragraph?
5. Can you think of writers of whom Faulkner's last three sentences in paragraph 3 are true? Who are they, and how does his comment fit them?
6. In the first sentence of paragraph 4, what does Faulkner mean by *as though he stood alone*? By *the end of man* in that sentence and the following sentence does Faulkner mean the literal end or destruction of the human race, or is his meaning different? Explain.
7. Comment on the structure and diction of the sentence in paragraph 4 beginning "It is easy enough . . . ."
8. What is the difference between *endure* and *prevail* as Faulkner is using the words? What does he believe to be the duty and the privilege of the writer?
9. Faulkner is addressing his remarks to young men and women interested

in writing. What does he say of concern to the nonwriter about human life and values?

10. Faulkner's speech has been highly praised for its content and style and severely criticized as a piece of pompous and empty rhetoric. What is your judgment of it, and why?

[36] *Ihab Hassan*: The Anti-Hero

IHAB HASSAN (1925–   ) is a professor of English at Wesleyan University. The following essay is from *Radical Innocence: Studies in the Contemporary American Novel*, published in 1961; footnotes are the author's.

[1] "In its essence literature is concerned with the self," Lionel Trilling writes in *Freud and the Crisis of Our Culture*, "and the particular concern of the literature of the last two centuries has been with the self in its standing quarrel with culture."[1] The image of the self in its standing, and recently embittered, quarrel with culture—indeed in its quarrel with itself, as Mr. Trilling neglects to say—comes to focus in the figure of the anti-hero.

[2] In fiction, the unnerving rubric "anti-hero" refers to a ragged assembly of victims: the fool, the clown, the hipster, the criminal, the poor sod, the freak, the outsider, the scapegoat, the scrubby opportunist, the rebel without a cause, the "hero" in the ashcan and "hero" on the leash. If the anti-hero seems nowadays to hold us in his spell, it is because the deep and disquieting insights revealed to us by modern literature often require that we project ourselves into the predicament of victims.

[3] The gradual process of atrophy of the hero may have begun with Don Quixote, or perhaps even Job, Orestes, and Christ. It enters the critical phase, however, only late in the eighteenth century. Goethe's Werther introduces the "tragic" Romantic hero who, in his inordinate conception of himself, severs the traditional bond between the hero and his society, and points the way to such extreme stances of alienation as were to find expression in the Byronic and Sadist hero, in the gothic and

From Ihab Hassan, *Radical Innocence: Studies in the Contemporary American Novel*. Reprinted by permission of Princeton University Press. Copyright © 1961 by Princeton University Press.

[1] Lionel Trilling, *Freud and the Crisis of Our Culture* (Boston, 1955), pp. 58 ff.

demonic protagonist, in werewolf, ghoul, and vampire. But as the new bourgeois order, which the Romantic hero rejected, became a powerful social reality, the strategy of oppositon changed. The characters of Stendhal, Balzac, and Flaubert often seem, as Raymond Giraud has recognized, "heroes of ironies" whose "ideals, desires, and feelings are in disharmony" with their "adult conception of reality."[2] Similarly, the subtitle for *Vanity Fair: A Novel Without a Hero*, suggests that Victorian fiction was quietly disposing of the heroic protagonist. The ambivalences of a bourgeois hero in an overwhelmingly middle-class society raise for him problems of estrangement and communion, sincerity and simulation, ambition and acquiescence, which we recognize as the patent themes of the great novels of the last century. The wretched fate of the lower-class hero, caught between malignant Heredity and crushing Environment in the *roman experimental* of Zola, and in the less experimental but more benign novels of the brothers Goncourt, reflects the familiar bias of Naturalism and marks a further stage in the disintegration of heroism. Victim to immitigable "cosmic laws," with little or no control over his fate in the world, man turns inward again. The next development is predictable. "The way was open from the realist to the intimist novel," Mario Praz concludes in *The Hero in Eclipse in Victorian Fiction*. "Disillusioned observation of life as it really was, led to the eclipse of the hero and the disclosure of man's swarming interior world, made up of disparate and contradictory things."[3]

[4] With the retrenchment of the individual, the drama of good and evil which the hero and villain once objectified in society becomes blurred. The traditional forms of moral conflict are so internalized that no victory or defeat, where self is divided against itself, can claim to be more than pyrrhic. Cunningly introspective, the modern novel redefines the identity of its central character and redirects his energies toward the virtues of love or self-discovery, virtues that are a good deal more personal than social. To become someone, to know who or what one is, to reach finally another human being with love, and to do so in terms that society may censure, this is the passionate, bitter concern of the modern antihero. But the modern identity proved an elusive thing to capture. "You mustn't look in my novel for the old stable *ego* of the character," D. H. Lawrence wrote to Edward Garnett. "There is another *ego*, according to whose action the individual is unrecognizable, and passes through, as it were, allotropic states...."[4] A new shifty ego, a new concept of man. The sad history of the anti-hero is nothing more than the history of man's changing awareness of himself. It is the record of his recoil.

[2] Raymond Giraud, *The Unheroic Hero* (New Brunswick, 1957), p. 189. See also Harry Levin, "From Priam to Birotteau," *Yale French Studies*, vi (1950), p. 76.

[3] Mario Praz, *The Hero in Eclipse in Victorian Fiction* (New York, 1956), p. 383.

[4] Aldous Huxley, ed., *The Letters of D. H. Lawrence* (London, 1956), p. 198.

[5] The encounter between the new ego and the destructive element of experience, we have insisted, lies at the dramatic center of the modern novel in Europe and America. The encounter is further illumined by some striking European images which define the modern idea of the self and clarify its responses. We shall view some concrete instances of the anti-hero—whom in hope and charity we may simply call "hero." These instances are taken from writers of very different age and background, yet they add to a remarkably persistent theme.

[6] To consider Dostoyevsky's *Notes from Underground*, 1864, modern is perhaps to stretch the idea of modernity to its permissible limit. The document so shrill and anxious, so full of spite and spleen, reveals, in any case, what the modern soul likes most to gnaw upon: itself. The dagger is turned inward, the most refined tortures are reserved for the self. Whom else are we really interested in? Listening for forty years from the crack under his floor, Dostoyevsky's hero looks at existence with a cringe and a snarl. He knows the intense pleasure of degradation and of despair and knows, while gnashing his teeth, that "there is no one even for you to feel vindictive against, that you have not, and perhaps never will have, an object for your spite. . . ."[5] Precisely the condition which Albert Camus calls, in *The Rebel*, metaphysical rebellion, and which our hero understands as a revolt against "the whole legal system of Nature."[6] But no one is to blame; "consequently there is only the same outlet left again —that is, to beat the wall as hard as you can."[7] This frenzy is not only meant to be a protest against the whole order of Nature, the terrible fact that "every sort of consciousness . . . is a disease," or merely a protest against the historical enemies of Dostoyevsky—rationalism, meliorism, and science, the coxcomb fact that two plus two equals four.[8] The frenzy, in the form of caprice, is also directed against our individuality. That Dostoyevsky's "insect" can establish his identity only by forcing himself to collide ignominiously with an arrogant officer who does not even recognize his existence is of no importance. The important thing is that it is *he* who *forces* the recognition. This is freedom.

[7] The grotesque image of this strange creature haunts modern literature and remains at the center of our dread. Its cracked reflections in some way or other penetrate the works of most European novelists. And its perverse truths, almost insupportable, infiltrate recent American fiction which does not stem only, as Hemingway claimed, from a book by Mark Twain called *Huckleberry Finn* but also from another, it may

[5] *The Short Novels of Dostoyevsky*, Introduction by Thomas Mann (New York, 1945), p. 137.
[6] *Ibid.*, p. 137.
[7] *Ibid.*, p. 140.
[8] *Ibid.*, p. 132.

be argued with equal pertinence, by Dostoyevsky called *Notes from Underground*. The image, taken up, modified, and recreated by later novelists deserves further attention.

[8] Conrad, we know, shared with Dostoyevsky more than the dubious heritage of a Slavic temper. His metaphysicial romances of the seven seas subject the idea of heroism to an ironic rhetoric which is peculiarly modern, and his abiding interest in the theme of the double—his *Secret Sharer* and Dostoyevsky's *The Double* come to mind—probes the distempers of the modern self in a way that seems now familiar. While no character of his strictly reminds us of the hero of the *Notes*, the state of immersion, the desperation felt in the heart of darkness or in the underground habitations of consciousness, the surrender to the "destructive element," compel our terrified assent in the novels of both authors. Kurtz, in *Heart of Darkness*, had perhaps immersed himself too deeply, there where victim and victimizer become one, till he could distinguish only the horror. But Kurtz creeping on all fours in the night-time jungle and Lord Jim erect and dazzling in spotless white are still two sides of the same image, two sides separated really by the enormous distance between action and heroic intention. Conrad does not repudiate human striving. In a celebrated passage from *Lord Jim* he simply points to the way of fulfillment. "A man that is born falls into a dream like a man who falls into the sea," Conrad writes. "If he tries to climb out into the air as inexperienced people endeavor to do, he drowns. . . . The way is to the destructive element submit yourself. . . ."[9] The unintelligent brutality of existence leaves man no other choice.

[9] It is, of course, the unintelligent brutality of existence that dominates the Dublin of Joyce's *Ulysses;* the city becomes a focus, in Eliot's famous words, to "the immense panorama of futility and anarchy which is contemporary history."[10] The proportions of the hero are further shrunken, his self pushed further underground in the world of memory and fantasy. The element to which Bloom submits himself, in humor and humility, is the ignominious element. Insult and pathos, loneliness and failure, are his familiars. Leopold Bloom, wandering Jew, mock Odysseus, and lowly Christ, finally appears to us, above all, as "Everyman or Noman."[11] He stands between Stephen Dedalus and Molly Bloom, between intelligence and nature, as a pathetic monument to the generosity of suffering. For intelligence, in the person of Stephen—he is Lucifer and Hamlet and Dedalus—can only cry: *Non serviam!* And Nature, in the person of Molly—Ceres, Hera, eternal Mother Earth—must endlessly

---

[9] Joseph Conrad, *Lord Jim* (New York, 1931), p. 214.
[10] T. S. Eliot, "Ulysses, Order and Myth," in John W. Aldridge, ed., *Critiques and Essays on Modern Fiction* (New York, 1952), p. 426.
[11] James Joyce, *Ulysses* (New York, 1946), p. 712.

murmur: Yes I will Yes. Man, meanwhile, goes clowning his sentimental way into eternity, unable to reconcile himself completely to one or the other.

[10] The two heroes of Joyce and of Dostoyevsky show that humility lies on the other side of spite. But the clown in man has many disguises. He is Bloom, "one lonely last sardine of summer."[12] He is also, as we shall see, an insect, a sentient tubercle, at best a shaggy wolf. The self in recoil cannot afford to be choosy.

[11] Dostoyevsky's metaphor of man as an insect inevitably calls to mind Kafka's story, "Metamorphosis," in which the narrator is transformed into a huge, hideous, and pathetic vermin. This, too, is self-degradation, a form of the self in recoil. This, too, is protest. The theme is everywhere in Kafka, in *The Castle*, in *The Trial*, in "The Penal Colony" or "The Judgment." Man is always judged, and found invariably guilty. He is the victim of an unappeasable power, a horrible and recurrent outrage, and even in his most serene moments he can only exclaim, like the Hunter Gracchus: "I am here, more than that I do not know, further than that I cannot go. My ship has no rudder, and it is driven by the wind that blows in the undermost regions of death."[13] The vision of man is as grotesque as that of Dostoyevsky; but it goes farther, denying man freedom, the sheer horror of choice, and denying him grace. Indeed, of man Kafka can only say, "He found the Archimedean point, but he used it against himself; it seems that he was permitted to find it only under this condition."[14] The lever which gives man mastery over his universe, moving worlds at the touch of a finger tip, is still the inbred dagger of the soul. In Kafka as in Dostoyevsky, the sense of compounded guilt and absurdity defines the point at which victimization and rebellion meet.[15]

[12] This view of the human predicament will no doubt seem to many both exigent and extreme. It borders, people argue, on disease. Exactly. In the panoramic view of Thomas Mann, whose sane vision did not prevent him from cultivating a lifelong interest in Kafka and Dostoyevsky, disease and even death become an ultimate response to life. The idea informs at least two of his masterpieces, *The Magic Mountain* and *Death in Venice*, and it hovers about his latest work, *The Confessions of Felix Krull*. Hans Castorp reflects, as if prompted by the hero of Dostoyevsky's *Notes*, "Disease was a perverse, a dissolute form of life. And life? Life

---

[12] *Ibid.*, p. 284.

[13] *Selected Stories of Franz Kafka*, Introduction by Philip Rahv (New York, 1952), p. 187.

[14] Franz Kafka, *Dearest Father* (New York, 1954), p 378.

[15] Parallels between the two novelists are well elaborated by Renato Poggioli, "Kafka and Dostoyevsky," in Angel Flores ed., *The Kafka Problem* (New York, 1946), pp. 97–107.

itself? Was it perhaps only an infection, a sickening of matter? . . . The first step toward evil, toward desire and death, was taken precisely then, when there took place that first increase in the density of the spiritual, that pathologically luxuriant morbid growth. . . ."[16] But the radical disease of consciousness, which the hero of Dostoyevsky resented to the end of his spite, and to which the Kafka hero finally submits in a lucid nightmare, is transmuted by Thomas Mann into a condition of spiritual refulgence. It is thus that Mann is able to claim, with Nietzsche and Dostoyevsky in mind, that "certain attainments of the soul and the intellect are impossible *without disease, without insanity, without spiritual crime,* and the *great invalids* are *crucified victims,* sacrificed to humanity and its advancement, to the broadening of its feeling and knowledge—in short, to its more *sublime health* [italics mine]."[17] Man, we see, pitches himself at the terrible limit of experience, as Lucifer did.

[13] Mann's statement reminds us that grace, if it is to be found at all, lies deep in the soft core of violence. The saint and the criminal stand back to back on either side of the demonic. Both are protestants, both victims. But pure violence, like the demonic, has no reality in the public realm, the domain of action. Pure violence, as we shall repeatedly observe in modern fiction, seems almost the ultimate form of introspection. That the saint and the criminal, the suppliant and psychopath—they are conjoined in the recent literature of hipsterism and in such enduring figures as Greene's Pinkie and Faulkner's Christmas—partake of violence compulsively is no surprise. For untrammelled violence is not an act, it is merely a state; it is the experience of world negation. As Miss Arendt saw, the saint and the criminal are both lonely figures: ". . . . the one being for, the other against, all men; they, therefore, remain outside the pale of human intercourse and are, politically, marginal figures who usually enter the historical scene in times of corruption, disintegration, and political bankruptcy. Because of its inherent tendency to disclose the agent together with the act, action needs for its full appearance the shining brightness we once called glory, and which is possible only in the public realm."[18]

[14] It is perhaps unnecessary to recover for our age the Corneillian idea of glory, but when the focus of moral energy moves so far from the center of human effort in the world, losing itself in the domain of holy silence or demonic violence, then it is time to give vent to our anxiety. The dissociation of action from intelligence, we remember, is manifest in Dostoyevsky's *Notes* whose hero openly contemns the active life. The consequences of this attitude are not limited to the cult of inactivity,

---

[16] Thomas Mann, *The Magic Mountain* (New York, 1927), pp. 285 ff.
[17] "Introduction," *The Short Novels of Dostoyevsky,* p. xv.
[18] Hannah Arendt, *The Human Condition* (Chicago, 1958), p. 180.

living in a hole, like the man from underground, or in a jar like the hero of Beckett's *The Unnamable,* living, if you will, in the "packing-box shanty on the city dump" thoughtfully reserved by the editors of *Life* for our most promising novelists. The consequences also involve the alienation of the moral and artistic imagination from things of this world, often leading to a criminal state of autonomy.

[15] The rebel-victim, we see, is also the outsider in search of truth.[19] Harry Haller, in Hermann Hesse's *Steppenwolf,* is still an isolate genius of suffering "whose fate it is to live the whole riddle of human destiny heightened to the pitch of a personal torture, a personal hell."[20] He is still grappling with the radical multiplicities of the human ego, oscillating not merely between the wolf and the man, not merely between two poles, such as the body and the spirit, the saint and the sinner, but between "thousands and thousands."[21] In the "Treatise on the Steppenwolf," however, the outsider is finally made to reckon with the fact that man may be nothing more than a temporary agreement between warring opposites, nothing more, in fact, than "a bourgeois compromise"—such as Bloom!

[16] The idea of man as a transient compromise in the universe entails the acceptance of permanent outrage. Harry Haller could find some redemption of that condition in love or art, or even in humor which reconciles all opposites, and in whose "imaginary realm the intricate and many-faceted ideal of all Steppenwolves finds its realization."[22] Other writers—Mauriac, Bernanos, Graham Greene—sought for their characters a solution more commensurate with their religious faith; for, as Colin Wilson has loudly noted, the problems of modern man, rebel, victim, or outsider, lend themselves to an intense religious apprehension which need not be specifically Christian.[23] Yet even the Christian novelists, so Jansenist they seem in their insistence on human depravity, manage to convey only the terrible intricacies of damnation. Thus, for instance, is the pursuit of damnation conceived in *Brighton Rock* as an appalling manifestation of the mercy of God. The modern Christian martyr, it seems, can aspire only to perdition.

[17] To the religious and the humanist solutions of man's plight in the universe must be added the Existentialist. The basic question here is still one of freedom, the search for identity under the aspects of violence or alienation. Freedom, we recall, is known to the hero of the *Notes* only

---

[19] See Colin Wilson, *The Outsider* (Boston, 1956), for an extended documentary more valuable for its recognition of the general problem and for its range of significant reference than for its particular insights into the crucial documents it uses.

[20] Hermann Hesse, *Steppenwolf* (New York, 1929), p. 28.

[21] *Ibid.,* p. 77.

[22] *Ibid.,* p. 73.

[23] *The Outsider,* p. 261. Also Colin Wilson, *Religion and the Rebel* (Boston, 1957).

as caprice; he understands that men, himself included, must seek freedom and must be repelled and horrified by it. The same ambivalence haunts the quest of Kafka's characters. Beginning with Gide, however, the ambivalence is seemingly resolved in favor of positive action. Man asserts his liberty in a gratuitous act of murder, as in Lafcadio's case, in acts of social repudiation, or ruthless heroism, as in the case of Michel and Theseus. Freedom consists of revolt, against morality, against the social order, against history. But the blood-curdling price is one that only heroes and supermen can afford. In this direction, the Existentialist novelists go farther than Gide was willing to go, and their view is correspondingly more special. Victory, in their novels, depends on the certainty of defeat, *is* the process of defeat. But unlike the heroes of classical tragedy, their protagonists act in full foreknowledge of their fatality, act *only* in *despite* of that fatality. And there is never any reconciliation.

[18] It is thus that Sartre understands man—a creature *condemned* to be free. Antoine Roquentin, in *The Nausea*, suffers from metaphysical disgust. His consciousness is like a decayed trap door through which the sordid impressions of his world endlessly sift. Nothing happens in his life, nothing begins or ends; Phenomena merely change, and Things, grotesque, obdurate, and unnamable, simply exist. Roquentin thinks: "I have only my body: a man entirely alone, with his lonely body, cannot indulge in memories; they pass through him. I shouldn't complain: all I wanted was to be free."[24] Thinking is his game, the famous Cartesian proof of existence his plaything. In Kafka's work, as Erich Heller perceived, a cursed Intelligence asserts its omnipresence; the Cartesian formula becomes: "I think, and therefore I am not."[25] Such negation of being is inadmissible to Sartre; the proper formula should read: "My thought is *me*. . . . At this very moment—it's frightful—if I exist, it is because I am horrified at existing."[26] The change is less of an improvement than it may seem. For as Roquentin comes to believe, existence is nothing if not superfluous. Everything is *de trop*, everything is rooted in the Absurd, the irreducible condition of all reality. Man, we see, is not only a clown or a transient compromise, he is a contingency of existence. The way to true being, seldom realized, lies through Nausea.

[19] Sartre's doctrine that existence precedes essence, carried to its atheistic conclusion, defines no limit to the idea of freedom and gives no value to the concept of being. Camus, a far more accomplished artist if not a more systematic thinker, starts with his "absurdist" philosophy of man and reaches, in *The Rebel* and *The Fall*, a more complex awareness of freedom. In his early novel, *The Stranger*, Meursault surrenders

[24] Jean-Paul Sartre, *Nausea* (Norfolk, Conn., n.d.,), p. 91.
[25] Erich Heller, *The Disinherited Mind* (New York, 1957), p. 202.
[26] *Nausea*, pp. 135 ff.

to the absurd, the destructive element, and loses his life, it seems, without ever finding it. In the following novel, *The Plague*, a small light of hope, even of redemption, flickers through the night of human victimization. Doctor Rieux says: "All I maintain is that on this earth there are pestilences and there are victims, and it's up to us, as far as possible, not to join forces with the pestilences. . . . I decided to take, in every predicament, the victim's side, so as to reduce the damage done. Among them, I can at least try to understand how one attains to the third category: in other words, to peace."[27] To join the victims is an act of rebellion against and alienation from the prevalent norm. But such an act is never purely nugatory. "Rebellion," Camus wrote, "though apparently negative, since it creates nothing, is profoundly positive in that it reveals the part of man which must always be defended."[28] Rebellion is therefore an aspiration to order, a means of lifting pain and evil from personal to collective experience. For the rebel-victim, the Cartesian argument par excellence is: "I rebel—therefore *we* exist [italics mine]."[29]

[20] The problem of the anti-hero is essentially one of identity. His search is for existential fulfillment, that is, for freedom and self-definition. What he hopes to find is a position he can take within himself. Society may modulate his awareness of his situation, but only existence determines his stand. The recoil of the modern self is its way of taking a stand. The retreat weakens its involvement in the living world. It leads it in the ways of violence and alienation, augments its sense of guilt and absurdity, and affords it no objective standard for evaluating the worth of human action. But living in the world exclusively, living in what Ortega y Gasset has called the Other, is also brutish and deadening. Complete immersion in the otherness of things is a ghastlier form of alienation: it is alienation from the self. "Without a strategic retreat into the self," Ortega rightly notes, "without vigilant thought, human life is impossible."[30] It is precisely in fear of the Other—total loss of selfhood—that the modern conscience has fallen back on its internal resources. The schizophrenic goes too far in that direction, the rebel-victim remains in the field of our vision.

[21] Camus' statement, "I rebel—therefore we exist," brings to surface a dialectic that has been implicit in all the works we have viewed. In its naked form, the dialectic can be seen as an interplay between the essential Yes and the radical No, two piercing utterances beyond which the human voice cannot rise. Such utterances may sometimes blend. It is only silence they equally abhor. In the modern novel, man seems to overcome the contradictions of his experience, its destructive or demonic

[27] Albert Camus, *The Plague* (Paris, 1948), p. 229.
[28] *The Rebel*, p. 19.
[29] *Ibid.*, p. 22.
[30] Ortega y Gasset, *The Dehumanization of Art* (New York, 1956), p. 185.

element, by assuming the role of the anti-hero, the rebel-victim. The rebel denies without saying No to life, the victim succumbs without saying Yes to oppression. Both acts are, in a sense, identical: they affirm the human against the nonhuman. The figure of modern man, when he chooses to assert his full manhood, always bears the brave indissoluble aspects of Prometheus and Sisyphus—the eternal rebel and the eternal victim. The paradox is resolved when man cries, in the ringing words of Jaspers, "Although I am an anvil, as a hammer I can consummate what I must suffer."[31] Sparks from the same anvil were struck when Christ said to his disciples, "For whosoever will save his life shall lose it; and whosoever will lose his life for my sake shall find it."[32]

[22] The condition of modern life may not be more desperate, as relativists sapiently remind us, than those which prevailed in any earlier age. Men, as usual, like to exaggerate their predicament to convince themselves, if nothing else, that they are still alive. All this is beside the point. It is certainly not the wretchedness of modern existence that we have sought to illustrate in this chapter, but rather man's peculiar awareness of his own situation. This awareness is both critical and adverse. The spirit of recoil in modern literature continues to affirm itself despite all our bounties.

COMMENT AND QUESTIONS

1. Some of Hassan's examples of the anti-hero may be unfamiliar to you. If this is so, do you find that the unfamiliar references make the essay unclear? Explain.
2. Consult your dictionary, if necessary, to determine the meaning in context of the following words: *rubric* (paragraph 2), *atrophy* (paragraph 3), *pyrrhic* and *allotropic* (paragraph 4), *meliorism* (paragraph 6), *exigent* (paragraph 12), *Jansenist* (paragraph 16), *Cartesian* and *contingency* (paragraph 18), *nugatory* (paragraph 19).
3. In what ways are the two opening paragraphs an effective beginning?
4. Paragraph 3 traces the disintegration of heroism, particularly from the late eighteenth century through the nineteenth century. What do the various kinds of heroes discussed in that paragraph have in common?
5. At the end of paragraph 4, what does the author mean by saying that the history of the anti-hero is the record of man's "recoil"?
6. Paragraph 5 is an introduction to concrete instances of the anti-hero. What is Hassan's purpose in starting with a full discussion of Dostoyevsky's hero?

[31] Karl Jaspers, *Man in the Modern Age* (New York, 1957), p. 205.
[32] Matthew 16:25.

7. How do you interpret Conrad's advice (paragraph 8) about submitting oneself to the "destructive element"? To what extent do you agree or disagree with it? Explain.
8. What relationship does Hassan see between the saint and the criminal?
9. What is the meaning of Camus' statement, quoted in paragraphs 19 and 21: "I rebel—therefore we exist"?
10. Examine paragraph 20, a summary of the problem of the anti-hero. To what extent do you agree or disagree with the statement that "living in the world exclusively . . . . is a ghastlier form of alienation"? Explain.
11. What is the meaning of Jaspers' statement, quoted near the end of paragraph 21? How is it related to the preceding material in the paragraph?
12. The author says in his closing paragraph that he has sought to illustrate man's peculiar, critical, and adverse awareness of his situation. To what extent do you share the view of life reflected in the literature Hassan has discussed? Or, what characters or authors discussed in the essay most nearly represent your own view?

[37] *Martin Esslin*: The Significance of the Absurd

MARTIN ESSLIN (1918–) is a London theatrical producer and director of drama for the B. B. C. A student of the theater in both Europe and America, Esslin has taught in the department of dramatic arts and speech at the University of California and is the author of *Brecht: The Man and His Work* and *The Theatre of the Absurd* (1961), from which the following selection is taken.

[1] When Nietzsche's Zarathustra descended from his mountains to preach to mankind, he met a saintly hermit in the forest. This old man invited him to stay in the wilderness rather than go into the cities of men. When Zarathustra asked the hermit how he passed his time in his solitude, he replied:

I make up songs and sing them; and when I make up songs I laugh, I weep, and I growl; thus do I praise God.

Zarathustra declined the old man's offer and continued on his journey:

But when he was alone, he spoke thus to his heart: "Can it be possible! This old saint in the forest has not yet heard that God is dead!"

[²] *Zarathustra* was first published in 1883. The number of people for whom God is dead has greatly increased since Nietzsche's day, and mankind has learned the bitter lesson of the falseness and evil nature of some of the cheap and vulgar substitutes that have been set up to take His place. And so, after two terrible wars, there are still many who are trying to come to terms with the implications of Zarathustra's message, searching for a way in which they can, with dignity, confront a universe deprived of what was once its center and its living purpose, a world deprived of a generally accepted integrating principle, which has become disjointed, purposeless—absurd.

[³] The Theatre of the Absurd is one of the expressions of this search. It bravely faces up to the fact that for those to whom the world has lost its central explanation and meaning, it is no longer possible to accept art forms still based on the continuation of standards and concepts that have lost their validity; that is, the possibility of knowing the laws of conduct and ultimate values, as deducible from a firm foundation of revealed certainty about the purpose of man in the universe.

[⁴] In expressing the tragic sense of loss at the disappearance of ultimate certainties the Theatre of the Absurd, by a strange paradox, is also a symptom of what probably comes nearest to being a genuine religious quest in our age: an effort, however timid and tentative, to sing, to laugh, to weep—and to growl—if not in praise of God (whose name, in Adamov's phrase, has for so long been degraded by usage that it has lost its meaning), at least in search of a dimension of the Ineffable; an effort to make man aware of the ultimate realities of his condition, to instill in him again the lost sense of cosmic wonder and primeval anguish, to shock him out of an existence that has become trite, mechanical, complacent, and deprived of the dignity that comes of awareness. For God is dead, above all, to the masses who live from day to day and have lost all contact with the basic facts—and mysteries—of the human condition with which, in former times, they were kept in touch through the living ritual of their religion, which made them parts of a real community and not just atoms in an atomized society.

[⁵] The Theatre of the Absurd forms part of the unceasing endeavor of the true artists of our time to breach this dead wall of complacency and automatism and to re-establish an awareness of man's situation when confronted with the ultimate reality of his condition. As such, the Theatre of the Absurd fulfills a dual purpose and presents its audience with a twofold absurdity.

[⁶] On the one hand, it castigates, satirically, the absurdity of lives lived unaware and unconscious of ultimate reality. This is the feeling of the deadness and mechanical senselessness of half-unconscious lives, the feeling of "human beings secreting inhumanity," which Camus describes in *The Myth of Sisyphus*:

In certain hours of lucidity, the mechanical aspect of their gestures, their senseless pantomime, makes stupid everything around them. A man speaking on the telephone behind a glass partition—one cannot hear him but observes his trivial gesturing. One asks oneself, why is he alive? This malaise in front of man's own inhumanity, this incalculable letdown when faced with the image of what we are, this "nausea," as a contemporary writer calls it, also is the Absurd.

[7] This is the experience that Ionesco expresses in plays like *The Bald Soprano* or *The Chairs*, Adamov in *La Parodie*, or N. F. Simpson in *A Resounding Tinkle*. It represents the satirical, parodistic aspect of the Theatre of the Absurd, its social criticism, its pillorying of an inauthentic, petty society. This may be the most easily accessible, and therefore most widely recognized, message of the Theatre of the Absurd, but it is far from being its most essential or most significant feature.

[8] Behind the satirical exposure of the absurdity of inauthentic ways of life, the Theatre of the Absurd is facing up to a deeper layer of absurdity—the absurdity of the human condition itself in a world where the decline of religious belief has deprived man of certainties. When it is no longer possible to accept simple and complete systems of values and revelations of divine purpose, life must be faced in its ultimate, stark reality. That is why, in the analysis of the dramatists of the Absurd in this book, we have always seen man stripped of the accidental circumstances of social position or historical context, confronted with the basic choices, the basic situations of his existence: man faced with time and therefore waiting, in Beckett's plays or Gelber's, waiting between birth and death; man running away from death, climbing higher and higher, in Vian's play, or passively sinking down toward death, in Buzzati's; man rebelling against death, confronting and accepting it, in Ionesco's *Tueur Sans Gages;* man inextricably entangled in a mirage of illusions, mirrors reflecting mirrors, and forever hiding ultimate reality, in the plays of Genet; man trying to establish his position, or to break out into freedom, only to find himself newly imprisoned, in the parables of Manuel de Pedrolo; man trying to stake out a modest place for himself in the cold and darkness that envelop him, in Pinter's plays; man vainly striving to grasp the moral law forever beyond his comprehension, in Arrabal's; man caught in the inescapable dilemma that strenuous effort leads to the same result as passive indolence—complete futility and ultimate death—in the earlier work of Adamov; man forever lonely, immured in the prison of his subjectivity, unable to reach his fellow man, in the vast majority of these plays.

[9] Concerned as it is with the ultimate realities of the human condition, the relatively few fundamental problems of life and death, isolation and communication, the Theatre of the Absurd, however grotesque, frivolous, and irreverent it may appear, represents a return to the original,

religious function of the theatre—the confrontation of man with the spheres of myth and religious reality. Like ancient Greek tragedy and the medieval mystery plays and baroque allegories, the Theatre of the Absurd is intent on making its audience aware of man's precarious and mysterious position in the universe. . . .

[10] In the "literary" theatre, language remains the predominant component. In the anti-literary theatre of the circus or the music hall, language is reduced to a very subordinate role. The Theatre of the Absurd has regained the freedom of using language as merely one—sometimes dominant, sometimes submerged—component of its multidimensional poetic imagery. By putting the language of a scene in contrast to the action, by reducing it to meaningless patter, or by abandoning discursive logic for the poetic logic of association or assonance, the Theatre of the Absurd has opened up a new dimension of the stage.

[11] In its devaluation of language, the Theatre of the Absurd is in tune with the trend of our time. As George Steiner has pointed out in two radio talks entitled *The Retreat from the Word*, the devaluation of language is characteristic not only of the development of contemporary poetry or philosophical thought but, even more, of modern mathematics and the natural sciences. "It is no paradox to assert," Steiner says, "that much of reality now begins *outside* language. . . . Large areas of meaningful experience now belong to non-verbal languages such as mathematics, formulae, and logical symbolism. Others belong to 'anti-languages' such as the practice of nonobjective art or atonal music. The world of the word has shrunk." Moreover, the abandonment of language as the best instrument of notation in the spheres of mathematics and symbolic logic goes hand in hand with a marked reduction in the popular belief in its practical usefulness. Language appears more and more as being in contradiction to reality. The trends of thought that have the greatest influence on contemporary popular thinking all show this tendency.

[12] Take the case of Marxism. Here a distinction is made between *apparent* social relations and the social *reality* behind them. Objectively, an employer is seen as an exploiter, and therefore an enemy, of the working class. If an employer therefore says to a worker; "I have sympathy with your point of view," he may himself believe what he is saying, but objectively his words are meaningless. However much he asserts his sympathy for the worker, he remains his enemy. Language here belongs to the realm of the purely subjective, and is thus devoid of objective reality.

[13] The same applies to modern depth psychology and psychoanalysis. Every child today knows that there is a vast gap between what is consciously thought and asserted and the psychological reality behind the words spoken. A son who tells his father that he loves and respects him is objectively bound to be, in fact, filled with the deepest Oedipal hatred

of his father. He may not know it, but he means the opposite of what he says. And the subconscious has a higher content of reality than the conscious utterance.

[14] The relativization, devaluation, and criticism of language are also the prevailing trends in contemporary philosophy, as exemplified by Wittgenstein's conviction, in the last phase of his thinking, that the philosopher must endeavor to disentangle thought from the conventions and rules of grammar, which have been mistaken for the rules of logic. "A *picture* held us captive. And we could not get outside it, for it lay in our language, and language seemed to repeat it to us inexorably. . . . Where does our investigation get its importance from, since it seems only to destroy everything interesting; that is, all that is great and important? (As it were, all the buildings, leaving behind only bits of stone and rubble.) What we are destroying is nothing but houses of cards, and we are clearing up the ground of language on which they stand." By a strict criticism of language, Wittgenstein's followers have declared large categories of statements to be devoid of objective meaning. Wittgenstein's "word games" have much in common with the Theatre of the Absurd.

[15] But even more significant than these tendencies in Marxist, psychological, and philosophical thinking is the trend of the times in the workaday world of the man in the street. Exposed to the incessant, and inexorably loquacious, onslaught of the mass media, the press, and advertising, the man in the street becomes more and more skeptical toward the language he is exposed to. The citizens of totalitarian countries know full well that most of what they are told is double-talk, devoid of real meaning. They become adept at reading between the lines; that is, at guessing at the reality the language conceals rather than reveals. In the West, euphemisms and circumlocutions fill the press or resound from the pulpits. And advertising, by its constant use of superlatives, has succeeded in devaluing language to a point where it is a generally accepted axiom that most of the words one sees displayed on billboards or in the colored pages of magazine advertising are as meaningless as the jingles of television commercials. A yawning gulf has opened between language and reality.

[16] Apart from the general devaluation of language in the flood of mass communications, the growing specialization of life has made the exchange of ideas on an increasing number of subjects impossible between members of different spheres of life which have each developed its own specialized jargon. As Ionesco says, in summarizing and enlarging on, the views of Antonin Artaud:

> As our knowledge becomes separated from life, our culture no longer contains ourselves (or only an insignificant part of ourselves), for it forms a "social" context into which we are not integrated. So the problem becomes that of bringing our life back into contact with our culture, making it a living culture

once again. To achieve this, we shall first have to kill "the respect for what is written down in black and white" . . . to break up our language so that it can be put together again in order to re-establish contact with "the absolute," or, as I should prefer to say, "with multiple reality"; it is imperative to "push human beings again toward seeing themselves as they really are."

[17] That is why communication between human beings is so often shown in a state of breakdown in the Theatre of the Absurd. It is merely a satirical magnification of the existing state of affairs. Language has run riot in an age of mass communication. It must be reduced to its proper function—the expression of authentic content, rather than its concealment. But this will be possible only if man's reverence toward the spoken or written word as a means of communication is restored, and the ossified clichés that dominate thought (as they do in the limericks of Edward Lear or the world of Humpty Dumpty) are replaced by a living language that serves it. And this, in turn, can be achieved only if the limitations of logic and discursive language are recognized and respected, and the uses of poetic language acknowledged.

[18] The means by which the dramatists of the Absurd express their critique—largely instinctive and unintended—of our disintegrating society are based on suddenly confronting their audiences with a grotesquely heightened and distorted picture of a world that has gone mad. This is a shock therapy that achieves what Brecht's doctrine of the "alienation effect" postulated in theory but failed to achieve in practice—the inhibition of the audience's identification with the characters on the stage (which is the age-old and highly effective method of the traditional theatre) and its replacement by a detached, critical attitude. . . .

[19] The madness of the times lies precisely in the existence, side by side, of a large number of unreconciled beliefs and attitudes—conventional morality, for example, on the one hand, and the values of advertising on the other; the conflicting claims of science and religion; or the loudly proclaimed striving of all sections for the general interest when in fact each is pursuing very narrow and selfish particular ends. On each page of his newspaper, the man in the street is confronted with a different and contradictory pattern of values. No wonder that the art of such an era shows a marked resemblance to the symptoms of schizophrenia. But it is not, as Jung has pointed out in an essay on Joyce's *Ulysses,* the artist who is schizophrenic: "The medical description of schizophrenia offers only an analogy, in that the schizophrenic has apparently the same tendency to treat reality as if it were strange to him, or, the other way around, to estrange himself from reality. In the modern artist, this tendency is not produced by any disease in the individual but is a manifestation of our time."

[20] The challenge to make sense out of what appears as a senseless

and fragmented action, the recognition that the fact that the modern world has lost its unifying principle is the source of its bewildering and soul-destroying quality, is therefore more than a mere intellectual exercise; it has a therapeutic effect. In Greek tragedy, the spectators were made aware of man's forlorn but heroic stand against the inexorable forces of fate and the will of the gods—and this had a cathartic effect upon them and made them better able to face their time. In the Theatre of the Absurd, the spectator is confronted with the madness of the human condition, is enabled to see his situation in all its grimness and despair, and this, in stripping him of illusions or vaguely felt fears and anxieties, enables him to face it consciously, rather than feel it vaguely below the surface of euphemisms and optimistic illusions. And this, in turn, results in the liberating effect of anxieties overcome by being formulated. This is the nature of all the gallows humor and *humour noir* of world literature, of which the Theatre of the Absurd is the latest example. It is the unease caused by the presence of illusions that are obviously out of tune with reality that is dissolved and discharged through liberating laughter at the recognition of the fundamental absurdity of the universe. The greater the anxieties and the temptation to indulge in illusions, the more beneficial is this therapeutic effect—hence the success of *Waiting for Godot* at San Quentin. It was a relief for the convicts to be made to recognize in the tragicomic situation of the tramps the hopelessness of their own waiting for a miracle. They were enabled to laugh at the tramps—and at themselves.

[21] As the reality with which the Theatre of the Absurd is concerned is a psychological reality expressed in images that are the outward projection of states of mind, fears, dreams, nightmares, and conflicts within the personality of the author, the dramatic tension produced by this kind of play differs fundamentally from the suspense created in a theatre concerned mainly with the revelation of objective characters through the unfolding of a narrative plot. The pattern of exposition, conflict, and final solution mirrors a view of the world in which solutions are possible, a view based on a recognizable and generally accepted pattern of an objective reality that can be apprehended so that the purpose of man's existence and the rules of conduct it entails can be deduced from it.

[22] This is true even of the lightest type of drawing-room comedy, in which the action proceeds on a deliberately restricted view of the world—that the sole purpose of the characters involved is for each boy to get his girl. And even in the darkest pessimistic tragedies of the naturalistic or Expressionist theatres, the final curtain enables the audience to go home with a formulated message or philosophy in their minds: the solution may have been a sad one, but it was a rationally formulated conclusion nevertheless. This, as I pointed out in the introduction, applies even to the thea-

tre of Sartre and Camus, which is based on a philosophy of the absurdity of human existence. Even plays like *Huis Clos* (*No Exit*), *Le Diable et le Bon Dieu* (*Lucifer and the Lord*), and *Caligula* allow the audience to take home an intellectually formulated philosophical lesson.

[23] The Theatre of the Absurd, however, which proceeds not by intellectual concepts but by poetic images, neither poses an intellectual problem in its exposition nor provides any clear-cut solution that would be reducible to a lesson or an apothegm. Many of the plays of the Theatre of the Absurd have a circular structure, ending exactly as they began; others progress merely by a growing intensification of the initial situation. And as the Theatre of the Absurd rejects the idea that it is possible to motivate all human behavior, or that human character is based on an immutable essence, it is impossible for it to base its effect on the suspense that in other dramatic conventions springs from awaiting the solution of a dramatic equation based on the working out of a problem involving clearly defined quantities introduced in the opening scenes. In most dramatic conventions, the audience is constantly asking itself the question "What is going to happen next?"

[24] In the Theatre of the Absurd, the audience is confronted with actions that lack apparent motivation, characters that are in constant flux, and often happenings that are clearly outside the realm of rational experience. Here, too, the audience can ask, "What is going to happen next?" But then *anything* may happen next, so that the answer to this question cannot be worked out according to the rules of ordinary probability based on motives and characterizations that will remain constant throughout the play. The relevant question here is not so much what is going to happen next but what *is* happening? "What does the action of the play represent?" . . .

[25] Ultimately, a phenomenon like the Theatre of the Absurd does not reflect despair or a return to dark irrational forces but expresses modern man's endeavor to come to terms with the world in which he lives. It attempts to make him face up to the human condition as it really is, to free him from illusions that are bound to cause constant maladjustment and disappointment. There are enormous pressures in our world that seek to induce mankind to bear the loss of faith and moral certainties by being drugged into oblivion—by mass entertainments, shallow material satisfactions, pseudo-explanations of reality, and cheap ideologies. At the end of that road lies Huxley's Brave New World of senseless euphoric automata. Today, when death and old age are increasingly concealed behind euphemisms and comforting baby talk, and life is threatened with being smothered in the mass consumption of hypnotic mechanized vulgarity, the need to confront man with the reality of his situation is greater than ever. For the dignity of man lies in his ability to face reality in all its senseless-

ness; to accept it freely, without fear, without illusions—and to laugh at it.

[26] That is the cause to which, in their various individual, modest, and quixotic ways, the dramatists of the Absurd are dedicated.

COMMENT AND QUESTIONS

1. The author refers, in paragraph 2, to "the falseness and evil nature of some of the cheap and vulgar substitutes" set up to take God's place in the world. What does he appear to mean by such "substitutes"?
2. Esslin several times uses the word *dignity*, although many of the characters of the Absurd dramatists lack the qualities we conventionally associate with this word. In what sense is the Theater of the Absurd concerned with human dignity?
3. What are the author's reasons for believing that the Theater of the Absurd represents a kind of religious quest? To what extent do you agree or disagree with his reasoning? Explain.
4. Paragraph 5, a transitional paragraph, introduces the two purposes or messages of the Theater of the Absurd. What are the two? How are they related? Why does Esslin consider the second message more important than the first?
5. "In its devaluation of language," Esslin says at the beginning of paragraph 11, "the Theatre of the Absurd is in tune with the trend of our time." What parts of the author's discussion of the divorce between language and reality (paragraphs 11–17) are most meaningful to you? Explain.
6. Summarize in your own words the values Esslin sees in the Theater of the Absurd.
7. If you have seen or read plays by Beckett, Ionesco, or other Absurd dramatists, discuss the applicability of Esslin's analysis to one or two of these plays.

[38] *Mary McCarthy:* Settling the Colonel's Hash

MARY MCCARTHY (1912–) is an American novelist, short story writer, and critic. Among her books are *Cast a Cold Eye, The Company She Keeps, The Groves of Academe, Memories of a Catholic Girlhood, The Stones of Florence,* and *The Group.* The following essay, written in 1954, is from a collection of essays, *On the Contrary,* published in 1961.

[1] Seven years ago, when I taught in a progressive college, I had a pretty girl student in one of my classes who wanted to be a short-story writer. She was not studying writing with me, but she knew that I sometimes wrote short stories, and one day, breathless and glowing, she came up to me in the hall, to tell me that she had just written a story that her writing teacher, a Mr. Converse, was terribly excited about. "He thinks it's wonderful," she said, "and he's going to help me fix it up for publication."

[2] I asked what the story was about; the girl was a rather simple being who loved clothes and dates. Her answer had a deprecating tone. It was just about a girl (herself) and some sailors she had met on the train. But then her face, which had looked perturbed for a moment, gladdened.

[3] "Mr. Converse is going over it with me and we're going to put in the symbols."

[4] Another girl in the same college, when asked by us in her sophomore orals why she read novels (one of the pseudo-profound questions that ought never to be put) answered in a defensive flurry: "Well, *of course* I don't read them to find out what happens to the hero."

[5] At the time, I thought these notions were peculiar to progressive education: it was old-fashioned or regressive to read a novel to find out what happens to the hero or to have a mere experience empty of symbolic pointers. But I now discover that this attitude is quite general, and that readers and students all over the country are in a state of apprehension, lest they read a book or story literally and miss the presence of a symbol. And like everything in America, this search for meanings has become a socially competitive enterprise; the best reader is the one who detects the most symbols in a given stretch of prose. And the benighted reader who fails to find any symbols humbly assents when they are pointed out to him; he accepts his mortification.

[6] I had no idea how far this process had gone until last spring, when I began to get responses to a story I had published in *Harper's*. I say "story" because that was what it was called by *Harper's*. I myself would not know quite what to call it; it was a piece of reporting or a fragment of autobiography—an account of my meeting with an anti-Semitic army colonel. It began in the club car of a train going to St. Louis; I was wearing an apple-green shirtwaist and a dark-green skirt and pink earrings; we got into an argument about the Jews. The colonel was a rather dapper, flashy kind of Irish-American with a worldly blue eye; he took me, he said, for a sculptress, which made me feel, to my horror, that I looked Bohemian and therefore rather suspect. He was full of the usual profound clichés that anti-Semites air, like original epigrams, about the Jews: that he could tell a Jew, that they were different from other people, that you couldn't trust them in business, that some of his best friends were Jews, that he distinguished between a Jew and a kike, and finally that, of course, he didn't agree with Hitler: Hitler went too far; the Jews were human beings.

[7] All the time we talked, and I defended the Jews, he was trying to get my angle, as he called it; he thought it was abnormal for anybody who wasn't Jewish not to feel as he did. As a matter of fact, I have a Jewish grandmother, but I decided to keep this news to myself: I did not want the colonel to think that I had any interested reason for speaking on behalf of the Jews, that is, that I was prejudiced. In the end, though, I got my comeuppance. Just as we were parting, the colonel asked me my married name, which is Broadwater, and the whole mystery was cleared up for him, instantly; he supposed I was married to a Jew and that the name was spelled B-r-o-d-w-a-t-e-r. I did not try to enlighten him; I let him think what he wanted; in a certain sense, he was right; he had unearthed my Jewish grandmother or her equivalent. There were a few details that I must mention to make the next part clear: in my car, there were two nuns, whom I talked to as a distraction from the colonel and the moral problems he raised. He and I finally had lunch together in the St. Louis railroad station, where we continued the discussion. It was a very hot day. I had a sandwich; he had roast-beef hash. We both had an old-fashioned.

[8] The whole point of this "story" was that it really happened; it is written in the first person; I speak of myself in my own name, McCarthy; at the end, I mention my husband's name, Broadwater. When I was thinking about writing the story, I decided not to treat it fictionally; the chief interest, I felt, lay in the fact that it happened, in real life, last summer, to the writer herself, who was a good deal at fault in the incident. I wanted to embarrass myself and, if possible, the reader too.

[9] Yet, strangely enough, many of my readers preferred to think of

this account as fiction. I still meet people who ask me, confidentially, "That story of yours about the colonel—was it really true?" It seemed to them perfectly natural that I would write a fabrication, in which I figured under my own name, and sign it, though in my eyes this would be like perjuring yourself in court or forging checks. Shortly after the "story" was published, I got a kindly letter from a man in Mexico, in which he criticized the menu from an artistic point of view: he thought salads would be better for hot weather and it would be more in character for the narrator-heroine to have a Martini. I did not answer the letter, though I was moved to, because I had the sense that he would not understand the distinction between what *ought* to have happened and what *did* happen.

[10] Then in April I got another letter, from an English teacher in a small college in the Middle West, that reduced me to despair. I am going to cite it at length.

[11] "My students in freshman English chose to analyze your story, 'Artists in Uniform,' from the March issue of *Harper's*. For a week I heard oral discussions on it and then the students wrote critical analyses. In so far as it is possible, I stayed out of their discussions, encouraging them to read the story closely with your intentions as a guide to their understanding. Although some of them insisted that the story has no other level than the realistic one, most of them decided it has symbolic overtones.

[12] "The question is: how closely do you want the symbols labeled? They wrestled with the nuns, the author's two shades of green with pink accents, with the 'materialistic godlessness' of the colonel. . . . A surprising number wanted exact symbols; for example, they searched for the significance of the colonel's eating hash and the author eating a sandwich. . . . From my standpoint, the story was an entirely satisfactory springboard for understanding the various shades of prejudice, for seeing how much of the artist goes into his painting. If it is any satisfaction to you, our campus was alive with discussions about 'Artists in Uniform.' We liked the story and we thought it amazing that an author could succeed in making readers dislike the author—for a purpose, of course!"

[13] I probably should have answered this letter, but I did not. The gulf seemed to me too wide. I could not applaud the backward students who insisted that the story has no other level than the realistic one without giving offense to their teacher, who was evidently a well-meaning person. But I shall try now to address a reply, not to this teacher and her unfortunate class, but to a whole school of misunderstanding. There were no symbols in this story; there was no deeper level. The nuns were in the story because they were on the train; the contrasting greens were the dress I happened to be wearing; the colonel had hash because he had

hash; materialistic godlessness meant just what it means when a priest thunders it from the pulpit—the phrase, for the first time, had meaning for me as I watched and listened to the colonel.

[14] But to clarify the misunderstanding, one must go a little further and try to see what a literary symbol is. Now in one sense, the colonel's hash and my sandwich can be regarded as symbols; that is, they typify the colonel's food tastes and mine. (The man in Mexico had different food tastes which he wished to interpose into our reality.) The hash and the sandwich might even be said to show something very obvious about our characters and bringing-up, or about our sexes; I was a woman, he was a man. And though on another day I might have ordered hash myself, that day I did not, because the colonel and I, in our disagreement, were polarizing each other.

[15] The hash and the sandwich, then, could be regarded as symbols of our disagreement, almost conscious symbols. And underneath our discussion of the Jews, there was a thin sexual current running, as there always is in such random encounters or pickups (for they have a strong suggestion of the illicit). The fact that I ordered something conventionally feminine and he ordered something conventionally masculine represented, no doubt, our awareness of a sexual possibility; even though I was not attracted to the colonel, nor he to me, the circumstances of our meeting made us define ourselves as a woman and a man.

[16] The sandwich and the hash were our provisional, *ad hoc* symbols of ourselves. But in this sense all human actions are symbolic because they represent the person who does them. If the colonel had ordered a fruit salad with whipped cream, this too would have represented him in some way; given his other traits, it would have pointed to a complexity in his character that the hash did not suggest.

[17] In the same way, the contrasting greens of my dress were a symbol of my taste in clothes and hence representative of me—all too representative, I suddenly saw, in the club car, when I got an "artistic" image of myself flashed back at me from the men's eyes. I had no wish to stylize myself as an artist, that is, to parade about as a symbol of flamboyant unconventionality, but apparently I had done so unwittingly when I picked those colors off a rack, under the impression that they suited me or "expressed my personality" as salesladies say.

[18] My dress, then, was a symbol of the perplexity I found myself in with the colonel; I did not want to be categorized as a member of a peculiar minority—an artist or a Jew; but brute fate and the colonel kept resolutely cramming me into both those uncomfortable pigeonholes. I wished to be regarded as ordinary or rather as universal, to be anybody and therefore everybody (that is, in one sense, I wanted to be on the colonel's side, majestically above minorities); but every time the colonel

looked at my dress and me in it with my pink earrings I shrank to minority status, and felt the dress in the heat shriveling me, like the shirt of Nessus, the centaur, that consumed Hercules.

[19] But this is not what the students meant when they wanted the symbols "labeled." They were searching for a more recondite significance than that afforded by the trite symbolism of ordinary life, in which a dress is a social badge. They supposed that I was engaging in literary or artificial symbolism, which would lead the reader out of the confines of reality into the vast fairy tale of myth, in which the color green would have an emblematic meaning (or did the two greens signify for them what the teacher calls "shades" of prejudice), and the colonel's hash, I imagine, would be some sort of Eucharistic mincemeat.

[20] Apparently, the presence of the nuns assured them there were overtones of theology; it did not occur to them (a) that the nuns were there because pairs of nuns are a standardized feature of summer Pullman travel, like crying babies, and perspiring businessmen in the club car, and (b) that if I thought the nuns worth mentioning, it was also because of something very simple and directly relevant: the nuns and the colonel and I all had something in common—we had all at one time been Catholics—and I was seeking common ground with the colonel, from which to turn and attack his position.

[21] In any account of reality, even a televised one, which comes closest to being a literal transcript or replay, some details are left out as irrelevant (though nothing is really irrelevant). The details that are not eliminated have to stand as symbols of the whole, like stenographic signs, and of course there is an art of selection, even in a newspaper account: the writer, if he has any ability, is looking for the revealing detail that will sum up the picture for the reader in a flash of recognition.

[22] But the art of abridgment and condensation, which is familiar to anybody who tries to relate an anecdote, or give a direction—the art of natural symbolism, which is at the basis of speech and all representation—has at bottom a centripetal intention. It hovers over an object, an event, or series of events and tries to declare what it is. Analogy (that is, comparison to other objects) is inevitably one of its methods. "The weather was soupy," i.e., like soup. "He wedged his way in," i.e., he had to enter, thin edge first, as a wedge enters, and so on. All this is obvious. But these metaphorical aids to communication are a far cry from literary symbolism, as taught in the schools and practiced by certain fashionable writers. Literary symbolism is centrifugal and flees from the object, the event, into the incorporeal distance, where concepts are taken for substance and floating ideas and archetypes assume a hieratic authority.

[23] In this dream-forest, symbols become arbitrary; all counters are interchangeable; anything can stand for anything else. The colonel's hash

can be a Eucharist or a cannibal feast or the banquet of Atreus, or all three, so long as the actual dish set before the actual man is disparaged. What is depressing about this insistent symbolization is the fact that while it claims to lead to the infinite, it quickly reaches very finite limits —there are only so many myths on record, and once you have got through Bulfinch, the Scandinavian, and the Indian, there is not much left. And if all stories reduce themselves to myth and symbol, qualitative differences vanish, and there is only a single, monotonous story.

[24] American fiction of the symbolist school demonstrates this mournful truth, without precisely intending to. A few years ago, when the mode was at its height, chic novels and stories fell into three classes: those which had a Greek myth for their framework, which the reader was supposed to detect, like finding the faces in the clouds in old newspaper puzzle contests; those which had symbolic modern figures, dwarfs, hermaphrodites, and cripples, illustrating maiming and loneliness; and those which contained symbolic animals, cougars, wild cats, and monkeys. One young novelist, a product of the Princeton school of symbolism, had all three elements going at once, like the ringmaster of a three-ring circus, with the freaks, the animals, and the statues.

[25] The quest for symbolic referents had as its object, of course, the deepening of the writer's subject and the reader's awareness. But the result was paradoxical. At the very moment when American writing was penetrated by the symbolic urge, it ceased to be able to create symbols of its own. Babbitt, I suppose, was the last important symbol to be created by an American writer; he gave his name to a type that henceforth would be recognizable to everybody. He passed into the language. The same thing could be said, perhaps, though to a lesser degree, of Caldwell's Tobacco Road, Eliot's Prufrock, and possibly of Faulkner's Snopeses. The discovery of new symbols is not the only function of a writer, but the writer who cares about this must be fascinated by reality itself, as a butterfly collector is fascinated by the glimpse of a new specimen. Such a specimen was Mme. Bovary or M. Homais or M. de Charlus or Jupien; these specimens were precious to their discoverers, not because they repeated an age-old pattern but because their markings were new. Once the specimen has been described, the public instantly spots other examples of the kind, and the world seems suddenly full of Babbitts and Charlus, where none had been noted before.

[26] A different matter was Joyce's Mr. Bloom. Mr. Bloom can be called a symbol of eternal recurrence—the wandering Jew, Ulysses the voyager—but he is a symbol thickly incarnate, fleshed out in a Dublin advertising canvasser. He is not *like* Ulysses or vaguely suggestive of Ulysses; he is Ulysses, circa 1905. Joyce evidently believed in a cyclical theory of history, in which everything repeated itself; he also subscribed in youth to the doctrine that declares that the Host, a piece of bread, is

also God's body and blood. How it can be both things at the same time, transubstantially, is a mystery, and Mr. Bloom is just such a mystery: Ulysses in the visible appearance of a Dublin advertising canvasser.

[27] Mr. Bloom is not a symbol of Ulysses, but Ulysses-Bloom together, one and indivisible, symbolize or rather demonstrate eternal recurrence. I hope I make myself clear. The point is transubstantiation: Bloom and Ulysses are transfused into each other and neither reality is diminished. Both realities are locked together, like the protons and neutrons of an atom. *Finnegans Wake* is a still more ambitious attempt to create a fusion, this time a myriad fusion, and to exemplify the mystery of how a thing can be itself and at the same time be something else. The world is many and it is also one.

[28] But the clarity and tension of Joyce's thought brought him closer in a way to the strictness of allegory than to the diffuse practices of latter-day symbolists. In Joyce, the equivalences and analogies are very sharp and distinct, as in a pun, and the real world is almost querulously audible, like the voices of the washerwomen of the Liffey that come into Earwicker's dream. But this is not true of Joyce's imitators or of the imitators of his imitators, for whom reality is only a shadowy pretext for the introduction of a whole *corps de ballet* of dancing symbols in mythic draperies and animal skins.

[29] Let me make a distinction. There are some great writers, like Joyce or Melville, who have consciously introduced symbolic elements into their work; and there are great writers who have written fables or allegories. In both cases, the writer makes it quite clear to the reader how he is to be read; only an idiot would take *Pilgrim's Progress* for a realistic story, and even a young boy, reading *Moby Dick*, realizes that there is something more than whale-fishing here, though he may not be able to name what it is. But the great body of fiction contains only what I have called natural symbolism, in which selected events represent or typify a problem, a kind of society or psychology, a philosophical theory, in the same way that they do in real life. What happens to the hero becomes of the highest importance. This symbolism needs no abstruse interpretation, and abstruse interpretation will only lead the reader away from the reality that the writer is trying to press on his attention.

[30] I shall give an example or two of what I mean by natural symbolism and I shall begin with a rather florid one: Henry James' *The Golden Bowl*. This is the story of a rich American girl who collects European objects. One of these objects is a husband, Prince Amerigo, who proves to be unfaithful. Early in the story, there is a visit to an antique shop in which the Prince picks out a gold bowl for his fiancée and finds, to his annoyance, that it is cracked. It is not hard to see that the cracked bowl is a symbol, both of the Prince himself, who is a valuable antique but a little flawed, morally, and also of the marriage, which represents

an act of acquisition or purchase on the part of the heroine and her father. If the reader should fail to notice the analogy, James calls his attention to it in the title.

[31] I myself would not regard this symbol as necessary to this particular history; it seems to me, rather, an ornament of the kind that was fashionable in the architecture and interior decoration of the period, like stylized sheaves of corn or palms on the façade of a house. Nevertheless, it is handsome and has an obvious appropriateness to the theme. It introduces the reader into the Gilded Age attitudes of the novel. I think there is also a scriptural echo in the title that conveys the idea of punishment. But having seen and felt the weight of meaning that James put into this symbol, one must not be tempted to press further and look at the bowl as a female sex symbol, a chalice, a Holy Grail, and so on; a book is not a pious excuse for reciting a litany of associations.

[32] My second example is from Tolstoy's *Anna Karenina*. Toward the beginning of the novel, Anna meets the man who will be her lover, Vronsky, on the Moscow-St. Petersburg express; as they meet, there has been an accident; a workman has been killed by the train. This is the beginning of Anna's doom, which is completed when she throws herself under a train and is killed; and the last we see of Vronsky is in a train, with a toothache; he is off to the wars. The train is necessary to the plot of the novel, and I believe it is also symbolic, both of the iron forces of material progress that Tolstoy hated so and that played a part in Anna's moral destruction, and also of those iron laws of necessity and consequence that govern human action when it remains on the sensual level.

[33] One can read the whole novel, however, without being conscious that the train is a symbol; we do not have to "interpret" to feel the import of doom and loneliness in the train's whistle—the same import we ourselves can feel when we hear a train whistle blow in the country, even today. Tolstoy was a deeper artist than James, and we cannot be sure that the train was a conscious device with him. The appropriateness to Anna's history may have been only a *felt* appropriateness; everything in Tolstoy has such a supreme naturalness that one shrinks from attributing contrivance to him, as if it were a sort of fraud. Yet he worked very hard on his novels—I forget how many times Countess Tolstoy copied out *War and Peace* by hand.

[34] The impression one gets from his diaries is that he wrote by ear; he speaks repeatedly, even as an old man, of having to start a story over again because he has the wrong tone, and I suspect that he did not think of the train as a symbol but that it sounded "right" to him, because it was, in that day, an almost fearsome emblem of ruthless and impersonal force, not only to a writer of genius but to the poorest peasant in the fields. And in Tolstoy's case I think it would be impossible, even for the most fanciful critic, to extricate the train from the novel and try to make it say

something that the novel itself does not say directly. Every detail in Tolstoy has an almost cruel and viselike meaningfulness and truth to itself that make it tautological to talk of symbolism; he was a moralist and to him the tiniest action, even the curiosities of physical appearance, Vronsky's bald spot, the small white hands of Prince Andrei, told a moral tale.

[35] It is now considered very old-fashioned and tasteless to speak of an author's "philosophy of life" as something that can be harvested from his work. Actually, most of the great authors did have a "philosophy of life" which they were eager to communicate to the public; this was one of their motives for writing. And to disentangle a moral philosophy from a work that evidently contains one is far less damaging to the author's purpose and the integrity of his art than to violate his imagery by symbol-hunting, as though reading a novel were a sort of paper-chase.

[36] The images of a novel or a story belong, as it were, to a family, very closely knit and inseparable from each other; the parent "idea" of a story or a novel generates events and images all bearing a strong family resemblance. And to understand a story or a novel, you must look for the parent "idea," which is usually in plain view, if you read quite carefully and literally what the author says.

[37] I will go back, for a moment, to my own story, to show how this can be done. Clearly, it is about the Jewish question, for that is what the people are talking about. It also seems to be about artists, since the title is "Artists in Uniform." Then there must be some relation between artists and Jews. What it it? They are both minorities that other people claim to be able to recognize by their appearance. But artists and Jews do not care for this categorization; they want to be universal, that is, like everybody else. They do not want to wear their destiny as a badge, as the soldier wears his uniform. But this aim is really hopeless, for life has formed them as Jews or artists, in a way that immediately betrays them to the majority they are trying to melt into. In my conversation with the colonel, I was endeavoring to play a double game. I was trying to force him into a minority by treating anti-Semitism as an aberration, which, in fact, I believe it is. On his side, the colonel resisted this attempt and tried to show that anti-Semitism was normal, and he was normal, while I was the queer one. He declined to be categorized as anti-Semite; he regarded himself as an independent thinker, who by a happy chance thought the same as everybody else.

[38] I imagined I had a card up my sleeve; I had guessed that the colonel was Irish (i.e., that he belonged to a minority) and presumed that he was a Catholic. I did not see how he could possibly guess that I, with my Irish name and Irish appearance, had a Jewish grandmother in the background. Therefore when I found I had not convinced him by reasoning, I played my last card; I told him that the Church, his Church,

forbade anti-Semitism. I went even further; I implied that God forbade it, though I had no right to do this, since I did not believe in God, but was only using Him as a whip to crack over the colonel, to make him feel humble and inferior, a raw Irish Catholic lad under discipline. But the colonel, it turned out, did not believe in God, either, and I lost. And since, in a sense, I had been cheating all along in this game we were playing, I had to concede the colonel a sort of moral victory in the end; I let him think that my husband was Jewish and that that "explained" everything satisfactorily.

[39] Now there are a number of morals or meanings in this little tale, starting with the simple one: don't talk to strangers on a train. The chief moral or meaning (what I learned, in other words, from the experience) was this: you cannot be a universal unless you accept the fact that you are a singular, that is, a Jew or an artist or what-have-you. What the colonel and I were discussing, and at the same time illustrating and enacting, was the definition of a human being. I was trying to be something better than a human being; I was trying to be the voice of pure reason; and pride went before a fall. The colonel, without trying, was being something worse than a human being, and somehow we found ourselves on the same plane—facing each other, like mutually repellent twins. Or, put in another way: it is dangerous to be drawn into discussions of the Jews with anti-Semites: you delude yourself that you are spreading light, but you are really sinking into muck; if you endeavor to be dispassionate, you are really claiming for yourself a privileged position, a little mountain top, from which you look down, impartially, on both the Jews and the colonel.

[40] Anti-Semitism is a horrible disease from which nobody is immune, and it has a kind of evil fascination that makes an enlightened person draw near the source of infection, supposedly in a scientific spirit, but really to sniff the vapors and dally with the possibility. The enlightened person who lunches with the colonel in order, as she tells herself, to improve him, is cheating herself, having her cake and eating it. This attempted cheat, on my part, was related to the question of the artist and the green dress; I wanted to be an artist but not to pay the price of looking like one, just as I was willing to have Jewish blood but not willing to show it, where it would cost me something—the loss of superiority in an argument.

[41] These meanings are all there, quite patent, to anyone who consents to look *into* the story. They were *in* the experience itself, waiting to be found and considered. I did not perceive them all at the time the experience was happening; otherwise, it would not have taken place, in all probability—I should have given the colonel a wide berth. But when I went back over the experience, in order to write it, I came upon these meanings, protruding at me, as it were, from the details of the occasion.

I put in the green dress and my mortification over it because they were part of the truth, just as it had occurred, but I did not see how they were related to the general question of anti-Semitism and my grandmother until they *showed* me their relation in the course of writing.

[42] Every short story, at least for me, is a little act of discovery. A cluster of details presents itself to my scrutiny, like a mystery that I will understand in the course of writing or sometimes not fully until afterward, when, if I have been honest and listened to these details carefully, I will find that they are connected and that there is a coherent pattern. This pattern is *in* experience itself; you do not impose it from the outside and if you try to you will find that the story is taking the wrong tack, dribbling away from you into artificiality or inconsequence. A story that you do not learn something from while you are writing it, that does not illuminate something for you, is dead, finished before you started it. The "idea" of a story is implicit in it, on the one hand; on the other hand, it is always ahead of the writer, like a form dimly discerned in the distance; he is working *toward* the "idea."

[43] It can sometimes happen that you begin a story thinking that you know the "idea" of it and find, when you are finished, that you have said something quite different and utterly unexpected to you. Most writers have been haunted all their lives by the "idea" of a story or a novel that they think they want to write and see very clearly: Tolstoy always wanted to write a novel about the Decembrists and instead, almost against his will, wrote *War and Peace;* Henry James thought he wanted to write a novel about Napoleon. Probably these ideas for novels were too set in their creators' minds to inspire creative discovery.

[44] In any work that is truly creative, I believe, the writer cannot be omniscient in advance about the effects that he proposes to produce. The suspense in a novel is not only in the reader, but in the novelist himself, who is intensely curious too about what will happen to the hero. Jane Austen may know in a general way that Emma will marry Mr. Knightley in the end (the reader knows this too, as a matter of fact); the suspense for the author lies in the how, in the twists and turns of circumstance, waiting but as yet unknown, that will bring the consummation about. Hence, I would say to the student of writing that outlines, patterns, arrangements of symbols may have a certain usefulness at the outset for some kind of minds, but in the end they will have to be scrapped. If the story does not contradict the outline, overrun the pattern, break the symbols, like an insurrection against authority, it is surely a still birth. The natural symbolism of reality has more messages to communicate than the dry Morse code of the disengaged mind.

[45] The tree of life, said Hegel, is greener than the tree of thought; I have quoted this before but I cannot forbear from citing it again in

this context. This is not an incitement to mindlessness or an endorsement of realism in the short story (there are several kinds of reality, including interior reality); it means only that the writer must be, first of all, a listener and observer, who can pay attention to reality, like an obedient pupil, and who is willing, always, to be surprised by the messages reality is sending through to him. And if he gets the messages correctly he will not have to go back and put in the symbols; he will find that the symbols are there, staring at him significantly from the commonplace.

COMMENT AND QUESTIONS

1. Comment on the four opening paragraphs. What do they contribute to the whole essay?
2. What devices for emphasis does the author use in paragraph 8? Can you tell, from the summary in paragraphs 6 and 7, why the writer "was a good deal at fault in the incident"? Explain.
3. Do the two letters (paragraphs 9–12) have anything in common, or is Mary McCarthy citing the first and quoting from the second to make two different points?
4. The author says in paragraph 13 that there were no symbols in her story; in paragraphs 14–20 she qualifies the statement and then, in effect, reaffirms it. What different meanings of *symbol* is she establishing?
5. Explain the meaning of the following terms: *recondite* and *Eucharistic mincemeat* (paragraph 19); *centripetal, centrifugal, archetypes,* and *hieratic* (paragraph 22); *banquet of Atreus* (paragraph 23).
6. What are the author's principal objections to the "literary symbolism" taught in schools and practiced by certain writers? How would you describe her language and tone in communicating her attitudes?
7. Examine the use of figurative language, especially in paragraph 24, the last half of paragraph 25, and paragraphs 27 and 28. Which figures seem to you most effective, and why?
8. What point is the author making with the examples of the golden bowl in James' novel and the train in *Anna Karenina*?
9. "Settling the Colonel's Hash," first given as a talk at the Breadloaf School of English in Middlebury, Vermont, is addressed both to readers and to writers or students of writing. Summarize Mary McCarthy's advice to readers in paragraphs 35–45; summarize her advice to students of writing. How does she connect the two kinds of advice?
10. In what ways are the last two paragraphs an effective ending?
11. Comment on the title of the essay. What does the title mean to you?

[39] *Deems Taylor*: The Monster

DEEMS TAYLOR (1885–1966) was a well-known American critic and music commentator and the composer of two operas and many symphonic poems and songs. "The Monster" is taken from one of his books of criticism, *Of Men and Music*, published in 1937.

[1] He was an undersized little man, with a head too big for his body—a sickly little man. His nerves were bad. He had skin trouble. It was agony for him to wear anything next to his skin coarser than silk. And he had delusions of grandeur.

[2] He was a monster of conceit. Never for one minute did he look at the world or at people, except in relation to himself. He was not only the most important person in the world, to himself; in his own eyes he was the only person who existed. He believed himself to be one of the greatest dramatists in the world, one of the greatest thinkers, and one of the greatest composers. To hear him talk, he was Shakespeare, and Beethoven, and Plato, rolled into one. And you would have had no difficulty in hearing him talk. He was one of the most exhausting conversationalists that ever lived. An evening with him was an evening spent in listening to a monologue. Sometimes he was brilliant; sometimes he was maddeningly tiresome. But whether he was being brilliant or dull, he had one sole topic of conversation: himself. What *he* thought and what *he* did.

[3] He had a mania for being in the right. The slightest hint of disagreement, from anyone, on the most trivial point, was enough to set him off on a harangue that might last for hours, in which he proved himself right in so many ways, and with such exhausting volubility, that in the end his hearer, stunned and deafened, would agree with him, for the sake of peace.

[4] It never occurred to him that he and his doings were not of the most intense and fascinating interest to anyone with whom he came in contact. He had theories about almost any subject under the sun, including vegetarianism, the drama, politics, and music; and in support of these theories he wrote pamphlets, letters, books ... thousands upon thousands of words, hundreds and hundreds of pages. He not only wrote these things, and published them—usually at somebody else's expense—but he would sit and read them aloud, for hours, to his friends and his family.

[5] He wrote operas; and no sooner did he have the synopsis of a story, but he would invite—or rather summon—a crowd of his friends to his

house and read it aloud to them. Not for criticism. For applause. When the complete poem was written, the friends had to come again, and hear *that* read aloud. Then he would publish the poem, sometime years before the music that went with it was written. He played the piano like a composer, in the worst sense of what that implies, and he would sit down at the piano before parties that included some of the finest pianists of his time, and play for them, by the hour, his own music, needless to say. He had a composer's voice. And he would invite eminent vocalists to his house, and sing them his operas, taking all the parts.

[6] He had the emotional stability of a six-year-old child. When he felt out of sorts, he would rave and stamp, or sink into suicidal gloom and talk darkly of going to the East to end his days as a Buddhist monk. Ten minutes later, when something pleased him, he would rush out of doors and run around the garden or jump up and down on the sofa, or stand on his head. He could be grief-stricken over the death of a pet dog, and he could be callous and heartless to a degree that would have made a Roman emperor shudder.

[7] He was almost innocent of any sense of responsibility. Not only did he seem incapable of supporting himself, but it never occurred to him that he was under any obligation to do so. He was convinced that the world owed him a living. In support of this belief, he borrowed money from everybody who was good for a loan—men, women, friends, or strangers. He wrote begging letters by the score, sometimes groveling without shame, at others loftily offering his intended benefactor the privilege of contributing to his support, and being mortally offended if the recipient declined the honor. I have found no record of his ever paying or repaying money to anyone who did not have a legal claim upon it.

[8] What money he could lay his hands on he spent like an Indian rajah. The mere prospect of a performance of one of his operas was enough to set him running up bills amounting to ten times the amount of his prospective royalties. On an income that would reduce a more scrupulous man to doing his own laundry, he would keep two servants. Without enough money in his pocket to pay his rent, he would have the walls and ceiling of his study lined with pink silk. No one will ever know—certainly he never knew—how much money he owed. We do know that his greatest benefactor gave him $6,000 to pay the most pressing of his debts in one city, and a year later had to give him $16,000 to enable him to live in another city without being thrown into jail for debt.

[9] He was equally unscrupulous in other ways. An endless procession of women marches through his life. His first wife spent twenty years enduring and forgiving his infidelities. His second wife had been the wife of his most devoted friend and admirer, from whom he stole her. And even while he was trying to persuade her to leave her first husband he was

writing to a friend to inquire whether he could suggest some wealthy woman—*any* wealthy woman—whom he could marry for her money.

[10] He was completely selfish in his other personal relationships. His liking for his friends was measured solely by the completeness of their devotion to him, or by their usefulness to him, whether financial or artistic. The minute they failed him—even by so much as refusing a dinner invitation—or began to lessen in usefulness, he cast them off without a second thought. At the end of his life he had exactly one friend left whom he had known even in middle age.

[11] He had a genius for making enemies. He would insult a man who disagreed with him about the weather. He would pull endless wires in order to meet some man who admired his work, and was able and anxious to be of use to him—and would proceed to make a mortal enemy of him with some idiotic and wholly uncalled-for exhibition of arrogance and bad manners. A character in one of his operas was a caricature of one of the most powerful music critics of his day. Not content with burlesquing him, he invited the critic to his house and read him the libretto aloud in front of his friends.

[12] The name of this monster was Richard Wagner. Everything that I have said about him you can find on record—in newspapers, in police reports, in the testimony of people who knew him, in his own letters, between the lines of his autobiography. And the curious thing about this record is that it doesn't matter in the least.

[13] Because this undersized, sickly, disagreeable, fascinating little man was right all the time. The joke was on us. He *was* one of the world's great dramatists; he *was* a great thinker; he *was* one of the most stupendous musical geniuses that, up to now, the world has ever seen. The world did owe him a living. People couldn't know those things at the time, I suppose; and yet to us, who know his music, it does seem as though they should have known. What if he did talk about himself all the time? If he had talked about himself for twenty-four hours every day for the span of his life he would not have uttered half the number of words that other men have spoken and written about him since his death.

[14] When you consider what he wrote—thirteen operas and music dramas, eleven of them still holding the stage, eight of them unquestionably worth ranking among the world's great musico-dramatic masterpieces—when you listen to what he wrote, the debts and heartaches that people had to endure from him don't seem much of a price. Eduard Hanslick, the critic whom he caricatured in *Die Meistersinger* and who hated him ever after, now lives only because he was caricatured in *Die Meistersinger*. The women whose hearts he broke are long since dead; and the man who could never love anyone but himself has made them deathless atonement, I think, with *Tristan und Isolde*. Think of the luxury

with which for a time, at least, fate rewarded Napoleon, the man who ruined France and looted Europe; and then perhaps you will agree that a few thousand dollars' worth of debts were not too heavy a price to pay for the *Ring* trilogy.

[15] What if he was faithless to his friends and to his wives? He had one mistress to whom he was faithful to the day of his death: Music. Not for a single moment did he ever compromise with what he believed, with what he dreamed. There is not a line of his music that could have been conceived by a little mind. Even when he is dull, or downright bad, he is dull in the grand manner. There is a greatness about his worst mistakes. Listening to his music, one does not forgive him for what he may or may not have been. It is not a matter of forgiveness. It is a matter of being dumb with wonder that his poor brain and body didn't burst under the torment of the demon of creative energy that lived inside him, struggling, clawing, scratching to be released; tearing, shrieking at him to write the music that was in him. The miracle is that what he did in the little space of seventy years could have been done at all, even by a great genius. Is it any wonder that he had no time to be a man?

COMMENT AND QUESTIONS

1. This essay is built on a pattern of contrast, with the first eleven paragraphs devoted to Wagner's unpleasant qualities and the last three, introduced by the turn in paragraph 12, to his genius. For an analysis of the essay, list in order the topic ideas in the first eleven paragraphs.
2. What is the reason for the sequence of ideas in these eleven paragraphs? Could the order be changed without loss?
3. How many of the unpleasant qualities discussed in the first section are referred to and justified in the last three paragraphs?
4. What does Taylor gain by withholding the "monster's" identity until paragraph 12?
5. The judgment of Wagner in the first eleven paragraphs is developed with a wealth of detail. In the absence of footnotes or sources introduced into the text, why do you think the reader is inclined to accept the detail and the characterization as authentic? How is the contrasting judgment in the last three paragraphs supported?
6. We have said in the "Introduction to Rhetorical Analysis" that proportion is a means of emphasis; that a writer ordinarily gives fullest development to the ideas he considers most important. In view of this general principle, can you account for the fact that Taylor devotes more than twice as much space to Wagner's unadmirable traits as to his genius?
7. Taylor's sentences are varied in structure and length, but he uses many

short sentences with a simple, conventional subject–verb–complement pattern and some short incomplete sentences which he might have attached to the preceding sentence. What is the effect of these numerous short sentences? Examine some of Taylor's longer and more complex sentences. Does he use them merely to avoid monotony, or are there in some cases other reasons for the change in sentence style?

8. The author slants his writing, first against and then in favor of Wagner, by selection of material, but also by use of charged words. Point out some examples of his attitudinal language. Does it seem to you appropriate and effective in this essay? Explain.

9. State in the form of a syllogism Taylor's argument in the last three paragraphs. Do you agree with his major premise?

[40] *DeWitt Parker*: The Intrinsic Value of Art

THE FOLLOWING selection discusses various forms of art—painting, sculpture, music, and literature—and the values they have in common. DeWitt Parker (1885–1949), who was a professor of philosophy at the University of Michigan, is the author of *Human Values, Analysis of Art*, and *The Principles of Aesthetics* (1946), from which this selection is taken.

[1] Our definition of art can be complete only if it enables us to understand the value of art. The reader might very well ask, however, what possible value expression could have when it becomes an end in itself. "I can understand its value," he might say, "when it has useful effects or conveys information, but what value can it possess of its own?" At this point, moreover, we are concerned with the value immediately realized in the experience of art, not with further values that may result from it. Art, no less than practical or scientific expression, may have beneficial effects on other experiences, which must be taken into account in measuring its total worth, but these we shall leave for investigation in our last chapters, after we have reached our fullest comprehension of art; we are interested now, in order to test and complete our definition, in the resident value only. That aesthetic expression does have this value follows directly from the spontaneous delight which artist and art lover take in it. The only problem, therefore, is its source, which, we shall find, is fed from many springs, some of them underground, and all intermingled.

[2] One source of value consists of the pleasures afforded by the

orderly media of expression—colors, lines and shapes, word sounds or tones, with their rhythms and relationships. As we have noted, there is no aesthetic expression without some values of this kind. These satisfactions we may call musical, because, taken by themselves, they have the vague, elusive quality of pure music. Outside of music, they are commonly fused with other satisfactions, for in literature and the plastic arts the sensuous media are symbols, verbal or representational, with definite meanings that may be agreeable; yet for purposes of analysis we can distinguish them. Thus we take pleasure in the yellow of Van Gogh's *Sunflowers*, partly because it is just that yellow, but partly because it is the color of a represented sunflower. Why we do enjoy the sensuous envelope of expression is a question we shall try to answer later; for the moment we are interested merely in setting it down as a universal spring of value in art.

[3] With this exception, the most obvious source of value in art is the imagination of objects and events which normally cause pleasure. Out of the meanings attached to his sensuous medium the artist may weave for us waking dreams of the things we like to see. We all enjoy perceiving the human form, so the sculptor offers a semblance of one; we like to see the ocean or flowers; here now is a shining vision by Winslow Homer or Van Gogh. The poet also is a magician, who may make of the meanings of words a happy dream:

> Gold wings across the sea!
> Moonlight from tree to tree,
> Sweet hair laid on my knee . . .

[4] In general, instincts and interests receive a partial satisfaction through imagining the objects, of which the perception or use might provide a full satisfaction. Both art and dream illustrate this principle.

[5] Similarly, through ideas of action or emotion suggested by the work of art, we are enabled imaginatively to perform actions, or to feel emotions, we should like to perform or feel. So, putting ourselves as it were into the represented body of the wrestler or dancer, we vicariously enjoy taking the proud poses or exerting the vigorous energies there suggested. Or, watching the play, we may find pleasure in fancying ourselves courting as eloquently as Romeo or being as charmingly responsive as Juliet. All aesthetic expression may thus become self-expression. We can understand how this is true if we remember that out of our own minds come the ideas and feelings which make up the content of the work of art; that all the artist does is to provide a set of stimuli or sensuous symbols which he hopes we will interpret as he intends. Self-expression is most readily the effect of the more subjective types of art, such as lyric poetry and music, because the emotions expressed are simple and uni-

versal; hence easily become anybody's experiences. Yet even the more objective types of art like the novel and drama, painting and sculpture, may become forms of self-expression, for we build up the worlds they contain in our imagination and emotion. We may then live in them, as it were, providing for ourselves imaginative modes of assuagement of our desires for action and passion.

[6] In the appreciation of the more objective types of art, however, the personality satisfied may not be the ordinary work-a-day one, but rather the self expanded by the imagination, under the suggestions of the artist. The acts represented in the landscape or genre picture, in the novel or play, may never have been performed by me; the opinions uttered may not be mine. And yet, as I look at the picture, it may be to me as if I were a shepherd moving with my sheep among the mountains or a peasant brawling with my companions. Or, watching the play, I may become as Anthony addressing the Romans or Hamlet soliloquizing on life and death. This is possible because each of us has capacities for action and emotion unrealized; the actual self is only one of many that might have been; hundreds of possible lives slumber in our souls. I remember George Herbert Palmer telling me when I was a student how many different professions he would have liked to pursue—that of ladies' tailor was one of them!—and I am sure he did not tell me all. No matter which life we may have chosen for our own, or have had forced upon us by our fate, we retain a secret longing for the others that have gone unfulfilled. Some of these—those that we deliberately rejected or that a turn of fate might have made ours—we may imagine vaguely; but many of them we have not the power to dream; yet they too beckon us from behind, and the artist provides us with their dream. Through art we may secure an imaginative realization of tendencies to think and act and feel, which, because incompatible with each other or with the conditions of our existence, cannot find free play in real life.

[7] Nevertheless, it must not be thought that the satisfactions of art are derived solely from the provision of substitute objects for the fulfillment of our own conscious or unconscious desires, through the simple process of identification with the world of persons and activities that we build up in the imagination under the artist's direction. Not all of art is "wish-fulfillment" in the ordinary sense. If the persons represented are too unlike ourselves we cannot without reservations place ourselves sympathetically within them; they therefore remain objects for us, not modes of ourselves. It would be hard for a man of simple, straightforward nature to identify himself with Hamlet or a normal woman to put herself in the place of Ophelia or [Lady] Macbeth. Even if we did identify ourselves with them imaginatively, their misfortunes were so great they would not provide us with a vicarious fulfillment of ordinary wishes: who could desire such a fate as theirs? Yet we do find satisfaction in works of art

of this kind. For, strange as it may seem at first thought, objects and persons that are foreign, or even opposed to us, may provide us with an assuagement of needs not of a personal, but of a general type, like pity or curiosity, or of a negative character, such as fear, horror, wrath, hate, indignation and scorn. And if real life does not offer opportunities in sufficient abundance and perfection for our appeasement—and how can life, since our needs are immoderate, almost infinite—we will seek them in art. . . .

[8] But just to express desire, quite apart from the provision of an imaginary object or activity through which it can be fulfilled, may be of value if it assists us to satisfy that desire which is deepest of all, for inner harmony or freedom.

> Oh, to be in England
> Now that April's there . . .

sang the poet and won for himself and for all who feel themselves into his verses, some appeasement, even though there is no hint of the assuagement of longing through a homecoming. No matter how poignant be a desire, the weight, the sting of it is lightened through expression, for it is drawn from the dark depths of the self to the clear and orderly surface of the work of art, where the mind can view and master it. Otherwise fluid and chaotic, or, when orderly, too busy with its ends to know itself, experience achieves the fixed outlines of a thing by being attached to a permanent form, and there can be retained and surveyed. Everyone has verified the clarifying effect of expression upon ideas, how they thus acquire definiteness and cohesion, so that even the mind that thinks them can hold them in review. Now, a similar effect upon feeling is no less certain. The unexpressed values of experience are vague strivings, embedded in disordered sensations and images; these expression sorts and organizes by attaching them to permanent ordered symbols. Even what is most intimate and fugitive becomes a stable object to which we may return again and again. When put into patterned words, the subtlest and deepest passions of a poet, which before were felt in a dim and tangled fashion, are brought out into the light. In music the most elusive moods, by being embodied in ordered sound, remain no longer subterranean. Through the novel or drama, the writer is able not only to enact his visions of life in the imagination, but by embodying them in external words and acts, to possess them for reflection. In painting, all that is seen or wondered at in nature is perceived with more delicacy and discrimination, and felt with greater freedom; or the vague fancies which a heated imagination paints upon the background of the mind come out better controlled when sketched with care upon a canvas.

[9] The most violent and unruly passions may be the material of art,

but once they are put into artistic form, they are mastered: "There is an art of passion but no passionate art"—Schiller. Through expression, the repression—the obstruction of feeling—is broken down; the mere effort to find a fitting artistic form diverts the attention and provides other occupation for the mind; an opportunity is given to reflect upon and digest the experience, through all these means bringing peace. It is impossible to cite too often the famous passage from Goethe's *Poetry and Truth:*

> And thus began that bent of mind from which I could not deviate my whole life through; namely that of turning into an image, into a poem, everything that delighted me or troubled me, or otherwise occupied my attention, and of coming to some certain understanding with myself thereupon . . . All the works therefore that have been published by me are only fragments of one great confession.[1]

[10] This effect of artistic expression belongs, as we have noted, to forms of expression outside of art. Every confidential outpouring of emotion, as between two friends, every confession in and outside of the confessional provides an example of the truth that to formulate feeling is to begin to be free with regard to it; not that we thereby get rid of it, but that we are able to find some place in our world where we can be on good terms with it. The greatest difficulty in bearing any disappointment or sorrow comes not from the frustration itself—for after all we have other things to live for—but from its effect upon the presuppositions of our entire being. The mind has an unconscious set of axioms or postulates which are assumed in the process of living; now anything that seems to contradict these, as a great calamity does, by destroying the logic of life, makes it seem meaningless and corrupts that faith in life which is the spring of action. In order for the health of the mind to be restored, the contradictory fact must somehow be reconciled with the mind's presuppositions, and the rationality of existence re-affirmed. But it is indispensable that we should clearly envisage and reflect upon the fact, viewing it in its larger relations where it will lose its overwhelming significance. Now precisely this transformation of experience may be achieved through expression. A fine illustration of this is Keats' sonnet ending

> . . . then on the shore
> Of the wide world I stand alone and think,
> Till love and fame to nothingness do sink.

[11] A great many works of art besides Goethe's, and some of them the greatest, like the *Divine Comedy,* so far as they spring intimately from the life of the artist, have had the salutary value of a confession for their

[1] English translation, edited by Park Godwin, Vol. I, p. 66.

creators. It is not always possible to trace the personal feelings and motives lying behind the artist's fictions, for the suffering soul covers its pain with subtle disguises; yet even when we do not know them we can divine them. We are certain that Watteau's gay picture visions were the projection and confession of his own disappointed dreams. In this respect, one great advantage of art over ordinary expression is its universality. Art is the confessional of the race. The artist provides a medium through which all men may confess themselves and heal their souls. Who does not feel a revival of some old or present despair of his own when he reads

>Un grand sommeil noir   Je ne vois plus rien,
>Tombe sur ma vie;   Je perds la mémoire
>Dormez toute espoir,   Du mal et du bien . . .
>Dormez toute envie!   O, la triste histoire!

yet who does not at the same time experience its assuagement? And this effect upon the reader is not confined to lyrical art; for, when in novel and drama we put ourselves in the place of the dramatis personae, we can pour our emotional experience into them and through them find relief for ourselves. Just so, Aristotle recognized the cathartic, or healing virtue of the drama as well as of music—"through pity and fear, effecting the proper purgation of these emotions."[2]

[12] The values that may result from expression which I have been describing pertain to generalizations of experience no less than to experiences of concrete objects and events. Many poems and some works of plastic art possess what I like to call "depth meanings"—meanings of universal scope underneath relatively concrete meanings or ideas. Thus in the following line of one of Frost's little poems

>Nothing gold can stay

the word "gold" has its usual surface meaning, but underneath that is its depth meaning, precious; so in addition to saying that nothing golden can endure, the poet is saying that nothing valuable can abide—a more universal statement. This is the same as one of the depth meanings in Shakespeare's

>Golden lads and girls all must
>As chimney sweepers come to dust . . .

although, of course, there is another meaning here—that of the equality in death of rich and poor. That there may be a multiplicity of meanings in a single work of art was recognized in the Renaissance, and even seems to have been regarded as essential to its purpose.[3] Sometimes

---

[2] *Poetics*, VI, 2. *Politics*, VIII, 7.

[3] Cf. Dante, *Convito*, Trattato Secundo; Leone Ebreo, *Dialoghi d'Amore*, pp. 99 and 100, Bari, Laterza, 1929.

the satisfaction in the expression of a generalization stems from the fact that the thought is one that we like to entertain, as in the so familiar

> God's in his heaven—
> All's right with the world!

but in other cases, as when the thought is not agreeable, it accompanies that adjustment to truth which arises as we look it squarely in the face, no longer struggling against it—"coming to some certain understanding with ourselves thereupon."

> You linger your little hour and are gone,
> And still the woods sweep leafily on,
> Not even missing the coral root flower
> You took as a trophy of the hour.

[13] All the other values of expression are enhanced through the fact that the medium is orderly and delightful. To imagine such objects as those suggested in the following lines

> Charmed magic casements, opening on the foam
> Of perilous seas, in faery lands forlorn

is pleasurable in itself, but more agreeable, and therefore more spontaneous, because of the melody of sound in which they are enveloped. And when the facts imagined are not pleasant, their expression in a delightful medium helps to induce us to make them our own and accept them notwithstanding. The medium becomes a charming net to hold us, and because of its allurements, we give ourselves the more freely to its spirit within. The following is not an agreeable thought

> Tomorrow and tomorrow and tomorrow
> Creeps in this petty pace from day to day,
> To the last syllable of recorded time;
> And all our yesterdays have lighted fools
> The way to dusty death.

yet the expression of this thought becomes a value in part because of the rhythmic charm of language. There is no incongruity between the fair form of a work of art and its content, however repugnant; for if we esteem the sympathetic vision of life—an imagination of it which provides some assuagement of our wishes, and in particular of our desire to be reconciled with it—we shall be glad of any means to this end.

[14] The contrast between the perfection of the work of art and the drab or difficult realities of nature and personal striving, serve also to make of beauty a consoler and healer. In place of a confused medley of sense impressions, art offers orderly colors and sounds and shapes; instead of an experience distracted and at loose ends, it offers one where each element serves the pervading purpose and where none are irrelevant or

distracting; instead of a life of duty hard to fulfill and ambitions painfully and only partially achieved, it provides an imagined life, which while imitating, and so appeasing, the interests of real life, remains free from its hazards and burdens. I would not base the value of art on the contrast between it and life; yet if life were not so bound and disordered, art would not seem so free and perfect; and very often those who suffer and struggle most love it best. The organic unity of the work of art, in which each element suggests another within its world, keeping you there and shutting you out momentarily from the real world to which you must presently return, and the sensuous charm of the medium, fascinating your eyes and ears, bring forgetfulness and a temporary release.

[15] The satisfactions which art provides are the greater because they are communicable; to possess them alone would be a good, but all values become enhanced when we add the joy of fellow feeling. Merely private and unutterable inspirations are not art. Beauty does for values what science does for intelligence; even as the one universalizes thought so the other universalizes feeling. In expressing himself the artist creates a form into which all similar experiences can be poured and out of which they can be shared. When we listen to the hymns of the church or read the poems of Horace the significance of our experience is magnified because we know that the feelings of millions have been there; we are in unison with a vast company living and dead. No thing of beauty is a private possession. All artists feed on one another, and into each of their products has gone the mind-work of the ages.

[16] But there are two types of universality—one by exclusion, the other by inclusion. Christian communists like Tolstoi demand that art express universal feelings only, such as the moral and religious; they would exclude all values that have not become those of the race. The aristocratic, the pathological, even the patriotic, are condemned as substance for art. But this is to diminish the importance of art; for it is art's privilege to make feelings common by providing a medium through which they can be communicated rather than merely to express those that are already common. Art is the more valuable because it encompasses the things which tend to separate and distinguish men than it would be if it were limited to those that unite them. There is nothing so bizarre that art may not express it, provided that thereby it may be communicated.

[17] The life of the imagination is, moreover, the only one that we can have in common. Actually to lead another's life would involve possessing his body, occupying his position, doing his work and so destroying him. But through the sympathetic imagination we can penetrate his life and leave him in possession. To do this thoroughly is possible, however, with the real life of a very few people, with intimates and friends. With the mass, we can share only ideal things like religion and patriotism, but

these also are matters largely of imagination. Now art widens the scope of this common life by creating a new, imaginary world to which we can all belong, where action and enjoyment do not involve competition or depend on mastery and possession.

[18] Finally, the values that art provides are relatively permanent. Art not only extends life and enables us to share it, but also preserves it. Existence has a leak in it, as Plato said; experience flows in and then flows on forever. Against this flux, our belief in progress comforts us; maturity is better than youth, we think, and each generation happier and more spiritual than the last. Yet the consolations of progress are partial. For even if it were true that we always go on to something better in the future, the past had its unique value, and that is lost ineluctably. The present repeats much of the form of the past—the essential aspects of human nature and institutions remain the same; but the distinctive bloom of each phase of personal life, and of each period of the world's history is transient. We cannot again become children or possess the strenuous freedom of the Renaissance, or the unclouded integrity attributed to the Greeks.

[19] In the life of the individual, however, the flux is not absolute; for through memory we preserve something of the unique value of our past. Its vividness, its fullness, the sharp bite of its reality go; but a subtle essence remains. And the worth that we attach to our personality depends largely upon it; for the instinct of self-preservation penetrates the inner world; we strive not only to maintain our physical existence in the present but our psychic past as well. In preserving the values of the past through memory we find a satisfaction akin to that of protecting our lives from danger. Through memory we feel childhood's joys and youth's sweet love and manhood's triumphs still our own, secure against the perils of oblivion.

[20] Now art does for the group what memory does for the individual. Only through expression can the past be preserved for all men and all time. When the individual perishes his memories go with him; unless he puts them into a form where they can be taken up into the consciousness of other men, they are lost forever. And just as the individual seeks a vicarious self-preservation by identifying himself with his children and his group, and finds compensation for his death in their continuance, so he rejoices when he knows that men who come after will appreciate the values of his life. We of the present feel ourselves enriched, in turn, as by a longer memory, in adding to the active values of our lives the imagined values of our forebears. Their desire to know themselves immortal is met by our desire to unite our lives with our whole past. Art alone makes this possible. History may tell us what men did, but only the poet or other artists can make us relive the values of their experience. For

through expression they make their own memories, or their interpretation of other men's memories, ours. Art is the memory of a people, the conserver of its values.

─◦⊰ COMMENT AND QUESTIONS ⊱◦─

1. Paragraph 1 limits the subject: the author is concerned in this discussion "with the value immediately realized in the experience of art, not with further values that may result from it." Does it seem to you that he is, at any time in the selection, talking about "further values that may result"? Explain.
2. Briefly summarize the principal values that Parker finds in art. Which of these values are most meaningful to you? Would you add other values to his enumeration?
3. To which of the values does Parker give emphasis by proportion and position? What do you think are the reasons for his emphasis? Explain.
4. The author uses a number of examples, many of them familiar to a general audience, some perhaps not familiar. Does the reader need to know the sources of the illustrations in order to understand the principles illustrated?
5. In paragraphs 5 and 6, what is the meaning of "self-expression"? What two forms of self-expression is Parker discussing here?
6. Initially, the author is concerned with the pleasures of seeing things in art that we like to see and imagining actions and emotions that we should like to experience. How does he later qualify the idea of the *pleasures* in art?
7. Parker suggests, especially in paragraphs 10 and 13, that art can help to reaffirm the rationality of existence and help us to fulfill our desire to be reconciled with life. What writers whom you have read would agree or disagree with the two assumptions that existence is rational and that we wish to be reconciled with life? To what extent do you agree or disagree? Explain.
8. In paragraphs 2, 8, 13, and particularly in paragraph 14, the author emphasizes the idea that art is orderly and that its order is a source of value. Martin Esslin, in "The Significance of the Absurd," describes the grotesqueness, the illogic, and the disorder in Absurd drama. Do you think that Parker could find in Absurd plays any of the values he assigns to art. Explain.
9. "History may tell us what men did, but only the poet or other artists can make us relive the values of their experience." Does this statement seem valid to you? Explain.

SCIENCE AND
THE MODERN WORLD

[41]   *J. Bronowski*: The Creative Mind

J. BRONOWSKI (1908–) is an English mathematician and writer, author of *The Face of Violence, The Commonsense of Science, William Blake and the Age of Revolution, The Poet's Defence,* and *The Identity of Man.* The following selection is the first of three essays in *Science and Human Values,* published in 1956 and revised in 1965. In paragraphs 8 and 9 of "The Creative Mind" Bronowski summarizes the aims and content of *Science and Human Values.*

– 1 –

[1] On a fine November day in 1945, late in the afternoon, I was landed on an airstrip in southern Japan. From there a jeep was to take me over the mountains to join a ship which lay in Nagasaki Harbor. I knew nothing of the country or the distance before us. We drove off; dusk fell; the road rose and fell away, the pine woods came down to the road, straggled on and opened again. I did not know that we had left the open country until unexpectedly I heard the ship's loudspeakers broadcasting dance music. Then suddenly I was aware that we were already at the center of damage in Nagasaki. The shadows behind me were the skeletons of the Mitsubishi factory buildings, pushed backwards and sideways as if by a giant hand. What I had thought to be broken rocks was a concrete power house with its roof punched in. I could now make out

the outline of two crumpled gasometers; there was a cold furnace festooned with service pipes; otherwise nothing but cockeyed telegraph poles and loops of wire in a bare waste of ashes. I had blundered into this desolate landscape as instantly as one might wake among the craters of the moon. The moment of recognition when I realized that I was already in Nagasaki is present to me as I write, as vividly as when I lived it. I see the warm night and the meaningless shapes; I can even remember the tune that was coming from the ship. It was a dance tune which had been popular in 1945, and it was called 'Is You Is Or Is You Ain't Ma Baby?'

[2] These essays, which I have called *Science and Human Values*, were born at that moment. For the moment I have recalled was a universal moment; what I met was, almost as abruptly, the experience of mankind. On an evening like that evening, some time in 1945, each of us in his own way learned that his imagination had been dwarfed. We looked up and saw the power of which we had been proud loom over us like the ruins of Nagasaki.

[3] The power of science for good and for evil has troubled other minds than ours. We are not here fumbling with a new dilemma; our subject and our fears are as old as the toolmaking civilizations. Men have been killed with weapons before now: what happened at Nagasaki was only more massive (for 40,000 were killed there by a flash which lasted seconds) and more ironical (for the bomb exploded over the main Christian community in Japan). Nothing happened in 1945 except that we changed the scale of our indifference to man; and conscience, in revenge, for an instant became immediate to us. Before this immediacy fades in a sequence of televised atomic tests, let us acknowledge our subject for what it is: civilization face to face with its own implications. The implications are both the industrial slum which Nagasaki was before it was bombed, and the ashy desolation which the bomb made of the slum. And civilization asks of both ruins, 'Is You Is Or Is You Ain't Ma Baby?'

– 2 –

[4] The man whom I imagine to be asking this question, wrily with a sense of shame, is not a scientist; he is civilized man. It is of course more usual for each member of civilization to take flight from its consequences by protesting that others have failed him. Those whose education and perhaps tastes have confined them to the humanities protest that the scientists alone are to blame, for plainly no mandarin ever made a bomb or an industry. The scientists say, with equal contempt, that the Greek scholars and the earnest cataloguers of cave paintings do well to wash their hands of blame; but what in fact are they doing to help direct the society whose ills grow more often from inaction than from error?

[5] This absurd division reached its *reductio ad absurdum*, I think,

when one of my teachers, G. H. Hardy, justified his great life work on the ground that it could do no one the least harm—or the least good. But Hardy was a mathematician; will humanists really let him opt out of the conspiracy of scientists? Or are scientists in their turn to forgive Hardy because, protest as he might, most of them learned their indispensable mathematics from his books?

[6] There is no comfort in such bickering. When Shelley pictured science as a modern Prometheus who would wake the world to a wonderful dream of Godwin, he was alas too simple. But it is as pointless to read what has happened since as a nightmare. Dream or nightmare, we have to live our experience as it is, and we have to live it awake. We live in a world which is penetrated through and through by science, and which is both whole and real. We cannot turn it into a game simply by taking sides.

[7] And this make-believe game might cost us what we value most: the human content of our lives. The scholar who disdains science may speak in fun, but his fun is not quite a laughing matter. To think of science as a set of special tricks, to see the scientist as the manipulator of outlandish skills—this is the root of the poison mandrake which flourishes rank in the comic strips. There is no more threatening and no more degrading doctrine than the fancy that somehow we may shelve the responsibility for making the decisions of our society by passing it to a few scientists armored with a special magic. This is another dream, the dream of H. G. Wells, in which the tall elegant engineers rule, with perfect benevolence, a humanity which has no business except to be happy. To H. G. Wells, this was a dream of heaven—a modern version of the idle, harp-resounding heaven of other childhood pieties. But in fact it is the picture of a slave society, and should make us shiver whenever we hear a man of sensibility dismiss science as someone else's concern. The world today is made, it is powered by science; and for any man to abdicate an interest in science is to walk with open eyes towards slavery.

[8] My aim in this book is to show that the parts of civilization make a whole: to display the links which give society its coherence and, more, which give it life. In particular, I want to show the place of science in the canons of conduct which it has still to perfect.

[9] This subject falls into three parts. The first is a study of the nature of the scientific activity, and with it of all those imaginative acts of understanding which exercise 'The Creative Mind.' After this it is logical to ask what is the nature of the truth, as we seek it in science and in social life; and to trace the influence which this search for empirical truth has had on conduct. This influence has prompted me to call the second part 'The Habit of Truth.' Last I shall study the conditions for the success of science, and find in them the values of man which science would have had to invent afresh if man had not otherwise known them: the values which make up 'The Sense of Human Dignity.'

[10] This, then, is a high-ranging subject which is not to be held in the narrow limits of a laboratory. It disputes the prejudice of the humanist who takes his science sourly and, equally, the petty view which many scientists take of their own activity and that of others. When men misunderstand their own work, they cannot understand the work of others; so that it is natural that these scientists have been indifferent to the arts. They have been content, with the humanists, to think science mechanical and neutral; they could therefore justify themselves only by the claim that it is practical. By this lame criterion they have of course found poetry and music and painting at least unreal and often meaningless. I challenge all these judgments.

— 3 —

[11] There is a likeness between the creative acts of the mind in art and in science. Yet, when a man uses the word science in such a sentence, it may be suspected that he does not mean what the headlines mean by science. Am I about to sidle away to those riddles in the Theory of Numbers which Hardy loved, or to the heady speculations of astrophysicists, in order to make claims for abstract science which have no bearing on its daily practice?

[12] I have no such design. My purpose is to talk about science as it is, practical and theoretical. I define science as the organization of our knowledge in such a way that it commands more of the hidden potential in nature. What I have in mind therefore is both deep and matter of fact; it reaches from the kinetic theory of gases to the telephone and the suspension bridge and medicated toothpaste. It admits no sharp boundary between knowledge and use. There are of course people who like to draw a line between pure and applied science; and oddly, they are often the same people who find art unreal. To them, the word useful is a final arbiter, either for or against a work; and they use this word as if it can mean only what makes a man feel heavier after meals.

[13] There is no sanction for confining the practice of science in this or another way. True, science is full of useful inventions. And its theories have often been made by men whose imagination was directed by the uses to which their age looked. Newton turned naturally to astronomy because it was the subject of his day, and it was so because finding one's way at sea had long been a practical preoccupation of the society into which he was born. It should be added, mischievously, that astronomy also had some standing because it was used very practically to cast horoscopes. (Kepler used it for this purpose; in the Thirty Years' War he cast the horoscope of Wallenstein which wonderfully told his character, and he predicted a universal disaster for 1634 which proved to be the murder of Wallenstein.)

[14] In a setting which is more familiar, Faraday worked all his life to link electricity with magnetism because this was the glittering problem of his day; and it was so because his society, like ours, was on the lookout for new sources of power. Consider a more modest example today: the new mathematical methods of automatic control, a subject sometimes called cybernetics, have been developed now because this is a time when communication and control have in effect become forms of power. These inventions have been directed by social needs, and they are useful inventions; yet it was not their usefulness which dominated and set light to the minds of those who made them. Neither Newton nor Faraday, nor yet Norbert Wiener, spent their time in a scramble for patents.

[15] What a scientist does is compounded of two interests: the interest of his time and his own interest. In this his behavior is no different from any other man's. The need of the age gives its shape to scientific progress as a whole. But it is not the need of the age which gives the individual scientist his sense of pleasure and of adventure, and that excitement which keeps him working late into the night when all the useful typists have gone home at five o'clock. He is personally involved in his work, as the poet is in his, and as the artist is in the painting. Paints and painting too must have been made for useful ends; and language was developed, from whatever beginnings, for practical communication. Yet you cannot have a man handle paints or language or the symbolic concepts of physics, you cannot even have him stain a microscope slide, without instantly waking in him a pleasure in the very language, a sense of exploring his own activity. This sense lies at the heart of creation.

- 4 -

[16] The sense of personal exploration is as urgent, and as delightful, to the practical scientist as to the theoretical. Those who think otherwise are confusing what is practical with what is humdrum. Good humdrum work without originality is done every day by everyone, theoretical scientists as well as practical, and writers and painters too, as well as truck drivers and bank clerks. Of course the unoriginal work keeps the world going; but it is not therefore the monopoly of practical men. And neither need the practical man be unoriginal. If he is to break out of what has been done before, he must bring to his own tools the same sense of pride and discovery which the poet brings to words. He cannot afford to be less radical in conceiving and less creative in designing a new turbine than a new world system.

[17] And this is why in turn practical discoveries are not made only by practical men. As the world's interest has shifted, since the Industrial Revolution, to the tapping of new springs of power, the theoretical scientist has shifted his interests too. His speculations about energy have

been as abstract as once they were about astronomy; and they have been profound now as they were then, because the man loved to think. The Carnot cycle and the dynamo grew equally from this love, and so did nuclear physics and the German V weapons and Kelvin's interest in low temperatures. Man does not invent by following either use or tradition; he does not invent even a new form of communication by calling a conference of communication engineers. Who invented the television set? In any deep sense, it was Clerk Maxwell who foresaw the existence of radio waves, and Heinrich Hertz who proved it, and J. J. Thomson who discovered the electron. This is not said in order to rob any practical man of the invention, but from a sad sense of justice; for neither Maxwell nor Hertz nor J. J. Thomson would take pride in television just now.

[18] Man masters nature not by force but by understanding. This is why science has succeeded where magic failed: because it has looked for no spell to cast over nature. The alchemist and the magician in the Middle Ages thought, and the addict of comic strips is still encouraged to think, that nature must be mastered by a device which outrages her laws. But in four hundred years since the Scientific Revolution we have learned that we gain our ends only *with* the laws of nature; we control her only by understanding her laws. We cannot even bully nature by any insistence that our work shall be designed to give power over her. We must be content that power is the byproduct of understanding. So the Greeks said that Orpheus played the lyre with such sympathy that wild beasts were tamed by the hand on the strings. They did not suggest that he got this gift by setting out to be a lion tamer.

- 5 -

[19] What is the insight with which the scientist tries to see into nature? Can it indeed be called either imaginative or creative? To the literary man the question may seem merely silly. He has been taught that science is a large collection of facts; and if this is true, then the only seeing which scientists need do is, he supposes, seeing the facts. He pictures them, the colorless professionals of science, going off to work in the morning into the universe in a neutral, unexposed state. They then expose themselves like a photographic plate. And then in the darkroom or laboratory they develop the image, so that suddenly and startlingly it appears, printed in capital letters, as a new formula for atomic energy.

[20] Men who have read Balzac and Zola are not deceived by the claims of these writers that they do no more than record the facts. The readers of Christopher Isherwood do not take him literally when he writes 'I am a camera.' Yet the same readers solemnly carry with them from their schooldays this foolish picture of the scientist fixing by some mechanical process the facts of nature. I have had of all people

a historian tell me that science is a collection of facts, and his voice had not even the ironic rasp of one filing cabinet reproving another.

[21] It seems impossible that this historian had ever studied the beginnings of a scientific discovery. The Scientific Revolution can be held to begin in the year 1543 when there was brought to Copernicus, perhaps on his deathbed, the first printed copy of the book he had finished about a dozen years earlier. The thesis of this book is that the earth moves around the sun. When did Copernicus go out and record this fact with his camera? What appearance in nature prompted his outrageous guess? And in what odd sense is this guess to be called a neutral record of fact?

[22] Less than a hundred years after Copernicus, Kepler published (between 1609 and 1619) the three laws which described the paths of the planets. The work of Newton and with it most of our mechanics spring from these laws. They have a solid, matter of fact sound. For example, Kepler says that if one squares the year of a planet, one gets a number which is proportional to the cube of its average distance from the sun. Does anyone think that such a law is found by taking enough readings and then squaring and cubing everything in sight? If he does, then, as a scientist, he is doomed to a wasted life; he has as little prospect of making a scientific discovery as an electronic brain has.

[23] It was not this way that Copernicus and Kepler thought, or that scientists think today. Copernicus found that the orbits of the planets would look simpler if they were looked at from the sun and not from the earth. But he did not in the first place find this by routine calculation. His first step was a leap of imagination—to lift himself from the earth, and put himself wildly, speculatively into the sun. 'The earth conceives from the sun,' he wrote; and 'the sun rules the family of stars.' We catch in his mind an image, the gesture of the virile man standing in the sun, with arms outstretched, overlooking the planets. Perhaps Copernicus took the picture from the drawings of the youth with outstretched arms which the Renaissance teachers put into their books on the proportions of the body. Perhaps he had seen Leonardo's drawings of his loved pupil Salai. I do not know. To me, the gesture of Copernicus, the shining youth looking outward from the sun, is still vivid in a drawing which William Blake in 1780 based on all these: the drawing which is usually called *Glad Day*.

[24] Kepler's mind, we know, was filled with just such fanciful analogies; and we know what they were. Kepler wanted to relate the speeds of the planets to the musical intervals. He tried to fit the five regular solids into their orbits. None of these likenesses worked, and they have been forgotten; yet they have been and they remain the stepping stones of every creative mind. Kepler felt for his laws by way of metaphors, he searched mystically for likenesses with what he knew in every strange corner of nature. And when among these guesses he hit upon his laws,

he did not think of their numbers as the balancing of a cosmic bank account, but as a revelation of the unity in all nature. To us, the analogies by which Kepler listened for the movement of the planets in the music of the spheres are farfetched. Yet are they more so than the wild leap by which Rutherford and Bohr in our own century found a model for the atom in, of all places, the planetary system?

– 6 –

[25] No scientific theory is a collection of facts. It will not even do to call a theory true or false in the simple sense in which every fact is either so or not so. The Epicureans held that matter is made of atoms two thousand years ago and we are now tempted to say that their theory was true. But if we do so we confuse their notion of matter with our own. John Dalton in 1808 first saw the structure of matter as we do today, and what he took from the ancients was not their theory but something richer, their image: the atom. Much of what was in Dalton's mind was as vague as the Greek notion, and quite as mistaken. But he suddenly gave life to the new facts of chemistry and the ancient theory together, by fusing them to give what neither had: a coherent picture of how matter is linked and built up from different kinds of atoms. The act of fusion is the creative act.

[26] All science is the search for unity in hidden likenesses. The search may be on a grand scale, as in the modern theories which try to link the fields of gravitation and electromagnetism. But we do not need to be browbeaten by the scale of science. There are discoveries to be made by snatching a small likeness from the air too, if it is bold enough. In 1935 the Japanese physicist Hideki Yukawa wrote a paper which can still give heart to a young scientist. He took as his starting point the known fact that waves of light can sometimes behave as if they were separate pellets. From this he reasoned that the forces which held the nucleus of an atom together might sometimes also be observed as if they were solid pellets. A schoolboy can see how thin Yukawa's analogy is, and his teacher would be severe with it. Yet Yukawa without a blush calculated the mass of the pellet he expected to see, and waited. He was right; his meson was found, and a range of other mesons, neither the existence nor the nature of which had been suspected before. The likeness had borne fruit.

[27] The scientist looks for order in the appearances of nature by exploring such likenesses. For order does not display itself of itself; if it can be said to be there at all, it is not there for the mere looking. There is no way of pointing a finger or a camera at it; order must be discovered and, in a deep sense, it must be created. What we see, as we see it, is mere disorder.

[28] This point has been put trenchantly in a fable by Karl Popper.

Suppose that someone wished to give his whole life to science. Suppose that he therefore sat down, pencil in hand, and for the next twenty, thirty, forty years recorded in notebook after notebook everything that he could observe. He may be supposed to leave out nothing: today's humidity, the racing results, the level of cosmic radiation and the stock-market prices and the look of Mars, all would be there. He would have compiled the most careful record of nature that has ever been made; and, dying in the calm certainty of a life well spent, he would of course leave his notebooks to the Royal Society. Would the Royal Society thank him for the treasure of a lifetime of observation? It would not. The Royal Society would treat his notebooks exactly as the English bishops have treated Joanna Southcott's box. It would refuse to open them at all, because it would know without looking that the notebooks contain only a jumble of disorderly and meaningless items.

– 7 –

[29] Science finds order and meaning in our experience, and sets about this in quite a different way. It sets about it as Newton did in the story which he himself told in his old age, and of which the schoolbooks give only a caricature. In the year 1665, when Newton was twenty-two, the plague broke out in southern England, and the University of Cambridge was closed. Newton therefore spent the next eighteen months at home, removed from traditional learning, at a time when he was impatient for knowledge and, in his own phrase, 'I was in the prime of my age for invention.' In this eager, boyish mood, sitting one day in the garden of his widowed mother, he saw an apple fall. So far the books have the story right; we think we even know the kind of apple; tradition has it that it was a Flower of Kent. But now they miss the crux of the story. For what struck the young Newton at the sight was not the thought that the apple must be drawn to the earth by gravity; that conception was older than Newton. What struck him was the conjecture that the same force of gravity, which reaches to the top of the tree, might go on reaching out beyond the earth and its air, endlessly into space. Gravity might reach the moon: this was Newton's new thought; and it might be gravity which holds the moon in her orbit. There and then he calculated what force from the earth (falling off as the square of the distance) would hold the moon, and compared it with the known force of gravity at tree height. The forces agreed; Newton says laconically, 'I found them answer pretty nearly.' Yet they agreed only nearly: the likeness and the approximation go together, for no likeness is exact. In Newton's sentence modern science is full grown.

[30] It grows from a comparison. It has seized a likeness between two unlike appearances; for the apple in the summer garden and the grave moon overhead are surely as unlike in their movements as two things

can be. Newton traced in them two expressions of a single concept, gravitation: and the concept (and the unity) are in that sense his free creation. The progress of science is the discovery at each step of a new order which gives unity to what had long seemed unlike. Faraday did this when he closed the link between electricity and magnetism. Clerk Maxwell did it when he linked both with light. Einstein linked time with space, mass with energy, and the path of light past the sun with the flight of a bullet; and spent his dying years in trying to add to these likenesses another, which would find a single imaginative order between the equations of Clerk Maxwell and his own geometry of gravitation.

– 8 –

[31] When Coleridge tried to define beauty, he returned always to one deep thought: beauty, he said, is 'unity in variety.' Science is nothing else than the search to discover unity in the wild variety of nature—or more exactly, in the variety of our experience. Poetry, painting, the arts are the same search, in Coleridge's phrase, for unity in variety. Each in its own way looks for likenesses under the variety of human experience. What is a poetic image but the seizing and the exploration of a hidden likeness, in holding together two parts of a comparison which are to give depth each to the other? When Romeo finds Juliet in the tomb, and thinks her dead, he uses in his heartbreaking speech the words,

> Death that hath suckt the honey of thy breath.

The critic can only haltingly take to pieces the single shock which this image carries. The young Shakespeare admired Marlowe, and Marlowe's Faustus had said of the ghostly kiss of Helen of Troy that it sucked forth his soul. But that is a pale image; what Shakespeare has done is to fire it with the single word honey. Death is a bee at the lips of Juliet, and the bee is an insect that stings; the sting of death was a commonplace phrase when Shakespeare wrote. The sting is there, under the image; Shakespeare has packed it into the word honey; but the very word rides powerfully over its own undertones. Death is a bee that stings other people, but it comes to Juliet as if she were a flower; this is the moving thought under the instant image. The creative mind speaks in such thoughts.

[32] The poetic image here is also, and accidentally, heightened by the tenderness which town dwellers now feel for country ways. But it need not be; there are likenesses to conjure with, and images as powerful, within the man-made world. The poems of Alexander Pope belong to this world. They are not countrified, and therefore readers today find them unemotional and often artificial. Let me then quote Pope: here he is in a formal satire face to face, towards the end of his life, with his own gifts. In eight lines he looks poignantly forward towards death and back to the laborious years which made him famous.

> Years foll'wing Years, steal something ev'ry day,
> At last they steal us from our selves away;
> In one our Frolicks, one Amusements end,
> In one a Mistress drops, in one a Friend:
> This subtle Thief of Life, this paltry Time,
> What will it leave me, if it snatch my Rhime?
> If ev'ry Wheel of that unweary'd Mill
> That turn'd ten thousand Verses, now stands still.

The human mind had been compared to what the eighteenth century called a mill, that is to a machine, before; Pope's own idol Bolingbroke had compared it to a clockwork. In these lines the likeness goes deeper, for Pope is thinking of the ten thousand Verses which he had translated from Homer: what he says is sad and just at the same time, because this really had been a mechanical and at times a grinding task. Yet the clockwork is present in the image too; when the wheels stand still, time for Pope will stand still for ever; we feel that we already hear, over the horizon, Faust's defiant reply to Mephistopheles, which Goethe had not yet written—'let the clock strike and stop, let the hand fall, and time be at an end.'

> Werd ich zum Augenblicke sagen:
> Verweile doch! du bist so schön!
> Dann magst du mich in Fesseln schlagen,
> Dann will ich gern zugrunde gehn!
> Dann mag die Totenglocke schallen,
> Dann bist du deines Dienstes frei,
> Die Uhr mag stehn, der Zeiger fallen,
> Es sei die Zeit für mich vorbei![1]

[33] I have quoted Pope and Goethe because their metaphor here is not poetic; it is rather a hand reaching straight into experience and arranging it with new meaning. Metaphors of this kind need not always be written in words. The most powerful of them all is simply the presence of King Lear and his Fool in the hovel of a man who is shamming madness, while lightning rages outside. Or let me quote another clash of two conceptions of life, from a modern poet. In his later poems W. B. Yeats was troubled by the feeling that in shutting himself up to write, he was missing the active pleasures of life; and yet it seemed to him certain that

---

[1] Should I say to the moment:
Do tarry! you are so beautiful!
Then you may throw me in chains,
Then I will gladly go to my perdition!
Then Death's knell may resound,
Then you shall be free of your service,
The clock may stop, the hour-hand drop,
Time may cease for me!

the man who lives for these pleasures will leave no lasting work behind him. He said this at times very simply, too:

> The intellect of man is forced to choose
> Perfection of the life, or of the work.

This problem, whether a man fulfills himself in work or in play, is of course more common than Yeats allowed; and it may be more commonplace. But it is given breadth and force by the images in which Yeats pondered it.

> Get all the gold and silver that you can,
> Satisfy ambition, or animate
> The trivial days and ram them with the sun,
> And yet upon these maxims meditate:
> All women dote upon an idle man
> Although their children need a rich estate;
> No man has ever lived that had enough
> Of children's gratitude or woman's love.

The love of women, the gratitude of children: the images fix two philosophies as nothing else can. They are tools of creative thought, as coherent and as exact as the conceptual images with which science works: as time and space, or as the proton and the neutron.

– 9 –

[34] The discoveries of science, the works of art are explorations—more, are explosions, of a hidden likeness. The discoverer or the artist presents in them two aspects of nature and fuses them into one. This is the act of creation, in which an original thought is born, and it is the same act in original science and original art. But it is not therefore the monopoly of the man who wrote the poem or who made the discovery. On the contrary, I believe this view of the creative act to be right because it alone gives a meaning to the act of appreciation. The poem or the discovery exists in two moments of vision: the moment of appreciation as much as that of creation; for the appreciator must see the movement, wake to the echo which was started in the creation of the work. In the moment of appreciation we live again the moment when the creator saw and held the hidden likeness. When a simile takes us aback and persuades us together, when we find a juxtaposition in a picture both odd and intriguing, when a theory is at once fresh and convincing, we do not merely nod over someone else's work. We re-enact the creative act, and we ourselves make the discovery again. At bottom, there is no unifying likeness there until we too have seized it, we too have made it for ourselves.

[35] How slipshod by comparison is the notion that either art or sci-

ence sets out to copy nature. If the task of the painter were to copy for men what they see, the critic could make only a single judgment: either that the copy is right or that it is wrong. And if science were a copy of fact, then every theory would be either right or wrong, and would be so for ever. There would be nothing left for us to say but this is so, or is not so. No one who has read a page by a good critic or a speculative scientist can ever again think that this barren choice of yes or no is all that the mind offers.

[36] Reality is not an exhibit for man's inspection, labelled 'Do not touch.' There are no appearances to be photographed, no experiences to be copied, in which we do not take part. Science, like art, is not a copy of nature but a re-creation of her. We re-make nature by the act of discovery, in the poem or in the theorem. And the great poem and the deep theorem are new to every reader, and yet are his own experiences, because he himself re-creates them. They are the mark of unity in variety; and in the instant when the mind seizes this for itself, in art or in science, the heart misses a beat.

COMMENT AND QUESTIONS

1. What is the purpose of the first section of Bronowski's essay? What images and figures of speech in the first three paragraphs seem to you effective in achieving the author's purpose? What does the name of the dance tune contribute?
2. The author is criticizing or rejecting a number of common attitudes toward science. What, specifically, is he criticizing, and what are the basic reasons for the criticism?
3. In paragraph 15 the author distinguishes between the two interests of the scientist. What is the main point of this distinction?
4. What idea is Bronowski emphasizing, at the end of paragraph 18, with his allusion to Orpheus, and why is he emphasizing it?
5. Sections 5 and 6 of the essay develop the thesis that scientific theory is not a collection of facts. What examples and reasons in these sections seem to you most effective in supporting the thesis? Explain.
6. In the discussion of Copernicus and Kepler (paragraphs 23 and 24) Bronowski touches on the idea of likenesses that reveal unity; at the end of paragraph 25 and the beginning of paragraph 26 he explicitly defines scientific activity: the search for unity in hidden likenesses. Where does he later return to this definition and for what purposes?
7. Section 8 is a discussion of art, chiefly of literature. How has this discussion been prepared for earlier in the essay?
8. In his concluding section, the author gives emphasis to an extension of his

ideas about creativity. State briefly the central idea of the last three paragraphs. Why do you think it is emphasized by the end-position?
9. If you have read DeWitt Parker's "The Intrinsic Value of Art," compare the ideas of Parker and Bronowski on the creative act and its values.
10. What seem to you the most important things the author says to the scholar or humanist who disdains science? What are the most important things he says to the scientist who finds poetry, music, and painting unreal or meaningless? Which of Bronowski's ideas are most convincing and which are least convincing to you? Explain.
11. Near the end of his long essay *Science and Human Values*, Bronowski says that science needs to teach us not its techniques but its spirit: "the irresistible need to explore." Does this statement seem consistent with what the author is saying in "The Creative Mind"? Explain.

[42] *J. Robert Oppenheimer*: Prospects in the Arts and Sciences

J. ROBERT OPPENHEIMER (1904–1967) was a distinguished American physicist who taught at the University of California at Berkeley, the California Institute of Technology, and Princeton University, and who was early known for his work at Los Alamos, New Mexico, as head of the project to develop the atomic bomb. He was director of the Institute for Advanced Study at Princeton, and in 1963 he received the Enrico Fermi Award for his work in theoretical physics. The following essay is from *The Open Mind*, published in 1960.

[1] The words "prospects in the arts and sciences" mean two quite different things to me. One is prophecy: What will the scientists discover and the painters paint, what new forms will alter music, what parts of experience will newly yield to objective description? The other meaning is that of a view: What do we see when we look at the world today and compare it with the past? I am not a prophet; and I cannot very well speak to the first subject, though in many ways I should like to. I shall try to speak to the second, because there are some features of this view which seem to me so remarkable, so new and so arresting, that it may be worth turning our eyes to them; it may even help us to create and shape the future better, though we cannot foretell it.

[²] In the arts and in the sciences, it would be good to be a prophet. It would be a delight to know the future. I had thought for a while of my own field of physics and of those nearest to it in the natural sciences. It would not be too hard to outline the questions which natural scientists today are asking themselves and trying to answer. What, we ask in physics, is matter, what is it made of, how does it behave when it is more and more violently atomized, when we try to pound out of the stuff around us the ingredients which only violence creates and makes manifest? What, the chemist asks, are those special features of nucleic acids and proteins which make life possible and give it its characteristic endurance and mutability? What subtle chemistry, what arrangements, what reactions and controls make the cells of living organisms differentiate so that they may perform functions as oddly diverse as transmitting information throughout our nervous systems or covering our heads with hair? What happens in the brain to make a record of the past, to hide it from consciousness, to make it accessible to recall? What are the physical features which make consciousness possible?

[³] All history teaches us that these questions that we think the pressing ones will be transmuted before they are answered, that they will be replaced by others, and that the very process of discovery will shatter the concepts that we today use to describe our puzzlement.

[⁴] It is true that there are some who profess to see in matters of culture, in matters precisely of the arts and sciences, a certain macrohistorical pattern, a grand system of laws which determines the course of civilization and gives a kind of inevitable quality to the unfolding of the future. They would, for instance, see the radical, formal experimentation which characterized the music of the last half-century as an inevitable consequence of the immense flowering and enrichment of natural science; they would see a necessary order in the fact that innovation in music precedes that in painting and that in turn in poetry, and point to this sequence in older cultures. They would attribute the formal experimentation of the arts to the dissolution, in an industrial and technical society, of authority—of secular, political authority, and of the catholic authority of the church. They are thus armed to predict the future. But this, I fear, is not my dish.

[⁵] If a prospect is not a prophecy, it is a view. What does the world of the arts and sciences look like? There are two ways of looking at it: One is the view of the traveler, going by horse or foot, from village to village to town, staying in each to talk with those who live there and to gather something of the quality of its life. This is the intimate view, partial, somewhat accidental, limited by the limited life and strength and curiosity of the traveler, but intimate and human, in a human compass. The other is the vast view, showing the earth with its fields and towns and valleys as they appear to a camera carried in a high-altitude rocket. In one sense this prospect will be more complete; one will see all branches of knowledge, one will see all the arts, one will see them as part of the vastness and complication of the whole of human life on earth. But one will miss a great deal; the beauty and warmth of human life will largely be gone from that prospect.

[6] It is in this vast high-altitude survey that one sees the general surprising quantitative features that distinguish our time. This is where the listings of science and endowments and laboratories and books published show up; this is where we learn that more people are engaged in scientific research today than ever before, that the Soviet world and the free world are running neck and neck in the training of scientists, that more books are published per capita in England than in the United States, that the social sciences are pursued actively in America, Scandinavia, and England, that there are more people who hear the great music of the past, and more music composed and more paintings painted. This is where we learn that the arts and sciences are flourishing. This great map, showing the world from afar and almost as to a stranger, would show more: It would show the immense diversity of culture and life, diversity in place and tradition for the first time clearly manifest on a world-wide scale, diversity in technique and language, separating science from science and art from art, and all of one from all of the other. This great map, world-wide, culture-wide, remote, has some odd features. There are innumerable villages. Between the villages there appear to be almost no paths discernible from this high altitude. Here and there passing near a village, sometimes through its heart, there will be a superhighway, along which windy traffic moves at enormous speed. The superhighways seem to have little connection with the villages, starting anywhere, ending anywhere, and sometimes appearing almost by design to disrupt the quiet of the village. This view gives us no sense of order or of unity. To find these we must visit the villages, the quiet, busy places, the laboratories and studies and studios. We must see the paths that are barely discernible; we must understand the superhighways and their dangers.

[7] In the natural sciences these are and have been and are likely to continue to be heroic days. Discovery follows discovery, each both raising and answering questions, each ending a long search, and each providing the new instruments for a new search. There are radical ways of thinking unfamiliar to common sense and connected with it by decades or centuries of increasingly specialized and unfamiliar experience. There are lessons of how limited, for all its variety, the common experience of man has been with regard to natural phenomena, and hints and analogies as to how limited may be his experience with man. Every new finding is a part of the instrument kit of the sciences for further investigation and for penetrating into new fields. Discoveries of knowledge fructify technology and the practical arts, and these in turn pay back refined techniques, new possibilties of observation and experiment.

[⁸] In any science there is harmony between practitioners. A man may work as an individual, learning of what his colleagues do through reading or conversation; he may be working as a member of a group on problems whose technical equipment is too massive for individual effort. But whether he is a part of a team or solitary in his own study, he, as a professional, is a member of a community. His colleagues in his own branch of science will be grateful to him for the inventive or creative thoughts he has, will welcome his criticism. His world and work will be objectively communicable; and he will be quite sure that if there is error in it, that error will not long be undetected. In his own line of work he lives in a community where common understanding combines with common purpose and interest to bind men together both in freedom and in co-operation.

[⁹] This experience will make him acutely aware of how limited, how inadequate, how precious is this condition of his life; for in his relations with a wider society, there will be neither the sense of community nor of objective understanding. He will sometimes find, in returning to practical undertakings, some sense of community with men who are not expert in his science, with other scientists whose work is remote from his, and with men of action and men of art. The frontiers of science are separated now by long years of study, by specialized vocabularies, arts, techniques, and knowledge from the common heritage even of a most civilized society; and anyone working at the frontier of such science is in that sense a very long way from home, a long way too from the practical arts that were its matrix and origin, as indeed they were of what we today call art.

[¹⁰] The specialization of science is an inevitable accompaniment of progress; yet it is full of dangers, and it is cruelly wasteful, since so much that is beautiful and enlightening is cut off from most of the world. Thus it is proper to the role of the scientist that he not merely find new truth and communicate it to his fellows, but that he teach, that he try to bring the most honest and intelligible account of new knowledge to all who will try to learn. This is one reason—it is the decisive organic reason— why scientists belong in universities. It is one reason why the patronage of science by and through universities is its most proper form; for it is here, in teaching, in the association of scholars and in the friendships of teachers and taught, of men who by profession must themselves be both teachers and taught, that the narrowness of scientific life can best be moderated, and that the analogies, insights, and harmonies of scientific discovery can find their way into the wider life of man.

[¹¹] In the situation of the artist today there are both analogies to and differences from that of the scientist; but it is the differences which are the most striking and which raise the problems that touch most on the evil of our day. For the artist it is not enough that he communicate with others who are expert in his own art. Their fellowship, their understanding, and their appreciation may encourage him; but that is not the end of his work, nor its nature. The artist depends on a common sensibility and culture, on a common meaning of symbols, on a community of experience and common ways of describing and interpreting it. He need not write for everyone or paint or play for everyone. But his audience must be man; it must be man, and not a specialized set of experts among his fellows. Today that is very difficult. Often the artist has an aching sense of great loneliness, for the community to which he addresses himself is largely not there; the traditions and the culture, the symbols and the history, the myths and the common experience, which it is his function to illuminate, to harmonize, and to portray, have been dissolved in a changing world.

[12] There is, it is true, an artificial audience maintained to moderate between the artist and the world for which he works: the audience of the professional critics, popularizers, and advertisers of art. But though, as does the popularizer and promoter of science, the critic fulfills a necessary present function and introduces some order and some communication between the artist and the world, he cannot add to the intimacy and the directness and the depth with which the artist addresses his fellow men.

[13] To the artist's loneliness there is a complementary great and terrible barrenness in the lives of men. They are deprived of the illumination, the light and tenderness and insight of an intelligible interpretation, in contemporary terms, of the sorrows and wonders and gaieties and follies of man's life. This may be in part offset, and is, by the great growth of technical means for making the art of the past available. But these provide a record of past intimacies between art and life; even when they are applied to the writing and painting and composing of the day, they do not bridge the gulf between a society, too vast and too disordered, and the artist trying to give meaning and beauty to its parts.

[14] In an important sense this world of ours is a new world, in which the unity of knowledge, the nature of human communities, the order of society, the order of ideas, the very notions of society and culture have changed and will not return to what they have been in the past. What is new is new not because it has never been there before, but because it has changed in quality. One thing that is new is the prevalence of newness, the changing scale and scope of change itself, so that the world alters as we walk in it, so that the years of man's life measure not some small growth or rearrangement or moderation of what he learned in childhood, but a great upheaval. What is new is that in one generation our knowledge of the natural world engulfs, upsets, and complements all knowledge of the natural world before. The techniques, among which and by which we live, multiply and ramify, so that the whole world is bound together by communication, blocked here and there by the immense synapses of political tyranny. The global quality of the world is new: our knowledge of and sympathy with remote and diverse peoples, our involvement with

them in practical terms, and our commitment to them in terms of brotherhood. What is new in the world is the massive character of the dissolution and corruption of authority, in belief, in ritual, and in temporal order. Yet this is the world that we have come to live in. The very difficulties which it presents derive from growth in understanding, in skill, in power. To assail the changes that have unmoored us from the past is futile, and in a deep sense, I think, it is wicked. We need to recognize the change and learn what resources we have.

[15] Again I will turn to the schools and, as their end and as their center, the universities. For the problem of the scientist is in this respect not different from that of the artist or of the historian. He needs to be a part of the community, and the community can only with loss and peril be without him. Thus it is with a sense of interest and hope that we see a growing recognition that the creative artist is a proper charge on the university, and the university a proper home for him; that a composer or a poet or a playwright or painter needs the toleration, understanding, the rather local and parochial patronage that a university can give; and that this will protect him from the tyranny of man's communication and professional promotion. For here there is an honest chance that what the artist has of insight and of beauty will take root in the community, and that some intimacy and some human bonds can mark his relations with his patrons. For a university rightly and inherently is a place where the individual man can form new syntheses, where the accidents of friendship and association can open a man's eyes to a part of science or art which he had not known before, where parts of human life, remote and perhaps superficially incompatible, can find in men their harmony and their synthesis.

[16] These, then, in rough and far too general words, are some of the things we see as we walk through the villages of the arts and of the sciences and notice how thin are the paths that lead from one to another, and how little in terms of human understanding and pleasure the work of the villages comes to be shared outside.

[17] The superhighways do not help. They are the mass media—from the loud-speakers in the deserts of Asia Minor and the cities of Communist China to the organized professional theater of Broadway. They are the purveyors of art and science and culture for the millions upon millions—the promoters who represent the arts and sciences to humanity and who represent humanity to the arts and sciences; they are the means by which we are reminded of the famine in remote places or of war or trouble or change; they are the means by which the great earth and its peoples have become one to one another, the means by which the news of discovery or honor and the stories and songs of today travel and resound throughout the world. But they are also the means by which the true human community, the man knowing man, the neighbor understand-

ing neighbor, the schoolboy learning a poem, the woman dancing, the individual curiosity, the individual sense of beauty are being blown dry and issueless, the means by which the passivity of the disengaged spectator presents to the man of art and science the bleak face of unhumanity.

[18] For the truth is that this is indeed, inevitably and increasingly, an open and, inevitably and increasingly, an eclectic world. We know too much for one man to know much, we live too variously to live as one. Our histories and traditions—the very means of interpreting life—are both bonds and barriers among us. Our knowledge separates as well as it unites; our orders disintegrate as well as bind; our art brings us together and sets us apart. The artist's loneliness, the scholar despairing because no one will any longer trouble to learn what he can teach, the narrowness of the scientist—these are unnatural insignia in this great time of change.

[19] For what is asked of us is not easy. The openness of this world derives its character from the irreversibility of learning; what is once learned is part of human life. We cannot close our minds to discovery; we cannot stop our ears so that the voices of far-off and strange people can no longer reach them. The great cultures of the East cannot be walled off from ours by impassable seas and defects of understanding based on ignorance and unfamiliarity. Neither our integrity as men of learning nor our humanity allows that. In this open world, what is there, any man may try to learn.

[20] This is no new problem. There has always been more to know than one man could know; there have always been modes of feeling that could not move the same heart; there have always been deeply held beliefs that could not be composed into a synthetic union. Yet never before today have the diversity, the complexity, the richness so clearly defied hierarchical order and simplification; never before have we had to understand the complementary, mutually not compatible ways of life and recognize choice between them as the only course of freedom. Never before today has the integrity of the intimate, the detailed, the true art, the integrity of craftsmanship and the preservation of the familiar, of the humorous and the beautiful stood in more massive contrast to the vastness of life, the greatness of the globe, the otherness of people, the otherness of ways, and the all-encompassing dark.

[21] This is a world in which each of us, knowing his limitations, knowing the evils of superficiality and the terrors of fatigue, will have to cling to what is close to him, to what he knows, to what he can do, to his friends and his tradition and his love, lest he be dissolved in a universal confusion and know nothing and love nothing. It is at the same time a world in which none of us can find hieratic prescription or general sanction for any ignorance, any insensitivity, any indifference. When a friend tells us of a new discovery we may not understand, we may not be able to listen without jeopardizing the work that is ours and closer to us; but we cannot find

in a book or canon—and we should not seek—grounds for hallowing our ignorance. If a man tells us that he sees differently than we, or that he finds beautiful what we find ugly, we may have to leave the room, from fatigue or trouble; but that is our weakness and our default. If we must live with a perpetual sense that the world and the men in it are greater than we and too much for us, let it be the measure of our virtue that we know this and seek no comfort. Above all, let us not proclaim that the limits of our powers correspond to some special wisdom in our choice of life, of learning, or of beauty.

[22] This balance, this perpetual, precarious, impossible balance between the infinitely open and the intimate, this time—our twentieth century—has been long in coming; but it has come. It is, I think, for us and our children, our only way.

[23] This is for all men. For the artist and for the scientist there is a special problem and a special hope, for in their extraordinarily different ways, in their lives that have increasingly divergent character, there is still a sensed bond, a sensed analogy. Both the man of science and the man of art live always at the edge of mystery, surrounded by it; both always, as the measure of their creation, have had to do with the harmonization of what is new with what is familiar, with the balance between novelty and synthesis, with the struggle to make partial order in total chaos. They can, in their work and in their lives, help themselves, help one another, and help all men. They can make the paths that connect the villages of arts and sciences with each other and with the world at large the multiple, varied, precious bonds of a true and world-wide community.

[24] This cannot be an easy life. We shall have a rugged time of it to keep our minds open and to keep them deep, to keep our sense of beauty and our ability to make it, and our occasional ability to see it in places remote and strange and unfamiliar; we shall have a rugged time of it, all of us, in keeping these gardens in our villages, in keeping open the manifold, intricate, casual paths, to keep these flourishing in a great, open, windy world; but this, as I see it, is the condition of man; and in this condition we can help, because we can love, one another.

COMMENT AND QUESTIONS

1. Oppenheimer, in his analysis of prospects in the arts and sciences, makes repeated use of contrast and comparison. Paragraph 1 briefly contrasts two meanings of *prospect* and states that the author will speak in terms of the second meaning—*view* rather than *prophecy*. Why does he, then, in paragraphs 2–4, discuss questions for the future and the theory of those

armed to predict the future? What is the relevance of these paragraphs to the whole essay?
2. Paragraph 5, contrasting two possible views of the world of arts and sciences, introduces the recurrent figure of travel and of the village. In paragraphs 5, 6, and later, what is the literal meaning of *villages*, of *paths*, and of *superhighways*?
3. Examine the language and the attitudes in paragraphs 5 and 6. What is gained and what is lost in each of the two views of the arts and sciences?
4. What is the function of the last two sentences of paragraph 6? Do they seem to you to effect a transition into the following paragraphs? Explain.
5. In what ways, according to the author, are the situations of the scientist and the artist comparable? In what ways do their situations differ? What does society at large lose by the "prospect" Oppenheimer is describing?
6. Summarize the author's ideas about the values of the universities as patrons of the arts and sciences. Is there a relationship between the universities and the figurative "paths" and "superhighways"? Explain.
7. This essay reflects a mind capable not only of highly intelligent analysis but also of fairness and reasonableness in seeing more than one side of a problem or question. The fairness accounts in part for the fact that many of Oppenheimer's paragraphs contain contrasting elements or are built on patterns of contrast. Re-read paragraphs 14, 17, 18, and 20, for example. What different kinds of contrast do you find in the four paragraphs?
8. What other traits of style are noticeable in paragraphs 14, 17, 18, and 20? Comment on the endings of these paragraphs.
9. Paragraph 21 suggests what we should and should not do in the world in which we live. To what extent do you agree with Oppenheimer's suggestions? Explain.
10. Examine paragraph 24. Is it an effective ending? If so, what makes it effective?
11. The tone of "Prospects in the Arts and Sciences"—particularly the author's attitude toward his subject—is complex. Do any of the following words seem to you to describe this attitude accurately: *pessimistic, despairing, hopeful, stoical, realistic, resigned*? Can you think of a description that seems to you more accurate than any one of these words?

[43] *Elting E. Morison*: It's Two-Thirds of a Century—We've Made It, So Far

THE FOLLOWING article, published in *The New York Times Magazine*, April 24, 1966, is not concerned solely with science; the author believes, however, that the rapid advance of scientific knowledge and the rapid application of scientific findings to human affairs are important causes of conditions and problems in the modern world. Elting E. Morison (1909–), author of *Admiral Sims and the Modern American Navy* and *Turmoil and Tradition*, is Sloan Fellows Professor of Industrial History at the Massachusetts Institute of Technology and chairman of the Social Studies Curriculum program of Educational Services, Inc.

[1] The main line of argument for this article was worked out on a 707 bound east from Los Angeles. Conditions for reflection upon the shape of things to come were almost perfect. Swirling gently around me was a current of cool air projected from a small spigot in the ceiling of the plane. Overhead also, from a small box, "a first-run movie" called, I believe, "From Moment to Moment," was steadily unwinding. In my earphones, in stereophonic sound, was the music of Verdi's "Requiem." I had been told I could watch Jean Seberg and listen to Verdi at the same time without mechanical complication and so I did. On the tray in front of me, ice-cold in a small cylindrical green bottle, was the first of two complimentary martinis. We were passing over the eastern slope of the Rocky Mountains on the way to Chicago.

[2] I had a great-grandfather who had taken somewhat the same route, the other way, from Illinois to California. He had driven out at the head of a wagon train in a buckboard drawn by two bay horses and had made about as much progress in one day, if it was a good day, as I was making between sips of the martini if I sipped fast. I reflected on this and on the fact that my ancestor looking upward, perhaps, from time to time on his westward journey would not have been able to tell very precisely what interesting uses we would be making of the empty skies.

[3] This is all by way of saying that it is hard to tell about the future. Indeed, the idea, as it was put to me, that a man who has spent time studying what has happened in the past two-thirds of a century should, as a result, be able to describe what will happen in the next one-third was probably never a very sensible idea. There is a difference between telling "where all past years are"—which John Donne thought was hard enough —and locating the years to come, let alone reporting on what they will look like.

[4] And today, when the rate and variety of change seem to approach infinity, the task of relating what went before to what will come after seems immeasurable. Any shrewd man would be willing to settle for the kind of prescience Carlyle had when he observed that there was thunder upon the horizon as well as dawn and let it go at that.

[5] Henry Adams went a good deal further. He made in fact something of an intellectual career out of his attempt to bring the future within a

foreseeable scheme and he produced, on the whole, some impressive results. Early in this century he said that the United States and Russia were the countries to watch—and that they should watch each other. He also told his brother Brooks in 1912 that a belt of dissolving society was stretched around the world from Peking to Sicily. In the next year, he believed, it would reach into the heart of civilization in Central Europe. At 75, he added, he was rotting to pieces in every sense, but "the damned world rots faster than I."

[6] In his minor calculation he was almost precisely right. Give or take a few months, the dissolving disease got to Sarajevo when he said it would. As for his larger divination, cast in the form of generalized calamity that increasingly attracted him as he got older, the evidence appears to offer considerable confirmation. Much of the world that Adams knew well has now, by rot or other means, disintegrated and most of the society he knew even better has dissolved. The far-flung battle lines that maintained the 19th-century order seem near the end of their long withdrawal and the peculiar fire of the time has almost sunk on all the dunes and headlands and even on the home grounds.

[7] To be more specific is hardly necessary. Everybody knows that things are not at all what they were at the beginning of this century; even the heart of society has shifted to some other not yet fully defined location. The intent here is not to describe the workings of the process—which Adams called a disease—but to discover if it has run its course.

[8] The answer is, "Probably not." For one thing, the figures of speech —disease, dissolution, rot—suggesting as they do decomposition ending in inert residues, are quite misleading. Some parts of the previous world did no doubt just fall apart or go to pieces. But more of it was torn, wrenched, blasted or blown asunder. From Verdun to Manchuria, from the Finland Station to the Sudetenland, from Omaha Beach to Hiroshima, to Dienbienphu and Vietnam, there has been a hectic destruction of ancient powers and principalities. Looked at this way, it could be said that the damned world was not so much rotting away as going to hell in a hack and hew.

[9] The energy in the system, in other words, has been tremendous. It still is. We are a long way from inert residues, but also some distance from tranquillity. The available energy has not yet been brought within any very orderly or stable scheme. In the first instance, it was turned against patterns and structures that had become antiquated, irrelevant, insufficient or just in the way. And no doubt for much of the two-thirds of a century just passed, the available energy was worked out in acts of violence designed by desperate men.

[10] But much of it, too, was put in the service of certain propositions, some old—all men are created equal; some new—any five-year plan—

that seemed to offer fuller promise for more lives. Working through the disorder, whether in Central Europe, Africa, India or Asia, there have been constructive intents and a purpose to reach useful accommodations politically and socially to conditions without precedent.

[11] To say that such intents are not yet fully realized, that from time to time and from place to place they have been and still are in open conflict with each other, is not the same as saying that the world is dissolving. It may well be the difference between galloping consumption and labor pains.

[12] Thus far, nothing new or very interesting has been said about either the past or the future. It amounts to little more than saying "our little systems have their day, they have their day and cease to be." It may speed things up somewhat to ask "What next?"—or more specifically: "May we soon be entering a time of much greater stability and harmony?"

[13] The answer must appear to be, "No, not in this century." In the way of creating new political arrangements to take the place of the old dispensations there seems to be unfinished business in India, Africa and throughout much of the Far East. It will no doubt take considerable time and much painful experiment to get things set right in these areas. And the uncertainties in these areas will be a continuing source of further perturbation in the larger system of international relations where Russia, China, the nations of Europe, and the United States will be seeking useful accommodations to each other.

[14] If all these foreseeable activities were to be played out within the old conventional schemes of time and energy, it would be possible perhaps to make some qualified prediction about when and how the dust would settle down, as in the previous century a man might with a show of confidence forecast some sort of schedule for the colonization of Africa or the disposition of the Shantung Peninsula. But not even a bold or rash man today would dare predict when and how the dust will settle in this disturbed world.

[15] For what is going on is not simply, as so often in the past, a reorganization of familiar elements, an attempt to give modified forms to fairly constant entities. In Africa, for instance, the cement has fallen out of the seams of empire, leaving small pieces; but the effort in Africa is not directed simply to putting the pieces together again in a fairly familiar context; it is directed to putting the pieces together to fit a set of novel and complicated conditions.

[16] What is true in Africa is true of all other places; even the most ancient structures are put under the rising pressure of novelty and complication. If one searches for the cause of this pressure within the whole

system, it can easily be discovered. It appears to derive from two things—the excitements produced by the steady advance of the ideas of science and the power introduced by the utilization of the scientific ideas in engineering. Indeed, the transcendent fact in the history of this century so far may well be the rapid development of a system that can produce a steadily enlarging flow of scientific findings and the increasingly rapid application of these findings to the affairs of men.

[17] By means of this system, man in the part of this century already passed has acquired an amazing domination over his natural or physical surrounding. Starting centuries ago on this effort to extend his control over his surrounding by steadily extending his skill as a tool-user, man is now close to the payoff of his long labors, the part where he can manipulate his environment to suit his own desires. Most of his progress, which has spread out over eons, is concentrated in the past two-thirds of a century.

[18] The extent and nature of this competence is, in fact, awesome; we can blow the world up, as we all know. But taken by itself, it is not a matter for unqualified pride. Thomas Huxley, who was in on the beginning of the great modern forward march, came to Baltimore near the end of the last century to say that he was not very much impressed by the existing plant—the dynamos, the open-hearth furnaces, the locomotives and all that. "The great issue," he went on, "about which hangs a true sublimity and the terror of overhanging fate is, what are you going to do with all these things?"

[19] In the short run—say 33⅓ years, to pick a figure at random—it is pretty clear what we will do and not do with some of these things. For instance, will we by the year 2,000 blow ourselves, or a considerable part of ourselves, up? The answer is almost certainly not. Indeed, it seems far more probable that the knowledge of the great destructive power we have at our disposal will tend to steady and stabilize the decision-makers.

[20] Will we have placed men upon the moon? The answer is almost certainly yes. But it is not clear that such first explorations will produce a constant flow of traffic between ourselves and that cold and blasted heath. Will we have so refined "the spare-parts deal" in modern medicine that the brains of one man will have been transplanted into the head of another? Quite probably. Will we have developed a vehicle to take us to London in two hours on a fairly predictable commuting schedule? Quite probably.

[21] Will we have so mastered the content and purpose of the nucleic acids that we will know far more fully than we do now how to manage the selection and development of human characteristics? Quite probably. And what of the computer? It will no doubt continue to extend its competence into many regions of man's thought and increasingly invade the sectors of routine management in technical and human systems.

[22] The putting of such questions and the supplying of such answers is really not a very profitable or even very interesting exercise. What it amounts to is saying that in the next few years we will without much doubt extend our technical competence. There is a slightly different kind of question which offers room for a little more stimulating speculation and for larger difference of opinion.

[23] Will there, for instance, be enough food, enough clothes, enough houses, even enough ground for the multiplying population in the year 2000? With due regard for the difficulty of deciding what "enough" may be, and recognizing that problems of distribution are perhaps greater than problems of production, it may be said that we seem to have it in our hands to supply the support required, if we put our minds to it. And, if we use our minds a little more, we will begin at the proper end and try to work with more understanding and system at the task of controlling the number of births.

[24] And, however many people there are, will they be put out of business by the machines? This seems very doubtful indeed. Historically at least, the more work the machinery does, the more work that machines can't do there seems to be. And what of leisure? More, one hopes than now, and better used and more opportunity for education continued episodically through life to keep up with the times—which will prove to be more upwardly mobile than the Joneses ever were.

[25] And what of the North, South, East and West; the town and the country; the old and the young, the rich and the poor; the King's English and the vernacular; the upper, the middle and the lower; the black, the white and the yellow—still all there no doubt, but with a leveling off of distinctions, a flattening out of differences.

[26] This, of course, is not at all what Huxley meant when he asked what we were going to do with all these things. He wanted to know, to what end will they be used? This is a hard question and the question that must precede it is little easier. It is the question of how or whether we can learn to handle or manage the system of ideas, forces, materials and things that we are busily constructing, whatever the end in view might be.

[27] The system at this moment is so powerful and so filled with interior change that any human organization resting upon it is subject to continuous change itself. That is why the social and political disequilibriums around the world from Cuba to Vietnam to the Congo will undoubtedly continue to perturb the equilibrium of the whole for some time to come. The task of creating a social and political structure firm enough to contain and flexible enough to be responsive to the scientific and technical changes will be difficult—and one not soon finished, because the exciting forces of science and engineering will be steadily changing as well.

[28] But one may hazard a guess that in the parts of the world where

"new" societies are emerging—and in the other parts of the world where older societies are attempting to modify familiar structures to meet the new conditions—real progress will be made in the next three decades towards useful accommodations both social and political. A further guess is that, to reach these accommodations, it will be necessary to reduce a little the circumference of the circle of freedom in which each man now stands.

[29] The extent to which a man has a sense of himself in our society depends to a considerable degree on the size of that circle and what goes on in it—specifically on the extent to which a man feels free and able to make independent choices among an array of alternative opportunities. During the next 33⅓ years, and probably thereafter, this space will in all probability serve as the theater for the most interesting and significant encounters that will occur in the period. An old associate of mine, a physiologist, says occasionally that man may be looked upon in time simply as "a node in a communication network." There are a growing number of other technical systems in which man can similarly be looked upon as a small point.

[30] And if others so consider him, it is but a step to his so considering himself. So one problem will be to discover how intricate systems can be managed not only in the interests of the general whole (across-the-board decisions) but can be so ordered that they may preserve a lively concern for the particular—the single individual.

[31] A lot in this process will depend upon the people who put the intricate system together, how sensitive they will remain to the claims of single men. But a lot, too, indeed much more, will depend on the single men. If they can figure out their legitimate claims and press them upon the public consciousness with persistence, it will do much to increase the sensitivity of those who may otherwise come to believe that—in putting together a great society—general rules, inclusive systems and across-the-board decisions are enough.

[32] And here, in the next third of a century, the load on single men will grow. For the size of the circle each man stands in as a single self is not only diminishing, but the space enclosed is filling up. The things which Emerson said were in the saddle and sufficient even in his time "to ride mankind" have now multiplied exponentially—even small and apparently insignificant things. Take what piles up in and around a seat in a 707—intercom, stereo, air conditioner, TV, and so forth. Almost all things are possible, even Miss Seberg and Giuseppe Verdi and Captain Jones' report on the weather at O'Hare all at the same time. How to sort things out and keep them in their proper places becomes a problem—too great a problem obviously in the case in point to be solved.

[33] These are, relatively, small and weak things compared with the machines and procedures creating the general surround a man stands in

today. These are powerful enough to set their own conditions and to determine their own environment if left untended. They may well do so unless the men in the environment can sort out and arrange things to suit themselves. In the old days when much that was desirable could not be done, one settled as a piece of ripe old wisdom for the possible. Today when so much is possible, the problem for the wise is to pick out from all the things that can be done what may be altogether fitting and proper—desirable to do.

[34] Such selection may be done in part by higher authority. We will go to the moon and cause Appalachia to flourish as the green bay tree, but we will resist the military application of nuclear energy. And it may be done in part by the influence of the general public in the body politic. But in the end, the decisions of higher authority and the opinion of the body politic will be determined by the mood of innumerable men standing in their own small circles.

[35] Their judgments will determine what kind of machines to build and what machines we can build that don't need to be built; what rules and regulations and moral codes shall govern the use of birth-control pills, nucleic acids and the procedures of the spare-parts deal; what kinds of technical systems and networks will preserve the largest play for human beings. It's a matter of selecting, as they say today, the proper targets of opportunity and designing the appropriate instrumentation to achieve the end in view.

[36] To fortify the single man as he seeks to make his judgments within his small circle he must have all kinds of support—some knowledge of the potential in each new idea and machine and network; as full a knowledge as possible of his own potential, historically conceived and currently understood; a set of definitions stating, among all the things that are possible, the things especially to be hoped for; and a set of criteria which, given his own potential and the potential in the machinery, will enable him to choose the best means to fulfill his hopes.

[37] Some part of this fortification will come no doubt from the decisions and aspirations set forth by those in authority and some part will certainly be found in the body of fact, attitude and timeless perception that makes up the Western culture. But more must in the future come from an educational process transformed to meet the new dispensation. In times without precedent, formal education, responsive to changing conditions, must assume much of the load borne in more static conditions by the familiar and sustaining cultures.

[38] And today when, as Whitehead said, the society that does not value the trained mind will perish, the imaginative development of new content and new forms in education has a very high priority. And finally, if the single man is to do his necessary work within his small circle, he must recover the feeling that he counts.

[39] In the creation of this feeling the support of the relevant parts of the old culture—the aspirations that may be defined for him by those in authority, the knowledge supplied by the new education—will all help. But in addition, he must have a sense that he has some hand in shaping the mechanical surround he will increasingly inhabit—that the character and quality of his life is not determined simply by the technically possible and economically feasible.

[40] How to give individual men the evidence they need to make sensible judgments about the kind of world they want to live in and how to give them the power to make their judgments stick, that is the unfinished business of the next third of the century.

COMMENT AND QUESTIONS

1. The first six paragraphs might be considered introductory; paragraph 7 states the author's purpose, or part of his purpose, in writing the article. What do the first paragraphs contribute?
2. What use does Morison make of the indirect and direct quotations from Henry Adams in paragraph 5? Of the quotation from Thomas Huxley in paragraph 18?
3. A question-to-answer pattern is recurrent in this essay. Summarize the author's reasons for saying "Probably not" in answer to the indirect question at the end of paragraph 7 and his reasons for saying "No, not in this century" in answer to the question at the end of paragraph 12.
4. Paragraphs 19–21 ask and answer a number of questions, and paragraph 22 makes a transition to a "slightly different kind of question." How do the questions in paragraphs 23–25 differ from those in paragraphs 19–21? To what extent do you agree with the author's comments in paragraphs 23–25?
5. At the end of paragraph 28, Morison introduces the figure of the circle of freedom. Explain what he means by his guess that it will be necessary to reduce a little the circumference of that circle. What examples can you give of ways in which the circle of freedom for the individual has already been reduced in this century?
6. The plane on which Morison was traveling offered him a number of free choices. What were they? How, then, is the further discussion of the plane, in paragraph 32, relevant to the circle of freedom?
7. In paragraph 33 and again in paragraph 39, the author uses *surround* as a noun. Neither *The Standard College Dictionary* nor *Webster's New World Dictionary* lists the word as a noun; *Webster's Seventh New Collegiate Dictionary* does list it as a noun and defines it: "something (as a border or edging) that surrounds." If you had been editing Morison's article, would you have suggested changing the word *surround* to the more generally used

word *surroundings?* Explain.
8. The author emphasizes a number of times the role of individual men in shaping the world they live in. Do you agree with what he says about the possible influence of individuals? Explain.
9. Does this article seem to you to offer a solution to the problem stated by Thomas Huxley and restated by Morison in paragraph 26? Explain.
10. Comment on the title "It's Two-Thirds of a Century—We've Made It, So Far." Does the title prepare the reader for the content of the article or emphasize what is most important in the article? Can you think of other possible titles?

[44] *Emmanuel G. Mesthene*: Learning to Live with Science

EMMANUEL G. MESTHENE is Executive Director of the Harvard University Program on Technology and Society. The following article appeared in the *Saturday Review*, July 17, 1965.

[1] It was Gilbert Murray who first used the celebrated phrase "the failure of nerve." Writing about ancient Greek religions, Murray characterized as a failure of nerve the change of temper that occurred in Hellenistic civilization around the turn of the era. The Greeks of the fifth and fourth centuries B.C. believed in the ultimate intelligibility of the universe. There was nothing in the nature of existence or of man that was inherently unknowable. They accordingly believed also in the power of the human intelligence to know all there was to know about the world, and to guide man's career in it.
[2] The wars, increased commerce, and infiltration of Oriental cultures that marked the subsequent period brought with them vicissitude and uncertainty that shook this classic faith in the intelligibility of the world and in the capacity of men to know and to do. There was henceforth to be a realm of knowledge available only to God, not achievable by human reason. Men, in other words, more and more turned to God to do for them what they no longer felt confident to do for themselves. That was the failure of nerve.
[3] I think things are changing. I doubt that there are many men today who would question that life will be produced in the laboratory, that psychologists and their personality drugs will soon reveal what really

makes men tick, that scientific prediction is a far more promising guide to the future than divination, and that the heavens cannot long remain mysterious in the face of our ability to hit the moon today and the stars tomorrow. In a recent article, Daniel Bell characterized this new-found faith as follows: "Today we feel that there are no inherent secrets in the universe . . . and this is one of the significant changes in the modern moral temper." I would say, indeed, that this is a major implication of our new world of science and technology. We are witnessing a widespread recovery of nerve.

WE FEAR THE MACHINES

[4] Paradoxically, this taking on of new courage is tending at the same time to produce an opposite reaction, vague but disturbingly widespread. At the same time that we admire the new machines we build—the ones that play chess, and translate Russian, and catch and correct their own mistakes, and tend each other—we also begin to fear them. We fear them in two ways—one that we talk about, and one that we joke about.

[5] We talk quite openly about our fear that machines may take away jobs, deprive people of work. But we dare only to joke about our fear that machines will replace people, not only as workers, but as people. Already they do arithmetic better than any of us. How much longer can it be before they make people obsolete? This fear is part of our technological world, but I see it only as derivative. I think it has its roots in a deeper, moral implication.

[6] Some who have seen farthest and most clearly in recent decades have warned of a growing imbalance between man's capabilities in the physical and in the social realms. John Dewey, for example, said: "We have displayed enough intelligence in the physical field to create the new and powerful instrument of science and technology. We have not as yet had enough intelligence to use this instrument deliberately and systematically to control its social operations and consequences." Dewey said this more than thirty years ago, before television, before atomic power, before electronic computers, before space satellites. He had been saying it, moreover, for at least thirty years before that. He saw early the problems that would arise when man learned to do anything he wanted before he learned what he wanted.

WHAT SHOULD WE DO?

[7] I think the time Dewey warned about is here. My more thoughtful scientific friends tell me that we now have, or know how to acquire, the technical capability to do very nearly anything we want. Can we transplant human hearts, control personality, order the weather that suits us, travel to Mars or to Venus? Of course we can, if not now or in five or 10 years, then certainly in 25, or in 50 or a 100. If each of us examined the

extent of his own restored faith in the essential intelligibility of the world, we might find that we have recovered our nerve to the point that we are becoming almost nervy. (I think, incidentally, that this recovery of nerve largely explains the current crisis of the churches. After 20 centuries of doing man's work, they are now having to learn how to do God's. The Ecumenical Council is evidence that the long but false war between religion and science is ended, and that we are once more facing Augustine's problem, to distinguish what is God's and what is man's.)

[8] If the answer to the question "What can we do?" is "Anything," then the emphasis shifts far more heavily than before onto the question "What should we do?" The commitment to universal intelligibility entails moral responsibility. Abandonment of the belief in intelligibility 2,000 years ago was justly described as a failure of nerve because it was the prelude to moral surrender. Men gave up the effort to be wise because they found it too hard. Renewed belief in intelligibility 2,000 years later means that men must take up again the hard work of becoming wise, And it is much harder work now, because we have so much more power than the Greeks. On the other hand, the benefits of wisdom are potentially greater, too, because we have the means at hand to *make* the good life, right here and now, rather than just to go on contemplating it in Plato's heaven.

[9] The question "What should we do?" is thus no idle one but challenges each one of us. That, I think, is the principal moral implication of our new world. It is what all the shouting is about in the mounting concern about the relations of science and public policy, and about the impact of technology on society. Our almost total mastery of the physical world entails a challenge to the public intelligence of a degree heretofore unknown in history.

[10] But how do we come to grips with the challenge? How do we pull together and learn to use the knowledge we already have, and in using it learn the other things we need to know? What do the implications of our great contemporary scientific and technical spurt forward add up to? I do not have the answers, but I should like to propose some hypotheses.

WHAT HAPPENS TO THE WORKER?

[11] My first hypothesis is that the time will come when machines will put most people permanently out of work. What will happen to people when there is no longer work for them to do? Consider the foreman in a steel plant. He brings thirty years' experience to one of the half-dozen really crucial jobs in the mill. At the critical point in the process, it is his trained eye that tells him the molten metal is ready to pour, and it is his well-developed sense of timing and steady hand that tip the cauldron synchronously with the processes that precede and follow. For this he is well paid, and can provide for his family perhaps better than the

average. For this, too, he is looked up to by his fellows. They seek him out as a friend. He has prestige at his work, status in the town, and the respect of his children. He belongs. He contributes. He is needed.

[12] Then you move in a machine that takes his job away, and does it better. What happens to this man? What happens to his many juniors at the mill whose aspiration was to an achievement like his? One of the pervasive characteristics of our civilization has been the identification of life's meaning with life's work. The evidence is strong in the problem of the aged: how do they fight the conviction that their life is done, that the world could do very well, perhaps better, without them? Are we heading toward a time when society will be burdened with a problem of the aged beginning in most cases at age 20, because there will no longer be work to enter upon, let alone retire from, at the age of 65?

[13] Among the suggestions for banishing this specter are two that do not impress me much. The first is essentially a cry of anguish. Stop automation! Stop making more and more complicated machines! What business have we going to the moon, or tampering with life and heredity? Life is difficult enough without going out of our way to make it more so.

[14] All the odds are against the success of that kind of solution. The technologies of the atom bomb, the automobile, the industrial revolution, gunpowder, all provoked social dislocations accompanied by similar demands that they be stopped. But there is clearly no stopping. Aristotle said a long time ago that "man by nature desires to know." He will probe and learn all that his curiosity leads him to and his brain makes possible, until he is dead. The cry of "stop" is the fear reaction I talked about earlier. It comes from those who have not yet recovered their nerve.

[15] A second suggestion, specifically aimed at the prospect of loss of work, is that we find better ways to employ leisure. There is a whole literature growing up on this theme, and I think it should be encouraged. Other things being equal, and given my own biases, it is better to read a good book than to watch television, or to play a Beethoven quartet than listen to the Beatles. But leisure activity, no matter how uplifting and educational, is not a substitute for work. The very concept loses meaning in the absence of the correlative concept of "work." No, I do not think that is the happiest solution.

[16] But then that may not be the problem either. My second hypothesis is that my first hypothesis is wrong. Machines might not in fact put a significant number of people out of work permanently. It might just be that machines will simply take over the kinds of work that people have done up to now, and that people will then be freed, not to become problems to themselves and to society, but to do entirely new kinds of work that have hardly been thought about seriously because there has not yet been a serious possibility that they could be done.

[17] It is often said, for example, that as work in agriculture and industry is progressively mechanized, job opportunities in the service sector of the economy will increase and absorb released manpower. I assume that production processes will not be mechanized except as machines prove more efficient than human labor. There should then follow a significant increment in wealth, which, adequately distributed, could buy more of the services already available, from babysitting to education and government and from better waiters to art and religion. The structure of the work force might thus be altered significantly.

[18] Even more exciting is the possibility that the nature of service itself might be altered. I suggest a trivial, perhaps ridiculous example. Doubled police forces and quadrupled sanitation forces could give us, for the first time, really safe and really clean cities. Put 20,000 people into the streets every day to catch the cigarette butts before they even hit the ground, and you might have a clean city.

[19] Inherently, there is nothing ridiculous about a clean city. If the suggestion makes one smile, it is rather because such use of people, by today's standards, is ridiculously uneconomical. People are more efficiently employed to produce the goods we consume. But if machines will be doing most of that, then maybe people can be employed to produce the services, such as street-cleaning or teaching, that we would like to have more of if we could.

[20] Consider another example. One of the genuinely new and exciting ideas of the Kennedy Administration, I think, was the Peace Corps, the idea that young Americans in large numbers could, by example, help less favored peoples to help themselves. Imagine a Peace Corps 50,000,000 strong in Africa, released by machines to pour the kind of sweat that machines will never pour. This is the kind of service that can anticipate, peacefully and constructively, the ugly danger that the have-nots of the world will resort to uncontrollable violence as the gap between their expectations and reality widens. It is also the kind of service that might provide to individuals a satisfaction and a goal to life undreamed of by today's assembly-line worker in Detroit, however fully employed. From such a perspective, the new machines and the new technologies may spell, not the end of the world, but the beginning of a new one. We might begin to see, for the first time, what God meant when he said that the meek shall inherit the earth.

[21] There has been a long tradition that divides work into creative and intellectual for the few, and routine and mechanical for the many. There has grown up around that distinction (although we are told that that was not yet true in the time of the Greeks) a moral judgment: that the first kind of work was for superior people, and the second for inferior people. There then occurred, I think, one of those curious inversions of

history whereby an effect is later seen as cause. The reason the majority of people did routine and mechanical work, we were told was that that was the only kind of work they were fit to do, because they were inferior.

[22] It seems to me much more plausible, however, that the reason the majority of people have done routine and mechanical work is that there has been a very great deal of routine and mechanical work to do. I am not denying that some people are more gifted than other people. But it seems to me that we have not yet been motivated to inquire sufficiently into how many people of what kinds can do what, because there has up to now been so much routine and mechanical work to do that most people have necessarily been impressed into doing it.

[23] I suggest also that it is this same imperative of a great deal of routine and mechanical work to do that has led to the ivory-tower syndrome on the part of creative, intellectual workers. I doubt that artists and scientists have typically detached themselves from the world because they liked it that way. The cry for application of knowledge, at least since Francis Bacon, and the essential need of the artist to communicate preclude that view. I suspect, rather, that there may be another reversal of cause and effect here: that the ivory tower may be symptomatic of a world by necessity too preoccupied with the routine and mechanical to generate a real demand for the product of the artist and the scholar. It is no accident that art and philosophy were the exclusive province of the freemen, not the slaves, in Greece, or that science, even in our own age, has for most of its history been indulged in by the gifted amateur who was rich in fact or by philanthropy.

NEW DEMAND FOR SCHOLARS AND ARTISTS

[24] And now machines will do the routine and mechanical work of the world. Very large numbers of human resources will be released and available for services to mankind beyond those required for subsistence. The need to discover the nature of this new kind of work, to plan it and to do it, just might overcome the traditional gap between the creative and the routine. The many will be challenged, as they have not been before, to rise to their maximum potentialities. The few—the scholars and the artists—may find that there is a new demand for them in the world, to muster, to shape, and to guide this new force. The two historical judgments that I have criticized as inverted, in other words, might become true from now on in: work could finally become the measure of man, and efficacy the measure of ideas.

[25] What will be the nature of this new work? What goals will it serve? How will it be done? What talents will be needed for it? I do not know the answers to these questions, either. Each, I think, provides an opportunity for imaginative inquiry still to be done. I have undertaken only to state a hypothesis, or, more accurately, to indicate a hunch that

precedes hypothesis. My hunch is that man may have finally expiated his original sin, and might now aspire to bliss. I think also that my hunch may hang together historically. Original sin was invented after, and to account for, the failure of nerve. With the recovery of nerve, we do not need the concept any more, and the advance of technology frees us from the drudgery it has imposed.

[26] But freedom from drudgery, as I have suggested, entails a commitment to wisdom. Consider, as one example, the staggering implications for education. Education (in foot-high letters on public billboards) has become a panacean word. But education for what? For whom? What kind of education? And when? There is very little small print on the billboards to answer those questions.

[27] The response of education to the new world of science and technology up to now has taken the form of five principal proposals or goals: 1) more education for more people, 2) educational booster shots in some form of continuing adult education, 3) increased production of scientists and engineers, 4) expanded vocational training, and 5) mid-career refresher training or retraining for a different specialty.

[28] It is hard to quarrel with more education, or with continuing education. With respect to the other three goals, however, one can raise the question "For how long?" To be sure, we need more scientists and engineers than we have now, but we already hear warnings that the demand will level off, and it is perhaps not too early to start thinking about a massive effort in the social sciences and the humanities.

[29] Similarly with vocational education. Training in a trade is desirable and useful. But in which trade? Certainly not in those doomed to extinction in the next 10 to 20 years. The informal experience of the young people who have recently been crusading in Mississippi and Alabama might prove a much more relevant vocational education for the future that lies ahead of us.

[30] Today's best educational judgments, in other words, might turn into tomorrow's worst mistakes, because they depend on forecasting successfully the shape of what is coming. Of course, the judgments must still be made today, despite the risk, despite the increased uncertainties of a world that changes shape rapidly and radically. This is a measure of the difficulty of the modern educator's task. Yet in this very change may lie a relative certainty, with a particular further implication for the job of education. I add a word about that.

WHAT IS REALITY?

[31] There were two ancient Greek philosophers, long before even Socrates haunted the streets of Athens, who had diametrically opposed views about reality. There was Parmenides, who argued that all change is illusory, transitory, imperfect, unreal. And later there was Heraclitus,

who saw reality as a flowing river, apparently the same but never the same, to whom all was constant flux and change, and who dismissed the permanent as unreal, as evidence of human imperfection, as a distortion of reality.

[32] I go back to those ancient thinkers, because each gave his name to a major and persistent theme in Western intellectual history. Parmenides, the apostle of the eternal, has had his emulators in Christian theology, in romantic idealism, and in 20th-century mathematics and logic. The followers of Heraclitus, who saw the world as flux, include the medieval nominalists, the 19th-century evolutionary philosophers, and today's existentialists.

[33] Are we Parmenidians or Heracliteans? In our social attitudes, we certainly lean to Parmenides. In our concept of work, the real is the career that holds together, makes sense, and lasts a lifetime. If a man changes jobs too often, we consider him a drifter, or, if we like him, we say he has not yet found his proper work. We see the change as unnatural, unreal, unwanted, and feel much more comfortable with the permanent, the stable.

[34] Similarly with our social institutions. Democracy, capitalism, socialism, the organized faiths—these are the real, the cherished, and any change is transitional, accidental, to be avoided, or dealt with as quickly as possible, to return to the stable, the familiar, the true.

[35] The evidence is becoming compelling that we are going to have to change these attitudes and comfortable habits. Careers are increasingly becoming shorter-lived than people. The complexities of national existence lead to an increasing and inevitable mixing-up of the public and the private. States' rights, that honored mark of 18th-century federalism, has become a slogan of those who would have us return to the 18th-century. The profit motive is being introduced into the Soviet economy, and the world's religions are beginning to talk to each other. All our familiar institutions, in other words, are changing so rapidly and so constantly that the change is becoming more familiar now than the institutions that are changing. The change is the new reality. We are entering an era that might aptly be called Social Heracliteanism.

[36] The challenge to education is indeed staggering. Teachers who have been brought up to cherish the stable must take the children of parents who have been brought up to cherish the stable, and try to teach them that the stable, the unchanging, is unreal, constraining, a false goal, and that they will survive in an age of change to the degree that they become familiar with change, feel comfortable with it, understand it, master and control it.

[37] When that task is done, the recovery of nerve will be complete, because our new technical mastery will have been supplemented by the wisdom necessary to harness it to human ends. John Dewey's dream will

have been realized. We will be the masters of our techniques instead of their slaves, and we might just become the first civilization since 500 B.C. to be able to look the Greeks in the face with pride, instead of just with wonder. I do not like to think of the alternative, which is that the people of a century from now will say of us: "Look at the trouble and woe they had with their technology, and look what ours has done for us."

COMMENT AND QUESTIONS

1. Explain clearly what Mesthene means by "recovery of nerve." What are the effects of this recovery, and what problems does it involve?
2. What is the meaning of the distinction in the second sentence of paragraph 5 between people as workers and people as people?
3. The author says, in paragraph 16, that his second hypothesis is that his first hypothesis is wrong; and he develops more fully and more emphatically the second hypothesis. What seem to be his reasons for including the first hypothesis and for giving it as much development as he does?
4. Comment on the examples of services in paragraphs 18–20. Are they well selected and well arranged for Mesthene's purposes? Explain.
5. State in your own words the reversals of cause and effect the author discusses in paragraphs 21–23. Does his reasoning seem to you to be clear and sound? Explain.
6. To what extent do you agree with Mesthene's ideas, in paragraphs 33–35, that we tend to be Parmenidians in our attitudes and that we need to change those attitudes?
7. Summarize the possible gains Mesthene sees for the individual and for society if his second hypothesis proves true. What are the principal problems to be solved before the gains can be realized?
8. Examine paragraph 37. In what ways is it an effective ending?
9. If you have read the article by Elting E. Morison, compare and contrast Morison's and Mesthene's views of the future.

[45]   Norman Cousins: The Computer and the Poet

NORMAN COUSINS (1912–   ) is the editor of the *Saturday Review* and author of many works, including *Modern Man Is Obsolete, Who Speaks for Man?, The Last Defense in a Nuclear Age,* and *In Place of Folly*. "The Computer and the Poet" is an editorial from the *Saturday Review* of July 23, 1966.

[1] The essential problem of man in a computerized age remains the same as it has always been. That problem is not solely how to be more productive, more comfortable, more content, but how to be more sensitive, more sensible, more proportionate, more alive. The computer makes possible a phenomenal leap in human proficiency; it demolishes the fences around the practical and even the theoretical intelligence. But the question persists and indeed grows whether the computer will make it easier or harder for human beings to know who they really are, to identify their real problems, to respond more fully to beauty, to place adequate value on life, and to make their world safer than it now is.

[2] Electronic brains can reduce the profusion of dead ends involved in vital research. But they can't eliminate the foolishness and decay that come from the unexamined life. Nor do they connect a man to the things he has to be connected to—the reality of pain in others; the possibilities of creative growth in himself; the memory of the race; and the rights of the next generation.

[3] The reason these matters are important in a computerized age is that there may be a tendency to mistake data for wisdom, just as there has always been a tendency to confuse logic with values, and intelligence with insight. Unobstructed access to facts can produce unlimited good only if it is matched by the desire and ability to find out what they mean and where they would lead.

[4] Facts are terrible things if left sprawling and unattended. They are too easily regarded as evaluated certainties rather than as the rawest of raw materials crying to be processed into the texture of logic. It requires a very unusual mind, Whitehead said, to undertake the analysis of a fact. The computer can provide a correct number, but it may be an irrelevant number until judgment is pronounced.

[5] To the extent, then, that man fails to make the distinction between the intermediate operations of electronic intelligence and the ultimate responsibilities of human decision and conscience, the computer could prove a digression. It could obscure man's awareness of the need to come to terms with himself. It may foster the illusion that he is asking fundamental questions when actually he is asking only functional ones. It may be regarded as a substitute for intelligence instead of an extension of it. It may promote undue confidence in concrete answers. "If we begin with certainties," Bacon said, "we shall end in doubts; but if we begin with doubts, and we are patient with them, we shall end in certainties."

[6] The computer knows how to vanquish error, but before we lose ourselves in celebration of the victory, we might reflect on the great advances in the human situation that have come about because men were challenged by error and would not stop thinking and probing until they found better approaches for dealing with it. "Give me a good fruitful error, full of seeds, bursting with its own corrections," Ferris Greenslet wrote. "You can keep your sterile truth for yourself."

[7] The biggest single need in computer technology is not for improved circuitry, or enlarged capacity, or prolonged memory, or miniaturized containers, but for better questions and better use of the answers. Without taking anything away from the technicians, we think it might be fruitful to effect some sort of junction between the computer technologist and the poet. A genuine purpose may be served by turning loose the wonders of the creative imagination on the kinds of problems being put to electronic tubes and transistors. The company of poets may enable the men who tend the machines to see a larger panorama of possibilities than technology alone may inspire.

[8] A poet, said Aristotle, has the advantage of expressing the universal; the specialist expresses only the particular. The poet, moreover, can remind us that man's greatest energy comes not from his dynamos but from his dreams. The notion of where a man ought to be instead of where he is; the liberation from cramped prospects; the intimations of immortality through art—all these proceed naturally out of dreams. But the quality of a man's dreams can only be a reflection of his subconscious. What he puts into his subconscious, therefore, is quite literally the most important nourishment in the world.

[9] Nothing really happens to a man except as it is registered in the subconscious. This is where event and feeling become memory and where the proof of life is stored. The poet—and we use the term to include all those who have respect for and speak to the human spirit—can help to supply the subconscious with material to enhance its sensitivity, thus safeguarding it. The poet, too, can help to keep man from making himself over in the image of his electronic marvels. For the

danger is not so much that man will be controlled by the computer as that he may imitate it.

[10] The poet reminds men of their uniqueness. It is not necessary to possess the ultimate definition of this uniqueness. Even to speculate on it is a gain.

—≼ COMMENT AND QUESTIONS ≽—

1. Parallel structures and sentences built on patterns of contrast are marked traits of style in this well-written essay. Point out examples that seem to you effective.
2. The first two paragraphs are concerned with human problems and needs that the author says are important. What are his reasons for believing that the computer may make it harder rather than easier for men to solve their problems and fulfill their needs? To what extent do you agree, first with Cousins' statement of values, and second with his ideas about computer technology as a possible hindrance to realizing the values?
3. In paragraph 5 Cousins speaks of man's illusion "that he is asking fundamental questions when actually he is asking only functional ones"; and in paragraph 7 the author says that we need "better questions and better use of the answers." What examples can you give to illustrate the difference between functional and fundamental questions? Does it seem to you possible for a computer to answer fundamental questions? Explain.
4. Do you think that Cousins is suggesting that the poet compose the questions given to the computer, or is his meaning different? Explain.
5. What is the meaning of the statement at the end of paragraph 9 concerning the danger of man imitating the computer? If man were to imitate the computer, what might be his attitudes toward himself and toward other men?
6. Cousins says in his last paragraph that it is not necessary to have "the ultimate definition" of man's uniqueness. What are some of the qualities of this uniqueness that he apparently sees and values?
7. What other writers whom you have read in this section, "Science and the Modern World," would agree wholly or in part with Cousins' ideas?

[46]   *Walter Sullivan*: What If We Succeed?

WALTER SULLIVAN (1918–   ) is Science Editor of the *New York Times* and author of *White Land of Adventure, Quest for a Continent,* and *Assault on the Unknown.* The following selection is the last chapter of *We Are Not Alone: The Search for Intelligent Life on Other Worlds,* published in 1964. In preceding chapters, Sullivan has explored the history of man's attempts to communicate with other worlds and the reasons for the belief of many scientists that intelligent life exists on other planets.

[1] On the night of October 30, 1938, there were manifestions of panic in widely scattered parts of the United States. They began shortly after Orson Welles, the actor and producer, sat in front of a microphone in the New York studios of the Columbia Broadcasting System to introduce an adaptation of *The War of the Worlds,* written in 1898 by H. G. Wells. Orson Welles told his nationwide audience how, in recent years, people on earth had gone about their daily lives in complacence: "Yet across an immense ethereal gulf, minds that are to our minds as ours are to the beasts in the jungle, intellects vast, cool and unsympathetic regarded this earth with envious eyes and slowly and surely drew their plans against us...."

[2] The dramatization that followed, consisting of simulated news bulletins, interviews and sometimes fearful sound effects, was so realistic that thousands believed Martians had, in fact, landed in New Jersey—hideous creatures that slew all opposing them with a sinister "heat-ray." People rushed into the streets only partially clothed or struck out aimlessly across open country. Cars raced wildly through crowded cities.

[3] Is this a hint of what might happen if we did, in fact, make contact with a superior civilization? Possibly so, according to a report submitted to the Federal government in 1960. For so dramatic an effect, the encounter would presumably have to be physical, but even radio contact would lead to profound upheavals, the report said. The document was a by-product of the historic action taken by Congress on the heels of the first Sputniks in establishing an agency for the exploration of space. The National Aeronautics and Space Act of July 29, 1958, called for "long-range studies" of the benefits and problems to be expected from space activities. Pursuant to this act, NASA set up a Committee on Long-Range

Studies and awarded a study contract to the Brookings Institution. More than 200 specialists were interviewed by a team led by Donald N. Michael, a social psychologist who later became Director of the Peace Research Institute in Washington. Pertinent portions of the resulting report were reviewed by such figures as Lloyd V. Berkner, head of the Space Science Board, Caryl P. Haskins, President of the Carnegie Institution of Washington, James R. Killian, Chairman of the Corporation of M.I.T., Oscar Schachter, Director of the General Legal Division of the United Nations, and Margaret Mead, the anthropologist.

[4] The document was submitted to NASA only a few months after Project Ozma's attempt to intercept signals from two nearby stars, and much in the minds of those who drafted it was the question of what would happen if we discovered another, far more advanced civilization. The report did not rule out the possibility of direct contact, such as the one so vividly dramatized by Orson Welles, and it suggested that artifacts left by explorers from another world "might possibly be discovered through our space activities on the Moon, Mars, or Venus." Nevertheless, it said, if intelligent life is discovered beyond the earth during the next twenty years, it most probably will be in a distant solar system and manifest itself by radio. Such circumstances, it added, would not necessarily rule out revolutionary effects:

Anthropological files [the report said] contain many examples of societies, sure of their place in the universe, which have disintegrated when they have had to associate with previously unfamiliar societies espousing different ideas and different life ways; others that survived such an experience usually did so by paying the price of changes in values and attitudes and behavior.

Since intelligent life might be discovered at any time via the radio telescope research presently under way, and since the consequences of such a discovery are presently unpredictable because of our limited knowledge of behavior under even an approximation of such dramatic circumstances, two research areas can be recommended:

1. Continuing studies to determine emotional and intellectual understanding and attitudes—and successive alterations of them if any—regarding the possibility and consequences of discovering intelligent extraterrestrial life.

2. Historical and empirical studies of the behavior of peoples and their leaders when confronted with dramatic and unfamiliar events or social pressures. . . .

[5] Such studies, the report continued, should consider public reactions to past hoaxes, "flying saucer" episodes and incidents like the Martian invasion broadcast. They should explore how to release the news of an encounter to the public—or withhold it, if this is deemed advisable. The influence on international relations might be revolutionary, the report concluded, for the discovery of alien beings "might lead to a greater unity

of men on earth, based on the 'oneness' of man or on the age-old assumption that any stranger is threatening."

[6] Much would depend, of course, on the nature of the contact and the content of any message received. Man is so completely accustomed to regarding himself as supreme that to discover he is no more an intellectual match for beings elsewhere than our dogs are for us would be a shattering revelation. Carl Gustav Jung, the disciple of Freud who later went his own psychological way, has said of a direct confrontation with such creatures: The "reins would be torn from our hands and we would, as a tearful old medicine man once said to me, find ourselves 'without dreams,' that is, we would find our intellectual and spiritual aspirations so outmoded as to leave us completely paralyzed."

[7] There has been some debate recently in scientific circles as to whether our new acquaintances would, in fact, be "nice people" or the monstrous villains depicted by Orson Welles. Much of the population has been conditioned by science-fiction tales of evil genius at work among the stars, of death rays and battles between galaxies. This may, in part, have accounted for the reaction to the Welles broadcast. Some of those concerned with the search for life in other worlds have sought to counter this attitude.

[8] Thus Philip Morrison, in one of his lectures, questioned whether any civilization with a superior technology would wish to do harm to one that has just entered the community of intelligence. If he were looking through a microscope, he said, and saw a group of bacteria spell out, like a college band, "Please do not put iodine on this plate. We want to talk to you," his first inclination, he said, would certainly not be to rush the bacteria into a sterilizer. He doubted that advanced societies "crush out any competitive form of intelligence, especially when there is clearly no danger."

[9] Ronald Bracewell, in his lecture at the University of Sydney, asked whether beings in another world could covet our gold or other rare substances. Do they want us as cattle or as slaves? He replied by pointing out the literally astronomical cost of transport between solar systems. Any civilization able to cover interstellar distances would hardly need us for food or raw material, which they could far more easily synthesize at home. "The most interesting item to be transferred from star to star," he said, "is information, and this can be done by radio."

[10] Edward Purcell, who forcefully argued the impracticality of travel between solar systems, said the relations between such widely separated civilizations must be "utterly benign." Maybe journeys over such distances could be made "by magic," he added, "but you can't get there by physics."

[11] Arthur C. Clarke, one of the most knowledgeable of all science-fiction writers, has pointed out the difficulty of administering a galactic

empire, be it benign or tyrannical, because the distances would make communications so very slow. Radio messages to our nearest neighbors would take a decade or more.

[12] Nevertheless there has been at least one dissent in the scientific community and its author, as might be expected, is among those who refuse to dismiss the possibility of travel between solar systems, particularly if one does not insist that the trip be completed within a human lifetime. The dissenter was Freeman Dyson, the brilliant young physicist at the Institute for Advanced Study in Princeton. In a letter to *Scientific American* in the spring of 1964 he questioned whether one was justified in assuming that the distant creatures with whom we may converse are moral by our standards.

[13] "Intelligence may indeed be a benign influence," he said, "creating isolated groups of philosopher-kings far apart in the heavens and enabling them to share at leisure their accumulated wisdom." On the other hand, he added, "intelligence may be a cancer of purposeless technological exploitation, sweeping across a galaxy as irresistibly as it has swept across our own planet." Assuming interstellar travel at moderate speeds, he said, "the technological cancer could spread over a whole galaxy in a few million years, a time very short compared with the life of a planet."

[14] What our detectors will pick up is a technological civilization, he argued, but it will not necessarily be intelligent, in the pure sense of the word. In fact, he continued, it may even be that the society we are inherently likely to detect is more probably "a technology run wild, insane or cancerously spreading than a technology firmly under control and supporting the rational needs of a superior intelligence." It is possible that a "truly intelligent" society might no longer feel the need of, or be interested in, technology. "Our business as scientists is to search the universe and find out what is there. What is there may conform to our moral sense or it may not. . . . It is just as unscientific to impute to remote intelligences wisdom and serenity as it is to impute to them irrational and murderous impulses. We must be prepared for either possibility and conduct our searches accordingly."

[15] This point of view is reflected in the questions of those who ask: Should we reply, if we hear someone calling? Since message travel times are long, a hasty reply would be uncalled for, but it seems to this writer hard to believe that we would hear from a race of villains or a civilization run amok. As noted in the chapter entitled "Is There Intelligent Life on Earth?" an achievement of lasting peace and stability seems to be an important element in qualifying for membership in the interstellar community. While Dyson is understandably dismayed at what technology and population growth are doing to the face of our planet, a society that could not bring such trends under control would probably suffer the disintegration envisioned by Fred Hoyle.

[16] In fact, the achievement of great stability and serenity would seem a prerequisite for a society willing to make the expensive and enormously prolonged effort required to contact another world.

[17] What, indeed, do we know about the roots of evil—of greed, aggressiveness and treachery? On earth they are clearly manifestations of a complex society that has not reached stability. Animals, as a rule, are aggressive only when necessary. The well-fed lion lies near the waterhole while his traditional victims, sensing his satiety, quench their thirst in peace. Man's inherent aggressiveness has made wars possible—though it does not necessarily initiate wars—but it would appear that if man is to survive, this aspect of his personality will have to be controlled—an achievement that in the past few years has seemed increasingly possible.

[18] Because we have information on only one form of intelligent, technological life we tend to think of such life elsewhere as resembling ourselves more closely than is probably justified. The creatures in which we are interested, besides having minds, must be able to move about and to build things. That is, they must have something comparable to hands and feet. They must have senses, such as sight, touch and hearing, although the senses that evolve on any given planet will be determined by the environment. For example, it may be that, for various reasons, vision in the infrared part of the spectrum will be more useful than sight in the wavelengths visible to human eyes. Creatures fulfilling such requirements might bear little resemblance to man. As Philip Morrison has put it, they may be "blue spheres with twelve tentacles." They may be as big as a mountain or as small as a mouse, although the amount of food available would set a limit on largeness and the fixed sizes of molecules must limit the extent to which the size of a complex brain can be compressed. Life spans in some worlds might be extremely great. The cells of our bodies (with a few exceptions, such as brain cells) are constantly replenishing themselves. It would appear that, barring accident or disease, this should continue indefinitely, but because of some subtle influence the replacement process is imperfect. This, the essence of aging, is now under intensive study. It is not inconceivable that it can be controlled. Progress in the transplantation of human organs and the manufacture of other body components (such as heart valves) is such that even the most sober medical men believe we may ultimately be able to extend lifetimes considerably. Lives measured in many centuries instead of barely one would make the slowness of interstellar signaling far more acceptable. Yet even life spans comparable to our own of today should not divert our interest in message exchanges. "Imagine," says Edward Purcell of Harvard, "that a reply to one of your messages was scheduled to be received forty years from now. What a legacy for your grandchildren."

[19] Otto Struve and others have said that the current awakening of mankind to the possible existence of intelligent life in other worlds is as

much a challenge to established ways of thought as was the Copernican revolution that displaced the earth from the center of the universe. The latter set in motion a religious and philosophical upheaval that only in recent decades has run its course. It will be recalled that Giordano Bruno, the Copernican protagonist, was burned at the stake and Martin Luther argued that, since Joshua, in the Bible, commanded the sun—not the earth—to stand still, the system of Copernicus must be false.

[20] By the mid-nineteenth century great changes had taken place. Father Angelo Secchi, the great Jesuit astronomer, was helping to lay the foundations of modern astrophysics—and worrying about the religious implications of the vast universe opening before him. Could it be, he asked, that God populated only one tiny speck in this cosmos with spiritual beings: ". . . It would seem absurd to find nothing but uninhabited deserts in these limitless regions," he wrote. "No! These worlds are bound to be populated by creatures capable of recognizing, honoring and loving their Creator."

[21] Both Protestant and Catholic theologians pursued this subject during the early decades of the twentieth century, many of them viewing it in terms of man's spiritual history as set forth in their dogma. It was proposed by Catholic authorities that beings in other worlds could be in a variety of "states."

[22] For example, they might be in a state of grace, such as that enjoyed by Adam and Eve before they succumbed to the serpent's temptation. They might be in the fallen state of mankind after the expulsion from Eden. They might have undergone these stages and been redeemed by some action of God. They might be in a "state of integral nature," midway between man and angel and immune to death; or they might have proved so evil that redemption was denied them. C. S. Lewis, the Anglican lay theologian, has proposed that the vast distances between solar systems may be a form of divine quarantine: "They prevent the spiritual infection of a fallen species from spreading"; they block it from playing the role of the serpent in the Garden of Eden. Father Daniel C. Raible of Brunnendale Seminary of the Society of the Precious Blood in Canton, Ohio, said in the Catholic weekly *America* that intelligent beings elsewhere "could be as different from us, physically, as an elephant is from a gnat." To be "human" in the theological sense they need only be "composites of spirit and matter." As God could create billions of galaxies, he reasoned, "so He could create billions of human races each unique in itself." To redeem such races, he said, God could take on any bodily form. "There is nothing at all repugnant in the idea of the same Divine Person taking on the nature of many human races. Conceivably, we may learn in heaven that there has been not one incarnation of God's son but many."

[23] The idea of God incarnate in some strange, if not grotesque, creature is to some Catholics unacceptable. Such a point of view was expressed

by Joseph A. Breig, a Catholic journalist, in a dialogue published in a 1960 issue of *America*. There can have been only one incarnation, one mother of God, one race "into which God has poured His image and likeness," he said.

[24] In reply Father L. C. McHugh, an associate editor of the magazine, wrote: "Does it not seem strange to say that His power, immensity, beauty and eternity are displayed with lavish generosity through unimaginable reaches of space and time, but that the knowledge and love which alone give meaning to all this splendor are confined to this tiny globe where self-conscious life began to flourish a few millennia ago?"

[25] Like the Catholics, the Protestants have been concerned with whether or not God could have taken on bodily form elsewhere. Paul Tillich, one of the foremost Protestant theologians, argues that there is no real reason why such incarnations could not have taken place: "Incarnation is unique for the special group in which it happens, but it is not unique in the sense that other singular incarnations for other unique worlds are excluded. . . . Man cannot claim to occupy the only possible place for Incarnation. . . . The manifestation of saving power in one place implies that saving power is operating in all places."

[26] Astronomy tells us that new worlds are constantly evolving and old ones are becoming uninhabitable. The lifetime of our own world is thus limited, he said, but this "leaves open other ways of divine self-manifestation before and after our historical continuum." Elsewhere he wrote, with characteristic boldness: "Our ignorance and our prejudice should not inhibit our thoughts from transcending our earth and our history and even our Christianity."

[27] The hint of Tillich that, though worlds come and go, spiritual life somewhere in the universe goes on forever has been carried further by John Macquarrie of the University of Glasgow, in lectures that he gave in 1957 at Union Theological Seminary in New York. He took his cue from the "steady state" theory proposed by Fred Hoyle, Hermann Bondi and Thomas Gold in which, although the universe is constantly expanding, there is continuous creation of new matter to fill the resulting voids. "It might well be the case," he said, "that the universe has produced and will continue to produce countless millions of . . . histories analogous to human history." The creation would be cyclical, in that it produces "the same kind of thing over and again in endless variations.

[28] "To attempt to draw ultimate conclusions about God and the universe from a few episodes of the history which has been enacted on this planet," he continued, "would seem to be a most hazardous if not impossible proceeding."

[29] Long before Project Ozma the British mathematician and physicist Edward A. Milne proposed that only one incarnation—that of Jesus—was necessary, because, when news of it reached other worlds via radio, they

too would be saved. This was challenged by E. L. Mascall, University Lecturer in the Philosophy of Religion at Oxford, who said redemption was, in effect, not exportable. Like a number of other theologians who have taken part in this dialogue, he cited the argument of Saint Thomas Aquinas in the thirteenth century that the Incarnation could have taken one of several forms: instead of God the Son appearing on earth, he said, it might have been God the Father or God the Holy Ghost. He reasoned that none of these alternatives was ruled out on theological grounds. If so, today's scholars argue, why could there not also be incarnations elsewhere?

[30] At the conclusion of this analysis, Mascall was almost apologetic for discussing such hypothetical problems: "Theological principles tend to become torpid for lack of exercise," he said, "and there is much to be said for giving them now and then a scamper in a field where the paths are few and the boundaries undefined; they do their day-to-day work all the better for an occasional outing in the country."

[31] Actually, such "outings" have been taken by churchmen as sober as William Ralph Inge, Dean of St. Paul's Cathedral in London and known as "the gloomy dean" for his criticism of modern life. Like Father Secchi, he considered it intolerably presumptuous to believe that spiritual life exists only on this one planet. In a series of lectures given at Lincoln's Inn Chapel in 1931–33 he discussed Plato's concept of a "Universal Soul," and its parallels with Christian views on the Holy Spirit. This, he said,

raises the question whether there is soul-life in all parts of the universe. I do not think we need follow Fechner in believing that every heavenly body has a soul of its own. [Gustav Theodor Fechner, the German experimental psychologist, preached a highly animistic philosophy.] But I would rather be a star-worshipper than believe with Hegel (if he was not merely speaking impatiently, which is likely enough) that the starry heavens have no more significance than a rash on the sky, or a swarm of flies. There may be, and no doubt are, an immense number of souls in the universe, and some of them may be nearer to the divine mind than we are.

[32] It is, perhaps, a sign of the times and of the convergence of Catholicism and Protestantism that theologians of both faiths have been moved by the discussion of the Incarnation in a poem, "Christ in the Universe," by the English turn-of-the-century poetess Alice Meynell:

> ... No planet knows that this
> Our wayside planet, carrying land and wave,
> Love and life multiplied, and pain and bliss,
> Bears, as chief treasure, one forsaken grave. ...
>
>   But, in the eternities,
> Doubtless we shall compare together, hear
> A million alien Gospels, in what guise
> He trod the Pleiades, the Lyre, the Bear.

O, be prepared, my soul!
To read the inconceivable, to scan
The million forms of God those stars unroll
When, in our turn, we show them a Man.

[33] There are some faiths that have long preached the existence of many worlds, and so for them the shock of discovery would be lessened. Notable among these are the Buddhists and Mormons. The doctrine of the latter, the Church of Jesus Christ of Latter-Day Saints, is set forth in a series of revelations including one entitled the "Visions of Moses, as revealed to Joseph Smith the Prophet, in June, 1830." This tells how Moses "beheld many lands; and each land was called earth, and there were inhabitants on the face thereof." God told Moses:

And worlds without number have I created. . . . But only an account of this earth, and the inhabitants thereof, give I unto you. For behold, there are many worlds that have passed away by the word of my power. And there are many that now stand, and innumerable are they unto man; but all things are numbered unto me, for they are mine and I know them. . . . And as one earth shall pass away, and the heavens thereof even so shall another come; and there is no end to my works, neither to my words.

[34] This is strikingly similar to the "steady state" concept advanced by such men as Tillich and Macquarrie.

[35] The holy books of Buddhism, in their own glittering way, speak of many worlds. Such a book is the *Saddharma-Pundarika* or *Lotus of the True Law*. The Lord appears before an assembly of Bodhisattvas, or wise men, gathered from countless worlds and numbering eight times the grains of sand in the river Ganges. He tells them of many worlds, of golden people, jeweled trees, perfumed winds, wafting showers of petals. To illustrate the great number of worlds, he says:

Let there be the atoms of earth of fifty hundred thousand myriads of kotis of worlds; let there exist some man who takes one of those atoms of dust and then goes in an eastern direction fifty hundred thousand myriads of kotis of worlds further on, there to deposit that atom of dust; let in this manner the man carry away from all those worlds the whole mass of earth, and in the same manner, and by the same act as supposed, deposit all those atoms in an eastern direction. Now, would you think, young men of good family, that any one should be able to imagine, weigh, count, or determine [the number of] those worlds?

[36] While the Hindus believe in the transmigration of souls into other bodies or spiritual states, their various cosmologies do not envisage other inhabited worlds. As for the Confucians, their attention has been centered on earthly matters, in particular the behavior of man, even though some early Chinese scholars spoke of other earths with their own heavens shining upon them.

[37] About a dozen centuries ago Jewish thinkers conceived of the cosmos in somewhat of a steady-state manner. This is reflected in one of the commentaries on the Bible, prepared long ago by scholarly Rabbis and entitled the *Midrash Rabba*. It states that, "The Holy One, blessed be he, builds worlds and destroys them." However, according to contemporary Jewish theologians there has not been much speculation on the religious implications of extraterrestrial life.

[38] While the Brookings report to NASA dwells on the stresses and strains that would follow our making contact with another planet, it is staggering to consider the potential gains. Life in another world would presumably be at a far more advanced stage of evolution—technological, biological and medical—than ours. Knowledge of such a civilization, its discoveries, its techniques might enable us to leap-frog thousands or even millions of years ahead along the path before us. The agonies of premature death, congenital deformity, insanity, as well as such diseases of our society as prejudice, hatred and war, might be eliminated long before otherwise possible. No matter how much another world differed from our own in superficial ways, we might learn from its history enough to understand better our own: what, for example, brought about the great revolutions in the development of life on earth, the extinction of the giant reptiles, the emergence of the mammals and finally of man.

[39] Alastair Cameron, the astrophysicist, in the introduction to his anthology on interstellar communication, describes the possibility of life in other worlds as "currently the greatest question in scientific philosophy." Already, he says, we are admitting "that there may be millions of societies more advanced than ourselves in our galaxy alone. If we can now take the next step and communicate with some of these societies, then we can expect to obtain an enormous enrichment of all phases of our sciences and arts. Perhaps we shall also receive valuable lessons in the techniques of stable world government."

[40] One question that has been raised by J. Robert Oppenheimer, the nuclear physicist, is whether or not the science of another civilization would be comprehensible to us. He cites the "uncertainty principle" first recognized a generation ago, which says that we have a choice as to which traits of an atomic system we wish to study and measure, but in any single case we cannot measure them all. For example, in an experiment, we can determine the location of a particle but, if we do so, we cannot find out its speed. Similarly our science has concentrated on asking certain questions at the expense of others, although this is so woven into the fabric of our knowledge that we are generally unaware of it. In another world the basic questions may have been asked differently.

[41] Thus, while the period of Isaac Newton taught us that scientific truth in the most distant corner of the universe is identical to that in any laboratory on earth, yet in this century it has been shown that there are

various ways in which we can seek this truth, and science in one world may be seeking it by means different from those in another. This would make it more difficult to understand the work of our distant neighbors, but it seems unlikely that such understanding would be impossible.

[42] Most exciting of all the prospects are the spiritual and philosophical enrichment to be gained from such exchanges. Our world is undergoing revolutionary changes. Our ancestors enjoyed a serenity denied to most of us. As we devastate our planet with industrialization, with highways, housing and haste, the restoration of the soul that comes from contemplating nature unmarred by human activity becomes more and more inaccessible. Furthermore, through our material achievements, we are threatened by what the French call "embourgeoisement"—domination of the world by bourgeois mediocrity, conformity and comfort-seeking.

[43] The world desperately needs a global adventure to rekindle the flame that burned so intently during the Renaissance, when new worlds were being discovered on our own planet and in the realms of science. Within a generation or less we will vicariously tread the moon and Mars, but the possibility of ultimately "seeing" worlds in other solar systems, however remote, is an awesome prospect. "The soul of man was made to walk the skies," the English poet Edward Young wrote in the eighteenth century:

> how great,
> How glorious, then, appears the mind of man,
> When in it all the stars and planets roll!
> And what it seems, it is. Great objects make
> Great minds, enlarging as their views enlarge;
> Those still more godlike, as these more divine.

[44] The realization that life is probably universal, however thinly scattered through the universe, has meaning for all who contemplate the cosmos and the mortality of man. George Wald, Professor of Biochemistry at Harvard and a long-time participant in the search for an understanding of life's origins, has said:

Life has a status in the physical universe. It is part of the order of nature. It has a high place in that order, since it probably represents the most complex state of organization that matter has achieved in our universe. We on this planet have an especially proud place as men; for in us as men matter has begun to contemplate itself. . . .

[45] Harlow Shapley, the astronomer, has likewise found spiritual wealth in the new discoveries. They have contributed, he said, "to the unfolding of a magnificent universe":

To be a participant is in itself a glory. With our confreres on distant planets; with our fellow animals and plants of land, air, and sea; with the rocks and waters of all planetary crusts, and the photons and atoms that make up the stars —with all these we are associated in an existence and an evolution that inspires respect and deep reverence. We cannot escape humility. And as groping philosophers and scientists we are thankful for the mysteries that still lie beyond our grasp.

[46] The universality of life also has meaning with regard to the mortality, not only of individuals on earth, but of our planet itself. Bertrand Russell has pointed out that "all the labours of the ages, all the devotion, all the inspirations, all the noonday brightness of human genius, are destined to extinction in the vast death of the solar system." Yet it seems that life, in a sense, may be eternal. Perhaps true wisdom is a torch—one that we have not yet received, but that can be handed to us by a civilization late in its life and passed on by our own world as its time of extinction draws near. Thus, as our children and grandchildren offer some continuity to our personal lives, so our communion with cosmic manifestations of life would join us with a far more magnificent form of continuity.

[47] The Spanish-American philosopher George Santayana, in his preface to a volume of Spinoza's works, discussed a form of immortality enjoyed by those who commune with the eternal: "He who, while he lives, lives in the eternal, does not live longer for that reason. Duration has merely dropped from his view; he is not aware of or anxious about it; and death, without losing its reality, has lost its sting. The sublimation of his interest rescues him, so far as it goes, from the mortality which he accepts and surveys."

[48] The universe that lies about us, visible only in the privacy, the intimacy of night, is incomprehensibly vast. Yet the conclusion that life exists across this vastness seems inescapable. We cannot yet be sure whether or not it lies within reach, but in any case we are a part of it all; we are not alone!

COMMENT AND QUESTIONS

1. This selection has a question-to-answer and cause–effect pattern: If we succeed in discovering intelligent extraterrestrial life, the author is asking, what will be the effects? What is the purpose of beginning the discussion with the account of Orson Welles' 1938 broadcast?
2. The author is informative and fair in presenting conflicting points of view and also skillful in emphasizing his own views. Examine the opinions presented in paragraphs 8–17 on the question of whether beings in another world would be "nice people" or villains. What is the logical and psychological order of presentation?

3. What is the function of paragraph 18—the speculations about what other forms of life might be like—in the development of the essay?
4. What are the principal religious and philosophical problems which arise from the possible existence of intelligent life in other worlds (paragraphs 19–32)? Does Sullivan appear, by selection and emphasis, to be slanting in favor of one theory or attitude?
5. Why are Catholic and Protestant theologians more concerned than members of other faiths about the religious implications of extraterrestrial life?
6. The last section of Sullivan's book (paragraphs 38–48) is devoted to the potential gains of our making contact with other planets. What kinds of gains does he foresee?
7. What is the purpose of including the question raised by Oppenheimer (paragraphs 40–41), and what is the reason for placing it here instead of in paragraph 38 or near the end of the selection?
8. What criticisms of society in our world does Sullivan make in the course of the selection? How are they related to his central idea of the possibilities inherent in communication with other worlds?

CURRENT PROBLEMS
AND ATTITUDES

[47] *Lewis Mumford*: The American Way of Death

LEWIS MUMFORD (1895–) is an American critic and author of a number of well-known studies of American life. Among his books are *Sticks and Stones, The Brown Decades, Technics and Civilization, The Culture of Cities,* and *The City in History*. The following article, from *The New York Review of Books*, April 28, 1966, is a review of two books—*Unsafe at Any Speed: The Designed-in Dangers of the American Automobile* by Ralph Nader, and *Safety Last: An Indictment of the Auto Industry* by Jeffrey O'Connell and Arthur Myers. The article is also Mumford's own indictment of the motor car industry and of some values of American society.

[1] As so often happens, when the minds of many people have been silently brooding over the same subject, there has recently been an outbreak of books, articles, and legislative investigations, all devoted to assessing the mechanical defects, the bodily hazards, and the mounting social disadvantages of the motor car. The tone of this discussion has been critical, not to say sacrilegious. Some of the critics have dared to say that the Sacred Cow of the American Way of Life is overfed and bloated; that the daily milk she supplies is poisonous; that the pasturage this species requires wastes acres of land that could be used for more significant human purposes; and that the vast herds of sacred cows, al-

lowed to roam everywhere, like their Hindu counterparts, are trampling down the vegetation, depleting wild life, and turning both urban and rural areas into a single smudgy wasteland, whose fancy sociological name is Megalopolis.

[2] The priesthood of the Sacred Cow, very sensitive to the mildest heresy, now shows definite signs of alarm, alternating plaintive moos with savage bellows; for in their religion, the cult of the Sacred Cow is closely affiliated with an older object of worship, the Golden Calf. With justified trepidation, the priestly establishment feels religion itself (capitalized) is being challenged—that religion for whose evidences of power and glory the American people, with eyes devoutly closed, are prepared to sacrifice some 45,000 lives every year, and to maim, often irreparably, more than a million and a half more. Only war can claim so many premature deaths; for the death rate from motor cars is greater than the combined death rate from falls, burnings, drownings, railroads, firearms, and poisonous gases, plus some two thousand other deaths from unidentifiable causes. And though only roughly half as many Americans were killed outright by autos in the last four-year period as were killed in our armed forces during a similar term in the Second World War, nearly three times as many were injured.

[3] The current uprising against the miscarriage of the horseless carriage has long been brewing; John Keats's *The Insolent Chariots* broke the painful silence as far back as 1958. Only childish petulance on the part of the car manufacturers and their allies makes them attribute this spreading dissatisfaction with their product to the outspoken criticisms of a few mischievous critics, since the latter, till now a sorry few, have had none of the auto industry's facilities for commanding public attention and suppressing debate. The roots of the current revolt spread over a wide area, and they go much deeper than even the most impassioned advocates of safer motor car design yet realize.

[4] If the temple of the Sacred Cow is crumbling, it is because the whole mode of existence for which it is the prime mover has become antagonistic to the genuine human needs it was once supposed to serve and enhance. The fact is that the great American dream of a nation on wheels, which began with the covered wagon, has come to a dreary terminus. The very success of the auto industry in fulfilling the mechanical conditions for that dream has turned it, ironically, into a nightmare. An essential part of the American's delight over the auto was a happy leftover from pioneer days: the ingratiating idea of private freedom, in the sense of being able to go anywhere one willed, at any time one willed, at any speed one willed, up hill and down dale exploring the great open spaces, and at least getting away from the familiar habitat, the daily round, the mechanical grind. In what has belatedly been called "auto-

mobility," now that we are losing it, the personal "auto" was even more essential than the mechanical "mobility."

[5] Until about 1930, this dream bore more than a faint resemblance to actuality. Even such a fastidious soul as Henry James hailed the aristocratic joys of travel by motor car, which opened up the landscape and refreshed the spirit; so much so, that such usual interruptions as a leaky tire or a boggy road, if not too frequent, only added an extra spice to the adventure. Unfortunately, one of the conditions for enjoying this freedom was the existence of other possible modes of transportation, to handle mass demands, such as the wonderful transportation network of railroads, electric trolleys, and steamboats that once spanned the country and not merely took up much of the travel load but met different human needs at different speeds. By now people have fallen into the habit of characterizing the pre-motor-car era as the "horse-and-buggy" age, as if fast transportation were unknown till the auto came. Actually, electric trolleys, in New England and the Middle West, travelled over their own rights of ways at speeds of fifty miles an hour: I cherish a picture post-card, c. 1910, showing such a trolleycar, sensibly streamlined, that served Indianapolis. As with the mass movement into suburbia, which coincided with the mass production of motor cars, the desired freedom depended upon creating a more complex pattern of both movement and settlement, maintaining and improving a balanced transportation system, and maintaining and improving old cities. Had those two essential factors been understood and respected, the motor car could have made an invaluable contribution in creating a regional distribution of population. As in the Netherlands today, this would give the countryside the social advantages of the city, and multiply the number of cities with easy access to the countryside, without the compulsive and wasteful routines that have now been developed to cope with the uncontrolled explosion of motor cars.

[6] The huge success of the auto industry, not merely in multiplying the number of cars, but in utilizing its quasi-monopolistic resources and public monies to elbow out competing forms of locomotion and transportation, has turned the dream of automobility into the anxiety nightmare it has become today. From that nightmare Americans are now belatedly struggling to awake: the nightmare of the air becoming toxic with poisonous exhausts, including the highly lethal carbon monoxide; of the water supply, polluted with deadly lead from gasoline exhausts already half way to the danger point even in the Arctic wastes; the nightmare of diurnal mass commutation by car, along freeways where speed is compulsory, where the constant tensions demonstrably produce higher blood pressure, where a single car, stopping in time to avert an accident, may trigger a succession of more serious accidents in the tail-

gateing cars behind, even when traveling at the usual drugged crawl of rush hours.

[⁷] The motor car, it goes without saying, has brought many pleasant and desirable benefits; and certain by-products, like the beautiful Taconic Parkway in New York, remain permanent contributions to amenity and esthetic delight. But the whole picture has become increasingly dismal, and the most attractive feature of the American dream, freedom of movement and settlement, is turning into a system of choiceless compulsion. Just as old Henry Ford graciously said the consumer could have a car of any color he wanted as long as it was black, so motor travel is reaching a point where the driver can go anywhere he wants to, at a high speed, so long as he demands no change in either the environment or the destination. G. K. Chesterton's epigram "Nothing fails like success" may yet prove the epitaph of the motor industry. Though danger and death have played a part in the awakening, frustration and boredom have perhaps played a greater part—if only because courting danger has unfortunately proved one of the chronic modes of faking real life and finding momentary relief from its emptiness and its grim routines.

[⁸] The signs of this revolt are multiplying. Just a few years ago the motor car owners of the San Francisco Bay region voted $750 million to rebuild the fast public transportation system which the worshippers of the Sacred Cow had cleverly scrapped only twenty years before. But even more significantly, at the moment I write, news comes from San Francisco that "an overflow crowd of spectators cheered wildly at the City Hall here . . . as the Board of Supervisors voted down two proposed freeways on which the Federal Government was willing to put up two hundred and eighty million dollars." Even worse, these delirious iconoclasts are demanding that the Embarcadero Freeway, whose construction, half-way through, was brought to an end by public demand, should be torn down. Is it not indeed time that Detroit began to pay a little attention to the feedback? If the current disillusion with the motor car keeps on growing, auto industry investments may not remain so profitable, unless Detroit's current representative in the Defense Department manages to involve the country in even more extensive military aggressions than Vietnam.

[⁹] But to go back to the American dream. In the 1920s when a score of small corporations still gave the color of "free enterprise" to the auto industry, the automobile was a crude but relatively honest machine: clumsy in its transmission system and gear shift, capricious in its starting devices, unreliable in its braking capability, decidedly old-fashioned in its reliance upon the gas engine, but still, for all its adolescent gawkiness, a functional machine, designed for transportation and recreation. Around 1930, just when the "new capitalism" suddenly slumped down to earth, the motor car industry picked itself up by exchanging economy for style.

General Motors led the way here, and even Ford was compelled to follow. In the new hierarchy of values, recreation, reliability, safety, efficiency, economy all took a lower place. Style and speed were what counted. At this point, the automotive engineer took his orders from beauty specialists, whose job was to give the car a new look every year, in order to make last year's model unfashionable, that is, prematurely obsolete. The pioneer's dream wagon entered Madison Avenue's fairyland.

[10] Within the next two decades, the motor car became a status symbol, a religious icon, an erotic fetish: in short, "something out of this world," increasingly voluptuous and tumescent, as if on the verge of an orgasm. What words other than Madison Avenue's can adequately describe these exciting confections, glittering with chrome, pillowed in comfort, sleepy-soft to ride in, equipped with mirrors, cigarette lighters, radios, telephones, floor carpeting; liquor bars and tape-recorders are still optional. But in achieving these delights the designers so far turned their backs on the sordid realities of life as to increase the dangers through accidents by displaying jutting knobs, projecting, often knife-edged, instrument panels, murderous wings, confusing shift levers, soft suspension coils, undersized wheels, flimsy hardtops, utterly inadequate front and rear fenders, such broad, barge-like hoods as to give the driver minimum visibility in passing or parking, not to mention sun-reflecting chrome on windshield wipers and window frames to blind either the driver or an approaching car.

[11] In the process of styling the motor car for flashy sales appeal, the designers not only increased the dangers but gratuitously cancelled out good features that earlier cars had had. By lowering its center of gravity, they made the car impossible to enter except by acrobatic maneuvers—this in an age that boasts more elderly people and more arthritic limbs than ever before. Likewise they reduced the six-person capacity that had been happily achieved by eliminating the running board, to a four-person size. To speak plainly, the present motor car has been the result of a secret collaboration between the beautician and the mortician; and according to sales and accident statistics both have reason to be satisfied.

[12] With all the vast resources available for fundamental engineering research, the American motor car industry has not succeeded in producing a single original over-all design since 1930, except the Army Jeep, an honest job unfortunately built with no attention to passenger comfort. In neither shapes nor sizes has it pioneered any car as sensible as the small Volkswagen or the VW autobus. While many able engineers doubtless remain in the automotive industry, they might stop the fashion parade if they came up with a car as rugged as a Rover; and if they sought to

make even bolder departures, they would be rated as unemployable. But fortunately there are still honest men in the industry, even at the upper levels, such as a vice-president of Ford who publicly admitted as late as 1964 that "the automatic transmission"—adopted on a mass production basis in 1939—"was the last major improvement." This changeover from working machines to beauty salon dummies bears the hallmark of the affluent society and its expanding economy: compulsive spending and conspicuous waste. Unfortunately, the waste extends to human lives.

[13] The motor car industry's studious indifference to safety, as a possible deterrent to marketability, has at last produced a public reaction; and a still greater one will possibly follow. The damning evidence against motordom, particularly against General Motors, which dominates the field, has now been marshalled together by two lawyers, Ralph Nader, who was an adviser to the Senate sub-committee investigating automobile hazards, and Jeffrey O'Connell, a professor of law at the University of Illinois, and erstwhile associate Director of the Automobile Claims Study at the Harvard Law School. Much of this evidence comes from public spirited physicians, faced with the dire human consequences of engineering negligence; and it is to the activity of a handful of zealous legislators, like New York State Senator Edward J. Speno and United States Senators Ribicoff and Gaylord Nelson, that we are indebted for the public airing of the auto industry's shocking behavior.

[14] Now to assault the integrity of the great motor car producers is almost as audacious an enterprise as challenging the military judgment of the Pentagon; and incidentally, if we value our lives, quite as essential. The three great corporations—General Motors, Ford, and Chrysler—have a virtual monopoly of the American market as pace-setters and tastemakers, so that Studebaker, American Motors, and Willis-Overland had to follow their bad examples or go under. These three corporations do not stand alone, but reach out into a whole series of ancillary industries, beginning with steel, rubber, and oil, which depend upon them for their existence: Likewise these giant enterprises spread their devastating glamor through go-go Highway Departments heavy with Federal Subsidies, and through all the current media of publicity and advertisement; while by judicious grants for "research" the auto industry does not a little to seduce the judgment and sully the objectivity of the research institutes and universities that accept their dubiously philanthropic support.

[15] In the face of this massive vested interest, it says something for the tough original fabric of American life, and not least for the Fathers of the Constitution, that any open discussion of this seemingly all-powerful megamachine can still take place. Yet, despite many early warning signals, the motor industry was so deeply entrenched, so assured of

popular approval by its mounting profits that the present criticism of its aims and its methods has caught it off guard. If motordom knew how to silence this discussion, it would do so. General Motors has already demonstrated, with a stupidity that amounts to genius, that it is prepared to go to any lengths to prevent a rational public assessment of the changes that must be made in the American motor car to ensure its safety on the road. If General Motors' position were not so vulnerable and damnable they would not have hired detectives in the hope of digging up something unsavory about the character of the young lawyer who wrote *Unsafe at Any Speed*. By this action, they not merely made a public confession of guilt, but added an extra count to the indictment: attempted character assassination with intent to kill.

[16] The reaction of the motor industry to criticism of its product shows that those in control exhibit the same weaknesses that General Matthew Ridgway, that gallant and intelligent officer, has pointed out in relation to the Vietnam-Chinese policy of the Pentagon: Their judgments are devoid of human understanding. And no wonder; for they issue from the same type of mind, the computer mind, programmed strictly for money and power. But since the subject of the motor car's deficiencies has been opened up there is no telling where the assault will stop: Even computers may come in for a ribbing.

[17] Now it is both the strength and the weakness of the two sober books under review that they are mainly concerned with a narrow segment of the motor car problem: the defects and dangers of bad mechanical design. Their positive value lies in their bringing together various suggestions, from engineers and physicians, for reducing the accident rate from mechanical defects, and for lessening the injuries that come from normal human error and from incalculable, uncontrollable incidents, such as a bee suddenly stinging the driver. These are indeed life-and-death matters; and the authors' common approach to the subject is probably the shortest and quickest way to open up the much larger problems that must sooner or later be faced.

[18] On the whole matter of safety, the evidence that both books summarize is both appalling and incontrovertible. Every device for increasing the safety of the motor car has been resisted by the manufacturers, even when, like the safety door catch, it has been finally accepted; while the most dangerous part of the car in a serious accident, the chief cause of fatalities, is the steering assemblage, which still has serious defects besides the tight squeeze that most cars inflict upon the driver. What is worse than the mere failure to take urgent safety measures, is the fact that even when the automotive engineers have provided them at an early stage of the design, they have been removed, either to reduce

costs, give emphasis to some meretricious selling point, or just to eliminate any concern for danger from the prospective buyer's mind.

[19] What both books reveal is that the great motor car corporations, with all the insolence born of their supreme financial position in the economy, have not merely been careless about essential safety features in design: They have been criminally negligent, to the point of being homicidal. If these facts were not solidly established, no publisher in his senses would dare to publish these books; for every chapter would give ground for libel.

[20] Since the authors cover nearly the same ground, use substantially the same evidence, and exhibit similar well-justified indignation over the auto industry's refusal to mend its ways, so long as those ways are profitable, I hardly know how to advise the reader as to making a choice of them; though I should warn him that the data in either book are warranted, for a week or two, to make even the loveliest motor ride taste a little gritty, as with sand in the spinach. With regard to the main points about safety and air pollution, these books are in general agreement; though since Myers is a journalist, he does not make Nader's rhetorical error of using the Corvair case as the opening argument, since such an extreme example of bad engineering and obstinate contempt for evidence serves best as a clincher to a more widely based indictment. If all motor cars were as bad as Chevrolet's early Corvairs (1960–1963) no one with any instinct for self-preservation would dare to put his foot into any machine. Apart from this, *Unsafe at Any Speed* is as well-balanced as *Safety Last;* but the first has an Index without a list of cited sources, while the other has lists of references with every chapter but no index.

[21] Both books are driven by the evidence to point to the ultimate source of the motor car's structural defects, namely, that the cars are built with a single thought uppermost in the mind of the manufacturers: What will make them sell? And by what pinching and paring on essentials can more money be spent on styling and on advertising the non-essentials, those glossy features that will catch the eye, flatter the ego, coddle a neurosis—and open the purse.

[22] What these books demonstrate is that most American motor cars, even of the latest vintage, are still unfit vehicles for coping with the normal mischances of the road. When one considers the wide range of competence in licensed drivers, at different ages with different road experience, and the wide daily fluctuations in their general health, their eyesight, their inner tensions and pressures, it is obvious that the one factor that can and should be standardized and normalized rigorously, and raised to the highest degree of mechanical efficiency and structural safety, is the vehicle itself. That is the responsibility of the motor car

companies, not of the motorist. And if the fulfillment of that responsibility means that the profits of General Motors must be cut down from a billion and a half dollars a year to as little as a third of that amount, this is still no reason why this responsibility should not be imposed—by legislation if necessary—as a mandatory condition for earning any profits whatever.

[23] In stressing the need for introducing every possible mechanical dodge to make the car and its occupants less vulnerable to accidents, both books carry their stern indictments to various sensible conclusions; and I would not, by what follows, lessen the sting of their indictment, qualify their arguments, or minimize the value of their recommendations: quite the contrary. Most of the structural changes they suggest are desirable; and some, like seatbelts, are so cheap and simple that one wonders why so much effort had to go into making them standard equipment.

[24] As if to show their open contempt for the whole safety argument, the manufacturers have lately souped up their cars and their advertising slogans in order to appeal to the least safe group of motor car drivers, the newly licensed adolescents and the perpetual adolescents; and they have underlined their incitement to calculated recklessness by giving the cars appropriate names, Thunderbirds, Wildcats, Tempests, Furies, to emphasize hell-bent power and aggressiveness, while their allies in the oil industry, for good measure, offer to place a tiger in the tank. Speed is the pep pill that the motor car manufacturers are now cannily offering to adolescents like any dope peddler; and since power and speed are both regarded as absolute goods by the worshippers of the Sacred Cow, both as good in themselves and as the surest way to expand the industry and maximize the profits, why should anyone suppose that any other human considerations will modify their homicidal incitements? Speed, marijuana, heroin, and lysergic acid, are all attempts to use a scientific technology to overcome the existential nausea that the lopsided development of this very technology is the main cause of. Have Messrs. Nader, O'Connell, and Myers sufficiently reckoned with the vast irrational opposition that their sound and rational arguments will encounter? Will safety alone appeal to a public that, in the face of indisputable cancer statistics, now consumes more cigarettes than ever before?

[25] But suppose the rational argument for safer cars nevertheless wins out. I don't think that the writers of these books fully realize where their proposals will ultimately lead them unless they place these essential changes within a much wider framework. Both the desire for safety and for the enjoyment of the motor car demand a broader restatement of the whole problem. What is the place of the motor car in a rational scheme of transportation? By what system of control at source can we handle the motor car explosion, which is as badly in need of birth control as the population explosion? And what measures are needed to restore to both

transportation and travel—including air travel—some of the humanly desirable qualities that an exclusive concern with speed has already robbed them of?

[26] As to the enjoyment of the motor car, some of the safety devices that have been suggested, crash helmets, shoulder straps as well as a seat belt, padded leg protection, may have unfortunate results in opposite directions; either by reducing the pleasurable sense of freedom, or by prompting those who submit to these constraints to seek a compensatory release in aiming at higher speeds with greater impunity—despite the fact that this in turn will raise the accident rate. Nothing could be worse in the long run for the auto industry than to eliminate the very things that made the automobile, at the beginning, so attractive: the sense of freedom and variety that motor travel once gave. In the interests of speed, the highway designers have steadily been taking away the visual pleasure and environmental stimulus of a long journey, and every other "improvement" conspires to the same end. The same compulsory high speed, the same wide monotonous road, producing the same hypnotic drowsiness, the same air-conditioned climate in the car, the same Howard Johnsons, the same clutter of parking lots, the same motels. No matter how fast he travels or how far he goes, the motorist never actually leaves home: Indeed no effort is spared to eliminate variety in the landscape, and to make famous beauty spots by mountain or sea into as close a counterpart of the familiar shopping center as the original landscape will permit. In short, automobility has turned out to be the most static form of mobility that the mind of man has yet devised.

[27] If speed and safety were the only considerations, there is no reason why the auto industry, once it awakened from its self-induced narcosis, should not "go with" this movement and make greater profits than ever. For it is easy to foresee the theoretic ideal limit toward which both the automotive engineer and the highway engineer have begun to move: to make the surface of this planet no better for any form of organic life than the surface of the moon. To minimize road accidents, the highway engineers have already advocated cutting down all trees and telegraph poles within a hundred feet of each side of the road. But that is only a beginning. To provide maximum safety at high speed, the car will either have to be taken out of the motorist's hands and placed under automatic control, as M.I.T. researchers have, on purely mechanical assumptions, worked out; or else turned into an armored vehicle, windowless, completely padded on the inside, with front and rear vision provided on a screen, and a television set installed to amuse the non-drivers, just as if they were in a jet-plane. Along those lines, the motor car in a not-too-distant future would become a space capsule, a mobile prison, and the earth itself a featureless asteroid. Meanwhile, a further consolidation of the megamachine, with autos, jet planes, and rockets forming a single

industry; the profits of that ultimate combine should exceed the wildest expectations of even General Motors.

[28] But who wants speed at that price or safety at that price? one is tempted to ask. Buckminster Fuller and Jacques Ellul will doubtless answer, Everyone: or at all events, that is what is coming, whether anyone wants it or not. This answer is naive, but not disarming. For these backward assumptions which are really the leftovers of the Victorian avant garde are precisely what must now be questioned. Beyond the area of safety and freedom of movement lies the need for a conception of what constitutes a valid human life, and how much of life will be left if we go on ever more rapidly in the present direction. What has to be challenged is an economy that is based not on organic needs, historic experience, human aptitudes, ecological complexity and variety, but upon a system of empty abstractions: money, power, speed, quantity, progress, vanguardism, expansion. The overvaluation of these abstractions, taken as goods in themselves, has produced the unbalanced, purposeless, sick-making, and ultimately suicidal existence we now confront.

[29] In short, the crimes and the misdemeanors of the motor car manufacturers are significant, not because they are exceptional but because they are typical. These indictments of the auto industry pin down the same evils as were exposed by Rachel Carson's survey of the chemical industry's proliferation of pesticides and herbicides, and by Senator Kefauver's exposure of the pharmaceutical industry. The insolence of the Detroit chariotmakers and the masochistic submissiveness of the American consumer are symptoms of a larger disorder: a society that is no longer rooted in the complex realities of an organic and personal world; a society made in the image of machines, by machines, for machines; a society in which any form of delinquency or criminality may be practiced, from meretriciously designed motor cars or insufficiently tested wonder drugs to the wholesale distribution of narcotics and printed pornography, provided that the profits sufficiently justify their exploitation. If those remain the premises of the Great Society we shall never be out of danger —and never really alive.

---§{ COMMENT AND QUESTIONS }§---

1. How would you describe the tone of this essay?
2. In paragraphs 1 and 2, what does Mumford mean by the Sacred Cow and the Golden Calf, and what is the effect of his sustained figure of speech?

3. The first sentence of paragraph 4 is a statement of the author's thesis. To what "genuine human needs" is the mode of existence developed in the essay antagonistic?
4. Examine Mumford's use of charged language in, for example, paragraphs 10, 15, 19, and 24. Where else do you find examples of highly emotive words? Comment on the purpose and the effectiveness of the author's charged language.
5. Mumford uses a generally formal vocabulary and some very informal expressions; examples of the latter are *go-go, digging up, souped up, hell-bent, "go with."* The words listed below are part of the author's formal vocabulary. If they are unfamiliar to you, examine them in their context (paragraph references are in parentheses after each word) and see if the context establishes their meaning; if the meaning is still unclear, look up the word in your dictionary. Can you justify Mumford's mixture of levels of language?

quasi-monopolistic (6)	fetish (10)	meretricious (18)
diurnal (6)	gratuitously (11)	mandatory (22)
amenity (7)	ancillary (14)	narcosis (27)
iconoclasts (8)	sully (14)	ecological (28)

6. Various methods of development are used in this essay. What use is made of contrast and comparison? Of cause–effect development?
7. Although Mumford praises the two books which are the springboard for his essay, he says that they are concerned with a narrow segment of the motor car problem. Why, in his opinion, are safer cars not the whole answer to the problem? What larger problems must be faced?
8. The authors of the two books Mumford comments on apparently describe and give convincing evidence of the structural defects of modern cars, and then make recommendations for remedying the situation. Does Mumford follow a similar procedure of describing, giving evidence, and suggesting remedies for a situation? Explain.
9. In this essay, the author is probably less concerned with cars than with values. What values does he attack as false or unworthy? What values does he approve?
10. The title of this review is the title of a widely read book, a criticism of the funeral industry in the United States, written by Jessica Mitford and published in 1963. Why do you think Mumford chose to use this well-known title? Does *death* in the title of the review have implications beyond the death rate on the highways? If so, what direct or indirect references to other kinds of death can you find in the selection?

[48] James Baldwin: Notes of a Native Son

JAMES BALDWIN (1924–   ) is an American novelist and essayist, author of *Go Tell It on the Mountain, Giovanni's Room, Another Country, Notes of a Native Son,* and *The Fire Next Time.* The following essay is from the book of the same name, a collection of essays published in 1955.

[1] On the 29th of July, in 1943, my father died. On the same day, a few hours later, his last child was born. Over a month before this, while all our energies were concentrated in waiting for these events, there had been, in Detroit, one of the bloodiest race riots of the century. A few hours after my father's funeral, while he lay in state in the undertakers's chapel, a race riot broke out in Harlem. On the morning of the 3rd of August, we drove my father to the graveyard through a wilderness of smashed plate glass.

[2] The day of my father's funeral had also been my nineteenth birthday. As we drove him to the graveyard, the spoils of injustice, anarchy, discontent, and hatred were all round us. It seemed to me that God himself had devised, to mark my father's end, the most sustained and brutally dissonant of codas. And it seemed to me, too, that the violence which rose all about us as my father left the world had been devised as a corrective for the pride of his eldest son. I had declined to believe in that apocalypse which had been central to my father's vision; very well, life seemed to be saying, here is something that will certainly pass for an apocalypse until the real thing comes along. I had inclined to be contemptuous of my father for the conditions of his life, for the conditions of our lives. When his life had ended I began to wonder about that life and also, in a new way, to be apprehensive about my own.

[3] I had not known my father very well. We had got on badly, partly because we shared, in our different fashions, the vice of stubborn pride. When he was dead I realized that I had hardly ever spoken to him. When he had been dead a long time I began to wish I had. It seems to be typical of life in America, where opportunities, real and fancied, are thicker than anywhere else on the globe, that the second generation has no time to talk to the first. No one, including my father, seems to have known exactly how old he was, but his mother had been born during slavery. He was of the first generation of free men. He, along with

thousands of other Negroes, came North after 1919 and I was part of that generation which had never seen the landscape of what Negroes sometimes call the Old Country.

[4] He had been born in New Orleans and had been a quite young man there during the time that Louis Armstrong, a boy, was running errands for the dives and honky-tonks of what was always presented to me as one of the most wicked of cities—to this day, whenever I think of New Orleans, I also helplessly think of Sodom and Gomorrah. My father never mentioned Louis Armstrong, except to forbid us to play his records; but there was a picture of him on our wall for a long time. One of my father's strongwilled female relatives had placed it there and forbade my father to take it down. He never did, but he eventually maneuvered her out of the house and when, some years later, she was in trouble and near death, he refused to do anything to help her.

[5] He was, I think, very handsome. I gather this from photographs and from my own memories of him, dressed in his Sunday best and on his way to preach a sermon somewhere, when I was little. Handsome, proud, and ingrown, "like a toe-nail," somebody said. But he looked to me, as I grew older, like pictures I had seen of African tribal chieftains: he really should have been naked, with war-paint on and barbaric mementos, standing among spears. He could be chilling in the pulpit and indescribably cruel in his personal life and he was certainly the most bitter man I have ever met; yet it must be said that there was something else in him, buried in him, which lent him his tremendous power and, even, a rather crushing charm. It had something to do with his blackness, I think—he was very black—with his blackness and his beauty, and with the fact that he knew that he was black but did not know that he was beautiful. He claimed to be proud of his blackness but it had also been the cause of much humiliation and it had fixed bleak boundaries to his life. He was not a young man when we were growing up and he had already suffered many kinds of ruin; in his outrageously demanding and protective way he loved his children, who were black like him and menaced, like him; and all these things sometimes showed in his face when he tried, never to my knowledge with any success, to establish contact with any of us. When he took one of his children on his knee to play, the child always became fretful and began to cry; when he tried to help one of us with our homework the absolutely unabating tension which emanated from him caused our minds and our tongues to become paralyzed, so that he, scarcely knowing why, flew into a rage and the child, not knowing why, was punished. If it ever entered his head to bring a surprise home for his children, it was, almost unfailingly, the wrong surprise and even the big watermelons he often brought home on his back in the summertime led to the most appalling scenes. I do not remember, in all those years, that one of his children was ever glad to see

him come home. From what I was able to gather of his early life, it seemed that this inability to establish contact with other people had always marked him and had been one of the things which had driven him out of New Orleans. There was something in him, therefore, groping and tentative, which was never expressed and was buried with him. One saw it most clearly when he was facing new people and hoping to impress them. But he never did, not for long. We went from church to smaller and more improbable church, he found himself in less and less demand as a minister, and by the time he died none of his friends had come to see him for a long time. He had lived and died in an intolerable bitterness of spirit and it frightened me, as we drove him to the graveyard through those unquiet, ruined streets, to see how powerful and overflowing this bitterness could be and to realize that this bitterness now was mine.

[6] When he died I had been away from home for a little over a year. In that year I had had time to become aware of the meaning of all my father's bitter warnings, had discovered the secret of his proudly pursed lips and rigid carriage: I had discovered the weight of white people in the world. I saw that this had been for my ancestors and now would be for me an awful thing to live with and that the bitterness which had helped to kill my father could also kill me.

[7] He had been ill a long time—in the mind, as we now realized, reliving instances of his fantastic intransigence in the new light of his affliction and endeavoring to feel a sorrow for him which never, quite, came true. We had not known that he was being eaten up by paranoia, and the discovery that his cruelty, to our bodies and our minds, had been one of the symptoms of his illness was not, then, enough to enable us to forgive him. The younger children felt, quite simply, relief that he would not be coming home anymore. My mother's observation that it was he, after all, who had kept them alive all these years meant nothing because the problems of keeping children alive are not real for children. The older children felt, with my father gone, that they could invite their friends to the house without fear that their friends would be insulted or, as had sometimes happened with me, being told that their friends were in league with the devil and intended to rob our family of everything we owned. (I didn't fail to wonder, and it made me hate him, what on earth we owned that anybody else would want.)

[8] His illness was beyond all hope of healing before anyone realized that he was ill. He had always been so strange and had lived, like a prophet, in such unimaginably close communion with the Lord that his long silences which were punctuated by moans and hallelujahs and snatches of old songs while he sat at the living-room window never seemed odd to us. It was not until he refused to eat because, he said, his family was trying to poison him that my mother was forced to accept

as a fact what had, until then, been only a unwilling suspicion. When he was committed, it was discovered that he had tuberculosis and, as it turned out, the disease of his mind allowed the disease of his body to destroy him. For the doctors could not force him to eat, either, and, though he was fed intravenously, it was clear from the beginning that there was no hope for him.

[9] In my mind's eye I could see him, sitting at the window, locked up in his terrors; hating and fearing every living soul including his children who had betrayed him, too, by reaching towards the world which had despised him. There were nine of us. I began to wonder what it could have felt like for such a man to have had nine children whom he could barely feed. He used to make little jokes about our poverty, which never, of course, seemed very funny to us; they could not have seemed very funny to him, either, or else our all too feeble response to them would never have caused such rages. He spent great energy and achieved, to our chagrin, no small amount of success in keeping us away from the people who surrounded us, people who had all-night rent parties to which we listened when we should have been sleeping, people who cursed and drank and flashed razor blades on Lenox Avenue. He could not understand why, if they had so much energy to spare, they could not use it to make their lives better. He treated almost everybody on our block with a most uncharitable asperity and neither they, nor, of course, their children were slow to reciprocate.

[10] The only white people who came to our house were welfare workers and bill collectors. It was almost always my mother who dealt with them, for my father's temper, which was at the mercy of his pride, was never to be trusted. It was clear that he felt their very presence in his home to be a violation: this was conveyed by his carriage, almost ludicrously stiff, and by his voice, harsh and vindictively polite. When I was around nine or ten I wrote a play which was directed by a young, white schoolteacher, a woman, who then took an interest in me, and gave me books to read and, in order to corroborate my theatrical bent, decided to take me to see what she somewhat tactlessly referred to as "real" plays. Theater-going was forbidden in our house, but, with the really cruel intuitiveness of a child, I suspected that the color of this woman's skin would carry the day for me. When, at school, she suggested taking me to the theater, I did not, as I might have done if she had been a Negro, find a way of discouraging her, but agreed that she should pick me up at my house one evening. I then, very cleverly, left all the rest to my mother, who suggested to my father, as I knew she would, that it would not be very nice to let such a kind woman make the trip for nothing. Also, since it was a schoolteacher, I imagine that my mother countered the idea of sin with the idea of "education," which word, even with my father, carried a kind of bitter weight.

[11] Before the teacher came my father took me aside to ask *why* she was coming, what *interest* she could possibly have in our house, in a boy like me. I said I didn't know but I, too, suggested that it had something to do with education. And I understood that my father was waiting for me to say something—I didn't quite know what; perhaps that I wanted his protection against this teacher and her "education." I said none of these things and the teacher came and we went out. It was clear, during the brief interview in our living room, that my father was agreeing very much against his will and that he would have refused permission if he had dared. The fact that he did not dare caused me to despise him: I had no way of knowing that he was facing in that living room a wholly unprecedented and frightening situation.

[12] Later, when my father had been laid off from his job, this woman became very important to us. She was really a very sweet and generous woman and went to a great deal of trouble to be of help to us, particularly during one awful winter. My mother called her by the highest name she knew: she said she was a "christian." My father could scarcely disagree but during the four or five years of our relatively close association he never trusted her and was always trying to surprise in her open, Midwestern face the genuine, cunningly hidden, and hideous motivation. In later years, particularly when it began to be clear that this "education" of mine was going to lead me to perdition, he became more explicit and warned me that my white friends in high school were not really my friends and that I would see, when I was older, how white people would do anything to keep a Negro down. Some of them could be nice, he admitted, but none of them were to be trusted and most of them were not even nice. The best thing was to have as little to do with them as possible. I did not feel this way and I was certain, in my innocence, that I never would.

[13] But the year which preceded my father's death had made a great change in my life. I had been living in New Jersey, working in defense plants, working and living among southerners, white and black. I knew about the south, of course, and about how southerners treated Negroes and how they expected them to behave, but it had never entered my mind that anyone would look at me and expect *me* to behave that way. I learned in New Jersey that to be a Negro meant, precisely, that one was never looked at but was simply at the mercy of the reflexes the color of one's skin caused in other people. I acted in New Jersey as I had always acted, that is as though I thought a great deal of myself—I had to *act* that way—with results that were, simply, unbelievable. I had scarcely arrived before I had earned the enmity, which was extraordinarily ingenious, of all my superiors and nearly all my co-workers. In the beginning, to make matters worse, I simply did not know what was happening. I did not know what I had done, and I shortly began to wonder what *anyone* could possibly do, to bring about such unanimous, active, and

unbearably vocal hostility. I knew about jim-crow but I had never experienced it. I went to the same self-service restaurant three times and stood with all the Princeton boys before the counter, waiting for a hamburger and coffee; it was always an extraordinarily long time before anything was set before me; but it was not until the fourth visit that I learned that, in fact, nothing had ever been set before me: I had simply picked something up. Negroes were not served there, I was told, and they had been waiting for me to realize that I was always the only Negro present. Once I was told this, I determined to go there all the time. But now they were ready for me and, though some dreadful scenes were subsequently enacted in that restaurant, I never ate there again.

[14] It was the same story all over New Jersey, in bars, bowling alleys, diners, places to live. I was always being forced to leave, silently, or with mutual imprecations. I very shortly became notorious and children giggled behind me when I passed and their elders whispered or shouted —they really believed that I was mad. And it did begin to work on my mind, of course; I began to be afraid to go anywhere and to compensate for this I went places to which I really should not have gone and where, God knows, I had no desire to be. My reputation in town naturally enhanced my reputation at work and my working day became one long series of acrobatics designed to keep me out of trouble. I cannot say that these acrobatics succeeded. It began to seem that the machinery of the organization I worked for was turning over, day and night, with but one aim: to eject me. I was fired once, and contrived, with the aid of a friend from New York, to get back on the payroll; was fired again, and bounced back again. It took a while to fire me for the third time, but the third time took. There were no loopholes anywhere. There was not even any way of getting back inside the gates.

[15] That year in New Jersey lives in my mind as though it were the year during which, having an unsuspected predilection for it, I first contracted some dread, chronic disease, the unfailing symptom of which is a kind of blind fever, a pounding in the skull and fire in the bowels. Once this disease is contracted, one can never be really carefree again, for the fever, without an instant's warning, can recur at any moment. It can wreck more important things than race relations. There is not a Negro alive who does not have this rage in his blood—one has the choice, merely, of living with it consciously or surrendering to it. As for me, this fever has recurred in me, and does, and will until the day I die.

[16] My last night in New Jersey, a white friend from New York took me to the nearest big town, Trenton, to go to the movies and have a few drinks. As it turned out, he also saved me from, at the very least, a violent whipping. Almost every detail of that night stands out very clearly in my memory. I even remember the name of the movie we saw because its title impressed me as being so patly ironical. It was a movie about the German

occupation of France, starring Maureen O'Hara and Charles Laughton and called *This Land Is Mine*. I remember the name of the diner we walked into when the movie ended: it was the "American Diner." When we walked in the counterman asked what we wanted and I remember answering with the casual sharpness which had become my habit: "We want a hamburger and a cup of coffee, what do you think we want?" I do not know why, after a year of such rebuffs, I so completely failed to anticipate his answer, which was, of course, "We don't serve Negroes here." This reply failed to discompose me, at least for the moment. I made some sardonic comment about the name of the diner and we walked out into the streets.

[17] This was the time of what was called the "brown-out," when the lights in all American cities were very dim. When we re-entered the streets something happened to me which had the force of an optical illusion, or a nightmare. The streets were very crowded and I was facing north. People were moving in every direction but it seemed to me, in that instant, that all of the people I could see, and many more than that, were moving toward me, against me, and that everyone was white. I remember how their faces gleamed. And I felt, like a physical sensation, a *click* at the nape of my neck as though some interior string connecting my head to my body had been cut. I began to walk. I heard my friend call after me, but I ignored him. Heaven only knows what was going on in his mind, but he had the good sense not to touch me—I don't know what would have happened if he had—and to keep me in sight. I don't know what was going on in my mind, either; I certainly had no conscious plan. I wanted to do something to crush these white faces, which were crushing me. I walked for perhaps a block or two until I came to an enormous, glittering, and fashionable restaurant in which I knew not even the intercession of the Virgin would cause me to be served. I pushed through the doors and took the first vacant seat I saw, at a table for two, and waited.

[18] I do not know how long I waited and I rather wonder, until today, what I could possibly have looked like. Whatever I looked like, I frightened the waitress who shortly appeared, and the moment she appeared all of my fury flowed towards her. I hated her for her white face, and for her great, astounded, frightened eyes. I felt that if she found a black man so frightening I would make her fright worth-while.

[19] She did not ask me what I wanted, but repeated, as though she had learned it somewhere, "We don't serve Negroes here." She did not say it with the blunt, derisive hostility to which I had grown so accustomed, but, rather, with a note of apology in her voice, and fear. This made me colder and more murderous than ever. I felt I had to do something with my hands. I wanted her to come close enough for me to get her neck between my hands.

[20] So I pretended not to have understood her, hoping to draw her closer. And she did step a very short step closer, with her pencil poised incongruously over her pad, and repeated the formula: ". . . don't serve Negroes here."

[21] Somehow, with the repetition of that phrase, which was already ringing in my head like a thousand bells of a nightmare, I realized that she would never come any closer and that I would have to strike from a distance. There was nothing on the table but an ordinary watermug half full of water, and I picked this up and hurled it with all my strength at her. She ducked and it missed her and shattered against the mirror behind the bar. And, with that sound, my frozen blood abruptly thawed, I returned from wherever I had been, I *saw*, for the first time, the restaurant, the people with their mouths open, already, as it seemed to me, rising as one man, and I realized what I had done, and where I was, and I was frightened. I rose and began running for the door. A round, potbellied man grabbed me by the nape of the neck just as I reached the doors and began to beat me about the face. I kicked him and got loose and ran into the streets. My friend whispered, *"Run!"* and I ran.

[22] My friend stayed outside the restaurant long enough to misdirect my pursuers and the police, who arrived, he told me, at once. I do not know what I said to him when he came to my room that night. I could not have said much. I felt, in the oldest, most awful way, that I had somehow betrayed him. I lived it over and over and over again, the way one relives an automobile accident after it has happened and one finds oneself alone and safe. I could not get over two facts, both equally difficult for the imagination to grasp, and one was that I could have been murdered. But the other was that I had been ready to commit murder. I saw nothing very clearly but I did see this: that my life, my *real* life, was in danger, and not from anything other people might do but from the hatred I carried in my own heart.

– II –

[23] I had returned home around the second week in June—in great haste because it seemed that my father's death and my mother's confinement were both but a matter of hours. In the case of my mother, it soon became clear that she had simply made a miscalculation. This had always been her tendency and I don't believe that a single one of us arrived in the world, or has since arrived anywhere else, on time. But none of us dawdled so intolerably about the business of being born as did my baby sister. We sometimes amused ourselves, during those endless, stifling weeks, by picturing the baby sitting within in the safe, warm dark, bitterly regretting the necessity of becoming a part of our chaos and stubbornly putting it off as long as possible. I understood her perfectly and congratulated her on showing such good sense so soon. Death,

however, sat as purposefully at my father's bedside as life stirred within my mother's womb and it was harder to understand why he so lingered in that long shadow. It seemed that he had bent, and for a long time, too, all of his energies towards dying. Now death was ready for him but my father held back.

[24] All of Harlem, indeed, seemed to be infected by waiting. I had never before known it to be so violently still. Racial tensions throughout this country were exacerbated during the early years of the war, partly because the labor market brought together hundreds of thousands of ill-prepared people and partly because Negro soldiers, regardless of where they were born, received their military training in the south. What happened in defense plants and army camps had repercussions, naturally, in every Negro ghetto. The situation in Harlem had grown bad enough for clergymen, policemen, educators, politicians, and social workers to assert in one breath that there was no "crime wave" and to offer, in the very next breath, suggestions as to how to combat it. These suggestions always seemed to involve playgrounds, despite the fact that racial skirmishes were occurring in the playgrounds, too. Playground or not, crime wave or not, the Harlem police force had been augmented in March, and the unrest grew—perhaps, in fact, partly as a result of the ghetto's instinctive hatred of policemen. Perhaps the most revealing news item, out of the steady parade of reports of muggings, stabbings, shootings, assaults, gang wars, and accusations of police brutality, is the item concerning six Negro girls who set upon a white girl in the subway because, as they all too accurately put it, she was stepping on their toes. Indeed she was, all over the nation.

[25] I had never before been so aware of policemen, on foot, on horseback, on corners, everywhere, always two by two. Nor had I ever been so aware of small knots of people. They were on stoops and on corners and in doorways, and what was striking about them, I think, was that they did not seem to be talking. Never, when I passed these groups, did the usual sound of a curse or a laugh ring out and neither did there seem to be any hum of gossip. There was certainly, on the other hand, occurring between them communication extraordinarily intense. Another thing that was striking was the unexpected diversity of the people who made up these groups. Usually, for example, one would see a group of sharpies standing on the street corner, jiving the passing chicks; or a group of older men, usually, for some reason, in the vicinity of a barber shop, discussing baseball scores, or the numbers, or making rather chilling observations about women they had known. Women, in a general way, tended to be seen less often together—unless they were church women, or very young girls, or prostitutes met together for an unprofessional instant. But that summer I saw the strangest combinations: large, respectable, churchly matrons standing on the stoops or the corners with their

hair tied up, together with a girl in sleazy satin whose face bore the marks of gin and the razor, or heavy-set, abrupt, no-nonsense older men, in company with the most disreputable and fanatical "race" men, or these same "race" men with the sharpies, or these sharpies with the churchly women. Seventh Day Adventists and Methodists and Spiritualists seemed to be hobnobbing with Holyrollers and they were all, alike, entangled with the most flagrant disbelievers; something heavy in their stance seemed to indicate that they had all, incredibly, seen a common vision, and on each face there seemed to be the same strange, bitter shadow.

[26] The churchly women and the matter-of-fact, no-nonsense men had children in the Army. The sleazy girls they talked to had lovers there, the sharpies and the "race" men had friends and brothers there. It would have demanded an unquestioning patriotism, happily as uncommon in this country as it is undersirable, for these people not to have been disturbed by the bitter letters they received, by the newspaper stories they read, not to have been enraged by the posters, then to be found all over New York, which described the Japanese as "yellow-bellied Japs." It was only the "race" men, to be sure, who spoke ceaselessly of being revenged—how this vengeance was to be exacted was not clear—for the indignities and dangers suffered by Negro boys in uniform; but everybody felt a directionless, hopeless bitterness, as well as that panic which can scarcely be suppressed when one knows that a human being one loves is beyond one's reach, and in danger. This helplessness and this gnawing uneasiness does something, at length, to even the toughest mind. Perhaps the best way to sum all this up is to say that the people I knew felt, mainly, a peculiar kind of relief when they knew that their boys were being shipped out of the south, to do battle overseas. It was, perhaps, like feeling that the most dangerous part of a dangerous journey had been passed and that now, even if death should come, it would come with honor and without the complicity of their countrymen. Such a death would be, in short, a fact with which one could hope to live.

[27] It was on the 28th of July, which I believe was a Wednesday, that I visited my father for the first time during his illness and for the last time in his life. The moment I saw him I knew why I had put off this visit so long. I had told my mother that I did not want to see him because I hated him. But this was not true. It was only that I *had* hated him and I wanted to hold on to this hatred. I did not want to look on him as a ruin: it was not a ruin I had hated. I imagine that one of the reasons people cling to their hates so stubbornly is because they sense, once hate is gone, that they will be forced to deal with pain.

[28] We traveled out to him, his older sister and myself, to what seemed to be the very end of a very Long Island. It was hot and dusty and we wrangled, my aunt and I, all the way out, over the fact that I had recently begun to smoke and, as she said, to give myself airs. But I

knew that she wrangled with me because she could not bear to face the fact of her brother's dying. Neither could I endure the reality of her despair, her unstated bafflement as to what had happened to her brother's life, and her own. So we wrangled and I smoked and from time to time she fell into a heavy reverie. Covertly, I watched her face, which was the face of an old woman; it had fallen in, the eyes were sunken and lightless; soon she would be dying, too.

[29] In my childhood—it had not been so long ago—I had thought her beautiful. She had been quick-witted and quick-moving and very generous with all the children and each of her visits had been an event. At one time one of my brothers and myself had thought of running away to live with her. Now she could no longer produce out of her handbag some unexpected and yet familiar delight. She made me feel pity and revulsion and fear. It was awful to realize that she no longer caused me to feel affection. The closer we came to the hospital the more querulous she became and at the same time, naturally, grew more dependent on me. Between pity and guilt and fear I began to feel that there was another me trapped in my skull like a jack-in-the-box who might escape my control at any moment and fill the air with screaming.

[30] She began to cry the moment we entered the room and she saw him lying there, all shriveled and still, like a little black monkey. The great, gleaming apparatus which fed him and would have compelled him to be still even if he had been able to move brought to mind, not beneficence, but torture; the tubes entering his arm made me think of pictures I had seen when a child, of Gulliver, tied down by the pygmies on that island. My aunt wept and wept, there was a whistling sound in my father's throat; nothing was said; he could not speak. I wanted to take his hand, to say something. But I do not know what I could have said, even if he could have heard me. He was not really in that room with us, he had at last really embarked on his journey; and though my aunt told me that he said he was going to meet Jesus, I did not hear anything except that whistling in his throat. The doctor came back and we left, into that unbearable train again, and home. In the morning came the telegram saying that he was dead. Then the house was suddenly full of relatives, friends, hysteria, and confusion and I quickly left my mother and the children to the care of those impressive women, who, in Negro communities at least, automatically appear at times of bereavement armed with lotions, proverbs, and patience, and an ability to cook. I went downtown. By the time I returned, later the same day, my mother had been carried to the hospital and the baby had been born.

– III –

[31] For my father's funeral I had nothing black to wear and this posed a nagging problem all day long. It was one of those problems,

simple, or impossible of solution, to which the mind insanely clings in order to avoid the mind's real trouble. I spent most of that day at the downtown apartment of a girl I knew, celebrating my birthday with whiskey and wondering what to wear that night. When planning a birthday celebration one naturally does not expect that it will be up against competition from a funeral and this girl had anticipated taking me out that night, for a big dinner and a night club afterwards. Sometime during the course of that long day we decided that we would go out anyway, when my father's funeral service was over. I imagine I decided it, since, as the funeral hour approached, it became clearer and clearer to me that I would not know what to do with myself when it was over. The girl, stifling her very lively concern as to the possible effects of the whiskey on one of my father's chief mourners, concentrated on being conciliatory and practically helpful. She found a black shirt for me somewhere and ironed it and, dressed in the darkest pants and jacket I owned, and slightly drunk, I made my way to my father's funeral.

[32] The chapel was full, but not packed, and very quiet. There were, mainly, my father's relatives, and his children, and here and there I saw faces I had not seen since childhood, the faces of my father's one-time friends. They were very dark and solemn now, seeming somehow to suggest that they had known all along that something like this would happen. Chief among the mourners was my aunt, who had quarreled with my father all his life; by which I do not mean to suggest that her mourning was insincere or that she had not loved him. I suppose that she was one of the few people in the world who had, and their incessant quarreling proved precisely the strength of the tie that bound them. The only other person in the world, as far as I knew, whose relationship to my father rivaled my aunt's in depth was my mother, who was not there.

[33] It seemed to me, of course, that it was a very long funeral. But it was, if anything, a rather shorter funeral than most, nor, since there were no overwhelming, uncontrollable expressions of grief, could it be called— if I dare to use the word—successful. The minister who preached my father's funeral sermon was one of the few my father had still been seeing as he neared his end. He presented to us in his sermon a man whom none of us had ever seen—a man thoughtful, patient, and forbearing, a Christian inspiration to all who knew him, and a model for his children. And no doubt the children, in their disturbed and guilty state, were almost ready to believe this; he had been remote enough to be anything and, anyway, the shock of the incontrovertible, that it was really our father lying up there in that casket, prepared the mind for anything. His sister moaned and this grief-stricken moaning was taken as corroboration. The other faces held a dark, non-committal thoughtfulness. This was not the man they had known, but they had scarcely expected to be confronted with *him;* this was, in a sense deeper than questions of fact, the

man they had not known, and the man they had not known may have been the real one. The real man, whoever he had been, had suffered and now he was dead: this was all that was sure and all that mattered now. Every man in the chapel hoped that when his hour came he, too, would be eulogized, which is to say forgiven, and that all of his lapses, greeds, errors, and strayings from the truth would be invested with coherence and looked upon with charity. This was perhaps the last thing human beings could give each other and it was what they demanded, after all, of the Lord. Only the Lord saw the midnight tears, only He was present when one of His children, moaning and wringing hands, paced up and down the room. When one slapped one's child in anger the recoil in the heart reverberated through heaven and became part of the pain of the universe. And when the children were hungry and sullen and distrustful and one watched them, daily, growing wilder, and further away, and running headlong into danger, it was the Lord who knew what the charged heart endured as the strap was laid to the backside; the Lord alone who knew what one *would* have said if one had had, like the Lord, the gift of the living word. It was the Lord who knew of the impossibility every parent in that room faced: how to prepare the child for the day when the child would be despised and how to *create* in the child—by what means?—a stronger antidote to this poison than one had found for oneself. The avenues, side streets, bars, billiard halls, hospitals, police stations, and even the playgrounds of Harlem—not to mention the houses of correction, the jails, and the morgue—testified to the potency of the poison while remaining silent as to the efficacy of whatever antidote, irresistibly raising the question of whether or not such an antidote existed; raising, which was worse, the question of whether or not an antidote was desirable; perhaps poison should be fought with poison. With these several schisms in the mind and with more terrors in the heart than could be named, it was better not to judge the man who had gone down under an impossible burden. It was better to remember: *Thou knowest this man's fall; but thou knowest not his wrassling.*

[34] While the preacher talked and I watched the children—years of changing their diapers, scrubbing them, slapping them, taking them to school, and scolding them had had the perhaps inevitable result of making me love them, though I am not sure I knew this then—my mind was busily breaking out with a rash of disconnected impressions. Snatches of popular songs, indecent jokes, bits of books I had read, movie sequences, faces, voices, political issues—I thought I was going mad; all these impressions suspended, as it were, in the solution of the faint nausea produced in me by the heat and liquor. For a moment I had the impression that my alcoholic breath, inefficiently disguised with chewing gum, filled the entire chapel. Then someone began singing one of my father's favorite songs and, abruptly, I was with him, sitting on his knee, in the hot,

enormous, crowded church which was the first church we attended. It was the Abyssinia Baptist Church on 138th Street. We had not gone there long. With this image, a host of others came. I had forgotten, in the rage of my growing up, how proud my father had been of me when I was little. Apparently, I had had a voice and my father had liked to show me off before the members of the church. I had forgotten what he had looked like when he was pleased but now I remembered that he had always been grinning with pleasure when my solos ended. I even remembered certain expressions on his face when he teased my mother—had he loved her? I would never know. And when had it all begun to change? For now it seemed that he had not always been cruel. I remembered being taken for a haircut and scraping my knee on the footrest of the barber's chair and I remembered my father's face as he soothed my crying and applied the stinging iodine. Then I remembered our fights, fights which had been of the worst possible kind because my technique had been silence.

[35] I remembered the one time in all our life together when we had really spoken to each other.

[36] It was on a Sunday and it must have been shortly before I left home. We were walking, just the two of us, in our usual silence, to or from church. I was in high school and had been doing a lot of writing and I was, at about this time, the editor of the high school magazine. But I had also been a Young Minister and had been preaching from the pulpit. Lately, I had been taking fewer engagements and preached as rarely as possible. It was said in the church, quite truthfully, that I was "cooling off."

[37] My father asked me abruptly, "You'd rather write than preach, wouldn't you?"

[38] I was astonished at his question—because it was a real question. I answered, "Yes."

[39] That was all we said. It was awful to remember that that was all we had *ever* said.

[40] The casket now was opened and the mourners were being led up the aisle to look for the last time on the deceased. The assumption was that the family was too overcome with grief to be allowed to make this journey alone and I watched while my aunt was led to the casket and, muffled in black, and shaking, led back to her seat. I disapproved of forcing the children to look on their dead father, considering that the shock of his death, or, more truthfully, the shock of death as a reality, was already a little more than a child could bear, but my judgment in this matter had been overruled and there they were, bewildered and frightened and very small, being led, one by one, to the casket. But there is also something very gallant about children at such moments. It has something to do with their silence and gravity and with the fact that one cannot

help them. Their legs, somehow, seem *exposed,* so that it is at once incredible and terribly clear that their legs are all they have to hold them up.

[41] I had not wanted to go to the casket myself and I certainly had not wished to be led there, but there was no way of avoiding either of these forms. One of the deacons led me up and I looked on my father's face. I cannot say that it looked like him at all. His blackness had been equivocated by powder and there was no suggestion in that casket of what his power had or could have been. He was simply an old man dead, and it was hard to believe that he had ever given anyone either joy or pain. Yet, his life filled that room. Further up the avenue his wife was holding his newborn child. Life and death so close together, and love and hatred, and right and wrong, said something to me which I did not want to hear concerning man, concerning the life of man.

[42] After the funeral, while I was downtown desperately celebrating my birthday, a Negro soldier, in the lobby of the Hotel Braddock, got into a fight with a white policeman over a Negro girl. Negro girls, white policemen, in or out of uniform, and Negro males—in or out of uniform—were part of the furniture of the lobby of the Hotel Braddock and this was certainly not the first time such an incident had occurred. It was destined, however, to receive an unprecedented publicity, for the fight between the policeman and the soldier ended with the shooting of the soldier. Rumor, flowing immediately to the streets outside, stated that the soldier had been shot in the back, an instantaneous and revealing invention, and that the soldier had died protecting a Negro woman. The facts were somewhat different—for example, the soldier had not been shot in the back, and was not dead, and the girl seems to have been as dubious a symbol of womanhood as her white counterpart in Georgia usually is, but no one was interested in the facts. They preferred the invention because this invention expressed and corroborated their hates and fears so perfectly. It is just as well to remember that people are always doing this. Perhaps many of those legends, including Christianity, to which the world clings began their conquest of the world with just some such concerted surrender to distortion. The effect, in Harlem, of this particular legend was like the effect of a lit match in a tin of gasoline. The mob gathered before the doors of the Hotel Braddock simply began to swell and to spread in every direction, and Harlem exploded.

[43] The mob did not cross the ghetto lines. It would have been easy, for example, to have gone over Morningside Park on the west side or to have crossed the Grand Central railroad tracks at 125th Street on the east side, to wreak havoc in white neighborhoods. The mob seems to have been mainly interested in something more potent and real than the white face, that is, in white power, and the principal damage done during the riot of the summer of 1943 was to white business establishments in Harlem. It might have been a far bloodier story, of course, if, at the hour

the riot began, these establishments had still been open. From the Hotel Braddock the mob fanned out, east and west along 125th Street, and for the entire length of Lenox, Seventh, and Eighth avenues. Along each of these avenues, and along each major side street—116th, 125th, 138th, and so on—bars, stores, pawnshops, restaurants, even little luncheonettes had been smashed open and entered and looted—looted, it might be added, with more haste than efficiency. The shelves really looked as though a bomb had struck them. Cans of beans and soup and dog food, along with toilet paper, corn flakes, sardines, and milk tumbled every which way, and abandoned cash registers and cases of beer leaned crazily out of the splintered windows and were strewn along the avenues. Sheets, blankets, and clothing of every description formed a kind of path, as though people had dropped them while running. I truly had not realized that Harlem *had* so many stores until I saw them all smashed open; the first time the word *wealth* ever entered my mind in relation to Harlem was when I saw it scattered in the streets. But one's first, incongruous impression of plenty was countered immediately by an impression of waste. None of this was doing anybody any good. It would have been better to have left the plate glass as it had been and the goods lying in the stores.

[44] It would have been better, but it would also have been intolerable, for Harlem had needed something to smash. To smash something is the ghetto's chronic need. Most of the time it is the members of the ghetto who smash each other, and themselves. But as long as the ghetto walls are standing there will always come a moment when these outlets do not work. That summer, for example, it was not enough to get into a fight on Lenox Avenue, or curse out one's cronies in the barber shops. If ever, indeed, the violence which fills Harlem's churches, pool halls, and bars erupts outward in a more direct fashion, Harlem and its citizens are likely to vanish in an apocalyptic flood. That this is not likely to happen is due to a great many reasons, most hidden and powerful among them the Negro's real relation to the white American. This relation prohibits, simply, anything as uncomplicated and satisfactory as pure hatred. In order really to hate white people, one has to blot so much out of the mind—and the heart—that this hatred itself becomes an exhausting and self-destructive pose. But this does not mean, on the other hand, that love comes easily: the white world is too powerful, too complacent, too ready with gratuitous humiliation, and, above all, too ignorant and too innocent for that. One is absolutely forced to make perpetual qualifications and one's own reactions are always canceling each other out. It is this, really, which has driven so many people mad, both white and black. One is always in the position of having to decide between amputation and gangrene. Amputation is swift but time may prove that the amputation was not necessary—or one may delay the amputation too long. Gangrene is slow, but it is impossible to be sure that one is reading one's symptoms right.

The idea of going through life as a cripple is more than one can bear, and equally unbearable is the risk of swelling up slowly, in agony, with poison. And the trouble, finally, is that the risks are real even if the choices do not exist.

[45] "But as for me and my house," my father had said, "we will serve the Lord." I wondered, as we drove him to his resting place, what this line had meant for him. I had heard him preach it many times. I had preached it once myself, proudly giving it an interpretation different from my father's. Now the whole thing came back to me, as though my father and I were on our way to Sunday school and I were memorizing the golden text: *And if it seem evil unto you to serve the Lord, choose you this day whom you will serve; whether the gods which your fathers served that were on the other side of the flood, or the gods of the Amorites, in whose land ye dwell: but as for me and my house, we will serve the Lord.* I suspected in these familiar lines a meaning which had never been there for me before. All of my father's texts and songs, which I had decided were meaningless, were arranged before me at his death like empty bottles, waiting to hold the meaning which life would give them for me. This was his legacy: nothing is ever escaped. That bleakly memorable morning I hated the unbelievable streets and the Negroes and whites who had, equally, made them that way. But I knew that it was folly, as my father would have said, this bitterness was folly. It was necessary to hold on to the things that mattered. The dead man mattered, the new life mattered; blackness and whiteness did not matter; to believe that they did was to acquiesce in one's own destruction. Hatred, which could destroy so much, never failed to destroy the man who hated and this was an immutable law.

[46] It began to seem that one would have to hold in the mind forever two ideas which seemed to be in opposition. The first idea was acceptance, the acceptance, totally without rancor, of life as it is, and men as they are: in the light of this idea, it goes without saying that injustice is a commonplace. But this did not mean that one could be complacent, for the second idea was of equal power: that one must never, in one's own life, accept these injustices as commonplace but must fight them with all one's strength. This fight begins, however, in the heart and it now had been laid to my charge to keep my own heart free of hatred and despair. This intimation made my heart heavy and, now that my father was irrecoverable, I wished that he had been beside me so that I could have searched his face for the answers which only the future would give me now.

COMMENT AND QUESTIONS

1. The title of Baldwin's essay echoes Richard Wright's novel *Native Son*, an attack on race prejudice in the United States. What are the connotations of *Notes*? Does the word seem well chosen to describe the form and structure of the essay?
2. The first paragraph associates the death of the author's father, the birth of his sister, and race riots. It therefore introduces some of the merging themes woven through the essay—oppositions of death–birth, blackness–whiteness, hate–love, parent–child, innocence–experience, and reality–unreality. Is paragraph 1 coherent?
3. How does paragraph 2 further develop some of the themes? What is the meaning of *codas* in that paragraph? Of *apocalypse*? Does the paragraph indicate what kind of apocalypse Baldwin experienced?
4. Paragraph 5 is interesting for its style as well as for its graphic picture of the author's father. Point out sentence structures, combinations of words, and repetitions of words and sounds that seem to you effective.
5. What is the function of paragraph 6?
6. How are recurrent themes stressed and developed in paragraphs 7–12? What is the purpose of developing fully the experience with the white schoolteacher?
7. During the year in New Jersey (paragraphs 13–22), experience replaces innocence; and, for the author, hate and the opposition of blackness–whiteness become one. What other theme recurs in these paragraphs? Why do you think Baldwin develops as fully as he does the episode in the restaurant, paragraphs 18–21? In the last sentence of section I, what is the meaning of "my *real* life"?
8. "Notes of a Native Son" is an example of narration which departs from chronological order. Analyze the time-structure of the essay. In what ways is this structure more effective for Baldwin's purposes than a setting down of events in the time-order in which they occurred?
9. Section II begins with the death–birth opposition. What other oppositions are woven into this part of the essay and in some respects changed?
10. Examine the imagery and the sentence structures in paragraph 30. What makes the paragraph a good section ending?
11. The opening paragraph of section III brings together death and birth in a different way, and the second sentence of the paragraph refers to "the mind's real trouble." What is this "real trouble"?
12. Paragraphs 33–41 further develop some of the basic themes. What changes in feeling and tone do these paragraphs establish?
13. How are the themes of reality–unreality and of hate–love associated, in paragraphs 42–44, with the riot in Harlem? What does Baldwin mean by saying, in paragraph 44, that the white world is "too ignorant and too innocent"?
14. By the end of the essay, some of the themes have coalesced; the opposi-

tions have been modified and have shifted into new oppositions. For the author, what realizations have emerged from the experience of his father's death?

15. Baldwin is, of course, writing about a Negro son, his Negro father, and the experience of being a Negro. In what ways do his experiences transcend the particular and his themes become universal themes?

[49] *Norman Podhoretz*: My Negro Problem— and Ours

NORMAN PODHORETZ (1930–), an American writer and critic, is the editor of *Commentary*. A collection of his articles, called *Doings and Undoings: The Fifties and After in American Writing*, was published in 1964; the following essay first appeared in the February, 1963, issue of *Commentary*. Footnotes are the author's.

> *If we—and . . . I mean the relatively conscious whites and the relatively conscious blacks, who must, like lovers, insist on, or create, the consciousness of the others—do not falter in our duty now, we may be able, handful that we are, to end the racial nightmare, and achieve our country, and change the history of the world.*—JAMES BALDWIN

[1] Two ideas puzzled me deeply as a child growing up in Brooklyn during the 1930's in what today would be called an integrated neighborhood. One of them was that all Jews were rich; the other was that all Negroes were persecuted. These ideas had appeared in print; therefore they must be true. My own experience and the evidence of my senses told me they were not true, but that only confirmed what a day-dreaming boy in the provinces—for the lower-class neighborhoods of New York belong as surely to the provinces as any rural town in North Dakota—discovers very early: *his* experience is unreal and the evidence of his senses is not to be trusted. Yet even a boy with a head full of fantasies incongruously synthesized out of Hollywood movies and English novels cannot altogether deny the reality of his own experience—especially when there is so much deprivation in that experience. Nor can he altogether gainsay the evidence of his own senses—especially such evidence of the senses as

comes from being repeatedly beaten up, robbed, and in general hated, terrorized, and humiliated.

[2] And so for a long time I was puzzled to think that Jews were supposed to be rich when the only Jews I knew were poor, and that Negroes were supposed to be persecuted when it was the Negroes who were doing the only persecuting I knew about—and doing it, moreover, to *me*. During the early years of the war, when my older sister joined a left-wing youth organization, I remember my astonishment at hearing her passionately denounce my father for thinking that Jews were worse off than Negroes. To me, at the age of twelve, it seemed very clear that Negroes were better off than Jews—indeed, than *all* whites. A city boy's world is contained within three or four square blocks, and in my world it was the whites, the Italians and Jews, who feared the Negroes, not the other way around. The Negroes were tougher than we were, more ruthless, and on the whole they were better athletes. What could it mean, then, to say that they were badly off and that we were more fortunate? Yet my sister's opinions, like print, were sacred, and when she told me about exploitation and economic forces I believed her. I believed her, but I was still afraid of Negroes. And I still hated them with all my heart.

[3] It had not always been so—that much I can recall from early childhood. When did it start, this fear and this hatred? There was a kindergarten in the local public school, and given the character of the neighborhood, at least half of the children in my class must have been Negroes. Yet I have no memory of being aware of color differences at that age, and I know from observing my own children that they attribute no significance to such differences even when they begin noticing them. I think there was a day—first grade? second grade?—when my best friend Carl hit me on the way home from school and announced that he wouldn't play with me any more because I had killed Jesus. When I ran home to my mother crying for an explanation, she told me not to pay any attention to such foolishness, and then in Yiddish she cursed the *goyim* and the *schwartzes*, the *schwartzes* and the *goyim*. Carl, it turned out, was a *schwartze*, and so was added a third to the categories into which people were mysteriously divided.

[4] Sometimes I wonder whether this is a true memory at all. It is blazingly vivid, but perhaps it never happened: can anyone really remember back to the age of six? There is no uncertainty in my mind, however, about the years that followed. Carl and I hardly ever spoke, though we met in school every day up through the eighth or ninth grade. There would be embarrassed moments of catching his eye or of his catching mine—for whatever it was that had attracted us to one another as very small children remained alive in spite of the fantastic barrier of hostility that had grown up between us, suddenly and out of nowhere. Nevertheless, friendship would have been impossible, and even if it had been

possible, it would have been unthinkable. About that, there was nothing anyone could do by the time we were eight years old.

[5]*Item:* The orphanage across the street is torn down, a city housing project begins to rise in its place, and on the marvelous vacant lot next to the old orphanage they are building a playground. Much excitement and anticipation as Opening Day draws near. Mayor LaGuardia himself comes to dedicate this great gesture of public benevolence. He speaks of neighborliness and borrowing cups of sugar, and of the playground he says that children of all races, colors, and creeds will learn to live together in harmony. A week later, some of us are swatting flies on the playground's inadequate little ball field. A gang of Negro kids, pretty much our own age, enter from the other side and order us out of the park. We refuse, proudly and indignantly, with superb masculine fervor. There is a fight, they win, and we retreat, half whimpering, half with bravado. My first nauseating experience of cowardice. And my first appalled realization that there are people in the world who do not seem to be afraid of anything, who act as though they have nothing to lose. Thereafter the playground becomes a battleground, sometimes quiet, sometimes the scene of athletic competition between Them and Us. But rocks are thrown as often as baseballs. Gradually we abandon the place and use the streets instead. The streets are safer, though we do not admit this to ourselves. We are not, after all, sissies—that most dreaded epithet of an American boyhood.

[6] *Item:* I am standing alone in front of the building in which I live. It is late afternoon and getting dark. That day in school the teacher had asked a surly Negro boy named Quentin a question he was unable to answer. As usual I had waved my arm eagerly ("Be a good boy, get good marks, be smart, go to college, become a doctor") and, the right answer bursting from my lips, I was held up lovingly by the teacher as an example to the class. I had seen Quentin's face—a very dark, very cruel, very Oriental-looking face—harden, and there had been enough threat in his eyes to make me run all the way home for fear that he might catch me outside.

[7] Now, standing idly in front of my own house, I see him approaching from the project accompanied by his little brother who is carrying a baseball bat and wearing a grin of malicious anticipation. As in a nightmare, I am trapped. The surroundings are secure and familiar, but terror is suddenly present and there is no one around to help. I am locked to the spot. I will not cry out or run away like a sissy, and I stand there, my heart wild, my throat clogged. He walks up, hurls the familiar epithet ("Hay, mo'f———r"), and to my surprise only pushes me. It is a violent push, but not a punch. A push is not as serious as a punch. Maybe I can still back out without entirely losing my dignity. Maybe I can still say, "Hey, c'mon Quentin, whaddya wanna do *that* for. I dint do nothin' to

you," and walk away, not too rapidly. Instead, before I can stop myself, I push him back—a token gesture—and I say, "Cut that out, I don't wanna fight, I ain't got nothin' to fight about." As I turn to walk back into the building, the corner of my eye catches the motion of the bat his little brother has handed him. I try to duck, but the bat crashes colored lights into my head.

[8] The next thing I know, my mother and sister are standing over me, both of them hysterical. My sister—she who was later to join the "progressive" youth organization—is shouting for the police and screaming imprecations at those dirty little black bastards. They take me upstairs, the doctor comes, the police come. I tell them that the boy who did it was a stranger, that he had been trying to get money from me. They do not believe me, but I am too scared to give them Quentin's name. When I return to school a few days later, Quentin avoids my eyes. He knows that I have not squealed, and he is ashamed. I try to feel proud, but in my heart I know that it was fear of what his friends might do to me that had kept me silent, and not the code of the street.

[9] *Item:* There is an athletic meet in which the whole of our junior high school is participating. I am in one of the seventh-grade rapid-advance classes, and "segregation" has now set in with a vengeance. In the last three or four years of the elementary school from which we have just graduated, each grade had been divided into three classes, according to "intelligence." (In the earlier grades the divisions had either been arbitrary or else unrecognized by us as having anything to do with brains.) These divisions by IQ, or however it was arranged, had resulted in a preponderance of Jews in the "1" classes and a corresponding preponderance of Negroes in the "3's," with the Italians split unevenly along the spectrum. At least a few Negroes had always made the "1's," just as there had always been a few Jewish kids among the "3's" and more among the "2's" (where Italians dominated). But the junior high's rapid-advance class of which I am now a member is overwhelmingly Jewish and entirely white—except for a shy lonely Negro girl with light skin and reddish hair.

[10] The athletic meet takes place in a city-owned stadium far from the school. It is an important event to which a whole day is given over. The winners are to get those precious little medallions stamped with the New York City emblem that can be screwed into a belt and that prove the wearer to be a distinguished personage. I am a fast runner, and so I am assigned the position of anchor man on my class's team in the relay race. There are three other seventh-grade teams in the race, two of them all Negro, as ours is all white. One of the all-Negro teams is very tall—their anchor man waiting silently next to me on the line looks years older than I am, and I do not recognize him. He is the first to get the baton and crosses the finishing line in a walk. Our team comes in second, but a few

minutes later we are declared the winners, for it has been discovered that the anchor man on the first-place team is not a member of the class. We are awarded the medallions, and the following day our home-room teacher makes a speech about how proud she is of us for being superior athletes as well as superior students. We want to believe that we deserve the praise, but we know that we could not have won even if the other class had not cheated.

[11] That afternoon, walking home, I am waylaid and surrounded by five Negroes, among whom is the anchor man of the disqualified team. "Gimme my medal, mo'f———r," he grunts. I do not have it with me and I tell him so. "Anyway, it ain't yours," I say foolishly. He calls me a liar on both counts and pushes me up against the wall on which we sometimes play handball. "Gimme my mo'f———n' medal," he says again. I repeat that I have left it home. "Le's search the li'l mo'f———r," one of them suggests, "he prolly got it *hid* in his mo'f———n' *pants*." My panic is now unmanageable. (How many times had I been surrounded like this and asked in soft tones, "Len' me a nickel, boy." How many times had I been called a liar for pleading poverty and pushed around, or searched, or beaten up, unless there happened to be someone in the marauding gang like Carl who liked me across that enormous divide of hatred and who would therefore say, "Aaah, c'mon, le's git someone else, *this* boy ain't got no money on 'im.") I scream at them through tears of rage and self-contempt, "Keep your f———n' filthy lousy black hands offa me! I swear I'll get the cops." This is all they need to hear, and the five of them set upon me. They bang me around, mostly in the stomach and on the arms and shoulders, and when several adults loitering near the candy store down the block notice what is going on and begin to shout, they run off and away.

[12] I do not tell my parents about the incident. My team-mates, who have also been waylaid, each by a gang led by his opposite number from the disqualified team, have had their medallions taken from them, and they never squeal either. For days, I walk home in terror, expecting to be caught again, but nothing happens. The medallion is put away into a drawer, never to be worn by anyone.

[13] Obviously experiences like these have always been a common feature of childhood life in working-class and immigrant neighborhoods, and Negroes do not necessarily figure in them. Wherever, and in whatever combination, they have lived together in the cities, kids of different groups have been at war, beating up and being beaten up: micks against kikes against wops against spicks against polacks. And even relatively homogeneous areas have not been spared the warring of the young: one block against another, one gang (called in my day, in a pathetic effort at gentility, an "S.A.C.," or social-athletic club) against another. But the Negro-white conflict had—and no doubt still has—a special intensity

and was conducted with a ferocity unmatched by intramural white battling.

[14] In my own neighborhood, a good deal of animosity existed between the Italian kids (most of whose parents were immigrants from Sicily) and the Jewish kids (who came largely from East European immigrant families). Yet everyone had friends, sometimes close friends, in the other "camp," and we often visited one another's strange-smelling houses, if not for meals, then for glasses of milk, and occasionally for some special event like a wedding or a wake. If it happened that we divided into warring factions and did battle, it would invariably be halfhearted and soon patched up. Our parents, to be sure, had nothing to do with one another and were mutually suspicious and hostile. But we, the kids, who all spoke Yiddish or Italian at home, were Americans, or New Yorkers, or Brooklyn boys: we shared a culture, the culture of the street, and at least for a while this culture proved to be more powerful than the opposing cultures of the home.

[15] Why, *why* should it have been so different as between the Negroes and us? How was it borne in upon us so early, white and black alike, that we were enemies beyond any possibility of reconciliation? Why did we hate one another so?

[16] I suppose if I tried, I could answer those questions more or less adequately from the perspective of what I have since learned. I could draw upon James Baldwin—what better witness is there?—to describe the sense of entrapment that poisons the soul of the Negro with hatred for the white man whom he knows to be his jailer. On the other side, if I wanted to understand how the white man comes to hate the Negro, I could call upon the psychologists who have spoken of the guilt that white Americans feel toward Negroes and that turns into hatred for lack of acknowledging itself as guilt. These are plausible answers and certainly there is truth in them. Yet when I think back upon my own experience of the Negro and his of me, I find myself troubled and puzzled, much as I was as a child when I heard that all Jews were rich and all Negroes persecuted. How could the Negroes in my neighborhood have regarded the whites across the street and around the corner as jailers? On the whole, the whites were not so poor as the Negroes, but they were quite poor enough, and the years were years of Depression. As for white hatred of the Negro, how could guilt have had anything to do with it? What share had these Italian and Jewish immigrants in the enslavement of the Negro? What share had they—downtrodden people themselves breaking their own necks to eke out a living—in the exploitation of the Negro?

[17] No, I cannot believe that we hated each other back there in Brooklyn because they thought of us as jailers and we felt guilty toward them. But does it matter, given the fact that we all went through an unrepresentative confrontation? I think it matters profoundly, for if we

managed the job of hating each other so well without benefit of the aids to hatred that are supposedly at the root of this madness everywhere else, it must mean that the madness is not yet properly understood. I am far from pretending that I understand it, but I would insist that no view of the problem will begin to approach the truth unless it can account for a case like the one I have been trying to describe. Are the elements of any such view available to us?

[18] At least two, I would say, are. One of them is a point we frequently come upon in the work of James Baldwin, and the other is a related point always stressed by psychologists who have studied the mechanisms of prejudice. Baldwin tells us that one of the reasons Negroes hate the white man is that the white man refuses to *look* at him: the Negro knows that in white eyes all Negroes are alike; they are faceless and therefore not altogether human. The psychologists, in their turn, tell us that the white man hates the Negro because he tends to project those wild impulses that he fears in himself onto an alien group which he then punishes with his contempt. What Baldwin does *not* tell us, however, is that the principle of facelessness is a two-way street and can operate in both directions with no difficulty at all. Thus, in my neighborhood in Brooklyn, *I* was as faceless to the Negroes as they were to me, and if they hated me because I never looked at them, I must also have hated them for never looking at *me*. To the Negroes, my white skin was enough to define me as the enemy, and in a war it is only the uniform that counts and not the person.

[19] So with the mechanism of projection that the psychologists talk about: it too works in both directions at once. There is no question that the psychologists are right about what the Negro represents symbolically to the white man. For me as a child the life lived on the other side of the playground and down the block on Ralph Avenue seemed the very embodiment of the values of the street—free, independent, reckless, brave, masculine, erotic. I put the word "erotic" last, though it is usually stressed above all others, because in fact it came last, in consciousness as in importance. What mainly counted for me about Negro kids of my own age was that they were "bad boys." There were plenty of bad boys among the whites—this was, after all, a neighborhood with a long tradition of crime as a career open to aspiring talents—but the Negroes were *really* bad, bad in a way that beckoned to one, and made one feel inadequate. *We* all went home every day for a lunch of spinach-and-potatoes; *they* roamed around during lunch hour, munching on candy bars. In winter *we* had to wear itchy woolen hats and mittens and cumbersome galoshes; *they* were bare-headed and loose as they pleased. *We* rarely played hookey, or got into serious trouble in school, for all our street-corner bravado; *they* were defiant, forever staying out (to do what delicious things?), forever making disturbances in class and in the halls, forever

being sent to the principal and returning uncowed. But most important of all, they were *tough*; beautifully, enviably tough, not giving a damn for anyone or anything. To hell with the teacher, the truant officer, the cop; to hell with the whole of the adult world that held *us* in its grip and that we never had the courage to rebel against except sporadically and in petty ways.

[20] This is what I saw and envied and feared in the Negro: this is what finally made him faceless to me, though some of it, of course, was actually there. (The psychologists also tell us that the alien group which becomes the object of a projection will tend to respond by trying to live up to what is expected of them.) But what, on his side, did the Negro see in me that made me faceless to *him*? Did he envy me my lunches of spinach-and-potatoes and my itchy woolen caps and my prudent behavior in the face of authority, as I envied him his noon-time candy bars and his bare head in winter and his magnificent rebelliousness? Did those lunches and caps spell for him the prospect of power and riches in the future? Did they mean that there were possibilities open to me that were denied to him? Very likely they did. But if so, one also supposes that he feared the impulses within himself toward submission to authority no less powerfully than I feared the impulses in myself toward defiance. If I represented the jailer to him, it was not because I was oppressing him or keeping him down: it was because I symbolized for him the dangerous and probably pointless temptation toward greater repression, just as he symbolized for me the equally perilous tug toward greater freedom. I personally was to be rewarded for this repression with a new and better life in the future, but how many of my friends paid an even higher price and were given only gall in return.

[21] We have it on the authority of James Baldwin that all Negroes hate whites. I am trying to suggest that on their side all whites—all American whites, that is—are sick in their feelings about Negroes. There are Negroes, no doubt, who would say that Baldwin is wrong, but I suspect them of being less honest than he is, just as I suspect whites of self-deception who tell me they have no special feeling toward Negroes. Special feelings about color are a contagion to which white Americans seem susceptible even when there is nothing in their background to account for the susceptibility. Thus everywhere we look today in the North, we find the curious phenomenon of white middle-class liberals with no previous personal experience of Negroes—people to whom Negroes have always been faceless in virtue rather than faceless in vice— discovering that their abstract commitment to the cause of Negro rights will not stand the test of a direct confrontation. We find such people fleeing in droves to the suburbs as the Negro population in the inner city grows; and when they stay in the city we find them sending their children to private school rather than to the "integrated" public school in the

neighborhood. We find them resisting the demand that gerrymandered school districts be re-zoned for the purpose of overcoming de facto segregation; we find them judiciously considering whether the Negroes (for their own good, of course) are not perhaps pushing too hard; we find them clucking their tongues over Negro militancy; we find them speculating on the question of whether there may not, after all, be something in the theory that the races are biologically different; we find them saying that it will take a very long time for Negroes to achieve full equality, no matter what anyone does; we find them deploring the rise of black nationalism and expressing the solemn hope that the leaders of the Negro community will discover ways of containing the impatience and incipient violence with the Negro ghettos.[1]

[22] But that is by no means the whole story; there is also the phenomenon of what Kenneth Rexroth once called "crow-jimism." There are the broken-down white boys like Vivaldo Moore in Baldwin's *Another Country* who go to Harlem in search of sex or simply to brush up against something that looks like primitive vitality, and who are so often punished by the Negro they meet for crimes that they would have been the last ever to commit and of which they themselves have been as sorry victims as any of the Negroes who take it out on them. There are the writers and intellectuals and artists who romanticize Negroes and pander to them, assuming a guilt that is not properly theirs. And there are all the white liberals who permit Negroes to blackmail them into adopting a double standard of moral judgment, and who lend themselves—again assuming the responsibility for crimes they never committed—to cunning and contemptuous exploitation by Negroes they employ or try to befriend.

[23] And what about me? What kind of feelings do I have about Negroes today? What happened to me, from Brooklyn, who grew up fearing and envying and hating Negroes? Now that Brooklyn is behind me, do I fear them and envy them and hate them still? The answer is yes, but not in the same proportions and certainly not in the same way. I now live on the upper west side of Manhattan, where there are many Negroes and many Puerto Ricans, and there are nights when I experience the old apprehensiveness again, and there are streets that I avoid when I am walking in the dark, as there were streets that I avoided when I was a child. I find that I am not afraid of Puerto Ricans, but I cannot restrain my nervousness whenever I pass a group of Negroes standing in front of a bar or sauntering down the street. I know now, as I did not know when I was a child, that power is on my side, that the police are working for me and not for them. And knowing this I feel ashamed and

[1] For an account of developments like these, see "The White Liberal's Retreat" by Murray Friedman in the January 1963 *Atlantic Monthly*.

guilty, like the good liberal I have grown up to be. Yet the twinges of fear and the resentment they bring and the self-contempt they arouse are not to be gainsaid.

[24] But envy? Why envy? And hatred? Why hatred? Here again the intensities have lessened and everything has been complicated and qualified by the guilts and the resulting over-compensations that are the heritage of the enlightened middle-class world of which I am now a member. Yet just as in childhood I envied Negroes for what seemed to me their superior masculinity, so I envy them today for what seems to me their superior physical grace and beauty. I have come to value physical grace very highly, and I am now capable of aching with all my being when I watch a Negro couple on the dance floor, or a Negro playing baseball or basketball. They are on the kind of terms with their own bodies that I should like to be on with mine, and for that precious quality they seem blessed to me.

[25] The hatred I still feel for Negroes is the hardest of all the old feelings to face or admit, and it is the most hidden and the most overlarded by the conscious attitudes into which I have succeeded in willing myself. It no longer has, as for me it once did, any cause or justification (except, perhaps, that I am constantly being denied my right to an honest expression of the things I earned the right as a child to feel). How, then, do I know that this hatred has never entirely disappeared? I know it from the insane rage that can stir in me at the thought of Negro anti-Semitism; I know it from the disgusting prurience that can stir in me at the sight of a mixed couple; and I know it from the violence that can stir in me whenever I encounter that special brand of paranoid touchiness to which many Negroes are prone.

[26] This, then, is where I am; it is not exactly where I think all other white liberals are, but it cannot be so very far away either. And it is because I am convinced that we white Americans are—for whatever reason, it no longer matters—so twisted and sick in our feelings about Negroes that I despair of the present push toward integration. If the pace of progress were not a factor here, there would perhaps be no cause for despair: time and the law and even the international political situation are on the side of the Negroes, and ultimately, therefore, victory—of a sort, anyway—must come. But from everything we have learned from observers who ought to know, pace has become as important to the Negroes as substance. They want equality and they want it *now*, and the white world is yielding to their demand only as much and as fast as it is absolutely being compelled to do. The Negroes know this in the most concrete terms imaginable, and it is thus becoming increasingly difficult to buy them off with rhetoric and promises and pious assurances of support. And so within the Negro community we find more and more people

declaring—as Harold R. Isaacs recently put it in these pages[2]—that they want *out:* people who say that integration will never come, or that it will take a hundred or a thousand years to come, or that it will come at too high a price in suffering and struggle for the pallid and sodden life of the American middle class that at the very best it may bring.

[27] The most numerous, influential, and dangerous movement that has grown out of Negro despair with the goal of integration is, of course, the Black Muslims. This movement, whatever else we may say about it, must be credited with one enduring achievement: it inspired James Baldwin to write an essay[3] which deserves to be placed among the classics of our language. Everything Baldwin has ever been trying to tell us is distilled here into a statement of overwhelming persuasiveness and prophetic magnificence. Baldwin's message is and always has been simple. It is this: "Color is not a human or personal reality; it is a political reality." And Baldwin's demand is correspondingly simple: color must be forgotten, lest we all be smited with a vengeance "that does not really depend on, and cannot really be executed by, any person or organization, and that cannot be prevented by any police force or army: historical vengeance, a cosmic vengeance based on the law that we recognize when we say, 'Whatever goes up must come down.'" The Black Muslims Baldwin portrays as a sign and a warning to the intransigent white world. They come to proclaim how deep is the Negro's disaffection with the white world and all its works, and Baldwin implies that no American Negro can fail to respond somewhere in his being to their message: that the white man is the devil, that Allah has doomed him to destruction, and that the black man is about to inherit the earth. Baldwin of course knows that this nightmare inversion of the racism from which the black man has suffered can neither win nor even point to the neighborhood in which victory might be located. For in his view the neighborhood of victory lies in exactly the opposite direction: the transcendence of color through love.

[28] Yet the tragic fact is that love is not the answer to hate—not in the world of politics, at any rate. Color is indeed a political rather than a human or a personal reality and if politics (which is to say power) has made it into a human and a personal reality, then only politics (which is to say power) can unmake it once again. But the way of politics is slow and bitter, and as impatience on the one side is matched by a setting of the jaw on the other, we move closer and closer to an explosion and blood may yet run in the streets.

[29] Will this madness in which we are all caught never find a resting-

[2] "Integration and the Negro Mood," December 1962.
[3] Originally published last November in the *New Yorker* under the title "Letter From a Region in My Mind," it has just been reprinted (along with a new introduction) by Dial Press under the title *The Fire Next Time.*

place? Is there never to be an end to it? In thinking about the Jews I have often wondered whether their survival as a distinct group was worth one hair on the head of a single infant. Did the Jews have to survive so that six million innocent people should one day be burned in the ovens of Auschwitz? It is a terrible question and no one, not God himself, could ever answer it to my satisfaction. And when I think about the Negroes in America and about the image of integration as a state in which the Negroes would take their rightful place as another of the protected minorities in a pluralistic society, I wonder whether they really believe in their hearts that such a state can actually be attained, and if so *why* they should wish to survive as a distinct group. I think I know why the Jews once wished to survive (though I am less certain as to why we still do): they not only believed that God had given them no choice, but they were tied to a memory of past glory and a dream of imminent redemption. What does the American Negro have that might correspond to this? His past is a stigma, his color is a stigma, and his vision of the future is the hope of erasing the stigma by making color irrelevant, by making it disappear as a fact of consciousness.

[30] I share this hope, but I cannot see how it will ever be realized unless color does *in fact* disappear: and that means not integration, it means assimilation, it means—let the brutal word come out—miscegenation. The Black Muslims, like their racist counterparts in the white world, accuse the "so-called Negro leaders" of secretly pursuing miscegenation as a goal. The racists are wrong, but I wish they were right, for I believe that the wholesale merging of the two races is the most desirable alternative for everyone concerned. I am not claiming that this alternative can be pursued programmatically or that it is immediately feasible as a solution; obviously there are even greater barriers to its achievement than to the achievement of integration. What I am saying, however, is that in my opinion the Negro problem can be solved in this country in no other way.

[31] I have told the story of my own twisted feelings about Negroes here, and of how they conflict with the moral convictions I have since developed, in order to assert that such feelings must be acknowledged as honestly as possible so that they can be controlled and ultimately disregarded in favor of the convictions. It is *wrong* for a man to suffer because of the color of his skin. Beside that clichéd proposition of liberal thought, what argument can stand and be respected? If the arguments are the arguments of feeling, they must be made to yield; and one's own soul is not the worst place to begin working a huge social transformation. Not so long ago, it used to be asked of white liberals, "Would you like your sister to marry one?" When I was a boy and my sister was still unmarried, I would certainly have said no to that question. But now I am a man, my sister is already married, and I have daughters. If I were to be asked

today whether I would like a daughter of mine "to marry one," I would have to answer: "No, I wouldn't *like* it at all. I would rail and rave and rant and tear my hair. And then I hope I would have the courage to curse myself for raving and ranting, and to give her my blessing. How dare I withhold it at the behest of the child I once was and against the man I now have a duty to be?"

COMMENT AND QUESTIONS

1. The author begins with the conflict between commonly accepted ideas and the evidence of his senses and his experience. Where and for what purpose does he discuss a similar conflict later in the essay?
2. The childhood experiences with Negroes are presented in great detail. Why does Podhoretz develop them so fully? What is gained by narrating the "items" in the present tense?
3. What is meant by "the culture of the street," near the end of paragraph 14?
4. The author asks a number of questions in his essay. Point out examples of the use of questions to introduce new aspects of the whole problem.
5. Podhoretz moves from his personal experience to generalizations about people, Negro and white. Does this shift from the particular to the general seem to you justifiable and logical? Explain.
6. Explain how Podhoretz thinks the "mechanism of projection" worked for him and probably for the Negro boys. How is this projection related to "the principle of facelessness"?
7. How does the author support his ideas that all Negroes hate whites and that all American whites are sick and twisted in their feelings about Negroes? Are the ideas convincing to you? Explain.
8. In paragraph 26 and later, Podhoretz expresses a despair about the push toward integration. Do you agree with his views? Explain.
9. What is the meaning of James Baldwin's statement, with which Podhoretz agrees, that color is not a human or personal reality but is a political reality? How is the statement related to the author's concluding paragraphs?
10. Paragraph 30 suggests what Podhoretz believes is the only solution to the Negro problem. What does paragraph 31 contribute to the essay? Comment on the effectiveness of the last sentence.
11. When "My Negro Problem—and Ours" was published in *Commentary*, it provoked sharply different reactions from readers. What is your reaction to the essay, and why?

[50] *John Fischer*: Substitutes for Violence

JOHN FISCHER (1910–   ) is an American writer and publisher, editor in chief of *Harper's Magazine* from 1953 to 1967. The following essay was published in that magazine in January, 1966. Footnotes are the author's.

Scoundrels and in some cases even ruffians terrified the citizens. Young mothers had to take their babies to Central Park in armored cars. Old women went to the theater in tanks, and no pretty woman would venture forth after dark unless convoyed by a regiment of troops . . . the police wore bullet-proof underwear and were armed with mortars and fifteen-inch howitzers . . . — JAMES RESTON
The New York Times, Oct. 29, 1965

[1] Like most fables, Mr. Reston's moral tale exaggerates a little. But not much; for all of us are uneasily aware that violence is becoming a central fact of American life. Year after year the official graph for crimes of violence—murder, rape, assault, robbery, and riot—inches a little higher.[*] Many of these crimes seem to be entirely senseless: a California sniper blazes away at random at passing motorists . . . Bronx youngsters pillage the Botanical Garden and wreck their own schoolrooms . . . a subway rider suddenly pulls a knife and starts slashing at his fellow passengers . . . a gang of roaming teen-agers comes across an old man drowsing on a park bench; they club and burn him to death without even bothering to rifle his pockets.

[2] It is hardly surprising, then, that violence is becoming a dominant concern in our politics, literature, and conversation. Every campaigning candidate promises to chase the hoodlums off the city streets. Murder and mayhem—usually aimless, inexplicable, "existential"—are a growing preoccupation of American novelists: witness the recent work of Norman Mailer, Nelson Algren, and a hundred less-publicized writers. And not only the novelists; one of the most memorable nonfiction books of the past year was Truman Capote's *In Cold Blood,* a factual account of the pecu-

[*] According to the annual reports of the Federal Bureau of Investigation. But its figures are based on voluntary reports by more than eight thousand local law-enforcement agencies, using different definitions of crime and widely varying statistical methods; therefore the FBI does not vouch for their accuracy. In fact, nobody knows precisely how much crime is committed in the United States, or its rate of increase, if any.

481

liarly brutal murder of the Clutter family by two young sadists. Significantly, the scene was not a city street but a Kansas farm.

[3] Nor is the carnage limited to the United States. As *The Economist* of London pointed out in a recent article (reprinted in the November issue of *Harper's*), rioting and hooliganism are on the rise in nearly every country, including England, Sweden, and Russia. Bloodshed in the big cities naturally gets most of the headlines, but it seems to be almost as widespread in predominantly rural areas—the Sudan, for example, India, the Congo, and Colombia, where *la violencia* has taken hundreds of thousands of lives during the last two decades.

[4] Explanations for all this are easy to come by, from nearly every clergyman, sociologist, and politician. Unfortunately they are seldom consistent. Some blame the miseries of slum life, others the breakdown of the family, or religion, or our national moral fiber. Racial and religious frictions apparently account for much free-floating hostility—in Watts and Calcutta, Capetown and Hué, even in Moscow and Peking, where African students report a lot of rough treatment from their hosts. Marxists, naturally, explain it all in terms of bourgeois decadence (although that would hardly account for the outbreaks in Prague and Novocherkassk, where the wicked bourgeoisie were liquidated long ago). While the Black Muslims decry police brutality, J. Edgar Hoover is prescribing more policemen, armed with wider powers. The Freudians suggest that sexual frustration may be the root of the trouble, while Billy Graham is just as sure that it is sexual laxity. Nearly everybody points an indignant finger at the dope peddlers, and William Buckley gets cheers whenever he proclaims that nothing will save us short of a universal moral regeneration.

[5] Perhaps there is some truth in all these explanations. But I am beginning to wonder whether, far beneath them all, there may not lie another, more primordial reason. Just possibly the global surge of antisocial violence may result from the fact that nearly all societies—especially those we describe as "advanced"—suddenly have been forced to change a key commandment in their traditional codes of behavior; and many people, particularly the young males, have not yet been able to adjust themselves to this reversal.

[6] That commandment was simple: "Be a fighter." Ever since human beings began to emerge as a separate species, something over a million years ago, it has been our first law of survival. For the earliest men, life was an incessant battle: against the hostile Pleistocene environment, against other mammals for food, against their own kind for a sheltering cave, a water hole, a hunting range, a mate. The fiercest, wiliest, and strongest lived to raise children. The meek, weak, slow, and stupid made an early breakfast—for a local tiger or, perhaps oftener, for a neighboring

family, since archaeological evidence suggests that cannibalism was common among primeval man. The result was that "our ancestors have bred pugnacity into our bone and marrow. . . ."*

[7] As civilization began to dawn, fighting became more organized—a community enterprise rather than a family one. In addition to their daily skirmishes with wolves, cattle thieves, and passing strangers, the able-bodied men of the village (or polis, kingdom, or pueblo) normally banded together at least once a year for a joint killing venture. The convenient time for settled farming people was early fall, after the harvest was in; then they had both enough leisure and enough surplus food to mount an expedition. So it was about September when the Assyrian swept down like a wolf on the fold, when Gideon smote the Philistines, when Vikings ravaged the Kentish coast, when the Greeks shoved off for Troy, when the Dorians swept into the Argive plain, irresistibly armed with that first mass weapon, the iron sword. (Because iron ore was much more plentiful than copper, it could be used—once the secret of smelting it was learned—to equip every man in the ranks. The victims of the Dorians, still lingering in the Bronze Age, normally armed only their officers with metal blades; the rest carried flint-tipped spears and arrows.) Tribes in the preagricultural stage sometimes found other seasons more suitable for rapine. The War Moon of the Great Plains Indians, for example, came in May—since the spring grass was then just high enough to graze the horses of a raiding party, and the full moon made it easy to travel fast at night. Regardless of timing, however, warfare was for centuries the main social enterprise, absorbing virtually all of the community's surplus time, energy, and resources. "History," as William James put it, "is a bath of blood . . . war for war's sake, all the citizens being warriors . . . To hunt a neighboring tribe, kill the males, loot the village, and possess the females was the most profitable, as well as the most exciting, way of living."

[8] As soon as warfare became socialized, the premium on belligerence was redoubled. Always highly favored by the processes of natural selection, it was now celebrated as a prime civic virtue as well. The Great Fighter was enshrined as the universal hero. His name might be Hercules or Rustum, Beowulf or David, Kiyomori or Hiawatha, but his characteristics remained the same: physical strength, reckless courage, skill with weapons, and a bottomless appetite for bloodshed. From earliest boyhood the males of the community were taught to emulate him. Their training for combat began as soon as they could lift a spear, and by eighteen they normally would be full-fledged warriors—whether in Athens or Cuzco—equally ready to defend their city's walls or to pillage a weaker neighbor.

---

* As William James put it in his classic essay, "The Moral Equivalent of War," published in 1910. His other comments on this grisly topic will be noted in a moment.

Success in battle was the basic status symbol. The best fighters were feted in victory celebrations, heaped with honors and plunder, endowed with the lushest women, both homegrown and captive. The weak and timid, on the other hand, were scorned by elders and girls alike, and in many societies cowardice was punished by death.

[9] For nearly all of human history, then, the aggressive impulse—so deeply embedded in our genes—had no trouble in finding an outlet. This outlet was not only socially acceptable; it was encouraged and rewarded by every resource at society's disposal.

[10] This remained true until roughly a hundred years ago. (When my grandfathers were boys, the martial virtues were still applauded about as much as ever, and both of them marched off to the Civil War with the joyous spirit of an Alcibiades bound for Syracuse.)

[11] Then, with stunning abruptness, the rules changed. Within about a century—a mere eye-blink in terms of evolutionary development—the traditional outlet for violence closed up. Fighting, so long encouraged by society, suddenly became intolerable.

[12] One reason, of course, was the industrialization of war. It not only made warfare ruinously expensive; it took all the fun out of it. Long before the invention of the atom bomb, farsighted men such as William James had come to see that war was no longer "the most profitable, as well as the most exciting, way of living"; and by 1918 the lesson was plain to nearly everyone. In retrospect, our Civil War seems to have been the last in which physical strength, raw courage, and individual prowess could be (sometimes, at least) decisive; perhaps that is why it is written about so much, and so nostalgically.

[13] For there is a certain animal satisfaction (as every football player knows) in bopping another man over the head. By all accounts, our ancestors thoroughly enjoyed hammering at each other with sword and mace; it exercised the large muscles, burned up the adrenalin in the system, relieved pent-up frustrations, and demonstrated virility in the most elemental fashion. But nobody can get that kind of satisfaction out of pulling the lanyard on a cannon, pointed at an unseen enemy miles away; you might as well be pulling a light switch in a factory. Indeed, in a modern army not one man in ten ever gets near combat; the great majority of the troops are cranking mimeograph machines, driving trucks, and tending the PX far to the rear. As a consequence, warfare—aside from its other disadvantages—no longer satisfies the primitive instinct for violence as it did for uncountable thousands of years.

[14] At about the same time—that is, roughly a century ago—the other socially approved outlets for pugnacity also began to close up. For example, so long as our society was mostly rural and small-town, a good deal

of purely personal, casual brawling was easily tolerated. When Lincoln was a young man, the main public amusement seemed to be watching (and often joining in) the donnybrooks which boiled up regularly in the village street; and during his New Salem days, Abe more than held his own. Our literature of the last century, from *Huckleberry Finn* to the story of the OK Wagon Yard, is studded with this kind of spontaneous combat. And our chronicles memorialize the violent men (whether fur trappers, river boatmen, forty-niners, lumberjacks, or cowboys) in the same admiring tone as the sagas of Achilles and Roland. As recently as my own boyhood, fist-fighting was considered a normal after-school activity, like marbles and run-sheep-run; nobody thought of us as juvenile delinquents, in need of a corps of Youth Workers to hound us into docility. A tight-packed urban society, however, simply can't put up with this kind of random combat. It disturbs the peace, endangers bystanders, and obstructs traffic.

[15] As we turned into a nation of city dwellers, we lost another traditional testing ground for masculine prowess: the struggle against nature. Since the beginning of history, when men weren't fighting each other they spent most of their time fighting the elements. To survive, they had to hack down forests, kill off predatory animals, battle with every ounce of strength and cunning against blizzards, droughts, deserts, and gales. When Richard Henry Dana came home after two years before the mast, he knew he was a man. So too with the striplings who rafted logs down rivers in a spate, drove a wagon over the Natchez Trace, pulled a fishing dory on the Grand Banks, or broke sod on the Nebraska prairies. Not long after he started shaving, my father went off alone to homestead a farm in what eventually became the state of Oklahoma. If he had been bothered by an "identity crisis"—something he couldn't even conceive—it would have evaporated long before he got his final papers.

[16] Today of course the strenuous life, which Theodore Roosevelt thought essential for a healthy man, has all but vanished. Probably not 5 per cent of our youngsters grow up to outdoor work, in farming, forests, or fisheries; and even for them, although the work may be hard, it is rarely either exciting or dangerous. (The modern cowboy does most of his work in a pickup truck, while Captain Ahab's successor goes to sea in a floating oil factory.) This final conquest of nature has had some results both comic and a little sad. Among the Masai tribesmen, for instance, when a boy comes of age it has always been customary for him to prove his manhood by killing a lion with a spear; but according to recent reports from Africa, there are no longer enough lions to go around.

[17] In our tamer culture, we have shown remarkable ingenuity in inventing lion-substitutes. The most fashionable surrogates for violence are the strenuous and risky sports—skiing, skin diving, surfing, mountain

climbing, drag racing, sailing small boats in rough weather—which have burgeoned so remarkably in recent years. When a middle-aged Cleveland copy editor crosses the Atlantic alone in a twelve-foot sloop, nobody accuses him of suicidal impulses; on the contrary, millions of sedentary males understand all too well his yearning for at least one adventure in life, however self-imposed and unnecessary. (Women, of course, generally do not understand; most of the wives I've overheard discussing the Manry voyage wondered, not how he made it, but why Mrs. Manry ever let him try.)

[18] But these devices serve only the middle class. For the poor, they ordinarily are too expensive. When Robert Benchley remarked that there was enough suffering in life without people tying boards on their feet and sliding down mountains, he missed the point; the real trouble with skiing is that slum kids can't afford it. Consequently, they try to get their kicks vicariously, by watching murder, football, boxing, and phony wrestling matches on television. When that palls, their next resort usually is reckless driving. That is why access to a car (his own, his family's, or a stolen one) is as precious to the adolescent male—rich or poor—in our culture as possession of a shield was in fifth-century Athens. It is a similar badge of manhood, the equipment necessary to demonstrate that he is a fearless and dashing fellow. (It also is the reason why insurance premiums are so high on autos driven by males under twenty-five years old.)

[19] Such games are socially useful, because they absorb in a relatively harmless way some of our pent-up aggressions. But they all have one great drawback: they are merely games. They are contrived; they are artificial adjuncts to life, rather than the core of life itself. When our ancestors harpooned a whale, pillaged a city, or held the pass at Thermopylae, they knew they were playing for keeps. When our sons break their legs on a ski slope or play "chicken" on the highway, they know that the challenge is a made-up one, and therefore never wholly satisfying. They still yearn for a genuine challenge, a chance to prove their hardihood in a way that really means something.

[20] Lacking anything better, some of them—a growing number, apparently—turn to crimes of violence. Gang fights, vandalism, robbery are, in an important sense, more "real" than any game. And for large groups of disadvantaged people, any form of antisocial violence is a way of striking back, in blind fury, at the community which has condemned them to disappointment and frustration. This is equally true, I suspect, of the Negro rioters in Watts and the poor whites of the South, who take so readily to the murders, church burnings, and assorted barbarities of the Klan.

[21] This sort of thing may well continue, on a rising scale, until we can discover what James called a "moral equivalent for war." He thought he

had found it. He wanted to draft "the whole youthful population" into a peacetime army to serve in "the immemorial human warfare against nature." What he had in mind was a sort of gigantic Civilian Conservation Corps, in which every youngster would spend a few years at hard and dangerous labor—consigned to "coal and iron mines, to freight trains, to fishing fleets in December . . . to road-building and tunnel-making." When he wrote, a half-century ago, this idea sounded plausible, because the need for such work seemed limitless.

[22] Today, however, his prescription is harder to apply. In many parts of the globe, the war against nature has ended, with nature's unconditional surrender. Automation, moreover, has eliminated most dangerous and physically demanding jobs; our mines and freight trains are overmanned, our roads are now built with earth-moving machines rather than pick and shovel.

[23] Nevertheless, so far as I can see James's idea is still our best starting point. And already an encouraging number of people are groping for ways to make it work, in the different and more difficult circumstances of our time.

[24] A few have found personal, unofficial answers. The young people who join the civil-rights movement in the South, for example, are encountering hardship, violence, and occasionally death in a cause that is obviously genuine; they aren't playing games. But The Movement can accommodate only a limited number of volunteers, and presumably it will go out of business eventually, when the white Southerners reconcile themselves to rejoining the United States. In the North, civil-rights work has often turned out to be less satisfying, emotionally, because The Enemy is harder to identify and the goals are less clear. As a result its young partisans sometimes have drifted into a kind of generalized protest, carrying placards for almost anything from SNCC to Free Speech to World Peace: that is, they have ended up with another form of game playing.

[25] President Kennedy, who understood thoroughly the youthful need for struggle and self-sacrifice, had the Jamesian principle in mind when he started the Peace Corps. It remains the most successful official experiment in this direction, and it led to the Job Corps and several related experiments in the domestic Antipoverty Program. How they will work out is still an open question, as William Haddad pointed out last month in *Harper's*. At least they are a public recognition that the country has to do *something*. If we don't—if we continue to let millions of young men sit around, while the adrenalin bubbles and every muscle screams for action, with no outlet in sight but a desk job at best and an unemployment check at worst—then we are asking for bad trouble. Either we can find ways to give them action, in some useful fashion, or we can look forward to a rising surge of antisocial violence. In the latter case we may, a decade

from now, remember the Fort Lauderdale beach riots as a mere boyish prank.

[26] What I am suggesting, of course, is that all of us—especially our businessmen, sociologists, and political leaders—ought to invest a good deal more effort, ingenuity, and money in the search for acceptable substitutes for violence. How many industries have really tried to create interesting and physically demanding jobs for young people? Have the paper companies, for instance, figured out how many foresters they might use, if they were to develop their timber reserves for camping, hunting, and fishing, as well as for wood pulp? And are they sure such a venture would not be profitable?

[27] To take care of the population explosion, we are going to have to duplicate all of our present college buildings within the next twenty years. Has any university looked into the possibility of using prospective students to do some of the building? Maybe every able-bodied boy should be required to labor on the campus for six months as a bricklayer or carpenter before he is admitted to classes?

[28] Cleaning up our polluted rivers is a task worthy of Paul Bunyan, and one we can't postpone much longer. What governor has thought of mobilizing a state Youth Corps to do part of the job? Has Ladybird Johnson calculated how many husky youngsters might be deployed, axes in hand, to chop down billboards along our highways and replace them with trees?

[29] The possibilities aren't as easy to spot as they were in William James's day, but even in our overcrowded and overdeveloped society some of them still exist. No single one of them will provide the kind of simple, large-scale panacea that James had in mind—yet if we can discover a few hundred such projects, they might add up to a pretty fair Moral Equivalent. In any case, the search is worth a more serious try than anyone has made yet.

[30] Why, my wife asks me, is all that necessary? Wouldn't it be simpler for you men to stop acting like savages? Since you realize that belligerence is no longer a socially useful trait, why don't you try to cultivate your gentler and more humane instincts? Are you saying that You Can't Change Human Nature?

[31] No, that isn't quite what I'm saying. I recognize that human nature changes all the time. Cannibalism, for example, is now fairly rare, and polygamy (at least in its more open form) has been abandoned by a number of cultures. Someday (I hope and believe) the craving for violence will leach out of the human system. But the reversal of an evolutionary process takes a long time. For a good many generations, then, the

Old Adam is likely to linger in our genes; and during that transitional period, probably the best we can hope for is to keep him reasonably quiet with some variant of William James's prescription.

⇥{ COMMENT AND QUESTIONS }⇤

1. The basic pattern of this essay might be called problem-to-solution: the problem of violence to ways of providing substitutes for violence. Where in the essay does Fischer also use patterns of narration, of contrast, and of cause and effect?
2. The author announces a thesis in paragraph 5 and clarifies it in paragraph 6. What are the purposes of the first four paragraphs? How would you describe the tone of paragraph 5?
3. How does Fischer make the survey of human history, in paragraphs 6–10, interesting?
4. Briefly summarize the author's main points about why advanced societies have been forced to change a traditional "key commandment."
5. Examine the last sentence of paragraph 14. What makes it an effective sentence?
6. What is the function in the essay of the report about the lions in paragraph 16? Of the comment on women's attitudes at the end of paragraph 17?
7. Some of our present substitutes for violence, the author says, are socially useful outlets for aggressiveness. What deficiencies does he see in them? To what extent do you agree or disagree with his analysis in paragraphs 17–20?
8. What is your reaction to Fischer's general proposal of a large-scale program to provide substitutes for violence? Comment on his particular suggestions in paragraphs 26–28. How many young men whom you know would probably like to participate in such a program? What might be the major difficulties in making it work?
9. If you have read John Dewey's essay "Does Human Nature Change?" what similarities do you see between Dewey's and Fischer's ideas?

[51]   *Leon H. Keyserling*: Something
for Everybody

THE FOLLOWING article, from *The New York Times Book Review* of February 27, 1966, is a review of a book edited by Robert Theobald and called *The Guaranteed Income: Next Step in Economic Evolution?* Since the reviewer does not wholly agree with the general thesis of the book, the article presents two attitudes toward a current question. Leon H. Keyserling (1908–   ), an attorney and economist, has been Chairman of the Council of Economic Advisers and President of the Conference on Economic Progress. His publications include *The Federal Budget and the General Welfare, Food and Freedom, Progress on Poverty,* and *Agriculture and the Public Interest.*

[1] The central proposition of the Preface and 10 essays in this book is that society, presumably starting in the United States, should guarantee to everyone a socially acceptable level of income. This guaranteed income would not be made available solely to those unable to work for reasons such as age or disability, or debarred from work by involuntary unemployment. It would extend to *all,* regardless of whether they are or should be "gainfully employed" in the production of goods and services as this term has come to be understood. It would include all who, for reasons of their own, prefer leisure to gainful employment.

[2] I assume that this guaranteed income should be far above the currently defined poverty-income ceiling of $3,000-plus for a family. For while only about 34 million Americans lived in poverty in 1964, another 49 million lived in deprivation, with incomes below the requirements for a "modest but adequate" budget. The concept of what is "modest but adequate" changes with advances in the industrial arts; today, it implies in the U.S. a family income of about $6,000.

[3] Interest in these essays is heightened by the Feb. 4 release of the long-awaited Report of the National Commission on Technology, Automation, and Economic Progress. This Report advocates guaranteed incomes for all, but evidently in the same context as this reviewer, rather than in the different context underlying these essays.

[4] The essays are valuable on several counts, aside from being very readable throughout. The espousal of a guaranteed annual income for all, while not entirely novel, has so little acceptance to date that it should

be rated as enterprising and courageous. We do need these virtues today. The position is unassailable that the U.S. economy is already powerful enough to assure a "modest but adequate" standard of living for all our people. In my view, we therefore have a moral obligation to furnish this assurance, and the authors are most commendable in bringing moral considerations to the forefront at a time when they are being seriously neglected in most approaches to economic problems.

[5] Still another merit is that the book brings together a wide range of disciplines; economic and related social policies are too important to be left, even in their technical or professional aspects, to economists alone. The authors' challenge to the conventional economics is telling, notably Meno Lovenstein's. The contributors include four economists (Robert Theobald, Clarence E. Ayers, Lovenstein and Ben B. Seligman); an anthropologist (Conrad M. Arensberg); a psychologist (Robert H. Davis); a psychiatrist (Erich Fromm); an administrator and scholar in the field of culture and technology (Marshall McLuhan); a social-welfare expert (Edward Schwartz); and a conservationist (William Vogt).

[6] My dissent from the general theme of the volume is partial but vital. When I join in the view that all of our people should be guaranteed a "modest but adequate" income and standard of living, I envisage this as stemming primarily from a full-employment policy coupled with adequate compensation, and secondarily from guaranteed incomes for those not qualified for gainful employment because of age or other disability. But the authors go far beyond this. With probably two exceptions (Mr. Ayers and Mr. Seligman) they appear to relegate far to the rear the goal of sustained full employment and the ever-increasing national output which would result from full utilization of a growing labor force plus an advancing technology. Most of them are mainly interested in incomes, not jobs.

[7] The economic basis of the case is stated simply and with candor by the book's editor, Mr. Theobald, in the Preface, consistently with his voluminous other writings on the same subject. He is a British socio-economist, formerly with the Organization for European Economic Cooperation and now living in New York. As he would have it, the onrush of technology, automation and cybernation is so overwhelming that massive unemployment is utterly unavoidable and full employment a pious dream. This presents to him no difficulties from the viewpoint of available output: advances in industrial techniques are such that, even with only a moderate fraction of the population of working age gainfully employed in the production of conventional goods and services, we will enjoy "an overwhelming abundance" of them. Under these assumptions, it is manifestly more desirable that everybody should live nicely on a guaranteed

income rather than that poverty should be the lot of those who cannot be gainfully employed.

[8] In evaluating this case, I am not particularly impressed with the standard argument that income without employment as customarily defined would for motivational and psychological reasons be corrosive of the human spirit. Fromm, McLuhan and Arensberg offer reasons at least worthy of careful consideration to the effect that freedom from the obligation to work, equating with the freedom of every individual to do what he thinks he likes best, might have real value in terms of individual development. Vogt adds the point that the guaranteed income for all would not accentuate the problem of overpopulation. And at least for those who cannot be gainfully employed, Schwartz castigates the "means test" along lines which should help to propel much-needed revision of the prevalent approaches to many current welfare programs which tend to encourage pauperization.

[9] Before going all the way with the authors, we must examine Mr. Theobald's proposition (which most of the others in the group seem to share) that sustained full employment and the ever-increasing production of goods and services which would result as technology advances are neither feasible nor highly desirable. The first difficulty with this proposition is that those among the authors (primarily Mr. Davis and Mr. Seligman) who pick up the task of giving us the facts do not in my view come through convincingly. They offer relevant data with respect to computers and other innovations, and valid evidence of long-term acceleration in the rate of increase in output per man-hour worked. But even if they are talking only about the U.S. and its domestic needs, they offer no comprehensive quantitative appraisal as to how long it would take us, even if fully employed, to turn out so much goods and services that we would no longer be concerned about the increased output which would result from sustained full employment.

[10] Let us look at some facts that seem to be most pertinent, first with respect to *when* we might be able to produce more than we would need or want. The average disposable per-capita income in the U.S. in 1965 was about $2,400, or about $7,500–8,000 on an average consumer-unit basis. I do not suppose that most of the professors and others who write books would regard a family income of about three times this as more than could be used wisely and well (and without corruption of soul) for the needs and niceties of life, including a trip to Europe now and then. Most of them would aspire toward achieving this income and living standard, if they have not already done so, before they would plunk for "retirement" on a guaranteed income of even $6,000 or thereabouts. In all probability, nonintellectuals would make the same choice with even more alacrity, although I have never noted that the intellectual community is congenitally opposed to more income and "material" things.

[11] During the years 1955–1965, U.S. per-capita disposable income in real terms increased less than 23 per cent. On this basis, allowing for compounding, it would take more than five decades for average U.S. incomes and living standards to reach levels which the professors and other writers certainly would not regard as "too high" even now. To attain these levels requires just that much more national production of goods and services on a per-capita basis.

[12] Besides, increased output must serve many purposes other than personal incomes and outlays. It must help to build plant and equipment; finance research; conserve and replenish our neglected natural resources; purify our polluted air and waters; modernize our obsolescent transportation systems; rebuild our decaying cities; rehouse the at least one-sixth of the total population who still live in urban and rural slums; generate the additional hospitals and personnel needed to bring adequate medical care to the two-fifths of our people who do not now obtain it at costs within their means. It must also help to overcome enormous deficiencies in educational plant and teachers, and enable to go to college the half of our young people who have the ability and ambition but lack the means; and support (as far as we can see ahead) immense outlays for defense and space exploration and international policies fraught with great uncertainties. This is not the whole list.

[13] All of these things are paid for, in the final analysis, not with money but with production. One of the writers in the volume, Mr. Ayers, does intimate that the guaranteed income for all would provide the purchasing power to stimulate full production and full employment. But this reverses the core theme of the volume: that the guaranteed income for all is essential because massive unemployment is in the cards, and because output per employed worker will soon be so fabulous that high employment will no longer be needed.

[14] And even if we in the U.S. should reach, 50 years hence, a situation where our production at full employment led to genuine saturation of needs and desires at home, what about the rest of the world? This brings us back to 1966, not forward to 2016. While the rich nations get richer, the poor get poorer. The widening gap threatens us no less than them. The prospect is that, by 1970, there will be a billion people in the world who are literally starving. What should we now and henceforth be doing to help them avoid this, not only with know-how, but also with exports of food and hardware and capital, in immensely increased amounts? Are Africa, Asia and South America shuddering at the prospect of an "overwhelming abundance" of goods and services? Is it the advance of technology which explains their massive unemployment?

[15] Before we even talk about dulling the greatest nonsecret weapon in the world, our soaring productive powers, we should reexamine and reconstruct our worldwide economic policies. The Administration has just

done much of this in qualitative terms. But we do not yet realize that the quality of what we do to help those who need help most is quantitative at its very foundation.

[16] In the full perspective of human needs, we have room and to spare for all we can produce at full employment, as far ahead as we can see. It would thus be one of the greatest tragedies in human history, if, when the prophets' dreams of abundance (not surfeit) are for the first time feasible in terms of our productive powers and potentials, we should bury these instead of using them to the hilt.

[17] Nor is there any merit in the argument that we have not the organizing skills, economic tools and experience to assure sustained full employment (and the full production that goes with it) in the U.S. Even with some very deficient policies, and despite the advances of the new technology, we have reduced unemployment from 6.7 per cent in 1961 to 4 per cent now. If 4 per cent, why not 3, or even 2?

[18] I project ahead at a more rapid rate than most other economists the likely advances in productivity, or output per man-hour worked, resulting from technological change. Even so, I estimate that we need, for the decade ahead, an average annual economic growth rate of only about 5 to 6 per cent to absorb all increases in productivity plus a rapidly growing labor force. This is far below the 9 per cent average annual rate of economic growth which we maintained for four years during World War II, despite the dislocation of wartime.

[19] The utilization of our burgeoning productive powers is not an insoluble problem. It is a relatively easy problem, if we apply to it, in the cause of winning the war against poverty at home and disaster overseas, with the added frosting of large material progress for the rest of us, a modicum of the energy and determination we applied during World War II.

[20] The question may legitimately be posed: If the authors are correct in the limited objective of a guaranteed annual income for those who really cannot be employed, what harm is done by going as much further as they do? My concern is that, by attempting to advance a thesis which seems indefensible when pushed so far, they are undermining their effectiveness in winning acceptance of their more limited and splendid theme: that the American economy is powerful enough, and should be socially-minded enough, to guarantee an American standard of living to all those who really cannot participate in the functioning economy, and also to those who are employed but at substandard wages.

[21] We are now paying to our senior citizens, more than three-quarters of whom live in abject poverty and who constitute about 27 per cent of all the U.S. poor, Social Security benefits averaging half of what they ought to be within five years. We are grossly neglecting the 25 per cent

of all the U.S. poor who live in fatherless families, with at least half headed by mothers who cannot or should not work. For these, we should establish decent systems of family allowances, similar to those in some European countries. We should commence, for the first time, to make large Federal contributions in the general welfare category. Also with Federal contributions, we should greatly improve our unemployment insurance and workmen's compensation systems.

[22] About 60 per cent of the poor are poor because their breadwinners are unemployed, or employed only part-time, or paid substandard wages when employed, or because of some combination of these situations. The remedy here is an adequate, national, full-employment-and-income policy. This type of "guarantee" was really the mandate of the Employment Act of 1946. But we have moved toward its full implementation only with mincing steps. Grafted upon this rather than pursued independently, guaranteed incomes to those who cannot or should not be employed is eminently desirable. This would also enlarge aggregate demand, and thereby stimulate employment to counteract the displacements due to technological advance.

[23] What I urge, in essence, is that we build upon what we have, more courageously and comprehensively than we are now doing. We really have in place the institutions, the machinery and even the stated purposes to build a Great Society, strong and just. We need only to use them.

[24] This seems to me more promising—economically, financially, politically, and psychologically—than to blur the dividing line between evolution and revolution. It may seem appealing to write an entirely new prescription on a white sheet of paper, but entirely "new approaches" are not meritorious per se.

[25] Even the current "war on poverty" suffers from too much bright new experimentalism. Poverty is not a new problem nor even a recent discovery. There is a wealth of revealed experience, both at home and abroad, bearing upon what works toward reducing poverty. The poor should not be made the victims of a farrago of "new approaches."

[26] Too much of the recent and current writing on economic and related social problems seems to manifest the sentiment that nobody will listen unless there are iconoclastic shockers in the story. We have plenty of real economic problems, some requiring drastic solutions, without ranging off into the wild blue yonder. My good friend John K. Galbraith, in his most famous book, "The Affluent Society," made a tremendous contribution in his plea for more attention to the "public sector." Unfortunately, he elected to spice up his text with forays to the effect that economic growth and full employment are no longer essential in an affluent society. I fear that the heritage of this mistake is reflected in the volume under review.

[27] Speculative but remote thinking and writing about the highly improbable would be more welcome were we not now confronted by so many unmet problems and so many aberrations in national policies that call for quick, precision readjustment. The 1967 Federal Budget makes it clear that we are willing, if need be, to cut back on nonessentials in order to finance an expanding war in Vietnam (I imply no dissent from that). But we are not yet willing, through tax increases, to cut back on scores of billions of dollars of wasteful private consumption (and the private investment designed to feed it), in order to finance adequately the most urgent of our domestic public priorities—the very bricks and mortar of a Great Society.

[28] The servicing of these priorities requires intense efforts to expand production, combined with unalloyed determination to allocate the product in accord with what we need most, not what we need least. We have gone too far already on the assumption that stimulating any kind of demand through incontinent tax reductions can turn the trick.

[29] The tasks ahead will require changes in the structure of the labor force and employment, but no surrender of the goal of full employment. It will require many alterations in the structure of demand, but even firmer commitment than we now have to a high enough level of total demand to expand total output even more rapidly than we are now doing.

[30] The development of the economic means suitable to these tasks, and the enlargement of the popular understanding and support which is so essential, call for the best that the intellectual community can offer. If we make long-range budgets of our needs and resources, and use fiscal and other policies sufficiently to redirect our energies in accord with our needs, we can create a Great Society at home, and do our full share toward spreading its seeds among the 3 billion people of the earth.

COMMENT AND QUESTIONS

1. Paragraph 1 explains the central proposition of the book the author is reviewing; paragraph 2 clarifies the meaning of "modest but adequate" income; and paragraphs 3–5 are generally commendatory of the interest and value of the book. Does anything in the first paragraph prepare for Keyserling's "partial but vital" dissent from the central thesis of the book?
2. With what ideas in the volume he is reviewing does the author apparently agree? What is his dissent and his own thesis?
3. In paragraph 7 and again in paragraph 9, the author summarizes the assumptions underlying *The Guaranteed Income:* (a) that technology and automation make massive unemployment inevitable, and (b) that ad-

vances in industrial techniques will, even with a small fraction of the population working, produce an overwhelming and even undesirable abundance of goods and services. What are Keyserling's main arguments against these assumptions? Which of his arguments seem most convincing to you, and why?
4. What is the function in the article of paragraph 12?
5. Later in his review, Keyserling is critical of the extremism in the book he is discussing and critical of "new approaches." What seem to be the reasons for his criticism and his concern?
6. As the author says, a standard argument against the kind of guaranteed income recommended in Theobald's book is that unearned income would be psychologically damaging and damaging to character. Does this seem to you a valid argument? Explain.
7. Robert Theobald, in a letter to *The New York Times Book Review* after Keyserling's review appeared, wrote that in his opinion everyone should have a right either to an income or to a job and that unless the income was absolutely guaranteed to everyone, rules for determining eligibility for a guaranteed income would be necessary; the administrators of the eligibility rules would then have an enormous and potentially dangerous power. Does this point seem to you to strengthen the case for the guaranteed income for all? Explain.
8. The following advertisement appeared in national magazines at about the time *The Guaranteed Income* was published. Comment on the language and the point of view.

WHEN WE ALL TAKE IN EACH OTHER'S WASHING UTOPIA WILL HAVE ARRIVED

Let's tax the whole country so New Yorkers won't have to pay as much as the true cost of their train rides. Let's all pay more for our breakfast coffee so the rich planters of South America will stay rich and won't have to pay the taxes you pay. Let's continue to forgive France the 4 billion dollars we lent them almost 50 years ago (plus the billions we have given them since) so they can drain away our gold. Let's all continue to pay more for gasoline taxes to build superhighways for states who refuse to build their own. Let's all keep on paying more for food than it costs to raise it, so some farmers can be paid billions they don't earn. Let's continue to pay billions to "veterans" who never saw a battle. Let's keep on paying more for our homes so building trades unionists can continue to get as much as $30 for a 6 hour day.

Who's kidding whom?

If we all did our own work, paid our own bills instead of insisting others pay them, we'd get more done, and save the billions of dollars every year in handling charges—charges that have so boosted our debt that *interest alone* is more than 11 billion dollars a year.

Sharing the wealth (i.e., socialism) is nothing but sharing the poverty, and don't let any politician steal your vote by telling you differently.

[52] *John Lear*: Men, Moonships, and Morality

JOHN LEAR (1909–) is an American writer and editor who, since 1956, has been science editor of the *Saturday Review*. The following article was published in the January 7, 1967, issue of that magazine.

[1] Three hundred and fifty-eight years ago Johannes Kepler—the great German mathematician who figured out how the earth and its sister planets orbit the sun—wrote the first scientific treatise on the problems man must solve in traveling to the moon. He considered the perils of the solar wind. He correctly described the influence of gravity in both the earthly and lunar phases of the voyage. He anticipated the use of inertial power. And he predicted that when earth was finally seen from the moon the geographical features of the planet would be recognizable.

[2] At the time Kepler wrote that manuscript, in the year 1609, the very idea of going to the moon so unsettled his superstitious contemporaries that his mother (who had been named allegorically in his script) was imprisoned as a witch and put on trial for her life.

[3] By the end of the month of September in the year 1967, the inertial power that Kepler foresaw will have been in use for ten years. Moonships designed to carry a crew of three men are already built and christened with the name *Apollo*. Considerably smaller and lighter craft have been rocketed to the moon's surface, and others have been placed in orbit around the moon. One of the latter, called *Orbiter I*, has photographed both hemispheres of the moon: the one earth never sees as well as the one that is continually in earthlings' sight. While pursuing its course around the moon, *Orbiter* I has also photographed the earth. The first of those pictures confirms Kepler's prediction of 358 years ago. Although not clearly distinguishable by the untrained eye, features discerned in the crescent image of the planet by photo-analysts of the National Aeronautics and Space Administration at Langley, Virginia, include the eastern coast of the United States, southern Europe, and Antarctica.

[4] The appearance of the earth from the moon, then, at 4:35 P.M. Greenwich Mean Time on August 23, 1966 (the date of the photograph), was not vastly different from what Kepler had expected from looking at the moon in 1609. But three and a half centuries of technological change had to intervene before confirmation of his vision became pos-

sible. During that interim, the art of transportation has undergone several successive revolutions. People today are able to move over long distances at speeds that would have been thought incredible in Kepler's day. Their political inventions have not kept pace with their growing mobility, but in the main kings have given way to popularly elected agents of the people, empires have crumbled into independent states, and nations have banded together in free associations of free individuals.

[5] What has been the fate of moral wisdom meanwhile?
[6] Dr. Robert S. Morison, director of Cornell University's Division of Biological Sciences, commented on this most fundamental of all human questions at the public celebration of California Institute of Technology's seventy-fifth birthday two months ago.
[7] "Compared to our views on the nature of matter, the origin of the seasons, the control of the weather, and even on the creation and nature of man himself," he said, "our views on private property, murder, rape, and adultery have changed very little since the time of Moses."
[8] Casting a long look backward into history, he continued:
"In earlier times, the repositories of knowledge, wisdom, and morals were inextricably intertwined. The high priests of the early riverine societies were the astronomers, the biologists, the philosophers, the lawyers, and the religious leaders all wrapped into one. To a large extent, scientific and theological knowledge coincided.
[9] "The rapid growth of scientific knowledge in our time has resulted in a greater and greater gulf between natural and theological knowledge and a considerable decline in interest in the latter. Ethics and morality occupy an uneasy position somewhere in between."

[10] Noting that the explosion in technological information in recent decades has left many parents unable to pass on to their children the practical knowledge the children need to confront the future confidently, Dr. Morison went on:
[11] "The astonishing thing is that the decline in respect for fathers, mothers, and priests as repositories of expert scientific knowledge has not been accompanied by more of a decline in respect for their moral influence."

[12] Only the first five pages of Dr. Morison's message at Caltech were concerned with the past and present state of morality, however. The remaining eleven pages spelled out a warning of impending change, "the social consequences of which are not easy to see." At the end of his remarks an inescapable question loomed:
Can the family survive as the fundamental reproductive cell of the great and sprawling body of civilization?

[13] Without going so far as to enunciate a flat negative answer, the Cornell biologist suggested three reasons for expecting at least a diminution in the family's social role:

[14] 1) While it is "a fine mechanism for transmitting conventional wisdom in a relatively static society," the family "is relatively poor at assimilating and transmitting new knowledge essential to survival" in a rapidly altering environment.

[15] 2) Birth control—now deemed necessary to give all earth's peoples enough food to eat, water to drink, and air to breathe—and growth of knowledge about genetically transmitted disease are together separating "the phenomena associated with sexual attraction and those involving reproduction *per se.*"

[16] Since "much of the conventional moral apparatus of almost all societies has been based on the assumption of an extremely close tie between the two," and since the family has been the traditional repository of the tie, it is prudent to try to evaluate what changes may come in the institution of the family "if sexual behavior and reproduction become completely separated from one another." Should such a final break occur, society "would have to struggle on the one hand with defining the nature of interpersonal relationships which have no long-term social point other than the satisfaction of the individuals concerned. On the other hand, it must seek new ways to ensure reasonable care for infants and children in an emotional atmosphere which lacks biological reinforcement through basic sexual and parental drives."

[17] 3) Our increasing knowledge of the biology and psychology of infancy and early childhood fortifies an old belief in the importance of shaping the first five or six years of a child's life.

[18] "These are the years which the child ordinarily spends in the bosom of his family, and the evidence is accumulating that it is this fact that is primarily responsible for the relative fixity of the socio-economic class structure of a country like the United States." And "just as a wider appreciation of the science of genetics has made a pleasant eighteenth century fantasy of the stirring phrase 'all men are created equal' . . . it is quite clear that it is idle to talk of a society of equal opportunity as long as that society abandons its newcomers solely to their families for their most impressionable years."

[19] Many will fear the effects on children of the accelerated erosion of parental responsibility for bringing up the children. The apprehensions spring from a conviction that freedom of the individual will be circumscribed and that the ultimate consequences will be a colorless, conformist society.

[20] Dr. Morison conceded the fears, but did not share them. Instead, he expressed his faith in "the almost infinite adaptability of the human

nervous system." He emphasized: "It is hard to see how enriching the environment and increasing the contacts of young children can do other than increase their capacity for intelligent choices later in life and thus free them from both external and internal constraints that normally limit personal freedom."

[21] Parents rather than children will be most likely to suffer deprivation from the decline of family influence, he predicted. Fathers and mothers will lose a sense of importance in relation to the future. And "if all this is even approximately right, it would seem essential to set about devising substitutes or sublimations. Somehow people must be made to expand their sense of loyalty and responsibility to include a larger share of the human race."

[22] Now directors of divisions of modern universities do not make pronouncements of this magnitude without due deliberation. Before drafting his Caltech birthday address, Dr. Morison not only consulted many fellow members of the Cornell faculty individually but gathered about him at night a gifted group with out-of-the-ordinary communicative ability. Among this party was a man who knows at least as much as and perhaps more than any other American scientist does about the changing role of the family in societies competitive with our own. This person was Urie Bronfenbrenner, Cornell professor of psychology and of child development and family relationships, a frequent professional visitor to the Soviet Union, chairman of the research advisory committee to UNESCO's cross-cultural study of prejudice, and member of the social science advisory board of the U.S. Disarmament and Arms Control Agency.

[23] Professor Bronfenbrenner during the half year prior to Dr. Morison's appearance at Caltech had been reporting on his Soviet experiences and observations at scientific symposia scattered from Moscow to Winnipeg to Miami to Boston. On each occasion he had told how the Communist society had been taking over traditional functions of the Russian family for the last decade. Following an order issued by Nikita Khrushchev in 1956, children were put into collective schools at the age of three months and brought up through nurseries, kindergartens, and boarding schools under conditions designed to create "the new Soviet man." Seven million boys and girls, almost 10 per cent of the present Soviet population of preschool and school age, are now being reared in these institutions; by 1970, one-third of all Soviet children will be involved; by the 1980's, all.

[24] The principles and methods employed in the collective schools were developed by a Communist social psychologist, A. S. Makarenko, who died in 1939 after setting up fantastically successful camps for rehabilitation of wild gangs of juvenile delinquents who pillaged the Russian

countryside in the 1920s. Makarenko's posthumous glory in the U.S.S.R. is so radiant that Professor Bronfenbrenner says the American equivalent can be arrived at only by imagining Dr. Benjamin Spock and John Dewey combined into one man.

[25] Makarenko's books have been best sellers throughout Russia for a quarter century. Thousands of copies have also been sold in eastern Europe, Cuba, and China. Mao's notorious Red Guards are an extreme example of the pitch to which youth can be disciplined by the Makarenko system. Virtually every language has its editions of Makarenko's works— English included. The United States is the only major nation on earth that has not published a translation.

[26] This last-mentioned omission will be corrected next month, when Doubleday, through an arrangement with the Am-Rus Literary Agency, will release an Americanized version of Makarenko's handbook for Russian parents under a new title: *The Collective Family*. An Anchor paperback original, translated by Robert Daglish, the volume will sell for $1.45 per copy.

[27] Professor Bronfenbrenner's introduction to *The Collective Family* will not be reassuring to American readers. For he reminds the forgetful that it was just ten years ago come October that Soviet technologists startled people everywhere by putting the first man-made moon into orbit around planet earth. *Sputnik I* stayed up until January 4, 1958, and *Sputnik II* was orbiting for two months with the dog Laika as passenger before American rocketeers lofted *Explorer I*, the first capitalist moon, on January 31, 1958.

[28] Ever since that traumatic humbling of American pride, curricula in American schools have been repeatedly shock-proofed against future anguish with the new math, the new physics, the new chemistry, and the new biology.

[29] So Professor Bronfenbrenner's message inevitably must come as a profoundly rude shock: During our ten-year preoccupation with the teaching of technical skill—accompanied, as it has been, with long-haired campus rebellions of sometimes riotous proportions—the Russians have been concentrating on the inculcation of character!

[30] The Soviet process begins at the age of three months, in collective playpens shared by six to eight infants. "Upbringers" (one for every four charges among the younger children) stimulate sensory, motor, mental, and social responses with special exercises. Devotion to the ideal of common ownership of property is fostered from the beginning through use of phrases like "mine is ours; ours is mine." By the time the children are eighteen months old, they control their excretory functions and wash,

dress, and feed themselves. As soon as they can talk, they are encouraged to judge and criticize each other's behavior from the group's perspective. It is the "upbringer's" job to see that individual and collective self-reliance develop together. In kindergarten, there is group play at keeping store, going to the doctor, and similar real-life simulations; there is actual responsibility for gardening and care of animals; and some kindergartens teach foreign languages. In the collective boarding schools, each student must choose a vocation (automotive mechanics, dressmaking, radio repair, computer programming are among subjects available) in which to receive daily training not only in school shops but in affiliated factories, institutes, and farms.

[31] "In the collective, by the collective, for the collective" was the motto Makarenko wrote to guide what Khrushchev later described as "engineering of the soul."

[32] What has Soviet collective schooling accomplished to date?

[33] Professor Bronfenbrenner has reported to his scientific colleagues on comparative studies of Soviet children and age-mates in the United States and Western Europe. The preschoolers, he said, "cry far less frequently, are more obedient, and appear to be better able to take care of themselves." Yet, although they are "clearly normal, and perhaps even advanced, physically and mentally," the Soviet children display "emotional blandness." Older children in the collective boarding schools "are well-mannered, attentive, and industrious. In informal conversations, they reveal strong motivation to learn, a readiness to serve their society, and what is perhaps best described as an idealistic and even sentimental attitude toward life."

[34] What implications has the Soviet schooling experiment for our own democratic society?

[35] Although research on the subject is still too limited to allow firm judgment, "a recently completed experiment . . . has yielded sobering results." More than 150 sixth-graders (six classrooms) in each country [U.S. and U.S.S.R.] were placed in situations revelatory of their readiness to engage in morally disapproved behavior such as cheating on an exam, denying responsibility for property damage, etc. The American children were "far more ready to take part in such actions."

[36] Now Soviet collective schooling was established deliberately for an ideological purpose. Soviet parents accepted it willingly because it freed living space in crowded homes, cut food costs (which run up to 70 per cent of the Russian family budget), raised family income by allowing mothers to work, and offered deprived children opportunities otherwise denied them.

[37] The American family meanwhile has been losing its traditional influence over the children by default. Mothers work to augment strained

domestic budgets, children are left on their own, and offspring of poorer families—particularly those of the Negro community—drop out of school and become delinquents.

[38] "The question therefore arises whether we cannot profit by taking to heart Makarenko's injunctions regarding the constructive influence of imposing communal responsibility within both family and peer-groups," the introduction to *The Collective Family* says. "This does not mean subscribing to his insistence on the primacy of the collective over the individual. It does mean giving the children, from early ages on, genuine responsibilities from which they learn the meaning of self-respect and respect for others. Such responsibilities can and must extend beyond the home to the neighborhood, the school, the community, and—in due course—the larger society. They should involve not only parents and friends but the full range of human beings who make up the society, including those who most need and deserve the service of others—old people, young children, the handicapped, and the underprivileged. . . . We, too, must teach morality . . . consistent with the welfare of all and the dignity of each."

--◄{ COMMENT AND QUESTIONS }►--

1. What seem to be the purposes of the first four paragraphs of Lear's article?
2. Examine paragraph 9. Do you agree that "ethics and morality occupy an uneasy position" somewhere between scientific and theological knowledge? Explain.
3. Paragraph 12 seems to shift from the idea of morality, and the question about the survival of the family as a dominant force may not at first seem relevant to the author's central theme. When does the discussion of the family become clearly relevant?
4. Comment on Dr. Morison's reasons, in paragraphs 14–18, for expecting some diminution in the family's role. Do the reasons seem to you logical? Explain.
5. What is the meaning of the statement at the end of paragraph 18 that "it is idle to talk of a society of equal opportunity as long as that society abandons its newcomers solely to their families for their most impressionable years"? To what extent do you agree with the statement, and why?
6. Paragraphs 27–29 bring into new relationship the men, moonships, and morality of Lear's alliterative title. Why do you think the author included, in paragraph 29, the reference to campus rebellions?
7. According to this article, what seem to be the significant advantages of the Russian system of collective schooling? Are any disadvantages suggested? Do you see disadvantages? Explain.

8. Examine the quotation in the last paragraph from Professor Bronfenbrenner's introduction to *The Collective Family*. Do his proposals seem reasonable and feasible to you? How, specifically, might they be put into effect?
9. If you have read "Substitutes for Violence" by John Fischer, do you think that some modified version of Russian collective schooling might provide the substitutes for violence that Fischer is recommending? Explain.

A Glossary of Rhetorical Terms

Abstract Words. Words which generally name qualities, concepts, and conditions. See pages 11–12.

Alliteration. The repetition of consonant sounds, usually at the beginnings of words: "The *furrow followed free*."

Analogy. A sustained comparison of two dissimilar ideas or situations.

Antithesis. A stylistic arrangement of opposed elements to heighten the contrast between them: "I wish to preach not the doctrine of ignoble ease, but the doctrine of the strenuous life."

Appositives and Appositive Structures. An appositive is a noun, pronoun, noun phrase, noun clause, or noun plus modifiers standing beside another noun and denoting the same person or thing: "The spring flowers, *daffodils and scillas*, brighten the yard." An apposed adjective is an adjective, or an expression used as an adjective, that occupies the same position as an appositive: "The dog, *playful and gay*, jumped over the fence."

Assumptions. What a communicator conjectures or takes for granted about his subject or about the interests, attitudes, and beliefs of his audience. See pages 5–6.

Attitudinal Language. Language which expresses the feelings or attitudes of a communicator toward himself, his audience, and his subject. See **Charged Language** and **Tone**.

Balance. See **Parallelism.** When parallel expressions are similar in length and rhythm as well as in grammatical construction, they are said to be *balanced*: "The world is *a comedy to those who think, a tragedy to those who feel*."

Charged Words and **Charged Language.** Words which carry strong emotional or attitudinal meaning are called charged words; and language intended to produce emotional charges—attractions or repulsions—in the hearer or reader is called charged language. See page 6.

Climactic Arrangement. The arrangement of sentence elements (or of elements in a paragraph or a whole composition) to build to a climax or strong ending. See page 13.

Complement. A noun or adjective structure that completes the thought and establishes the meaning of a verb: "Bert is *chairman;* he looks *tired.*

Concrete Words. Words which generally refer to things that exist in the physical world, on the nature and meaning of which people can agree. See pages 11-12.

Connotation. The implied or associated meanings of a word. "Home," for example, carries suggestions of comfort and security; "house" does not.

Context. The surrounding words or circumstances which establish the meaning of a particular expression.

Denotation. The factual meaning of a word used to identify something by naming it. See **Connotation.**

Direct Discourse. Quotation of a person's exact words.

Dominant Impression. In narrative or descriptive writing, the unified effect to which details contribute.

Economy. A trait of good style, achieved by avoiding unnecessary and verbose expressions, cutting weak clauses to phrases or single words, and using exact words.

>WORDY: She rendered a vocal selection.
>
>REVISED: She sang.
>
>WORDY: The wind which blew through the cracks made a whistling sound.
>
>REVISED: The wind whistled through the cracks.
>
>WORDY: He lifted the stick that he uses to conduct the orchestra.
>
>REVISED: He lifted his baton.

Emphasis. Stress on important words and ideas by means of position, proportion, repetition, and other techniques. See pages 10, 12–14.

Figurative Language. Language in which words are used nonliterally. See pages 11–12.

Formal and Informal Style. Formal English, more often written than spoken, is likely to have the following characteristics: long sentences, parallel and balanced constructions, a wide and exact vocabulary, the absence of contractions (*can't, don't*), and an impersonal tone. In informal English, the sentences are likely to be shorter and to have the rhythms and uncomplicated constructions of speech, and the tone is more often personal than impersonal. For examples of formal and informal style, see pages 7–8.

Heavy Words. Formal or pretentious words used unnecessarily in an informal context. They have too much bulk or weight for the situation.

Indirect Discourse. Statement of what a person said without quotation of his exact words: "He said that he did not approve."

Inversion or **Inverted Order.** A departure from the normal subject–verb–object order of English sentences: "The solstice he does not observe, the equinox he knows as little." *Inversion* is sometimes used to refer to the moving of any sentence element from its most normal or common position: "Desperately he struggled, but to no avail."

Irony. A manner of expression in which the real meaning is different from, sometimes the opposite of, the apparent or literal meaning.

Loose Sentence. A sentence which continues after the main idea has been expressed: *"They returned to camp* after a long and exhausting walk through the woods." See **Periodic Sentence.**

Motif. A repeated detail (sound, visual image, sensation, or condition) used to give texture and unity to a piece of writing.

Normal Order. The conventional pattern of English sentences in which the subject precedes the verb and the object or complement follows the verb.

Pace. The movement of a piece of writing. Pace depends, in narrative writing, on the balance between summary and presentation of material. In non-narrative writing it may depend on the fullness of development and detail. See pages 13–14.

Paradox. A statement that seems contradictory or unbelievable but that may in fact be true: "My life closed twice before its close."

Parallelism. The principle of usage which requires that coordinate elements in a compound construction be given the same grammatical form: "The world will little note nor long remember what we say here; but it can never forget what they did here." For further examples, see pages 8–10.

Periodic Sentence. A sentence, more characteristic of formal than of informal style, in which the meaning is suspended until the end: "About his disappointments, his anxieties, and the reasons for his action, *we have little knowledge.*"

Persona. The "voice," role, or personality which a speaker or writer adopts in a particular communication. See pages 6–7.

Premise. An assertion or previous statement that is the basis of an argument. See **Syllogism.**

Repetition. In skillful writing, a means of emphasizing important words and ideas, of binding together the sentences in a passage, and of creating emotional effects. See pages 10-11.

Slanting. The process of selecting facts, words, and emphasis to achieve the communicator's intention.

> *Slanting by selection of facts:*
>
>> FAVORABLE: Tom is an honor student.
>> UNFAVORABLE: Tom hasn't shaved for two weeks.
>
> *Slanting by selection of charged words:*
>
>> FAVORABLE: Jean is a slender blonde.
>> UNFAVORABLE: Jean is a skinny girl with brassy hair.
>
> *Slanting by emphasis:*
>
>> MORE FAVORABLE: Although Tom hasn't shaved for two weeks, he is an honor student.
>> LESS FAVORABLE: Tom may be an honor student, but he hasn't shaved for two weeks.

Style. A quality of excellence or distinction. See pages 7-14.

Subordination. Expressing in dependent clauses, or phrases, or single words, ideas which are not significant enough to be expressed in a main clause or an independent sentence.

> LACKING SUBORDINATION: The quarterback was tired. He was also battered. He was determined to win.
>
> SUBORDINATION: The quarterback, though tired and battered, was determined to win.

Syllogism. In formal logic, the pattern in which a deductive argument is expressed: All men are mortal (major premise). John is a man (minor premise). Therefore John is mortal (conclusion). See page 15.

Symbol. A particular object, person, experience, or situation which stands for, or is associated with, some larger relationship or idea.

Tone. The manner of verbal expression; the expression of a communicator's attitudes toward himself, his audience, and his material. See pages 5-7.

Topic Sentence. A sentence which expresses the central idea of a paragraph.

Transitions. Words, phrases, sentences, or even paragraphs, which show the reader the connections between the writer's ideas. See page 5.

Triad. A sequence of three parallel constructions: ". . . to defend our island home, to ride out the storm of war, and to outlive the menace of tyranny. . . ."

Variety. Variation in the length and construction of sentences to avoid monotony and to suit style to sense. See pages 8–10.

Vitalizing. Bringing people and scenes to life. Vitalizing a person usually involves showing him in some typical pose or activity. Vitalizing a scene means carrying the reader into it by providing him with some of the sights, sounds, and other sense impressions that are part of experiencing that scene.

Index to Authors and Titles

(FOR AN INDEX TO RHETORICAL TERMS, SEE THE GLOSSARY, page 507–11.)

Agnosticism and Christianity, by Thomas Henry Huxley, 208
Alienation: Quantification, Abstractification, by Erich Fromm, 64
American Way of Death, The, by Lewis Mumford, 438
Anti-Hero, The, by Ihab Hassan, 338
Apology, the, by Plato, 99
Baldwin, James
  Notes of a Native Son, 450
Becker, Carl L.
  The Ideal Democracy, 83
Bronowski, J.
  The Creative Mind, 383
Calculating Machine, by E. B. White, 308
Computer and the Poet, The, by Norman Cousins, 422
Conrad, Joseph
  Preface to *The Nigger of the Narcissus*, 331
Cousins, Norman
  The Computer and the Poet, 422
Creative Mind, The, by J. Bronowski, 383
Crisis of American Masculinity, The, by Arthur M. Schlesinger, Jr., 73
Crowther, Geoffrey
  Two Heresies, 24
Dewey, John
  Does Human Nature Change? 238
Dictionary as a Battlefront, The, by Mario Pei, 299
Dixon, W. Macneile
  Human Nature and the Human Situation, 246
Does Human Nature Change? by John Dewey, 238
Edman, Irwin
  A Reasonable Life in a Mad World, 284
Einstein, Albert
  Science and Religion, 221

Enlargement of Mind, by John Henry Newman, 152
Epictetus
  The Quiet Mind, 187
Epicurus
  Letter to a Friend, 183
Esslin, Martin
  The Significance of the Absurd, 348
Evans, Bergen
  Grammar for Today, 291
Excellence: The Ideal of Individual Fulfillment, by John W. Gardner, 168
Existentialism, by Jean-Paul Sartre, 227
Fascination of Style, On the, by F. L. Lucas, 321
Faulkner, William
  Remarks on Receiving the Nobel Prize, 336
Fischer, John
  Substitutes for Violence, 481
Fromm, Erich
  Alienation: Quantification, Abstractification, 64
Gardner, John W.
  Excellence: The Ideal of Individual Fulfillment, 168
Genesis of a Mood, The, by Joseph Wood Krutch, 260
Grammar for Today, by Bergen Evans, 291
Hassan, Ihab
  The Anti-Hero, 338
Human Nature and the Human Situation, by W. Macneile Dixon, 246
Huxley, Thomas Henry
  Agnosticism and Christianity, 208
Ideal Democracy, The, by Carl L. Becker, 83
Idea of a Multiversity, The, by Clark Kerr, 161
Intrinsic Value of Art, The, by DeWitt Parker, 373

It's Halfway to 1984, by John Lukacs, 54
It's Two-Thirds of a Century—We've Made It, So Far, by Elting E. Morison, 404
James, William
  Religious Faith, 213
Jesus
  Sermon on the Mount, 220
Kerr, Clark
  The Idea of a Multiversity, 161
Keyserling, Leon H.
  Something for Everybody, 490
Krutch, Joseph Wood
  (headnote, 260)
  The Genesis of a Mood, 260
  Life, Liberty, and the Pursuit of Welfare, 272
Lear, John
  Men, Moonships, and Morality, 498
Learning to Live with Science, by Emmanuel G. Mesthene, 413
Letter to a Friend, by Epicurus, 183
Liberty of Thought and Discussion, On the, by John Stuart Mill, 128
Life, Liberty, and the Pursuit of Welfare, by Joseph Wood Krutch, 272
Lucas, F. L.
  On the Fascination of Style, 321
Lukacs, John
  It's Halfway to 1984, 54
Marcus Aurelius
  from the *Meditations,* 193
McCarthy, Mary
  Settling the Colonel's Hash, 357
Meditations, excerpts from the, by Marcus Aurelius, 193
Men, Moonships, and Morality, by John Lear, 498
Mesthene, Emmanuel G.
  Learning to Live with Science, 413
Mill, John Stuart
  On the Liberty of Thought and Discussion, 128
Monster, The, by Deems Taylor, 369
Morison, Elting E.
  It's Two-Thirds of a Century—We've Made It, So Far, 404
Mumford, Lewis
  The American Way of Death, 438
My Negro Problem—and Ours, by Norman Podhoretz, 468
Myth of the Cave, The, by Plato, 121

Newman, John Henry
  Enlargement of Mind, 152
Notes of a Native Son, by James Baldwin, 450
Oppenheimer, J. Robert
  Prospects in the Arts and Sciences, 396
Opportunity for Change, The, by Nils Y. Wessell, 33
Orwell, George
  The Principles of Newspeak, 310
  Why I Write, 46
Parker, DeWitt
  The Intrinsic Value of Art, 373
Pei, Mario
  The Dictionary as a Battlefront, 299
Plato
  (headnotes, 99, 121, 176)
  Apology, 99
  Symposium, excerpt from, 176
  The Myth of the Cave, 121
Podhoretz, Norman
  My Negro Problem—and Ours, 468
  Preface to *The Nigger of the Narcissus,* by Joseph Conrad, 331
Principles of Newspeak, The, by George Orwell, 310
Prospects in the Arts and Sciences, by J. Robert Oppenheimer, 396
Quiet Mind, The, by Epictetus, 187
Reasonable Life in a Mad World, A, by Irwin Edman, 284
Religious Faith, by William James, 213
Remarks on Receiving the Nobel Prize, by William Faulkner, 336
Sartre, Jean-Paul
  Existentialism, 227
Schlesinger, Arthur M., Jr.
  The Crisis of American Masculinity, 73
Science and Religion, by Albert Einstein, 221
Sermon on the Mount, by Jesus, 220
Settling the Colonel's Hash, by Mary McCarthy, 357
Significance of the Absurd, The, by Martin Esslin, 348
Something for Everybody, by Leon H. Keyserling, 490
Stoic View, The, 186
Substitutes for Violence, by John Fischer, 481
Sullivan, Walter
  What If We Succeed? 425
Symposium, excerpt from, by Plato, 176

Taylor, Deems
   The Monster, 369
Thurber, James
   Which, 23
Two, Heresies, by Geoffrey Crowther, 24
Walden, 1939, by E. B. White, 39
Wessell, Nils Y.
   The Opportunity for Change, 33

What If We Succeed? by Walter Sullivan, 425
Which, by James Thurber, 21
White, E. B.
   (headnote, 39)
   Calculating Machine, 308
   Walden, 1939, 39
Why I Write, by George Orwell, 46